10⁰⁰

K

Solving Problems
On
Concurrent Processors

"Mirror, mirror, on the wall, who's the fastest of them all?"

Snow White's stepmother poses the fundamental question in concurrent computation. The right mirror shows many small microprocessors - each a MOTOROLA 68020. The left mirror shows a CRAY-XMP (photo courtesy of CRAY Research, Inc.). Small microprocessors form the basis of the hypercubes and similar concurrent computers studied in this book. The CRAY-XMP is one of the fastest conventional supercomputers. It features four identical central processing units sharing eight or sixteen million 64-bit words of ECL bipolar central memory. The XMP/4 mainframe consists of 12 columns arranged in a 270° arc requiring just 64 square feet (6 square meters) of floor space. The frontispiece was composed by J. Goldsmith who used a ray-tracing method requiring several hours of computation on the 128-node Mark II hypercube.

Solving Problems
On
Concurrent Processors

Volume I

General Techniques and
Regular Problems

Geoffrey C. Fox, Mark A. Johnson, Gregory A. Lyzenga,
Steve W. Otto, John K. Salmon, David W. Walker

California Institute of Technology

Prentice Hall, *Englewood Cliffs, New Jersey 07632*

Library of Congress Cataloging-in-Publication Data

Fox, Geoffrey C.
    Solving problems on concurrent processors.

    Includes index.
    Contents: v. 1. General techniques and regular
problems.
    1. Parallel processing (Electronic computers)
2. Multiprocessors. I. Title.
QA76.5.F627 1988   004'.35   87-7288
ISBN 0-13-8230226 (v. 1)

Editorial/production supervision: *Barbara A. Marttine*
Cover design: *Lundgren Graphics*
Manufacturing buyer: *Richard Washburn*

The frontispiece photo shows a picture of a CRAY/XMP Supercomputer with four processing elements. The CRAY XMP/4 system offers performance up to ten times that of the CRAY-1. It features four identical central processing units sharing eight or sixteen million 64-bit words of ECL biopolar central memory. The XMP/4 mainframe (center) consists of 12 columns arranged in a 270° arc requiring just 64 square feet (6 square meters) of floor space. To the left is the XMP's I/O Subsystem. (Picture courtesy of Cray Research Inc.)

Printed in the United States of America

10 9 8 7 6 5 4

ISBN 0-13-823022-6

Prentice-Hall International (UK) Limited, *London*
Prentice-Hall of Australia Pty. Limited, *Sydney*
Prentice-Hall Canada Inc., *Toronto*
Prentice-Hall Hispanoamericana, S.A., *Mexico*
Prentice-Hall of India Private Limited, *New Delhi*
Prentice-Hall of Japan, Inc., *Tokyo*
Simon & Schuster Asia Pte. Ltd., *Singapore*
Editora Prentice-Hall do Brasil, Ltda., *Rio de Janeiro*

Contents

Preamble

This book has an unusual emphasis: it is a blend of computer science and natural sciences which reflects the thrust of our research project at Caltech. We are attempting to derive fundamental computer science insights by analyzing and generalizing the results of explicit concurrent implementations of mainly scientific algorithms. For the lack of a better term, we can call our problem-driven approach computational science. We hope that this book will encourage others to perform research along similar lines. Further, we hope that the book contains results that will interest both computer scientists and computer users. Maybe some users will be convinced that the increase in computer performance promised by concurrent processing can be exploited in fields that up to now have not made major use of computer simulations. Huge performance increases lie in the future and their realization will lead to crucial breakthroughs in both old and new fields.

Most of our knowledge has been gained from use of hypercube concurrent computers built at Caltech. We have tried to present the lessons learned from this research in a fashion that generalizes to other machines. We have also tried to give credit to the important work of other groups on other machines. However, we are not going to be completely successful, and our book is clearly biased to the hypercube and somewhat unfair to other types of machines. For this we apologize.

This book concentrates on practically motivated model problems which serve to illustrate generic algorithmic and decomposition techniques. We have also confined ourselves to reasonably "regular" problems for which straightforward techniques can yield good concurrent performance. In the rest of this preamble, we shall present a cursory summary of the contents of this volume and the Software Supplement which comprises Vol. 2.

Chapter 1 is at an elementary level and illustrates the ideas of concurrency in fields outside computation. Chapter 2 describes the technological driving forces and choices and issues for concurrent computation. The introduction concludes with a discussion in Chap. 3 of the particular approach used in this book. These three initial chapters form a self-contained overview of concurrent computation which may be read independently of the rest of the volume. Where appropriate, these chapters make reference to later chapters which incorporate more detailed treatments. The bulk of this book is aimed at the level of a graduate or advanced undergraduate student in an engineering or scientific discipline. We assume that the reader has some experience in programming conventional (sequential or Von Neumann) computers; however no previous knowledge of parallel or concurrent computation is assumed.

Chapters 4, 5, and 6 contain simplified descriptions of a software (programming) environment, while introducing some of the basic algorithmic issues involved in using concurrent computers. This discussion is presented in the context of a "virtual machine" and ignores practical constraints that arise from using any real hardware and software system.

The example of the numerical solution of a wave equation is used in these chapters. We present sample software in both the FORTRAN and C programming languages, and also make use of a less detailed but clearer "pseudocode", which will prove useful in discussing the more complicated algorithms of later chapters. The pseudocode is explained in Appendix A. Although most of the original research upon which this book is based employed the C language, we believe that any modern high-level language can be used in our approach to concurrent computation. We will only show preference to C in the operating systems discussions of Chaps. 4, 6, 14, and 15. Otherwise, we will attempt to employ C or FORTRAN equally in our illustrative discussions.

Chapters 7 through 13 explain several key examples involved in the numerical solution of partial differential equations, matrix problems, particle dynamics, Fourier transforms, and Monte Carlo or statistical algorithms.

In Chap. 14, we present a practical implementation of our model computing environment on a hypercube concurrent computer. This introduces our standard Crystalline Operating System, CrOS III, which has been implemented on a number of machines including the hypercubes constructed at Caltech. Appendix E contains a summary definition of CrOS III for C and FORTRAN. CrOS III does not incorporate all of the features one could hope for in a concurrent environment; however, it is characterized by generally high performance and it is easy to use. In Chap. 15, we discuss the implementation of the CUBIX library first introduced in Chap. 6, which builds upon CrOS III to provide an attractive user environment incorporating many features associated with UNIX[†] file handling and other input/output and system capabilities. These specific software tools allow us to discuss more advanced topics in Chaps. 16 through 22. Chapter 16 is our first discussion of an intrinsically irregular problem–that of molecular dynamics with a short- or medium-range force. This is much more complicated than the long-range force problem covered in Chap. 9, and can make use of the full power of a general asynchronous message-passing operating system. However, we have chosen here to implement this problem under the CrOS III synchronous communication environment. This approach serves to illustrate the surprising power and usefulness of the comparatively simple CrOS III environment. Chapter 17 discusses a complicated problem arising in the study of population dynamics, which is also characterized by dynamic irregularity. This example allows us to discuss important load-balancing techniques that were first surveyed in Chap. 3. In Chaps. 18 and 19, sorting and tree algorithms are presented. We discuss these two interesting problems in which the decomposition must be carefully tailored to the hypercube and is expected to be significantly different on machines of other topologies. In Chaps. 20 and 21, we discuss some of the most important matrix algorithms, treating the specific case of the solution of banded matrix equations. The tools developed in Chap. 21 are used to extend the algorithm in Chap. 19 and provide a utility library that constitutes an important adjunct to CrOS III. The techniques developed in Chap. 22 allow one to implement the hardware independent virtual machine introduced earlier in Chap. 4. In Chap. 23, we summarize the volume by discussing how

---

[†] UNIX is a trademark of AT&T.

the hypercube can be used as a supercomputer in a wide variety of fields. Here we follow a science-based rather than the algorithm-based approach of the rest of the book.

The second volume is the Software Supplement which contains a set of computer programs that explicitly realize the algorithms and software discussed in the main text. This also describes a simulator that runs on many sequential machines and which will execute the example programs. The Software Supplement is described in more detail in Appendix B of this volume.

There are now several concurrent computers available commercially, including machines with the hypercube topology for which our work is particularly relevant. We are able to supply software at a nominal cost to allow our programs to run on some of these commercial machines. We can also supply the software presented in the Software Supplement on diskette. Information on this service may be obtained by returning the form included with this book or the supplement. If the form is not available, please write to

C^3P Requests
Caltech Concurrent Computation Program, 206-49
California Institute of Technology
Pasadena, CA 91125
Electronic Mail Address:
C3PREQUEST @ HAMLET.CALTECH.EDU for ARPANET
C3PREQUEST @ HAMLET for BITNET

A videotaped course is available which is loosely based on this book and has been taken by many beginning hypercube users at Caltech and JPL.

Information Request Form for

SOLVING PROBLEMS ON CONCURRENT PROCESSORS
Geoffrey C. Fox, Mark A. Johnson, Gregory A. Lyzenga,
Steve W. Otto, John K. Salmon, David W. Walker
Published by Prentice Hall

Name:
Address:
Telephone:
Electronic Mail:

Please send me information on available software and available C^3P reports.
Cost $2.50   YES   NO

Please place me on the mailing list for C^3P Technical Bulletin -
Cost $30.00 per year   YES   NO

Please send me the following C^3P documents (give numbers as listed in references as C^3P -nnn).
Cost $2.50 per report.

Please send me the following videotapes (circle required numbers, or "ALL"):
1.   Concurrent Computing: an Overview
2.   The Family of Hypercubes at JPL/CIT: How to Use Them
      Optimization of Programs for the Mark III Hypercube
3.   How to Write C Programs in CrOS III and CUBIX
4.   How to Write FORTRAN Programs in CrOS III
5.   The One-Dimensional Wave Equation and Elliptic Equations on the Hypercube
6.   Matrix Operations on the Hypercube
7.   The Fast Fourier Transform and the Many-Body Problem
8.   Sorting and the Traveling Salesman Problem
9.   Hypercube Applications in Science and Engineering
ALL. The complete set of above 9 videotapes

Costs: In order to cover reproduction and mailing costs it is necessary to charge for the above items as follows:
     1. C^3P Bulletin $30.00 per year
     2. C^3P documents $2.50 per document
     3.   Videotapes $7.00 per tape
Please enclose payment with this order form and send to:
C^3P Requests
Caltech Concurrent Computation Program, 206-49
California Institute of Technology
Pasadena, CA 91125
This information may also be sent electronically to
C3PREQUEST @ HAMLET.CALTECH.EDU   (Arpanet)
or
C3PREQUEST @ HAMLET   (Bitnet)

Acknowledgments

We would like to thank the many people and organizations without whose support and help our fledgling research would not have flourished. A colloquium by Carver Mead started our interest in this field. The generous help of Chuck Seitz and others in the Caltech Computer Science Department was essential to the construction of the first hypercube and served to teach us the rudiments of computer science. Robbie Vogt taught us what a project is and his friendship and help continues to be invaluable. Our project has benefited from substantial outside support which has been essential for the research reported here. Specific sponsors are the Department of Energy, the Joint Tactical Fusion Program Office, NASA, the National Security Agency, and the Electronic Systems Division of the USAF in the federal government; the Parsons and System Development Foundations; ALCOA, General Dynamics, General Motors, Hitachi, IBM, INTEL, Lockheed, MOTOROLA, NCUBE, SANDIA, and Shell were corporate supporters. We would like to thank personally Don Austin, Jerry Danburg, Sandy Frey, Ed Oliver, Emil Sarpa, Charles Smith, Gil Wiegand, Dan Wiener, and Bob Woods for daring to support our work at an early stage. At Caltech, R. Clayton, B. Hager, P. Haff, H. Keller, A. Kuppermann, and T. Tombrello were the first to be swayed by our arguments.

We would like to thank Jim Bower and Wojtek Furmanski for help in preparing parts of the text. The comments of Bill Buzbee, Gary Montry, John Palmer, Dave Rogstad, and Lisa Quinones on an early draft were very valuable.

Caltech's Jet Propulsion Laboratory (JPL) has provided invaluable engineering and intellectual support since 1983, and T. Cole, D. Curkendall, C. Kukkonen, J. Peterson, D. Rapp, and D. Rogstad started the fruitful collaboration between JPL and Campus. Finally, the unwavering help of the Caltech and JPL administration is acknowledged.

The untiring and careful efforts of Marc Goroff and Mary Maloney in preparing the manuscript were essential.

1

Well-Known Concurrent Processors

1-1 Introduction

The first three chapters are designed to fulfill two goals. Firstly, they form a self-contained survey of concurrent computation which may be studied by the reader independently of the more detailed discussion in the rest of the book. Secondly, they give an overview of the approach used in the rest of the book so that these initial, more descriptive chapters may serve as a unifying theme for the diverse topics encountered in working through Chaps. 4 through 22.

In this chapter we ignore the classical digital computers and consider some homely examples to show that the concepts and challenges of concurrent processing are well known and have been a key driving force in the development of societies and other complex systems. In Sec. 1-2, we discuss general principles, and in Sec. 1-3 we analyze the task of constructing a long wall, which rather effectively illustrates most of the issues in concurrent computing. In Sec. 1-4, we find a similar analogy in the division of land for farming. In the last two sections of Chap. 1, we discuss nature's approach to concurrent processing in the operation of the brain and other organizations.

Chap. 2 is a traditional discussion of the central issues in concurrent computation. We discuss both the technological driving forces and the many possible choices and issues facing us in the form of algorithms, hardware, and software. In Chap. 3, we consider the general framework developed by our research group at Caltech. This underlies the philosophy used in the following chapters. The hardware is specialized to be a Multiple-Instruction Multiple-Data (MIMD) computer; concurrent algorithms come from domain decomposition, and we adopt an intuitive approach to software that lets the user develop the decomposition "by hand" in a conventional high-level language. This is not the only possible approach to concurrent computation, but it is one that we have found fruitful.

Those with experience in concurrent computation will probably skip Chap. 1 and parts of Chap. 2. However, the overview of our approach in Chap. 3 will be helpful to most readers.

1-2 What Is Concurrent Processing?

Concurrent processing has been a contributory factor in the formation and development of societies on earth and is, as such, already familiar to the reader. A computer is a man-made device that has been developed to solve certain classes of problems. These problems are typically numerical in nature, although there is a growing and correct interest in using computers to address problems of artificial intelligence. The latter includes areas such as language and learning, or more generally, those tasks which mankind still does better than computers. As the problems have become harder and harder (or what is often equivalent, larger and larger), computers have been refined, gaining continuously in speed and data storage (memory) capabilities. Unfortunately, there appears to be no realistic approach to substantially increasing the performance of individual computers in the future; technology is already nearing limits set by the speed of light and quantum physics effects. There is now general agreement that the only route to significantly increased performance is through *concurrent computation*–the use of many computers together to solve the same problem.

We will define *concurrent processing* as the use of several working entities (either identical or heterogeneous), working together toward a common goal. In concurrent computation, the entities are computers and the goal might be a large scientific calculation (such as weather prediction), or an artificial intelligence application (such as winning the world chess championship or controlling a nation's defense).

Consider the beginning of time when mankind was facing a tough battle to survive the harsh world in which it found itself. Presumably, survival required advancement on at least two fronts. First was to increase the performance of the basic entity as defined above; this would involve training and education for individual men and women. A second and potentially more powerful (and perhaps easier) approach was to use concurrency. People gathered together into societies of gradually increasing size in which groups of men and women were able to solve problems together that were beyond the capabilities of any one individual. We may also speculate that just as today there are some who doubt the viability of concurrent computation, there may have existed prehistoric skeptics who concluded that perhaps 4, then 64, or just conceivably 1024 represented the absolute upper limit to the number of people in a useful society. Indeed Plato in his laws (Sec. 9, The Foundation of the New State) postulated 5040 as the upper limit for the size of a reasonable society. Many today would conclude that such skeptics were proved wrong as individuals formed families, then villages, then towns, and then countries. By analogy, concurrent computation will be initially difficult, and will require the identification of reasonable architectures (organization in the society analogy). We feel, however, that we can confidently predict success for arbitrarily large numbers of computers so that concurrency becomes the generally accepted approach to large computations!

1-3 The Construction of Hadrian's Wall

We now wish to draw a more detailed analogy to concurrent computation by studying a non-numerical concurrent processing problem and showing how it illustrates the key issues and lessons relevant in concurrent computation [Messina 87]. Consider the problem of constructing a large wall in a short length of time. For definiteness we may consider Hadrian's Wall–a structure 120 kilometers in length and 2 meters high constructed to separate England from Scotland (Encyclopedia Brittanica). We can use this to illustrate several key issues in concurrent processing:

- Domain Decomposition.
- Size (in terms of number of *members*) of the problem domain.
- Relation of the processor topology (architecture) to that of the problem.
- Difficulties encountered in irregular domains.
- Even more difficulties encountered in inhomogeneous domains.
- The distinct *speedups* possible with local (as in a CRAY computer) and global (as in hypercube) parallelism.
- Concurrent input (output) devices.

In our analogy, the *domain* is the wall which is itself made up of a large number of independent members, namely bricks. The members are the basic indivisible or atomic entities which make up the domain.

1-3.1 Domain Decomposition of Hadrian's Wall

A natural way to speed up the construction of the wall is to use several bricklayers to build it. As illustrated in Fig. 1-1, we divide the wall up into sections assigning each bricklayer equal lengths of the wall. Naturally, each section can be built concurrently so that we expect to obtain a *speedup S* that is roughly equal to the number N of bricklayers assigned to the job. We assume that our idealized bricklayers lay bricks at an equal rate, and so are correctly allocated equal lengths of wall. This is not very accurate for human workers but is reasonable for the analogous computers.

Concurrent construction of a wall using N = 8 bricklayers.
Decomposition by vertical section.

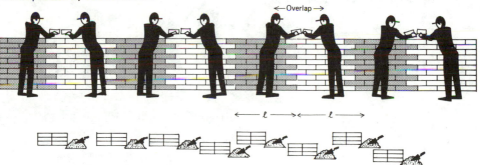

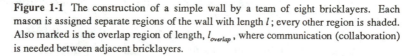

Figure 1-1 The construction of a simple wall by a team of eight bricklayers. Each mason is assigned separate regions of the wall with length l; every other region is shaded. Also marked is the overlap region of length, $l_{overlap}$, where communication (collaboration) is needed between adjacent bricklayers.

We note that the wall could in fact be divided either by horizontal or vertical sections. We chose the latter since it exhibits the most natural concurrency, whereas as shown in Fig. 1-2, one cannot easily assign separate bricklayers to individual horizontal courses of the wall. The latter decomposition corresponds to an inherently sequential formulation of the algorithm, which can only yield a useful speedup by using the masons in the "pipeline" scheme shown in Fig. 1-2.

If we consider Fig. 1-1 again, we note that there is some interruption of work where neighboring sections assigned to different bricklayers are to be joined. Let us define an *efficiency* ε by:

$$\varepsilon = \frac{S}{N} \tag{1-1}$$

where N is the number of bricklayers used to build the wall S times faster than a single bricklayer.

We may note that an obviously necessary condition to obtain high efficiency (ε ~1) is that the section assigned to an individual bricklayer is "large enough." Let l be the length of such a section. Further assume that we can quantify the amount of "overhead" (communication, collaboration, or confusion between neighboring masons) in the definition of a characteristic length $l_{overlap}$ centered on the section joints. In this notation, we can write:

$$\varepsilon \sim 1 - \frac{c \; l_{overlap}}{l} \tag{1-2}$$

where the constant c, of order unity, depends on the nature of the overlap problem. One might estimate that $l_{overlap}$ is about one meter.

Concurrent Construction of a wall using N = 8 bricklayers.
Decomposition by horizontal section.

Figure 1-2 The masons working in a pipeline to build the wall decomposed by horizontal sections; adjacent courses, assigned to separate bricklayers, are shaded.

We can now summarize the key issues in the concurrent construction of Hadrian's Wall.

· Concurrency is achieved by dividing the wall into a number of smaller walls, each assigned to an individual bricklayer. Typically, construction of long walls can use a very high degree of concurrency.

· The decomposition will be efficient as long as each bricklayer builds a wall whose length is greater than some minimum value l_{min}. In the notation of Eq. (1-2), we can estimate:

$$l_{min} \sim 10c \; l_{overlap} \tag{1-3}$$

to obtain at least 90% efficiency. Note that this criterion is independent of the number N of bricklayers.

- Each bricklayer is performing a job similar to the one that he or she would have undertaken for the task of building the whole wall. However, as illustrated in Fig. 1–3, the work differs from the latter in two ways. Firstly, one is building a different (smaller) wall, and secondly, the small wall has unusual edge conditions. Instead of the usual straight edges, we have novel edge (boundary) conditions involving a jagged join and requiring communication with the neighboring bricklayers in order to coordinate the joining process.

The complete problem.

The sub task performed by an individual bricklayer.

Figure 1-3 A comparison of the full problem (completion of all of the wall) with the subproblem (the part built by an individual layer) in the decomposition of Fig. 1-1.

The three features of our analogy above correspond to three very general features of concurrent computation. A typical computation consists of an algorithm applied to a large dataset which we consider as forming a *domain* which includes many *members*.

- Concurrency is achieved by domain decomposition. The underlying dataset is divided up into parts or *grains* and one grain is assigned to each computer.
- Large speedups can be obtained as long as each computer contains a grain of large enough size. We can usually quantify this through a relation (like Eq. (1-2)) between the efficiency (speedup divided by the number N of computers) and the grain size.
- Each computer uses an algorithm similar to that employed in the conventional (sequential) approach. There are two key differences. Firstly, each node involves an underlying dataset that is quantitatively different, as it corresponds to only a part of the domain and not the full domain. Secondly, the boundary conditions on the algorithm tend to involve communication with neighboring computers.

In Chap. 3, we will give a simple example from image processing of the validity of the analogy and the proposed general principles of concurrent computation. Chap. 5 and successive chapters will give many confirming and more detailed examples. It is somewhat remarkable how close an analogy may be drawn between concurrent computation and "mundane" human problems. The analogy deepens in the following subsections.

1-3.2 The Concurrent Architecture for the Construction of Hadrian's Wall

In Fig. 1-4, we illustrate the organizational structure needed for our problem. Each bricklayer needs to communicate with his or her neighbor, and we may further need a foreman who is able to send or receive information to and from all the people on the job. Naturally, if the supervisory function gets too large, we will replace the single foreman by a hierarchically organized management team.

Topology of bricklayers is one dimensional - the same as the wall.

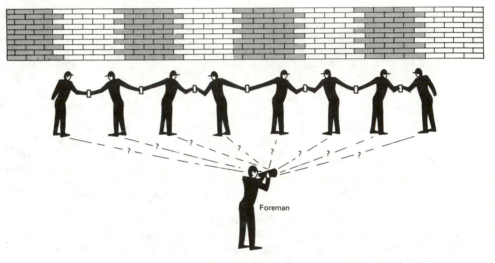

Foreman

Figure 1-4 The one dimensional topology needed by the team of masons; the foreman's interaction with the team could be either broadcast (with a megaphone) or communicated to one mason and passed down the line.

It is apparent that the needed architecture or topology is that of a one-dimensional line. This topology is naturally identical to that of the wall itself. A recurring theme in this book is that the topology or architecture of the concurrent processor should match as closely as possible the topology of the problem it is designed to solve.

The hypercube topology was chosen for the machines built at Caltech because it is a "rich" topology that includes or matches the structure of many interesting problems. Our bricklayer analogy has been designed to illustrate concurrent computers (like the hypercube) in which each node of the machine has its own memory. However, the foreman as described above could be regarded as a kind of shared memory bank, and in fact our bricklaying example is perhaps more easily mapped into machines like the RP3, under construction at the IBM Yorktown research lab, which incorporate both distributed and shared memory [Pfister 85]. It has been found that in practical problems, one can easily add the "foreman" concept to a hypercube of identical workers; in Chap. 4, we will assign this supervisory role to a *control process* (*or*), which in the Caltech machines is embodied in a separate computer distinct from the "nodes" of the hypercube. The control mechanism can and often should be more elaborate. The computers can have both "worker" and/or supervisory (control) roles. As in the human example, one can have several foremen to increase the communication between the workers and management. For instance, in the Mark II and III hypercubes built at Caltech that will be discussed in Sec. 2-9, we use a control processor for every 32 "worker computers"; a 128-node machine has four control computers.

1-3.3 Irregularities in Hadrian's Wall

The decomposition in Fig. 1-1 is particularly simple, since we assumed that the wall is of uniform height and that each worker lays bricks at the same rate. Let us retain the latter assumption but relax the condition of wall uniformity. In Fig. 1-5, we show a wall with variable height. In order to balance the work between the different bricklayers, we must still assign them equal numbers of bricks, but this no longer corresponds to equal lengths of the wall. Workers assigned to locations where the wall is higher are responsible for shorter lengths of it. This leads to increased difficulties in the overlap region (between workers) as adjacent bricklayers are on different courses at a given time. Nevertheless, in spite of the additional planning necessary, the height irregularities do not pose any fundamental problem.

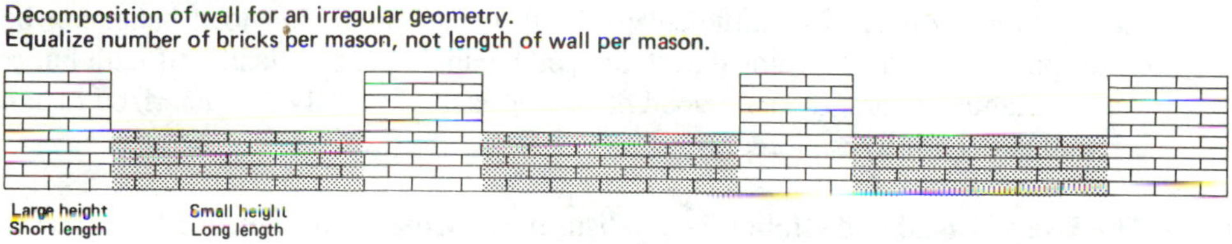

Decomposition of wall for an irregular geometry.
Equalize number of bricks per mason, not length of wall per mason.

Large height   Small height
Short length   Long length

Figure 1-5 A wall of irregular geometry; again the shading indicates a possible decomposition.

In concurrent computation, we will also find geometrically *regular* problems to be the easiest. These are analogous to the wall with constant height. The decomposition usually corresponds to simple geometrical partitions which minimize the volume of required communication. *Irregular* geometries, typified by the wall with varying height, require more sophisticated techniques for problem decomposition which we will discuss in several examples later in the book.

1-3.4 Inhomogeneities in Hadrian's Wall

In Fig. 1-6, we propose a further (hypothetical) complication in the wall-building task, by adding a set of gargoyles at irregular intervals. Now we have an *inhomogeneous* problem containing more than one distinct type of member (here bricks and gargoyles). Furthermore, the different members may be associated with very different construction times (which may be unpredictable). Now the planning process and the assignment of workers becomes much more difficult. As different gargoyles are associated with different and unpredictable amounts of work, and possibly even different types of workers, we may need to employ *dynamic planning* in which workers are assigned to projects as they become needed.

An inhomogenous wall with decoration.
Best decomposition uncertain.

Figure 1-6 An inhomogeneous wall; the presence of the gargoyles suggests the need for a complicated and perhaps dynamic decomposition in order to equalize the work for each mason.

In concurrent computation, inhomogeneous problems are again the hardest, and require an adaptive planning process that is called *dynamic load balancing*. We will survey our current knowledge of this in Sec. 3-8. It is not yet known how well dynamic load balancing will work in general and therefore how broadly applicable concurrent computation may be to inhomogeneous problems. This is in some contrast with the irregular problems discussed in the last subsection. Such problems only require *static balancing* or *decomposition*; it is sufficient to do all the planning and load balancing before the computation starts. It seems that static load balancing is practically difficult but conceptually straightforward; dynamic load balancing is not as easily characterized in general and remains to be fully explored.

1-3.5 The Use of Local and Global Parallelism in the Construction of Hadrian's Wall

The use of multiple bricklayers (or more generally, domain decomposition) is an example of a *global parallelism*. However, we can also realize *local* speedup if individual workers can perform several tasks at the same time. For instance, one worker might hold the brick with one hand and the mortar and trowel with the other. Many such trivial examples of *local parallelism* can easily be listed.

The simplest microprocessors employ little local parallelism; each instruction is executed sequentially, with each one finishing before the next can begin. However, more sophisticated and powerful computers incorporate increasing degrees of local parallelism. For instance, new instructions can be fetched while the others are being interpreted and executed. The INTEL 8086 used in the Caltech Cosmic Cube and Mark II hypercube concurrent computers uses some local parallelism, while machines like the CRAY supercomputer take particular advantage of local parallelism with their *pipelined* arithmetic units. It seems clear that future concurrent computers will be constructed from nodes incorporating pipelined arithmetic. As in the human example, the goal should be to exploit both local and global parallelism. Local and global parallelism yield speedups that are largely independent of one another.

For those with programming experience, we can contrast local and global parallelism in a different way. The former corresponds to concurrency in the operations executed within the innermost DO or FOR loop of the program; the latter to the outer DO or FOR loop being run concurrently. Typically, an outer loop runs over members of the domain and so gives rise to the domain decomposition that we have described. An inner loop often runs over internal indices labeling each member and only manipulates one or a few members of the domain. These ideas are illustrated in the symbolic computer code below.

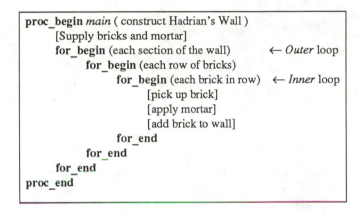

```
proc_begin main ( construct Hadrian's Wall )
      [Supply bricks and mortar]
      for_begin (each section of the wall)        ← Outer loop
            for_begin (each row of bricks)
                  for_begin (each brick in row)   ← Inner loop
                  [pick up brick]
                  [apply mortar]
                  [add brick to wall]
            for_end
      for_end
      for_end
proc_end
```

Code 1-1 Pseudocode describing the construction of Hadrian's wall. Domain decomposition corresponds to the loop labeled *Outer* and local parallelism to that labeled *Inner*.

1-3.6 External Input/Output and Hadrian's Wall

The question of I/O (Input/Output) has always been a thorny one with regard to computers. Any problem involving the analysis of data (perhaps those collected by some instrument) usually requires high bandwidth data transfer with some external storage device, as well as large computational power. Displays of the results of a calculation also typically require the rapid output of large amounts of data.

In Fig. 1-7, we see that Hadrian's Wall requires some large amount of "input bandwidth" to deliver the necessary bricks and mortar. Our domain decomposition allows one to achieve this naturally with each bricklayer being supplied by a separate truck. We note that current truck technology is reasonably well matched to the supply needs of people. If we had alternately chosen to build the wall with a single superhuman being, we would also have had to develop a supertruck capable of supplying bricks and mortar at the appropriate "super" rate.

We encounter the same issues with concurrent computers. It is possible to obtain high I/O bandwidth by using separate input/output channels to each node of the system. One achieves an increase by a factor N (the number of nodes) in the bandwidth. The

Concurrent brick delivery - high bandwidth connection to "outside world."

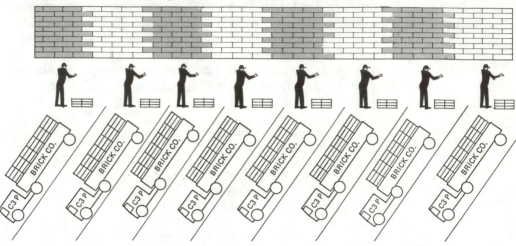

Figure 1-7   An example of concurrent data acquisition; delivery of bricks to the masons.

initial hypercube class machines are constructed of modest nodes for which it is easy to
find I/O devices of commensurate performance. On the other hand, the use of very
powerful sequential computers like those comprising the CRAY-XMP make it difficult to
match the processing speed to the usually slower data storage devices.

1-4 Farming as a Two-Dimensional Decomposition

For millenia, society has found it necessary to farm large areas of land to be able to
grow necessary food. Predictably this problem is also solved by domain decomposition.
The land is subdivided, first into farms and then into fields, with separate workers in each
farm. As illustrated in Fig. 1-8(b), it is usual to divide the domain into subblocks that are
roughly square. We might assume that this is chosen over, say, the one-dimensional
choice also shown in Fig. 1-8(a) because it minimizes edge (communication) effects.
Such square subblock decompositions will be discussed later in the book and shown to be
natural for a wide range of two-dimensional problems including partial differential equations, particle dynamics, matrices, and image processing.

We can quantify the difference between Figs. 1-8(a) (one-dimensional) and 1-8(b)
(two-dimensional) decomposition. Suppose we have N farms, with $N = 16$ in the figure,
and that each farm has one field with an area of n square miles. In the two-dimensional
case, the fields are of size $\sqrt{n}$ by $\sqrt{n}$ miles and in a one-dimensional decomposition $\sqrt{nN}$
by $\sqrt{n/N}$ miles. We see that for large N, the total length of the roads running around the
fields is $N\sqrt{nN}$ in 1-8(a) and $2N\sqrt{n}$ in 1-8(b). Thus, we find that the ratio of lengths is:

$$\frac{\text{road length in one-dimensional case}}{\text{road length in two-dimensional case}} = \frac{\sqrt{N}}{2} \qquad (1\text{-}4)$$

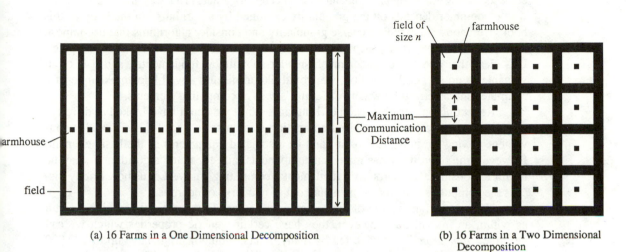

(a) 16 Farms in a One Dimensional Decomposition

(b) 16 Farms in a Two Dimensional Decomposition

Figure 1-8 Farmland divided by roads or property lines (solid lines) in either a one or two dimensional decomposition. Communication costs are minimized by the two dimensional choice.

This can be interpreted as a quantitative measure of the increased communication cost for the one-dimensional case. We will find exactly the same ratio when comparing different matrix decompositions in Chap. 10. The generalization of the ratio in Eq. (1-4) for arbitrary systems will be discussed in Sec. 3-5.

Contrasting the farming example with Hadrian's Wall, we see that workers are organized with a two-dimensional communication mesh in the former case and with a one-dimensional mesh in the latter. Human beings constitute a "node" for society that is quite flexible; individual humans are capable of communicating within a variety of network topologies. Extending this analogy to the case of the hypercube, a machine was built that could be matched to a variety of topologies. Although its communication capabilities are underutilized for many problems, the flexibility of the hypercube represents a reasonably general purpose design.

1-5 The Brain

Current digital computers are constructed from macroscopic components–chips, circuit boards, etc.–that are themselves made from very many (more) fundamental units. High density memory and microprocessor chips currently contain 100,000 to one million transistors, and a reasonable (but still uncertain) extrapolation of current technology is expected to lead to future chips with factors of a hundred *more* transistors. Depending on the scale or granularity with which we view digital computers, we can find very different basic entities. At the small scale, we find transistors. These are organized modularly into chips, several chips form a circuit board, and these are joined together to form a conventional sequential computer. Finally, a concurrent computer like the hypercube consists of several sequential machines connected together. The way that we view the whole computer depends on the granularity exploited by algorithms. In the body of this book, we choose to exploit a coarse granularity and consider algorithms that decompose problems into large grains, each of which can be calculated by a conventional computer. It is clear that one can consider much smaller subunits as fundamental, and it is often valuable to do so. In this section, we would like to discuss a well-known example of a computer characterized by widely differing "sizes" of computing elements.

Reflecting on our discussion of Hadrian's Wall, we could have looked at different scales and seen very different-sized computing elements. In Sec. 1-3, we found it convenient to view an individual brain (and its associated equipment) as the basic element. However, the brain itself has many subcomponents, and for many algorithms it may be useful to consider the neuron as a fundamental computing entity. Let us now briefly discuss the computers constructed by nature out of networks of neurons.

Neurons and the nature of their interconnects vary from species to species, as well as within an individual. However, they have certain generic properties which we can describe. A *neuron* is a device fed by many inputs. Some neurons have up to 100,000 such inputs via an antenna-like structure referred to as a *dendrite*. The connections are usually close appositions between neurons across which chemical signal carriers diffuse. This type of connection is called a chemical *synapse*. Each neuron connects to some number of downstream neurons via its *axon* (extending several meters in some cases). Axons are used both to convey information to other neurons and to forward sensory data from the various input devices used by the brain to gather information. Each of these components is seen clearly in a drawing of several neurons made in 1888 by the famous neuroanatomist Ramon y Cajal, and reproduced in Fig. 1-9. A neuron performs a complicated analog calculation based upon its input, which in its simplest form may perhaps be idealized as a weighted sum of the form $r_i = \sum_j w_{ij} \, n_j$, where r_i is response of neuron i to all those neurons j connected to it. The neuron-to-neuron signal n_i can be thought of as digital, with a single binary value. A signal travels down the axon if and only if n_i "spikes," or exceeds a certain threshold Th_i. Thus we can write:

$$n_i = \theta \left(\sum_j w_{ij} n_j - Th_i \right) \qquad (1\text{-}5)$$

where the θ function takes value 1 or 0 depending on whether its argument is positive or negative.

One finds neuron-based computers, systems relying on the simultaneous activity of many neurons, performing a variety of functions–memory, sensory, pattern recognition, control, and "higher" reasoning. In effect, therefore, the nervous system is a concurrent processor. In many of the functions it performs, it is vastly superior to that of current digital computers. So in neural networks, we find a flexible, powerful concurrent computer which is in many cases the most sophisticated implementation of concurrent processing yet discovered. The specific algorithms used by the brain are the subject of intense theoretical and experimental study and are outside the scope of this book. In Fig.

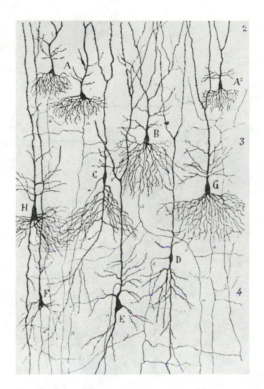

Figure 1-9 A drawing of ten neurons showing nuclei with a tangle of dendrites, axons, and collaterals emanating from them drawn by Ramon y Cajal in 1888.

1-10, we see a "wiring diagram" for the parts of the brain used in interpretation of some sensory information from a rat. We see that just as we group transistors into various chips, nature has grouped together collections of neurons into macroscopic modules which are interconnected in a complicated way. It is interesting to note that at whatever level we look, a collection of bricklayers, a collection of neural modules, or at neurons themselves, we observe separate and distinct computing elements communicating with each other by messages.

In contrasting chips with neural networks, we see both differences and similarities. Chips run at a cycle time of from 10^{-7} seconds (nowadays) to an "ultimate" 10^{-9} seconds. Neurons are much slower, operating at a maximum frequency of about 1000 hertz, or a cycle time of 10^{-3} seconds. Chips are characterized by a very regular interconnect between transistors, and typically tolerate no errors. It seems that neural networks show much more variety, both in interconnect and speed. Moreover, the brain is found to be fault tolerant and continues to function even if neurons or their connections die or are "incorrect." Neurons have a remarkable multiplicity of connections, sometimes as many as 100,000, although it is worth noting that an axon acts in some sense like a bus,

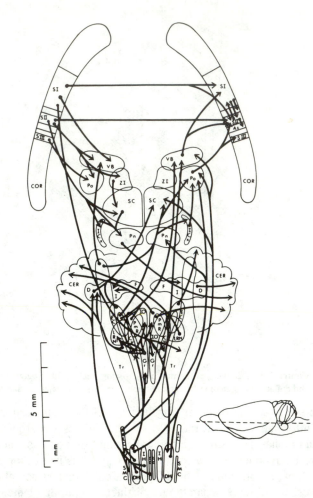

Figure 1-10 The brain of a rat showing its division into modules (cortex and nuclei) with a complicated interconnect; each module contains very many neurons. The "wiring diagram" is determined experimentally for the interpretation of tactile sensory data (W. Walker, unpublished).

broadcasting information to all neurons swept out by it and its collaterals. In Chaps. 9 and 10, we will discuss algorithms requiring full or partial broadcasts, and in Sec. 3-5 we will see that in some sense they are characterized by a counterintuitive low system dimension characterizing information flow. Comparing total system sizes is difficult; perhaps we will eventually design and build a digital computer network of some 10^{13} transistors. Estimates of the number of neurons in the brain vary; $10^{11} - 10^{14}$ or more neurons in total have been estimated. What about performance? Even if we avoid software and algorithmic issues, it is hard to compare even raw speeds! The digital computer is much faster per component, but how do we correctly include a factor in the neural network's performance corresponding to the number of interconnects? This could increase the estimated performance of the brain by a factor of 10^5. We need to better understand the algorithms used by the brain. There are also differences in architecture; the brain consists of many specialized devices: a portion of the cortex specializes in vision, a portion on audition, etc. This is one of many possible architectures for a digital computer. It would seem fair to say that future digital concurrent computers could have a performance in the same league as that of the brain—a challenging if disquieting expectation.

1-6 Nature's Concurrent Processors

There are many challenging questions to be answered about nature's computer—the brain—and its fundamental element—the neuron.

- What algorithms are used by the brain and why is it so good at some problems (e.g., pattern recognition) and so bad at others (e.g., arithmetic)?
- How is fault tolerance built into the algorithm or the "hardware"?
- Is the size of the brain determined by algorithmic, evolutionary, or physiological issues?

At a crude level, some of the algorithms used by the brain are similar to those found in this book. Nature makes extensive use of domain decomposition or "place encoding." In vision, the separate pixels recorded by the eye are spatially distributed in the brain just as in the image-processing example that will be shown in Sec. 3-3. However, nature goes further by distributing the domains formed by separate orientations, velocity, and colors of objects over the neural network. Studies of the hearing system show that separate frequencies, phases, and amplitudes detected by the ear are similarly decomposed. So we can use domain decomposition whether we are decomposing a wall over masons or an individual's field of view over the cortex.

Let us compare two ways of increasing the size of nature's computer by a factor N: in the first, we consider N humans and in the second, a single being whose brain has N times as many neurons as normal. In principle, the second choice has much greater computing power because all parts of the brain retain high bandwidth communication. Any two humans can communicate, but usually at a bandwidth that is a few bits per second (higher if we exchange visual information with movies), whereas internally, the brain must be capable of bandwidths that are at least a factor of 10^{12} better! To illustrate this point, consider recognition of a particular pattern in a picture. We divide the picture in two and allow two humans to each see just one half; the two partners must converse (exchange information) in order to complete the pattern recognition. Clearly, this method is clumsier and slower than using a single human for this problem. However, the computer formed from several individuals, although suffering from low internal bandwidth, does have the advantage of increased bandwidth for the receipt of external data. When we compare small grain-size (roughly neuronlike) silicon computers to large grain-size (roughly brainlike) computers, we do *not* find the same communication problem; large grain-size silicon computers can be built with high enough internode communication bandwidth that one can decompose arbitrary problems over the large grain-size units. In particular, one can expect that pattern recognition will not slow down when one increases the number of computers as it did in the example above with several humans compared to one. Concurrent computers can obtain speedups comparable to the number of nodes for problems of pattern recognition. This discussion calls attention to the importance of node to node bandwidth in concurrent processors.

If we consider colonies of bees, ants, or other such insects, we see examples in which many rather small brains are joined together in tightly organized societies that can tackle problems that are insoluble for an individual. This society is kept in place by communication between its elements, the individual bees or ants. This communication is again of very low bandwidth, with local transmission of messages occurring through chemical signals. We might expect that the modest computing power of each element and the low interelement bandwidth fundamentally limits the power of this concurrent computer. Even if we were to match the total number of neurons, a collection of ants could presumably never match a human brain.

Nature has shown us several interesting analogies. We see many different concurrent computers, each employing message-passing between elements and incorporating a form of domain decomposition as the algorithmic technique. In this view, communication bandwidth between elements can be crucial in determining the problems and decompositions that may be profitably addressed. We find it useful to look at hierarchies of computers whose fundamental entities have very different grain sizes. In nature, these range from neurons to complete brains; while in concurrent computers, the range is from a simple node of the Connection Machine to an individual CPU of the CRAY-XMP.

2

General Issues in Concurrent Computing

2-1 The Driving Forces for Concurrent Computation

The recent excitement in computer science concerning concurrent computation stems from the happy confluence of a need and an opportunity. The need is for increased computing performance in a wide variety of fields in pure and applied university research, in industry, and in defense applications. The opportunity is the VLSI revolution which is expected to lead to dramatic cost-performance gains, particularly when exploiting concurrency. We will elaborate on these issues in Sec. 2-2 and 2-3. In Sec. 2-4 through 2-9, we review some of the many possible approaches to concurrent computing from the hardware, algorithmic, and software points of view. We note that some of these sections describe the forefront of a rapidly advancing technology, and may be only of historical interest when this book is published. We include this transitory material in order to provide a proper background for the rest of the volume. We urge the reader to supplement the reading of this chapter with some of the many excellent articles that regularly appear in the popular technological and professional scientific journals [Bell 85, Dongarra 87, Frenkel 86, Haynes 82, and Karplus 87].

We will use the generic term *supercomputer* to describe very high performance computers [Karin 87, Lazou 87]. This term has no precise definition; it is currently operationally defined as any machine with performance comparable to or greater than the line of computers offered by CRAY, CDC, ETA, and Japanese vendors for the price range of $10–30M. Clearly, the performance of a supercomputer thus defined, increases with time. Furthermore, as new concurrent architectures become established, one may see other kinds of machines setting the standard of performance.

2-2 The Need for and Use of Increased Computer Performance

The need for supercomputers has now become generally recognized; it has been documented by government committees who find increasing use of supercomputers by industry, universities, and the federal government. Recently, the National Science Foundation established a program with an annual budget of approximately $50M to provide supercomputer access to university researchers. In Japan, the well-advertised "fifth-generation project" is developing supercomputers primarily targeted at problems of artificial intelligence. Fujitsu, Hitachi, and NEC have each introduced commercial super-computers that compete directly with U.S. counterparts such as CRAY and ETA. In the United Kingdom, a recent report proposed an initiative similar to one already started by the NSF in the U.S. [Forty 85]. An increasing number of universities in the U.S., Japan, and Europe have or will soon purchase supercomputers [Duff 84, Duff 87].

Currently, commercial supercomputers are essentially fast sequential computers employing relatively little concurrency. One purpose of this book is to encourage the more cost-effective and potentially much more powerful approach to supercomputing based on concurrency. However, independent of questions of architecture, the increasing sales and demand for very fast sequential machines is an important indicator of the need for very high performance computers.

In scientific calculations–whether in university, industry, or government laboratory–this need is relatively easy to document and quantify [Wilhelmson 87]. Surprisingly common, for example, is the need to solve sets of three-dimensional partial differential equations defined over a large domain which is discretized into a total of 10^6 to 10^8 points [Peterson 85b]. Such problems require computers with gigabytes of total memory and several gigaflop performance (i.e., capable of several billion floating-point operations each second). Other scientific algorithms requiring supercomputer performance include simulations of nuclear explosions, many-body problems, and Monte Carlo approaches to problems in chemistry and physics [Kalos 86, Schilling 87, and Wallace 84]. Fields in which major scientific computer simulations are of great importance include:

Aerodynamics	Design of new aircraft.
Astrophysics	Evolution of galaxies, stellar and black hole dynamics.
Biology	Modeling of new genetic compounds, simulation of neural networks.
Computer Science	Simulation of chips and other circuits.
Chemistry	Prediction of reaction rates.
Engineering	Structural analysis, combustion calculations.
Geophysics	Seismic exploration and continuum physics simulation.
High Energy Physics	Calculation of properties of fundamental particles.
Material Science	Simulation of new composite materials.
Meteorology	Accurate prediction of the weather in real time.
Nuclear Physics	Weapon simulation.
Plasma Physics	Simulation of fusion reactions.

In fact, many observers now talk about a three-pronged approach to science, with theory and experiment being joined by computer simulation as complementary approaches to a problem [Buzbee 87, Goddard 85]. Indeed, it is being increasingly recognized in industry that computer simulation is an attractive alternative to conventional experimental tests. In this sense, a computer can be viewed in context as an "electronic wind tunnel" or as a complement to expensive structural testing of buildings and machines.

Supercomputing is perceived to be of great importance in the oil industry (the largest computer user outside the federal government), and to automobile and pharmaceutical companies. As another example, we find that supercomputers are now being used in Hollywood to create graphics for films and advertisements.

We can expect new scientific and industrial fields to be opened up by the advent of supercomputers. An obvious example is found in robotics; the availability of small supercomputers should allow the development of "serious" robots whose abilities are competitive with those of humans and which begin to realize the dreams of many science fiction writers. On a larger scale, we can imagine advanced supercomputers controlling a nation's defensive and offensive weapons. Such a concept is central to the much debated American Strategic Defense Initiative (SDI). Political questions aside, this research project is a good example of one which can never be adequately tested experimentally! SDI must rely on computer simulations of unparalleled complexity to verify its correctness. The sheer magnitude of this particular simulation has led some to doubt that the Strategic Defense Initiative can meet its goals. We should note that such uses of supercomputers will likely require major developments in the area of artificial intelligence, a field that is paced as much by algorithm and software issues as by limitations of hardware performance. However, in spite of these uncertainties, supercomputers are believed to be already central to many areas of the nation's defense effort. Such reliance includes both weapon simulation and the gathering and interpretation of data from worldwide sensors.

2-3 The Technical Opportunities

The past quarter century has been witness to remarkable progress in microelectronics. From the first integrated circuits in 1959, we have progressed to the chips that today contain up to one million separate components. Manifested in the form of 256 kilobit to 1 megabit memory chips and modern microprocessors (like the INTEL 80386, MOTOROLA 68020, and NATIONAL 32032), these chips allow the manufacture of single, printed circuit computers, incorporating several megabytes of memory and the ability to execute one to ten million instructions per second. It is this technology that has allowed the cost-effective construction of concurrent computers like the hypercube illustrated in Fig. 2-3. We attempt here to point out some implications of this technological trend [Seitz 84a, 84b, Dally 86].

The increasing density and corresponding functionality of chips improves the performance of computers in two distinct and important ways. The decreasing distance between components within a chip reduces signaling time and hence increases the speed at which it can run. However, the higher density also decreases the net cost per component, and although this does not directly boost performance, it reduces the dollar cost of obtaining that performance. This constitutes a fundamental motivation behind concurrent processing; if we can get the same performance at one-hundredth the previous cost, we should be able to use 100 such units together to get 100 times the performance at the original cost. One can relate both the higher density and shorter travel time to the gradually decreasing feature size of the gates and signal times on a chip. The feature size λ is currently between one and three μm in commercial chips. This size may be expected to decrease by an order of magnitude in the future. We note that the increasing performance obtained from lower travel time is at best inversely proportional to λ. However, the gain in cost effectiveness from increasing density is inversely proportional to λ^2 for current two-dimensional layouts. We see that one can expect more gain in performance per dollar from the higher density and concurrent computation (which is inversely proportional to λ^2) than from the greater speed of the chips (which is naively inversely proportional to λ). Thus it appears that concurrent computation will be crucial in exploiting this technology.

The successful reduction of feature size has been the subject of intense industrial and government research, such as that embodied in the VHSIC program. Technical aspects involved include the lithography method (electron beams may be needed below 1 μm) and the purity of the wafers from which the chips are fabricated. Feature size is by no means the only issue affecting the performance of chips. Some of the speed increase of recent chips such as the MOTOROLA 68020 and the new RISC architecture chips come simply from improved design of the microprocessor and its support chips. An extremely important advance in this field can be expected to come from the use of improved materials. Significant speed increases may result from the substitution of gallium arsenide for the currently used silicon and germanium. GaAs has an order of magnitude better electronic mobility than Si/Ge. Although challenging, the use of GaAs coupled with further decreases in feature size should be expected. This could lead to the upgrading of chips (currently with 2 μm feature size in Si and a clock speed of 100 ns) to attain clock times of order 1ns with 0.2 μm features in GaAs. We may thus project roughly a factor of 10,000 improvement in cost-performance, coming from a factor of 100 in clock speed, and another factor of 100 in the increased density. Apart from these "conventional" improvements, we may further anticipate a renewed interest in low temperature and superconducting devices which offer increased electron mobility and decreased waste heat production.

So far, we have discussed the technological opportunity offered by improvements in the chip technology. In order to build useful computers, we must be able to communicate between these devices. In fact, the size of today's large concurrent computers is limited by the ability to build reliable high speed communication, or in other words, by the technology required to wire the backplane [Palmer 86]. Communication is needed for transferring data from external devices as well as between chips. The latter is clearly crucial if we are to be able to use many–eventually tens of thousands–of these chips together in a concurrent computer. It is intuitively reasonable that if the chip can execute typical instructions in t_{instr} seconds, then one needs to be able to communicate information at the same rate, e.g., a computer which executes a 32-bit instruction in 1 μsec needs a communication bandwidth of approximately 32 megabit/sec. A future GaAs "miracle chip" executing a 64-bit instruction in 1ns would require 64 gigabit/sec bandwidth. The need for such communication speeds will become increasingly apparent through the detailed discussions in the rest of the book. It is interesting that these speeds are attainable through reasonable extrapolations of today's optical fiber technology. The current bottleneck is not the fiber itself but the availability of cost–effective optical–digital computer interfaces. There is, however, no reason to believe that these technological problems will not be solved.

2-4 The Computer Revolution–A Disquieting Dream

In the previous subsection, we suggested that one might be able to construct an *optically interconnected concurrent computer* of great power. Such a machine would consist of 10^4 to 10^5 individual sequential computers, which we call *nodes*. One or more complete nodes would be fabricated on a chip and would consist of a GaAs central processing unit with a clock speed of 1ns and with an associated memory capacity of some 10^8 bits. The resultant computer would have 10^{13} bits of total memory and be capable of 10^{14} (64-bit) operations per second. As already discussed in Sec. 1-5, this computational power rivals that attributed to the brain. In Sec. 2-5, we will note that this is not the only possible realization of the technological advances forecast in Sec. 2-3. One could also build machines consisting of a larger number of simpler nodes. These could be capable of many more (albeit simpler) operations per second.

Exploiting these technological opportunities requires corresponding advances in fault tolerance, algorithms, and software. We hope that this book will hasten the development of relevant concurrent algorithms and software. Our experience is limited to a modest number of problems implemented on machines with at most 1024 nodes. It is a bold extrapolation, but we see no reason to believe that society will not learn how to use these amazing future machines. As is the case with all technological advances, they offer the potential for great positive effect, or conversely, misapplication. As these technological advances are probably inevitable, our larger collective task may be to see that the developments actually prove to be a boon to mankind. In any case, we can predict a new computer revolution with parallel or concurrent machines of great power permeating life in future societies.

2-5 Choices in Concurrent Computing

Up to now, we have considered concurrent processing from a general point of view stressing the analogies between computation and more familiar examples. Now we wish to concentrate on concurrent computation and survey some of the issues that seem to be important. In Sec. 2-6, 2-7, and 2-8, respectively, we will discuss the hardware, algorithmic, and software issues. One of the goals is to indicate the limitations of the approach taken in this book. Our approach has been arrived at through a number of choices between exclusive alternatives. Some of these choices have been dictated by the concurrent systems with which we have experience and others by a desire to "get going" with the available limited tools. The general remarks in Sec. 2-6 to 2-8 are contrasted with choices made for this book in Chap. 3.

In the final section of this chapter, we will discuss some of the commercially available super or mini-supercomputers, with a bias to concurrent machines, and indicate to what extent the ideas presented in the book can be used on currently available machines.

2-6 Architecture and Topology

In the preceding discussion we have considered some very different kinds of concurrent processors. The brain, consisting of very many small elements (neurons) with a complex interconnection, was one example. A team of masons comprised of sophisticated elements (individual bricklayers) and a simple one-dimensional interconnection, is another.

With computers, we are faced with similar choices. We can choose either a large or small node as the basic processing element, and we refer to this measure as the *grain size* of the concurrent computer.

Small grain-size machines currently have memories with upwards of about 1000 bytes per processing element. Commercial machines with this type of node include the ICL DAP in England [DAP 79], the Goodyear MPP at NASA's Goddard Space Flight Center [Batcher 85], and the Connection Machine from Thinking Machines Corporation [Hillis 85]. The first Connection Machine CM-1 consists of 65536 very small nodes, each having a one-bit arithmetic unit and 4096 bits of storage. It is clearly not practical to store a significant program in such a node and so these machines operate in so-called SIMD mode, or *Single Instruction Multiple Data* [Frenkel 86, Gabriel 86, Hillis 87, and Siegel 79]. In SIMD mode, the same program instructions are executed simultaneously by every node. This is a more general approach than one might think at first, since the common instruction may lead to different results through the dependence on the data stored at each node. In addition, such machines allow individual nodes to ignore selected broadcast instructions based on the local value of flag variables. We will refer to small grain SIMD machines as *cellular computers*. An important class of SIMD small grain-size machines include *systolic arrays*. These are characterized by topology and node elements specialized for a particular application. Systolic arrays have been developed for matrix operations, but currently the most important applications for systolic arrays seem to be in the initial stages of image processing.

The brain may be an example of a cellular computer. Each element is a neuron which (in a very oversimplified fashion) we can consider to be repeatedly executing the simple instruction "if sum of inputs is greater than my threshold and no inhibitions are set, then output a spike." Neurons are, in fact, very complex and this may not be a very realistic model. Current work on neural networks may lead to man-made cellular computers with an architecture more similar to the brain than current digital computers. However, this possibility is outside the scope of this book.

The next class of computers includes those with a *large grain size*. These typically have at least 100K bytes of memory at each node. There are many machines of this class which we will discuss in Sec. 2-9. Such machines may be conceived as SIMD with common instructions, or as MIMD, *Multiple-Instruction Multiple-Data*, with each node executing a separate program or instruction stream. Typically, large grain machines are MIMD, since the MIMD approach provides more flexibility at little additional cost. Nature's MIMD processors were typified by the team of masons in Sec. 1-3, with each processing element represented by an "independent" worker. This example implies an interesting generalization. The node of an MIMD machine may itself consist of an MIMD collection of smaller subunits (the brain is divided into several cortex regions), or pushing the analogy farther, each node (or subunit of a node) might consist of a concurrent computer with SIMD elements such as the neuron. We might expect to find such a hierarchical arrangement (concurrent processors of concurrent processors) in silicon computers. The CEDAR project at Illinois [Kuck 86] is a good example of this kind of hierarchy. We noted in Sec. 1-6 that there is a good reason that the most powerful processors are either small grain-size SIMD or large grain-size MIMD. The intermediate case, modest memory MIMD, has insufficient memory to be a flexible computer and is not intrinsically as powerful as the cellular computer which maximizes its computing capability at the expense of memory. We will analyze this issue in Sec. 3-6. One could further divide the large grain concurrent machines *into medium grain-size* computers like the current hypercubes or *large grain-size* computers like the CRAY-XMP. However, we will not need to make use of this refinement in the present discussion.

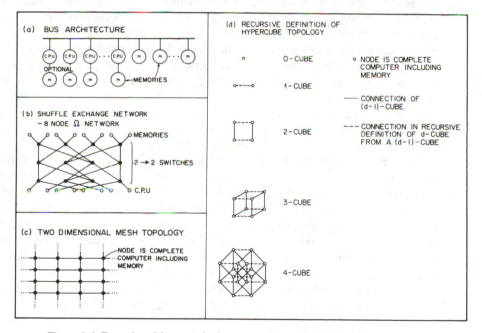

Figure 2-1 Examples of four popular interconnection topologies for concurrent computers: (a) A common Bus, (b) An omega network switch connecting several CPU's (processing unit for program execution and arithmetic calculation) to a bank of shared memories. In (a) and (b), one generally has both shared and local (distributed) memories. The other two diagrams show designs with solely distributed memory, (c) A two dimensional mesh, (d) Hypercube topologies of dimensions up to 4.

In addition to grain size, another relevant variable is the nature or topology of the interconnection between the processing elements. Some of the possible choices are illustrated in Fig. 2-1. An important class of concurrent computers makes use of *shared memory*. These machines feature a common memory that can be accessed by all the processing elements. The simplest design of this class is shown in Fig. 2-1(a) and uses a common bus, or communication channel, to allow the individual processing elements to access the shared memory. This design is particularly appropriate if N, the number of processing elements, is small. However, since the effective bus communication time in this approach is proportional to N, the design becomes inadequate for large N. We will learn in Sec. 3-5 that many important algorithms require a communication bandwidth per processor that is independent of the number of processors. A more sophisticated shared memory design is typified by 2-1(b) and involves a switch connecting the processing units to the shared memory. The so-called omega network switch in Fig. 2-1(b) has a communication time that increases in proportion to $\log N$ with increasing system size [Hockney 81b]. In Figs. 2-1(c) and 2-1(d), we illustrate a different class of machine characterized by a *distributed memory*. In pure distributed memory machines, the basic processing element includes local memory to the exclusion of shared or global memory. We are faced with the choice between topologies like the two- or three-dimensional mesh, in which the number of channels needed per node is independent of N, or alternatively, architectures like the hypercube in which the number of channels per node grows logarithmically. Distributed memory machines go hand-in-hand with the message-passing model for concurrent computation. It is interesting that all of our examples of "concurrent processors" seen in nature use the message-passing technique. Shared memory machines can be used in this fashion by using the common memory to implement a *full interconnect*, through which messages can be sent directly between any two processing elements. In the distributed memory architecture, messages can only be *directly* exchanged between pairs of nodes sharing a hardware connection; other messages can be sent but must be forwarded by intermediate elements. Shared memory machines have an attractive generality, but it can be a nontrivial challenge to arrange the algorithm or hardware to avoid memory "conflicts," or bottlenecks caused by the need for several processors to simultaneously access a common memory unit [Frenkel 86]. This problem can be alleviated by both a well designed network and by providing each processing node with its own local memory or cache, leading to a hybrid design approach incorporating features of both the shared and distributed memory classes.

A final salient feature in the classification of concurrent computers involves the nature of the node itself. We have already seen the distinction between small and large grain size which impacts the nature of the node processor. However, in either case, one can choose the architecture of the node itself to optimize its performance for particular algorithms. One may build nodes optimized for certain calculations. Examples might be nodes designed specifically for artificial intelligence, databases, or high energy physics. These particular choices have been made respectively in the Nonvon machine from Columbia [Gabriel 86 and Shaw 84], the commercial Teradata database engine [Schemer 84], and the specialized two-dimensional mesh built, again at Columbia, for lattice gauge theory calculations [Christ 86]. One will sometimes tailor the machine architecture or topology as, for instance, in the systems designed by Kunz and Nash for analysis of high energy physics experimental data [Gaines 86, Gaines 87]. Another choice may be to enhance the node for floating-point or scientific calculations. This would typically involve the use of local parallelism with vector or pipelined arithmetic units. This choice is implemented in the current American and Japanese supercomputers, including the CRAY machines that will be discussed in Sec. 2-9.

In summary, we have classified concurrent computers by four important attributes:
- Small grain-size SIMD versus large grain MIMD.
- Shared versus distributed memory.
- Topology of the interconnect between nodes.
- Features and specialization of the node.

The hypercube, which constitutes a major focus of this book, is a large grain-size MIMD, distributed memory, hypercube topology machine with a general purpose node.

The large number of possible hardware choices is a major factor in the current uncertainty and confusion in the field of concurrent computation.

2-7 Algorithms

It may be correctly argued that concurrent algorithms represent the centerpiece of the field of concurrent computation. There are two important provisos in this assertion. First we are somewhat sloppy in talking just about algorithms; we should more properly consider the combination of a problem and its associated algorithm. This is important, because as we will discuss in Sec. 3-1, interesting problems are a small subset of all possible problems, and we are surely only interested in algorithms that are relevant to real problems. A second caveat also concerns the "reality" of our research; we would like the hardware to be, where possible, driven by the problems and not vice versa. In reality, however, the dependency works both ways, and one need only study algorithms for which it is reasonable to build the hardware. Perhaps the appropriate strategy is first to study the hardware in general and then to motivate the specific hardware realization by detailed lessons from the algorithms. We can see this in the Caltech hypercube research; the initial algorithm work was motivated by the first hypercube hardware [Fox 84a], but the design of the next generation machines was strongly affected by lessons from the early algorithm work.

In most scientific fields there is currently very little understanding of the importance of considering concurrent algorithms. Researchers propose and evaluate techniques without considering their implementation on a concurrent computer. It is clearly essential to change this approach because independent of the controversy over the optimal architecture, there is no doubt that concurrency is the only route to high performance computation.

It is hard to find discussion of algorithms for large grain-size MIMD machines in the computer science literature. Some results from the pioneering Cm* project are surveyed in [Gehringer 87]. We hope that this book and the growing availability of commercial hypercubes will lead to a more widespread discussion of algorithms for these machines. As illustrated in Sec. 1-3 and discussed in depth in the body of the book, the natural approach involves dynamic domain decomposition. We note that domain decomposition fits algorithmically more naturally with distributed rather than shared memory machines. The concurrent algorithm divides an underlying data domain into parts in which each part is placed in the local memory of a node. On the other hand software considerations give strong motivation for the shared memory approach.

One can find more discussion of small grain-size algorithms in the literature. Much of this work is centered on systolic arrays and implementations for machines such as the DAP. These algorithms are often closely related to the large grain-size algorithms. In fact, although we will only explicitly discuss the large grain-size algorithms in this book, the techniques are, in fact, often applicable to small grain-size SIMD machines with straightforward changes as long as one specializes to regular problems. Dynamic and irregular algorithms such as those discussed in the later chapters of this book will often not be applicable to SIMD machines. The discussion of sorting in Chap. 18 will be an example in which SIMD and MIMD machines have very different optimal algorithms.

The discussions of finite difference and finite element problems in Chaps. 7 and 8 will illustrate an interesting point. For small problems, in one or two dimensions, the best algorithms involve explicit matrix inversion. This approach is impractical, however, for large (three-dimensional) problems where the preferred approach is to use iterative techniques. On sequential machines, this change is dictated by the outrageous memory requirements of the direct inversion method. It is interesting that although direct matrix inversion can be implemented quite well on a concurrent processor, the iterative techniques fit even more beautifully on such machines and offer the most "natural" concurrent algorithms. So we see that a quite general consideration regarding the best algorithm for a large problem incidentally yields an algorithm that is also better suited for concurrent implementation.

In summary, we must admit that there is no consensus stating which algorithms and problems are suitable for concurrent computers. In this book we will concentrate on those appropriate for distributed memory, large grain-size machines. We have, in fact, found only one essential requirement for successful concurrent algorithms: that the problem must be "large" in the sense we described in Sec. 1-3. The algorithms for shared memory or SIMD architectures are often closely related to those presented in this book, but we will not discuss them explicitly. We will, however, try to present our outlook in a manner independent (where possible) of the particular interconnection of the distributed memory computer. Shared memory machines can, as explained in Sec. 2-6 and 14-9, often be used in a way that emulates a fully interconnected machine. In this restricted sense, our algorithms and the corresponding explicit programs are fully applicable to shared memory concurrent computers.

2-8 Software

Software issues are closely related to those involving the algorithms and hardware. We believe that software should be the follower and not leader of these issues, and that the software environment and tools should be adapted to best match the algorithms and hardware. We are only just starting to learn about the latter two areas. As a natural consequence, current progress and understanding of software issues on distributed memory machines is not very advanced. We have taken an approach in this book that we believe to be sensible and necessary at this time, but it is born of expediency rather than careful study. We are motivated by the desire to learn about algorithms by implementing real problems on real machines. This motivation has required us to build a software environment whose development did not dominate the overall project.

The path we have followed in this book is to take a standard sequential software environment and modify it for the concurrent machines. In particular, we have written our programs in a conventional high-level language with the addition of subroutine calls to support the message-passing between processing elements.

An approach that has been very successful for local parallelism (such as vectorization on CRAYs) is the development of compilers that automatically decompose conventional sequential (e.g., FORTRAN) code. This is attractive since it allows one to run existing programs on the new concurrent machines [Athens 87, Dongarra 87, and Frenkel 86]. Although this approach has had success in many applications on shared memory machines, we believe that it cannot be the complete picture. Algorithms are often very different in their sequential and concurrent forms, and compilers cannot be expected to deal with such basic restructuring.

Although we are skeptical about the prospects for general decomposing compilers for distributed memory machines, we do believe that it is possible to build decomposing *packages* or high-level program development environments that greatly aid the user in specific fields. Examples might be software packages that automatically decompose matrix or finite element problems. These packages would differ from compilers as they are of limited scope and would incorporate or assume substantial algorithmic information. We see these packages as one of the ways in which the new concurrent machines will first be made generally accessible. We hope that the emerging availability of concurrent hardware will prompt new entrepreneurial software efforts aimed at developing concurrent packages for a wide variety of scientific, business, and industrial applications. A particularly ambitious project of this type is led by Ken Wilson who has pioneered the use of advanced computing ideas in science [Wilson 86].

There has been major computer science research into new concurrent languages. This is clearly important, and we need not only natural languages in which to program, but also natural ways to represent the mathematics of concurrent algorithms. A barrier to concurrency in conventional languages is often encountered in the form of global constructs such as *common blocks* (in FORTRAN) or *external variables* (in C). It is clearly attractive to consider languages in which processing and variables are localized into modules. This has motivated the development of so-called *object orientated*, or *functional* (applicative) languages. These styles of programming have received comparatively little practical use in scientific computation. A particularly interesting approach is called *dataflow*, and several groups have explored languages and hardware to implement it [Arvind 87, Dennis 74, Dongarra 87, Vegdahl 84]. In fact, the approach taken in this book could be regarded as *large grain-size dataflow*, since we employ processes whose execution is triggered (resumed) by the receipt of messages from other processes. Most dataflow research relies on hardware enhancements to optimize the concurrent execution of processes. We expect that another attractive approach will be to allow the combination of user and software aids, related to those for load balancing that we will discuss in Sec. 3-8, to schedule dataflow processes. We only have experience in the large grain-size case, but we expect that small grain-size dataflow can also be implemented well in distributed memory machines like the hypercube.

Although our approach provides comparatively little algorithmic motivation for shared memory machines, it is clearly easier to develop concurrent software for shared rather than distributed memory machines. Examples are the successful ALLIANT Shared Memory Concurrent Computer and, for instance, the recent work on compilers from IBM, Illinois, and Rice reported at the 1987 Supercomputer Conference at Athens [Athens 87]. Further, it is easier to automatically balance the load on shared memory machines. Although the current hypercube program development environment is clumsy, we have not found either software development or load balancing to be a limiting difficulty in our current work on the hypercube. It will require much more research and experience to evaluate software development as a possibly crucial advantage of shared memory machines.

In summary, there are many important and interesting software choices to be explored and practiced. In this particular exploration, we have made simple expedient choices which are further explained in Chaps. 4, 6, 14, and 15.

2-9 Today's Concurrent Supercomputers

The importance of concurrency in obtaining high performance has been recognized by many computer manufacturers. The most popular architecture has been the shared memory design with a common bus linking a modest number (from 4 to 32) of processing elements. This is a sensible architecture as it is feasible to build a bus capable of serving a few processors. Furthermore, such machines lend themselves to use as either multiprocessors (several jobs on machine; each job only occupies one node) or concurrent processors (one job spread over many nodes). Machines of this type are manufactured by CRAY, ETA, ALLIANT, ELXSI, ENCORE, SEQUENT, and FLEX to mention a few of the current vendors. The CRAY-XMP and CRAY-2, each incorporating four very powerful processors, are illustrated in the frontispiece and Fig. 2-2, respectively. A successful research machine of this type is LCAP developed at IBM, Kingston [Clementi 87] consisting of an IBM mainframe controlling several high-performance FPS array processors which are the nodes of this concurrent computer.

The shared memory design only scales to a large number of nodes if switches like that illustrated in Fig. 2-1(b) are employed. Such a connection is used in the BBN Butterfly machine whose node is based on the MOTOROLA 68000/68020 microprocessors [Schmidt 87]. A more sophisticated machine of this type, capable of extension to 512 nodes, is under construction at IBM's T. J. Watson research laboratories. This research computer, RP3, is based on ideas developed at New York University [Schwartz 80, Pfister 85, Gottlieb 86, and Dongarra 87].

We have already mentioned in Sec. 2-6 some of the very powerful small grain-size machines. The other major class of high performance concurrent machines commercially available use the hypercube topology, whose utility was first demonstrated in research at Caltech. There are currently four available commercial hypercube machines varying in maximum practical size from 128 to 1024 nodes [Rattner 85, Palmer 86]. These characteristics are compared in Table 2-1 and the machines themselves are shown in Fig. 2-3. This figure also includes some of the early hypercubes built at the Caltech Campus and the Jet Propulsion Laboratory [Seitz 85, Tuazon 85, Peterson 85a]. We have achieved a reasonable understanding of the issues that determine the performance of hypercubes and Table 2-1 only gives values for parameters which we will find to be important later in the book [Kolawa 85, Grunwald 87].

In Fig. 2-4 we show a recent distributed memory concurrent computer from MEIKO which is built around an innovative chip designed by INMOS. The T800 transputer chip has approximately 1 megaflop performance and four built-in communication channels [Askew 86, Barron 83, Pritchard 87]. It is similar to the chip used in the proprietary NCUBE hypercube but it has higher performance albeit with less onboard communication channels. The transputer has optimized support for OCCAM which has language constructs based on Hoare's CSP [Hoare 78], and which naturally supports a version of the loosely synchronous environment discussed in this book. We expect that essentially all the parallel algorithms and much of the explicit code developed in this book will be useable on transputer arrays. Another distributed memory computer SUPRENUM is under development at the GMD laboratory in Germany and is described in several articles in [Athens 87]. It has a crossed bus interconnection with a node similar to that of the Mark IIIfp hypercube.

As we will discuss in Sec. 3-5 and illustrate in many of the later chapters, the ratio t_{comm}/t_{calc} characterizing typical communication and calculation times is crucial to the performance of the hypercube. We have only listed this ratio for the hypercubes built at Caltech, because the value is very sensitive to factors that are certain to change shortly for the commercial machines. t_{comm} is strongly dependent on the software environment; the more functional the operating system the slower is the communication speed! The crystalline operating system used in this book, CrOS III, has been carefully developed so as to allow reasonable functionality without sacrificing performance. We may expect commercial machines to eventually offer a mix of high performance production "operating" environments coexisting with high functionality "debugging" systems. We should note that the ratio t_{comm}/t_{calc} is also highly dependent on the floating-point hardware used. As noted in the table, several hypercubes incorporate high performance ($\sim$ 10 megaflop per node) floating-point accelerators. These machines are characterized by large values of t_{comm}/t_{calc}. It is not known at present which algorithms can make use of these high performance units and what demands they will place on the communication system.

It is interesting to compare representatives of three current approaches to supercomputers.

- CRAY-XMP, large grain-size MIMD, 1-4 processors each with 8.5ns cycle time per node. Total memory can be up to 1024 megabytes with the SSD solid state storage device.
- Mark IIIfp hypercube, medium grain-size MIMD, 8-128 nodes, each with 60ns cycle time per node and up to 512 megabytes of total memory.
- Connection Machine CM-1, small grain size, SIMD, 65536 processors each with 250 ns cycle time per node and up to 32 megabytes of total memory.

These machines are based upon very different architectures, but each delivers supercomputer performance on *some* problems. The three different machines are optimal for different kinds of problems, but each can execute about 1000 MIPS (millions of instructions per second), and has from 100–1000 megaflops floating-point performance. It will be interesting to see how these fundamentally different approaches evolve.

Table 2-1: COMPARISON OF MULTICOMPUTERS
(As explained in the text, the table omits some items marked ...)

	Caltech (Seitz) Cosmic Cube	Caltech (JPL) Mark II	INTEL iPSC/1	AMETEK S14	Caltech (JPL) Mark IIIfp	NCUBE /10	Floating Point Systems T Series	INTEL iPSC/2	AMETEK S2010**	MEIKO Computing Surface**
Main Processor	INTEL 8086 5 Mhz	INTEL 8086 8 Mhz	INTEL 80286 8 Mhz	INTEL 80286 8 Mhz	MOTOROLA 68020 16 Mhz	Custom 7 Mhz	INMOS Transputer T414, 15 Mhz	INTEL 80386 16 Mhz	MOTOROLA 68020 25 Mhz	INMOS Transputer T800, 20 Mhz
Maximum Nodes/Machine	64	128	128	256	128	1024	128*	128	~1000	~1000
Memory/Node (Megabytes)	0.125	0.25	0.5	1	4	0.5	1	1→8	1→8	0.25→48
Maximum Machine Memory (Megabytes)	8	32	64	256	512	512	128	1024	~8000	~4000
Floating Point Processor	INTEL 8087	INTEL 8087	INTEL 80287	INTEL 80287	MOTOROLA 68882	Custom	None	INTEL 80387	MOTOROLA 68882	T800
Is Fast Floating Point Coprocessor(~10mflop Per node) available	No	No	Yes	No	Yes	No	Yes (Standard Equipment)	Yes	Yes	No
Typical 64-bit Floating Point Performance without fast coprocessor (flops/node)	20K to 30K	30K to 45K	30K to 45K	30K to 45K	150K	100K	...	250K	250K	500K
Measured Node to Node Communication Bandwidth (incl. software ovhd.) (Megabit/sec)	0.5	0.8	...	...	15	...	...	...	...	
t_{comm}/t_{calc} (see Sec. 3-5)	1.5 to 3	1.5 to 3	...	...	0.4 to 20 (20 with FP coprocessor board)	...	...	...	...	...

* Largest configuration delivered. Architecture can be extended.

** Not hypercube topology but rather mesh topology and no natural limit to system size.

Figure 2-2 The multiprocessor CRAY-2 Computer System incorporates major innovations in computer architecture and technology, including the largest common memory and fastest internal clock offered on a commercially available computer system. The CRAY-2 also makes use of an innovative new cooling technology. (Picture courtesy of Cray Research Inc.)

Figure 2-3
Hypercube Heaven—Pictures of hypercubes either constructed at Caltech or commercially:
(a) The Cosmic Cube with 64 nodes constructed by Chuck Seitz in the Caltech Computer Science Department

Figure 2-3 (b) A Mark II single node and the packaging into a 128-node system constructed at the Caltech Jet Propulsion Laboratory (JPL)

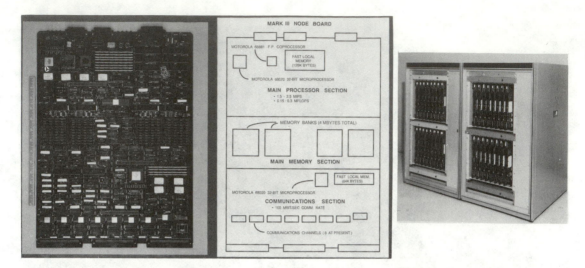

Figure 2-3 (c) A Mark III single node and the packaging into a 32-node system built at JPL

Figure 2-3 (d) A 16-node INTEL iPSC system with vector node enhancement. The node pictures show two boards; the basic iPSC node and the vector add-on. (Pictures courtesy of INTEL)

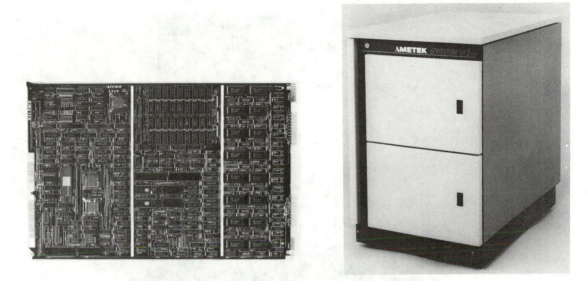

Figure 2-3 (e) A single board and its packaging into a 32-node AMETEK S14/32 system (Picture courtesy of AMETEK)

Figure 2-3 (f) A single board node for the FPS T Series Hypercube. The largest configuration delivered has 128 such nodes. (Picture courtesy of FPS)

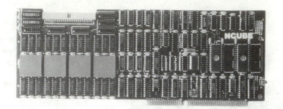

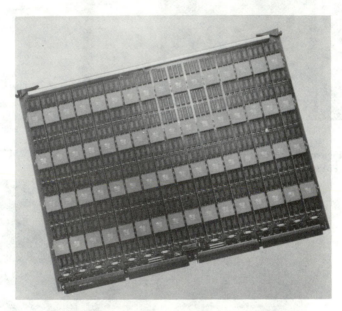

Figure 2-3 (g) A 4 node NCUBE PC hypercube add-on, a 64 node board and its packaging into a NCUBE/TEN system with 1024 nodes (Pictures courtesy of NCUBE)

Figure 2-3 (h) An 8 node, 68010-based hypercube built as an EE91 class project at Caltech by undergraduates S. Karlin and B. Suggs [Karlin 85]

Figure 2-3 (i) The PCcube array of IBM Personal Computers connected as a hypercube [Breaden 86]

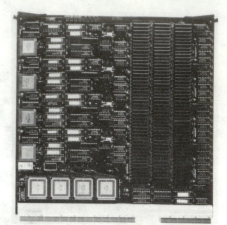

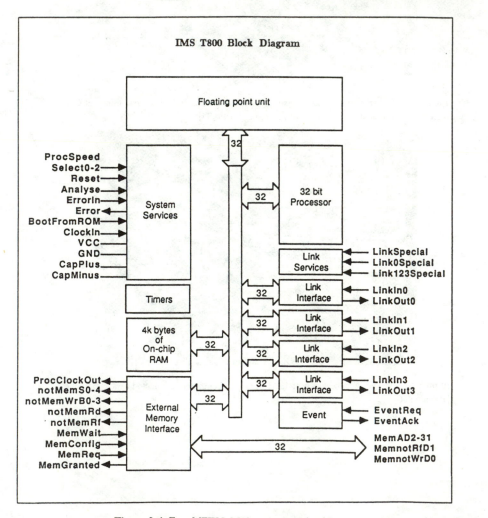

IMS T800 Block Diagram

Floating point unit

32

32 bit Processor

System Services

ProcSpeed
Select0-2
Reset
Analyse
ErrorIn
Error
BootFromROM
ClockIn
VCC
GND
CapPlus
CapMinus

Link Services — LinkSpecial, Link0Special, Link123Special

32 — Link Interface — LinkIn0, LinkOut0

Timers

32 — Link Interface — LinkIn1, LinkOut1

4k bytes of On-chip RAM

32

32 — Link Interface — LinkIn2, LinkOut2

32 — Link Interface — LinkIn3, LinkOut3

ProcClockOut
notMemS0-4
notMemWrB0-3
notMemRd
notMemRf
MemWait
MemConfig
MemReq
MemGranted

External Memory Interface

32

Event — EventReq, EventAck

32 — MemAD2-31, MemnotRfD1, MemnotWrD0

Figure 2-4 Four MEIKO M40 systems each with a total of 160 transputer based nodes. We also show a basic 4 node board and a schematic of the T800 transputer [Askew 86, Barron 83].

3

A Particular Approach
to Concurrent Computing

3-1 The Theory of Complex Problems and Complex Computers

In Chap. 1, and especially in Sec. 1-3, we have shown that the essential issues in concurrent computing have been known for a long time. We suggest that one of the reasons that the field is controversial and confusing at present is that concurrent computing is not usually discussed in a general framework. In other words, we believe that it will be fruitful to abstract the issues in concurrent computation, and then attempt to isolate the fundamental principles behind this general field. Some of our colleagues, in particular Wolfram at Illinois and Gell-Mann and Hopfield at Caltech, have pointed out that one can usefully discuss the idea of the theory of complex systems. We will briefly discuss this concept below and indicate its general usefulness [Fox 86a]. Some of our definitions will be necessarily vague or simplified; this reflects the tentative nature of the theory and its lack of an accepted structure.

A *complex system* is a large collection, in general, of disparate entities. These entities share a set of mutual dynamic connections. A dynamic complex system evolves according to a statistical or deterministic set of rules which relate the system at a later time to its state at an earlier time. Examples include the earth's atmosphere, in which the basic entities could be regarded as air density, pressure, velocity, etc., and in which the connections would be defined by the basic equations of motion. Another example of a complex system is a human society comprised of individual men and women (the entities) and governed by a rather more complicated connection set than in the global weather example. In this example, a given entity is typically connected to his or her family and friends, with other, often weaker, connections to business and recreational colleagues. In this case, the strongest connections are typically associated with spatially nearby individuals with, however, some "long-range" connections. By contrast, in the global weather example, the connections would only exist between neighboring points. As a final example, consider the complex system consisting of the set of coefficients for the infinite series defined by:

$$e^x = \sum_{n=0}^{\infty} a_n \, x^n \; ; a_n = \frac{1}{n!} \tag{3-1}$$

In this example, the operation of series multiplication $e^{2x} = e^x \cdot e^x$ constitutes a connection between the entities of the system which we identify with the coefficients of the series. These three sample complex systems are illustrated in Fig. 3-1.

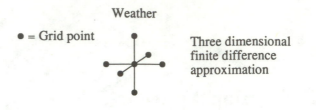

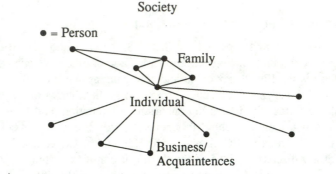

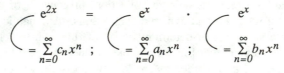

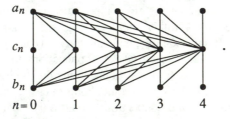

Figure 3-1 An illustration of the fundamental entities (grid points, people, coefficients) in three sample complex systems (weather, society, mathematics). We show the interconnection between different entities.

A concurrent processor is also an example of a complex system. In Figs. 1-9 and 1-10, we showed one such *complex processor* –namely the brain–viewed at two different scales. Another example is the hypercube, a *complex computer*, shown in Fig. 2-3. The fundamental task in concurrent processing is the use of one complex system to "solve," "calculate," or "simulate" another complex system. We will refer to the former system as the *processor* and the latter as the *problem*. In concurrent computation, the processor is a man-made device, the complex computer, whereas in other settings, the processor might consist of a complex system of people, neurons, ants, etc. As described in Chap. 2, complex computers can be and have been designed and built with a wide variety of fundamental entities (i.e., the basic computer nodes) and a wide variety of interconnection schemes.

Among our aims is to determine which complex computers are best applied to the various classes of complex problems. Mathematically, concurrent computing can be viewed as a mapping between one system (the problem) and another (the computer). In order to make this mapping concrete, we need to develop a means of classifying systems so that we can objectively parameterize our generalized problems and processors. Our goal is to find general results of the form:

"Complex computers with system parameters and properties of *such and such values* can be used to compute problems with *this and that values* for its respective defining parameters."

Very little work has been done in this area, but it is possible to describe some techniques that have proven useful in this context [Fox 86a]. We have chosen to make use of formalisms and ideas from mathematics and physics which are fields that study particular large complex systems.

An important subset of the properties of a complex system are those which characterize its geometrical or topological structure. This will be discussed further in Sec. 3-5. We will find that problems can be handled effectively as long as the computing system has a topology that contains, or is richer, than that of the problem system. Systems with significant static or dynamic inhomogeneities or variations can be usefully classified by parameters, such as temperature, used in statistical physics. Such inhomogeneous problems will only be briefly discussed in this book, mainly in Chaps. 16 and 17, because they require sophisticated tools somewhat beyond the scope of the present volume. In dealing with distributed memory MIMD computers like the hypercube, such inhomogeneous problems typically involve issues of load balancing. A short review of load balancing is given in Sec. 3-8.

The remainder of this chapter will focus on a single subclass of complex computers, the hypercube and its derivatives. In the context of the foregoing discussion in this section, the hypercube embodies three crucial features:

- The rich set of node-to-node connections ensures that the hypercube is appropriate for modeling systems with a wide variety of topological and geometrical structures.
- The flexible node–with a general purpose computing environment–allows use of the hypercube to address systems with essentially arbitrary basic entities; the computer may not be optimal for any particular problem, but with appropriate software it suffices to simulate most problem entities.
- The large amount of memory available to each node permits a "large" enough subproblem to be contained within each node, so that connections between nodes are relatively less important than connections mapped entirely within a single node. This is important when a close correspondence does not exist between the

structures of the problem and the machine. In this case of a topology mismatch, connections between machine nodes can be "costly" in a sense to be quantified in Sec. 3-5.

Thus we do not advocate the hypercube as a perfect or optimal machine, but rather one that is "good enough" to address and to begin to investigate a wide variety of problems. We are optimistic that this pragmatic approach serves to clarify the general concepts and issues in using all kinds of complex computers. We would suggest that progress in concurrent computation requires the consideration of "real problems." At first this seems inconsistent, for we have maintained that an "abstract" or "theoretical" understanding of the properties of complex systems is crucial to bringing order and general agreement to the field of concurrent computation. Why then should we build expensive hardware and software? Why not first retire to a desert island and "solve" these fundamental issues? A key difficulty with this purely theoretical approach is that we are not really interested in the most general system; we are interested in complex computers that can be built by man or grown by nature. We are fundamentally interested in those complex problems that arise from the works of nature, man, or his inventions. We conjecture that these particular complex computers and problems are a restricted subset of some larger space of complex systems. We further speculate that concurrent computation would be either very hard or impossible for the most general problem. However, the interesting, natural or man-made (and eventually computer-made), complex problems tend to be organized in a modular fashion so as to be handled in a straightforward manner on a concurrent computer. Thus we believe it is essential to base a meaningful study of concurrent computation on the study of real problems with real machines.

3-2 Large Grain-Size Message-Passing Computers

In Chap. 2, we surveyed possible concurrent architectures, and both there and in Sec. 3-1 we suggested why the hypercube is an interesting machine. To use the hypercube, we are forced to make certain choices. In the decomposition of a problem, we are required to divide it into large "pieces." In the design of an algorithm and its implementation, provision must be made for these pieces to communicate via message-passing. Each piece of the problem will be controlled by a separate computer program or *process*; one can have one or more processes running in each node of the hypercube. In this book, we will retain the simplicity of a single process resident in each processor. In Chaps. 4 and 22, we will generalize this with a virtual machine with one process for each of its nodes; however, when the virtual machine is mapped onto real hardware, there may be many virtual nodes on each physical node. We can classify the resulting computing environment as LAPMP or *Large Asynchronous Processes with Message Passing*, which is an important specialization used throughout this book. An alternative characterization of our programming methodology, explained in Sec. 3-4, is *large grain-size dataflow*. The algorithms and programs can be employed in similar form on machines other than the hypercube as long as they support a LAPMP environment. As discussed in Sec. 2-4, shared memory machines can support LAPMP, although this programming methodology does not fully exploit the special advantages of this hardware architecture. We can note that shared memory machines typically achieve their algorithmic concurrency from the same domain decomposition used on distributed machines like the hypercube. However, in the latter case one must make this domain decomposition explicit and this leads to LAPMP. A shared memory allows the decomposition to be implicit for the data, i.e., one must decompose the algorithm over the processors, but the data can be left undivided in the shared memory. This leads to the greater ease of programming for shared memory machines, even though there is typically no algorithmic need for the shared memory.

3-3 Decomposition and the Example of Image Processing

In discussing our subject in general, we encounter a difficulty with terminology. As stressed in Sec. 3-1, we are basically studying a wide variety of complex systems from many different problem areas. Unfortunately this leads to a plethora of possible names for the key concepts of system. We will introduce here a set of conceptual definitions in the hope of unifying our subsequent discussions. A similar choice was required in Sec. 1-3 in the discussion of Hadrian's Wall.

Each complex system is assumed to have associated with it a *domain* of objects or data. The first step in concurrent computation consists of *decomposing* this domain into several grains–one *grain* to be associated with each processor in the concurrent computer. As discussed in Sec. 3-2, one can, in fact, further divide the domain with each grain being formed of several granules. Each *granule* is then associated with a separate process and is controlled by a conventional sequential program. We will usually not distinguish grains from granules in this book. We have already used the term grain when we described the hypercube as having a large grain-size architecture.

Every domain is made up of "atomic" or basic entities which cannot be usefully decomposed further. We will define these basic entities as the *members* of the domain. Each grain of the system may contain many members. By definition, a system of large grain size is comprised of grains containing large numbers of members. Each member is typically labeled by one or more variables. If the domain is a box and the members are atoms contained in the box, then the members could be labeled by the position and velocity of the atoms. We will term the set of labels as the *components* of each member. Typically, one has relatively few components per member; the components might be called degrees of freedom for physical systems.

Other useful definitions concern the nature of the domain. A domain is called *homogeneous* if each of its members involves identical amounts of computation; otherwise, it is *inhomogeneous*. Hadrian's Wall was homogeneous as long as each brick was identical; the addition of ornaments rendered it inhomogeneous. A domain is called *regular* if its geometry is in some sense simple, e.g., a rectangular mesh; otherwise it is *irregular*. Clearly, each of these definitions admits some degree of subjectivity, and their precise applicability in a particular system may not always be clear. Section 1-3.3 included an example of geometrical irregularities in Hadrian's Wall. Table 3-1 illustrates these concepts for a variety of complex systems discussed in this book.

Another crucial property of the problems discussed in this book is not well known and we will coin the term *loosely synchronous* for it. We refer to a class of problems where there is some parameter which can be used to synchronize the different grains of the decomposed computation. This computational parameter corresponds to, for instance, time in physical simulations and iteration count in the solution of systems of equations by relaxation. Loosely synchronous problems are divided into cycles by this parameter which can be used to synchronize the different nodes working on the problem. We will explain this term by example as all problems discussed in this book fall into this class. We believe, in fact, that the majority of large scale computations are loosely synchronous and this is an essential property in ensuring that large concurrent processors perform well. Note that this synchronization refers to a property of the algorithm or problem and not to the machine as we will always consider the nodes to operate asynchronously, in the hardware sense, between the rendezvous' at the end of cycles.

Consider next the simple example illustrated in Fig. 3-2. This diagram shows a simple picture digitized as a square array of pixels. This image forms a two-dimensional data domain which is naturally decomposed for a 16-node concurrent processor as a 4×4 two-dimensional mesh with each node holding an 8×8 pixel subarray. It should be clear that strictly speaking, this is not a "real problem." A serious image-processing problem might involve a 4096×4096 pixel array with a large number of possible intensity or color values associated with each pixel. However, we can illustrate some important basic ideas with this example.

Given the domain in Fig. 3-2(a), we could consider various tasks such as:

(a)   Geometrical corrections if the image had been distorted when projected onto the pixel plane.

(b)   Convolutions used to filter the image. In Fig. 3-2(b), we illustrate a very simple noise elimination algorithm; any "on" pixel completely surrounded by "off " pixels is reset to "off."

(c)   Feature extraction or pattern recognition, e.g., recognizing the presence of the flag.

In tasks of the type (b), a common approach involves Fourier analysis. The decomposition in Fig. 3-2 is well suited to this technique when the underlying concurrent processor has a hypercube topology. This point is further explained in Chap. 11. Here however, we will discuss simpler convolution algorithms such as that illustrated in Fig. 3-2(b) or its generalization defined in 3-2(c). In the latter case, the processed value of the pixel at any point depends on its previous value as well as that of those other pixels that are adjacent in the array. This is a two-dimensional *nearest-neighbor* algorithm.

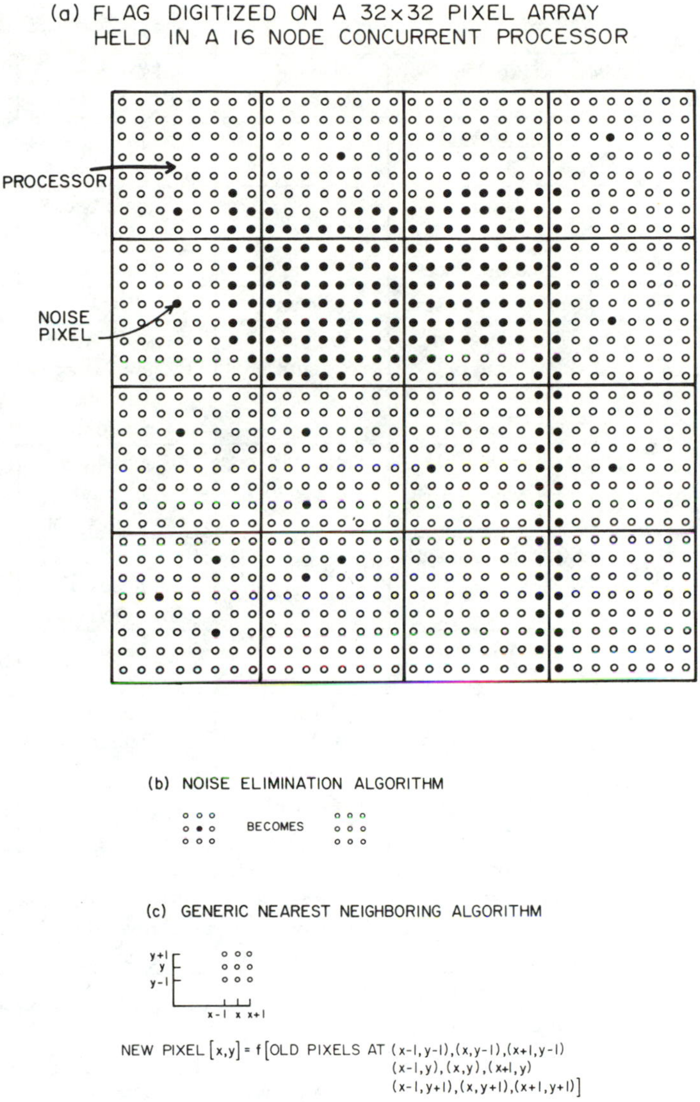

(a) FLAG DIGITIZED ON A 32×32 PIXEL ARRAY
HELD IN A 16 NODE CONCURRENT PROCESSOR

PROCESSOR

NOISE
PIXEL

(b) NOISE ELIMINATION ALGORITHM

BECOMES

(c) GENERIC NEAREST NEIGHBORING ALGORITHM

y+1
y
y-1

x-1 x x+1

NEW PIXEL [x,y] = f [OLD PIXELS AT (x-1,y-1),(x,y-1),(x+1,y-1)
(x-1,y),(x,y),(x+1,y)
(x-1,y+1),(x,y+1),(x+1,y+1)]

Figure 3-2 (a) A flag digitized onto a 32 × 32 pixel plane and decomposed onto a 16 node concurrent processor. There are also a few noise pixels, (b) A simple algorithm to remove the noise, (c) Generic nearest neighbor algorithm with Cartesian coordinate system labeling pixels.

Table 3-1: Complex Systems and the Nature of Their Associated Data Domain

Related Chapter in Book	Problem	Domain	Members	Typical Algorithm
1	Construction of Wall	Wall	Bricks	Hard Working Masons
1	Farming	Midwest	Square Feet of Soil	Sowing and Harvesting
1	Neuroscience	Brain	Neurons	Intelligence
3	Image Processing	Picture	Pixel	Convolution
5	Exploration Geophysics	Region of Earth	Seismic Wave Pressure, Velocity Values at Grid Points	Time Evolution of Wave Equations
7	Electric Field Calculation	Parallel Plate Capacitor	Electrostatic Potential at a Grid Point	Finite Differences
8	Structural Analysis	Dam	Stress and Strain at nodes of finite elements	Finite Element
9	Gravitational Dynamics	Globular Cluster	Star	Time Evolution
10, 20, 21	Matrices	Two-Dimensional Display of Elements	Matrix Elements	Multiplication Inversion Eigenvalues
10	Updating Spread Sheets	Two-Dimensional Set of Cells	Cells	Calculating Subtotals
11	Evolution of Universe	Universe and its Fourier Transforms	Galaxies and Fourier Coefficients of Gravitational Potential	Solution of Poisson's Equation and Time Evolution
13, 16	Phase Transitions	Solid	Molecules	Monte Carlo
16	Molecular Dynamics	Gas Volume or Protein	Molecules	Time Evolution
17	Population Dynamics	Ocean	Sharks and Minnows	Nature's Laws
18	Sorting	List	Character Strings	Quicksort
19	Reasoning	Knowledge	Ideas, Laws	Tree Search
19	Computer Algebra	Expression and Operations	Variables	Simplifications
22	Circuit Simulation	Chip	Transistors	Time Evolution

3-4 The Programming Model

We have already touched upon our software model in Sec. 2-8 and 3-2, but we can now clarify the picture with the specific example of image processing introduced in the last section. We will first consider the nearest-neighbor algorithm described in Sec. 3-3 and in Figs. 3-2(b) and (c). Figure 3-3 shows the subproblem to be tackled by one of the processors (that on the left in the second row). We can see that just as in the example of Hadrian's Wall, (Sec. 1-3), each node is confronted with a problem similar to that facing a sequential machine solving the whole problem. The principal difference is that the node needs only to update the 64 pixels assigned to its subdomain, rather than the full 1024 of the sequential case. Beyond this difference, the 22 pixels on three of four edges need special treatment. Each of these "special" pixels requires information contained in other nodes in order to complete the convolution. Thus the key features of the software in this example are:

- The essential algorithm is identical to that for a sequential machine except that each node has special geometry constraints corresponding to the restriction of the algorithm to the grain contained in the given node.
- At the edges of the cell contained within each node, there occur "unusual" boundary conditions. In Fig. 3-3, these boundary conditions on the north, south, and east edges amount to an instruction of the form: "Please communicate with a neighboring node to perform the convolution for an edge pixel."

THE SUBPROBLEM

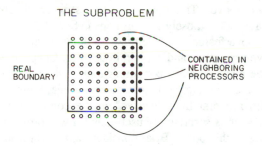

Figure 3-3 A typical subproblem associated with the decomposition illustrated in Fig. 3-2.

For this particularly simple problem, it is not difficult to see how to construct software sufficiently general that it runs on both sequential and concurrent machines. In this and other more complicated problems, it is generally advisable to write the program in a modular fashion, so that geometry and boundary value sections are carefully separated from the rest of the code.

We should also take note of the data- or communication-driven nature of the computation. The convolution update of the edge pixels must await communication of data from the neighboring nodes before the pixel update can be performed. It is in this sense that we term this programming style a form of *large grain-size dataflow*. Usually the term dataflow implies other characteristics—such as "the absence of side effects"—which are not present in our approach. So the large grain-size dataflow terminology should only be taken qualitatively. This relationship between communicating processes is called a rendezvous in the language ADA.

One characteristic of the software solution proposed for this example is that each node runs identical program code. The nodes perform different instructions, however, because the code incorporates data-dependent branching. This will be a common characteristic of all the programming examples in this book:

- Each node runs identical code but at any given time different nodes will typically be executing different instructions, because of data-dependent branches. This kind of branching occurs in the boundary condition phase of the image-processing example, and for some convolution algorithms in the basic pixel update itself.

Two aspects of the communications required for this example have not yet been emphasized, but are very important. The points are that:

- It is possible to structure the code so when any given node writes a message intended for another, the destination node "expects" the message and will take actions necessary to read it in any contingency presented by data-dependent branching. In this scheme, the arrival of a message is made known to the application program through a flag that may be "polled" at the program's leisure, rather than by interrupting the process upon message receipt. It is also true that most of the communication between nodes occurs for a hypercube implementation over channels that are directly connected in hardware . As we will comment below this is less important than the *loose synchronization* of receiving and transmitting nodes defined above. This communication structure is appropriate for problems which we have called loosely synchronous in Sec. 3-3.

The above features characterize a communication system to which we will apply the adjective *crystalline* and explain in detail in Chaps. 4 and 14. We define a crystalline system to be a synchronous communication system which we apply to loosely synchronous problems. The simple nature of crystalline communication allows it to be implemented with minimal time "wasted" in the communication software. The crystalline operating system is surprisingly useful, and it will prove to be sufficiently flexible for all the examples in this book. Brief consideration might lead one to expect that this system would only "work" for simple nearest-neighbor problems like the image-processing case discussed above. One of the global "morals" of this book, however, is that it is much more general. The structure of communications can still be very dynamic and data dependent in a crystalline system. All that is required is that if a certain data-dependent branch changes the communication structure, then this change must be made known to all relevant nodes. As an example, the choice of a pivot row and column dramatically changes the communication patterns in a matrix-inversion algorithm. This approach is consistent with crystalline communication as long as the pivot information is broadcast to all nodes. Non-nearest-neighbor communication is also possible in a crystalline environment, as long as there is the loose synchronization–the possibility of a message is expected by intermediate forwarding and destination nodes–as explained above. Examples of this application of crystalline communication will be included in Chaps. 10, 20,

21, and 22. Sections 22-2 to 22-5 are particularly important in stressing the surprising generality of the crystalline environment. The language OCCAM builds in a synchronous communication model that is crystalline by our definition.

A more general operating system allows messages to be sent between arbitrary nodes and allows for these messages to interrupt the destination node. In fact, such an operating environment has been very popular, as in the standard system for the INTEL and NCUBE commercial hypercubes. We believe that the utility of a crystalline environment has been underrated and so we have deliberately not adopted a more general *asynchronous* communication system in this book. Crystalline communication is natural in loosely synchronous problems because these have some sort of global synchronization between the nodes; this is true of all the problems in this book where either some overall iteration count or simulation time naturally synchronizes all the nodes. Note that crystalline communication is quite adequate for irregular problems and not just applicable to simple geometries. Another advantage of the crystalline system is its simplicity, which allows it to be relatively easy to implement on different hardware with good performance characteristics. The asynchronous environment is essential for applications such as event-driven simulations, computer chess, and other artificial intelligence problems where there is only local synchronization. These problems also tend to need other sophisticated tools, such as load balancing. Recently we have introduced hybrid systems combining high functionality asynchronous systems with high performance synchronous communication. These features can provide a friendly user environment (including asynchronous debugging) and run production (synchronous) codes with little communication overhead.

Chapter 4 introduces *crystalline* communications within the context of a *virtual concurrent processor* in which arbitrary node-to-node connections are permitted. In Chaps. 5 through 13, we will explore some simple examples which require only a subset of these connections. The required connections turn out to be those corresponding to mesh or hypercube topologies. Because the hypercube includes all of these topologies, we will repeatedly turn to the hypercube as a point of reference for concrete implementation. The bulk of Chap. 14 will describe CrOS III, the implementation of the crystalline operating system on the hypercube. CrOS III is a proposed standard crystalline communication system which has been implemented on a selection of concurrent computers in general use. The adoption of simple standards should encourage the development of concurrent computation by facilitating portability of codes between machines. Appendix E contains a formal definition of CrOS III. Chapters 6 and 15 will describe an enhancement to CrOS III that allows an attractive UNIX-like input/output environment within each node process.

In Chap. 22 and especially Sec. 22-5 we introduce the *virtual machine loosely synchronous communication system* which is, we believe, an appropriate general programming model for loosely synchronous problems. This realizes the abstract model introduced in Chap. 4 and can be implemented within either a crystalline or an asynchronous communication environment.

3-5 Communication and the Geometric Properties of Systems

In Sec. 2-9, we described some hypercubes and gave in Table 2-1 values for some of the key hardware parameters. Two of these parameters are particularly important to the analysis of machine performance:

* t_{calc}: The typical time required to perform a generic calculation. For scientific problems, this can be taken as a floating point calculation

$$a = b*c$$

or $a = b+c$

* t_{comm}: The typical time taken to communicate a single word between two nodes connected in the hardware topology.

Both t_{calc} and t_{comm} are somewhat vaguely defined here. The magnitude of t_{calc} depends upon both the nature of the floating-point operation and upon such things as the storage location of b and c: are they in the node memory, a possible cache, or in registers? Even if we specialize to crystalline communications, t_{comm} depends upon the number of words being transferred between the nodes, since the communication hardware and software incur significant startup times. We will address some of these issues in Chaps. 4 and 14, but for the present we will note that for crystalline communication and the machines listed in Table 2-1, t_{comm} or t_{calc} are not generally affected by the above issues by more than a factor of two. Both t_{calc} and t_{comm} are illustrated in Fig. 3-4.

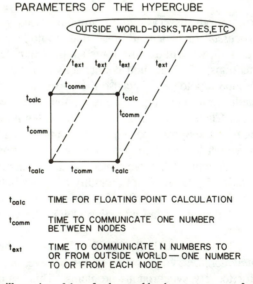

PARAMETERS OF THE HYPERCUBE

t_{calc}	TIME FOR FLOATING POINT CALCULATION
t_{comm}	TIME TO COMMUNICATE ONE NUMBER BETWEEN NODES
t_{ext}	TIME TO COMMUNICATE N NUMBERS TO OR FROM OUTSIDE WORLD — ONE NUMBER TO OR FROM EACH NODE

Figure 3-4 An illustration of three fundamental hardware parameters for hypercube concurrent computers. We show t_{calc}, t_{comm}, t_{ext} discussed in Sections 3-5, 3-6, and 3-7.

If we now analyze the convolution problem posed in Fig. 3-2(c), we note that an update of all pixels in each node requires times given by:

$$T_{calc} \sim 9n \; t_{calc} \tag{3-2}$$

$$T_{comm} \sim 4(\sqrt{n}+1) \; t_{comm} \tag{3-3}$$

where we have generalized the specific problem, illustrated in Fig. 3-2(a), to one in which each node of the concurrent processor holds n pixels stored as a $\sqrt{n} \times \sqrt{n}$ array. In Fig. 3-2(a), we show the case $n = 64$. We further define N to be the total number of nodes. Thus the full image-processing problem involves a total of Nn pixels comprising a $\sqrt{Nn} \times \sqrt{Nn}$ array.

In Eq. (3-3), T_{comm} is the total time needed to communicate all the needed pixel values between neighboring nodes. This is illustrated in Fig. 3-3, which shows that communication is required for the pixels stored at each edge. Equation (3-3) is written for the typical node in the middle of the domain which is engaged in communication on all four edges (the number of edges is the origin of the 4 in Eq. (3-3).) The node shown in Fig. 3-3 actually performs less communication since one edge is an exterior boundary and needs no communication. For our purposes, the maximum (over nodes) communication time, as recorded in Eq. (3-3), is most relevant.

Taking the ratio of Eqs. (3-3) and (3-2), we obtain f_C, the fractional communication overhead, which takes the form for large n:

$$f_C \sim \frac{constant}{\sqrt{n}} \cdot \frac{t_{comm}}{t_{calc}} \tag{3-4}$$

The alert reader will note that the *constant* in Eq. (3-4) is 4/9; however the exact value is unimportant at present. As discussed above, t_{comm} and t_{calc} are already somewhat indeterminate. Of principal relevance is the fact that the *constant* in Eq. (3-4) is a number of order unity.

As we will see in the next section, f_C may be interpreted as the fraction of the total run time spent on communication. We might expect, therefore, that a necessary condition for good performance of a concurrent processor and algorithm is a reasonably small value of f_C.

Equation (3-4) has several interesting implications:

- f_C only depends on the hardware through the ratio $\frac{t_{comm}}{t_{calc}}$, which as shown in Table 2-1 has a value of order 2 for the Caltech Cosmic Cube and Mark II hypercubes. As discussed in Sec. 2-3, the use of optical communications should allow the hardware ratio $\frac{t_{comm}}{t_{calc}}$ to remain at around this value even as the speed of the calculational processor is upgraded.

- f_C only depends on the size of the domain through the grain size n. For fixed n, f_C is independent of the number of processors. *It does not grow with increasing number of processors.*

In Chap. 5 and subsequent chapters, we will examine measured values of f_C for particular problems implemented on the Caltech hypercube. This formalism leads to an interesting generalization of the specific case given in Eq. (3-4). If the underlying domain of the complex system is characterized by a topological dimension d, then

$$f_C \sim \frac{c}{n^{1/d}} \frac{t_{comm}}{t_{calc}} \tag{3-5}$$

This form can be easily understood in the context of nearest-neighbor algorithms in a space of dimension d. In that case, f_C just represents a generalized surface-to-volume ratio which is always proportional to $n^{-1/d}$ for a grain size (volume) of n. The constant c in Eq. (3-5) remains dependent on the algorithm, as in the case of Eq. (3-4), but experience leads us to expect it to fall in the range

$$0.1 \leq c \leq 10 \tag{3-6}$$

For such familiar problems as partial differential equations solved in d dimensions it is typically found that c is approximately 1.

The only departures from Eq. (3-5) that will be discussed in this book involve problems of sorting in Chap. 18 and the Fast Fourier Transform (FFT) in Chap. 11. The generalization of Eq. (3-5) for the FFT assumes the modified form:

$$f_C \sim \frac{c}{\log n} \frac{t_{comm}}{t_{calc}} \tag{3-7}$$

Equation (3-7) may be considered as the limit of Eq. (3-5) for a system of infinite dimension. Equations (3-5) and (3-7) correspond to implementations on a hypercube or a complex computer with infinite ($\log_2 N$ as $N \rightarrow \infty$) dimension. In Eq. (3-5), c is independent of N but in Eq. (3-7), c increases logarithmically with N. In practice, however, c still satisfies the inequality of Eq. (3-6), and the logarithmic increase does not seem to be numerically important.

It should be emphasized that the dimension d appearing in (3-5) need not always correspond to the topological dimensionality of the underlying domain. This will be most clearly illustrated by the long-range force problem of Chap. 9, which is characterized by dimension $d = 1$ regardless of the topology of the underlying space. This point may be illustrated by modifying our image-processing example. Consider changing the local algorithm illustrated in Fig. 3-2(c) to one in which the updated value of the pixel at any point is a function of all other pixels in the image. In this case, Eqs. (3-2) and (3-3) are changed to :

$$T_{calc} = n \cdot nN \cdot t_{calc} \tag{3-8}$$

where n is number of pixels in the node and nN the number of pixels in the image. The optimal implementation leads to a total communication time of:

$$T_{comm} = n(N-1)t_{comm} \tag{3-9}$$

In this expression, $n(N-1)$ is the number of pixels stored outside the node. We find in this case that the communication overhead takes the form:

$$f_C = \frac{T_{comm}}{T_{calc}} \approx \frac{1}{n} \cdot \frac{t_{comm}}{t_{calc}} \tag{3-10}$$

This expression has the form of Eq. (3-5) with a dimension of $d = 1$. We can easily understand the form of Eq. (3-10) by recognizing that every pixel communicated from another node is used in the update of n pixels; n calculations are performed for each communication. The comparison of Eqs. (3-4) and (3-10) illustrates an important point. The communication overhead f_C depends on the ratio of communication to calculation and not simply on the amount of communication. The nearest-neighbor algorithm leading to Eq. (3-4) involves a minimal absolute amount of communication but it also requires minimal calculation. As the result, f_C is not particularly small. The fully connected algorithm analyzed in Eqs. (3-8, 9, 10) involves much more communication, but even more calculation. Thus we find that the ratio f_C is very small. It is worth emphasizing that the overhead in this case is inversely proportional to n, rather than following the relation

$$f_C \sim \frac{t_{comm}}{t_{calc}} \tag{3-11}$$

that one might expect for the computation of a fully connected system. Equation (3-11) holds in the case that the pixels are repeatedly communicated as needed for the update of each individual pixel without exploiting the fact that each communicated pixel can be used n times. This multiple use of communicated pixels makes all the difference between Eq. (3-10) with $d = 1$ and Eq. (3-11) which corresponds to infinite dimensionality! A less thoughtful implementation could have lead to Eq. (3-11).

Referring back to Sec. 1-3, we see that the construction of Hadrian's Wall can be analyzed similarly. The overhead due to communication between masons yields the l^{-1} (l is the length of wall assigned to each mason) dependency in Eq. (1-2). This is quite analogous to Eq. (3-5) with $d = 1$. The correspondence is not unexpected since we employed a simple one-dimensional decomposition in Sec. 1-3.

Consider the computation of irregular complex systems for which the connection pattern is neither that of the simple nearest-neighbor structure of Eq. (3-3) nor of the general broadcast illustrated in Eq. (3-9). Instances of this connection structure can occur in the simulation of integrated circuits, in neural networks (as illustrated in Figs. 1-9 and 1-10), or in war games and other simulations of human society. Such complex systems are characterized by an irregular connectivity, and in these cases we will define a generalized *system dimension* by simply inverting (3-5):

$$n^{\frac{1}{d}} \sim \frac{c}{f_C} \cdot \frac{t_{comm}}{t_{calc}} \tag{3-12}$$

The resultant dimension d will in general depend upon the grain size n. However, this grain-size dependence will often prove to be weak. A useful example is found in the case of computer circuits, in which the empirical rule discovered by Rent can be stated in our notation as

$$d_{circuit} \approx 3 \tag{3-13}$$

This is an interesting result, since circuits are typically laid out in two rather than three dimensions [Landman 71, Mandelbrot 79, Donath 79].

An interesting relationship exists between f_C and the dimension d_c and d_p of respectively the complex computer and the complex problem. The definition of Eq. (3-12) can be applied to any complex system if it is written in the form:

$$\text{Communication through} \atop \text{surface of grain} = \left[\begin{array}{c} \text{volume or} \\ \text{calculational} \\ \text{complexity} \\ \text{of grain} \end{array} \right]^{1-1/d} \tag{3-14}$$

Now let us consider a specific case:

$$f_C = \frac{1}{\sqrt{n}} \frac{t_{comm}}{t_{calc}} \tag{3-15}$$

for a two-dimensional decomposition with $d_c = d_p = 2$. On the other hand, if a one-dimensional decomposition is employed, one can show that f_C takes the form:

$$f_C = \frac{\sqrt{N}}{2} \frac{1}{\sqrt{n}} \frac{t_{comm}}{t_{calc}} \tag{3-16}$$

corresponding to $d_c = 1$, but still $d_p = 2$. The one-dimensional decomposition is realized in the case of a two-dimensional matrix problem by storing complete rows or columns of a matrix in each node of the concurrent computer. This is discussed further in Chap. 10. We also found the analogues of Eqs. (3-15) and (3-16) when discussing farming in Sec. 1-4. We can interpret the growth of f_C in Eq. (3-16) with N, the number of nodes of the computer, as a direct reflection of inadequate dimensionality in the underlying complex computer. It has been conjectured [Fox 86a] that in general:

If $d_c \geq d_p$, then:

$$f_C = \frac{constant}{n^{1/d_p}} \frac{t_{comm}}{t_{calc}} \tag{3-17}$$

Whereas if $d_c < d_p$, then:

$$f_C = N^{(1/d_c - 1/d_p)} \frac{constant}{n^{1/d_p}} \frac{t_{comm}}{t_{calc}} \tag{3-18}$$

From this point of view, the hypercube appears as a good architecture because it has high system dimension.

Further discussions of complex systems have been published [Fox 85a, Fox 86a, and Flower 86]. Here we will be satisfied to note that this approach to the analysis of communication overhead has shown the importance of two fundamental parameters of the complex system. One is the *size* of the system as embodied in the grain size n when the system is to be mapped onto a concurrent computer. The second important parameter is the system dimension d. The values of d in the systems comprising the problem and the computer are important determinants of the effectiveness of the computational mapping. Note that d can be equal to, greater than, or less than the natural topological dimension. We have seen examples of these three cases in Eqs. (3-4), (3-13), and (3-10) respectively.

3-6 Performance Analysis

An important measure of the performance of a concurrent computer is the *speedup* factor S associated with a particular calculation. The speedup is defined as the ratio of the time required to complete a given calculation on a single-node processor to the equivalent calculation performed on a concurrent processor. This definition must be taken with a grain of salt, since for instance it may not be possible in practice to fit the "full problem" within the memory of the single-node computer. This is more than an academic issue in defining the speedup but rather a manifestation of an interesting characteristic of concurrent machines, especially those with distributed memory. That is, it is technically easier to provide large total memory on concurrent rather than on sequential machines. This constitutes an important advantage of concurrent machines which is not addressed by the speedup analysis to be considered next.

Let us define $T_{conc}(N)$ to be the time elapsed on a concurrent processor with N nodes, and denote the sequential computer time T_{seq} by:

$$T_{seq} = T_{conc}(1) \qquad (3\text{-}19)$$

It follows that the speedup S depends upon N, the number of nodes, and is given by:

$$S(N) = \frac{T_{seq}}{T_{conc}(N)} \qquad (3\text{-}20)$$

If T_{seq} cannot be measured directly, then it can usually be found by running a small problem on the sequential machine and then extrapolating to the real problem by using the predicted or measured dependence on problem size.

As we will find, it is sometimes useful to introduce the concurrent *efficiency* ε, defined by:

$$\varepsilon = \frac{S}{N} \qquad (3\text{-}21)$$

The speedup S is reduced from its ideal value of N (the efficiency is bounded from above by one) for one or more of four causes:

·   Nonoptimal Algorithm or Algorithmic Overhead
    It may not be possible to find an algorithm for the concurrent machine that is as good as that for the sequential computer. The best example in this book corresponds to the case of sorting in Chap. 18 in which we found it necessary to develop new algorithms for the hypercube.

- Software Overhead

  In Chaps. 9, 10, and 20 we show that even with a completely equivalent algorithm software overhead arises in the concurrent implementation. This may, for example, involve additional index calculations necessitated by the manner in which data are "split up" among processors.

- Load Balancing

  The speedup is generally limited by the speed of the slowest node. Thus, an important consideration is to ensure that each node performs the same amount of work. This important topic is covered in Sec. 3-8 and will be discussed further in Chap. 17.

- Communication Overhead

  Any time spent in communication constitutes a penalty on the overall performance as compared with the sequential case. Viewing communication as a penalty is an oversimplification. For instance, it might be argued that we should be comparing communication costs in concurrent machines with virtual memory costs in sequential machines. In this simple discussion, we will neglect this point.

The sorting problem mentioned above demonstrates algorithmic inefficiency. The more irregular problems discussed in Chaps. 16, 17, 19, 20, 21, and 22 will illustrate load imbalance issues. Apart from these cases, the speedup behaviors of the remaining examples covered in this book are dominated by issues of communication. In fact, communication cost constitutes the dominant efficiency issue in all of the examples in this book except sorting.

In the remainder of this section, we will discuss the effects of communication on the performance of a particular family of actual machines–the 8086-based Mark I (Cosmic Cube) and Mark II computers constructed at the Caltech Campus and JPL [Fox 85c, Quinlan 87]. These machines do not allow any overlap of calculation and communication; any time spent communicating directly degrades the speedup. The more sophisticated Caltech Mark III and commercial designs allow some communication to proceed concurrently with the calculation and for such advanced hypercubes, the following analysis would require modification [Fox 87]. Similar analyses have been developed at CMU and applied to the Cm* system which included distributed and/or shared memory [Gehringer 87].

If calculation and communication cannot be overlapped, then the effect of communication overhead on the speedup can be immediately written down as:

$$T_{conc}(N) = \frac{T_{seq}}{N}(1 + f_C) \tag{3-22}$$

or

$$S = \frac{N}{1 + f_C} \tag{3-23}$$

and

$$\varepsilon = \frac{1}{(1 + f_C)} \approx 1 - f_C \tag{3-24}$$

where the final result in (3-24) is only valid when, as we usually find in our practical examples, the overhead f_C is small compared to unity. The formulae (3-22, 23, 24) give a good description of the examples in this book except the problems from Chaps. 16 through 22, which involve additional sources of inefficiency. It will be most convenient in subsequent discussions to work with the overhead f_C, whose relationship to efficiency is simply:

$$\frac{1}{\varepsilon} - 1 = f_C \qquad (3\text{-}25)$$

The result of Eq. (3-24) has an interesting interpretation,when we regard efficiency as the speedup per node. Combining Eq. (3-5) with Eq. (3-24), we find that speedup per node is independent of N, the number of nodes. Instead, it simply depends on the node characteristics t_{comm} and t_{calc} and n, the amount of data stored at each node. This result relates local properties of the computer to local properties of the complex system being computed. We will find in later chapters that the simple forms of Eqs. (3-5), (3-23) correctly describe the observed speedups that have been measured on the Caltech hypercubes. *The success of these simple model equations is important, since their lack of explicit N dependence implies that concurrent computers with large numbers of nodes can be efficiently used.* This forms the basis of our conviction that very large concurrent computers will be successful in the future.

In the above discussion we have ignored a point commonly considered important to analysis of concurrency. This is sometimes referred to as *Amdahl's law*, and states that if an inherently sequential component of the problem takes fraction α of the time on a single node, then one can never realize a speedup factor greater than α^{-1} [Amdahl 67]. This is a valid argument, but it must be tempered by the observation that for most (perhaps all interesting) large problems, α is very small and represents no serious limit to the speedup [Fox 84c]. A major reason for this is that we are assuming a programming model in which the concurrent algorithm is designed and written "from scratch." If one is constrained to the limited modification of existing programs via currently limited parallelizing tools, then the effective value of α can be (and often is found to be) rather large ($\sim$ 10%). This may be regarded, however, as a defect to the "modification of existing dusty decks" approach to parallelization, and not an intrinsic feature of concurrent computation. In the approach to concurrency adopted here, we still encounter inherently sequential tasks in essentially all problems. Possible examples would be the printing of a final answer or calculation of a global scalar product. The latter problem is discussed in detail in Chaps. 14 and 19. Similar tasks are part of the matrix algorithms of Chap. 20. These examples of sequential components correspond to stages of the computation which involve a small number of degrees of freedom. We suggest here that all inherently sequential parts of an effective concurrent algorithm should involve relatively few degrees of freedom or members. In the scalar product of Chap. 19, it will be shown that for a hypercube architecture, the time required for such a "bottleneck" step is limited by:

$$T_{global} \leq const. \ \log_2 N \qquad (3\text{-}26)$$

for either communication or calculation. Let us now interpret n in Eq. (3-5) as the

number of members present in the largest part of the calculation. We may now note that
(3-26) is usually unimportant, since the communication overhead described in Eq. (3-5)
takes a much longer time. Node-to-node communication increases with grain size at
least as fast as $n^{1-1/d}$ and the calculation within the node increases at least as fast as n.
Typically n and $n^{1-1/d}$ are large compared to $\log_2 N$ and in our practical examples we
find the effects contained in Eq. (3-26) to be unimportant. For the interesting values of
n, both the calculation and the communication described by Eq. (3-5) are much larger
than the inherently sequential component time typified by Eq. (3-26). Amdahl's law is
correct but the sequential fraction α decreases, often like n^{-1} as n increases, and large
speedups are possible for large problems.

In Fig. 3-5, we show typical plots of the speedup as a function of N, the number of
nodes. In Fig. 3-5(a), we show an extrapolation for fixed grain size n. To be precise, the
plot corresponds to implementations which satisfy:

$$f_C \text{ reasonably small or} \tag{3-27}$$

$$n^{\frac{1}{d}} \gg const. \frac{t_{comm}}{t_{calc}}$$

as well as negligible global or inherently sequential components. For an algorithm in
which the basic calculation cost grows in proportion to n, the latter corresponds to the
constraint:

$$n \gg const. \log_2 N \tag{3-28}$$

We can make this clearer by considering the concrete example of a two-
dimensional finite element problem like that discussed in Chap. 8. In this case we will
find that on the Caltech Cosmic Cube and Mark II hypercubes:

$$f_C \sim \frac{1}{\sqrt{n}} \tag{3-29}$$

and for $n \geq 100$, the constraints of Eqs. (3-27 and 28) are satisfied.

For three-dimensional problems, Eq. (3-29) becomes:

$$f_C \sim n^{-1/3} \tag{3-30}$$

and we require $n \sim 1000$ in order to satisfy Eqs. (3-27 and 28).

In general, we can say that each problem class is characterized by a minimum grain
size n_{min} below which the overheads become large. As long as n is greater than n_{min}, the
speedup is linear in N with a corresponding high efficiency, and $S \geq 0.8N$ for machines
with similar performance characteristics to the Caltech hypercubes, i.e., machines with
$t_{comm}/t_{calc} \sim 2$. Fig. 3-5(a) can now be interpreted as a plot of the speedup for a suite of
problems in which as N increases, the grain size n is always kept "large enough." Note
that this extrapolation requires that any problem run on a machine with N nodes contain
Nn_{min} members. In other words, the size of the minimal problems for a given machine
grows in proportion to N. It is sufficient that n remains constant, so that the problem size
is directly proportional to N, but it is evident that a slower growth in problem size will

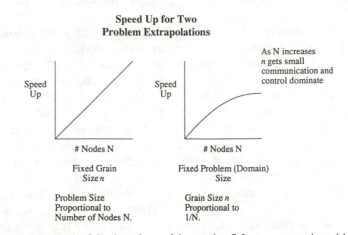

Figure 3-5 A sketch of the dependence of the speedup S for two assumptions: (a) fixed grain size, (b) fixed problem size,

also lead to an essentially linear speedup. This is an important point. Large concurrent computers are applicable to the simulation of large problems. In this view, small problems are best handled by small machines. The discussion above quantifies the meanings of "large" and "small." In the language of Sec. 3-5, the above analysis is only valid if the dimensionality of the computer is larger than or equal to that of the simulated system. Otherwise, the N dependence in Eqs. (3-16) and (3-18) spoil the extrapolation to large N and the speedup will not scale as predicted in Fig. 3-5(a). In Fig. 3-5(b), we illustrate what happens to the speedup at fixed problem size. Now, the overheads grow with N. For fixed overall problem size, Eq. (3-5) becomes:

$$ f_C \sim \frac{const.}{(total\ size)^{1/d}} \cdot \frac{t_{comm}}{t_{calc}} \cdot N^{1/d} \qquad (3\text{-}31) $$

The overhead f_C now grows with increasing N and, as shown in Fig. 3-5(b), the overheads eventually dominate as the speedup levels off when plotted against N.

Our experience indicates that most applications that need increased computer performance are characterized by being significantly larger than current implementations. It is reasonable to expect this trend to continue so that Fig. 3-5(a) rather than Fig. 3-5(b) should represent the relevant predictor for the speedup to be realized in the application concurrent computers to these future large problems.

Let us return to Eq. (3-22) and see how we can use it to design an "optimum" concurrent processor. We will consider a fixed problem for which Eq. (3-5) holds with particular values of coefficient c and dimension d. Combining the two equations yields:

$$ T_{conc}(N,n) = \frac{T_{seq}(n)}{N} \left[1 + \frac{\beta}{n^{1/d}} \right] \qquad (3\text{-}32) $$

where we have introduced $\beta = c\,(t_{comm}/t_{calc})$. We will assume the particular values $\beta = 1$ and $d = 3$ when needed for illustration.

The definition of an "optimal" machine will naturally depend on one's computational goals and constraints. Consider first a world in which there are no fiscal or hardware limits—where we have the goal of minimizing the execution time $T_{conc}(N,n)$. This is achieved in the degenerate limit of $n = 1$ and the number of nodes equal to the total number of members. This does not necessarily lead to advocacy of the small grain-size SIMD approach described in Chap. 2. The problem under consideration could well require an MIMD structure. We note that minimizing T_{conc} has led us to the scenario of Fig. 3-5(b); a very large speedup in a region in which the incremental cost is high and S only increases slowly with N. This optimization has led to an expensive solution: a very large machine used inefficiently.

Another interesting and perhaps more realistic goal is to maximize the cost-effectiveness of the machine. In this approach it would be worth building a machine which ran the problem twice as fast, just so long as the machine cost less than a factor of two more to build. Suppose the problem of interest fully utilizes all the memory associated with each node. We can propose a simple model for the cost C of a concurrent computer of the form:

$$C = \text{Cost}(N, n) = N(n+\delta) \cdot \text{const} \qquad (3\text{-}33)$$

Here we have modeled each node as consisting of memory plus calculation and communication modules. In Eq. (3-33), n measures the cost of the memory and δ the cost of everything else. We have neglected the N dependence of δ which might arise in a machine like a hypercube from a logarithmic increase in the number of communication channels.

We now seek to maximize the speedup per dollar, or equivalently, to minimize the normalized product TC defined by:

$$TC = \frac{T_{conc}(N, n) \cdot \text{Cost}(N, n)}{\delta\, T_{seq}(n)} = (1 + \frac{n}{\delta})\,(1 + \frac{\beta}{n^{1/d}}) \qquad (3\text{-}34)$$

It is interesting that this function is independent of N and depends only upon the grain size n. Identifying n as the number of nodal points in a finite element problem, we may roughly estimate that $n = 1000$ would correspond to a few megabytes of memory. Taking the Caltech Mark III hypercube as an example, we can estimate the value $\delta = 10,000$, in these peculiar units of nodal points. To be explicit, this value of δ implies that in a node with 10 megabytes of memory, half of the cost of the machine is associated with the memory. For this value of δ, TC is plotted in Fig. 3-6. This cost function displays a minimum at $n \sim 400$. This example is only illustrative; a machine like the commercial NCUBE hypercube has a much lower value for δ.

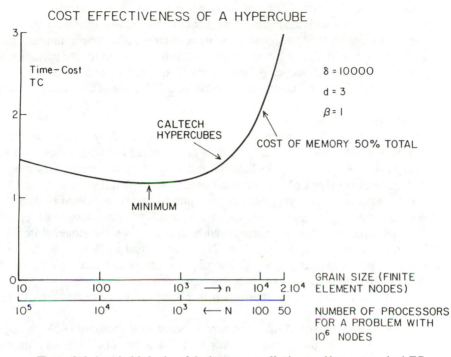

COST EFFECTIVENESS OF A HYPERCUBE

Time-Cost
TC

δ = 10000

d = 3

β = 1

CALTECH
HYPERCUBES

COST OF MEMORY 50% TOTAL

MINIMUM

| 10 | 100 | 10^3 $\longrightarrow n$ | 10^4 2.10^4 | GRAIN SIZE (FINITE ELEMENT NODES) |

| 10^5 | 10^4 | 10^3 $\longleftarrow N$ | 100 50 | NUMBER OF PROCESSORS FOR A PROBLEM WITH 10^6 NODES |

Figure 3-6 A typical behavior of the inverse cost effectiveness (time-cost product) TC defined in Sec. 3-6. The graph is drawn for the parameter values $d = 3$, $\beta = 1$, and $\delta = 10000$.

The analytic expression for this minimum is obtained by differentiating Eq. (3-34), yielding:

$$n^{1+\frac{1}{d}} + \beta(1-\frac{1}{d})\, n = \frac{\delta\beta}{d}$$

or

$$n \approx (\frac{\delta\beta}{d})^{\frac{d}{(d+1)}} \tag{3-35}$$

For the case $\delta = 10,000$, $\beta = 1$ and $d = 3$, the approximation Eq. (3-35) gives a minimum value $n = 439$. At the minimum, we find that the communication overhead f_c is approximately 0.14 while the fraction of cost devoted to memory is n/δ or 0.04.

Unlike the earlier minimization, the result of Eq. (3-35) corresponds to a large grain size with the speedup in the linear regime shown in Fig. 3-5(a).

The result of Eq. (3-35) is interesting as a quantification of the trade-off between memory and calculational power. As memory per node increases, the cost of the node increases, but so does the speedup as the result of decreasing communication overhead. We hasten to add that there are many other factors which may influence memory size.

Among these factors might be memory necessary to implement sophisticated operating systems, which is an issue that we have not discussed at all. Currently operational hypercubes are deliberately designed with more memory than the minimum configuration shown in Fig. 3-6. The minimum of Eq. (3-35) is only valid for the particular application parameters discussed above. A "superoptimal" quantity of memory allows some flexibility in a general-purpose computer intended for a full range of complicated problems.

3-7 External Sources of Data

A large number of major computations involve not only substantial calculations but also high bandwidth access to large data banks stored on disks, tapes, or other external storage devices. Examples include the full range of commercial database applications and scientific analysis of experimental data. The exploration of this class of problems using "research class" hypercubes (as at Caltech) has been limited to date. This limitation has been largely due to the lack of time and funds necessary to develop high-speed external input/output (I/O) channels rather than due to a fundamental deficiency of the hypercube approach to this problem class. Theoretical studies, however, lend credence to the expectation that many I/O intensive problems can run well on the hypercube. Among the representative examples that have been examined are:

(1)   An image-processing application involving the Fast Fourier Transform technique [Solomon 84].

(2)   A problem involving the concurrent search of a database [Kolawa 86]. This was examined for the special case in which all the data fits in memory, but these results may be extrapolated to a distributed database stored on disks. This analysis is not definitive, because the result depends not only on algorithmic issues but also the hardware architecture of a concurrent I/O system—an area which does not seem to have been studied in depth.

(3)   The analysis of data from a high energy physics experiment [Fox 84b]. This was successful although the full hypercube node interconnection topology was not necessary.

Let us briefly consider the first problem—image processing via the Fast Fourier Transform—in somewhat more detail. As shown in Fig. 3-4, the performance of a hypercube in I/O operations is characterized by a new parameter t_{ext} which is defined according to the following:

• t_{ext}:   One word of data is transferred to or from each node of the concurrent computer (N words in total) in time t_{ext} .

It is natural to connect each node of the concurrent computer to an external device using a channel constructed similarly to that used for the node-to-node connections. This leads to the equality

$$t_{ext} = t_{comm} \tag{3-36}$$

so that,

$$t_{ext} \sim t_{calc} \tag{3-37}$$

where Eq. (3-37) relies on the hardware satisfying the relation $t_{comm}/t_{calc} \sim 1$, as discussed in the previous sections. This model is incomplete because it ignores the serious issues regarding the packaging and reliability of practical concurrent I/O systems. We have further ignored the constraints arising from the speed of the external device. Such a device could be a slow disk or a fast real-time data acquisition system.

With regard to machines like the Caltech Mark II and III hypercubes, Eq. (3-36) represents the largest possible external bandwidth. Channels are provided on each node, but in the current packaging of these machines, we only connect one node in each module of 32 nodes to an external device. Thus these machines actually have performance governed by:

$$t_{ext} = 32 t_{comm} \qquad (3\text{-}38)$$

This value has proven adequate for the calculation intensive problems so far considered for hypercube applications at Caltech.

Returning to the image-processing application, we use the decomposition illustrated in Fig. 3-2 and store n pixels in each node. As described in Chap. 11, the Fast Fourier Transform (FFT) can be efficiently implemented on a hypercube, requiring a total time proportional to $n \log n \; t_{calc}$. This should be contrasted with the time proportional to $n \, t_{ext}$ which is needed to load and unload the image. We can now introduce, analogously to the internal f_C, a new fractional external I/O overhead f_E, defined as the ratio of external I/O time to calculation time. For the FFT example we find

$$f_E = \frac{constant}{\log n} \cdot \frac{t_{ext}}{t_{calc}} \qquad (3\text{-}39)$$

where in the explicit example of implementation on the Caltech hypercube, the *constant* in Eq. (3-39) assumes the value 0.05. We observe an interesting similarity to the internal communication overhead f_C; comparing Eqs. (3-7) and (3-39), we see that f_C and f_E differ only by a numerical constant and the substitution of t_{ext} for t_{comm}.

We can interpret f_C^{-1} or f_E^{-1} as the average numbers of calculations performed per communicated word via internal or external channels respectively. The high performance of large grain-size hypercubes corresponds to low overheads f_C and f_E. As long as each node contains a large grain, it can be expected that each communication will be associated with substantial amounts of calculation. This qualitative generalization is realized in the application investigated so far, and should serve as a reasonably general rule of thumb.

We will not discuss external data storage further in this book, but the above remarks are intended to be indicative of the applicability of this overall approach to problems requiring substantial communication bandwidth to external devices. We note that high performance I/O is now becoming available on the commercial hypercubes. This will allow better tests of the ideas presented here.

3-8 Load Balancing and the Statistical Properties of Systems

As described in Sec. 3-6, the balancing of the workload among the nodes of a concurrent computer is central to achieving high performance. This load-balancing problem is central to all approaches to concurrent processing. As explained below, the problems discussed in this book are sufficiently simple that the user can rather easily find decompositions that adequately balance the load. However, more complex problems, such as irregular simulations and artificial intelligence, require more powerful techniques and so investigation of automatic load-balancing methods is central to research in concurrent computation [Fox 86a, 85a, 86d, 86g, 86h, 86i; Flower 86, Krämer 87]. We will briefly review this work at the end of this section.

An important feature of the problems described here is that they are generally homogeneous. By this, we mean that each member of the underlying data domain is associated with a similar calculational time. This definition will be slightly modified in Chap. 17 in which there exist different "species" with different corresponding calculation times. Homogeneous problems can in principle be load balanced by placing equal numbers of members in each node. Even the homogeneous case is not easy in practice if the members are irregularly distributed in the domain. This is illustrated in Fig. 3-7, which shows an astrophysics problem of the type discussed in Chap. 16. In Fig. 3-7(a) the large scale universe is shown at an initial time at which the galaxies (are assumed to) have a uniform spatial distribution. Load balance is achieved by assigning equal volumes of space to each node. This technique is similar to that used in most of the examples in this book. In Fig. 3-7(b), we show the universe evolved forward to a later time. As might have been anticipated, gravitation causes the galaxies to clump together. The assignment of equal spatial volumes to each node no longer balances the load. The problem now is to devise a method to reallocate the workload in such a manner as to maintain the initial high efficiency.

The pattern recognition problem illustrated in Fig. 3-2(a)–identification of the nation whose flag is flying–is inhomogeneous. Any decomposition of the problem will lead to each node doing very different types of work. One node could be identifying a flagpole while another is busy counting the stars on the flag.

The examples in Chaps. 5 through 13 are all "naturally" well balanced while the more challenging problems in Chaps. 16 through 22 display degrees of inherent load imbalance. Of these latter problems, the population dynamics problem of Chap. 17 is perhaps most dominated by load-balancing considerations. Chapter 17 incorporates a discussion of some of the factors involved in the general problem of inhomogeneous load balancing.

The example shown in Fig 3-7, like the problems to be discussed in Chaps. 16 and 17, has a balance that changes with time. The "load balancer" must run on a continuing basis in order to update the load distribution. A much simpler case is that of *static load balancing* such as might arise with an irregular geometry finite element problem of the type discussed in Chap. 8 [Flower 86]. Here, one needs only to balance the load at the start of the problem and it is better to term this process as automatic problem decomposition. In most cases, it is possible to implement the balancer concurrently with the

LOAD IMBALANCE IN EVOLUTION OF UNIVERSE
PROJECTION OF "GALAXIES" ON 16-NODE PROCESSOR

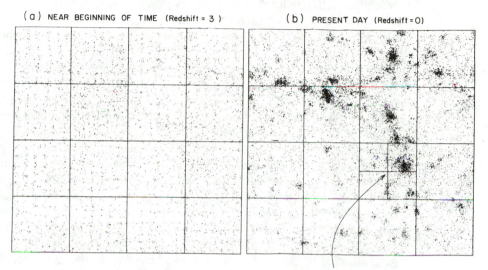

(a) NEAR BEGINNING OF TIME (Redshift = 3)   (b) PRESENT DAY (Redshift = 0)

Further subdivision
accentuates inhomogenities

Figure 3-7 The distribution of galaxies in the universe from a theoretical simulation. We
show the galaxies at early times in (a) and after evolution to present day in (b). We also
illustrate a decomposition over 16 nodes with an inset to 64 in (b). The load imbalance is
enhanced as the number of nodes increases.

application on the same concurrent computer. This approach is, in general, essential for
the design of a *dynamic load balancer* [Fox 86h].

Automatic load balancing or decomposition can be viewed as a problem in optimization. One wishes to minimize the total execution time of the implementation on the
given concurrent computer. Viewed in this fashion, we see that load balancing is very
similar to many other resource allocation problems. Analogous are:

- Automatic load balancing or decomposition on a highly coupled concurrent com-
  puter like the hypercube.
- Optimizing compilers for vector supercomputers like the CRAY.
- Scheduling tasks in a multiuser environment.
- Allocation of phone lines or more general communication links in real world com-
  munication system.
- Battle management systems.

The first class of methods for automatic load balancing are heuristic and typically
only apply to a subset of concurrent problems. We can mention:

1) The *scattered decomposition* originally developed for matrices [Fox 84d] is described for this application in Chap. 20. It is a simple passive method that can be shown to be optimal for certain very irregular or rapidly changing problems [Fox 86a]. This method has also been used on the hypercube for graphics ray tracing [Goldsmith 86, 87], finite element problems [Morison 86], and in Chap. 17, we will show how it can be used in ecological simulations.

2) In the *self-scheduling* method, one views the concurrent computer as a pool of processors which process work as it becomes available. Slave processes demand work from their masters when it becomes available. This simple technique is very generally useful in shared memory machines. It is appropriate for hypercube implementation of certain hierarchical problems with few "spatial" connections between the fundamental *members*. It has been successfully used for a computer chess program on the hypercube [Felten 86a].

3) In many simulations, one can view load balancing as a graph partitioning problem [Fox 86d, 86h, 86i]. In the language of Sec. 3-3, the nodes of the graph correspond to the members of the complex system and the edges of the graph to the connections between the members. In [Fox 86d], it is shown that one can use rather general graph theoretical techniques, in particular, the distance between nodes of the graph, to approximately decompose many problems. We use the concept of the graphical distance to divide a problem into grains containing nearby points. This is a generalization of the orthogonal recursive bisection described in Sec. 22-3 for circuit simulation. All realistic decomposition methods are inherently approximate as the load-balancing problem is NP complete. However, the graphical method is not only approximate but unlike, say, the simulated annealing method described later, cannot easily be improved if its natural decomposition is inadequate. It makes up for this inherent approximation by its speed in performing the decomposition.

4) A second class of load-balancing techniques use more analytic methods. The first step is to define a so-called objective or energy function which is to be minimized. Typically this is taken not as:

$$E_1 = \max_{processors} \; (\text{work per processor}) \qquad (3\text{-}40)$$

which is precisely related to the execution time on the concurrent computer but rather we replace E_1 by E_2 defined by:

$$E_2 = \sum_{processors} (\text{work per processor})^2 \qquad (3\text{-}41)$$

There are many possible forms of (3-41) depending on the exact nature of the hardware and the relative importance of calculation and communication. However, in each case, E_2 retains its characteristic least squares formulation. The most straightforward application of (3-41) interprets E_2 as the energy of a physical system whose particles are the members of the complex system. As described in [Fox 86a] this mapping into a physics problem is quite deep and allows one to introduce the ideas of temperature and phase transitions for general dynamic complex systems. One can show that the required decomposition corresponds to the ground state of the physical system. This can be found by the techniques of statistical physics where the optimization method is called simulated annealing [Kirkpatrick 83, Fox 85a, 86a, Flower 86]. This technique is further discussed in Chap. 17.

An alternative approach to minimizing Eq. (3-41) uses an idea introduced by Hopfield and Tank [Hopfield 86]. This maps the complex system into a biological or neural network in which one can consider each member being represented by a set of neurons [Fox 86i].

Both the simulated annealing and neural network methods seem very powerful [Fox 86g], and we are currently implementing them in a dynamic load balancer running on the hypercube [Fox 86h]. Both optimization methods can run concurrently with good speedup. Initial tests suggest that they will allow the hypercube to automatically "follow" very complex and dynamic problems. However, we need substantially more experience before we can make definite statements and consider decomposition or load balancing as a solved or even as a soluble problem.

As indicated above, this field is a subject of intense research and for this reason we will only consider it in passing in the later chapters of this book. We emphasize that many and perhaps the majority of large-scale scientific problems can be straightforwardly decomposed by elementary techniques and so their concurrent implementation can be rigorously treated before the load-balancing issue is fully understood.

4

A Simple Concurrent
Programming Environment

4-1 Introduction

This chapter describes a concurrent programming environment within which the algorithms of subsequent chapters may be implemented. This environment is discussed in the context of a *virtual* concurrent processor, and is based on the hypercube crystalline operating system, CrOS III, described in detail in Chap. 14.

To call CrOS III an operating system is something of a misnomer, since in fact it is just a collection of routines which may be called by application programs, largely for interprocessor communication. In this respect, CrOS III differs from operating systems such as UNIX which provide a full user environment, with facilities for I/O, debugging, editing, and so on. Clearly, to provide an adequate environment for the user, CrOS III must be embedded in a higher-level operating environment. Such an environment should be multi-user, and at the very least, provide debugging, editing, graphics and I/O facilities. By making CrOS III available as a part of a more general operating system, the user can take advantage of the speed of CrOS III, while retaining the additional functionality needed for program development.

With this limited goal in mind, we now go on to describe a version of the CrOS III environment that will allow us to discuss the concepts and methods of concurrent computation in concrete terms, rather than abstract generalities. Since we do not wish to limit our discussion unnecessarily by our choice of the programming environment, we will define and describe in this chapter a virtual concurrent processor to which the discussion of concurrent algorithms in Chaps. 5 through 13 will be applied. By considering a very general programming environment, we do not mean to imply that the system we define should be used in its full generality to implement concurrent algorithms on a real machine. Rather, we will start with a very general system and examine which features of the system are actually needed for each algorithm. Since we do not want to limit our programming environment to what is easy to implement before we have even discussed the algorithms that use the environment, we call the concurrent processor virtual to remind ourselves that we are giving the system more generality than a real concurrent processor is likely to have. In Sec. 22-5 we show how to emulate the virtual concurrent processor on various hardware architectures, and give details of its implementation on a hypercube by means of the CrOS III *crystal_router*.

The virtual concurrent processor is an ensemble of independent processing elements communicating with each other by exchanging messages. Each of the independent processors executes its own instruction stream and operates on a separate set of data;

69

such an ensemble is known as a Multiple-Instruction Multiple-Data (MIMD) machine. An environment in which the processors communicate by transmitting and receiving data items is known as a *message-passing* system. We use message-passing exclusively in the virtual concurrent processor and make no explicit use of any shared memory facilities. However, the virtual environment imposes no restrictions on how a message-passing environment might be implemented on a real machine. After examining several concurrent algorithms in subsequent chapters, we will present a specific hardware system and the implementation of a restricted version of the virtual environment in Chap. 14. A full virtual environment for hypercubes, called the virtual machine loosely synchronous communication system, is presented in Sec. 22-5.

4-2 The Virtual Concurrent Processor

This section discusses the virtual concurrent processor, following which we present the routines that allow interprocessor communication. This is followed with a few comments on the implementation of the communication routines on a real concurrent processor. However, a detailed discussion of machine-specific issues will be deferred until Chap. 14. This chapter concludes with two examples to illustrate the use of the communication routines.

The virtual concurrent processor is a collection of identical processing elements, also called nodes or processors. Such an ensemble of identical nodes is frequently referred to as a homogeneous machine. Though concurrent processors can be composed of a variety of different nodes, such machines are often designed for specialized applications and will not be considered here. As stated above, the nodes comprise an MIMD machine with no shared memory facilities. All communication between nodes is accomplished by passing messages through communication channels.

The individual processors are assumed to incorporate sufficient computational power and memory capacity to be capable of running application codes of an interesting size. What constitutes an interesting minimum problem size varies from application to application, but typically ranges upward from the capability of modern microcomputer systems. The individual processors may or may not have a sophisticated operating system.

Several features of the programming environment of a node distinguish it from a sequential computer. The most important difference is that a node has some number of communication channels that allow it to communicate with other nodes in the ensemble. A communication channel implements point-to-point communication between two nodes. Another feature of the node environment is a unique identifying number, the processor number, which will be referred to as *procnum*. Since a copy of the same program is typically loaded into each of the nodes of the concurrent processor, the processor number is very important for referring to a specific node within the ensemble. Another useful parameter of the node environment is the total number of nodes used by the application, which will be referred to as *nproc*.

Considered collectively, the processors which comprise the ensemble machine are connected by a communication network composed of the communication channels connecting pairs of nodes. As illustrated in Fig. 4-1, a large number of possible interconnection schemes could be used, each with its own special properties. The fully interconnected network offers the greatest generality of interprocessor communication, but implementing such a network in hardware is clearly impractical for more than a relatively small number of processors. More restricted networks such as lattices or trees trade a reduction in the number of direct connections for greater simplicity of implementation.

Examples of Interconnection Topologies

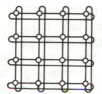
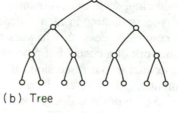

(a) Grid   (b) Tree

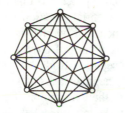
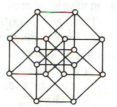

(c) Fully Interconnected   (d) 4 Dimensional
                                                Hypercube

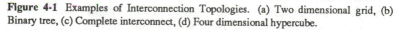

Figure 4-1 Examples of Interconnection Topologies. (a) Two dimensional grid, (b) Binary tree, (c) Complete interconnect, (d) Four dimensional hypercube.

Since we would like to avoid having the interconnection topology of the concurrent processor become an issue before we even discuss specific algorithms, we choose to consider the most general case, the fully interconnected topology. Such a topology serves as a good model for shared memory, multiprocessor machines. Since we are discussing a virtual concurrent processor these problems will be overlooked for now. As various concurrent algorithms are presented in subsequent chapters, we will note that the generality of the fully interconnected topology is not needed. After learning what restrictions can be imposed on the interconnection topology, we will return to the implementation issues of the communication network in Chap. 14.

In the fully interconnected topology, a *communication channel* connects each pair of nodes in the concurrent processor. In order to identify a specific communication channel, an identifying number is associated with each channel. A convenient way of numbering the communication channels in the virtual concurrent processor is for the channel number to correspond to the processor number of the node at the other end of the channel. While such a numbering scheme for communication channels is not always the most useful, we will use it in the virtual concurrent processor because of its simplicity when the fully interconnected topology is used.

So far we have not mentioned how processes map onto the nodes of the concurrent machine. The virtual concurrent processor allows us to discuss environments in which there are many processes per node. However, for concreteness we will assume a one-to-one mapping between processes and nodes. Having a multitasking environment in each node is necessary for some advanced applications, but for the applications we shall be considering, such an environment would only add unneeded complexity. In addition to the process running in each node, the concurrent processor has a special process, called the control process, that handles tasks that do not otherwise conveniently fit into the framework of a concurrent processor. We shall leave the location of the control process unspecified in our discussion. It could reside in its own special processor or in a host computer. Alternatively, it could run in one of the nodes, in addition to the process that runs in each of the nodes. In order for the nodes to be able to refer to the control process, it is assigned its own unique value of *procnum*, even though we have not specified the node in which the control process actually resides.

The main reason for creating a special control process is that concurrent algorithms typically have some tasks that are inherently sequential. Section 3-6 describes why such components do not, in general, lead to large concurrent overheads. While any one of the nodes could handle the sequential tasks, having a control process allows the sequential components to be considered as conceptually separate from the concurrent tasks of the algorithm. The additional process conveniently handles tasks that do not fit into the symmetry of processes running in the nodes of the ensemble. The control process is appropriately named because one of its major tasks in a typical application program is the coordination and monitoring of the concurrent processor. Since the proper handling of the sequential components of an algorithm is essential for efficient implementation, the concept of a distinct control process will be important in the design of concurrent algorithms. We note that because of its special role, the control process has very little computation to perform in a good algorithm, a feature that further distinguishes it from the node processes which handle the bulk of the computational load. The concept of a control process is refined in Chaps. 6 and 15 in which a general-purpose control process called CUBIX is discussed.

4-3 Basic Communication Routines

Having introduced the virtual concurrent processor that we shall use to explore concurrent programming techniques, we now define the communication routines which will be used to program the virtual concurrent processor. As mentioned previously, communication between nodes or processes is implemented by sending discrete messages on the communication channels that connect pairs of nodes. All communications between processes are implemented through reciprocal operations involving coordinated transmitting and receiving by the participating processes. Having communications implemented by pairs of complementary routines allows us to avoid making unnecessary machine-dependent assumptions about the communication channels. By requiring that the transmits and receives be coordinated by the participating nodes, we limit the application programs to using *expected* communications. Expected communications means that a node cannot write to another node unless the destination node is prepared to receive the message. This type of communication model is also termed *loosely synchronous*. Although in Chap. 14 we consider a more general method of providing communication capabilities to the nodes, we have found that the majority of scientific calculations fall into this loosely synchronous category.

We do not specify the language used in programming the virtual concurrent processor. However, for ease of programming and portability it is essential that high-level languages, such as C and FORTRAN, should run in the nodes. Throughout this chapter the basic communication routines of the virtual concurrent processor will be specified in sections of pseudocode. This pseudocode is representative of the high-level language used in a particular implementation. A full description of the pseudocode used in this book is given in Appendix A.

We begin by introducing a complementary pair of communication routines that provide the capability of transmitting and receiving messages between pairs of nodes connected by a channel. The routines are *vm_write* and *vm_read*, and are defined in Code 4-1.

```
int_fun vm_write ( buf, proc, nbytes )
declare_buf buf;
declare_int proc;
declare_int nbytes;


int_fun vm_read ( buf, proc, nbytes )
declare_buf buf;
declare_int proc;
declare_int nbytes;
```

Code 4-1 Primitive Routines for Interprocessor Communication

The routine *vm_write* causes *nbytes* bytes of data stored in *buf* to be written to the communication channel indicated by *proc*. Since we have labeled the communication channels of the virtual concurrent processor by the processor number of the node on the other side of the channel, we will use channel number and destination processor interchangeably.

The complementary routine, *vm_read*, causes at most *nbytes* of data to be read from the communication channel *proc* and stored in *buf*. The number of bytes actually read is determined by the number written by the transmitting node, so the transmitting node and the receiving node do not have to use the same value of *nbytes*. However, if the length of the message sent by the transmitting node is greater than the maximum set by the receiving node, an error is generated. If an error occurs while reading or writing a message, *vm_read* or *vm_write* returns an error code. Otherwise, the number of bytes read or written is returned.

In addition to defining the routines that perform the reading and writing operations on the communication channels, we must examine how the communications affect application programs so that we can use them effectively. When *vm_read* is called by a program, the processor checks whether a message is ready to be read from the indicated channel. If no message is ready, the processor continues to check for a message until one is available. The message is then read into the buffer and *vm_read* returns the number of bytes read. If the source processor does not send a message *vm_read* will not return, and execution of the application program cannot continue.

In a similar fashion, *vm_write* checks whether the indicated channel is ready for a message to be written. As with *vm_read*, if the channel is not ready, *vm_write* continues to check it until it is ready. When the channel is ready, the message is written and *vm_write* returns the number of bytes written. Since the channel typically has some capacity to buffer data and we do not want the behavior of *vm_write* to depend on the size of the channel buffer, *vm_write* waits until the destination node calls *vm_read* before returning. When we discuss a specific implementation of *vm_read* and *vm_write* in Chap. 14, we will explain the importance of requiring that *vm_write* not return until the destination node calls *vm_read*. For now we simply postulate the behavior of *vm_write* and note that it is consistent with requiring that a call of *vm_write* be complemented with a call of *vm_read* in the destination node.

Both *vm_read* and *vm_write* are known as *blocking* communication routines, and may be implemented by continually polling the channel until it is ready. Using blocking communications in an application program has an important synchronizing effect on the processors. As we have mentioned, the nodes comprise an MIMD machine in which the node processes are running asynchronously. However, when a node calls *vm_read* to receive data from another node, it cannot continue until the message is received, and the message cannot be received until the source processor has written the message. Thus, *vm_read* has imposed a strong synchronizing condition; it blocks further computation until the source node reaches its call to *vm_write*. If the source node has also called *vm_read* by mistake, neither node can become unblocked and *deadlock* occurs. However, deadlock can always be avoided by correctly complementing *vm_read* with *vm_write* and vice versa. Likewise, a node that calls *vm_write* to send data to another node suspends execution of its program until the destination node calls *vm_read*, and thus imposes a similar synchronizing condition along with the attendant possibility of deadlock. It remains true that between communication calls the processors run asynchronously, perhaps executing entirely different instructions. In Sec. 22-5 non-blocking versions of *vm_read* and *vm_write* are discussed, and lead to the requirement of an explicit synchronization routine, *vm_comsync*.

The synchronizing condition imposed by the blocking communication routines, *vm_read* and *vm_write*, is an example of a *rendezvous*, and has important consequences for application programs. Since all the communication routines that will be presented in this chapter for the virtual concurrent processor are blocking, we mention some of the consequences now, leaving the details for the chapters which present specific concurrent algorithms.

The most important effect of the synchronization imposed by the communication routines is that the nodes are forced to execute their programs in a loose synchronization. However, the synchronization, or lockstep, is imposed by the application program through its use of the communication routines, not by the nodes actually running synchronously. Since the synchronization is imposed only when the communication routines are called, the lockstep may be sloppy, with the nodes proceeding at their own pace between communications. If one node has less computation to perform than nodes with which it must communicate, it wastes time while waiting to read or write. Thus, an efficient concurrent algorithm must carefully balance the computational loads of nodes that communicate. Balancing the loads between every communication step in the algorithm is essential because the slowest node always determines the amount of time taken by each computational step.

We shall refer to the collection of blocking communication routines as a *crystalline* operating system since they are most useful for algorithms which incorporate a high degree of regularity and predictability in the tasks performed concurrently. The problems must be regular in the sense that the communications can be expected by the participating nodes and that the computational loads are well balanced, so that the algorithm is not adversely affected by the synchronizing effects of the blocking communications.

In Chap. 22 we show how to implement *vm_read* and *vm_write* on machines like the hypercube, which do not have a full interconnect between nodes. This is possible with one additional restriction. As defined above, *vm_read* and *vm_write* only require loose synchronization between source and destination nodes. An implementation using the efficient CrOS III *crystal_router*, described in Sec. 22-2, further requires that the loose synchronization be shared between all nodes traversed by the message as it travels from source to destination. On the hypercube, the basic CrOS III system provides the most efficient communication using channel addressing to nearest neighbor nodes, while the virtual concurrent processor system, built on top of CrOS III provides loosely synchronous, node-addressed communication, with additional software overhead in the message transmission.

4-4 Collective Communication Routines

The two crystalline communication routines introduced in the previous section are adequate for all communications needs, at least within the limitations of the virtual concurrent processor as we have defined it. A node can communicate directly with any other node in the ensemble using *vm_read* and *vm_write*. However, we have argued that the fully interconnected communication network we use in the virtual concurrent processor would be difficult to implement in a real machine. With the goal of imposing restrictions on which pairs of nodes are directly connected by a communication channel, we would like to group commonly used communication sequences into conceptual units.

Additional communication routines are then added to the crystalline operating system that reflect the conceptual grouping. The resulting collective communication routines have the advantage of guiding our thinking toward concurrency while casting the communications operations in a form which may be efficiently implemented on actual machines.

As the simplest example of collective communication, consider two nodes that need to exchange data with each other. Such an exchange can be easily implemented by having one node write while the other reads and then switching roles. But how does the programmer specify which node should write first? A simple method uses the processor numbers of the nodes. The node whose processor number is greater calls *vm_write* first while the other node calls *vm_read* first. However, now consider the slightly more complicated case of a subset of nodes that write to one node and read from a different node in such a way that data is shifted one step around a ring. Determining which nodes should write first and which should read first is not as simple as when only two nodes exchange data.

Presumably an algorithm could be devised that would correctly specify the order of the reading and writing operations. However, the application programmer should not have to explicitly perform the ordering every time. Furthermore, situations in which data is both read and written frequently occur when crystalline communications are used, because the applications are usually symmetric. Thus, if one node needs to receive data from another node, all the nodes typically need to receive data from some other node, so all the nodes must also transmit data. Clearly, a new communication routine should be added to the crystalline operating system that performs a collective write and read of data.

The new communication routine that we introduce is *vm_shift*, which causes data to be both written and read and is complementary to itself. Thus, all nodes involved in the collective communication call *vm_shift* concurrently.

```
int_fun vm_shift ( inbuf, sourceproc, inbytes, outbuf, destproc, outbytes )
declare_buf inbuf;
declare_int sourceproc;
declare_int inbytes;
declare_buf outbuf;
declare_int destproc;
declare_int outbytes;
```

Code 4-2 Routine for Collective Ensemble Communication

The arguments of *vm_shift* are exactly the same as the combined arguments of *vm_read* and *vm_write*. It causes at most *inbytes* bytes of data to be read from processor *sourceproc* and stored in *inbuf*. In addition, *outbytes* bytes of data are written from *outbuf* to the node indicated by *destproc*. As with *vm_read*, if *sourceproc* sends more than *inbytes* bytes of data, an error code is returned. Otherwise, *vm_shift* returns the number of bytes read.

Let us now examine another commonly used form of collective communication, a broadcast to a subset of the nodes. We will see in Chap. 10 that partial broadcasts are frequently needed to program matrix algorithms. While the source node could use *vm_write* to write a message to each of the nodes in the subset of the ensemble, we anticipate the possibility that a partial broadcast could be implemented on a real concurrent processor more efficiently as a collective unit. In addition, by creating a special broadcast routine, we have again provided a conceptual grouping of several communication operations which should make understanding the principles of concurrent programming easier.

A partial broadcast routine should be complementary to itself (as in the case of *vm_shift*) for ease of use. The nodes participating in the broadcast must be indicated by some method and the source node must also be specified. One method of indicating which nodes are involved in the broadcast is by listing their processor numbers in an array and passing this array to the broadcast routine as an argument. While an array of processor numbers may not be the optimal way to indicate the participating nodes in a real implementation, it is easy to understand and is adequate for the virtual concurrent processor.

```
int_fun vm_bcast ( buf, sourceproc, num, nodes, nbytes )
declare_buf buf;
declare_int sourceproc;
declare_int num;
declare_buf nodes; ( an integer array of num elements )
declare_int nbytes;
```

Code 4-3 Routine for Broadcast from a Node to Other Nodes

The new communication routine we add to the crystalline operating system is *vm_bcast*. The routine *vm_bcast* causes *nbytes* bytes of data stored in *buf* in the processor *sourceproc* to be written to all other nodes listed in the array *nodes*. The total number of nodes listed in *nodes* is *num*. For nodes other than the source node, at most *nbytes* will be read from the source node and stored in *buf*. The nodes involved in the broadcast do not have to use the same value of *nbytes*, but if a node uses a smaller value of *nbytes* than the source node, an error code is returned. Otherwise, the number of bytes read is returned, except in the source node, in which the number of bytes written is returned. All nodes involved in the broadcast must list the same nodes in *nodes* and use the same values of *sourceproc* and *num*.

As a third example of collective communication, consider an algorithm in which each node obtains a partial result that must be combined with the results of the other nodes. For example, each node may calculate a result which is to be added to the results of the other nodes. Although such a combining operation could be implemented using *vm_write* and *vm_read* interspersed with arithmetic operations, we shall postulate a new communication routine that groups the necessary communication operations into a unit.

The resulting routine is somewhat different in nature from the other two collective communication routines we have presented. In addition to communication between nodes to exchange the data, calculation is required to combine the data. However, regardless of the type of calculation used to combine the data, the communication operations needed to exchange the data remain the same.

Since the necessary communications are not affected by the method of combining the data, we do not want any particular method programmed into the collective communication routine. Otherwise, a separate routine would be required to provide each desired method. Fortunately, high-level languages such as C and FORTRAN allow function names to be passed to routines via the routine's argument list. Thus, the particular method of combining the data can be specified by an argument of the communication routine.

A standard format is needed for the combining function that is flexible enough for it to be used in a wide variety of situations. An important requirement of the format should be that it be applicable regardless of the types of data items being combined. Any type of data can be passed by reference to the combining function by means of a buffer. The combining function knows the type of data on which it operates, and the communication routine that uses the combining function need only know the size of the data items. Therefore, the required argument format for the combining function should include two buffers. The combining function should return its result by overwriting the first buffer. In addition, a third argument gives the size of the data objects, which may be useful in some cases as we will see when we discuss an actual implementation in Chap. 14. We do not want the result to depend upon the order in which the combining function is applied to pairs of partial results in the nodes, so we require the combining function to be both associative and commutative.

The new collective communication routine is called *vm_combine*, which causes *nitems* data items to be taken from *buf* and combined with the data items from all other nodes in the ensemble. Each data item is *size* bytes in length. They are combined in pairs by the function *func*. The contents of *buf* are overwritten with the result of the combining operation. All nodes must call *vm_combine* and all must use the same combining function and the same values of *size* and *nitems*. The examples in Sec. 4-8 will illustrate the use of *vm_combine* and the definition of a simple combining function.

```
int_fun vm_combine ( buf, func, size, nitems )
declare_buf buf;
function func;
declare_int size;
declare_int nitems;
```

Code 4-4 Routine for Collective Combination of Data from Nodes

4-5 Communications between Nodes and Control Process

We now return to our discussion of the control process and its relationship to the processes running in the nodes of the concurrent processor. We have assigned to the control process the conceptually distinct task of coordinating and monitoring the ensemble and executing the inherently sequential components of an algorithm. Even though the control process could communicate with the node processes using the communication routines as we have presented them, such direct communication would blur the distinctive features of the control process. As in the previous section, we would like to introduce collective communication routines through which the control process and the node processes communicate. Such routines will serve to maintain the intended distinction of the control process.

Collective communications between the control process and the nodes are implemented as reciprocal operations involving pairs of communication routines. One of the routines is called by all of the nodes in the ensemble, while the other is called by the control process. Two modes of communication are supported, one which allows the control process to send data to the nodes, and one which allows the nodes to send data to the control process. Both modes cause separate messages to be communicated between the control process and the nodes.

The mode of communication from the control process to the nodes causes the control process to send a separate message to each of the nodes. The routines, *vm_loadelt* and *vm_loadcp*, are called in the ensemble and the control process, respectively. Here, and elsewhere in this volume, the suffix *elt* is used to refer to the elements (or nodes) of the concurrent processor. The suffix *cp* refers to the control process.

```
int_fun vm_loadelt ( bufelt, nbytes )
declare_buf bufelt;
declare_int nbytes;

int_fun vm_loadcp ( bufcp, bufmap )
declare_buf bufcp;
declare_buf bufmap; ( an integer array )
```

Code 4-5 Routines for Transfer of Data from Control Process to Nodes

The routine *vm_loadelt* causes at most *nbytes* bytes of data to be read from the control process and placed in *bufelt*. All nodes must call *vm_loadelt*, but they may use different values of *nbytes*. Each node receives a separate message from the control process and the messages may have different lengths. If the message a node receives is longer than the maximum length specified by *nbytes*, an error code is returned. Otherwise, the number of bytes read is returned.

The routine *vm_loadcp* causes a separate message to be sent to each node in the ensemble according to the specification in the array *bufmap* , which contains the value of *nproc* followed by the length of the message in bytes for each node. The messages are taken from *bufcp* and are assumed to be concatenated in order of processor number, so that the first message goes to processor number 0, the second to processor number 1, and so forth. If the value of *nproc* obtained from *bufmap* is different than the current value of *nproc* , then *vm_loadcp* returns an error code. The examples in Sec. 4-8 illustrate the use of *vm_loadelt* and *vm_loadcp* .

The second mode of collective communication between the nodes and the control process performs the inverse function of the *load* routines. The routines *vm_dumpelt* and *vm_dumpcp* allow separate messages to be sent from each of the nodes to the control process. The *load* and *dump* routines are inverses in the sense that data which is written to the control process with the *dump* routines can be restored to the nodes with the *load* routines.

```
int_fun vm_dumpelt ( bufelt, nbytes )
declare_buf bufelt;
declare_int nbytes;

int_fun vm_dumpcp ( bufcp, nbytes, bufmap )
declare_buf bufcp;
declare_int nbytes;
declare_buf bufmap; ( an integer array )
```

Code 4-6 Routines for Transfer of Data from Nodes to Control Process

The routine *vm_dumpelt* causes *nbytes* bytes of data to be written from *bufelt* to the control process. All nodes must call *vm_dumpelt*, but they may use different values of *nbytes*. The routine *vm_dumpcp* causes a maximum of *nbytes* bytes of data to be read from each of the nodes in the ensemble and stored in *bufcp*. The array *bufmap* is created with the same format that *vm_loadcp* expects: the current value of *nproc* followed by the length of the message from each of the nodes. The messages are concatenated into *bufcp* in order of their processor numbers, which is also the order expected by *vm_loadcp*. If any of the messages from the nodes is longer than the maximum length specified by the control process, *vm_dumpcp* returns an error code.

The collective communications involving the nodes and the control process are crystalline communication routines just like the routines introduced in Sec. 4-3 and 4-4. Thus, the same limitations apply to the collective routines as discussed in Sec. 4-3. In particular, the participating nodes are synchronized by the communication operations. So when a collective communication routine affects all nodes and the control process, all processes are blocked until the slowest process executes its call to the communication routine. Again we see the importance of having communicating processes perform tasks that take nearly the same length of time between communication operations.

We have thus far proposed communication routines that allow the two-way transmission of *distinct* data between the ensemble nodes and the control process. It is natural at this point to complete the set of control/ensemble functions by introducing routines to handle the transmission of *common* messages in this context. The functions needed to handle these tasks are obtained as extensions of the routines *vm_bcast* and *vm_combine* introduced previously.

The two new routines *vm_bcastcp* and *vm_bcastelt* are defined in Code 4-7. Their usage is entirely analogous to that of the *vm_loadcp/vm_loadelt* pair, except that the entire contents of the argument buffer of *vm_bcastcp* is sent to all nodes, rather than breaking it up. In this case, the broadcast is assumed to be global, so there occurs no argument in either routine specifying the participating nodes.

```
int_fun vm_bcastcp ( buf, nbytes )
declare_buf buf;
declare_int nbytes;


int_fun vm_bcastelt ( buf, nbytes )
declare_buf buf;
declare_int nbytes;
```

Code 4-7 Broadcast Routines between Nodes and Control Process

In Code 4-8, we define *vm_combcp* and *vm_combelt* as the control/ensemble routines analogous to *vm_combine*. Again, the usage of these routines follows directly from their predecessors, and in this case, the control process receives a single message which is the result of the ensemble-wide combination of messages determined by the combining function.

```
int_fun vm_combcp ( buf, size, nitems )
declare_buf buf;
declare_int size;
declare_int nitems;


int_fun vm_combelt ( buf, func, size, nitems )
declare_buf  buf;
function func;
declare_int size;
declare_int nitems;
```

Code 4-8 Combine Routines between Nodes and Control Process

4-6 Mapping a Decomposition Topology onto the Concurrent Processor

So far we have presented a variety of routines that implement communication between processes of the virtual concurrent processor. The communication routines require either a source or a destination processor number, except when the source or destination is implied, as in the routines that implement collective communication between the nodes and the control process. However, when an actual application is programmed on a concurrent machine, the problem is usually decomposed into subproblems that are connected by some communication topology without explicitly assigning a particular node to each region.

For example, in a problem involving a large matrix, the matrix might be decomposed into square submatrices, so that each submatrix could be assigned to a node. Such a decomposition results in a *decomposition topology* that is a two-dimensional grid of submatrices. While the algorithm can easily specify the necessary communications in terms of the decomposition topology, the communication routines require that processor numbers be used to refer to the source and destination nodes.

In order for a concurrent algorithm to specify the source and destination processor numbers conveniently, it needs a mapping of the nodes in the concurrent processor onto the regions in the decomposition topology. The last set of routines we introduce in this chapter maps the nodes of the ensemble onto a particular decomposition topology. Although the mapping routines are not communication routines, we include them with the discussion of the communication routines because they provide a convenient utility for effectively using the communication routines. In addition, the set of mapping routines anticipate that not all schemes for mapping the concurrent processor onto a decomposition topology will be equally efficient on a given machine.

While many types of mappings are possible, the mapping function that we present here is a particular instance of the mapping concept that is limited to decomposition topologies which are Cartesian grids. We refer to this particular mapping function as *gridmap*, which is implemented by a set of three routines. While *gridmap* is not strictly necessary in a fully interconnected machine topology, we introduce it here so that more restricted hardware configurations can also be used.

The first routine, *vm_gridinit*, takes the dimensionality of the grid and the number of nodes in each dimension as arguments and performs the necessary initializations for the other two *gridmap* routines.

```
int_fun vm_gridinit ( dim, num )
declare_int dim ;
declare_buf num ; ( an integer array )
```

Code 4-9 Routine to Set Up Processor-To-Mesh Mapping

The routine *vm_gridinit* maps the nodes of the ensemble onto a *dim*–dimensional Cartesian grid. The array *num* contains the number of nodes in each dimension of the grid. If *vm_gridinit* cannot perform the requested mapping on the ensemble it returns an error code. The routine *vm_gridinit* must be called before the other two *gridmap* routines are called.

The other two *gridmap* routines, *vm_gridcoord* and *vm_gridproc*, return information to the application program about the decomposition topology indicated by the arguments of *vm_gridinit*.

```
int_fun vm_gridcoord ( proc, coord )
declare_int proc;
declare_buf coord; ( an integer array )

int_fun vm_gridproc ( coord )
declare_buf coord; ( an integer array )
```

Code 4-10 Routines to Obtain Mapping Between Processors and Mesh Coordinates

The routine *vm_gridcoord* stores the Cartesian coordinates of the node whose processor number is *proc* in the array indicated by *coord*. The coordinates in each dimension are numbered consecutively starting with 0, and the array *coord* must have as many elements as the dimensionality of the decomposition topology. If the specified node is not part of the decomposition topology, or if *vm_gridinit* has not yet been called, *vm_gridcoord* returns an error code. The routine *vm_gridproc* performs the inverse of the mapping performed by *vm_gridcoord*. Given an array containing the coordinates of a node in the decomposition topology, *vm_gridproc* returns the processor number of the node. If the coordinates are not within the bounds of the mapping as specified in *vm_gridinit*, then *vm_gridproc* instead returns an error code.

4-7 Comments on Real Concurrent Processors

In the preceding sections, we have made several references to the possibility of restricting the communications available on the virtual concurrent processor to allow an efficient implementation on a real machine. If the communication channels are implemented in hardware, having every node connected to every other node by a channel is impractical, except when the number of nodes is small. However, the fully interconnected topology is interesting because it allows us to consider implementing algorithms without being constrained by the interconnection topology of a specific machine.

One method of reducing the number of communication channels needed by a real concurrent processor relies on the concept of collective communication routines. Collective communications, such as those that allow communication between the control process and the nodes, need not require that all nodes be able to communicate directly with the control process. By defining collective routines, we not only provide a conceptual grouping that clarifies the discussion of algorithms but also allow a machine-dependent implementation of the collective routines. A machine-dependent implementation is allowed because the machine dependencies are isolated from the application programs by the collective routines. Hiding machine dependencies through the use of collective communication routines is an important means of allowing an efficient, but reasonably general and easily used communication system.

As algorithms are presented in the following chapters, we show that the full generality of the fully interconnected machine is not needed for a rich variety of problems. In addition to showing how the algorithms are implemented using the crystalline communication routines of the virtual concurrent processor, we give actual performance measurements for the algorithms. We obtained the performance measurements by running the algorithms on a real concurrent processor that was designed and built at Caltech. The actual implementations use a specific version of the crystalline operating system, CrOS III, that will be presented in Chap. 14. The interconnection topology used in Caltech's concurrent processor is that of a hypercube, which was introduced in Chaps. 2 and 3 and will be further described in Chap. 14.

We discuss the effectiveness of the concurrent algorithms in the following chapters by calculating and then measuring their efficiencies. Although we have not discussed the communication speed or the computational speed of the virtual concurrent processor, both are important issues in a real concurrent processor and must be known in order to estimate an algorithm's efficiency. Figure 4-2 illustrates the communication speed as a function of message length on the Caltech Mark II and INTEL iPSC hypercube concurrent processors. The time required for a basic communication operation (consisting of writing and reading a 32-bit word) is around 60 μsec. The nodes of both hypercubes, which use the Intel 8087 floating-point coprocessor, perform floating-point operations in about 30 μsec. Both characteristic times will be important in discussions of the efficiencies of the algorithms presented in subsequent chapters. These times were defined in Sec. 3-5 and listed in Table 2-1 [Kolawa 85, Quinlan 87].

4-8 Some Simple Examples

In this section, the usage of the communication routines will be illustrated in two simple example programs. The examples should serve to clarify the manner in which a typical concurrent application is structured and managed, setting the stage for the discussion in subsequent chapters. The structure of the two examples is similar and is typical of concurrent programs managed by a control process. The control process first sends the element code to each of the nodes and initiates execution. The control process may then send some input data to each node. These data are processed by the nodes which return their results to the control process, where they are output. Listings of the source code for the examples of this section are given in C and FORTRAN, although in principle any high-level language could be used. In the case of the FORTRAN programs the requirement that all function and variable names contain no more than six characters has led to the modification or truncation of some names. To avoid confusion wherever such an abridged name is mentioned in the ensuing discussion, the FORTRAN name is given in parentheses.

In addition to the communication routines discussed earlier in this chapter, reference is made in the example programs to two additional routines. The first is *vm_downld* (VMDOWN). This routine, which is called in the control process program, loads the node program into each of the nodes and initiates execution. In the node programs, the number of processors, *nproc*, and the processor number, *procnum* (PROCNU), are declared in the C versions as external integers, whereas in the FORTRAN versions they are placed in a COMMON block. The values of these variables are assigned in the routine *vm_init* (VMINIT).

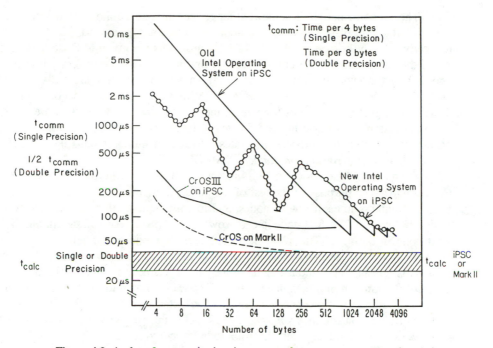

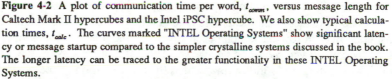

Figure 4-2 A plot of communication time per word, t_{comm}, versus message length for Caltech Mark II hypercubes and the Intel iPSC hypercube. We also show typical calculation times, t_{calc}. The curves marked "INTEL Operating Systems" show significant latency or message startup compared to the simpler crystalline systems discussed in the book. The longer latency can be traced to the greater functionality in these INTEL Operating Systems.

The C program run in the control process for the first example is shown in Code 4-11. The program executed in each node of the virtual concurrent processor is given in Code 4-12. The corresponding FORTRAN programs are shown in Code 4-13 and Code 4-14. In the examples considered here, the number of processors, *nproc*, is fixed at 32. This value is assigned in the control process by means of a *define* statement in the C code, and by a PARAMETER statement in the FORTRAN code. The first action of the control process is to call the routine *vm_downld* (VMDOWN), which loads the node program into each of the nodes and initiates execution. As may be seen from Code 4-12 (4-14), each node evaluates the square of its unique processor number, *procnum* (PROCNU), and then calls the routine *vm_combine* (VMCOMB) to find the sum over all processors. After calling *vm_combine* (VMCOMB), each node is left with the sum of the squares of the processor numbers residing in the variable *sum*. Each node then transfers the square of its processor number and the global sum of squares to a buffer and sends this to the control process using the routine *vm_dumpelt* (VMDMPE). The program in the nodes then terminates. Returning to Code 4-11 (4-13) we see that these results are read in the control process by the routine *vm_dumpcp* (VMDMPC). The control process then outputs the results from each processor, and the program terminates.

The second example is somewhat lengthier but is still quite straightforward. The C code for the control process and the node programs are given in Code 4-15 and 4-16, respectively. The corresponding FORTRAN programs are given in Code 4-17 and 4-18. As in the first example, the control process first loads the node program into the nodes and initiates execution. Code 4-16 (4-18) shows that each node calls the routines *vm_gridinit* (VMGINT) and *vm_gridcoord* (VMGCRD) to map the nodes into a two-dimensional grid consisting of 8 nodes in the x-direction and 4 nodes in the y-direction. Each node stores the Cartesian coordinates of its position in the grid in the array *coord*. Meanwhile, the control process generates 32 random numbers, and then sends one to each node using the routine *vm_loadcp* (VMLODC).

Each node reads the random number sent to it with the routine *vm_loadelt* (VMLODE). The purpose of the rest of the node program is to find the maximum of the random numbers in each row of nodes, and to communicate this value to the rest of the nodes in the row. The first node in each row sends the value of its random number to the next node in the row. This node then compares its random number with that received from the first node, and passes on the larger of the two to the next node in the row. This process is repeated until the last node in the row is reached, at which point the maximum value of the random numbers in each row of nodes is known to the last node in that row. All of the communications between nodes are effected by means of the basic interprocessor communication routines *vm_read* (VMREAD) and *vm_write* (VMWRIT). This type of process, in which data is moved from node to node down a line of nodes, is known as a *pipe* and will be used again in the matrix algorithms of Chaps. 10 and 20.

The next stage of the example is to communicate the maximum value stored in the last node in each row back along each row to all the other nodes in that row. This is also done by calls to *vm_read* and *vm_write*. The last node in each row passes the maximum value to the next node in the row, which then passes it on to the next, and so on. Each node then communicates the maximum value for its row, and its Cartesian position in the grid, to the control process by means of two calls to *vm_dumpelt* (VMDMPE). The program in each of the nodes then terminates. The control process reads the results from the nodes using the routine *vm_dumpcp* (VMDMPC) and outputs them. The program in the control process then terminates.

After each call to a communications routine in the control process, the value returned by the routine is checked for errors. If an error is detected the routine *cp_abort* (CPABRT) is called. This outputs an appropriate message and then terminates execution of the program. It is good programming practice to also check the values returned by communications routines in the node program, and to return a flag to the control process when an error occurs. However, for the sake of conciseness, no such checks are made in the node programs listed in Code 4-12 (4-14) and 4-16 (4-18). The Software Supplement contains a version of these programs in which the return status of communication routines in the node programs is checked for errors, and the reader is referred to that volume for a fuller version of the programs discussed here.

```
#include <stdio.h>
#define ERROR -1
#define nproc 32

main()
{
        int i,nbytes,status,buffer[2*nproc],bufmap[1+nproc];

        status = vm_downld(nproc,"example1ELT");
        if(status==ERROR) cp_abort("vm_downld");

        nbytes = 2*sizeof(int);
        status  = vm_dumpcp(buffer,nbytes,bufmap);
        if(status==ERROR) cp_abort("vm_dumpcp");
        for(i=0;i<nproc;++i)
                printf(" \n Processor number %2d : n*n = %3d, sum of n*n = %5d",
                i, buffer [2*i], buffer [2*i + 1]);
        printf ( " \n \n");
        exit(0);
}

cp_abort(s)
char s[40];
{
        fprintf(stderr," \n \n An error occurred in %s - program terminated \ n",s);
        exit(1);
}
```

Code 4-11 C Version of Control Processor Program for Example 1

```
extern int procnum;

main()
{
      int nbytes,status,n_squared,sum,nitems,buffer[2],int_add();

      status    = vm_init();
      n_squared = procnum*procnum;
      sum       = n_squared;
      nbytes    = sizeof(int);
      nitems    = 1;
      status = vm_combine(&sum,int_add,nbytes,nitems);

      buffer[0] = n_squared;
      buffer[1] = sum;
      nbytes *= 2;
      status    = vm_dumpelt(buffer,nbytes);
}

int int_add(ptr1,ptr2,size)
int *ptr1, *ptr2,size;
{
      *ptr1 += *ptr2;
      return 0;
}
```

Code 4-12 C Version of Node Program for Example 1

```
      PROGRAM EX1CP
      INTEGER ERROR
      PARAMETER (NPROC=32,ERROR=-1,INTSIZ=4)
      INTEGER BUFFER(2*NPROC),BUFMAP(1+NPROC),STATUS,VMDMPC,VMDOWN
      STATUS = VMDOWN(NPROC,"EXAMPLE1ELT")
      IF(STATUS.EQ.ERROR) CALL CPABRT("VMDOWN")
      NBYTES = 2*INTSIZ
      STATUS = VMDMPC(BUFFER,NBYTES,BUFMAP)
      IF(STATUS.EQ.ERROR) CALL CPABRT("VMDMPC")
      DO 10 I=1,NPROC
         WRITE(*,100)I-1,BUFFER(2*I-1),BUFFER(2*I)
 10      CONTINUE
      STOP
100   FORMAT(/'Processor number ',I2,' : n*n = ',I4', sum of n*n = ',I5)
      END

      SUBROUTINE CPABRT(S)
      CHARACTER*6 S
      WRITE(*,100)S
      STOP
100   FORMAT(//' An error occurred in ',A,' - program terminated'/)
      END
```

Code 4-13 FORTRAN Version of Control Processor Program for Example 1

```
PROGRAM EX1ELT
PARAMETER (INTSIZ=4)
INTEGER SUM,BUFFER(2),PROCNU,VMINIT,VMCOMB,VMDMPE,STATUS
COMMON/PARAM/NPROC,PROCNU
CALL VMINIT
NSQURD = PROCNU*PROCNU
SUM    = NSQURD
NBYTES = INTSIZ
NITEMS = 1
STATUS = VMCOMB(SUM,INTADD,NBYTES,NITEMS)
BUFFER(1) = NSQURD
BUFFER(2) = SUM
NBYTES = 2*INTSIZ
STATUS = VMDMPE(BUFFER,NBYTES)
STOP
END

INTEGER FUNCTION INTADD(INT1,INT2,SIZE)
INTEGER INT1,INT2,SIZE
INT1 = INT1 + INT2
INTADD = 0
RETURN
END
```

Code 4-14 FORTRAN Version of Node Program for Example 1

Processor number	0 :	n * n =	0,	sum of n * n = 10416
Processor number	1 :	n * n =	1,	sum of n * n = 10416
Processor number	2 :	n * n =	4,	sum of n * n = 10416
Processor number	3 :	n * n =	9,	sum of n * n = 10416
Processor number	4 :	n * n =	16,	sum of n * n = 10416
Processor number	5 :	n * n =	25,	sum of n * n = 10416
Processor number	6 :	n * n =	36,	sum of n * n = 10416
Processor number	7 :	n * n =	49,	sum of n * n = 10416
Processor number	8 :	n * n =	64,	sum of n * n = 10416
Processor number	9 :	n * n =	81,	sum of n * n = 10416
Processor number	10 :	n * n =	100,	sum of n * n = 10416
Processor number	11 :	n * n =	121,	sum of n * n = 10416
Processor number	12 :	n * n =	144,	sum of n * n = 10416
Processor number	13 :	n * n =	169,	sum of n * n = 10416
Processor number	14 :	n * n =	196,	sum of n * n = 10416
Processor number	15 :	n * n =	225,	sum of n * n = 10416
Processor number	16 :	n * n =	256,	sum of n * n = 10416
Processor number	17 :	n * n =	289,	sum of n * n = 10416
Processor number	18 :	n * n =	324,	sum of n * n = 10416
Processor number	19 :	n * n =	361,	sum of n * n = 10416
Processor number	20 :	n * n =	400,	sum of n * n = 10416
Processor number	21 :	n * n =	441,	sum of n * n = 10416
Processor number	22 :	n * n =	484,	sum of n * n = 10416
Processor number	23 :	n * n =	529,	sum of n * n = 10416
Processor number	24 :	n * n =	576,	sum of n * n = 10416
Processor number	25 :	n * n =	625,	sum of n * n = 10416
Processor number	26 :	n * n =	676,	sum of n * n = 10416
Processor number	27 :	n * n =	729,	sum of n * n = 10416
Processor number	28 :	n * n =	784,	sum of n * n = 10416
Processor number	29 :	n * n =	841,	sum of n * n = 10416
Processor number	30 :	n * n =	900,	sum of n * n = 10416
Processor number	31 :	n * n =	961,	sum of n * n = 10416

Output from Example 1

```c
#include <stdio.h>
#define ERROR -1
#define SEED  1
#define nproc 32

main()
{
      int i,nbytes,status,coord[2*nproc],bufmap[1+nproc];
      double buffer[nproc],max_num[nproc],drand();

      status = vm_downld(nproc,"example2ELT");
      if(status == ERROR) cp_abort("vm_downld");

      nbytes = sizeof(double);
      randset(SEED);
      bufmap[0] = nproc;
      for(i=0;i<nproc;++i){
            bufmap[i+1] = nbytes;
            buffer[i]   = drand();
      }
      status = vm_loadcp(buffer,bufmap);
      if(status == ERROR) cp_abort("vm_loadcp");

      status = vm_dumpcp(max_num,nbytes,bufmap);
      if(status == ERROR) cp_abort("vm_dumpcp");
      nbytes = 2*sizeof(int);
      status = vm_dumpcp(coord,nbytes,bufmap);
      if(status == ERROR) cp_abort("vm_dumpcp");
      printf("\n\nProcessor  x position  y position  Value    Row maximum");
      for(i=0;i<nproc;++i)
            printf("\n%6d %11d %11d %11.4f %11.4f",i,coord[2*i],
                  coord[2*i+1],buffer[i],max_num[i]);

      printf("\n\n");

      exit(0);
}
```

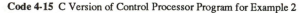

Code 4-15 C Version of Control Processor Program for Example 2

```
extern int procnum;

main()
{
    int nbytes,status,sourcepos[2],destpos[2],coord[2],num[2];
    int sourceproc,destproc,temp_proc;
    double max_num,temp;

    status = vm_init ();
    num[0] = 8;
    num[1] = 4;
    status = vm_gridinit(2,num);
    status = vm_gridcoord(procnum,coord);
    nbytes = sizeof(double);
    status = vm_loadelt(&max_num,nbytes);

    if( coord[0] != 0 ){
        sourcepos[0] = coord[0] - 1;
        sourcepos[1] = coord[1];
        sourceproc  = vm_gridproc(sourcepos);
        status = vm_read(&temp,sourceproc,nbytes);
        max_num = (max_num > temp) ? max_num : temp;
    }
    if( coord[0] != 7 ){
        destpos[0]  = coord[0] + 1;
        destpos[1]  = coord[1];
        destproc    = vm_gridproc(destpos);
        status = vm_write(&max_num,destproc,nbytes);
    }

    temp_proc = sourceproc;
    if( coord[0] !=7 ){
        sourceproc  = destproc;
        status = vm_read(&max_num,sourceproc,nbytes);
    }
    if( coord[0] !=0 ){
        destproc    = temp_proc;
        status = vm_write (&max_num,destproc,nbytes);
    }

    status = vm_dumpelt(&max_num,nbytes);
    nbytes = 2*sizeof(int);
    status = vm_dumpelt(coord,nbytes);
}
```

Code 4-16 C Version of Node Program for Example 2

```
PROGRAM EX2CP
INTEGER ERROR, DPSIZ, SEED
PARAMETER (NPROC=32,ERROR=-1,INTSIZ=4,DPSIZ=8,SEED=1)
INTEGER STATUS,VMDMPC,VMLODC,VMDOWN,
INTEGER BUFMAP (1 + NPROC), COORD (2*NPROC)
DOUBLE PRECISION RAND,BUFFER(NPROC),MAXNUM(NPROC)
STATUS = VMDOWN(NPROC,"EXAMPLE2ELT")
IF (STATUS.EQ.ERROR) CALL CPABRT("VMDOWN")
NBYTES = DPSIZ
CALL RNDSET(SEED)
BUFMAP(1) = NPROC
DO 10 I=1,NPROC
   BUFMAP(I+1) = NBYTES
10    BUFFER(I)  = RAND(0)
STATUS = VMLODC(BUFFER,BUFMAP)
IF (STATUS.EQ.ERROR) CALL CPABRT("VMLODC")
STATUS = VMDMPC(MAXNUM,NBYTES,BUFMAP)
IF (STATUS.EQ.ERROR) CALL CPABRT("VMDMPC")
NBYTES = 2*INTSIZ
STATUS = VMDMPC(COORD,NBYTES,BUFMAP)
IF (STATUS.EQ.ERROR) CALL CPABRT("VMDMPC")
WRITE(*,100)
DO 20 I=1,NPROC
   J2 = 2*I
   J1 = J2-1
   WRITE(*,101)I-1,COORD(J1),COORD(J2),BUFFER(I),MAXNUM(I)
20    CONTINUE
STOP
100  FORMAT(//' Processor x position y position   Value   Row maximum')
101  FORMAT(I8,I12,I12,F12.4,F12.4)
END
```

Code 4-17 FORTRAN Version of Control Processor Program for Example 2

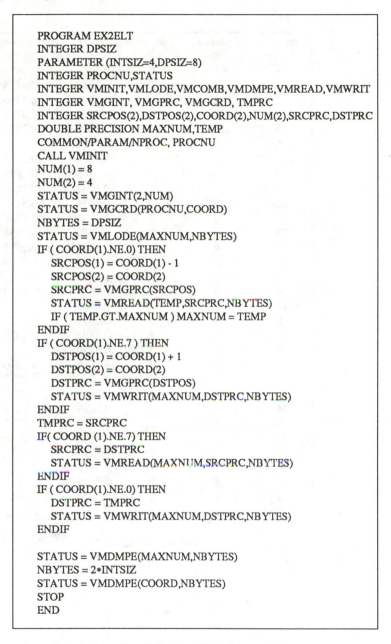

```
PROGRAM EX2ELT
INTEGER DPSIZ
PARAMETER (INTSIZ=4,DPSIZ=8)
INTEGER PROCNU,STATUS
INTEGER VMINIT,VMLODE,VMCOMB,VMDMPE,VMREAD,VMWRIT
INTEGER VMGINT, VMGPRC, VMGCRD, TMPRC
INTEGER SRCPOS(2),DSTPOS(2),COORD(2),NUM(2),SRCPRC,DSTPRC
DOUBLE PRECISION MAXNUM,TEMP
COMMON/PARAM/NPROC, PROCNU
CALL VMINIT
NUM(1) = 8
NUM(2) = 4
STATUS = VMGINT(2,NUM)
STATUS = VMGCRD(PROCNU,COORD)
NBYTES = DPSIZ
STATUS = VMLODE(MAXNUM,NBYTES)
IF ( COORD(1).NE.0) THEN
   SRCPOS(1) = COORD(1) - 1
   SRCPOS(2) = COORD(2)
   SRCPRC = VMGPRC(SRCPOS)
   STATUS = VMREAD(TEMP,SRCPRC,NBYTES)
   IF ( TEMP.GT.MAXNUM ) MAXNUM = TEMP
ENDIF
IF ( COORD(1).NE.7 ) THEN
   DSTPOS(1) = COORD(1) + 1
   DSTPOS(2) = COORD(2)
   DSTPRC = VMGPRC(DSTPOS)
   STATUS = VMWRIT(MAXNUM,DSTPRC,NBYTES)
ENDIF
TMPRC = SRCPRC
IF( COORD (1).NE.7) THEN
   SRCPRC = DSTPRC
   STATUS = VMREAD(MAXNUM,SRCPRC,NBYTES)
ENDIF
IF ( COORD(1).NE.0) THEN
   DSTPRC = TMPRC
   STATUS = VMWRIT(MAXNUM,DSTPRC,NBYTES)
ENDIF

STATUS = VMDMPE(MAXNUM,NBYTES)
NBYTES = 2*INTSIZ
STATUS = VMDMPE(COORD,NBYTES)
STOP
END
```

Code 4-18 FORTRAN Version of Node Program for Example 2

Processor	x position	y position	Value	Row maximum
0	0	0	0.5139	0.9476
1	1	0	0.1757	0.9476
2	3	0	0.3087	0.9476
3	2	0	0.5345	0.9476
4	7	0	0.9476	0.9476
5	6	0	0.1717	0.9476
6	4	0	0.7022	0.9476
7	5	0	0.2264	0.9476
8	0	1	0.4948	0.9834
9	1	1	0.1247	0.9834
10	3	1	0.0839	0.9834
11	2	1	0.3896	0.9834
12	7	1	0.2772	0.9834
13	6	1	0.3681	0.9834
14	4	1	0.9834	0.9834
15	5	1	0.5354	0.9834
16	0	3	0.7657	0.8230
17	1	3	0.6465	0.8230
18	3	3	0.7671	0.8230
19	2	3	0.7802	0.8230
20	7	3	0.8230	0.8230
21	6	3	0.1519	0.8230
22	4	3	0.6255	0.8230
23	5	3	0.3147	0.8230
24	0	2	0.3469	0.9315
25	1	2	0.9172	0.9315
26	3	2	0.5198	0.9315
27	2	2	0.4012	0.9315
28	7	2	0.6068	0.9315
29	6	2	0.7854	0.9315
30	4	2	0.9315	0.9315
31	5	2	0.8699	0.9315

Output from Example 2

5

Introduction to Decomposition and Concurrent Algorithms: Wave Equation

5-1 General Principles

The purpose of this chapter is to introduce the methods used in designing an efficient concurrent algorithm to solve an important class of concrete computational problems. We shall attempt to incorporate the general ideas of concurrency illustrated in previous chapters by utilizing the terminology and programming constructs already introduced. The result is a simple template for the decomposition of an easily grasped example which prepares the reader for the more complex examples of later chapters.

In the opening chapters, we described two examples in some detail. These examples were the construction of Hadrian's Wall by a team of masons, and image processing by a concurrent computer. As a first example of the actual implementations of these ideas, we have chosen the numerical solution of a one-dimensional wave equation, which might describe the vibrations of a uniform string. The wave equation example poses problems for concurrent decomposition that are closely analogous to those in the earlier qualitative discussions. For this reason, we have attempted to maintain continuity of terminology with the earlier chapters. While strictly speaking the only prerequisite for understanding the present example is a review of the programming conventions of Chapter 4, the wave equation illustration is intended to follow naturally from the descriptive material of the opening chapters, and to lead into the more detailed subsequent chapters.

We previously introduced the general idea of a problem domain and its decomposition. The domain is composed of many members and most decompositions assign large numbers of members to each node. In the case of the Hadrian's Wall example, the domain was the wall itself and the members were the individual bricks. The wall was divided into grains comprised of vertical sections. In the case of the wave equation, the domain is the physical extent of the string, and the displacement $\psi(x, t)$ is a function of the distance x and time t representing the unknown solution. Figure 5-1 shows a decomposition of this problem for an 8-node concurrent computer. The particular numbering order of nodes illustrated in Fig. 5-1 derives from the connection architecture of a hypercube machine, but is not central to the present example. For any particular concurrent computer, this numbering order need only be constrained by the availability of the requisite internode virtual links.

The grid points of this problem consist of discrete nodal points at which ψ is to be evaluated. By analogy with the example of Hadrian's Wall, we decompose the string into contiguous sections. In an earlier discussion, we noted the importance of the domain

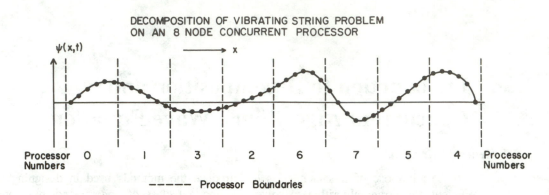

Figure 5-1 The vibrating string with a typical decomposition onto an 8-node concurrent computer. This example shows each node containing six grid points at which ψ is defined. The processors are numbered as they would be for a hypercube.

topology (which is one-dimensional for both Hadrian's Wall and the string) and the grain size of the decomposition. Figure 5-1 has only six grid points, together comprising a grain, in each processor for the sake of clarity in this simple illustration. One would normally prefer a larger number of points per node, for reasons of concurrent efficiency. This matter is further elaborated in Sec. 5-4.

In the next section, we will detail the decomposition of the wave equation and the natural concurrency inherent in the discrete solution approach. In some sense, the ease with which concurrency is extracted from this problem is related to a basic concurrency in the physical system that it describes. The concurrent solution of processor domain regions parallels the concurrent dynamical evolution of elements of an actual string.

Section 5-3 examines the structure of the example software, consisting of a *control process program* and *element programs* which run in each node of the concurrent computer. In this example, the nodes execute identical programs but take differing actions and obtain different results by acting on different data. A parallel to this situation in the Hadrians's Wall example would be to supply each mason with identical sets of instructions that are sufficiently general to cover any peculiar circumstances a particular worker might encounter.

Chapter 5 closes with sections devoted to discussion of the quantitative performance and further generalizations of this simple illustrative case.

5-2 The One-Dimensional Wave Equation

The time-dependent motion of a simple vibrating string is described by the hyperbolic partial differential equation:

$$\frac{1}{c^2} \frac{\partial^2 \psi}{\partial t^2} - \frac{\partial^2 \psi}{\partial x^2} = 0 \tag{5-1}$$

The solution $\psi(x,t)$ is the vibration amplitude expressed as a function of position and time. The problem becomes fully posed with the addition of boundary conditions on the spatial domain, and initial position and velocity distributions. While an analytic solution may be obtained by elementary methods, we shall solve the problem by a numerical method which lends itself to a natural concurrent decomposition. This may not be the best way to solve such a simple problem, but it serves as a useful example for the solution of larger or more difficult problems that are not as amenable to analytic methods. Our program for the numerical solution of this equation will be to propose a uniform discretization of the spatial and temporal domains, and approximate the partial differential equation of Eq. (5-1) by a finite difference expression. If Δx and Δt represent the space and time step sizes respectively, and ψ_i represents the approximate solution at the ith nodal point in the spatial discretization, then the second order finite difference equation becomes:

$$\frac{\psi_i(t-\Delta t) - 2\psi_i(t) + \psi_i(t+\Delta t)}{c^2\Delta t^2} - \frac{\psi_{i-1}(t) - 2\psi_i(t) + \psi_{i+1}(t)}{\Delta x^2} = 0 \qquad (5\text{-}2)$$

Neglecting issues of solution stability, the straightforward scheme for solving this system involves stepping sequentially from one time step to the next using the relation:

$$\psi_i(t+\Delta t) = 2\psi_i(t) - \psi_i(t-\Delta t) + \tau^2[\psi_{i-1}(t) - 2\psi_i(t) + \psi_{i+1}(t)] \qquad (5\text{-}3)$$

where $\tau = c\,\Delta t/\Delta x$.

The question now arises how best to divide the problem domain for effective concurrent solution. With such a simple example, the answer is obvious because of the close analogy between our problem and the Hadrian's Wall example. If we were to propose giving each processor some subset of the time steps to calculate, this would correspond to assigning bricklayers to work on successive horizontal layers of the wall. Such a temporal decomposition would allow no concurrent speedup, since each processor would be required to wait until the completion of all earlier time intervals.

As anticipated in Fig. 5-1, the correct decomposition in this case is based upon the assignment of spatial groups of nodal points to processors. With such a decomposition, the processors are allowed to evolve their subdomains forward in time quasi-simultaneously. If we neglect for the moment the necessity for neighboring spatial regions to exchange data, this choice of domain decomposition shows ideal concurrency, with no sequential dependence of one processor's calculation on another's.

Actual departures from ideality arise because the two "end" nodal points in any particular processor require a nodal value from the neighboring processor in order to be updated according to Eq. (5-3). Since this requires a communication step to be interpolated between the ordinary computational steps of updating the mesh, the relative amounts of time spent in computation and communication (or any other kind of "idle activity", for that matter) during an update step determines the concurrent efficiency of the algorithm. The efficiency of a given calculation is adversely impacted by relatively large amounts of communication, as well as by idle time spent waiting for processors with differing work loads to "catch up" with one another.

Again, the solutions to these problems are apparent in the present example. The problem of communication inefficiency is ameliorated by maximizing the grain size of the decomposition. Translated into the terminology of our specific example, we should strive to assign large numbers of nodal points to each processor. As the number of points contained within a processor becomes large compared with two (the number of end points), the fractional cost of communication overhead becomes small. As for the problem of idle time, since the amount of work associated with updating most of the nodes is identical (the problem is homogeneous), load balancing is assured by simply assigning equal numbers of nodal points to each processor.

The foregoing brief discussion of the factors influencing concurrent efficiency has tacitly assumed that somehow the total problem size is a variable degree of freedom to be varied in order to obtain maximum efficiency. In fact, with many "real world" problems one is confronted with a fixed problem size and is interested in minimizing computation time, rather than maximizing efficiency. The concept of algorithmic concurrent efficiency as discussed here and in Sec. 5-4 is, therefore, not so useful in connection with a given fixed problem as it is in describing the effectiveness of a given decomposition approach to a range of problems. A decomposition such as that just presented, for which efficiency is maximized for large grain size, makes "best use" of concurrent computation in the limit of large problem size, although for any actual problem, the bottom-line cost will be the more relevant benchmark.

The final issue to be dealt with in this section is the question of decomposition topology. We must determine the interprocessor connection network necessary to effect the required communications. As with the previous issues of concurrency, the simple geometry of the problem affords a straightforward intuitive answer. Not surprisingly, a one-dimensional lattice or chainlike connectivity among processors gives all the communication links necessary to do one-dimensional finite difference updating. As Fig. 5-2 shows schematically, this simple mapping requires each processor to communicate with a "left" and "right" neighbor during the course of an update step.

We may summarize the basic algorithm put forward in this section by the following sequence of operations in each processor:
1.   Initialize starting values.
2.   Identify neighbor communication channels required for linear topology.
3.   Exchange end nodal values with neighbors.
4.   Perform update $\psi_i(t) \rightarrow \psi_i(t+\Delta t)$ on all nodal points.
5.   Go to 3; repeat until done.

In the following section, we will translate this simple algorithm into example code, making use of the programming constructs defined in Chap. 4.

5-3 Example Software Structure

Our task in this section is to employ the virtual concurrent processor defined in the previous chapter to construct an example implementation of the vibrating string algorithm. This example is sufficiently simple that we can conveniently present much of the programming detail which is omitted in subsequent examples. In all cases, however, the

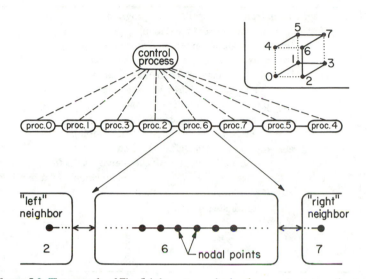

Figure 5-2 The example of Fig. 5-1 drawn to emphasize the processor connection topology. As the blow-up of processors 2, 6 and 7 illustrates, the update of "boundary" nodal points in each processor requires communication with nearest neighbor processors in a one-dimensional chain, which is a subset of the connections available in a hypercube (shown in inset).

Software Supplement to this volume provides a full implementation of the illustrative text examples.

We begin by presenting the control process program. The purpose of this program, which runs only in the control processor, is to act as coordinator of collective ensemble operations and to mediate such external input/output activity as is required. In this example, the control process program obtains as input data the information needed to set up the decomposed domain and initial conditions. It then instructs the ensemble to complete the desired number of time steps, and finally receives the results.

An examination of the pseudocode implementation in Code 5-1 (and the corresponding FORTRAN and C programs given in Appendix D) shows that the control process program initiates actions in the ensemble by issuing global communications to which the node programs respond. We may note in passing that if the number of nodal points in the problem domain is not evenly divisible by N, the number of processor nodes, the calculation cannot be perfectly load balanced. In such a case, the best that can be done is to distribute the load such that there exists no more than a one-point difference between the loads in any pair of nodes. This load imbalance condition will enter into our efficiency discussion in Sec. 5-4. During the main task of update computation, the control process simply waits for the completion of the task and thus has no impact upon the concurrent efficiency. Finally, dumping and printing of the final solution occurs via control/ensemble communication. Although this might not be the best way to solve the wave equation in practice, it provides a useful illustration of the important issues involved in such a problem.

```
proc_begin  main (run the control process program)
    for_begin (interactive command loop)
            [read command from terminal or standard input]
            [vm_bcastcp–broadcast command to ensemble]
            if_begin (command is INITIALIZE) then
                    proc_call initialize_problem (signal ensemble to set starting values)
            else_if (command is UPDATE) then
                    [read number of steps, k]
                    [vm_bcastcp–broadcast k to ensemble]
            else_if (command is OUTPUT) then
                    proc_call output_results (receive results from ensemble using
                                                     vm_dumpcp  and direct it to output stream)
            else_if (command is STOP) then
                    [terminate program]
            if_end
    for_end
proc_end
```

Code 5-1 Control Process Pseudocode Program for Wave Equation Solver

We next turn our attention to the ensemble node program. The node program has a structure which complements that of the control process program. During the setup and output phases of the programs, control process "write" calls are balanced by corresponding node "read" calls, and vice versa. The node program, however, contains as its most important part the section that performs the time step calculation. Communications calls in this part are for the mutual exchange of data between ensemble processors, and do not involve the control process.

The node program outlined in Codes 5-2 and 5-3 runs independently in each of the processors. The processors take requested action depending upon the values of the parameters passed to them from the control process and their neighbors.

The node program begins by defining the communication links required for the linear decomposition topology of this problem. Following this preparatory step, the node program receives data from the control process necessary to generate the initial configuration of the vibrating string. Once all the starting values are obtained, the nodes begin their update steps. During this "working" phase, the control process is not involved and only communication between nodes occurs. After the specified number of updates, the node program may receive the request to forward its results through the control process.

Essentially all of the interesting action associated with the problem solution occurs within this node program. Its flow centers on the central solution algorithm, and is punctuated by its points of contact with the control process, and with its "sibling" node processes.

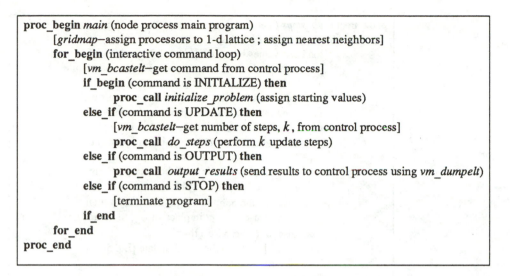

```
proc_begin main (node process main program)
    [gridmap—assign processors to 1-d lattice ; assign nearest neighbors]
    for_begin (interactive command loop)
        [vm_bcastelt—get command from control process]
        if_begin (command is INITIALIZE) then
            proc_call initialize_problem (assign starting values)
        else_if (command is UPDATE) then
            [vm_bcastelt—get number of steps, k, from control process]
            proc_call do_steps (perform k update steps)
        else_if (command is OUTPUT) then
            proc_call output_results (send results to control process using vm_dumpelt)
        else_if (command is STOP) then
            [terminate program]
        if_end
    for_end
proc_end
```

Code 5-2   Main Node Program for Wave Equation Solver

The above example program serves to illustrate the practical issues associated with implementing a particular problem decomposition within the virtual machine environment defined in Chap. 4. Further practical details may be found in Appendix D which includes explicit C and FORTRAN control and node programs respectively.

It may be seen in this example that the communication calls unique to the concurrent computation environment are infrequent enough that the basic structure of the corresponding sequential algorithm is more or less preserved. On the other hand, the intricate "handshaking" required between the control process and node programs in order to accomplish global data manipulations presents something of an obstacle to the reader trying to trace the flow of information and control.

The positive and negative aspects of this example serve as motivations for the developments to follow in subsequent chapters. In particular, we will expand upon the themes of "natural" concurrent decomposition while introducing programming extensions (in Chap. 6) which remove much of the clutter caused by explicit control process communication tasks.

```
proc_begin  do_steps ( perform k update steps )
     for_begin (a total of k loops)
          [load end values into l_neighbor and r_neighbor]
          [vm_shift–send r_neighbor to processor on right while
            receiving into l_point from processor on left]
          [vm_shift–send l_neighbor to processor on left while
            receiving into r_point from processor on right]
          for_begin (number of points in subdomain, i )
               if_begin  (the point is a global endpoint ) then
                    [ the value remains zero ]
               else_if  (the point is a left boundary ) then
                    [ use l_point in place of ψ_{i-1} to do update (Eq. 5-3) ]
               else_if  (the point is a right boundary ) then
                    [ use r_point in place of ψ_{i+1} to do update (Eq. 5-3) ]
               else_if  (otherwise ) then
                    [ perform the usual update (Eq. 5-3) ]
               if_end
          for_end
          [replace previous and current step values for next step]
     for_end
proc_end
```

Code 5-3 Updating Subroutine for Wave Equation Solver (Node Program)

5-4 Concurrent Efficiency in the Wave Equation Example

We have already given a qualitative discussion of the factors influencing the concurrent efficiency of the vibrating string calculation under a linear decomposition. In this section, we will quantify the treatment somewhat, in order to give a feeling for the kinds of performance to be expected in practice.

We should recall the definition of efficiency within the context of the current problem. Suppose that $T_1(M)$ is the machine time required to perform an update cycle over M nodal points within a single (sequential) processor. This serves as our baseline for comparison with the concurrently computed case. We shall denote by $T_N(M)$ the time required to update the same M points within a concurrent ensemble of N processors. In this case the efficiency ε is given by:

$$\varepsilon = \frac{T_1(M)}{NT_N(M)} \tag{5-4}$$

As mentioned earlier, there are distinct factors that cause $T_N(M)$ to measurably exceed $N^{-1}T_1(M)$ in an actual calculation. It is possible, however, to lump together the distinct sources of inefficiency into the net concurrent *overhead, f* which we encountered in Chap. 3. The overhead is defined such that

$$f = \frac{1}{\varepsilon} - 1 = \frac{NT_N(M) - T_1(M)}{T_1(M)} \tag{5-5}$$

The concept of overhead is useful because components of the overhead arising from different effects simply combine additively to determine the overall efficiency. Thus, we can separately analyze the two important influences on efficiency in our particular example.

We first consider the inefficiency due to communication overhead. In order to quantify this effect, we must have values for t_{calc} and t_{comm}, the calculation and communication times of a single member of our program.

Although the actual magnitudes of these times may be of interest, for the discussion of efficiency we shall be principally interested in their ratio, t_{comm}/t_{calc}. As discussed in Secs. 2-9 and 4-7, the value of t_{comm}/t_{calc} for actual machines depends upon issues of hardware-resident software as well as message size. Extrapolation of current trends in concurrent computer development suggests that t_{comm}/t_{calc} values near unity will be typical in the near future. In our illustrative calculations in the present chapter, we will consider the two values of 0.1 and 10, in order to bracket the probable range of actual machine characteristics.

The contribution of communication overhead to concurrent inefficiency is simply expressed:

$$f_C = \left[\frac{2N}{M} \right] \frac{t_{comm}}{t_{calc}} \tag{5-6}$$

This expression assumes that the decomposition places equal numbers of points in each processor (M/N is an integer) and that every processor contains two "communicated" points. Thus for every M/N update calculations, there occur two communication operations within a given node.

The treatment of cases for which the processors have unequal loads requires modification of Eq. (5-6). The example implementation of the last section yields a load imbalance if M/N is noninteger. In the imbalanced case, there exists a one point difference between the loads of the processors. In this case, we add an overhead term equal to N/M, which is the fraction of ideal run time spent waiting for the overloaded processor(s) to catch up. The net overhead now consists of communication and load balance components:

$$f = f_C + f_L = \left[\frac{2N}{M} \right] \frac{t_{comm}}{t_{calc}} + \left[\frac{N}{M} \right] \left\lceil \frac{M \bmod N}{N} \right\rceil \tag{5-7}$$

Here, the quantity within the ceiling function $\lceil \rceil$ in the latter term is zero when M/N is an integer and unity otherwise.

Now the concurrent efficiency is obtained directly from Eq. (5-7) via the definition:

$$\varepsilon = (1 + f)^{-1} \tag{5-8}$$

The result of evaluating these expressions for the two example values of t_{comm}/t_{calc} is shown in the plot of Fig. 5-3. It is apparent that with increasing grain size ($n = M/N$), the load-balanced efficiency asymptotes to unity. Furthermore, the "sawtooth" effect caused by load imbalance when M is not evenly divisible by N (8 in this case) diminishes as grain size grows. The upper envelope of each sawtooth curve corresponds to the case of perfect load balance, while the lower envelope delineates the imperfectly balanced case.

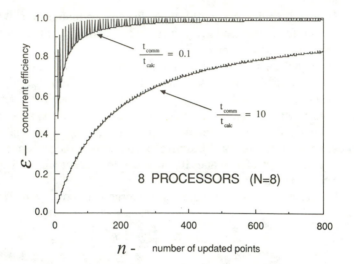

Figure 5-3 Plots of concurrent efficiency as a function of total problem size, for an 8-processor ensemble. Shown are cases for two values of the ratio t_{comm}/t_{calc}.

Figure 5-4 presents the same calculated performance trends as Fig. 5-3, but in a manner which makes clearer the functional relationship between efficiency and grain size. As stated above, the quantity $\varepsilon^{-1} - 1$ represents the net communication/imbalance overhead fraction. It may be seen from Eq.(5-6) that for a fixed value of t_{comm}/t_{calc}, this overhead is inversely proportional to the grain size, $(n = M/N)$. As a result, a plot of $\varepsilon^{-1} - 1$ versus M^{-1} should fall between envelopes that are straight lines passing through the origin. The slopes of the envelopes marking best- and worst-case load balance are determined by the magnitudes of t_{comm}/t_{calc} and N.

Superimposed on the calculated plots of Fig. 5-4 are measured values for the wave equation problem solved on eight processors of the Caltech Mark II hypercube. It is apparent from these results that our efficiency calculations are valid, with a t_{comm}/t_{calc} ratio of approximately 3.7.

5-5 Summary

The example put forward in this chapter is quite simple in terms of its root equations and implementation. It does, however, serve to illustrate many of the characteristics common to applications written for the ensemble/control process architecture. The homogeneous problem exemplified by our discrete update algorithm serves to highlight the importance of the factors of communication overhead, topology, and load balance in determining performance. From this point we may move on to the consideration of problems that are more complex from one or more of these standpoints.

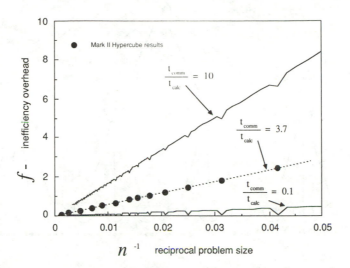

Figure 5-4 Plots of inefficiency overhead as a function of reciprocal problem size. Machine parameters are as in Fig. 5-3. Points represent actual timings of calculations on eight nodes of the Mark II hypercube. The measured values are for load balanced configurations which correspond to the lower envelope of the sawtooth curve.

We emphasize that the domain decomposition used in this chapter and discussed in Chap. 1 and 3 is very simple but general. A preview of the range of applications for this method to be discussed in subsequent chapters is illustrated in Fig. 5-5.

Chapters 7 through 13 will deal with physically motivated computational problems that introduce the issues of higher dimensional decomposition topologies as well as more diverse solution methods. In later chapters, further problems associated with load balancing and concurrent algorithms are pursued.

The next chapter, however, will deal with another consideration in practical implementation. We have seen that while the structure of the ensemble program in our example follows in a straightforward manner from its sequential equivalent, the overall clarity is obscured somewhat by the necessity for two enmeshed application programs to handle the control and node processes respectively. The following chapter introduces an augmentation of the programming environment which precludes the necessity for rewriting a control program for each new application. This environment, built up from the already described operating system primitives, provides a clearer programming style for most problems. At the cost of imposing a slightly thicker layer of "management" software, we will realize a relatively great gain in algorithmic clarity and transportability.

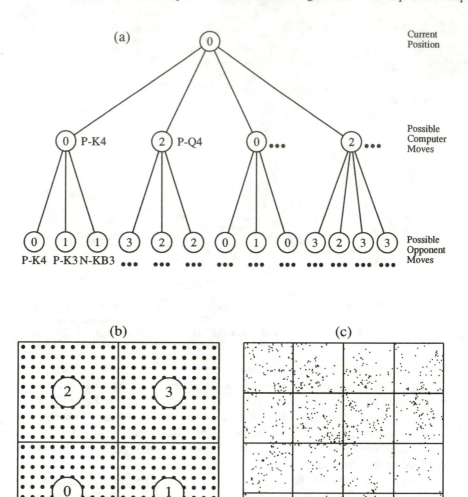

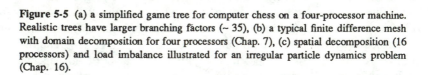

Figure 5-5 (a) a simplified game tree for computer chess on a four-processor machine. Realistic trees have larger branching factors (~ 35), (b) a typical finite difference mesh with domain decomposition for four processors (Chap. 7), (c) spatial decomposition (16 processors) and load imbalance illustrated for an irregular particle dynamics problem (Chap. 16).

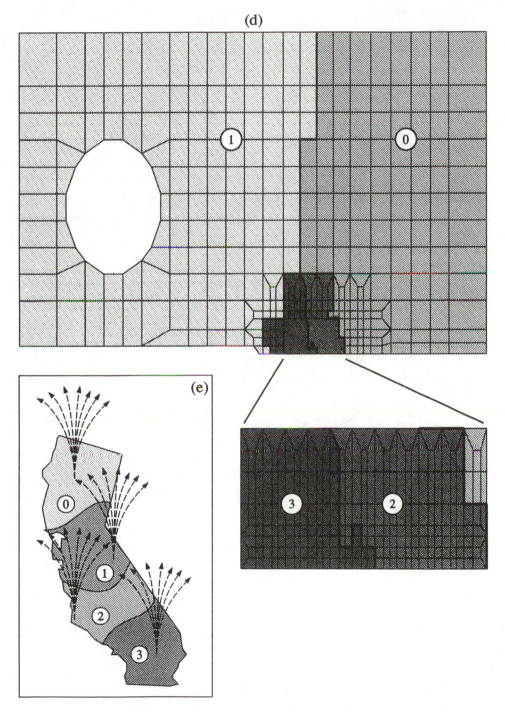

Figure 5-5 (d) domain decomposition for four processors of an irregular finite element mesh using methods discussed in Sec. 3-8 and Chap. 8, (e) a decomposition of the problem of tracking multiple targets [Gottschalk 87].

6

An Approach to the Concurrent Input/Output Problem: CUBIX and the Wave Equation

6-1 Introduction

In Chap. 5, we used the example of a vibrating string to illustrate some of the general concepts involved in constructing a concurrent application. When designing a parallel program to treat a specific problem, we encountered the necessity to write two programs. The first of these, running in the control processor, is the *control program*, while the other, running in the nodes of the parallel machine, is the *node program*. The control program manages the program's interaction with the outside world and coordinates the global actions of the parallel program. This style of programming is a natural one to apply to distributed memory, large node, message-passing parallel computers because they frequently provide no direct facility for parallel I/O, except indirectly through the *control processor*. This I/O isolation of the node processes represents a serious impediment to robust programming. Application programs in this model are considerably longer and more error-prone than would be the case if direct I/O involving node processes were possible. A related difficulty arises from the fact that the application consists of two tightly coupled programs, which must communicate in a rigidly coordinated manner. In the indirect I/O model, unanticipated I/O activity on the part of any or all processes most often results in the complete breakdown of the program. Maintenance, modification, and debugging of programs is clearly very difficult in such an environment.

In this chapter, we present an alternative to the control program/node program methodology, in which the control program becomes an unchanging part of the system, and the only thing that changes from one application to the next is the node program. This approach becomes possible if we provide a library of routines for node programs which permits each application node process to engage in I/O activities analogous to those associated with an ordinary sequential process.

6-2 Introductory Input/Output Formatting

The purpose of this chapter is to introduce the general principles and framework of a concurrent I/O subroutine library. This generic approach to the concurrent I/O problem was first implemented in the C language on the Caltech Mark II hypercube, under the name of CUBIX. A detailed discussion of CUBIX within the CrOS III Crystalline Operating System, will be given in Chap. 15. For the present, however, we will discuss

111

CUBIX in only the degree of detail necessary to illustrate its basic utility.

A problem arises here in attempting to present this environment in a language-independent way. Whereas the C language handles I/O through subroutine calls, FORTRAN incorporates I/O tasks and their associated formatting functions as parts of the language definition. This means that if we propose a subroutine-based CUBIX system, it will give the appearance of being biased in favor of C over FORTRAN. While the C programmer can simply make use of CUBIX versions of the familiar *printf* and *scanf* functions, the WRITE and READ statements familiar to the FORTRAN programmer are useless without language/compiler extensions. Of course, the FORTRAN programmer may simply adopt the subroutine-based I/O approach with CUBIX, but it will be at the cost of sacrificing some of the language independence of our concurrent programming approach.

In this chapter, we will adopt the perhaps inelegant expedient of casting all CUBIX I/O operations in a C-like syntax. While this choice will be comforting to the ingrained C programmer, the FORTRAN devotee may feel quite abandoned. For this reason, we devote this section to the definition of CUBIX I/O formatting conventions. In most particulars, the conventions follow the standard C library definitions [ANSI 87]. As described in Appendix C, we will apply these ideas to FORTRAN as extensions to the conventional WRITE and READ statements.

Formatted data is read from the standard input device, usually a terminal, through calls of the *scanf(format, arg1, ...)* function. In the simplest usage, the first argument is a character string specifying the format of the data to be read. Among the valid possible contents of the format string are:

- the substring "%d", which indicates that an integer should be read, and
- the substring "%f", which indicates that a floating-point number should be read.

A number of such tokens may be concatenated within a single format string. The format string is scanned from left to right. As the data are read and interpreted, they are placed at the addresses specified by subsequent arguments *arg1, arg2,....* Since these arguments must be addresses, it is common practice in the C language to use the address-of operator, '&,' prepended to a variable name.

Formatted output is produced with the *printf(format, arg1, ...)* function. The first argument is also a character string in which the same two character tokens may be used to identify integer and floating-point numbers in the argument list. The format string can also contain other characters, which are printed without modification in the output stream. The string "\n" may be used to insert a new-line character in the output at the corresponding point.

Finally, we will need to refer to specific output streams. The name *stdin* can be used to refer to the standard input stream, i.e., the place from which *scanf* reads, and the name *stdout* can be used to refer to the standard output stream, i.e., the place to which *printf* writes.

Code 6-1 illustrates the basic use of *scanf* and *printf* in a C program.

```
main()
{
        int i;
        float x;
        printf("Enter an integer and a floating-point number.\n");
        scanf("%d%f", &i, &x);
        printf("You entered %d and %f\nBye.\n", i, x);
        exit(0);
}
```

Code 6-1 Example of C-Language Formatted I/O

The following transcript, in which italics indicate user input, shows the result of an invocation of Code 6-1:

> Enter an integer and a floating-point number.
> *42 3.14*
> You entered 42 and 3.140000
> Bye.

The analogous FORTRAN program would follow directly from this example. Format strings would be passed via character variables, and because FORTRAN arguments are passed by address, variable names would replace the addresses of the C example.

6-3 The CUBIX Library Functions and Modes

The aim of the CUBIX system is to provide a reasonably general concurrent I/O environment which in its "sequential limit" reverts to an appearance and function as close as possible to conventional sequential I/O functionality. Code 6-1 illustrates a set of generic I/O tasks whose meaning and aim is clear for a single-processor machine. What then is the meaning of the program in Code 6-1 when executed under CUBIX in the processors of a concurrent ensemble? The answer to this question depends upon the programming context, and is tied up with the new concept of concurrent I/O *modes*.

We can imagine a context in which all processors of the ensemble have identical values for the variables i and x to send to an output stream. In this case, the sensible action for the system to take would be to print a *single* output stream corresponding to the identical outputs of the node processes. This mode of concurrent I/O handling will be referred to as the *singular mode*, and represents the default mode in CUBIX.

The use of singular mode I/O is subject to a few simple but important restrictions. Firstly, it should be clear that each node of the ensemble must concurrently execute identical I/O operations. A second restriction has to do with the meaning of *concurrent* I/O operations. This restriction follows by close analogy with the restrictions imposed upon crystalline communications in Chap. 4. In fact, the similarity stems directly from the fact that CUBIX routines are built up from the crystalline communication primitives. As with those primitives, the CUBIX routines must be called in *loose synchronization*.

While the calls need not occur perfectly simultaneously in real time, the node processes cannot proceed beyond the CUBIX subroutine call until all processors have arrived at the rendezvous point. Since communication takes place within the CUBIX subroutine, no node may have read or write operations pending at the time of the call.

Concurrent I/O would clearly be rather trivial and uninteresting if the singular mode were the only option. We instead recognize the need to exchange distinct data with different processors of the ensemble, and introduce the *multiple* I/O mode to this end.

When an input or output stream is operating in multiple mode, the individual processes may invoke CUBIX library routines with different arguments or data. The distinct data are in this case routed sequentially to or from the I/O device in order of increasing processor number. The CUBIX system provides for the switching of a stream between singular and multiple modes through a pair of loosely synchronous subroutine calls.

An I/O stream can be switched between multiple and singular modes with the functions *fmulti* and *fsingl*. These functions require a single argument which identifies the stream to be switched, e.g., *stdin* or *stdout*. Code 6-2 illustrates the use of multiple and singular I/O as a means of manipulating "common" and "private" processor data. The structure *ce*, the file *cros.h* and the function *cparam* are part of the CrOS III communication system. They will be discussed further in Chap. 14. They are used here so that the processor can identify itself.

```
#include <cros.h>
#include <stdio.h>

main()
{
        int n, i;
        struct cubenv ce;
        cparam (&ce);
        printf ("CUBIX is now in singular mode.\n");
        printf("Please enter a number.\n");
        scanf("%d", &n);
        printf ("CUBIX now switching to multiple mode.\n");
        printf("Enter %d numbers.\n", ce.nproc);
        fmulti(stdin);
        scanf("%d", &i);
        fmulti(stdout);
        printf("You gave %d and %d to processor %d.\n", n, i, ce.procnum);
        if(ce.procnum == 0)
                printf ("This unique message came from processor zero.\n");
        exit(0);
}
```

Code 6-2 Program Illustrating CUBIX Singular and Multiple Modes

An interactive session involving the program of Code 6-2 on a concurrent processor with eight nodes would have the following pattern:

> CUBIX is now in singular mode.
> Please enter a number.
> *42*
> CUBIX now switching to multiple mode.
> Please enter 8 numbers.
> *2 3 5 7 11*
> *13 17 19*
> You gave 42 and 2 to processor 0.
> This unique message came from processor zero.
> You gave 42 and 3 to processor 1.
> You gave 42 and 5 to processor 2.
> You gave 42 and 7 to processor 3.
> You gave 42 and 11 to processor 4.
> You gave 42 and 13 to processor 5.
> You gave 42 and 17 to processor 6.
> You gave 42 and 19 to processor 7.

We can see from this simple example how in multiple mode some of the restrictions associated with singular mode are relaxed. As already noted, there is no longer the need for all processors to issue identical calls. Furthermore, in multiple mode there is no need for processors to produce output in loose synchronization. This is because output is buffered separately in the nodes. Writing into these distinct processor buffers with *printf* may proceed completely asynchronously. Flushing of the buffers, by calling *fflush*, *fclose* or *exit*, however, must be accomplished with loosely synchronous calls. In multiple output mode, buffers are never flushed automatically, so the application program must explicitly call *fflush* in order for the user to see the output. When flushed, the contents of the buffers belonging to each node appear in the output stream in order of increasing processor number.

To demonstrate the advantage of using the CUBIX library, we will consider a modification of the wave equation solver of Chap. 5, using the CUBIX system. This time there is no need for a control program. Code 6-3 outlines in pseudocode all of the user-written node programming needed in order to accomplish the same tasks as the Chap. 5 example. Appendix D contains complete implementations of this same example problem in both C and FORTRAN.

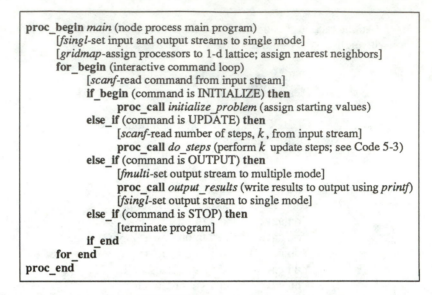

```
proc_begin main (node process main program)
        [fsingl-set input and output streams to single mode]
        [gridmap-assign processors to 1-d lattice; assign nearest neighbors]
        for_begin (interactive command loop)
                [scanf-read command from input stream]
                if_begin (command is INITIALIZE) then
                        proc_call initialize_problem (assign starting values)
                else_if (command is UPDATE) then
                        [scanf-read number of steps, k, from input stream]
                        proc_call do_steps (perform k update steps; see Code 5-3)
                else_if (command is OUTPUT) then
                        [fmulti-set output stream to multiple mode]
                        proc_call output_results (write results to output using printf)
                        [fsingl-set output stream to single mode]
                else_if (command is STOP) then
                        [terminate program]
                if_end
        for_end
proc_end
```

Code 6-3 Main CUBIX Program for Wave Equation Solver

The user-written code required to implement the CUBIX example of Code 6-3 is somewhat more lengthy than the corresponding element program of the previous chapter. It is significant, however, that the program is very much shorter than the combined element and control programs of Chap. 5. Furthermore, the clarity and ease of modifying the program is greatly enhanced using CUBIX, since there is no longer the need for the user to explicitly coordinate the control and element processes.

A further advantage of the CUBIX approach stems from its previously mentioned compatibility with standard sequential I/O operations. The programs presented in Appendix D could be compiled and run on a conventional computer without modification. The specialized concurrent library routines such as *shift, gridinit, fmulti*, and so on need only be implemented in such a manner as to give the correct (or null) results in the limit of a single processor. This backward compatibility of CUBIX-style applications with sequential computers offers many advantages in the task of program development. Initial development and debugging of the nonconcurrent body of a program is invariably easier within a mature sequential environment, and the applicability of a single programming style to a variety of machine types makes it all the more attractive as a general purpose approach.

The applications to be developed in the remainder of this book will make use of the CUBIX style of concurrent programming for the reasons cited above. The detailed implementation of CUBIX within the CrOS III crystalline communication system is deferred until Chap. 15. While it is good to retain an awareness of the importance (and limitations) of the control process as an intermediary for communication with the nodes of our concurrent computer, we will find that concealing this dependence as much as possible proves to be a fruitful approach to a wide variety of computational problems.

7

Elliptic Problems in Two Dimensions I:
Solution of Laplace's Equation
by Finite Difference

7-1 Introduction

In this chapter we extend our treatment of concurrent computational problems to the case of simple elliptic partial differential equations. The examples discussed in previous chapters generally involve the use of concurrency in sufficiently natural ways that the choice of decomposition strategy is fairly obvious. In the current discussion, we will explore the concurrent implementation of algorithms with a somewhat less clean-cut parallel structure, while also considering higher-dimensional topologies for decomposition.

An attempt is made here to use relatively simple illustrative methods, and to avoid the complications of more sophisticated numerical approaches. As elsewhere in this volume, the general principles of concurrent decomposition and algorithm structure sketched out below should serve to guide the further development of more generally useful and powerful programs. Insofar as the main issues of this chapter have little to do with the basic control process tasks discussed in the earlier examples, the examples of this and succeeding chapters are presented in the form of CUBIX applications. This choice of example structure improves the clarity of the concurrent algorithms.

For the purpose of this discussion we shall consider techniques for solving the two-dimensional Laplace equation:

$$\nabla^2 \phi = \frac{\partial^2 \phi}{\partial x^2} + \frac{\partial^2 \phi}{\partial y^2} = 0 \qquad (7\text{-}1)$$

While we might as easily treat other elliptic operators or three-dimensional cases, the present problem is sufficiently challenging to demonstrate a number of salient points regarding concurrent decomposition.

We seek solutions for the unknown potential, ϕ, within some finite spatial domain, given fixed boundary solution values. In pursuing an approximate numerical solution to (7-1), one common approach is to consider a spatial discretization of the problem domain, so that the problem becomes one of finding values of ϕ at a finite number of nodal locations. Note that here, as in Chap. 5, the term "nodal point" refers to the domain discretization, and should not be confused with the processor node of the concurrent ensemble. This approach is an extension of the one-dimensional spatial discretization employed in Chap. 5 to solve the wave equation. In the one-dimensional hyperbolic case, it was a straightforward matter to algebraically solve the finite difference expression to obtain a simple update prescription for the solution. In the case of an elliptic problem such as (7-1), the simultaneous solution of the difference equations connecting the discrete ϕ_i leads formally to a matrix problem. The difficulty of solving this matrix system is closely tied to the structure and sparsity of the matrix.

While a one-dimensional elliptic problem would give rise to a simple tridiagonal matrix, higher-dimensional operators yield more complicated matrix structures. We might attack any of these matrices with direct methods derived from Gaussian elimination. In this and in the next chapter, however, we will emphasize iterative solution methods. This choice is made for both pedagogic and practical reasons. Iterative methods are preferable for the illustration in this chapter because they involve concurrent decompositions with a comparatively obvious correspondence to the physical dimensionality of the problem domain. In contrast, direct matrix methods generally require a decomposition based upon the two-dimensional row/column world of the matrix. These row/column-oriented concurrent matrix operations will be covered in Chaps. 10 and 20. On the practical side, iterative methods assume importance in large higher-dimensional problems, where the cost of direct techniques increases with problem size much faster than the cost (per iteration) of iterative methods. It is likely that iterative techniques will predominate for the large three-dimensional problems to which concurrent processing is increasingly being applied.

Both this and the following chapter deal with methods of solving the matrix systems arising from discretized elliptic problems. At the level of the matrix problem, the difference between this chapter (finite difference) and the next chapter (finite elements) lies in the regularity of the matrix structure.

Because the method of finite differences yields matrices with a more predictable structure than the finite element method, this chapter will deal with iterative solvers that do not require the full system matrix to ever be assembled. This will contrast with the finite element equation solver discussed in Chap. 8, which assumes less about the matrix structure, but might be applied to finite difference systems as well.

7-2 The Finite Difference Formulation

In the simplest application of the finite difference method, the problem domain is covered with a uniformly-spaced square mesh of nodal points, so that all points, except those on boundaries, have four equidistant nearest neighbors. We may designate a node's neighbors by the subscripts $\pm x$ and $\pm y$. The first-order finite difference equation corresponding to Laplace's equation (7-1) is:

$$4\,\phi_i - \phi_{i-x} - \phi_{i-y} - \phi_{i+x} - \phi_{i+y} = 0 \qquad\qquad (7\text{-}2)$$

where i is an index running over all M nodal points. This leads to M simultaneous equations for the ϕ_i, and a matrix problem characterized by a symmetric, diagonally dominant sparse system.

Perhaps the simplest iterative technique applicable to this system is Jacobi iteration, also known as the method of simultaneous corrections. In this method, the trial value $\phi_i^{(k)}$

at the kth iteration is obtained by solving the ith equation for ϕ_i, using the values from the previous iteration at the other nodes. Inspection of (7-2) shows that this corresponds intuitively to replacing the unknown value ϕ_i at each node with the average of its neighbors' values from the previous iteration. The Jacobi update procedure for step k may be written:

$$\phi_i{}^{(k)} = \frac{1}{4}[\phi_{i-x}{}^{(k-1)} + \phi_{i-y}{}^{(k-1)} + \phi_{i+x}{}^{(k-1)} + \phi_{i+y}{}^{(k-1)}] \qquad (7\text{-}3)$$

The Jacobi iteration scheme represents one of the class of stationary iterative methods [Jennings 77], the members of which are distinguished by the correction technique applied at each update. In the case of Jacobi iteration, trial solution values are updated simultaneously. In another stationary method known as Gauss-Seidel iteration, the trial values ϕ_i are updated in sequence. For example, the value $\phi_i{}^{(k)}$ is obtained from the $i-1$ newly obtained values for step k and the remaining $M-i$ "old" values from step $k-1$.

It should be clear that when considering concurrent implementations of these methods, the Jacobi scheme is the most straightforward because it imposes no sequential order on corrections to nodal values. Therefore, neglecting communication steps, the Jacobi algorithm can be carried out completely in parallel without modification. This contrasts with the Gauss-Seidel case, which assumes a particular update sequence, which if observed in the concurrent case would require processors to work on regions of the domain sequentially instead of in parallel.

Unfortunately, the Jacobi method is of much less practical importance than the so-called nonsimultaneous methods because of its relatively slow convergence. At this point we might go forward with development of the concurrent Jacobi scheme despite its comparatively poor performance. However, this would not serve to illustrate much that has not already been discussed, since the update method simply amounts to a two-dimensional extension of the simultaneous updating used to evolve the wave equation forward in time in Chap. 5. Instead, we shall discuss the problem of concurrent successive over-relaxation, of which the Gauss-Seidel method is a special case.

In the case of successive over-relaxation (SOR) we replace the update prescription of (7-3) with:

$$\phi_i{}^{(k)} = \frac{\omega}{4}\left[\phi_{i-x}{}^{(k)} + \phi_{i-y}{}^{(k)} + \phi_{i+x}{}^{(k-1)} + \phi_{i+y}{}^{(k-1)}\right] + (1-\omega)\phi_i{}^{(k-1)} \qquad (7\text{-}4)$$

In the above formula, ω is the over-relaxation parameter, which generally lies in the range $1 < \omega < 2$ for optimum convergence. In the case that $\omega = 1$, the SOR method is identical with Gauss-Seidel [Jennings 77].

It should be noted that Eq. (7-4) has been written assuming that the $\phi_i{}^{(k)}$ are updated in order of increasing x and y coordinates. In fact, for a sequential algorithm, any particular update order might be used, and newly updated values could be simply written over their predecessor values in memory. While alternative update orders might affect the convergence rate, there would be no fundamental difference in the necessary programming aside from indexing. When we turn to a concurrent implementation of

SOR however, update order becomes a more important consideration. In order for two (or more) subsets of points to be updated concurrently, neither subset may have an influence on the result of the update step in the other. More formally, this means that any two points may be updated concurrently only if their mutual matrix element is zero. In the context of our first-order finite difference problem, it means that no two regions with adjacent edges may be updated in parallel. This restriction forces us to adopt the modified update order described in the following section. It is interesting to note that if our coefficient matrix were full (i.e., all nodal points interacting) there would be no possibility of a concurrent decomposition based upon spatial regions, and an alternative "long-range" decomposition like that of Chap. 9 would be required.

7-3 Concurrent Decomposition

The task of obtaining a concurrent decomposition for our finite difference/SOR problem centers about two related considerations: domain partitioning and update ordering. The first of these considerations determines to some extent the second, so we shall consider it first.

The finite difference formulation selected for this chapter restricts us to consideration of uniformly-spaced meshes of nodal points. While we could easily imagine the use of such a locally uniform mesh to approximately cover a nonrectangular domain, it will be convenient for the present example to consider the simple square domain illustrated in Fig. 7-1.

As was the case in Chap. 5, intuition provides an adequate means of selecting a good domain decomposition for multiple processors. In the two-dimensional case, we are required to select processor regions which balance the workload and minimize the communication overhead. Since communication occurs along interprocessor boundaries, the latter requirement seeks to minimize the perimeters of the subdomain boundaries. A convenient approximation to the best decomposition is obtained by breaking the square domain into congruent square subdomains. While intuition serves well here, the optimal solution for more convoluted meshes could be much less obvious. In such cases, we may choose to employ optimization methods of the kind discussed in Chaps. 13 and 17 in order to obtain a decomposition.

In Fig. 7-1, one particular processor region of a 16-node decomposition has been highlighted for the purpose of illustrating the flow of data within and between regions. A grid point which does not lie within the shaded boundary strip of the region requires only data "local" to its own processor node in order to be updated. In contrast, the shaded edge points require one or two values from neighboring processors in order to be updated. Thus these shaded points constitute the two-dimensional analog of the communicated end points given in the wave equation example of Chap. 5. In three dimensions, these communicated points would occupy the six faces and twelve edges of a parallelepiped.

If we were doing a simple simultaneous update scheme (Jacobi iteration), the algorithm would simply consist of steps that concurrently update the processor subregions, separated by communication steps that involve the swapping of edge values between

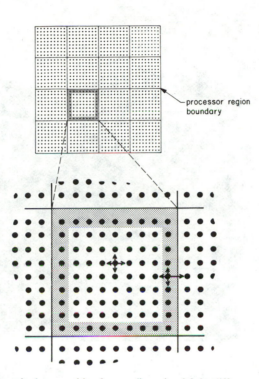

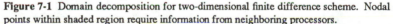

Figure 7-1 Domain decomposition for two-dimensional finite difference scheme. Nodal
points within shaded region require information from neighboring processors.

neighboring processors. An additional complication is introduced, however, by the consideration of consistent update ordering for nonsimultaneous corrections.

Given the rectangular decomposition shown in Fig. 7-1, the requirement of nonadjacent concurrent updating may be satisfied by invoking the so-called *red/black* or *checkerboard* ordering scheme of Fig. 7-2 (see for example [Ortega 85]). Each square (or rectangular) subregion is in turn subdivided into four regions of two kinds. For the sake of definiteness, we refer to these partitions as "red" and "black," by analogy with the squares of a checkerboard.

Inspection of Fig. 7-2 shows that no red or black partition of any subregion is adjacent to a partition of the same color in a neighboring processor. Thus, a fully parallel SOR update may be realized by first updating all red points, then all black points, and so on. A sufficient condition to guarantee the consistency of this update approach is to make certain that all processors have completed one color update cycle before any start on the next color.

Strictly speaking, this ordering is different from that of standard sequential SOR, in which the update sweep proceeds unidirectionally across the global grid. The definition of SOR, however, only requires that there is *some* update order, but cannot say what that

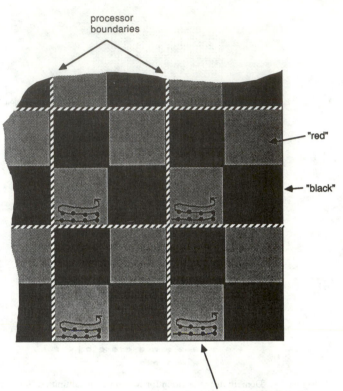

Figure 7-2 "Red/black" checkerboard domain partitioning required for concurrent implementation of the SOR algorithm. Points in red regions are updated first, and following
processor synchronization, black points are updated. This partition allows sequential
SOR cycles to run concurrently in the processor nodes.

order is, since it depends in detail on the specific problem. The reader may object at this
point that since the concurrent algorithm presented is no longer strictly equivalent to the
original sequential scheme, we have little justification for calling it true SOR. Indeed,
from a practical standpoint, the programmer may wish to dispense altogether with the
bother of maintaining a consistent update sequence and simply perform parallel SOR in
the subregions without regard for the updates occurring in neighboring processors. This
approach would amount to a kind of hybrid between the Jacobi and SOR methods, and
would scarcely introduce a greater corruption of the "pure" SOR scheme than we have
already inflicted. We will stay, however, with the red/black SOR approach in order to
illustrate the issues involved in adapting an inherently sequential update for concurrent
application.

In the next section, we will detail the implementation of this example in our virtual
concurrent processor environment. The main structure of the parallel algorithm we will

implement is briefly summarized by the following steps:

1. exchange edge values with neighboring processors.
2. perform SOR update on all red points in sequence to obtain $\phi_i^{(k)}$.
3. exchange edge values with neighboring processors.
4. perform SOR update on all black points in sequence to obtain $\phi_i^{(k)}$.
5. advance step $k \rightarrow k+1$.
6. if finished, stop. Otherwise, go to 1.

As was the case in the example of Chap. 5, the algorithm involves a highly predictable and homogeneous allocation of computation and communication tasks, so that load balancing is straightforward. Also, the individual processors, while not running strictly in lockstep, are kept in the loose synchronization required for update consistency by the communication calls interspersed between update cycles.

7-4 Example Implementation

We have thus far presented the concurrent finite difference algorithm in a somewhat abstract manner. In this section, we will attempt to clarify the implementation of this scheme with a pseudocode example. As elsewhere in the book, this example of pseudocode correlates with real examples in the Software Supplement.

We will present selected portions of the node programs designed to implement the algorithm in the CUBIX environment (cf. Chap. 6). For the sake of brevity and clarity, not all of the subroutines called are fully described, particularly when their function is tangential to the principal algorithmic issues.

The main module of this example program is given in Code 7-1. The main procedure begins by using grid-mapping routines (Chap. 4) to establish communication paths with up to four nearest neighbors in a two-dimensional processor mesh. Next, a loop is entered which accepts user commands via the CUBIX singular input functions.

Within the command loop, the appropriate option is executed through a subroutine call. In this very rudimentary example, the only options provided are those required to read in the starting data, to perform a specified number of updates, and to dump the result via CUBIX multiple I/O routines. Clearly, any really useful program of this kind would incorporate more features, such as those necessary to check for convergence.

The initialization and dumping portions of the program are not central to the present discussion, and have therefore not been described in detail. Their principal functions are to manage the allocation of domain points and fixed boundary points to subregions, and to set up the necessary bookkeeping to identify neighboring values for each relaxed point.

Of more immediate interest is the implementation of the update cycle, which constitutes the real heart of the program. Code 7-2 contains the pseudocode outline of this update cycle. As described in the previous section, each full cycle consists of a communication and computation phase for each of two colors of points in a processor. Strictly speaking, during the "red" phase of a cycle, edge data need only be received from neighboring black points, and need only be sent to neighboring red points. The reverse is true during the "black" phase. In the illustrated implementation, we have skirted the issue that

```
proc_begin  main (CUBIX node program for finite difference/SOR example)
        [gridmap ensemble onto two-dimensional plane]
        [identify 2-d neighboring processors]
        for_begin (interactive command loop)
                [read command from standard input]
                if_begin (command is INITIALIZE) then
                        proc_call get_data (read in boundary data to each processor)
                else_if (command is UPDATE) then
                        [read number of cycles, k ]
                        proc_call update_SOR (perform k  update cycles)
                else_if (command is DUMP) then
                        [dump solution values from each processor]
                else_if (command is STOP) then
                        [terminate program]
                if_end
        for_end
proc_end
```

Code 7-1 Main Driver Module for Finite Difference Example

only half of the edge values need be communicated during any call to *get_edge*. An intelligent implementation of *get_edge* should be designed to recognize whether the current phase is red or black, and communicate only the needed values.

Glossing over this detail, the function *get_edge* in Code 7-2 illustrates a method for systematically exchanging edge values among the processor nodes. Each node program requires storage space for the values at each of its own domain points, plus a single layer or "guard ring" of points needed to update the interior values. These slots are to be filled with values supplied by interprocessor communication.

In our rectangular decomposition geometry, the exchange is accomplished by four successive calls to *vm_shift*. First, a processor's values falling along the right edge are copied into a communication buffer and sent to the right neighbor while complementary left edge data arrives from the left neighbor. These data are stored in the appropriate guard ring locations, and the "right-shift" pass is ended. This is followed by analogous "left-," "up-," and "down-shift" passes, after which the guard rings of all processors have been filled with up-to-date values. We have made use here of the ability of *vm_shift* to transparently handle nonexistent neighbors in the case of processors with fewer than four two-dimensional neighbors.

Following the completion of the *get_edge* communication step, each processor independently performs a sequential SOR update on its red points, according to the prescription of Eq. (7-4). In this sequential process, each nodal value is immediately overwritten by its updated value. The communication step is then repeated, followed by an update of all black points.

This example serves to illustrate the relative simplicity with which a concurrent implementation of a finite difference solver may be designed. A more generally useful concurrent SOR program could be expected to follow the general pattern outlined above, although the adaptation of this decomposition approach to irregularly shaped domains or higher-order differencing schemes may present significant additional programming challenges.

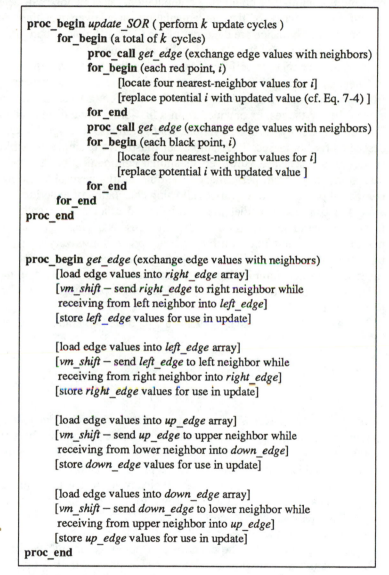

```
proc_begin update_SOR ( perform k update cycles )
    for_begin (a total of k cycles)
            proc_call get_edge (exchange edge values with neighbors)
            for_begin (each red point, i)
                    [locate four nearest-neighbor values for i]
                    [replace potential i with updated value (cf. Eq. 7-4) ]
            for_end
            proc_call get_edge (exchange edge values with neighbors)
            for_begin (each black point, i)
                    [locate four nearest-neighbor values for i]
                    [replace potential i with updated value ]
            for_end
        for_end
proc_end


proc_begin get_edge (exchange edge values with neighbors)
        [load edge values into right_edge array]
        [vm_shift − send right_edge to right neighbor while
         receiving from left neighbor into left_edge]
        [store left_edge values for use in update]

        [load edge values into left_edge array]
        [vm_shift − send left_edge to left neighbor while
         receiving from right neighbor into right_edge]
        [store right_edge values for use in update]

        [load edge values into up_edge array]
        [vm_shift − send up_edge to upper neighbor while
         receiving from lower neighbor into down_edge]
        [store down_edge values for use in update]

        [load edge values into down_edge array]
        [vm_shift − send down_edge to lower neighbor while
         receiving from upper neighbor into up_edge]
        [store up_edge values for use in update]
proc_end
```

Code 7-2 SOR Update Module for Finite Difference Example

7-5 Performance in Practical Applications

In designing and evaluating any practical application similar to the example just presented, a number of competing computational cost factors will determine the overall concurrent efficiency of the implementation on a given machine. Among the factors influencing performance are the order of the finite difference approximation (as discussed in the next section) and the dimensionality of the mesh.

While the relative performance relations may be derived theoretically, as was done in Chap. 5, it is useful at this point to consider *actual* performance figures that emerge from implementing a two-dimensional finite difference solver on a real machine. We present below the results obtained from a first-order finite difference program run on the Caltech Mark II hypercube in various configurations. The specific example cited here is described further in Sec. 7-7. Unlike our illustrative example, it employs a simultaneous spatial update scheme. However, its similar communication structure makes it a useful case study in program performance. Timing results were obtained as problem size and number of processors were varied, allowing calculation of experimental efficiencies.

We can easily predict the load-balanced efficiency dependence on problem size from considerations discussed in the previous chapters. The ratio of computation to interprocessor communication for a given update step is very nearly proportional to the ratio of total number of nodal points per processor, n, to the number of points per processor involved in communication. In other words, this ratio varies, in the two-dimensional case, as the ratio of the area to the perimeter of the processor region, or as $n^{1/2}$ for large n [Fox 85c, Reed 87].

The $n^{1/2}$ ratio immediately yields the predicted communication overhead

$$f_C = cn^{-1/2} \tag{7-5}$$

which in turn leads to the expected efficiency

$$\varepsilon = (1 + f_C)^{-1} \approx 1 - cn^{-1/2} \tag{7-6}$$

In the above expressions, c is a constant factor dependent in part upon the machine-specific ratio t_{comm}/t_{calc}. This constant is of some interest in the present experimental efficiency analysis, since it also depends upon the number of processors in the ensemble, which is variable in the benchmark results presented below.

In presenting the experimental efficiency results, it is useful to plot the quantity $-\log(1-\varepsilon)$ as a function of $\log n$. According to Eq. (7-6) such a plot should yield a family of parallel lines each with a constant slope of 1/2.

In Fig. 7-3, the experimental points [Meier 84] are plotted along with the line corresponding to $c = 1$. The experimental points group into families on lines of slope 1/2. The families of timings employing fewer processors fall on systematically higher efficiency trends than those for larger numbers of processors. The systematics of the variations in efficiency may be understood by considering the varying amounts of communication overhead for various numbers of processors at constant n. All ensemble configurations show an asymptotic trend to unit efficiency with increasing n. However, at constant n, different numbers of processors entail different communication overheads.

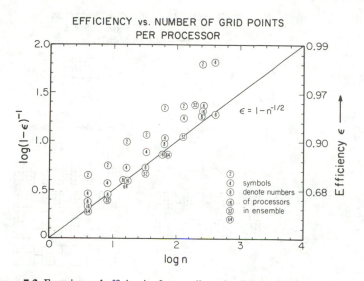

Figure 7-3 Experimental efficiencies for two-dimensional finite difference scheme with variable number of processors [Meier 84]. Although run on a hypercube, these results depend only upon a two-dimensional mesh connection.

When the ensemble consists of two processors, as shown in Fig. 7-4, communication involves only those nodal points along one edge of each processor. A four-node configuration involves twice as much communication at fixed n. With eight processors, the most burdened (and therefore speed-limiting) processors have three edges involved in communication. Finally, for configurations of 16 processors and more, the communication load becomes "saturated," with some processors communicating on all four boundaries. The results of Fig. 7-3 confirm this expectation.

This example demonstrates quantitatively the magnitude of the penalty imposed by communication overhead in a typical two-dimensional mesh problem. In this particular example all configurations achieve efficiencies in excess of 90% for $n \geq 100$.

It is also interesting to consider the significance of the experimentally determined values for c. As shown in Fig. 7-3, the efficiency results for Mark II hypercubes with 16 or more processors are well predicted by Eq. (7-6) with $c \approx 1$. This implies that for the machine and algorithm described, the times required to update and to communicate a single nodal point are roughly equal (to within a factor of order unity). It follows that the results in Fig. 7-3 may be approximately applied to machines with different assumed communication overhead costs through an additive adjustment of magnitude $\sim\log(t_{comm}/t_{calc})$.

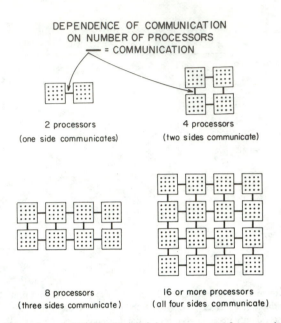

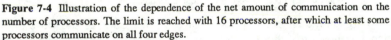

Figure 7-4 Illustration of the dependence of the net amount of communication on the number of processors. The limit is reached with 16 processors, after which at least some processors communicate on all four edges.

7-6 Higher-Order Differencing Schemes

One obvious generalization of the simple example discussed in the earlier sections of this chapter is to consider a higher-order finite difference scheme. Operationally, this means that more than nearest-neighbor nodal points are used to update the potential at a point. An extended update stencil clearly increases the number of arithmetic operations required, whether the update is performed sequentially or concurrently.

In the case of a concurrent algorithm, the larger numbers of boundary values communicated between processors also impacts the communication cost. However, the overall concurrent efficiency of the higher-order update scheme may actually be increased at fixed problem size, since the computational operations increase by a larger factor than the number of communicated data items. The actual effect in any specific case must depend upon the ratio of calculation to communication times and the scaling of communication overhead costs with message size. We can quantify these remarks using the communication overhead f_C introduced in Chap. 3. The efficiency discussed in the last section, takes the form:

$$\varepsilon = (1 + f_C)^{-1} \approx 1 - f_C \tag{7-7}$$

The basic issues are summarized in Fig. 7-5. Consider first Fig. 7-5(a), which illustrates the first-order problem described in the opening sections of this chapter. Using n as before to denote the maximum number of nodal points stored in each processor, we see that there are

$$4n \quad \text{floating-point calculations (cf. Eq. (7-3))}$$

and

$$4\sqrt{n} \quad \text{words to be communicated}$$

Here we have considered the general case of 16 or more processors in which communication is required on all four edges (cf. Fig. 7-4). This leads to a communication overhead given by

$$f_C = \frac{1}{\sqrt{n}} \frac{t_{comm}}{t_{calc}} \tag{7-8}$$

Combining Eqs., (7-7) and (7-8), we observe that the Mark II hypercube results of Fig. 7-3 are consistent with the result $c=1$ in Eq. (7-6) if

$$\frac{t_{comm}}{t_{calc}} \sim 1$$

This result falls in the expected range for machines and applications of this kind, for which it has been noted earlier that t_{comm} and t_{calc} can vary by factors of up to two.

Now consider a higher-order differencing scheme shown in Fig. 7-5(b) for which Eq. (7-3) is replaced by:

$$\phi_i^{(k)} = \frac{1}{60}[16\phi_{i-x}^{(k-1)} + 16\phi_{i-y}^{(k-1)} \tag{7-9}$$

$$+ 16\phi_{i+x}^{(k-1)} + 16\phi_{i+y}^{(k-1)}$$

$$- \phi_{i-2x}^{(k-1)} - \phi_{i-2y}^{(k-1)}$$

$$- \phi_{i+2x}^{(k-1)} - \phi_{i+2y}^{(k-1)}]$$

Here, we encounter $9n$ calculations and approximately $4(2\sqrt{n}) = 8\sqrt{n}$ words to be communicated. Even though communication has increased, f_C decreases by a factor of 1.1 from Eq. (7-8). In Fig. 7-5(c), we show what happens when off-diagonal terms are added to the stencil. Now f_C is decreased by a factor of 2 compared with Eq. (7-8). One way of understanding this decrease is to note that in Fig. 7-5(a) each communicated word is only used in a single update; for Fig. 7-5(b) some are used once and some twice; while in Fig. 7-5(c), each communicated word is typically used in three updates.

In Fig. 7-5(d) it is shown that as the update stencil increases in size, we obtain a value of $f_C = c/\sqrt{n}$ where c steadily decreases as the stencil increases in size. There is an interesting limit when the stencil grows so big that it covers the full domain. Now f_C takes the form:

$$f_C \approx \frac{const}{n} \frac{t_{comm}}{t_{calc}} \tag{7-10}$$

Expressed in words, $c/\sqrt{n}$ (c decreasing) tends to the limit $1/n$ as the stencil increases in size.

STENCIL DEPENDENCE OF CALCULATION
AND COMMUNICATION
illustrated for n=16

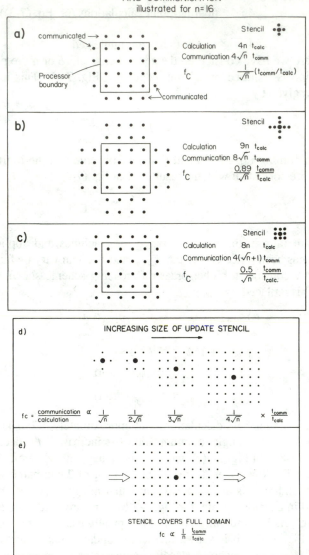

Figure 7-5 Illustration of the stencil dependence of the communication overhead f_c. (a) Shows the simple formula corresponding to equation (7-2) while (b) through (e) show stencils of increasing complexity.

The overhead described by Eq. (7-10) is identical to that of the long range force problem discussed in detail in Chapter 9. It is worth noting that one may think of Figs. 7-5(d) and (e) as applying to particle dynamics problems with a force of successively increasing range.

The discussion of higher-order differencing in this section has dealt only with simultaneous update schemes, rather than the successive relaxation methods illustrated earlier in this chapter. As mentioned above, the extended stencil of higher-order update schemes enlarges the border overlap between processors. In Sec. 7-3, we saw that a successive update scheme like SOR could be performed concurrently on a decomposed domain if each processor region was subdivided into two colors, so that no two adjacent regions in different processors were updated simultaneously.

For the extended stencil of Fig. 7-5(b) this analysis still holds, since no communication occurs across processor diagonals. Stencils like Fig. 7-5(c), however, with diagonal connections, require more than two colors to preserve a consistent successive update scheme. In this case, the four subrectangles of each processor region (Fig. 7-2) are assigned four distinct colors, and four phases are required to update all points in a processor. Figure 7-6 illustrates this modification.

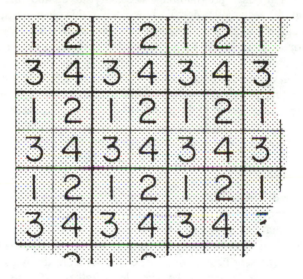

Figure 7-6 A four-color checkerboard sequence to handle stencils with diagonal connections in successive updating.

This result reinforces a growing appreciation that concurrent computers can be applied to algorithms more general than the simple nearest-neighbor procedures typified by Fig. 7-5(a). The simpler algorithms minimize communication, but also minimize calculation, so that the crucial communication/calculation ratio is not particularly small for this class of examples. The seemingly less attractive algorithms of Figs. 7–5(b), (c), (d), and (e) actually perform as well or better even though they deviate from the pure nearest-neighbor case.

One additional topic not yet discussed is the need for non-nearest neighbor interprocessor communication links in order to handle higher-order update stencils. A stencil such as that of Fig. 7-5(c) calls for update information from diagonally displaced neighboring processors, as well as those displaced only horizontally or vertically. In order to update a corner nodal point, a given processor will need to communicate with diagonally neighboring nodal points, as well as with its Cartesian nearest neighbors. This presents no particular difficulty for our virtual concurrent processor as set forth in Chap. 4, since any processor in the ensemble may be specified as a partner in a communication call. In an actual machine and operating system (e.g., a hypercube), however, the diagonal next-nearest neighbor connection between processors may not be directly available. In this case, corner nodal points must be treated specially, being communicated once in the vertical direction and once horizontally in order to arrive at the desired destination. While this small number of "special" nodal points should have no serious impact on performance, it can increase the complexity of writing the program, since the operations needed to pass a value around the corner must be coordinated among all involved processors.

The additional programming necessary to handle diagonal passing is actually minimal in the rectangular domain illustrated in this chapter. Since any corner grid point in a subregion which has a diagonal neighbor always has rectilinear neighbors as well, the diagonal communication is achieved "for free" by performing the up/down and left/right communication steps in succession. While this approach is completely robust for domains whose decomposition is topologically equivalent to a rectangular tiling, it is not applicable, in general, to less regular decompositions such as might be dictated by irregularly shaped or multiply connected domains. The issues associated with diagonal passing are discussed further in Chap. 8, in which the finite element method, which virtually always involves non-nearest neighbor communication, is discussed.

7-7 Scientific Applications

Finite difference algorithms of the kind described in this chapter have proven useful for solving a variety of differential equations that arise in scientific problems. While many combinations of update procedures, stencils, and equations remain to be explored, some experience has been gained in the solution of systems with nontrivial scientific interest. We present here a couple of examples from the work with which we are familiar on the Caltech hypercube. A great deal of other exciting science is being or could be addressed on concurrent computers using the techniques described in this chapter.

An early application which goes beyond the simple elliptical Laplacian problem is the solution by Meier [Meier 84] of the equations governing two-dimensional hydrodynamic flow. In the absence of magnetic, gravitational, and radiation fields, the problem becomes one of solving the coupled system:

$$\frac{\partial \rho}{\partial t} + \nabla \cdot (\rho \underline{v}) = 0 \qquad \text{(continuity)} \qquad (7\text{-}11a)$$

$$\frac{\partial (\rho \underline{v})}{\partial t} + \nabla \cdot (\rho \underline{v} \underline{v}) = -\nabla p \qquad \text{(momentum)} \qquad (7\text{-}11b)$$

$$\frac{\partial E}{\partial t} + \nabla \cdot (E \underline{v}) = -\nabla \cdot (p \underline{v}) \qquad \text{(energy)} \qquad (7\text{-}11c)$$

Here, ρ, p, ν, and E represent mass density, pressure, velocity, and energy density, respectively. This system has been solved on the Mark II hypercube as a means of simulating flow phenomena in astrophysics.

In a manner similar to the wave equation example of Chap. 5, the spatial domain serves as the basis for a two-dimensional decomposition, with centered spatial differencing used for mesh updating. Temporal differencing again occurs synchronously in all processors, so that the concurrent efficiency is governed by the same considerations which governed the Laplace equation example.

Another field in the applied sciences to which concurrent finite difference algorithms have been profitably applied is that of acoustic and elastic wave propagation. Clayton [Clayton 84] and Frankel and Clayton [Frankel 86] have also employed the Mark II hypercube to solve the acoustic wave equation in inhomogeneous media for seismological investigations. The second-order finite difference update scheme in two dimensions again requires a spatial update stencil which encompasses only Cartesian nearest neighbors. As in the above example, the efficiency analysis for the time-dependent problem carries through from the Laplace case, and the results of Clayton and Frankel have confirmed this expectation. The earlier use of numerical simulations to study seismic propagation and scattering employing sequential computers has been generally limited to relatively small two-dimensional domains. The encouraging results with concurrent processors may portend an extension of such work to larger and finer meshes, as well as to three dimensions.

8

Elliptic Problems in Two Dimensions II: The Finite Element Method

8-1 Introduction

The previous chapter was concerned with the numerical solution of an elliptic boundary value problem through domain discretization. It was this discretization in the sequential problem which formed the basis for a concurrent formulation of the method. In the present chapter we will consider the same basic problem, the solution of Laplace's equation, but make use of an alternative technique, the finite element method.

To the reader unfamiliar with the distinction between finite elements and finite differences, it may be unclear why both methods should be discussed. In fact, some who are familiar with the subject may raise the same question! Our reasons are twofold, having to do with the different contexts of applicability of the two methods, and with differences in the issues of concurrency involved.

In most cases, the finite element formulation of a boundary value problem entails a greater amount of programming and computational effort than a comparable finite difference application. The justification for this greater complexity lies principally in the facility with which the finite element method can be used to handle discrete grids with an irregular or complicated distribution of points. Such domain discretizations, which arise commonly from the need to model "real world" domains or to resolve phenomena over a range of spatial scales, are addressed in a natural and general way by the finite element method. The fact that finite elements are central to many modern scientific and engineering simulations therefore constitutes the first half of our justification for their consideration here.

The second rationale is based upon some of the new algorithmic issues raised by extending our treatment to finite elements. In the previous chapter we obtained a very simple finite difference matrix structure from the regular spacing of nodal points in the discretized domain. This simple structure allowed the implementation of stationary iterative solvers without the need for any explicit reference to global matrix indices.

In the case of finite elements, the analogous matrix of linear equation coefficients lacks the regular, predictable structure characteristic of the finite difference problem. This circumstance will force us to consider solution schemes that accommodate more general matrices. While the stationary methods discussed in the last chapter may be formally generalized to handle finite element matrices, such an implementation would prove to be awkward and inefficient in practice. It is therefore opportune at this point to discuss

135

a different class of iterative solvers, which handle such matrices by design. The so-called *gradient* methods to be discussed below are proposed as an effective approach to concurrent finite element analysis, although it should be noted that nothing prevents their effective use in the finite difference setting of Chap. 7. [Ortega 85] discusses the application of various iterative methods including the gradient methods to a range of vector and parallel computer architectures. Our specific problem of iterative solution of finite element systems in a MIMD environment was pioneered in the work of [Adams 82, 84] using the NASA ICASE Finite Element Machine.

8-2 The Finite Element Formulation

The method of finite elements is the subject of a large number of textbooks and research papers, ranging in their approaches from mathematically theoretical to pragmatic and heavily applied. It will be impractical in this brief discussion to do justice to a description of the method, but we will attempt to assemble the most basic concepts needed to discuss our Laplace equation example. It is hoped that this will provide the reader unfamiliar with finite elements an appreciation of the basic issues as they relate to concurrency, rather than a complete introduction to the subject.

We begin by considering a spatial domain on which we seek approximate solutions of the original equation

$$\nabla^2\phi = 0 \qquad\qquad\qquad (8\text{-}1)$$

subject to boundary conditions as in Chap. 7. The method of approaching this problem again calls for the determination of an approximate solution for ϕ at a finite number of discrete points in the domain. Figure 8-1 shows a typical finite element discretization of a two-dimensional domain.

It is apparent from Fig. 8-1 that the typical finite element grid does not have an evenly spaced or rectilinear structure. As in the finite difference case, we seek to construct a system of linear equations whose unknowns ϕ_i comprise the desired approximate solution. The following discussion outlines the construction of this system.

Besides the geometric complexity, the important new concept illustrated in Fig. 8-1 is that of the *element*, a domain area (or volume) delineated by line segments (or curves) between grid points. Every grid point is a part of at least one element, and in the finite element formulation there exists a nonzero matrix element connecting any two unknowns ϕ_i and ϕ_j whose points share a common element. From this it may be seen that the task of computing matrix elements may be broken up into the computation of element matrix contributions which may be subsequently assembled into the global matrix system, given a knowledge of the geometric arrangement of elements.

It is the proper computation of the element matrices that is one of the principal topics of finite element treatises, and determines in part the accuracy of the resulting solution. At the heart of this problem is the recasting of the governing differential equation in the form of a variational equation or so-called "weak form." Variational formulations of this type are often referred to as virtual work principles, particularly in mechanics.

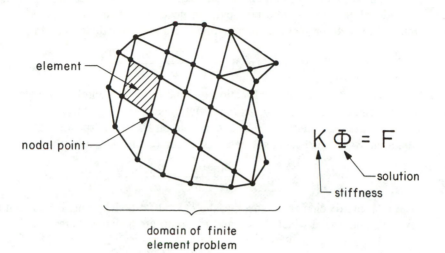

Figure 8-1 The finite element method involves solving for nodal degrees of freedom whose interaction is based upon element interpolation functions.

Standard finite element references such as [Hughes 87] or [Bathe 82] describe the application of this variational principle to the discrete problem. Broadly speaking, the space of acceptable solutions is assumed to be adequately represented by an M-dimensional space of basis functions (sometimes called "shape functions") where M is equal to the number of grid points. In the discrete problem (under the Bubnov-Galerkin approximation), we use these basis functions η_i to construct a trial solution.

The function η_i has the useful property of vanishing at all grid points except the ith point, at which it equals unity. This property facilitates the element-wise breaking up of computations related to the matrix elements. In practice, basis functions are usually chosen which have a simple linear or polynomial variation within an element. Our approximate solution $\tilde{\phi}$ is assumed to be given by the expansion:

$$\tilde{\phi} = \sum_{i=1}^{M} \phi_i \, \eta_i \qquad (8\text{-}2)$$

where as before, the coefficients ϕ_i are the approximate nodal values. When the variational principle is applied to this representation of the solution space, a linear system of equations or equivalently, a matrix problem is the result.

If we use Φ as shorthand notation for the vector of unknowns ϕ_i, the matrix problem may be expressed in the form

$$\mathbf{K} \, \Phi = \mathbf{F} \qquad (8\text{-}3)$$

In this equation, the matrix of coefficients $\mathbf{K}$ is commonly referred to as the "stiffness" matrix, and the right-hand side vector $\mathbf{F}$ contains "driving" terms originating in the boundary conditions.

The form of a general entry in the stiffness matrix is determined by the governing variational principle of the problem. In general, a matrix element K_{ij} consists of an integral over the problem domain involving the basis functions η_i and η_j:

$$K_{ij} = \int f(\eta_i, \eta_j, \frac{\partial \eta_i}{\partial x}, \frac{\partial \eta_j}{\partial x}, \frac{\partial \eta_i}{\partial y}, \frac{\partial \eta_j}{\partial y}, ...) dx\ dy \qquad (8\text{-}4)$$

The fact that the shape function η_i is nonzero only within those elements of which nodal point i is a part allows us to restrict the above integral to the area of a single element to obtain the element stiffness contribution k_{ij}^e. In the specific case of the Laplacian equation (8-1), the element stiffness matrix can be shown to have the form:

$$k_{ij}^e = \int (\frac{\partial \eta_i}{\partial x} \frac{\partial \eta_j}{\partial x} + \frac{\partial \eta_i}{\partial y} \frac{\partial \eta_j}{\partial y}) dx\ dy \qquad (8\text{-}5)$$

The total matrix element connecting the ith and j^{th} nodal points is obtained by summing over all elements of which the ith and j^{th} points are both members:

$$K_{ij} = \sum_e k_{ij}^e \qquad (8\text{-}6)$$

We have now sketched out the construction of the left-hand side of the matrix equation (8-3), and it remains to define the generalized force vector, **F**. In general, the treatment of driving terms in the finite element method is also connected with the variational form of the problem, but in the case of simple specified value (Neumann) boundary conditions, the form of **F** is relatively easy to demonstrate.

Consider the system of Eq. (8-3) to include equations for the specified boundary values, as well as for the *bona fide* unknowns. These "fixed" degrees of freedom are removed from the linear system by moving all terms involving such values to the right-hand side. Thus, if the fixed boundary potential at point i is denoted by g_i, we may write the contribution from a given element to the right-hand side vector **F** as:

$$f_i^e = -\sum_{j \neq i} k_{ij}^e g_j \qquad (8\text{-}7)$$

Here, k_{ij}^e is the element stiffness of Eq. (8-5), and the summation runs over all nodal points j in element e at which Neumann boundary conditions apply. As with the stiffness, the global right-hand side **F** is obtained through assembly of element contributions after the manner of Eq. (8-6).

All of the foregoing discussion has been concerned with the matter of constructing the linear system (8-3). While it is this task that is most specialized and specific to the finite element method, it is really somewhat tangential to our principal topic of concurrency. We will be concerned with the setup and structure of the stiffness matrix and right-hand side of (8-3) mainly as these influence the task of solving the system.

Our relative emphasis on solving Eq. (8-3) rather than the details of constructing it is based upon two observations. First, although calculating the required matrix elements from Eq. (8-5) by numerical integration is not an entirely trivial computational cost, it is in many practical cases a small cost compared with that of inverting **K**. Although this is not universally true, the solution step represents the main obstacle to extending finite element methods to large domains in many applications.

The second reason for skirting the issue of matrix setup is that the concurrent decomposition of this task is comparatively trivial to implement. Since both the matrix **K** and vector **F** naturally separate into independent element contributions, the processors of a concurrent ensemble can construct the element quantities for different elements in parallel, without the need for any interprocessor communication. Therefore, this step of equation setup has a concurrent implementation identical to that for a sequential machine. One potential complication would appear to arise from the need to combine element contributions from different processors into a global matrix equation. As we shall see in the next section, however, our choice of solution technique will allow us to do without this global assembly step.

8-3 The Equation Solver–Conjugate Gradient Method

As mentioned in the introduction to this chapter, iterative equation solvers called gradient methods, exist which are applicable in the case of finite element equations. It will be useful to start by briefly describing the basic approach of gradient methods before detailing a particular one.

Consider the task of iteratively solving M simultaneous equations. We may regard this problem as equivalent to finding the M-dimensional vector which minimizes some residual error quantity defined on the M-dimensional space. A gradient method makes use of trial values for the variable at step i to generate new values at step $i+1$ corresponding to a reduced value of the error function. By successively moving "downhill" toward the error minimum, the method converges toward the desired solution. Different gradient methods differ in their technique for choosing descent directions. For the discussion in this chapter, we will examine the *conjugate gradient* method [Jennings 77], which employs descent direction vectors that are mutually orthogonal relative to an inner product weighted by the stiffness matrix.

We begin by defining the quantities used in the conjugate gradient algorithm. The stiffness matrix **K** and "force" vector **F** are assumed to have been already constructed, and will remain unchanged by the algorithm. The remaining quantities are three M-vectors and two scalars whose contents are changed with each iteration. The iteration number to which a given M-vector applies will be indicated by a superscript. Thus, $\Phi^{(0)}$ denotes the starting trial solution, which in many practical cases is simply zero.

The other two M-vectors required are $\mathbf{r}^{(k)}$, the residual vector, and $\mathbf{p}^{(k)}$, the conjugate search direction. The conjugate gradient algorithm begins by initializing these M-vectors:

$$\mathbf{r}^{(0)} = \mathbf{p}^{(0)} = \mathbf{F} - \mathbf{K}\,\Phi^{(0)} \tag{8-8}$$

Then, the following iterative loop labelled by k is performed:

1. $\quad \alpha_k = \dfrac{(\mathbf{r}^{(k)} \cdot \mathbf{r}^{(k)})}{(\mathbf{p}^{(k)} \cdot \mathbf{K}\mathbf{p}^{(k)})}$

2. $\Phi^{(k+1)} = \Phi^{(k)} + \alpha_k \mathbf{p}^{(k)}$

3. $\mathbf{r}^{(k+1)} = \mathbf{r}^{(k)} - \alpha_k \mathbf{K}\mathbf{p}^{(k)}$ (8-9)

4. $\beta_k = \dfrac{(\mathbf{r}^{(k+1)} \cdot \mathbf{r}^{(k+1)})}{(\mathbf{r}^{(k)} \cdot \mathbf{r}^{(k)})}$

5. $\mathbf{p}^{(k+1)} = \mathbf{r}^{(k+1)} + \beta_k \mathbf{p}^{(k)}$

6. $k = k+1$; *go to* 1. (*continue until converged*)

The iterations are terminated when $\Phi^{(k)}$ has converged to within some desired accuracy, as determined by the magnitude of the vector of residuals, $\mathbf{r}$.

This algorithm does not depend upon any particular column or band structure, but it does require the matrix $\mathbf{K}$ to be symmetric and positive definite. Both of these conditions are satisfied by the finite element matrix of the present problem. It is significant that the only use that is made of $\mathbf{K}$ in this algorithm is to form its product with an M-vector. In order to perform this product, it is not necessary to assemble the element contribution matrices into a global $\mathbf{K}$, since the element contributions to any such product may be computed separately and summed afterward. This approach to computing a stiffness product is not of great importance for a conventional sequential computer in which the entire matrix $\mathbf{K}$ is readily available. In the concurrent implementation, however, a given processor may need access to parts of $\mathbf{K}$ residing in another processor. In this context, the element-wise modular approach to calculating products is vital.

8-4 Concurrent Decomposition

In order to see how best to implement this algorithm concurrently, let us look again at the operations carried out in Eq. (8-9). The iterative loop includes two basic kinds of operations: the vector inner product (such as $\mathbf{r}^{(k)} \cdot \mathbf{r}^{(k)}$), and the matrix-vector product $\mathbf{K}\mathbf{p}^{(k)}$. Each of these operations may be cast in a parallel form, as outlined below.

In the case of the vector inner product, the decomposition is easily seen. Each processor of the concurrent ensemble is given responsibility for a subset of the degrees of freedom which comprise a vector such as $\mathbf{r}$ or $\mathbf{p}$. Each processor concurrently calculates its contribution to the dot product, and the final result is obtained by summing the processor contributions via a collective combination step. If we neglect the single collective communication needed to assemble the inner product, this calculation involves no exchange of data between processors, and is limited in its concurrent efficiency essentially only by load balancing. As long as the processors are given equal numbers of degrees of freedom, the concurrent efficiency of this part of the calculation is close to unity.

We might assume at this point that the manner in which degrees of freedom are grouped for partitioning among processors is irrelevant. While this would be true for the vector dot product alone, the need to work with the stiffness matrix **K** dictates an element-based spatial decomposition, similar to that employed in the finite difference case. As stated above, a given row (or column) of this matrix contains nonzero elements only between degrees of freedom corresponding to points that share a common element. Consequently, a given entry of the **Kp** product vector only makes use of information that is spatially local to the corresponding grid point. Thus, it makes sense to group the degrees of freedom in processors according to contiguous spatial groupings of elements.

At this point, we can see the importance of the fact that it is not necessary to assemble the matrix **K** in its global form. The elements of the **Kp** vector may be constructed from the individual element "pieces" of **K** given in Eq. (8-5). Special consideration is required in dealing with degrees of freedom which fall on the boundary of a processor's region of responsibility. Since such an "internal boundary" point requires stiffness contributions from elements residing in more than one processor, it becomes necessary to exchange data between neighboring processors.

The calculation of the **Kp** product is handled by first performing computations for all elements internal to a given processor. This is followed by a communication cycle which brings in the boundary **Kp** contributions. The communication cycle must be designed in such a way as to additively accumulate all element contributions to a given degree of freedom and then to distribute the result to all processors which share that nodal point. We satisfy this requirement by invoking a two-pass sequence of communication between processors.

According to our definition of a processor region, each finite element belongs unambiguously to one processor, but the nodal points along outside edges are shared. We shall designate the edge points along the -x and -y boundaries of a given processor to be accumulated within that processor (Fig. 8-2). Conversely, the remaining +x and +y edges are designated as sent degrees of freedom, which are to have their contributions to the **Kp** product accumulated within the neighboring processor.

In this way each nodal point is accumulated in one and only one processor. The +xy corner nodal point is special in that its accumulation destination is in the processor located diagonally to the upper right. In the present discussion, this contribution reaches its destination through two successive communication steps. First, a left-to-right shift and accumulation is performed. Then, a down-to-up step is performed which leaves complete values of the **Kp** result in the destination slots. Since each processor needs a copy of the **Kp** result for subsequent calculation, the communication cycle is completed by reversing the direction of passing. An up-to-down pass followed by a right-to-left pass distributes the result to all processors. It is important that in the reverse pass the communication steps deliver copies, as opposed to performing additive accumulation as in the forward pass. The passing of corner values could be accomplished directly within the capabilities assumed for our virtual concurrent processor environment. In the present example, however, we use the two-step process to illustrate a means of implementing the method on machines such as hypercubes with restricted interprocessor links.

Figure 8-2 might suggest that this scheme for performing boundary communications requires a regular rectilinear arrangement of elements and nodal points in order to

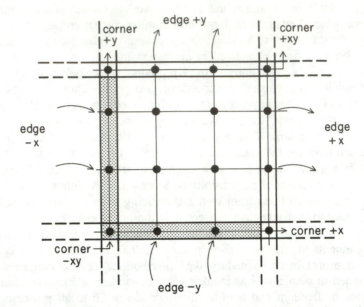

Figure 8-2 Processor regions overlap on the outer layer of nodal points. Accumulated degrees of freedom (shaded) are a processor's local responsibility, while the other edges and corners are under neighboring processors' jurisdiction.

work. In fact, it is irrelevant in this scheme whether the processors contain regular or congruent arrangements of elements. The only requirement in this regard is that neighboring processors agree on the number and kind of shared boundary nodes along their common edges. Aside from this consideration, it is only necessary to ensure that roughly equal numbers of degrees of freedom are contained within each processor to achieve a good load balance.

The generality of problems which can be handled by the above described scheme depends on machine-specific communication considerations. A grid such as that in Fig. 8-3(a), which is easily mapped onto a simple two-dimensional processor mesh, will work under even the restrictive assumption of a machine that supports only nearest-neighbor mesh communications. On the other hand, a grid which is used to model multiply connected or "dendritic" regions as in Fig. 8-3(b), may be difficult to map efficiently onto a machine with only hardwired mesh connections. Such problems may be more effectively handled by concurrent processors with the capability of more general interprocessor communication. In the final section of this chapter, we briefly discuss the use of crystalline communication routing utilities in this regard. In such cases, the details of the passing scheme described above for a simple mesh would no longer hold, but the concepts of accumulated and sent degrees of freedom within the conjugate gradient algorithm would remain valid. An alternative approach to handling irregular meshes within a restricted communication topology is the scattered decomposition [Morison 86] which is used in a related context in Chapter 17 for decomposing an inherently irregular problem.

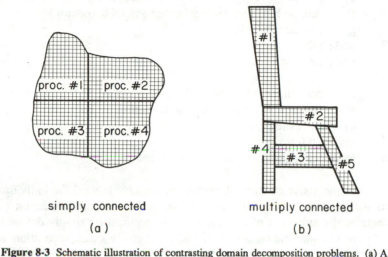

simply connected   multiply connected

(a)   (b)

Figure 8-3 Schematic illustration of contrasting domain decomposition problems. (a) A simply connected region is easily accommodated by mesh processor communication. (b) Multiply connected domain requires more communication flexibility or the scattered decomposition.

8-5 Example Implementation

The following examples of pseudocode serve to illustrate the concurrent conjugate gradient algorithm outlined in the previous section. Much of the programming needed to accomplish such tasks as interactive control, grid setup, and input/output may be similar in form to that already given in the case of finite differences. For this reason, we focus the following examples on the conjugate gradient algorithm and its associated communication operations.

We will examine here the structure of the node subroutine *conj_grad*, which performs the central task of solving the linear system of Eq. (8-3). This subroutine would normally be called from the main-level program following the steps of data input and matrix generation. The overall structure of the routine follows that of the iterative loop in Eq. (8-9). The loop is punctuated at intervals by communication calls needed to exchange neighboring data or to combine results across the ensemble. The modified conjugate gradient algorithm has the following form:

1.

    a)   perform $\mathbf{r} \cdot \mathbf{r}$ product within nodes (calc.)

    b)   sum $\mathbf{r} \cdot \mathbf{r}$ contributions across ensemble (comm.)

    c)   perform $\mathbf{Kp}$ product within nodes (calc.)

    d)   accumulate neighbor contributions to **Kp** (comm.)

    e)   perform **p** · **Kp** product within nodes (calc.)

    f)   sum **p** · **Kp** contributions across ensemble (comm.)

    g)   calculate α (calc.)

2.   update Φ (calc.)

3.   update **r** (calc.)

4.

    a)   perform new **r** · **r** product (calc.)

    b)   sum new **r** · **r** across ensemble (comm.)

    c)   calculate β (calc.)

5.   update **p** (calc.)

6.   increment iteration counter and continue

In the above concurrent algorithm, we have labeled the individual steps according to their function as either a calculation (calc.) or communication (comm.) task. The sequential counterpart of this algorithm is regained by simply deleting the steps labeled as pure communication steps. Thus, a relatively clean separation between functions specific to the concurrent algorithm and those of the conjugate gradient method proper is apparent. Code 8-1 contains the pseudocode implementation of this loop, and is indicative of the programming necessary to implement the conjugate gradient solver within a typical hypercube or other message-passing machine environment.

In this example, the iterative loop is "primed" by initially calculating the norm of the starting residual vector **r**$^{(0)}$. Concurrent calling of the subroutine *dot_global* results in the calculation of the global scalar product of vectors whose elements are distributed among the ensemble processors. The details of this subroutine will be discussed below in connection with Code 8-2 and Fig. 8-4.

The iterative loop itself makes use of similar constructs. The intermediate scalar products of **p** · **Kp** and **r** · **r** are also obtained through calls to *dot_global*. The remainder of the loop simply follows the sequential algorithm of Eq. (8-9).

The routine *K_p_product* is not described in detail here, because its structure does not involve any explicit issues of concurrency. As indicated in our earlier discussion, all that is important for our example is that *K_p_product* is designed to obtain the product of the stiffness matrix **K** with an M-vector, using an element-wise additive decomposition of **K**. In calling this routine, each processor obtains its contributions to the product vector as if the elements contained in other processors do not exist. The overlapping contributions to **Kp** from neighboring processors are subsequently accumulated in the *globalize* call.

Before dropping the subject of the formation of **Kp**, it should be noted that in an application on a given concurrent processor, the choice of an optimal strategy for handling the stiffness matrix is quite important, being impacted by such machine-dependent factors as the amounts of fast memory available to each processor. Alternate strategies may be formulated to minimize either the storage requirements or arithmetic operation count in obtaining **Kp**, depending upon the machine-imposed constraints.

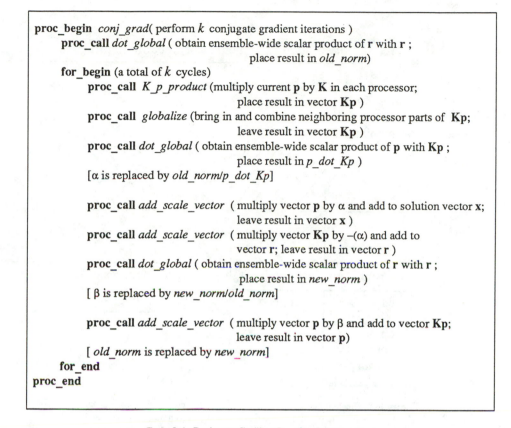

```
proc_begin conj_grad( perform k conjugate gradient iterations )
    proc_call dot_global ( obtain ensemble-wide scalar product of r with r ;
                                    place result in old_norm)
        for_begin (a total of k cycles)
            proc_call K_p_product (multiply current p by K in each processor;
                                    place result in vector Kp )
            proc_call globalize (bring in and combine neighboring processor parts of Kp;
                                    leave result in vector Kp )
            proc_call dot_global ( obtain ensemble-wide scalar product of p with Kp ;
                                    place result in p_dot_Kp )
            [α is replaced by old_norm/p_dot_Kp]

            proc_call add_scale_vector ( multiply vector p by α and add to solution vector x;
                                    leave result in vector x )
            proc_call add_scale_vector ( multiply vector Kp by −(α) and add to
                                    vector r; leave result in vector r )
            proc_call dot_global ( obtain ensemble-wide scalar product of r with r ;
                                    place result in new_norm )
            [ β is replaced by new_norm/old_norm]

            proc_call add_scale_vector ( multiply vector p by β and add to vector Kp;
                                    leave result in vector p)
            [ old_norm is replaced by new_norm]
        for_end
proc_end
```

Code 8-1 Conjugate Gradient Iterative Solver

We next examine the two routines *dot_global* and *globalize*, which incorporate the interprocessor communication step vital to the concurrent implementation. The implementations of both of these routines make use of an assumed ordering of the degrees of freedom within a given M-vector. This structure is illustrated schematically in Fig. 8-4.

In the construction of intermediate vectors such as r or **Kp**, we have chosen to order the entries so that the sent and accumulated degrees of freedom are grouped separately in memory. Such an ordering simplifies the task of selectively manipulating quantities of different communication type. As an example, the vector product operation of *dot_global* must take care not to "double-count" the contributions to the product which come from shared nodal points. In the illustrated scheme, the first *ndof_sends* entries of the M-vector correspond to those degrees of freedom for which some other processor has responsibility. Therefore, the *dot_global* routine is simply required to perform a dot product on the last *ndof_total−ndof_sends* entries of the multiplicand vectors. This step is followed by a global sum of the node contributions. Code 8-2 contains the pseudocode implementation of this routine.

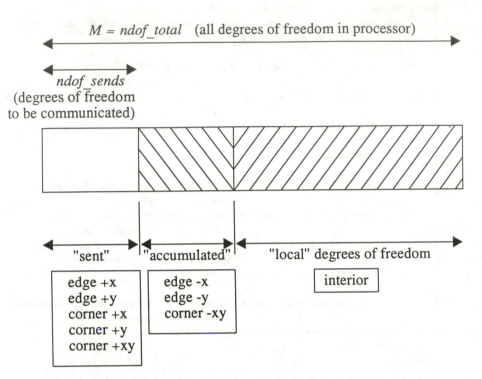

Figure 8-4 The numbering order of degrees of freedom within each processor is contrived to simplify the handling of communication. Accumulated and sent nodal points are stored as contiguous blocks so that they may be moved en masse during interprocessor communication. Shaded blocks represent local processor responsibility.

Also illustrated in Code 8-2 is the implementation of *globalize*. Whereas *dot_global* is used to obtain and distribute a global scalar quantity, the *globalize* subroutine is required to obtain neighboring processor contributions to a global M-vector built up from element pieces.

The *globalize* routine utilizes the two-pass cyclic communication scheme discussed above in connection with Fig. 8-2. Neighboring processors exchange and accumulate shared edge values via the communication buffers *right_buf*, *left_buf*, *up_buf*, and *down_buf*. Implicit in this treatment is the assumption that adjoining processors agree on the mapping between items communicated through these buffers and their ultimate destinations in the M-vector. In practice, such a mapping can be accomplished by indexing of the buffers, or in complicated geometries by explicitly passing a global index with each value. The latter alternative entails a greater communication cost, but may be necessary in cases where it is impractical to enforce a matching of local indices across processor boundaries, as might easily occur with complicated grids.

```
proc_begin dot_global ( obtain ensemble-wide scalar product of vector a with vector b )
    for_begin (loop over degrees of freedom in processor's jurisdiction ;
                    k running from ndof_sends to ndof_total )
        [ multiply kth element of a by kth element of b and sum in result ]
    for_end
    [ vm_combine — add values of result across ensemble and replace result ]
proc_end ( return result )


proc_begin globalize (bring in and combine neighboring processor contributions to vector a )
    [ place a entries to be sent to right neighbor in right_buf buffer ]
    [ vm_shift — send right_buf to right neighbor; receive from left neighbor into left_buf ]
    [ add entries of left_buf to corresponding entries of a, replacing them ]

    [ place a entries to be sent to upper neighbor in up_buf buffer ]
    [ vm_shift — send up_buf to upper neighbor; receive from lower neighbor into down_buf ]
    [ add entries of down_buf to corresponding entries of a, replacing them ]

    [ replace summed a entries from lower neighbor in down_buf buffer ]
    [ vm_shift — send down_buf to lower neighbor; receive from upper neighbor into up_buf ]
    [ replace entries of a with corresponding entries of up_buf just received ]

    [ replace summed a entries from left neighbor in left_buf buffer ]
    [ vm_shift — send left_buf to left neighbor; receive from right neighbor into right_buf ]
    [ replace entries of a with corresponding entries of right_buf just received ]
proc_end
```

Code 8-2 Communication Routines for Conjugate Gradient Solver

The routines outlined in Code 8-1 and Code 8-2 comprise the core of our conjugate gradient finite element solver. This particular example presents a somewhat special case, in that we have treated only two-dimensional problems and limited our discussion of complicated domains to general remarks. Nevertheless, the above implementation should serve to illustrate the central concepts common to more sophisticated programs, and to indicate some of the directions in which this work might be readily extended.

8-6 Performance of the Finite Element Example

As in the discussion of a finite difference application in the previous chapter, we now present the results of implementing our finite element/conjugate gradient algorithm on the Caltech Mark II hypercube. Much of the discussion in Chap. 7 relating to the theoretical efficiency of the concurrent algorithm is directly applicable here. The communication load varies as the number of perimeter nodal points per processor, while the computational load (which is dominated by matrix-vector products) is approximately proportional to the total number, n_{el}, of elements per processor. As a result, we would expect the two-dimensional lattice efficiency dependence given in Chap. 7:

$$\varepsilon \approx 1 - cn_{el}^{-1/2} \qquad (8\text{-}10)$$

We should expect detailed differences in the communication and computation tasks to be reflected in different values of c for the finite element and finite difference examples. Coincidentally, these differences approximately cancel to yield a value of $c \approx 1$ in Eq. (8-10), as obtained earlier for finite differences. In Fig. 8-5, the concurrent efficiencies are plotted on a logarithmic scale to illustrate the dependence of efficiency on problem size and number of processors.

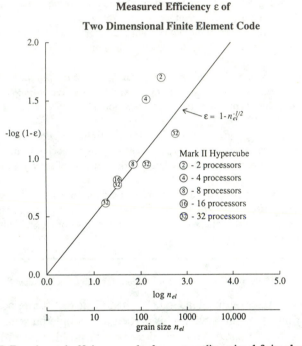

Measured Efficiency ε of

Two Dimensional Finite Element Code

Figure 8-5 Experimental efficiency results from a two dimensional finite element program running on Caltech Mark II hypercube. Solid line indicates theoretical efficiency trend Eq. (8-10).

As was noted in Chap. 7, configurations of fewer than 16 processors fall on higher parallel efficiency trends. The 32-node configuration, which involves processors communicating on all four sides, yields efficiencies lying close to the $c = 1$ line. We may conclude that the finite element implementation presented in this chapter shows good agreement with theoretical efficiency predictions and yields useful concurrent speedup on actual machines for more than about 10 finite elements per processor. A performance analysis of finite element problems on a shared memory ELXSI 6400 and comparison with the hypercube will be found in [Walker 86] and [Montry 87].

8-7 Extensions and Scientific Applications

The basic approach to solving finite element systems on concurrent processors outlined in this chapter has been employed to solve a number of scientifically interesting problems in continuum mechanics. This approach also forms the basis for ongoing work with the goal of solving more challenging problems [Nour-Omid 87a, b].

The concurrent conjugate gradient algorithm described above has been used [Lyzenga 85] to solve finite element systems arising from linear elastostatic boundary value problems. The form of the operator and resulting stiffness matrix is somewhat more complicated than those in the Laplacian example. The governing equation is given in tensor index notation by:

$$\sigma_{ij,j} = -f_i \qquad (8\text{-}11)$$

Here, f_i denotes a vector body force (such as gravitation) and σ_{ij} is the Cauchy stress tensor which is related to material displacements, u_i, by:

$$\sigma_{ij} = \lambda u_{k,k}\delta_{ij} + \mu(u_{i,j} + u_{j,i}) \qquad (8\text{-}12)$$

where λ and μ are the Lamé elastic constants for an isotropic medium. We employ the usual conventions here of commas for differentiation, repeated indices for summation, and δ_{ij} for the Kronecker delta unit tensor.

This equation gives rise to a problem similar to the Laplacian case, in that it involves only second derivatives of the dependent variables u_i, and yields a symmetric, positive-definite matrix. In work performed on the Mark II hypercubes, the conjugate gradient solver has been adopted unchanged, except for the addition of a simple preconditioner based upon a rescaling of the matrix by its diagonal elements. This problem has been solved for both the two-dimensional domain discussed above, and for three-dimensional domains.

The matter of preconditioning for iterative equation solvers is an important one if such techniques are to find broad practical application. While iterative methods like conjugate gradient are characterized by comparatively modest computational costs per iteration, the number of iterations required to obtain a solution to within a desired accuracy can be highly problem-dependent.

In general, matrix systems with widely varying magnitudes of eigenvalues present a problem for gradient methods. In such cases, when working with finite numerical precision, the solver may become "lost" in trying to find a residual minimum in M-space, since the shapes of level surfaces in this space are extremely nonspherical. Preconditioning amounts to the application of some transformation to the original matrix system which is intended to render it more tractable for the iterative solver.

In the finite element matrix, the diagonal elements are proportional to the areas (or volumes) of the elements associated with each degree of freedom. Therefore, one source of ill-conditioning in finite elements is any strong variation in grid refinement. Such ill-conditioning may be alleviated to some extent by rescaling the system so that the magnitudes of the diagonal elements are constant. In practice, this kind of diagonal preconditioner can substantially accelerate the convergence of the conjugate gradient method.

However, it may be of limited usefulness with other sources of ill-conditioning. For example, large contrasts in matrix elements within the same row or column of the stiffness will not be remedied by diagonal scaling.

In general, the more closely a preconditioning transformation approximates the actual inverse of the matrix, the more successful it will be in accelerating convergence. A number of promising approaches to this problem are applicable to the concurrent case. One such approach represents the approximate matrix inverse by a product of local element matrix inverses [Muller 85]. This element-by-element preconditioner can offer good performance for some classes of problems, but it also involves a sequential matrix factoring scheme which must be performed in a consistent manner on a concurrent processor.

By analogy with our discussion of the inherently sequential SOR update scheme in Chap. 7, it becomes necessary to apply the element-by-element preconditioning step in spatially disjoint subregions of adjoining processor regions. Since the finite element method yields diagonal connections between grid points as well as nearest neighbors, the four-color isolation scheme illustrated in Fig. 7-6 is needed.

Although not formally regarded as a preconditioner, the multigrid method offers yet another approach to increasing the robustness of iterative finite elements. In the multigrid method, a succession of meshes of progressively greater refinement is used. The solution obtained on a coarse grid at modest computational cost is projected onto the next finer grid as input to the next approximation to the ultimate solution.

Under some circumstances, this process of projecting the "low-frequency" solutions onto progressively finer meshes has the effect of giving the ultimate iterative solution step an easier system to solve. The application of this approach to large granularity concurrent processing is straightforward, as it involves the same domain decomposition schemes already discussed. The projection and interpolation of solutions between grids of different refinement involves concurrent vector/matrix operations completely analogous to those treated above in the discussion of simple conjugate gradients. A basic multigrid scheme has been implemented on the Caltech hypercube machines [Cisneros 87; Van de Velde 87a, b].

At first glance, it might seem that the multigrid method is not easily implemented on concurrent computers because of the involvement of steps using a coarse grid which allow little concurrency and hence constitutes a sequential bottleneck. This is not true, however, and the point provides an interesting comment on the relevance of Amdahl's law to concurrent computing [Amdahl 67, Chan 87, Fox 84c]. Let us consider a multigrid method in which the finest grid incorporates n nodal points per processor node. In its simplest form, the method is comprised of successive stages labelled by k, each involving $n_k = n/2^k$ members. We see that the total calculation time is:

$$T_{calc} \sim \sum_k n_k\, t_{calc} \qquad\qquad (8\text{-}13)$$

while the communication time is given by:

$$T_{comm} \sim \sum_k n_k^{1/2}\, t_{comm} \qquad\qquad (8\text{-}14)$$

Extending the k-sums to infinity we find:

$$T_{calc} \sim n\,(1 + 1/2 + 1/4 + ...) = 2n \qquad (8\text{-}13a)$$

and

$$T_{comm} \sim n^{1/2}(1 + 1/\sqrt{2} + 1/2 + ...) = 3.4n^{1/2} \qquad (8\text{-}14a)$$

In other words, we obtain a value for the communication overhead f_C that is increased by a factor of 1.7 as compared with Eq. (8-10), but is still proportional to $n^{-1/2}$. Here n is the grain size on the finest grid. The presence of the coarse grids with less concurrency only gives rise to the factor 1.7 and does not qualitatively change the efficiency behavior. The point is the same as that discussed in Section 3-6; the stages involving coarse grids (small n_k) have high overheads but they don't take very long, so that the net performance is dominated by the high efficiency stages on the fine grid. An improved multigrid formalism for the hypercube with less overhead on the coarse grids is presented in [Frederickson 87].

Our discussion of finite element problems in this chapter has tended to emphasize two-dimensional grids with a comparatively regular and simply connected structure. Such simple grids aid in the explanation and visualization of interprocessor communication paths. A critical issue, however, in the applicability of these ideas to finite element problems of practical importance is their generalization to higher-dimensional and irregular grids.

Consider first the extension to three dimensions. As shown in Fig. 8-6, whereas the two-dimensional protocol requires keeping track of eight distinct "types" of communicated degrees of freedom, in three dimensions there are 26 types of face, edge, and corner nodal points which must be shuttled between processors. This increase in complexity alone might be enough to suggest that simple mesh communication schemes are cumbersome in three dimensions. In fact, such schemes are not difficult to implement until irregular grids are considered.

As long as the modeled domain can be mapped by a topologically rectangular decomposition with no holes or niches, all shared degrees of freedom in a three-dimensional grid are guaranteed to reach their proper destinations after six communication steps (one in each spatial coordinate with each sign). This elegant method of routing edges, which is robust in a simply structured domain, forms a central part of the particle dynamics algorithm discussed in Chap. 16. Complications occur, however, when we consider more general kinds of finite element domains.

As we pointed out at the beginning of the chapter, a principal advantage of the finite element method is its facility in handling irregular domains. Thus a practically useful concurrent finite element program should not be limited to simple grids. It is a difficult programming task, however, to design a neighbor-passing procedure sufficiently general to handle every possible contingency of routing around "holes" in a complicated grid. General message routing systems provide the solution to this problem.

Non-nearest neighbor communication as provided by the *crystal_router* utility (Chap. 22) or by interrupt-driven systems (Sec. 14-8) can provide the robust communications needed for general finite element problems, though at some additional communication cost. In such a scheme, the original distinction between "accumulated" and "sent" degrees of freedom is retained, but explicit specification of routing directions with relative addresses such as "right" and "up" is abandoned. Instead, communicated degrees of freedom are accompanied by absolute addresses corresponding to their destination processors(s) and the routing system takes care of the rest.

Of course, the decomposition and routing utilities in such a system should be designed in order to take best advantage of the direct communication channels of a particular machine. As long as this is true, the performance of the finite element program with routed communications should not be much worse than optimal, since the number of nodal points requiring long-distance forwarding will be small.

Distinct Types of Communicated
Nodal Points in 2 and 3 Dimensions

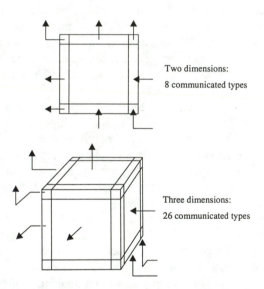

Two dimensions:

8 communicated types

Three dimensions:

26 communicated types

Figure 8-6 Comparison of the communicated degrees of freedom in two- and three-dimensional finite element implementations.

Another problem of importance in the concurrent finite element field is the automation of the domain decomposition task. While this issue does not deal directly with concurrency in the finite element solution process, it is important because it determines how much more difficult for the end user the concurrent program will be to use than its sequential equivalent. In formulating automated domain decomposition procedures, the communication protocol and data organization should be designed in such a manner as to minimize the user's awareness of the particular concurrent processor's communication restrictions. Significant progress has been made in the context of a two-dimensional example problem [Flower 86, Nour-Omid 87b] and powerful techniques are reviewed in Sec. 3-8 [Fox 86g]. We expect that the tasks of domain decomposition and mesh generation may well be combined in future systems. The emerging generation of computers will be capable of handling the extremely large finite element problems for which automatic decomposition will be a necessity.

9

Long Range Interactions

9-1 Introduction

In this chapter we consider algorithms in which a nontrivial computation must be performed on all pairs of objects in a data base. Many situations arise in which this type of calculation is necessary. In molecular dynamics calculations, such an algorithm is needed when the intermolecular force law has a Coulombic or other long-range component. A similar situation arises in Newtonian gravitational n-body simulations, in which the force law also has infinite range. Computing the product of two large polynomials is also a long-range problem because every pair of monomials must be combined to produce a term in the result. By definition, a long-range algorithm is characterized by a running time proportional to the number of pairs, or roughly, the square of the number of objects. Thus, long range problems with more than a few thousand objects pose significant challenges for even the fastest computers.

In order to present the important components of the long-range force algorithm without obscuring the ideas with unnecessary detail, this chapter is divided into several sections. Each of these sections presents a successively more complicated version of the algorithm. In this way, the most fundamental ideas are developed relatively cleanly, and the progression to more complex problems is accomplished by adding features to the fundamental framework. In Sec. 9-2, we consider the problem of computing the potential energy of a collection of particles which interact by a pairwise potential. This subproblem disregards Newton's third law. In Sec. 9-3, we take advantage of Newton's third law to reduce the necessary work by half, as is normally done in the sequential case. In Sec. 9-4, we compute a unique force for every particle in the system, and in Sec. 9-5, we comment on the application of the algorithm to the calculation of correlation functions.

9-2 Total Potential Energy

In order to introduce the basic communication strategy and to outline the approach, we begin with a computation of the total potential energy of a system of particles that interact via a pair potential. This is very much simpler than computing the forces on all the particles because the final result will be a single number rather than a different force for every particle. For the rest of this chapter the number of processors is denoted by N, and the number of particles is N_p. A particle is an aggregate data structure containing all the information necessary to describe the state of a physical particle in the simulation. For example, mass, charge, position, velocity, acceleration, etc.

The total potential energy of a system of such particles is given by

$$U = \frac{1}{2}\sum_{i=1}^{N_p}\sum_{j=1}^{N_p}\phi(\vec{x}_i, \vec{x}_j)$$

(9-1)

In Code 9-1, the function *pot_seq* computes the double summation in Eq. (9-1) for an array of particles. We use the auxiliary function *pot_2arr*, which uses two arrays of particles, in anticipation of the requirements of the parallel algorithm. The function *pair_potential* contains the physics of the computation, and returns the potential energy contribution, ϕ, of its two arguments. For example, *pair_potential* might compute the Newtonian potential of two massive objects.

$$\phi(\vec{x}_i, \vec{x}_j) = -\frac{Gm_i m_j}{|\vec{x}_i - \vec{x}_j|}$$

(9-2)

```
proc_begin pot_seq (sequential evaluation of potential energy, U, of particles P )
declare_buf Q; (copy of buffer P)
      [copy P to Q]
      proc_call pot_2arr (find potential energy, U, between particles in P and particles in Q)
proc_end

proc_begin pot_2arr ( find potential energy, U, between particles in buffers P and Q )
      [set U=0]
      for_begin ( each particle, P_i, in P )
            for_begin ( each particle, Q_j, in Q )
                  proc_call pair_potential ( find potential energy, U_ij, between P_i and Q_j )
                  [U←U+U_ij]
            for_end
      for_end
      [U←U/2]
proc_end
```

Code 9-1 Sequential Evaluation of Potential Energy

9-2.1 Parallel Decomposition

First we observe that the positions of all particles must eventually be communicated to every processor. If there are N_p particles, and N_{local} are stored in some processor, then that processor must somehow obtain the attributes of N_p-N_{local} particles and compute $N_{local}N_p$ pairwise interactions. The time spent in computation is thus:

$$T_{comp} \approx \max(N_{local}) N_p\, t_{pair}$$

(9-3)

where t_{pair} is the time required to compute the interaction potential of a pair of particles. We take an optimistic view and assume that we can do the communication without bottlenecks and that all data transfers are equally fast. Then the number of attributes read by any given processor provides an estimate of the communication time

$$T_{comm} \approx \max(N_p - N_{local}) \, t_{exchg} \qquad (9\text{-}4)$$

where t_{exchg} is the time required to communicate the attributes of one particle to a neighboring processor. In Eqs. (9-3) and (9-4) max(x) refers to the largest value of x in any processor in the system. If $t_{exchg} \approx t_{pair}$, then From Eqs. (9-3) and (9-4) we see that computation is more time consuming than communication, by a factor which grows approximately linearly max(N_{local}). Thus, the optimum decomposition will minimize T_{comp} and will be such that max(N_{local}) is minimized. In other words, an equal number of particles is stored in every processor. By definition, there is no locality in long-range problems, so the decomposition need not be concerned with the proximity of particles in space. All decompositions which balance the load are equally good. Assigning particles to processors at random, with the constraint that an equal number is assigned to each processor, is a perfectly good way to decompose long range problems.

Unfortunately, the number of particles is often fixed by considerations other than algorithmic convenience, and this number might not be divisible by the number of processors. In any case, the difference in N_{local} between any two processors can be made to be either one or zero. Our subsequent discussion assumes that all processors have exactly the same number of particles. The more general case is essentially the same, and can be treated with minimal cost by placing dummy particles in some processors.

9-2.2 Communication Structure: The Ring Topology

The discussion in the previous section relied on the optimistic assumption that the communication could be done without bottlenecks. In this section we discuss a very simple interconnection topology which verifies that assumption.

In order to evaluate all of the pair potentials, every pair of particles must meet in some processor at some time in the calculation. In other words, every particle must visit every processor, and while there, its interactions with all the particles in that processor must be tallied. We propose to connect the processors in a ring, as in Fig. 9-1. Every particle can visit all the processors in the ring by taking N-1 steps in either the clockwise or counterclockwise direction. Crucial to the practicality of this approach is that the communications can be done concurrently. Therefore, we can think of the ring as a pipeline. In a single time interval of duration, t_{exchg}, it is possible to transfer N particles one step around the ring, with each processor transmitting and receiving exactly one particle.

Now we ask: How much time does it take, in communication alone, to have every particle visit every processor? Since the communication is done concurrently, this interval is equal to the time required for a single processor to transmit and receive all N_p particles. This time is simply $N_p t_{exchg}$. This estimate, however, is based upon the additional assumption that no processor will finish its own work and fall idle waiting for its neighbor to send more particles. If all processors contain the same number of particles at all times, then such a load imbalance will not occur. With equal numbers of particles in each processor, the computational load between communication steps is exactly the same

(a)

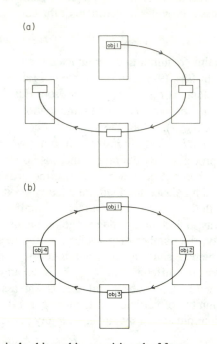

(b)

Figure 9-1 (a) A single object, obj_1, can visit each of four processors by following the path denoted by the arrows, (b) By performing the communication in parallel, four objects, obj_1 through obj_4, can each visit the same four processors in the same amount of time. In each step, each processor writes its object in the direction of the outgoing arrow and reads a new object from the direction of the incoming arrow. After only three steps (three units of time), all four objects have visited all four processors.

in all processors, so there need be no waiting for communication. As soon as one processor is ready to read, its neighbor should be ready to write.

In considering the parallel algorithm, we have already concluded that we must move particles from processor to processor, computing the interactions between two arrays of particles, those which started in a given processor, and those which are passing through. We can use *pot_2arr* from Code 9-1 to compute the interactions between these two arrays. In Code 9-2, *pot_par* is a procedure that computes the potential in parallel.

The procedure *pot_par* contains three procedure calls and a loop not found in *pot_seq*. The first procedure is *ring_setup* which maps the abstract ring topology, in which each processor has a clockwise and counterclockwise neighbor, onto the virtual machine. Since a ring is really a one-dimensional grid, *ring_setup* can obtain this information from the decomposition routines described in Sec. 4-6. The ring is closed by connecting the processors at locations 1 and N.

The **for** loop in the function *pot_par*, which runs over each processor in the ring, contains a call to *rotate*, which is the basic communication operation for this algorithm. *Rotate* moves all of the particles in the array, Q, around the ring by an amount of one processor in the clockwise direction. The contents of the array are replaced by the particles obtained from the counterclockwise neighbor. *Rotate* is easily implemented using *vm_shift* of Sec. 4-4.

```
proc_begin pot_par ( parallel evaluation of potential energy U )
declare_buf Q; ( array for particles being rotated around processor ring )
declare_float U_loc ; (contribution to potential energy from this processor )
      proc_call copy ( copy P to Q )
      proc_call ring_setup ( decompose system as a ring of processors )
      [set U_loc = 0]
      for_begin ( each processor in the ring )
            proc_call pot_2arr ( find potential energy, U_PQ , between particles in P
                                             and particles in Q )
            [U_loc ← U_loc + U_PQ]
            proc_call rotate ( send buffer Q to next processor in ring and replace with
                        corresponding buffer from previous processor )
      for_end
      proc_call global_add ( sum contributions, U_loc, of all processors to give
                                              total potential energy U )
      [U ← U /2]
proc_end
```

Code 9-2 Parallel Evaluation of Potential Energy

Finally, we find the subroutine *global_add*. Before the call to *global_add*, each processor has accumulated only a fraction of the total of all pair interactions. To obtain the total, we must compute an overall sum of all the partial sums stored in each processor. The function *vm_combine* , also introduced in Sec. 4-4, is used in *global_add* to sum the contributions from each processor.

9-2.3 Efficiency of the Algorithm

Problems involving long range forces seem to be ill-suited to parallel processing. After all, isn't the communication overhead extremely high, since every particle must visit every processor? The answer is that algorithms for long-range problems do, indeed, require considerable communication. The computational time, however, is so much larger that the communication overhead is relatively unimportant. The quantity of interest is not the total time spent communicating, but rather the speedup obtained by use of the concurrent processor.

Let $T_N(N_p)$ be the time to compute the potential energy in an N_p-body problem on N processors. The overhead, f , of the implementation has been defined in Eq. (5-5) as:

$$f = \frac{N T_N(N_p) - T_1(N_p)}{T_1(N_p)} \tag{9-5}$$

The parallel program *pot_par* has a running time given by:

$$T_N(N_p) \approx N(t_{pot\_2arr} + t_{rot}) \qquad (9\text{-}6)$$

where t_{pot_2arr} is the time to complete a call to *pot_2arr* and t_{rot} is the time to complete a call to *rotate*. These are expressed in terms of t_{exchg} and t_{pair} as

$$t_{pot\_2arr} \approx N_{local}^2 t_{pair} = \left(\frac{N_p}{N}\right)^2 t_{pair} \qquad (9\text{-}7)$$

and

$$t_{rot} \approx N_{local} t_{exchg} = \frac{N_p}{N} t_{exchg} \qquad (9\text{-}8)$$

The overhead is given approximately by:

$$f \approx \frac{N}{N_p} \frac{t_{exchg}}{t_{pair}} = \frac{1}{N_{local}} \frac{t_{exchg}}{t_{pair}} \qquad (9\text{-}9)$$

The overhead approaches zero if

$$\frac{1}{N_{local}} \frac{t_{exchg}}{t_{pair}} << 1 \qquad (9\text{-}10)$$

Thus, the algorithm will perform efficiently as long as N_{local} is large, i.e., as long as the amount of computation assigned to each processor is large. Increasing the number of processors with a fixed problem size reduces the efficiency, but the perhaps more likely scenario in which problem size grows with machine size leaves the efficiency approximately constant.

9-3 Symmetry of the Pair Potential

The discussion, until now, has overlooked one crucial fact: that the pair potential function ϕ often satisfies the symmetry relation:

$$\phi(\vec{x}_1, \vec{x}_2) = \phi(\vec{x}_2, \vec{x}_1) \qquad (9\text{-}11)$$

In dynamics problems, Eq. (9-11) is a consequence of Newton's Third Law. Even in nondynamical problems, such as the computation of correlation functions, a similar symmetry can be used to reduce the required amount of computation by half. Unless we can use Eq. (9-11) in the parallel algorithm, it will be impossible to achieve a *true* efficiency greater than 50%, because the parallel algorithm will always do twice as much work as the optimal sequential algorithm. It is easy to incorporate the symmetry of Eq. (9-11) into the sequential program. The subroutine *pot_sym_2arr* illustrated in Code 9-3 makes use of the symmetry, and may replace *pot_2arr* in Code 9-1.

```
proc_begin pot_sym_2arr ( find potential energy, U, between particles in buffers P and Q )
      [set U = 0]
      for_begin ( each particle, P_i, in P )
            for_begin ( each particle, Q_j, in Q for which j > i )
                  proc_call pair_potential ( find potential energy, U_ij, between P_i and Q_j )
                  [U ← U + U_ij]
            for_end
      for_end
proc_end
```

Code 9-3 Sequential Evaluation of Potential Energy Exploiting Symmetry of Potential Function

The subroutine *pot_sym_2arr* is called by a sequential program in exactly the same way as *pot_2arr*. The idea here is to take each particle, P_i, in array P and compute its interaction with those particles in Q starting at $i+1$. All pairs interact exactly once in this way, and self-interactions are never computed.

In the parallel program, it is harder to avoid computing self-interactions. The ith particle in the moving array must interact with the ith particle in the stationary array at least some of the time. If the interaction between two such congruent particles is computed every time, however, it will be computed independently in two processors and incorrectly counted twice in the total energy. We must introduce a function, *should_self_interact*, which sets the flag *self_interact* to 1 (YES) when the interaction should be computed between two congruent particles and to 0 (NO) otherwise. The function *pot_sym_par2* in Code 9–4 is a parallel version of *pot_sym_2arr*, i.e., it computes the interaction between two arrays of particles in a parallel context, properly accounting for the interactions of congruent pairs. It may replace the call to *pot_2arr* in Code 9-2.

Now we turn to the details of *should_self_interact*, in Code 9-5. Consider two processors with ring locations p_a and p_b, and assume $p_b > p_a$. We will compute the interaction between congruent pairs in p_a and, hence, not in p_b, if $(p_b - p_a) < N/2$. Conversely, if $(p_b - p_a) > N/2$, we compute the interaction in p_b. If $(p_b - p_a)$ is equal to $N/2$, we must use some criterion other than their separation to decide when to compute the self-interaction. Furthermore, to avoid the possibility of idle processors when $(p_b - p_a) = N/2$, we would like each processor to compute exactly half of the interactions. One possibility is to compute the interactions between even-numbered pairs in p_a and to compute those between odd-numbered pairs in p_b.

Note that this version of *should_self_interact* does not allow for computation of bona fide self-interactions. It always returns NO for the interaction of a particle with itself, i.e., when step is 0. This is most often desirable, especially in dynamics problems in which the self-energy is irrelevant, and often divergent. Nevertheless, it is sometimes useful to compute the self-interactions. This is accomplished by exchanging YES and NO in the first two **if** clauses of Code 9-5.

The discussion of the efficiency in Sec. 9-2.3 applies to the improved algorithm with little modification. We have reduced the computation by half, both in the sequential and parallel cases. Nevertheless, the communication costs have remained constant.

```
proc_begin pot_sym_par2 ( find potential, U_loc, between particles in buffers P and Q )
    [set U_loc = 0]
    for_begin ( each resident particle, P_i )
        proc_call should_self_interact ( set self_interact flag if interaction
                                    between P_i and Q_i is included )
        if_begin (self_interact = YES) then
            proc_call pair_potential ( find the potential energy, U_ii,
                                    between P_i and Q_i )
            [U_loc ← U_loc + U_ii]
        if_end
        for_begin (each particle, Q_j, in Q for which j > i )
            proc_call pair_potential (find the potential energy, U_ij,
                                    between P_i and Q_j )
            [U_loc ← U_loc + U_ij]
        for_end
    for_end
proc_end
```

Code 9-4 Parallel Evaluation of Potential Energy Exploiting Symmetry of Potential Function

```
proc_begin should_self_interact (set self_interact flag if interaction between
                            P_i and Q_i is included.)
    if_begin (Q has been rotated less than halfway round the ring ) then
        [self_interact = NO]
    else_if (Q has been rotated more than halfway round the ring ) then
        [self_interact = YES]
    else_if ( this processor is located less than halfway round the ring ) then
        [self_interact is YES if i even, NO if i odd]
    else
        [self_interact is YES if i odd, NO if i even]
    if_end
proc_end
```

Code 9-5 The Routine *should_self_interact*

Thus, the bulk of the program runs almost twice as fast, but the speedup is slightly reduced. The new overhead is

$$f \approx 2 \frac{N}{N_p} \frac{t_{exchg}}{t_{pair}} \qquad (9\text{-}12)$$

9-4 Force Calculations

We now generalize the algorithm of the previous section to compute and record the force felt by every particle rather than simply to calculate the total potential energy. We assume the physics of the problem is taken care of in a subroutine, *pair_force*, which computes the force between two particles, and adds it to the total force stored in each.

The parallel program *force_par* in Code 9-6 differs from *pot_par* in Code 9-2, in two ways. First, it calls *force_sym_par2*, which is the same as *pot_sym_par2*, except that *pair_force* is used to compute the interactions between particles. Second, the function *global_add* is replaced by the function *recombine*. In the force calculation, the moving particles have felt the effects of some of the particles, while the stationary array has felt the effects of the others. Clearly, we must bring these two arrays back together in the original processor and combine the results.

Bringing them back together is easy. At the end of the calculation, after N calls to *rotate*, the moving array has traveled all the way around the ring and is back where it started. The ring topology has returned the moving data without any extra effort. The combining operation is also simple. It is only necessary to add the force accumulated by each particle in the moving array to that accumulated by the corresponding particle in the stationary array. The procedure *recombine* achieves this.

```
proc_begin force_par ( parallel evaluation of force on each particle in P )
declare_buf Q; ( copy of buffer P )
     [initialize force on all particles in P to zero]
     proc_call copy ( copy P to Q )
     proc_call ring_setup ( decompose hypercube as a ring of processors )
     for_begin ( each processor in the processor ring )
          proc_call force_sym_par2 ( find forces between particles in P and Q )
          proc_call rotate ( send buffer Q to next processor in ring and replace
                             with corresponding buffer from previous processor )
     for_end
     proc_call recombine ( add force on each particle in Q to force on corresponding
                          particle in P )
proc_end
```

Code 9-6 Parallel Evaluation of the Mutual Force Exerted by a System of Particles

9-5 Calculation of Correlation Functions

One practical use of the ideas in this chapter was motivated by the study of experimental data taken from studies of turbulent plasmas in a Tokamak [Zweben 83]. An algorithm proposed by Grassberger and Procaccia for computing the correlation dimension associated with a dynamical system [Grassberger 83] was adapted for use in a parallel processor [Theiler 86]. This dimension is given by the power-law behavior of what is called the correlation integral.

For a dynamical system with time dependence, $x(t)$, the correlation integral, $C(r)$, measures the probability that a given pairwise distance $r_{ij} = |\vec{x}(t_i) - \vec{x}(t_j)|$ will satisfy $r_{ij} < r$. To estimate the correlation integral from experimental data consisting of N_o discrete measurements of $\vec{x}(t)$ requires the construction of a histogram of all N_o^2 values of r_{ij}.

We construct the histogram in parallel as follows. Two copies, one stationary and one moving of $N_o/N = N_{local}$ values of $\vec{x}_i$ are stored at each node of the hypercube. Also, at each node is a separate histogram. As the moving copies travel around the loop, the pairwise distances between the moving and stationary vectors at each node are computed, and the local histograms are updated. After the moving copy of the data has traveled all the way around the ring, the separate histograms in each node must be combined. This can be performed either by the sophisticated technique that will be described in Chap. 19 or by using the function *vm_combine* function discussed in Sec. 4-4. In any case, this last step takes a negligible amount of time, and a high performance concurrent calculation of the correlation integral is achieved.

Recently the basic sequential correlation algorithm has been improved, reducing the N_0^2 time complexity to $N_0 \log N_0$ [Theiler 87]; this new algorithm has not yet been implemented on a concurrent machine. It is interesting to note that it uses a similar clustering technique to that introduced by Barnes and Hut [Barnes 86] for the N_p body problem discussed in Secs. 9-1 to 9-4. As discussed in Sec. 23-4.5, this fast N_p body algorithm is currently being implemented on the hypercube.

9-6 Conclusion

The techniques described in this chapter apply to any problem that requires the examination of every pair of objects in a data base. The general outline for treating such problems in parallel is shown in Code 9–7.

```
proc_begin n_squared_problem ( parallel examination of pairs of objects in a database )
declare_buf Q ( copy of buffer P )
        [perform initializations]
        proc_call copy ( copy P to Q )
        proc_call ring_setup ( decompose hypercube as a ring of processors )
        for_begin ( each step, i, in the processor ring, i = 1,...,N )
                [compute interaction between data in P and Q]
                proc_call rotate ( send buffer Q to next processor in ring and replace
                        with corresponding buffer from previous processor )
        for_end
        [combine and/or accumulate results]
proc-end
```

Code 9-7 General Algorithm for Examining Every Pair of Items in a Database

Large problems of this type can be treated very efficiently with parallel computers. Large only means that the number of objects in the data base is much larger, say by a factor of 50 for a typical machine, than the number of processors. The high efficiency of long-range problems is quite surprising, since they are among the most communication intensive of regular problems. Although the amount of communication is indeed large, it still represents only a small fraction of the very costly calculation, and, thus, long-range algorithms perform very efficiently on parallel computers. An additional result is that the necessary communication topology is extremely simple; a ring of processors in which each processor has only two neighbors is all that is needed for an efficient implementation. Objects can be communicated around a ring of processors concurrently, making additional connectivity superfluous.

10

Matrix Algorithms I:
Matrix Multiplication

10-1 Introduction

The numerical solution of many problems reduces in part or fully to various matrix operations. Typical of these operations are multiplication of matrices and vectors, inversion or LU decomposition, and the determination of eigenvalues and vectors. These operations can be further classified by the characteristics of the matrix. The matrix can be "full" (i.e., with an insignificant number of zero matrix elements), banded (nonzero elements clustered about the diagonal), or sparse with a more complicated structure in the location of the nonzero elements. We find that matrix algorithms generally run well on concurrent computers and that the hypercube, in particular, is well suited to essentially all of these algorithms. In this volume, we will discuss three cases in detail: multiplication of full matrices in this chapter; the LU decomposition of banded matrices in Chap. 20; and matrix-vector multiplication in Chap. 21. Chapter 21 will also survey the key issues in some of the other matrix algorithms. The aim of presenting these three particular topics is to illustrate the typical issues in the use of concurrent computers to solve matrix problems.

The algorithms in this chapter are intended to be applicable to arbitrary concurrent computers, but as in previous chapters, the explicit performance measurements given in Sec. 10-5 correspond to a specific hypercube implementation. The Software Supplement to this volume contains detailed listings of the hypercube code for several matrix algorithms including those covered here and in Chaps. 20 and 21.

After these preliminary remarks, we turn our attention to the problem at hand: full matrix multiplication which constitutes one of the simplest matrix problems. In Chap. 21, we will discuss the case of matrix-vector multiplication, which might have been expected to be simpler but, in fact, for the most interesting sparse matrix cases, can require sophisticated techniques.

This chapter treats the following issues related to concurrent matrix multiplication: 10-2, parallel decomposition of the problem; 10-3, the specific case of square subblock decomposition; 10-4, rectangular and column decompositions; 10-5, results and practical considerations; and 10-6, a summary. Section 10-7 concludes with a comment on the use of concurrent processors to calculate spreadsheets. The work covered here is based on the discussion in [Fox 85b] and related research is covered in [Kung 80], [Sameh 85] and [Johnsson 87].

10-2 Decomposition of the Matrix Multiplication Problem

As in earlier chapters, the design of our concurrent algorithm is based upon the assumption of each node running a single process, with those processes communicating via messages. Decomposition involves breaking up the underlying data–in this case initial and final matrices–into parts and associating a part of each matrix with each processor. We will find that the algorithm will require substantially more movement of data than the previous examples in this book.

For the main discussion, we will need only to make use of processor interconnections which define a two-dimensional periodic mesh. This contrasts with the choice made in Chap. 7 for the case of the iterative sparse matrix solution of systems arising from partial differential equations. In that case, the necessary processor topology was governed by the spatial dimension of the underlying physical system. In the present case, the two-dimensional "world" of matrix rows and columns forms the basis for the decomposition. We will examine in Sec. 10-3.2 a part of the algorithm in which the performance of the concurrent algorithm could be improved by a richer node connectivity than that provided by a two-dimensional mesh.

We are interested in performing the multiplication:

$$C = A \cdot B \tag{10-1}$$

where C, A, and B are full $M \times M$ matrices. For simplicity, we will only discuss the multiplication of square matrices.

We begin by assuming that matrices A and B are identically decomposed into subblocks as shown in Fig. 10-1. We will demand that the resultant product, C, has the same decomposition so that it could serve as input for further processing steps. The algorithm will first be described for the case of square subblocks. The extension of the algorithm to rectangular subblocks and their extreme limit, a pure-row or column decomposition, will follow in Sec. 10-4. Among our eventual goals in this chapter will be to show that the choice illustrated in Fig. 10-1 is preferable to rectangular decompositions.

$\hat{A}^{00}$	$\hat{A}^{01}$	$\hat{A}^{02}$	$\hat{A}^{03}$
$\hat{A}^{10}$	$\hat{A}^{11}$	$\hat{A}^{12}$	$\hat{A}^{13}$
$\hat{A}^{20}$	$\hat{A}^{21}$	$\hat{A}^{22}$	$\hat{A}^{23}$
$\hat{A}^{30}$	$\hat{A}^{31}$	$\hat{A}^{32}$	$\hat{A}^{33}$

Figure 10-1 The square subblock decomposition of a matrix, A, onto a 4×4 mesh of processors. The hats refer to submatrices: $\hat{A}^{lk}$ contains the elements A_{ij} with $\frac{M}{4} l \le i < \frac{M}{4}(l+1), \frac{M}{4} k \le j < \frac{M}{4}(k+1)$.

We will assume that the multiplicand matrices, A and B, already reside in the memory of the ensemble processors, distributed piecewise in the two-dimensional fashion described. Our subsequent performance analyses do not consider the costs associated with the loading of A or B. This is not unreasonable if A and B came from previous processing steps of some larger algorithm within the concurrent processor. On the other hand, if one is interested in using the ensemble as a "flow-through" matrix multiplier, attention must be paid to the potentially significant costs of ensemble I/O. This is a general problem of essentially all parallel computers and can in principle be solved by a parallel I/O disk system or other special purpose devices for the rapid parallel loading and dumping of data. The cost of the matrix calculation grows in proportion to M^3, while the I/O cost is proportional to M^2; in principle, both can be speeded up by a factor that approaches N, the number of processors. The following discussion, however, will analyze the specific problem of direct matrix operations, without further consideration of the application and hardware dependent issues of data pre- and postprocessing.

10-3 Square Subblock Decomposition for Matrix Multiplication

10-3.1 The Basic Algorithm for Square Subblocks

The fundamental steps of the algorithm are illustrated schematically in Fig. 10-2 for the case of a 4×4 mesh of processors. The square submatrices are denoted by hats: e.g., $\hat{C}^{00}$ denotes the matrix subblock of C_{ij} for which $0 \le i < M/4, 0 \le j < M/4$. In general, $\hat{C}^{lm}$ is comprised of the elements of C_{ij} for which $lM/4 \le i < (l+1)M/4$, $kM/4 \le j < (k+1)M/4$. Square submatrices can be manipulated as if they were single elements of the matrix. That is

$$\hat{C}^{lk} = \sum_n \hat{A}^{ln} \cdot \hat{B}^{nk} \tag{10-2}$$

where the multiplication in the sum is actually matrix multiplication of the square submatrices, $\hat{A}^{ln}$ and $\hat{B}^{nk}$.

The concurrent matrix multiplication proceeds as follows:

Step 1: (Fig. 10-2a)

The diagonal subblocks of A are successively communicated in a horizontal direction so that all processors in the first "row" receive a copy of $\hat{A}^{00}$, all processors in the second "row" receive a copy of $\hat{A}^{11}$, and so on. In the terminology of Chap. 4, the diagonal subblocks of A are *broadcast* along each row of processors.

Step 2: (Fig. 10-2b)

The broadcast A subblocks are multiplied by the B subblocks currently residing in each processor and stored in C subblocks.

Step 3: (Fig. 10-2c)

The B subblocks of each processor are *shifted* to the "upper" neighboring processor and replaced by the corresponding B subblock from the "lower" neighbor. The periodic mesh connection is used to "roll" the topmost row into the bottommost row.

(a)

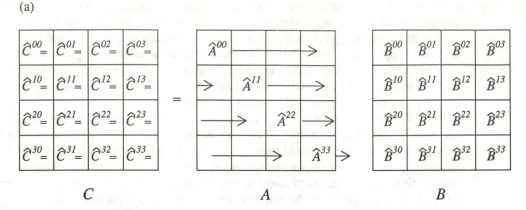

Figure 10-2(a) Step one of the square subblock algorithm for a 4×4 machine. See the text for an explanation of each step.

(b)

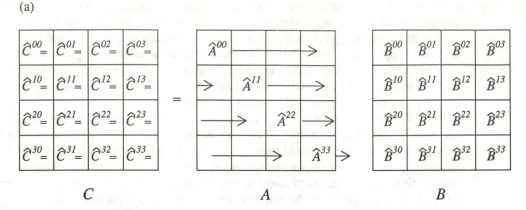

Figure 10-2(b) Step two of the square subblock algorithm for a 4×4 machine. See the text for an explanation of each step. The matrix T holds the block of A utilized at this stage of the algorithm.

Step 4: (Fig. 10-2d)

The A subblocks located in the processors one position to the right of the diagonal are now broadcast throughout the corresponding row, as in Step 1.

Step 5: (Fig. 10-2e)

The copied A subblocks are again multiplied by the B subblocks, with the results added to the partial results in the C subblocks. The above pattern of rolling blocks and performing block multiplications is continued until the B subblocks have returned to their original processors. At the completion of this cycle, the C subblocks contain the complete product matrix, distributed in the same manner as A and B.

(c)

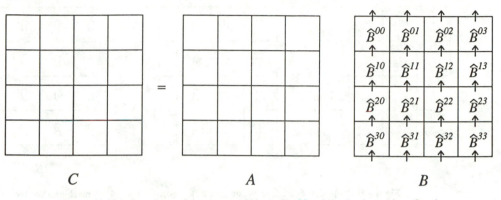

Figure 10-2(c) Step three of the square subblock algorithm for a 4×4 machine. See the text for an explanation of each step.

(d)

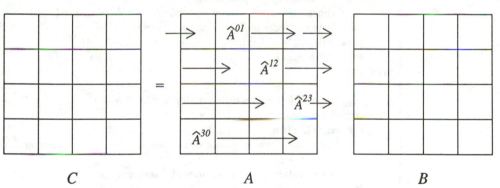

Figure 10-2(d) Step four of the square subblock algorithm for a 4×4 machine. See the text for an explanation of each step.

(e)

$\hat{A}^{00}\hat{B}^{00}$ $+$ $\hat{A}^{01}\hat{B}^{10}$	$\hat{A}^{00}\hat{B}^{01}$ $+$ $\hat{A}^{01}\hat{B}^{11}$	$\hat{A}^{00}\hat{B}^{02}$ $+$ $\hat{A}^{01}\hat{B}^{12}$	$\hat{A}^{00}\hat{B}^{03}$ $+$ $\hat{A}^{01}\hat{B}^{13}$
$\hat{A}^{11}\hat{B}^{10}$ $+$ $\hat{A}^{12}\hat{B}^{20}$	$\hat{A}^{11}\hat{B}^{11}$ $+$ $\hat{A}^{12}\hat{B}^{21}$	$\hat{A}^{11}\hat{B}^{12}$ $+$ $\hat{A}^{12}\hat{B}^{22}$	$\hat{A}^{11}\hat{B}^{13}$ $+$ $\hat{A}^{12}\hat{B}^{23}$
$\hat{A}^{22}\hat{B}^{20}$ $+$ $\hat{A}^{23}\hat{B}^{30}$	$\hat{A}^{22}\hat{B}^{21}$ $+$ $\hat{A}^{23}\hat{B}^{31}$	$\hat{A}^{22}\hat{B}^{22}$ $+$ $\hat{A}^{23}\hat{B}^{32}$	$\hat{A}^{22}\hat{B}^{23}$ $+$ $\hat{A}^{23}\hat{B}^{33}$
$\hat{A}^{33}\hat{B}^{30}$ $+$ $\hat{A}^{30}\hat{B}^{00}$	$\hat{A}^{33}\hat{B}^{31}$ $+$ $\hat{A}^{30}\hat{B}^{01}$	$\hat{A}^{33}\hat{B}^{32}$ $+$ $\hat{A}^{30}\hat{B}^{02}$	$\hat{A}^{33}\hat{B}^{33}$ $+$ $\hat{A}^{30}\hat{B}^{03}$

$=$

$\hat{A}^{01}$	$\hat{A}^{01}$	$\hat{A}^{01}$	$\hat{A}^{01}$
$\hat{A}^{12}$	$\hat{A}^{12}$	$\hat{A}^{12}$	$\hat{A}^{12}$
$\hat{A}^{23}$	$\hat{A}^{23}$	$\hat{A}^{23}$	$\hat{A}^{23}$
$\hat{A}^{30}$	$\hat{A}^{30}$	$\hat{A}^{30}$	$\hat{A}^{30}$

$\hat{B}^{10}$	$\hat{B}^{11}$	$\hat{B}^{12}$	$\hat{B}^{13}$
$\hat{B}^{20}$	$\hat{B}^{21}$	$\hat{B}^{22}$	$\hat{B}^{23}$
$\hat{B}^{30}$	$\hat{B}^{31}$	$\hat{B}^{32}$	$\hat{B}^{33}$
$\hat{B}^{00}$	$\hat{B}^{01}$	$\hat{B}^{02}$	$\hat{B}^{03}$

$$C \qquad\qquad T \qquad\qquad B$$

Figure 10-2(e) Step five of the square subblock algorithm for a 4×4 machine. See the text for an explanation of each step. The matrix T holds the block of A utilized at this stage of the algorithm.

```
proc_begin main ( run parallel matrix multiply program to find C = AB )
        [let N be the number of processors]
        [map concurrent computer onto array of √N × √N processors]
        [distribute subblocks of A and B to processors]
        proc_call mat_mult (perform matrix multiplication C = AB )
        [output the result]
proc_end

proc_begin mat_mult (perform matrix multiplication C = AB )
        [initialize subblock matrix, Ĉ, to zero]
        for_begin (i = 0 to (√N −1 ))
                proc_call bcast_A (broadcast appropriate Â along rows, store in T̂ )
                [Ĉ ← Ĉ + T̂B̂]
                proc_call roll_B (roll columns of B̂ upward)
        for_end
proc_end
```

Code 10-1 Matrix Multiplication Algorithm

The pseudocode for this algorithm is contained in Code 10-1.

10.3.2 Performance Analysis for Square Subblocks

Suppose that we multiply an $M \times M$ matrix on an $\sqrt{N} \times \sqrt{N}$ array of processors in the manner described in the previous section. The size of the subblock in each processor is $\hat{m} \times \hat{m}$, where $\hat{m} = M/\sqrt{N}$. The "broadcast-multiply-roll" cycle of the algorithm is repeated $\sqrt{N}$ times. For each cycle we need to broadcast an A submatrix across each row of processors. It is implemented using the *broadcast* collective communication routine introduced in Chap. 4. This implementation is illustrated in Code 10-2.

```
proc_begin bcast_A (broadcast appropriate Â along rows, store in T̂)
        [determine which row of processor array this processor is in]
        [determine the source processor in this row for the broadcast]
        if_begin (this processor is the source processor) then
                [broadcast Â]
                [copy Â to T̂]
        else_if (this processor is a destination processor) then
                [receive sub-block from source processor and store in T̂ ]
        if_end
proc_end
```

Code 10-2 Naive Broadcast Algorithm

On some actual machines, including Mark II hypercubes, this approach is not the most effective since such a broadcast requires time of order $\hat{m}^2(\sqrt{N}-1)\,t_{comm}$, and the initiating node in each row constitutes a sequential bottleneck. This estimate assumes that although the broadcast subblocks are identical, they must be separately sent to each destination node. On more advanced machines (e.g., the Caltech/JPL Mark III hypercube) provision may exist for hardware assist in such a broadcast to a subcube of the hypercube ensemble. However, we shall here consider a simple algorithm for hardware which has no broadcast enhancement to improve upon the above theoretical performance. We will instead set up a pipeline as shown in Fig. 10-2(d) with the originating node on each row just sending the subblock to one other node. Here we need one and not $\sqrt{N}-1$ copies of each message to be made in the originating node. This subblock is then successively forwarded $\sqrt{N}-1$ steps along the entire row. Such an algorithm requires a time for each cycle given by:

$$\hat{m}^2\,t_{comm} + (\sqrt{N}-2)\,t_{start} \tag{10-3}$$

Here, as usual, t_{comm} is the time required to pass a floating-point word between processors and t_{start} is the startup time of the pipeline per step of the pipe. Typically, t_{start} is comparable in value to t_{comm} and the first term in Eq. (10-3) dominates as usually $\hat{m}^2 >> (\sqrt{N}-2)$. In Chap. 20, we will study an example in which the t_{start} term is relatively more important as one is communicating fewer ($\hat{m}$ not $\hat{m}^2$) numbers, and the pipeline startup time will be apparent in the measured hypercube performances. We emphasize that the exact form of Eq. (10-3) depends on the details of the hardware, and it is written for the special case of the Caltech Mark II hypercube. This transmits messages in small (64-bit) packets with low latency. Further it takes approximately equal times ($1/2\ t_{comm}$) to read or write a message. In this case, $t_{start} \sim 2t_{comm}$ (32-bit) = t_{comm} (64-bit) is the time taken to read and write a single packet.

This modified algorithm for subblock pipelining is illustrated in Code 10-3.

```
proc_begin pipe_A (pipe appropriate Â along rows, store in T̂)
      [determine the source processor for the pipe]
      [determine the last processor in the pipe]
      if_begin (this processor is the source processor) then
            [copy Â to T̂]
            [send T̂ to processor on the right]
      else_if (this processor is not the last processor in pipe) then
            [receive T̂ from processor on left]
            [send T̂ to processor on the right]
      else_if (this processor is the last processor in pipe ) then
            [receive T̂ from processor on left]
      if_end
proc_end
```

Code 10-3 Pipe Broadcast Algorithm

Optimal broadcast algorithms on particular concurrent machines are important and surprisingly nontrivial. Two papers studying them for the hypercube architecture are [Fox 86b] and [Ho 86a]. One can reduce the coefficients of both t_{comm} and t_{start} but these refinements are not important unless $\hat{m}$ is very small or t_{comm} very large. This issue will be discussed in more detail in Chap. 21.

The time taken to roll B is:

$$\hat{m}^2 t_{comm} \qquad (10\text{-}4)$$

Note that in both Eqs. (10-3) and (10-4), we have assumed a negligible latency for initiating a message between two processors, as is actually the case for such machines as the Mark II Caltech hypercube. We will comment on this assumption at the end of Sec. 10-6.

Finally, the time required to compute the submatrix product for contribution to C is:

$$2\hat{m}^3 t_{calc} \qquad (10\text{-}5)$$

where, as usual, t_{calc} is the time required for a floating-point multiply or add. Therefore, the total computation time of the matrix multiplication is given by:

$$T = \sqrt{N} \; (2\hat{m}^3 t_{calc} + 2\hat{m}^2 t_{comm} + (\sqrt{N} - 2)t_{start}) \qquad (10\text{-}6)$$

or

$$T = \frac{2M^3 t_{calc}}{N} + \frac{2M^2 t_{comm}}{\sqrt{N}} + \sqrt{N}\,(\sqrt{N} - 2)t_{start} \qquad (10\text{-}7)$$

The first term of (10-7) corresponds to a concurrent speedup of magnitude N while the last two terms represent communication overhead. Before presenting actual timing results for this algorithm, we will generalize the discussion to the case of rectangular sub-blocks and its extreme limit of column decomposition.

10-4 Rectangular Subblock Decomposition for Matrix Multiplication

10-4.1 The Rectangular Block Algorithm

We now extend the previous algorithm to the case in which the submatrices in each processor are no longer square. The situation is illustrated in Fig. 10-3. An $M \times M$ matrix is decomposed onto an $N_0 \times N_1$ processor array where, for simplicity of presentation, we restrict ourselves to the case $N_0 \le N_1$. The submatrix in each processor is $\hat{m}_0 \times \hat{m}_1$ where $\hat{m}_0 = M/N_0$ and $\hat{m}_1 = M/N_1$. Furthermore, we assume that the aspect ratio, $r = \hat{m}_0/\hat{m}_1$, is an integer, so that an integral number of square subblocks of size $\hat{m}_1 \times \hat{m}_1$ fits in each processor. The issue of padding a matrix which may not perfectly fit within this decomposition is discussed in Sec. 10-5.

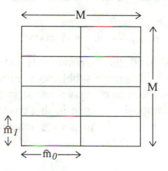

Figure 10-3 An $M \times M$ matrix decomposed onto a 2×4 processor mesh $(N_0 = 2, N_1 = 4)$. $\hat{m}_0 = M/N_0 = M/2$; $\hat{m}_1 = M/N_1 = M/4$.

The rectangular algorithm proceeds by a strategy similar to the square case. The only difference is that now each processing node splits its time among several square subblocks.

10-4.2 Performance Analysis for Rectangular Subblocks

The broadcast-multiply-roll cycle of the algorithm is repeated N_1 times. For each such cycle, the time required for the horizontal broadcast is:

$$\hat{m}_1^2 \, t_{comm} + (N_0 - 2) \, t_{start} \tag{10-8}$$

The time to multiply subblocks is:

$$r \, 2\hat{m}_1^3 \, t_{calc} = 2\hat{m}_1^2 \hat{m}_0 t_{calc} \tag{10-9}$$

and the time to roll vertically is:

$$\hat{m}_1 \hat{m}_0 t_{comm} \tag{10-10}$$

Therefore, the total computation time for the rectangular subblock algorithm is:

$$T = N_1[2\hat{m}_1^2 \hat{m}_0 t_{calc} + t_{comm}(\hat{m}_1^2 + \hat{m}_1 \hat{m}_0) + (N_0 - 2)t_{start}] \qquad (10\text{-}11)$$

or

$$T = \frac{2M^3 t_{calc}}{N} + N_1 [t_{comm}(\hat{m}_1^2 + \hat{m}_1 \hat{m}_0) + (N_0 - 2)t_{start}] \qquad (10\text{-}12)$$

We would naturally like to determine the optimal choice of the aspect ratio, r, holding the total number of processors $N_0 N_1 = N$ and the matrix size M fixed. The communication overhead from (10-12) is contained in the term:

$$N_1 t_{comm}(\hat{m}_1^2 + \hat{m}_1 \hat{m}_0) + N_1(N_0 - 2) t_{start} \qquad (10\text{-}13)$$

If 2 is negligible compared with N_0, the pipeline startup time only depends on $N_1 N_0 = N$ and is independent of r. Under this assumption, our task is to minimize the remaining term:

$$t_{comm} N_1 (\hat{m}_1^2 + \hat{m}_1 \hat{m}_0) = t_{comm} M (\hat{m}_1 + \hat{m}_0) \qquad (10\text{-}14)$$

Since M is held fixed, the minimum is found at $\hat{m}_1 = \hat{m}_0$, or $r = 1$. In other words, matrix multiplication with square subblocks is most efficient. This conclusion does not extend at this point to the case of a pure-row storage algorithm which would utilize one-dimensional ring decomposition since in that case the timing formula Eq. (10-11) does not hold. For pure-row or column-storage schemes, there is no broadcast step in the algorithm, so that Eq. (10-11) takes the modified form:

$$T_{row, column} = \frac{2M^3}{N} t_{calc} + N t_{comm} \frac{M^2}{N} \qquad (10\text{-}15)$$

10-4.3 Comparison of Square Subblocks with Row/Column

To complete the theoretical analysis, we will write down the concurrent efficiencies as defined in Chap. 5 for the square subblock and the pure-row algorithms.

For the subblock algorithm, the efficiency obtained from Eq. (5-5) is:

$$\varepsilon_{block} = \frac{1}{1 + f_{block}} = \frac{1}{1 + \frac{1}{\sqrt{n}} \frac{t_{comm}}{t_{calc}} + \delta} \qquad (10\text{-}16)$$

where, as usual, n denotes the grain size which is in this case the number of matrix elements per node ($n = M^2/N$). In (10-16), δ is typically a small term proportional to t_{start} and is due to the pipeline startup time. In the same notation, the efficiency for the pure-row scheme obtained from (10-15) is:

$$\varepsilon_{row} = \frac{1}{1 + f_{row}} = \frac{1}{1 + \frac{1}{\sqrt{n}} \frac{t_{comm}}{t_{calc}} \frac{1}{2}\sqrt{N}} \qquad (10\text{-}17)$$

The overhead f_{row} associated with the pure-row algorithm is larger by a factor $\sqrt{N}/2$, where N is the number of processing nodes.

10-5 Timing Results for Matrix Multiplication on the Caltech Hypercube

10-5.1 Load-Balanced Decompositions

To verify the validity of the preceding theoretical analysis of matrix multiplication algorithms, we examine the performance of matrix multiplication via the subblock and row techniques when run on the Caltech/JPL Mark II hypercubes. To serve as an efficiency baseline, a third program was run on a single-node processor multiplying matrices via the usual sequential algorithm. This baseline measurement yields the time on a single processor $T_1(M)$ needed in Eq. (5-4). Similar programming optimization steps were taken in the design of the three test programs. For example, indexing overheads and related activity were reduced to a minimum in each case so as to yield a fair comparison of the algorithms.

Timings for the sequential algorithm running on a single-node processor are shown in Fig. 10-4. The times are fit very well by the functional dependence:

$$T_1(M) = T_{single\ node} = 119\mu sec\ M^2 + 123\mu sec\ M^3 \tag{10-18}$$

for $M \times M$ matrix multiplication. This result was obtained using single precision, 32-bit arithmetic throughout the algorithm. The quadratic term (which is manifested in Fig. 10-4 as the very small but nonzero y-intercept) reflects the times taken to initialize the matrix C to zero at the beginning of the multiplication and to do some simple index arithmetic. As much index arithmetic as possible was removed from the innermost loops of the program.

Figure 10-5 shows timing results for a hypercube mapped to a 4×4 mesh and running the square subblock algorithm. Plotted in Fig. 10-5 is T/M^2 versus M, so that the asymptotic floating-point speed (the cubic term of Eq. (10-7)) plots as a linearly increasing term; communication overhead appears as a constant (nonzero y-intercept). The pipeline startup time of the algorithm appears as a $1/M^2$ term at small M. Examination of the plot shows that this implementation of concurrent matrix multiplication is quite efficient. Even for modest matrix sizes such as 16×16 or 32×32 (total matrix size) on a 4×4 machine, the pipeline startup time and communication overhead are small effects. A linear fit to the points representing timings for the larger matrix sizes is also shown in Fig. 10-5. The slope derived from this fit is 7.64 μ sec, almost exactly one sixteenth of 123 μ sec, the coefficient of M^3 in Eq. (10-18).

An alternative presentation of the 4×4 timing data is given in Fig. 10-6 in which we plot $1/\varepsilon - 1$ versus $1/\sqrt{n}$. As in the discussion of Chap. 5, this is done so as to reveal the overhead terms of Eq. (10-16) . The linear behavior for small $1/\sqrt{n}$ (large matrices) shows that the functional form of Eq. (10-16) holds. A linear fit yields the coefficient of $1/\sqrt{n}$ and the result:

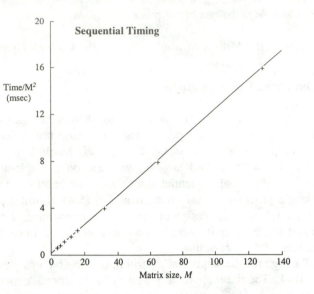

Figure 10-4 Matrix multiplication timings for a single node processor running the standard, sequential algorithm. The times normalized by M^2 are plotted for clarity. Also shown is the fit given in Eq. (10-18).

$$\frac{t_{comm}}{t_{calc}} = 1.39 \tag{10-19}$$

This is a reasonable figure for the crystalline operating system on the Mark II hypercube machine discussed in Chaps. 4 and 14. One must bear in mind, however, that some of what we have lumped into the category of "communication overhead" (quadratic, M^2, terms in the timing equation (10-7)) are actually attributable to other costs such as index initialization, which are dependent upon the details of user-written code. The lesson to be learned from this is that if one tries to write fast code by removing as much index arithmetic as possible from the innermost loop of the program, the sequential and concurrent implementation are both speeded up, but the coefficient of $1/\sqrt{n}$ in the hypercube overhead is increased. Thus the strategy lowers the coefficient of the cubic term (giving a faster code) but increases the quadratic terms which have dependencies on n and N identical to that of "real" communication overhead. This will be further illustrated below.

To show that the result of Eq. (10-16) is universal, i.e., independent of total machine size and dependent only upon the grain size, n, we examine different ensemble sizes. Fig. 10-7 is similar to the plot of Fig. 10-6, but with 8×8 machine results added. For $n > 100$ (a 10×10 submatrix in each node), the behavior is almost exactly universal. The deviation from the universality at small n is due to the larger pipeline startup time on the larger machine.

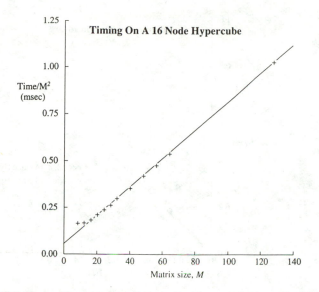

Figure 10-5 Timings for the square subblock algorithm on a 4×4 machine. Times are normalized by M^2, as in Fig. 10-4.

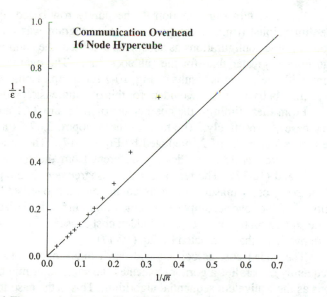

Figure 10-6 The same timings as in Fig. (10-5), but plotted as overhead ($1/\varepsilon - 1$) versus $1/\sqrt{n}$ (n is the grain size or the number of matrix elements per node).

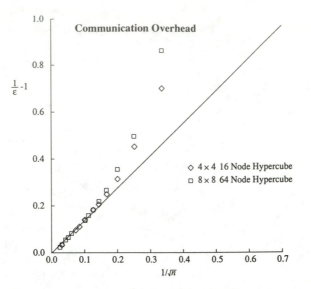

Figure 10-7 The same as Fig. (10-6), but with timings from a 8×8 machine added, showing universal behavior.

We next turn our attention to the purely row-based algorithm which requires a one-dimensional (ring) decomposition. This program was timed using the same hyper-cube machine configurations as above. As expected, the communication overhead for this algorithm is greater than for the subblock case. The overheads are shown in Fig. 10-8 along with the previous results of Fig. 10-7 for comparison. A breakdown in the universal scaling behavior is quite evident for this one-dimensional decomposition.

From these timings, the coefficients of $1/\sqrt{n}$ are 3.61 and 7.49 for the 16- and 64-node cases, respectively. The ratio of these slopes, 2.07, is in excellent agreement with the theoretical value of 2, predicted by Eq. (10-17). The ratio of 3.61 to 1.39 (Eq. (10-19)), however, is 2.6, significantly different from the factor of 2 expected from Eqs. (10-16) and (10-17). The reason for this disagreement is the previously discussed effect of indexing costs masquerading as communication overhead. Due to the large aspect ratio, r, of the row decomposition, much more index initialization work is required than in the square subblock case. This hidden cost causes the row decomposition to have even more overhead than predicted by Eq. (10-17).

The added cost associated with such index operations is a common occurrence. Frequently, a parallel algorithm executes the same total number of floating-point operations as the equivalent sequential algorithm. This is the case for all of the algorithms discussed in this chapter. Communication overhead and load imbalance give rise to overt performance degradations, which reduce the concurrent efficiency. This other type of degradation, however, is rooted in the integer arithmetic associated with the indexing of

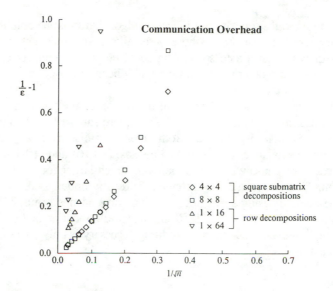

Figure 10-8 The same as Fig. (10-7), but with timings from the one-dimensional column algorithm added. The large communication overhead and non-universal behavior obtained with this decomposition are significant.

the various arrays involved. A typical matrix algorithm incorporates inner loops constructed as follows:

for (i running over $\hat{m}_0$ rows){

    Do some index arithmetic dependent upon decomposition to find associated columns for the processor.

    for (j running over $\hat{m}_1$ columns) {

        Inner loop identical to sequential code so that asymptotic efficiency is 1

        }}

The parallel algorithm requires more indexing operations than the sequential algorithm, leading to a new type of overhead to which we will refer as *software overhead*. As indicated above, the software and communication overheads have similar dependencies on n and N. Though typically a small effect, it should be kept in mind in any attempt to rigorously account for concurrent efficiencies. We will comment on this again in Chap. 20 for another matrix algorithm.

These experimental timing results confirm the theoretical assertion that the row decomposition scheme is less efficient than the subblock decomposition and that the size of the overhead increases with machine size as $\sqrt{N}$, in accordance with Eq. (10-17).

10-5.2 Padding for Arbitrary Matrix Size–Load Imbalance

Any practical matrix multiplication algorithm must be able to multiply matrices of arbitrary size–not just those whose order allows an exact mapping onto the concurrent processor with each processor having equal numbers of matrix elements. The simplest remedy for this problem is to pad the multiplicand matrices with a unit matrix block, in order to fill out the mapping.

Figures 10-9 and 10-10 present the results of the padding algorithm, examining a continuous range of matrix sizes M. The square subblock and column cases were run on a Mark II 64-node hypercube. Both algorithms display sawtooth performance curves whose upper envelopes are described by Eqs. (10-16) and (10-17). It is noteworthy that the severity of the sawtooth degradation is much larger for the one-dimensional decomposition. The reason for this difference is readily understood. If we set out to multiply 65×65 matrices using a row decomposition on a 64-node ring, it requires padding by 63 rows up to a matrix rank of 128. If the same multiplication is done blockwise on an 8×8 machine, however, the amount of padding necessary is only 7 rows, resulting in a 72×72 multiplication.

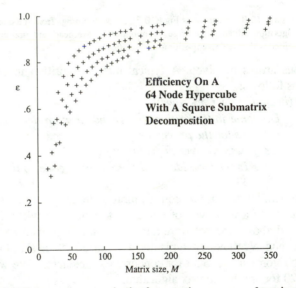

Figure 10-9 Efficiency versus matrix size for a continuous range of matrix sizes, illustrating "sawtooth" inefficiency effect. The square subblock algorithm on a 8×8 machine is illustrated.

The sawtooth effect may in some cases be a much more important practical consideration governing the choice between the two algorithms than Eqs. (10-16) and (10-17), although the amplitude of the effect diminishes for large matrices.

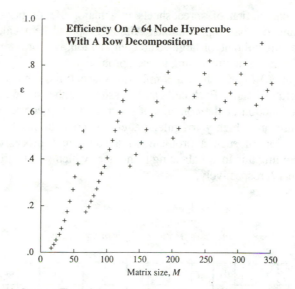

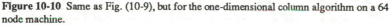

Figure 10-10 Same as Fig. (10-9), but for the one-dimensional column algorithm on a 64 node machine.

10-6 Summary of Matrix Multiplication

In the previous sections, we have demonstrated a simple but efficient method for implementing matrix multiplication based upon a generalized block decomposition scheme. Both theoretical and experimental performance analyses suggest that low-aspect ratio block decompositions offer the most favorable concurrent performance characteristics.

It is significant to note that purely row (or column) based algorithms may be more easily adapted from sequential programs, due to the simpler communication topology. Whether the additional costs incurred by the selection of such a nonoptimal method are justified may be application-dependent or may even depend upon the manner in which matrices are stored and handled by the programming language. For example, it may be expedient to make use of FORTRAN's natural treatment of column-based algorithms into which substantial optimization effort has been placed over many years. It is unfortunate that such algorithms are nonoptimal for concurrent decompositions.

In the performance analysis of Sec. 10-3 and 10-4, we have ignored any latency in the communication system, i.e., we have assumed that t_{comm} is independent of message size. As seen in Fig. 4-2, this is a good approximation on the Caltech hypercubes but not on the INTEL iPSC. Note that row/column storage involves the transmission of fewer messages (by a factor of 2) but in total more bytes (by a factor of $\sqrt{N}/2$) than the square subblock decomposition. Thus, on machines with substantial latency it can, in fact, be best to use row or column storage [Geist 86, Moler 86].

10-7 Comments on the Decomposition of Spreadsheets

The calculation of spreadsheets is a major use of personal computers for both financial and database applications. Although spreadsheet calculation is not generally regarded as the epitome of large-scale computation, it is of interest to consider the applicability of concurrent processing to such problems.

In Fig. 10-11, we show a simple spreadsheet; the typical structure is that of a rectangular array of cells. Each cell can be assumed either to be fixed (i.e., entered as data) or to be a function of the contents of other cells. In general, such a functional dependence results in a highly irregular pattern of connections between cells. The proper implementation of such a problem on a concurrent processor requires sophisticated message-routing and load-balancing techniques which will be discussed further in Chaps. 21, 22, and 17, respectively.

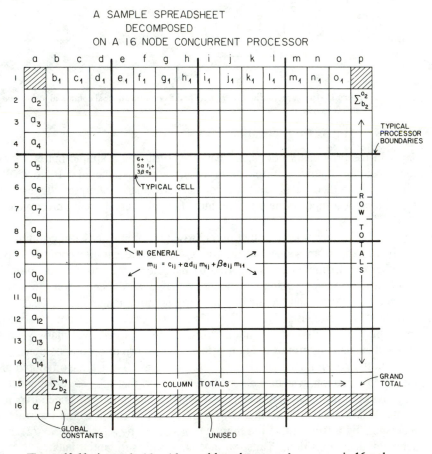

Figure 10-11 A sample 16×16 spreadsheet decomposed on a generic 16 node concurrent processor with 16 cells in each node.

Here we will be satisfied to observe that as in the matrix case, the spreadsheet encompasses a domain which is two-dimensional; however, it does not necessarily incorporate nearest-neighbor interactions. In general, we might expect the same optimal decomposition schemes as for the case of matrices. In this situation, the scattered square decompositions discussed in Chap. 20 are likely to be best. For simplicity, however, Fig. 10-11 only shows the simpler contiguous block decomposition which we have used in this chapter for matrix multiplication. Our example considers the basic cell operation to be:

$$M_{ij} = c_{ij} + \alpha\, d_{ij} M_{1j} + \beta e_{ij} M_{i1} \qquad (10\text{-}20)$$

where M_{1j} and M_{i1} store overall properties of the given columns and rows, respectively. This calculation may be performed concurrently after global broadcast of the constants α and β. The row and column parameters M_{1j} and M_{i1} need to be piped along columns and rows just as we saw for the matrix $\hat{A}$ in the multiplication algorithm of Sec. 10-3.2.

Often in spreadsheet calculation one needs to form partial or full sums of all cells in a row or column. If, for example, the rows denote people, the columns years, and the cells annual expenditures, then the subtotals represent the total expenditure in a given year or an individual's expenditure summed over all years. Operations of this kind are straightforward in their adaption and perform well on a hypercube concurrent processor; the best such special algorithm for this task will be described in Chap. 19 and Sec. 21-3.4.

The above discussion leads us to expect the typically efficient concurrent implementation, with overhead proportional to $1/\sqrt{n}$, where n cells reside in each node. The only real difficulty with practical concurrent spreadsheet calculation is in the load imbalance caused by inhomogeneity (differences) of the cell definitions. Such load-balancing problems will be treated in Chap. 17.

It would appear that, in principle, concurrent processors are well suited to spreadsheet applications, and recognition of this point could even motivate the generation of real code. With this possibility in mind, it may not be unreasonable to expect a future generation of personal computers or workstations built around a concurrent architecture.

11

The Fast Fourier Transform

11-1 Introduction

In 1965 Cooley and Tukey [Cooley 65] described an algorithm for computing the discrete Fourier transform (FT) of a series in a number of operations of order $M \log M$, where M is the number of points in the series. This algorithm provided a tremendous improvement over the order M^2 algorithms previously used. This algorithm and its variants are known as Fast Fourier Transforms (FFTs). The FFT is one of the principal algorithmic tools used for signal processing, image processing, and solving differential equations. Fourier transforms can be used to compute convolutions, analyze spectra, and smooth and identify features in images. In many cases, the reduction in computation from order M^2 to order $M \log M$ has changed the Fourier transform from a theoretical abstraction to a powerful numerical tool.

In this chapter we will consider finite, complex Fourier transforms. This is not an unduly restricted class, since the bulk of numerical FFTs are of this type. Infinite transforms are extremely important, but they must invariably be approximated by finite transforms before being treated numerically. We will also restrict ourselves to the binary FFT, in which the number of points is a power of two. Other algorithms, which actually perform better than the ones discussed here exist to treat the more general case. Such algorithms have been shown to work extremely well on parallel processors [Aloisio 87], and are discussed briefly in Sec. 22–3.2, in the context of the *crystal_router*.

11-2 The FFT Algorithm

The FFT can be cast as either a recursive or an iterative algorithm. Most scientific applications use the iterative algorithm because of its slightly enhanced speed, not to mention the practical fact that FORTRAN does not support recursion. The recursive algorithm is easier to understand and program, but is usually slower because of the overhead for the additional subroutine calls. Since simplicity is more important in this illustrative discussion than speed, we will discuss a parallel implementation of the recursive FFT algorithm in this chapter. The issues involved are essentially the same in both cases, and a clear understanding of this chapter should allow one to adapt an iterative version of the algorithm to a parallel machine. The Software Supplement contains implementations of both the iterative and recursive algorithms.

We will start by deriving the recursive FFT algorithm. Consider a sequence of M complex values, $(x_0, x_1, ..., x_{M-1})$, and define their Fourier transform as

$$\tilde{x}_k = \sum_{j=0}^{M-1} x_j \exp\left(2\pi i \frac{jk}{M}\right) \tag{11-1}$$

For reasons that will become clear, M is taken to be a power of two. It is possible to compute this sum precisely as it is written; compute $\tilde{x}_k$ for each k from zero through $M-1$ as a sum of M terms, in a total time proportional to M^2. However, if we split the summation into two parts, with one containing the even elements of x and the other containing the odd, a dramatic reduction in time is realized. To effect this improvement, we begin by writing:

$$\tilde{x}_k = \sum_{j'=0}^{\frac{M}{2}-1} x_{2j'} \exp(2\pi i \frac{2j'k}{M}) + \sum_{j'=0}^{\frac{M}{2}-1} x_{2j'+1} \exp(2\pi i \frac{(2j'+1)k}{M}) \tag{11-2}$$

We now make the following definitions:

$$M' = \frac{M}{2} \tag{11-3}$$

$$e_i = x_{2i} \qquad \text{(the even elements of } x\text{)} \tag{11-4}$$

and

$$o_i = x_{2i+1} \qquad \text{(the odd elements of } x\text{)} \tag{11-5}$$

and write Eq. (11-2) as

$$\tilde{x}_k = \sum_{j'=0}^{M'-1} e_{j'} \exp(2\pi i \frac{j'k}{M'}) + \exp(2\pi i \frac{k}{M}) \sum_{j'=0}^{M'-1} o_{j'} \exp(2\pi i \frac{j'k}{M'}) \tag{11-6}$$

Next, restrict consideration to $k < \dfrac{M}{2}$, and write Eq. (11-6) as:

$$\tilde{x}_k = \sum_{j'=0}^{M'-1} e_{j'} \exp(2\pi i \frac{j'k}{M'}) + \exp(2\pi i \frac{k}{M}) \sum_{j'=0}^{M'-1} o_{j'} \exp(2\pi i \frac{j'k}{M'})$$

$$\tilde{x}_{k+\frac{M}{2}} = \sum_{j'=0}^{M'-1} e_{j'} \exp(2\pi i \frac{j'k}{M'}) - \exp(2\pi i \frac{k}{M}) \sum_{j'=0}^{M'-1} o_{j'} \exp(2\pi i \frac{j'k}{M'}) \tag{11-7}$$

which can be expressed in terms of $\tilde{e}$ and $\tilde{o}$, the transforms of e and o.

$$\tilde{x}_k = \tilde{e}_k + \exp(2\pi i \frac{k}{M})\tilde{o}_k$$

$$\tilde{x}_{k+\frac{M}{2}} = \tilde{e}_k - \exp(2\pi i \frac{k}{M})\tilde{o}_k \tag{11-8}$$

Thus, to compute an M point FT, we compute two $M/2$ point FTs, $\tilde{e}$ and $\tilde{o}$, and combine them. The combination requires $M/2$ complex multiplications and M complex additions. If we let $T(M)$ be the time required to perform an M point FT, then:

$$T(M) = 2\,T(M/2) + M\,(t_{\pm} + \frac{t_*}{2}) \tag{11-9}$$

where t_* is the time required for a complex multiplication, and $t_{\pm}$ is the time required for a complex addition. The $M/2$ point FTs can be computed recursively, terminating when M is equal to 1. Since the one-point FT requires no work at all, $T(1) = 0$. The recursion relation, Eq. (11-9), can then be solved for $T(M)$, giving

$$T(M) = (t_{\pm} + \frac{t_*}{2})M \log_2 M \qquad (11\text{-}10)$$

11-3 Sequential Implementation

The program *fft_1* in Code 11-1 implements the recursive algorithm just described, on a sequential computer. To avoid unnecessary data movement, the routine acts on "arrays" that are not stored in contiguous memory locations. The elements of the array x are understood to be stored at x[0], x[p], x[2p], ... , x[(M-1)p], where p is initially 1 at the zeroth level of recursion. Thus, the FT of the even elements of x is computed by doubling the increment, p, and halving M, while that of the odd elements is obtained by starting at x[p], and doing the same. Upon completion x holds the FT of the input array. The original values are lost. The sequence of procedure calls for an 8-point recursive FFT is shown, diagramatically in Fig.11-1.

```
proc_begin fft_1 ( find M point FFT of complex data array, x )
    if_begin ( M = 1 ) then
            [return]
    else
            proc_call fft_1 ( find ẽ , the M/2 point FFT of even elements of x )
            proc_call fft_1 ( find õ , the M/2 point FFT of odd elements of x )
            proc_call fft_combine ( combine ẽ and õ to give M point FFT )
            [return]
    if_end
proc_end
```

Code 11-1 The Sequential Recursive FFT

As shown in Code 11-2, *fft_combine* combines the two $M/2$ point FTs, $\tilde{e}$ and $\tilde{o}$, producing the M point FT. It assumes that the input vector, x, contains the elements of $\tilde{e}$ and elements of $\tilde{o}$ at alternate locations. However, the order of the elements of $\tilde{e}$ and $\tilde{o}$ is permuted. Schematically, we can write the vector x as:

$$x = (\tilde{e}_{i_0} \tilde{o}_{i_0} \tilde{e}_{i_1} \tilde{o}_{i_1} \cdots \tilde{e}_{i_{M/2-1}} \tilde{o}_{i_{M/2-1}}) \qquad (11\text{-}11)$$

where $(i_0 i_1 \cdots i_{M/2-1})$ is a permutation of $(0\ 1 \cdots M/2-1)$. In order to properly evaluate Eq. (11-8), we require the function, *permute* which maps 0 into i_o, 1 into i_1, etc., and which is discussed further in Sec. 11-7.

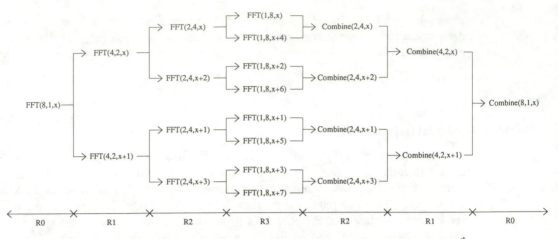

Figure 11-1 Schematic representation of an 8-point recursive FFT. Rn refers to the nth level of recursion. The notation FFT(N,p,x+m) indicates that the N data points x[m], x[p+m], x[$2p$+m],..., x[(N-1)p+m] are to be transformed. Thus m is the offset from the start of the data array, and p is the increment between the data points. The notation for the combine routine is similar.

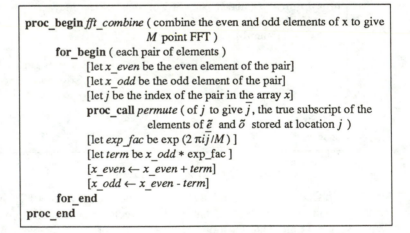

proc_begin *fft_combine* (combine the even and odd elements of x to give
                     M point FFT)
      for_begin (each pair of elements)
           [let *x_even* be the even element of the pair]
           [let *x_odd* be the odd element of the pair]
           [let *j* be the index of the pair in the array *x*]
           proc_call *permute* (of j to give $\bar{j}$, the true subscript of the
                   elements of $\tilde{e}$ and $\tilde{o}$ stored at location j)
           [let *exp_fac* be exp ($2\pi i j/M$)]
           [let *term* be *x_odd* $*$ exp_fac]
           [*x_even* $\leftarrow$ *x_even* + *term*]
           [*x_odd* $\leftarrow$ *x_even* - *term*]
      for_end
proc_end

Code 11-2 Routine to Combine the Even and Odd Partial FFTs in the Sequential Algorithm

11-4 Parallel Decomposition

     Now we turn to the parallel decomposition of the FFT algorithm. The natural space over which to decompose is that of the elements of x. In this approach, we divide the M elements of x equally among N processors. While not strictly necessary, simplicity dictates that N, the number of processors, be a power of 2 so that each processor holds an equal number of elements. The simplest such decomposition involves storing the first M/N elements in processor 0, the next M/N elements in processor 1, and so on. As the algorithm proceeds, the computed FT involves progressively fewer points. Eventually, there remains only one point in each processor. At even deeper levels of recursion, the number of points in each transform is less than the number of processors. At this point, several transforms are computed independently, and simultaneously, in disjoint subsets of the processors. In such cases, if the first element of any given sub-problem is stored in processor p, then the next corresponding element is found in processor $p + N/M$, and so on.

With this data decomposition, the parallel algorithm is straightforward. It must take account of three distinct cases:

- If M is 1, stop the recursion.
- If M is less than or equal to the number of processors, then only one point of the array to be transformed is stored locally. The processor assists in computing either $\tilde{e}$ or $\tilde{o}$, according to whether the single element is even or odd. Then, interprocessor communication brings $\tilde{e}$ and $\tilde{o}$ together in the same processor, and Eq. (11-8) is evaluated.
- If M is greater than the number of processors, the computation is the same as in the sequential case, but extends only over the values stored locally.

Code 11-3 displays *fft_2*, a parallel version of *fft_1*. The subroutine *fft_combine_2* in Code11-4 is almost identical to *fft_combine*, which was used in the sequential implementation. The only difference is that the inner loop spans only those elements of the array stored on a single processor.

Interprocessor communication enters only in the subroutine *fft_combine_comm*, shown in Code 11-5. This routine performs the combination operation for an M point FFT when the number of processors is equal to or less than the number of points in the transform. It must decide whether it holds an even or odd element and which processor holds the complementary element. Then it must exchange a complex value with that processor, carry out the complex arithmetic, and store the result.

With the addition of routines for complex arithmetic and index permutation, Codes 11-3, 11-4, and 11-5 form a complete module for computing FFTs in parallel. Neither the sequential routines, *fft_1* and *fft_combine*, nor the parallel ones have been optimized. Precisely the same optimizations can be applied to both. These include avoiding the subroutine overhead associated with complex arithmetic by in-line expansion, avoiding repeated calls to *permute* by using a look-up table for the complex roots of unity which are keyed to the global index, avoiding the subroutine overhead of the recursive algorithm by switching to the iterative algorithm, and making use of the regular properties of the 2nd, 4th, and 8th roots of unity to avoid redundant floating-point operations using a radix-8 algorithm. These optimizations neither restrict nor hinder the parallelization or the decomposition developed so far.

```
proc_begin fft_2 ( find M point FFT of distributed complex data array, x )
    if_begin ( M = 1 ) then
        [return]
    else_if (M ≤ number of processors ) then
        ( only one element of x is stored locally )
        proc_call fft_2 ( find M /2 point FFT of x )
        proc_call fft_combine_comm ( combine local value of x
                    with value from complementary processor )
        [return]
    else
        proc_call fft_2 ( find M/2 point FFT of even elements of x )
        proc_call fft_2 ( find M/2 point FFT of odd elements of x )
        proc_call fft_combine_2 ( combine the even and odd elements of x
                    within the same processor )
        [return]
    if_end
proc_end
```

Code 11-3 The Concurrent Recursive FFT

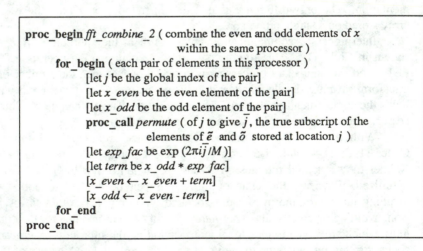

Code 11-4 Routine to Combine the Even and Odd Partial FFTs

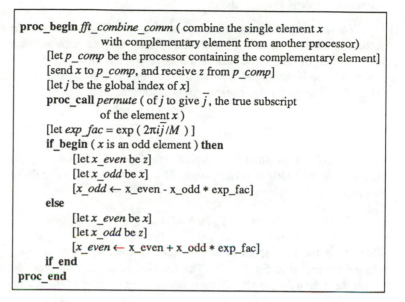

```
proc_begin fft_combine_comm ( combine the single element x
                  with complementary element from another processor)
[let p_comp be the processor containing the complementary element]
[send x to p_comp, and receive z from p_comp]
[let j be the global index of x]
proc_call permute ( of j to give j̄, the true subscript
                  of the element x )
[let exp_fac = exp ( 2πij̄/M ) ]
if_begin ( x is an odd element ) then
    [let x_even be z]
    [let x_odd be x]
    [x_odd ← x_even - x_odd * exp_fac]
else
    [let x_even be x]
    [let x_odd be z]
    [x_even ← x_even + x_odd * exp_fac]
if_end
proc_end
```

Code 11-5 Routine to Exchange and Combine Elements of x in the Concurrent Algorithm

11-5 Communication Structure

The parallel routine exchanges data between processors. In order to implement this operation in a real program, the virtual machine function *vm_shift* would be used. To determine how well the algorithm will work on a given real machine, we must know whether the virtual connections used by *vm_shift* are present in hardware. If they are present, we can expect the algorithm to perform very well. Thus, it is important to know exactly which processors are connected in the algorithm and what hardware topology is necessary to provide these links directly.

When *fft_combine_comm* is first called, the number of elements involved in the transform is equal to the number of processors. Thus, there is an element in each processor, and even and odd elements are stored in processors with adjacent processor numbers. At the next level of recursion, a point is stored in every second processor, and even and odd elements are stored in processors whose processor numbers differ by two. Proceeding deeper, we find that even and odd elements are stored in processors whose processor numbers differ by four, eight, sixteen, etc. In other words, a processor requires communication with those processors whose processor numbers differ by exactly one, two, four, eight, etc. This connectivity is precisely that of the hypercube. Thus, in order to avoid message forwarding in the FFT algorithm, the hardware communication graph should contain a hypercube as a subset. The use of the hypercube for FFTs was explored quite early by Allakhverdiyev and Sarafaliyeva [Allakhverdiyev 81].

11-6 Performance on the Hypercube

To simplify the performance analysis, we will assume that the machine interconnection topology contains a hypercube. Under this assumption, an exchange requires a fixed amount of time in each of two processors, and no other processors are affected, as they would be if messages required forwarding. Following the discussion in Chap. 5, we define the communication overhead, f, according to:

$$f = \frac{NT_N(M) - T_1(M)}{T_1(M)} \tag{11-12}$$

where $T_N(M)$ is the time to complete an M-point FFT on N processors. The parallel algorithm splits neatly into two stages, $M > N$ and $M \le N$. The following recursion relation holds for $M > N$:

$$T_N(M) = 2\,T_N(\frac{M}{2}) + \frac{M}{2N}\,\tau_> \tag{11-13}$$

where $\tau_>$ is the time spent in one iteration of the loop in *fft_combine_2*. Note that this relation is similar to Eq. (11-9). The solution is slightly different because the recursion terminates when the number of points equals the number of processors, i.e. when $N = M$.

$$T_N(M) = \frac{M}{N}(T_N(N) + \frac{\tau_>}{2}\,\log_2\frac{M}{N}) \tag{11-14}$$

For $M \le N$ we have

$$T_N(M) = T_N(\frac{M}{2}) + \tau_< \tag{11-15}$$

where $\tau_<$ is the time spent in a single call to *fft_combine_comm*. The solution of Eq. (11–15) is

$$T_N(M) = \tau_<\,\log_2 M \tag{11-16}$$

In particular, $T_N(N) = \tau_<\log_2 N$, which can be substituted into Eq. (11-14) giving

$$T_N(M) = \frac{M}{2N}(\tau_>\,\log_2 M + (2\tau_< - \tau_>)\,\log_2 N) \tag{11-17}$$

Thus, the overhead is given by:

$$f = \frac{2\tau_< - \tau_>}{\tau_>}\,\frac{\log_2 N}{\log_2 M} \tag{11-18}$$

The effects due to details of the implementation and the particular machine's architecture are contained in $\tau_>$ and $\tau_<$. On most parallel computers, floating-point arithmetic is much more costly than integer arithmetic, so we make the following generalizations about $\tau_>$ and $\tau_<$:

$$\tau_> = t_* + 2t_\pm \approx 10\,t_{calc} \tag{11-19a}$$

$$\tau_< = t_* + t_\pm + t_{shift} \approx 8t_{calc} + 2t_{comm} \qquad (11\text{-}19b)$$

where t_* and $t_\pm$ are the typical times for complex multiplication and addition operations, respectively, and t_{shift} is the time required to shift a complex value, equal to twice the value of t_{comm} as defined in Sec. 3-5. Note that when $N=1$, Eq. 11–19 and Eq. 11–17 are equivalent to Eq. 11–10. With the approximations of Eq. 11–19, the overhead is

$$f = \frac{2t_{comm} + 3t_{calc}}{5t_{calc}} \frac{\log_2 N}{\log_2 M} \qquad (11\text{-}20)$$

The overhead decreases slowly to 0 if M is increased with N fixed. Figure 11-2 is a plot of f vs. $\log_2 N/\log_2 M$, as measured on the Caltech Mark II hypercube. The points form a straight line corresponding to a value of $t_{comm}/t_{calc} = 3.3$ and show excellent agreement with the model.

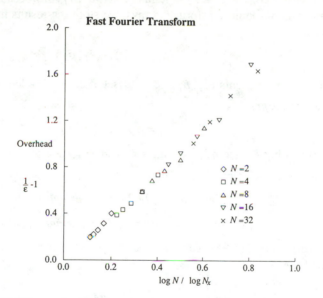

Figure 11-2 The overhead $f = 1/\varepsilon - 1$ defined in Eq. (11-12) and discussed in Sec. 11-6. The points come from measurements on the Caltech/JPL Mark II hypercube [Noerdlinger 86].

Even with $t_{comm} \approx 0$ the overhead does not vanish. This is a because both the processor and its complement compute the complex product in Code 11-5. Thus, we have introduced a small amount of *algorithmic overhead* in addition to the communication overhead. This overhead cannot be removed simply by computing the product in the odd processor, and transmitting only the result. In that case, although the even processor does no work, it is idle while the odd processor does the computation. A solution to this problem does exist for the iterative algorithm (which appears in the Software Supplement). The difficulty in the recursive algorithm is that there is really nothing else for the even processor to do while the odd processor computes the product. In the iterative algorithm, the two processors can agree each to compute half of the products at any given stage of the computation.

11-7 Permutation of the Indices by the FFT Algorithm

In Sec. 11-1, we postulated a function *permute* which mapped the offset from the beginning of the partially transformed array, *x*, into the index of the element stored at that location. In this section, we derive the details of *permute*.

We begin by giving a recursive description of *permute* (j, M), where M is the number of items in the permutation. The simplest case occurs when $M = 1$. Since there is only one item in the permutation, there is only one possible result:

$$permute\ (j, 1) = 0 \tag{11-21}$$

We can write *permute* $(j, 2M)$ in terms of *permute* (j, M) because when combining the even and odd M-point transformed arrays, we store the results in the $2M$-point array as follows:

$$(\tilde{x}_{i_0}, \tilde{x}_{i_0 + M}) \leftarrow (\tilde{e}_{i_0}, \tilde{o}_{i_0}) \tag{11-22}$$

Let the pair of elements $(\tilde{e}_{i_0}, \tilde{o}_{i_0})$ be at offset j in the M-element array. Then, by the definition of *permute*,

$$i_0 = permute\ (j, M) \tag{11-23}$$

After combining $\tilde{e}_{i_0}$ and $\tilde{o}_{i_0}$, the values $\tilde{x}_{i_0}$ and $\tilde{x}_{i_0 + M}$ are at offsets $2j$ and $2j+1$, respectively, in the $2M$-element array. Thus,

$$permute\ (2j, 2M) = i_0 = permute\ (j, M) \tag{11-24}$$

$$permute\ (2j+1, 2M) = i_0 + M = permute\ (j, M) + M \tag{11-25}$$

Eq. (11-24) and (11-25) can be recast as a recursion formula for computing *permute* (j, M).

$$permute\ (j, M) = \begin{cases} permute\ (\dfrac{j}{2}, \dfrac{M}{2}) & \text{if j is even} \\[2em] permute\ (\dfrac{j-1}{2}, \dfrac{M}{2}) + \dfrac{M}{2} & \text{if } j \text{ is odd} \end{cases} \tag{11-26}$$

Finally, we can translate the operations of Eq. (11-26) into words:

1) Set the high-order bit (the one corresponding to the value of $M/2$) in the result to be the same as the low-order bit in *j*.

2) Compute the rest of the bits by shifting both j and M one bit to the right and repeating the procedure.

This procedure selects bits from j, starting at the right, and inserts them into the result, starting at the left. It simply reverses the bits of j.

11-8 Inverting the Permutation in Parallel

One consequence of the permutation of indices is that elements of the final result are also permuted. Thus, $\tilde{x}_k$ is not found at an offset of k from the beginning of the array, x, after the completion of the FFT program. Instead, $\tilde{x}_k$ is found at an offset given by $permute\,(k,M)$, which is equal to the bit-reversal of the binary representation of k, as described in the previous section. The fact that $\tilde{x}_k$ is not where one might expect is usually not a problem because it is simple enough to determine its true location. On the other hand, sometimes it is useful to invert the permutation and rearrange the elements of $\tilde{x}_k$ in order of increasing k. A sequential program which does this is trivial because *permute* is its own inverse. For each value of k, one simply exchanges the two elements at offsets k and $permute\,(k,M)$.

The task is somewhat more complicated in the parallel case. Recall that the array, x, is distributed over all the nodes of the parallel processor. In Sec. 11-5, we found that the necessary communication topology for computation of the FFT is that of a hypercube. Thus, we restrict ourselves to a hypercube in the following discussion. The goal is to take the array, $\tilde{x}$, after the FFT has been performed, and to rearrange it so that $\tilde{x}_k$ is found at offset $k\ mod\ n$, in processor k/n, where n is the grain size, $n=M/N$. We divide the task into two parts: 1) Get the correct elements into the correct processors, regardless of order; and 2) Rearrange them locally without need for further communication.

To place elements in the correct processors, we need a way to identify the home processor of a given element. Recall that we want the number of the processor in which x_k is stored to correspond to the high bits of k, and that after the completion of the FFT, the high bits of k can be found, reversed, in the low bits of the offset of x_k. Thus, elements destined for processor p are those with offsets from the beginning of their home processor whose low bits correspond to the bit-reversal of p. The bit-reversal is denoted by $\bar{p}$. These elements are evenly spaced in memory, separated by N elements. They are always at offsets $\bar{p}, \bar{p}+N, \bar{p}+2N, \cdots$.

Slightly trickier is determining the route that a given set of elements will follow to reach their destination. Remember that we are restricted to using the hypercube communication channels. As can be readily verified, destinations are not necessarily nearest neighbors in the hypercube topology. We must find a way to route the messages through several nodes, and we must be sure that the intermediate nodes are prepared to forward the data properly. This problem can be solved by insisting that all elements being transferred at any given time are taking the same route, where a route is defined as a sequence of traversed hypercube channels. A route can be uniquely identified by an integer, r, in the range $0 \le r \le (N-1)$. Each bit in the binary representation of the integer represents a channel that is part of the route. Since all processors make use of the same route simultaneously, and hence the same channels, the polled communication scheme is perfectly adequate. Furthermore, since all processors are simultaneously working on the same route, there is no load imbalance or idle time. At any given time all the processors are active forwarding data to different final destinations. Organizing a long-range communication problem by enumeration of routes is a powerful idea that will be considered further in Chap. 21, where it is called the method of *ordered cube geo-desics*. The *index* algorithm of Chap. 21-3.2 is very similar to the algorithm of Code 11–6. In fact, Code 11-6 could be replaced by a local permutation followed by a call to *index*.

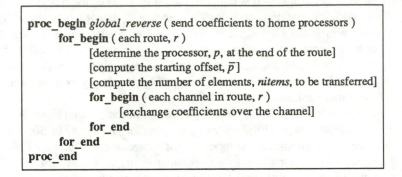

proc_begin *global_reverse* (send coefficients to home processors)
    for_begin (each route, *r*)
        [determine the processor, *p*, at the end of the route]
        [compute the starting offset, $\bar{p}$]
        [compute the number of elements, *nitems*, to be transferred]
        for_begin (each channel in route, *r*)
            [exchange coefficients over the channel]
        for_end
    for_end
proc_end

Code 11-6 The Routine *global_reverse*

With the communication phase complete, all that remains is to invert the permutation locally. While straightforward in principle, the local permutation requires considerable bit-oriented arithmetic to reverse bits, identify low-order and high-order bits, etc. Both C and FORTRAN implementations of this set of operations appear in the Software Supplement.

The cost of inverting the permutation is quite high. Almost every element of the array, x, must be transmitted over a long distance through the hypercube. The average distance traveled is half the diameter of the hypercube, or $(\log_2 N)/2$. We can estimate the time taken by Code 11-6 by counting the number of data transmissions. We find that each node executes $(N \log_2 N)/2$ exchanges, each one of M/N^2 complex numbers, so that the total time taken is given approximately by:

$$T_{invert} = \frac{M \log_2 N}{N} t_{comm} \tag{11-27}$$

The overhead due to inversion, f_{invert}, which is a form of algorithmic overhead, is given by

$$f_{invert} = \frac{T_{invert}(M)}{T_1(M)} = \frac{t_{comm}}{10 t_{calc}} \frac{\log_2 N}{\log_2 M} \tag{11-28}$$

Equation 11-28 has the same dependence on N and M as Eq. 11-20. Thus, the overhead due to permutation of indices in a parallel FFT has the same effect as slightly degraded communication speed. It does not affect the performance scaling with N or M except to modify the effective communication speed.

11-9 Multidimensional Transforms

Multidimensional Fourier transforms are extremely useful in a wide variety of differential equation and image-processing problems. In a multidimensional transform (we will consider two dimensions for illustrative purposes), the input vector and the output transform are objects carrying two indices. The two-dimensional transform, with M_1 points in direction 1 and M_2 points in direction 2 is defined by:

$$\tilde{x}_{jk} = \sum_{l=0}^{M_1-1} \sum_{m=0}^{M_2-1} x_{lm} \exp\left(2\pi i\left(\frac{jl}{M_1} + \frac{km}{M_2}\right)\right) \tag{11-29}$$

We can factor the exponential and use the standard rules for removing a constant from a summation to obtain

$$\tilde{x}_{jk} = \sum_{l=0}^{M_1-1} \exp\left(2\pi i\left(\frac{jl}{M_1}\right)\right) \sum_{m=0}^{M_2-1} x_{lm} \exp\left(2\pi i\left(\frac{km}{M_2}\right)\right) \tag{11-30}$$

The inner summation in Eq. (11-30) requires the computation of M_1 one-dimensional FTs, with one for each value of l, each involving M_2 points. Similarly, the outer summation requires the computation of M_2 one-dimensional FTs, one for each value of k, each over M_1 points. The total time predicted for these operations has the dependence:

$$T \propto M_1(M_2\log_2 M_2) + M_2(M_1\log_2 M_1) = M\log_2 M \tag{11-31}$$

In this expression,

$$M = M_1 M_2 \tag{11-32}$$

is the total number of points in the two-dimensional mesh. The total time required for the multidimensional transform of Eq. (11-29) is exactly the same as for the one-dimensional case. The algorithm simply applies the one-dimensional algorithm many times in sequence, first to evaluate the inner summation and then to evaluate the outer summation.

To compute multidimensional transforms in parallel, we still need a hypercube communication structure. We may consider a hypercube of dimension d to be a product, in a topological sense, of smaller hypercubes. The sum of the dimensions of the smaller cubes, d_1 and d_2, in a two dimensional problem, must be equal to the dimension of the whole hypercube, d. When computing the inner summation, we use the d_1 communication channels associated with the first subcube. Then, to compute the outer summation, we use the d_2 communication channels associated with the second subcube. A detailed analysis shows that the results of Sec. 11-6 are unchanged for multidimensional Fourier transforms. In the formulas of Sec. 11-6, M should be considered as the total number of elements in the transform, regardless of the number of dimensions.

An alternative decomposition for multi-dimensional transforms is the row decomposition. Again, for simplicity, consider a two-dimensional transform. We begin with one or more entire rows of the array stored within a single processor. The transforms of the rows can be computed using any sequential algorithm available. There is no communication within the transform phase. Then rows and columns of the partially transformed array are transposed, so that complete columns are now stored within a single processor. Finally, the columns are transformed, again without communication. This approach has some important advantages.

-       Any sequential transform algorithm can be used. Non-binary transforms, as well as algorithms tailored especially to known properties of the data like real-valuedness, may be used without difficulty.

-       All communication is isolated into a single phase which can be optimized independently of the transform. Additionally, some advantage may be gained by transmitting large amounts of data at one time rather than in several small chunks.

The algorithm to effect the transpose of the data is very similar to that used in Sec.11–8 to invert the bit-reversed transform. Each processor loops over routes through the hypercube, and sends data destined for the processor at the end of the route. As in Sec.11–8, the time needed for such communication is

$$T_{transpose} = \frac{M \log_2 N}{N} t_{comm} \tag{11-33}$$

Since there is no other source of overhead, the total overhead in a row decomposed multi-dimensional FFT is given by

$$f = \frac{t_{comm}}{10 t_{calc}} \frac{\log_2 N}{\log_2 M} \tag{11-34}$$

This overhead is functionally the same as all others encountered in this chapter. However, by performing all the communication at once, we have achieved a reduction in the coefficient of t_{comm}/t_{calc} that appears in the expression. This can be quite important on systems with a poor communication speed. Consolidating the communication can also be achieved for one-dimensional transforms, using the generalized collective communication routine *index* described in Chap. 21-3.2.

12

Monte Carlo Methods and the
Generation of Random Numbers

12-1 Introduction

Many important algorithms in engineering and the sciences are of the Monte Carlo type. This means that they employ pseudo-random number generators to simulate physical systems which are inherently probabilistic or statistical in nature [Knuth 73b]. A typical example of such an algorithm is the simulation of the neutrons emitted by a nuclear reactor. In the laboratory, one can measure the properties of the interactions of neutrons with various materials, such as those found in the walls of the reactor. These experimental measurements are used to obtain a set of probabilities, which convey information such as: "If a neutron of velocity v hits material x at angle θ, then there is a probability of y that the neutron will be absorbed (damaging the material) and there is a probability density $z(\phi)$ of it being scattered by angle ϕ." These probability functions can in turn be used to simulate processes in the nuclear reactor and to help in making engineering decisions regarding the design of the system.

This type of Monte Carlo computation proceeds by directly simulating the histories of individual neutrons, from production in the core of the reactor to eventual absorption in some material. For each neutron, the effects on the reactor (damage to walls and so forth) are tabulated. Once a large number of neutrons has been simulated, a reasonably accurate picture of the simulated system emerges (assuming, of course, that the initial modeling of the system was correct). We conventionally call the history of an individual neutron an event or path. We will refer to this type of algorithm as an event-tracing Monte Carlo method.

In this chapter we discuss a reliable method of generating concurrent random numbers. Chapter 13 will describe two application areas (simulated annealing, lattice gauge theories) which make use of the method.

12-2 Overview of the Generation of Random Numbers

At each decision step of the neutron path problem introduced in Sec. 12-1, random numbers are employed to make the decision in accordance with the probability function representing whatever it is that the neutron has run into. Strictly speaking, the random numbers used in computer algorithms are not really random at all. They are generated by some definite method, and if the algorithm is run a second time, with identical starting conditions, exactly the same "random" numbers will be produced. These generators are therefore called pseudo-random number generators which produce a sequence of numbers that appears to be random. One could conceive of attaching some specialized device to a computer to give truly random numbers, such as a Geiger counter measuring radioactive decays of a piece of uranium. Even if we ignore the implications for the reliability of our computer, this random number generator would be undesirable for reasons of reproducibility. Suppose we make a modification to the code (speeding up a certain subroutine, for example), and we wish to demonstrate that the algorithm has survived this modification without any bugs introduced. With the pseudo-random number generator, this is easy: we start with some standard initial condition and then put the program through its paces, exercising all relevant parts of the program. If the results are identical, we can be reasonably confident that no bugs have been introduced into the program.

When Monte Carlo algorithms with their associated random number generators are adapted for a parallel computer, questions immediately arise concerning correlations among the various parallel random number sequences (e.g., the random number sequence of each node of the parallel computer). If the sequences are correlated in some way, several severe problems present themselves. At the very least, if there are correlations, the effective speed of the algorithm may be much less than the naive speedup of the concurrent processor. This is because if correlations are present, much of the information coming from the various processing nodes will be redundant and will not help to improve the statistical accuracy of the overall computation. Even more dangerous is the fact that in many types of Monte Carlo computations, correlations will lead to actual biases, and incorrect results will be obtained. In the nuclear reactor algorithm, for example, if more neutrons end up going to the north than the south, due to some correlation of the random numbers, one may falsely conclude that the south side of the plant is correctly or incorrectly engineered.

It is important to realize that even in the sequential case, the question of correlations is a nontrivial one. A given pseudo-random number generator may be such that the nth and the $n+18$th number are correlated in some way, leading to the problems mentioned above. In the normal sequential case, ways of generating random numbers which are largely free of correlations have been found. If we could somehow reduce the parallel case to something equivalent to the sequential method, we would be satisfied. For the most popular method of generating pseudo-random numbers, this is possible. There is a modified, parallel method which can be used so that the parallel computer exactly mimics what a sequential machine would do in the same computation. All questions regarding correlations among the parallel random number sequences are thereby reduced to those applying to the sequential case which has been extensively studied. In this approach it may be said, "If you were happy with the sequential algorithm and the correlations among the pseudo-random numbers in that case, you will be happy with the parallel algorithm."

Another important feature of the method is that the parallel and sequential algorithms can be made to match exactly; therefore, debugging of complex parallel codes is greatly simplified.

Before plunging into the details of the parallel method and examples, let us mention some references. The fundamental formula appears in [Knuth 73b] and ideas related to those discussed here are treated in [Frederickson 83]. The parallel method is explicitly put forth in the context of vector computers in [Brown 83, Barkai 84].

12-3 Algorithm for Parallel Random Number Generation

We employ the most popular type of generator of pseudo-random numbers: the linear congruential algorithm. It is defined by:

$$X_{n+1} = (aX_n + c) \bmod m \qquad (12\text{-}1)$$

where X_i is the ith member of the sequence and a, c, and m are chosen in order to make the members of the sequence appear as random as possible (see Knuth 73b, p. 102, for a table of good choices for a, c and m).

A fundamental relation is that, given Eq. Eq. (12-1), it is easy to write down the $n+k$th member of the sequence in terms of the nth:

$$X_{n+k} = (A\, X_n + C)\, \bmod\, m \qquad (12\text{-}2)$$

with

$$A = a^k \qquad (12\text{-}3)$$

$$C = c(1 + a + a^2 + \cdots + a^{k-1}) = \frac{c(a^k - 1)}{a - 1}$$

Of course, $(a^k - 1)/(a - 1)$ is, typically, difficult to compute in practice (a is usually a very large number). It is usually simpler to use the more direct expression of Eq. (12-3), and to compute C by summing the powers of a directly using Horner's Rule. Equation (12–2) shows that the $n+k$th member of the sequence is related to the nth through the same kind of relation as Eq. (12-1), with just a different value of a and c.

Consider a generic concurrent processor, consisting of N processing nodes connected by some communication network. It does not matter here if the concurrent processor is MIMD or SIMD. The idea is to have each node compute random numbers using Eq. (12-2), with $k = N$ (A and C in Eq. (12-2) are calculated only once and stored). The nodes are given a staggered start, so that their sequences don't overlap. Let the seed, or 0th random number, be denoted by Y_0. Using this as a seed, a sequential computer would compute the sequence:

$$Y_0 = Y_0 \qquad (12\text{-}4)$$

$$Y_1 = (aY_0 + c) \bmod m$$

$$Y_2 = (aY_1 + c) \bmod m$$

$$\vdots$$

The seeds in the nodes of the concurrent ensemble are set as follows (subscripts denote position in the random number sequence, superscripts denote processing node):

$$X_0^{(0)} = Y_0 \qquad\qquad (12\text{-}5)$$

$$X_0^{(1)} = (aY_0 + c) \bmod m = Y_1$$

$$\cdot$$
$$\cdot$$
$$\cdot$$

$$X_0^{(N-1)} = Y_{N-1}$$

This defines the staggered start. The nodes now use Eq. (12-2) to compute the next member of each of their sequences, with $k=N$. Therefore

$$X_1^{(0)} = Y_{0+N} \qquad\qquad (12\text{-}6)$$

$$X_1^{(1)} = Y_{1+N}$$

$$\cdot$$
$$\cdot$$
$$\cdot$$

$$X_1^{(N-1)} = Y_{N-1+N}$$

and,

$$X_2^{(0)} = Y_{0+2N} \qquad\qquad (12\text{-}7)$$

$$X_2^{(1)} = Y_{1+2N}$$

$$\cdot$$
$$\cdot$$
$$\cdot$$

$$X_2^{(N-1)} = Y_{N-1+2N}$$

and so on. The method is illustrated in Fig. 12-1 for the case $N=4$. As is clear from the picture, the idea of the parallel method is to put the processing nodes into a staggered start and then to have them leapfrog one another using Eq. (12-2). The interleaved sequence corresponds exactly to the single sequence of random numbers that would be obtained on a sequential computer.

The simple pseudocode for a sequential (31-bit) random number generator is given in Code 12-1. The routine *rand_set* initializes the constants a and c (as given in Knuth, for example) and starts the random number sequence off with seed *ran_seed*.

The parallel random number generator, *prand*, and setup routine, *prand_set*, are outlined in Code 12-2. The routine *prand* is of the same form as *rand*, except that the multiplier and summand that it uses will be chosen to produce the large hops of N down the sequence of random numbers. The setup routine *prand_set* does most of the hard work of the parallel random number generator. It computes the correct multiplier and summand, A and C of Eq. (12-3), which produce the large hops of N steps. It also sets up the necessary staggered start determined by *ran_seed*. More specifically, in the

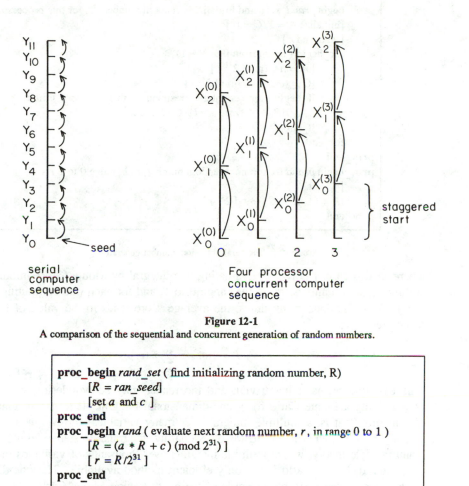

Figure 12-1
A comparison of the sequential and concurrent generation of random numbers.

```
proc_begin rand_set ( find initializing random number, R)
     [R = ran_seed]
     [set a and c ]
proc_end
proc_begin rand ( evaluate next random number, r, in range 0 to 1 )
     [R = (a * R + c) (mod 2³¹) ]
     [ r = R /2³¹ ]
proc_end
```

Code 12-1 The sequential random number generator

processing node whose *procnum* is equal to i, R will be set to the ith random number after the seed (Y_i of Eq. (12-4)). Note that the order of the computation of r and R are reversed in *rand* and *prand*. This is intentional and is done to get exact matching of the parallel and sequential sequences.

12-4 Example 1: Simple Event Tracing Monte Carlo

Our first example will be computing a one-dimensional integral by the Monte Carlo method. We will evaluate the definite integral:

$$I = \int_0^1 f(x) \, dx \qquad (12\text{-}8)$$

```
proc_begin prand_set ( find initializing random number, R, for this processor )
        [initialize A = 1, C = 0 ]
        [set a and c ]
        for_begin ( count from 0 to N − 1)
                [ A = aA (mod 2³¹ ) ]
                [C = (aC + c ) (mod 2³¹ ) ]
                if_begin ( loop counter corresponds to this processor ) then
                        [R = (A *ran_seed + C ) (mod 2³¹ ) ]
                if_end
        for_end
proc_end
proc_begin prand (return next random number, r, in range 0 to 1 )
        [r = R /2³¹ ]
        [R = (A *R + C ) (mod 2³¹ ) ]
proc_end
```

Code 12-2 The parallel random number generator

where in this case, $f(x) = x^2$. Evaluating this integral by Monte Carlo amounts to generating random numbers, r_i, in the range 0 to 1, and for each one computing the score, $f(r_i)$. If this is done many times, the average score tends to the value of the integral. More precisely:

$$I = \lim_{L \to \infty} \frac{1}{L} \sum_{i=1}^{L} f(r_i) \qquad (12\text{-}9)$$

This example seems rather trivial, and the reader may be wondering why we would bother doing a Monte Carlo for a one-dimensional integral. It turns out that in higher dimensions (that is, a multiple integral over many variables) the Monte Carlo method actually becomes an efficient means of evaluating integrals. In statistical mechanics and quantum field theory, where multiple integrals over thousands of variables (at least) are encountered, Monte Carlo is the only efficient method available. The one-dimensional integral also forms a simple example of the event tracing Monte Carlo. The events are just the generation of the random numbers themselves. The score (the summation of Eq. (12-9)) is analogous to keeping track of the interaction of each neutron with the reactor walls. The pseudocode which correlates with Eq. (12-9) (for the case $f(x) = x^2$) is listed in Code 12-3.

The parallel code for this problem is simple. We have already resolved the correlation problem among the random numbers. In addition, the events are completely independent of one another. The parallel algorithm, therefore, involves having each node generate events and keep its own estimate of the average score. At the end, the N scores are averaged and printed. The individual scores of each event could be accumulated as the algorithm runs, but this would generate much needless communication in the concurrent processor, leading to a less efficient implementation. By combining scores only at the end, the nodes are completely decoupled during the actual computation. If each

```
proc_begin main ( run sequential 1-D Monte Carlo integrator )
      [ receive number of trails ]
      [ receive random number seed, ran_seed ]
      proc_call rand_set ( find initializing random number, R )
      [ initialize score = 0 ]
      for_begin ( each trial )
                  proc_call rand ( return next random number, r, in range 0 to 1 )
                  [ score = score + r*r ]
      for_end
      [integral = score/(number of trials)]
      [output integral]
proc_end
```

Code 12-3 Code to compute $\int_{0}^{1} x^2\, dx$

node generates many events (the typical case), the algorithm will achieve a speedup very close to the perfect value of N. Code 12-4 contains the pseudocode for the concurrent version of the Monte Carlo integrator.

```
proc_begin main ( run Monte Carlo integrator program in each processor )
      [ receive number of trials to be executed in this processor ]
      [receive random number seed, ran_seed ]
      proc_call prand_set ( find initializing random number, R for this processor )
      [initialize score = 0 ]
      for_begin ( each trial )
                  proc_call prand ( evaluate next random number, r, in range 0 to 1 )
                  [ score = score + r*r ]
      for_end
      [ sum score over all processors ]
      [ integral = score /(total number of trials) ]
      [ output integral ]
proc_end
```

Code 12-4 Parallel version of 12-3

12-5 Example 2: Calculation of π via Monte Carlo

In this example we will compute an estimate for π via the "dartboard" algorithm. Consider a circle of unit radius centered at the origin with a square circumscribed about it (the corners of the square are at the points $(-1,-1)$, $(1,-1)$, $(1,1)$, and $(-1,1)$). This circle forms the dartboard. We now throw darts at the board, but in a rather special way. They are thrown so that they always hit the square, but have an equal probability of hitting any part of the square. During this process, we keep a score which is incremented by 1 for each dart inside the unit circle, and 0 for darts outside the circle. If we then divide the total score by the total number of darts thrown, we obtain an estimate of the ratio of the area of the circle to the area of the square, since the darts have equal probability of hitting any part of the square. The ratio of the areas is $\pi/4$, so that the total score divided by the total number of trials ($\times 4$) yields an estimate of π.

As in Example 1, the events (the throws of the darts) are independent and so we will have each node of the concurrent processor run its own dartboard simulation and make its own estimate of π. At the end, the N estimates will be globally combined. There is, however, a somewhat nontrivial aspect of this example as compared with the previous one. In fact, this is our main motivation for presenting it–there are, after all, better ways of computing π!

The complication arises from the fact that each event depends on two random numbers. As each event is processed in one of the nodes, two consecutive calls to *prand* will give numbers N steps apart in the fundamental sequence of random numbers, while the sequential program calls *rand* and so gives two consecutive random numbers, Y_i and Y_{i+1}. We have therefore lost the one-for-one matching of events between the parallel and sequential codes. Fixing this is easy: in a simple generalization of the previous prescription for parallel random numbers, we merely need to generate the numbers (on the concurrent processor) in pairs, (Y_i, Y_{i+1}) and then do a large hop down the sequence of $2N-1$ steps. This will restore the exact match with the sequential computation.

We present in Code 12-5 the modified random number generator and setup routine.

```
proc_begin prand_setB ( find initial random number, R , and multipliers and summands
              for this processor )
    [ initialize big jump multiplier and summand A = 1, B = 0 ]
    [ initialize small jump multiplier and summand a , c to one hop values ]
    for_begin ( count from 0 to 2N-1 )
        A = aA ( mod 2^31 )
        C = (aC + c )( mod 2^31 )
        if_begin ( loop counter equals 2 × processor number ) then
              [R = A *ran_seed + C ( mod 2^31 )]
        if_end
    for_end
proc_end
```

Code 12-5 The initializer for the "big jump" random number generator

We see that *prand_setB* produces two sets of multipliers and summands, one set, A, C for the big jumps of $2N-1$ steps, and the other set, a, c the usual pair for steps of size 1 or the small jumps. As a result, we need two different random number routines, *prandB* and *prandS* which follow the pseudocode of Code 12-6. With this issue resolved, the rest of the parallel code (Code 12-7) is simple. The structure is very similar to that of Example 1. The nodes execute the same algorithm to generate the events as in the sequential case, with the only difference being to first call *prandS*, producing the small jump, then *prandB*, giving the big jump.

```
proc_begin prandB ( evaluate next random number, r, in range 0 to 1 using big step )
     [ r = R /2³¹ ]
     [ R = (A *R + C ) ( mod 2³¹ ) ]
proc_end
proc_begin prandS ( evaluate next random number, r, in range 0 to 1 using small step )
     [ r = R /2³¹ ]
     [ R = (a *R + c ) (mod 2³¹ ) ]
proc_end
```

Code 12-6 The big and small jump random number generators

```
proc_begin main ( run parallel "dartboard" estimation of π in processor )
     [ receive number of darts to be thrown by this processor ]
     [ receive random number seed, ran_seed ]
     proc_call prand_setB ( find initial random number, R and multipliers and summands
                     for this processor )
     [ initialize score = 0 ]
     for_begin ( each dart thrown by this processor )
          proc_call prandS ( evaluate next random number, r, in range 0 to 1
                          using small skip )
          [ set x_coord = 2r - 1 ]
          proc_call prandB ( evaluate next random number, r, in range 0 to 1
                          using big skip )
          [ set y_coord = 2r - 1 ]
          if_begin ( dart has landed inside circle ) then
                  [ increment score by 1 ]
          if_end
     for_end
     [ sum score over all processors ]
     [ π = 4 * score/ ( total number of darts thrown by all processors) ]
     [ output π ]
proc_end
```

Code 12-7 A parallel program to compute π

12-6 Remarks on the Use of *prand*

In the examples, we have seen how to employ the parallel set of random numbers to robustly perform Monte Carlo calculations on the concurrent computer. Before concluding this chapter, it will be useful to say a few words about more realistic, complex algorithms and the issue of exact matching between the sequential and concurrent programs.

In Example 2, we saw that even if the events of the Monte Carlo problem depended upon multiple random numbers, we could modify the concurrent code to provide exact matching. In realistic cases, this strategy can break down. To illustrate, let us go back to the example of neutrons flowing out of a nuclear reactor and interacting with the surrounding environment. An event consists of the entire history of a single neutron. One possible way of decomposing this problem onto the concurrent processor is to have each node run its own simulation of the entire reactor and at the very end combine the results. The fundamental problem here is that the number of calls to the random number generator made by each event is inherently unpredictable. The number of calls to *prand*, in fact, depends upon the values of previous random numbers. A certain value for the first call may send a neutron into some lead, absorbing it and so ending that event. However, a different value for the first call to *prand* may cause the neutron to miss the lead, and hence have a much longer history, involving many more calls to *prand*. This results in a problem for the concurrent machine: each node, when it wants to process its next event, and therefore make a big jump in the random number sequence to avoid the random numbers already used by the other nodes, needs to know how large of a jump to make. This would mean that at the end of each event, all the nodes would have to communicate to determine how many random numbers each of them used, to find the proper size of the big jump, and to find the correct values of A and C to produce this jump.

Besides involving much overhead (recomputing new values for A and C each time) such a solution could give rise to a severe load imbalance on the concurrent machine. Some events will take much longer to process than others. If we resynchronize at every event, we will virtually guarantee this imbalance, but if we let the nodes stay decoupled through the processing of many events, computational load fluctuations will tend to average out, producing a much more load-balanced computation. A much more attractive alternative therefore suggests itself. Instead of modifying the concurrent code in some drastic way, we should slightly modify the sequential code. The philosophy is to have the sequential code simulate the concurrent machine insofar as the random numbers are concerned.

Suppose we wish to have the sequential algorithm exactly match the same computation on a concurrent machine of N processing nodes. On the concurrent machine, we use the simple parallel set of random numbers as shown in Example 1. This insures that no random numbers will overlap on the concurrent processor. On the sequential machine, we run the usual sequential program, but with a modified set of random numbers. N independent streams of random numbers are set up (e.g., turn the R of Code 12-1 into an array of length N) and the multiplier and summand for all N streams are the values A and C given in Eq. (12-3). These streams are given the same staggered start as in the concurrent case. Then, in the simulation of the first event, the first stream is used, in the simulation of the second event the second stream is used, and so on. This represents a fairly simple change in many sequential codes, and causes it to exactly match the concurrent result.

Finally, we should say that this is not the end of the story. Linear congruential pseudo-random numbers are often not random enough, and one may wish to use more powerful algorithms such as linear shift register methods. A parallel version of these seems problematical and to our knowledge has not been done. Recent research in parallel random numbers appears in [Percus 87].

13

Applications of Monte Carlo Methods: Traveling Salesman and QCD

13-1 Introduction

A reliable technique for generating pseudo-random numbers on a parallel machine was described in the previous chapter. Here we will describe some applications of this method. Two examples will be discussed: the Traveling Salesman optimization problem and the use of Monte Carlo methods for studying quantum field theories.

The Traveling Salesman application may seem at first to be an esoteric toy problem, but it serves to introduce the important subject of simulated annealing whose use in concurrent decomposition and load balancing of complex problems will be discussed in Chap. 17. Quantum field theory simulations are important in physics, and we will also find that they lead to an interesting approach to general finite difference algorithms on a MIMD concurrent computer.

The applications in this chapter will be described within the restricted context of hypercube architectures, because it is with this class of machines that the authors have experience. This specialization should not, however, significantly limit the applicability of the algorithms of this chapter to other parallel machine architectures.

13-2 The Traveling Salesman Problem

The classic Traveling Salesman Problem (TSP) is that of finding the shortest tour for a traveling salesman so that he visits each of a set of cities exactly once, and then returns to his initial city. The difficulty of this problem is illustrated by the immense number of possible tours: $(N-1)!/2$ for N cities. As this number grows faster than any finite power of N, one is limited to small problems if applying a brute force search of all candidates.

The TSP is a simple example of a difficult optimization problem and is NP-complete. Examples with more practical importance include circuit layout and wire placement, resource allocation, and logistical problems. In this chapter we will discuss the simulated annealing approach to the solution of these problems. Graph theoretic and linear programming techniques are covered (for sequential computation) in [Luenberger 84] and [Papadimitriou 82]. Important early work on the TSP appears in [Lin 65, 73], the branch and bound approach is covered in [Held 70, 71] and a parallel version of branch and bound is given in [Felten 87]. A promising approach to optimization, that of neural nets, is first given in [Hopfield 86].

The simulated annealing method [Kirkpatrick 83] is a Monte Carlo approach to solving the TSP. The algorithm samples a small number of the $(N-1)!/2$ possible tours to find a good solution. The method does not in general find the optimal solution, but rather an approximation to the best solution. In many practical contexts this near-optimal solution is quite adequate, so that simulated annealing represents a viable approach.

As mentioned above, we will discuss the TSP in terms of its implementation on a hypercube concurrent processor. This is to provide some specificity to our discussion and also to reflect work that has actually been done [Felten 85b]. As will be seen, the technique generalizes to MIMD machines of many other possible topologies. The hypercube is, as we've seen, well suited for mesh problems–those of a regular geometric nature. The TSP does not fall into this class of problems and this provides further motivation for studying it. It is of interest to learn how effectively concurrent processors of regular architecture can be applied to such a seemingly irregular class of problems.

The cities of the TSP are assumed to be arbitrarily positioned on a two-dimensional plane. An attempted physical or equal area decomposition of the problem would likely lead to load imbalance, with some processors of the ensemble having significantly more work to do than others. This load imbalance would be a major source of inefficiency. The correct decomposition is found by realizing that the topology of the TSP matches that of a ring. Since the traveling salesman visits each city exactly once before returning to the initial city, there exists a ringlike connectivity between cities in a given tour. Hypercubes include rings (see Fig. 13-1) as topological subsets, so that the problem maps nicely onto such a machine. The same is true of architectures based upon periodic meshes. By assigning each processing node an equal number of cities, we can minimize load imbalance. Each processor is assumed to store a list of cities. We begin by assuming there are 2^d processing nodes and N cities, and that the tour starts with the first city on the list in node 0. The candidate tour follows in sequence the list of $N/2^d$ cities in that node, and then continues with the list in node 1. After going through each of the nodes the tour returns to the first city in node 0. This is a decomposition based upon city labeling. As the optimization algorithm runs, the cities will be shuffled between nodes of the concurrent processor, eventually reaching their proper location in the optimal tour.

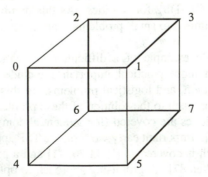

Figure 13-1 A three-dimensional cube with the ring emphasized.

13-3 Simulated Annealing as an Optimization Technique

A possible approach to solving the TSP is that of iterative improvement. This method starts with some initial configuration (initial tour) of the system and then changes are made to the system. The simplest kind of basic change that can be applied to perturb a tour is to swap pairs of cities. These swaps are not necessarily limited to adjacent pairs. Changes that decrease the tour length are accepted, while those that increase it are rejected as shown in Fig. 13-2. The process is repeated in some sequence until no further changes are accepted.

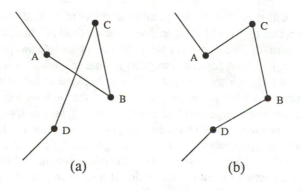

Figure 13-2 Adjacent swap algorithm. (a) initial tour (b) tour obtained by swapping B and C in the tour order.

Let us call the length of the tour the *objective function*. This function is defined over the space of all possible tours. It goes by this name since the objective of the TSP is to find the location of the minimum of this function. At this point, it is easy to see why iterative improvement is not a viable method for solving the TSP. Changes that decrease the objective function are always accepted, while those which increase the objective function are always rejected. For almost all initial tours, therefore, iterative improvement will rapidly get trapped in a local minimum, far above the true global minimum. To avoid getting caught in local minima, the algorithm should be allowed to conditionally accept some increases in the objective function. One achieves this by using the simulated annealing algorithm, which employs an analogy with statistical mechanics.

As with iterative improvement, we start with some initial tour and make changes to it. As before, changes which lower the objective function are always accepted, but instead of rejecting all moves which raise the objective function, we accept them with conditional probability $e^{-\Delta g/T}$, where Δg is the amount of increase in the objective function (tour length), and T is a parameter that is subject to control. In the statistical mechanics analogy the objective function is the energy of the system and the parameter T is the temperature. By occasionally accepting increases in the objective function the system can climb out of local minima. In the physical analogy, iterative improvement corresponds to the algorithm with $T=0$ and freezes the system very rapidly. This produces a metastable configuration usually far above the ground state (optimal tour) of the system. By lowering the temperature slowly, one anneals the system–the system is given time to escape from metastable configurations.

One problem with this approach is in developing adequate annealing schedules. An annealing schedule is the prescription for the number of iterations required at each temperature as the temperature is gradually lowered. Typically, the system is susceptible to freezing at a certain temperature (or temperatures). As a result, the temperature must be lowered very slowly through these points so as to avoid trapping in metastable states.

13-4 Concurrent Implementation of the Traveling Salesman Problem

We will now discuss the parallel implementation of simulated annealing for the TSP. A crucial aspect of the algorithm is the method of introducing random changes into the tour. Initially, we might consider the use of simple swaps of adjacent cities as our move strategy. Using adjacent swaps as the move method is reasonable at low temperatures, but not at high temperatures. This is because at high temperatures the goal is to find the correct global large-scale structure of the optimal tour. It takes many adjacent swaps to generate large-scale structure changes in the tour, so this does not work efficiently. We will ignore this point for now, but return to it later.

Using adjacent swaps has the advantage that Δg can be computed locally. That is, for most of the cities in a given node of the ensemble, the information necessary to compute Δg is already resident on that node. If a node has cities A, B, C and D and we are considering swapping B and C (see Fig. 13-2) then:

$$\Delta g = (\overline{AC} + \overline{BD}) - (\overline{AB} + \overline{CD}) \tag{13-1}$$

where $\overline{AC}$ is the distance between A and C. Each node stores a part of the tour. A cycle of the algorithm begins by having each node perform adjacent swaps of the cities away from the boundaries of the tour pieces. Once these are completed, the nodes communicate in a ring in order to complete adjacent swaps of the cities on ends of the tour segments. This sequence comprises one iteration. The process is repeated, allowing cities to move throughout the concurrent processor, eventually finding their proper locations in the optimal tour.

This algorithm is very efficient, but only when compared with the same (adjacent swap) algorithm on a sequential machine (see Table 13-1). The main difficulty, as mentioned above, is that this algorithm is inefficient in making large-scale improvements. When the system reaches a local minimum, it sometimes requires a large conspiracy of simple adjacent swaps to climb back out of the minimum. In order to speed up this process, we will at this point exploit the richer set of communication channels available in the hypercube architecture.

The improved algorithm is the same as before, except that it uses a more complex method of moving cities around the tour in addition to the adjacent swap. By using the extra communication channels we can move a city a longer distance through the tour during a single step. In Fig. 13-3, a 2^5 cube (32 processors) is shown in such a manner as to make the embedded ring obvious. In the adjacent swap algorithm, only those communication channels along the circumference are used. Clearly, if a city needs to move from node 16 to node 24, it would be much faster to move it directly.

Table 13-1

Adjacent Swap Efficiency 256 Cities Arranged in a Circle			
d	time/iteration(ms)	Speedup	Efficiency
0	639.1	1.00	1.00
1	332.2	1.92	0.96
2	167.3	3.82	0.96
3	84.8	7.54	0.94
4	43.1	14.82	0.93
5	22.2	28.80	0.90
6	11.6	54.92	0.86

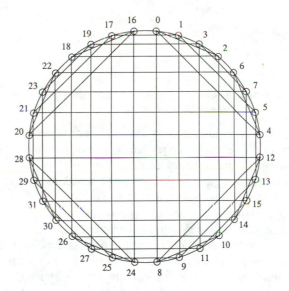

Figure 13-3 Even though it is not obvious, this is a 5 cube drawn in such a way so as to show the embedded ring. The small circles represent processors; the lines are communication channels. The channels going clear across the ring are those used during "hyperswaps" and allow cities to make very large moves in the tour.

To describe this nonadjacent swap between two nodes, let us designate the involved nodes by x and y. Assume that node x has cities labeled A_x, B_x, and C_x and node y has cities labeled A_y, B_y, and C_y. If we propose to swap B_x with B_y (see Fig. 13-4) then

$$\Delta g = \left[\overline{A_x B_y} + \overline{B_y C_x} + \overline{A_y B_x} + \overline{B_x C_y} \right] \\ - \left[\overline{A_x B_x} + \overline{B_x C_x} + \overline{A_y B_y} + \overline{B_y C_y} \right]$$

(13-2)

A reasonable implementation of the required calculation involves node x sending A_x, B_x and C_x to node y. Node y then computes Δg, decides whether or not to accept the swap, and so sends back to node x either B_x or B_y. This "hyperswap" algorithm gives the kth city in each node the option of swapping with the kth city in any of that node's "hyperneighbors" within the hypercube.

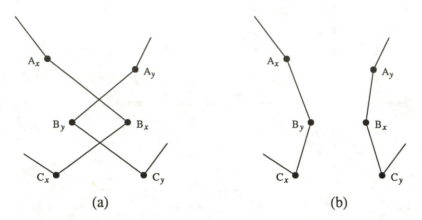

(a)   (b)

Figure 13-4 Hyperswap algorithm. (a) initial tour (b) tour obtained by swapping B_x and B_y in the tour order.

The hyperswap algorithm is less "efficient" than the pure adjacent swap method because every city is on the edge–that is, requires communications. On the other hand, the hyperswap is much better from a standpoint of obtaining the solution quickly, because it is less sensitive to the annealing schedule chosen and is several times more effective than using only adjacent swaps. The best algorithm may be a mixture of adjacent and hyperswaps, with fewer hyperswaps at low temperatures, since most of the large-scale structure of the system has locked in.

There is nothing special about the hypercube topology of the hyperswap algorithm. The aim is simply to allow cities to make large moves within the tour in single steps. On a parallel machine of lower connectivity than a hypercube, the large steps could be implemented via message forwarding. Conversely, on a shared-memory machine, large-step swaps could be implemented with even more freedom than in the hypercube example. Other types of moves which can be more effective than long-range swaps are discussed in [Kirkpatrick 83].

Because the optimal sequential annealing algorithm is not known, we cannot meaningfully discuss the efficiency of the concurrent program as we have done for other problems. In using (5-4), one should in fairness always use the best sequential program as a baseline for efficiency calculation, rather than a degenerate sequential version of the parallel algorithm.

13-5 An Example Traveling Salesman Problem

A 64-city problem, organized as 4 groups of 16 cities each positioned on a unit square, is shown in Fig. 13-5. The illustrated solution was found using a 64-node Caltech Mark I hypercube. The cities were grouped in order to observe the hierarchical nature of the solution process. After running at high temperature T, the four links connecting the groups were discovered by the optimizer and frozen in. The small-scale structure within the groups was then discovered by annealing at lower temperature. Since there still remain a few crossings within the groups, we surmise that we have not found the absolutely optimal path–further running at low temperature would be necessary to remove these defects.

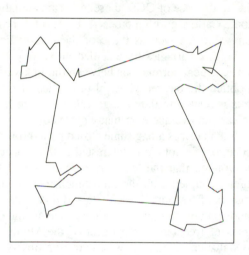

Figure 13-5 An approximate solution to a 64 city problem, with the 64 cities grouped as 4 clusters of 16 each.

13-6 Quantum Field Theories

Quantum chromodynamics (QCD) is the theory of quarks and gluons and how they interact. One would (well, at least a theoretical physicist would!) like to solve this theory and derive its predictions for such things as the force law between quarks. Furthermore, it is of interest to compute the theoretical properties of bound states of quarks and glue for comparison with the real world–protons, neutrons, and the like. If one can actually match all the observed properties in a simple, elegant way, then this will provide some indication that QCD is, in some sense, the correct theory.

QCD seems to be impossible to solve by analytic means. Not only is the relevant physics inherently quantum mechanical (so that semiclassical approximations are useless), but the fundamental interactions of the theory are nonlinear. The approach to the solution of QCD, and other quantum field theories by numerical means [Creutz 83] has only been realized in recent years. This approach (lattice gauge theories) is actually a numerical realization of Feynman's path integral formulation of quantum mechanics [Feynman 65].

13-7 The Monte Carlo Approach to Lattice Gauge Theory

The reader interested in a detailed description of the Monte Carlo technique in lattice gauge theories should consult the references; here we will simply sketch what goes on and point out those algorithmic features of interest in this discussion. We begin by setting up a four-dimensional grid or lattice. This lattice represents a volume of space-time. Associated with the sites of the lattice are variables which represent the quarks. On the connecting bonds or links between the sites reside other variables which represent the glue fields. In the case of QCD, these terms are actually SU(3) matrices.

The Monte Carlo algorithm proceeds by cycling through all the links and randomly changing their values as well as those of the nearby link variables (the interaction is local). Once the link variables have settled into a physically correct pattern of random walks, various statistical correlations between the link variables are evaluated, which are then used to obtain the desired physical properties of QCD. As an example, the force between quarks is related to the average value of large loops of link matrices. By average value is meant an average over many cycles of the Monte Carlo algorithm; a loop is the product of link matrices along some closed path through the lattice.

In practice, one is not really interested in the properties of QCD in a finite box, so the spacetime volume that the lattice represents should be made as large as possible. This requirement, coupled with the four-dimensional nature of the lattice and the large number of degrees of freedom at each site and link, make for large memory and computational demands on any computer. Lattice gauge Monte Carlo simulations often contain 10^6–10^7 degrees of freedom. As a result of the Monte Carlo statistical approach, the answers have statistical uncertainties. Interesting observables, such as the closed loops mentioned above, tend to have very unfavorable signal-to-noise ratios. The very long runs needed to resolve vanishingly small correlations further increase the demands upon the computer. It would appear that even current supercomputers are not up to this task in general. As a result, lattice gauge theories have provided strong motivation for the development of extremely high-performance, special-purpose parallel supercomputers [Christ 86, Beetem 86, Marinari 86, Gaines 86, 87, Schilling 87].

Figure 13-6 shows the result of an early lattice gauge computation on a hypercube computer [Otto 84a, Brooks 84]. The plotted result is the mutual potential energy of a pair of quarks, as a function of their separation distance. This is the QCD analog of the Coulomb force law between electrons. The error bars represent statistical errors due to the Monte Carlo method. The computed force law turns out to yield agreement with the expected qualitative behavior of QCD. At short distances, we observe Coulomb-like behavior (potential $\sim 1/r$), which accords well with the limit of asymptotic freedom. At long distances, a different term dominates the potential, which grows linearly with distance, r. This again agrees with previous expectations of the behavior of QCD at large distances. The linearly increasing potential corresponds to the formation of a flux tube between the quarks, leading to quark confinement.

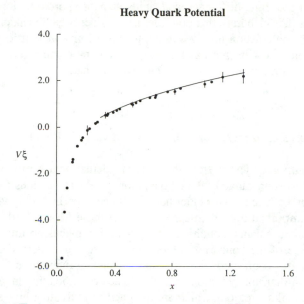

Figure 13-6 The heavy quark potential result as described in [Otto 84a]. The ordinate label $V\xi$ refers to the potential energy of the quark, anti-quark system: the force law between quarks is given by the negative derivative of the potential. The abscissa label x refers to the distance between the quarks. In absolute units, $x = 0.4$ roughly corresponds to 10^{-14} cm.

The above described computation was performed on a $12^3 \times 16$ lattice mapped onto a six-dimensional hypercube (64 nodes). The hypercube was mapped onto a $4 \times 4 \times 4$ three-dimensional mesh. As a result, each node was responsible for the update or evolution of a $3^3 \times 16$ sublattice of the entire problem. The concurrent efficiency of the computation was measured as 95%. The 5% inefficiency is accounted for by a 2% loss due to load imbalance (not all processors doing the same amount of work) and a 3% loss due to communication overhead. It is significant that this low communication overhead is not due to the short range of interaction between the degrees of freedom, as shown in the traditional lattice problems of Chaps. 7 and 8. In fact, most of the variables in the $3^3 \times 16$ sublattice are communicated at least once during an update cycle. The overhead is low because of the proportionally greater amount of computation required for each variable.

We can quantify these remarks by noting that the communication component of the concurrent overhead for this problem on the Caltech/JPL Mark I, II hypercubes follows the relation:

$$f = 1/\varepsilon - 1 = \frac{0.25}{n^{1/3}} \qquad (13\text{-}3)$$

where $n = 3^3 \times 16$ is the grain size. The coefficient of $n^{-1/3}$ is somewhat lower than the value of unity found in Chaps. 7 and 8 for iteratively solved elliptic problems. The lower coefficient reflects the increased calculational complexity of the QCD algorithm compared with the finite-difference and finite-element approximations to the Laplacian. In order to further elaborate this point, let us consider a QCD calculation for SU(m) gauge theory. The calculation involves multiplication of $m \times m$ matrices and has an associated computational cost proportional to m^3; the communication cost is proportional to the number of matrix elements or m^2. Thus, we find that:

$$1/\varepsilon - 1 \quad \propto \quad \frac{1}{m} \frac{1}{n^{1/3}} \frac{t_{comm}}{t_{calc}} \tag{13-4}$$

and decreases as m increases. The measured value in Eq. (13-3) corresponds to the case $m=3$.

An important lesson from the issue of calculational complexity is that one need not be limited to short-ranged interactions; more nonlocal versions (which do occur in practice) are also efficient. This latter point has been experimentally verified–see [Otto 84b].

An important algorithmic constraint on these Monte Carlo calculations is the so-called detailed balance condition. This condition places an important restriction on the update cycle of the concurrent algorithm. In order to satisfy detailed balance, any two points that are "connected" through the fundamental interaction (Lagrangian) must not be updated simultaneously [Otto 84b]. The basic decomposition involves division of the lattice into equal subregions which are assigned to individual nodes. Concurrency is realized by performing parallel Monte Carlo changes of the field within each processor so that N points are being updated at any one time. During this concurrent update, care must be taken to ensure that none of these points are linked in the interaction. This is easily accomplished for QCD by requiring that any two updated points are separated by at least one lattice point that is unchanged at the current step. There arises an analogous constraint in condensed matter Monte Carlo simulations and these require a somewhat more subtle algorithm [Johnson 86] to ensure detailed balance. The simulation of a liquid with irregularly distributed particles affords no obvious method of assuring that adjacent processors do not simultaneously try to move two mutually interacting molecules. In Monte Carlo calculations involving long-range force fields, detailed balance precludes the update of any two particles simultaneously. In such a case, concurrency must be sought not in simultaneous updates but through decomposition of the calculations associated with a single update. This approach has been applied to Coulomb force fields, and has proven quite successful [Fucito 85].

13-8 The "Walking Program"

Before concluding this chapter, it will be useful to discuss an important method of structuring the QCD algorithm in order to simplify the application code. As is the case in much practical programming, there is a right way and a wrong way to write the code.

The issue of concern relates to the previously mentioned loops. The fundamental variables of the calculation are matrices and a loop is a product of these matrices along some closed path through the lattice. On a distributed memory machine such as the hypercube, the encoding of these can become quite difficult since the loop can overlap more than one processor subdomain. Explicitly keeping track of where a given loop crosses processor boundaries is a daunting task, especially in four dimensions!

An effective way to deal with this problem is to devise a walking program for the calculation of loops. Figure 13-7 shows how to describe the shapes of arbitrary loops. A loop is specified by a string of symbols, each of which gives the direction for a single step along the loop. The loop shown is specified by the string: $(+\hat{x}, +\hat{y}, +\hat{x}, +\hat{y}, -\hat{x}, -\hat{x}, -\hat{y}, -\hat{y})$. To compute the loop, we feed the walker routine a starting location and this string as input. The walker reads the first entry of the string, takes a step through the lattice in that direction, and sets a matrix, *answer*, equal to the matrix it finds there. It then reads the next string entry, steps in that direction, and multiplies the matrix it finds there by *answer*. This process continues until the end of the string is reached. At this point, the walker will have walked completely around the loop and *answer* will finally contain the desired result. The walker travels around the loop, carrying the partial answer along with it.

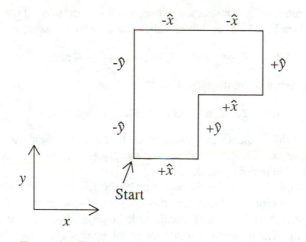

Figure 13-7 The loop corresponding to the walker string $(+\hat{x}, +\hat{y}, +\hat{x}, +\hat{y}, -\hat{x}, -\hat{x}, -\hat{y}, -\hat{y})$.

The beauty of this technique is twofold. Firstly, given a general walker routine, loops of all sizes and shapes are handled with equal ease. All that is required is to construct the appropriate string for the loop. Secondly, this algorithm translates quite easily into a parallel environment. All that needs to be added is a check, at each step, to determine whether a processor boundary is being crossed. If so, the partial result and the remaining string are passed to the appropriate processor. Once a processor passes along its work in this manner, it checks to see if any work requests (consisting of partial answers and strings) have entered its domain. If so, it processes them. Since the loops close, we are insured that once the dust settles, the loop answers will reside in their correct processors. That is, a final answer will land in the processor which contains the start of the loop.

The parallel walker routine allows the computation of loops of arbitrary shape and size to proceed, simply by specifying loop strings. Since the entire QCD algorithm is based on loops, the routine allows the high-level coding of the algorithm to be transparent to issues involving processor boundaries.

13-9 Finite Differences and the Walker Method

It turns out that the walker methodology helps tremendously in writing the QCD code. Can similar ideas be applied elsewhere? The answer seems to be yes. An example is found in finite difference codes, typified by the Laplace relaxation algorithm, described in Chap. 7. In that case, the fundamental step replaces a field variable with the average of its neighbors:

$$\phi_{i,j} \leftarrow \frac{1}{4}\left[\phi_{i+1,j} + \phi_{i,j+1} + \phi_{i-1,j} + \phi_{i,j-1} \right] \qquad (13\text{-}5)$$

A walker program can be constructed to perform this operation. It could start at the center of the stencil (see Fig. 13-8) and then walk according to the string:

$$\left[+\hat{x}, \text{fetch}, -\hat{x}, +\hat{y}, \text{add}, -\hat{y}, -\hat{x}, \text{add}, +\hat{x}, -\hat{y}, \text{add}, +\hat{y} \right]$$

Another string for accomplishing the same task is:

$$\left[+\hat{x}, \text{fetch}, +\hat{y}, -\hat{x}, \text{add}, -\hat{x}, -\hat{y}, \text{add}, -\hat{y}, +\hat{x}, \text{add}, +\hat{y} \right]$$

The entries "fetch," "add" indicate the action to be taken on the field variable(s) at the current site. Note that, in this case, the walker simply passes over some of the sites without using the variable residing there.

The use of this approach would allow coding of the Laplace solver without explicit reference to boundary points. Admittedly, this may represent overkill for the simple finite difference Laplacian problem, and entails added overhead associated with processing of the walker string. The potential importance of the method, however, becomes clear when one realizes that it allows modification of the differential operator and/or the differencing scheme (to arbitrarily complex templates) during execution of the program. For more complex operators and differencing schemes, the overhead of interpreting the string becomes a progressively less important consideration.

The programming methodology described in this section has quite general applicability. By properly designing the parallel implementation we have hidden the processor subdomain boundaries from view (allowing the solver to be easily coded). An added benefit is the enhanced adaptability and potential functionality of the overall program.

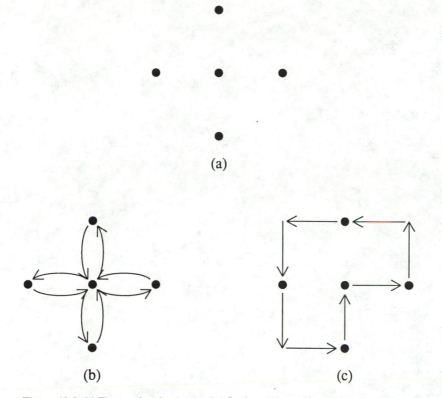

Figure 13-8 (a) The template for the simplest Laplace solver. (b) and (c) are equivalent walker strings for this template.

14

CrOS III: A Specific Implementation of the Programming Environment

14-1 Introduction

In Chap. 4 we presented a virtual concurrent processor so that we could discuss concurrent algorithms in concrete terms. The virtual concurrent processor was made very general to avoid restricting the discussion of the algorithms. However, the virtual concurrent processor was not designed to be implemented efficiently as a real machine, so the implementation issues were intentionally ignored. In this chapter we resume the discussion of communications in a concurrent processor and examine in detail a specific implementation of a crystalline communication system on a practical machine.

We shall give implementations in the C programming language of many of the routines discussed in Chap. 4. The C routines are meant to illustrate the algorithms used to implement the collective routing of data through the concurrent processor. However, the routines as presented are not necessarily the optimal or fullest possible implementations on a real machine. Some features, such as the handling of errors, are treated superficially since a more detailed treatment would detract from the discussion of the algorithms without providing any important benefits. In particular, no effort is made to correctly set the external integers *errno* and *errcnt* that are introduced in Sec. 14-3.

The crystalline operating system that we present in this chapter is called CrOS III. It was designed at Caltech to run efficiently on a specific concurrent processor - the Mark III hypercube described in Chap. 2 - and so will have some features and routines that were not discussed in Chap. 4. In addition to the discussion in this chapter, Appendix E provides a concise definition of CrOS III in the form of manual pages for each of the routines. We begin this chapter with a detailed description of a hardware implementation of the communication channels. Following the discussion of the channels, we discuss in detail the implementation of the basic crystalline communication routines. The implementation of the basic routines will not refer to any particular interconnection topology. Although CrOS III was motivated by a particular design of hypercube, it has been designed to be easily implemented on other machines. Currently it runs on essentially all hypercubes and the shared-memory BBN Butterfly.

Before we can proceed to the implementations of the collective communication routines, we must select an interconnection topology for the ensemble. The fully interconnected topology is impractical for a real machine and is not needed for the applications we have examined in previous chapters. After comparing the features of several topologies, we conclude that the hypercube topology is both adequate for all the applications we have examined and practical to build. In addition, we assume that the control process, whose location has been left unspecified until now, will reside in a separate processing element that will be known as the control processor. Having specified the topology encompassing the nodes of the ensemble and the control processor, we proceed to the discussion of routines that implement collective communications on a hypercube. Emphasis is placed on the algorithms used by the routines rather than other important, but less interesting, details of the implementations.

We then return to the issue raised in Sec. 4-6 of assigning nodes in the ensemble to regions of the decomposition topology. The issue is much more important now, since the hypercube does not have channels connecting all pairs of nodes and we would like adjacent regions of the decomposition topology to be connected by communication channels. We describe an algorithm for assigning nodes to a restricted class of Cartesian grids.

The chapter concludes with some comments on the limitations of the crystalline communication system and introduces a new method of implementing communications, the interrupt-driven approach, which overcomes some of the limitations of the crystalline system. Since none of the applications we examine in this book require an interrupt-driven communication system, a more detailed treatment of the subject is not given here. Finally, a few comments are made on the application of the topics discussed in this chapter to concurrent processors operating in a shared-memory rather than a message-passing environment.

14-2 Implementation of Communication Channels

Before we can discuss the implementation of the crystalline communication system, we must examine some of the details of the communication channels that will be used by the system. The channels provide the only means of communication between the nodes of the ensemble. Only two nodes can be connected by a single channel, so all communications are point-to-point. In contrast, if many nodes resided on a common bus, broadcast communications could be a primitive function. The channels that we consider are implemented in the node hardware and consist of a transmitting component and a receiving component. The transmitting component of one node is connected to the receiving component of the other node and vice versa.

While the transmitting and receiving components of a channel can be implemented in many ways, we will illustrate the important features of a channel by considering one particular implementation based on that used in the Caltech/JPL Mark I, II, and III hypercubes. In this implementation, each receiving component of a channel is associated with a buffer. The transmitting node can write into the channel buffer and the receiving node can read from it. However, the transmitting node must not write into the buffer if it contains data that has not yet been read. Likewise, the receiving node should not attempt to read from a buffer that does not contain valid data. Thus, the channel hardware must provide information on the status of the channel buffer to both the transmitting and receiving nodes.

In the hardware implementation that we are considering, two interrupt lines provide the channel's status information, where one of the lines is connected to the transmitting node and the other to the receiving node. A channel's interrupt lines can either be polled by the processor or cause the processor to be interrupted; in the current implementation we will always use the lines in polled mode. The channel hardware sets the transmit interrupt line when its associated channel buffer is empty, and clears the line otherwise. Similarly, the channel hardware sets the receive interrupt line when its channel buffer is full, and clears the line otherwise. In this implementation of the communication channels, all data must be sent in fixed-length packets whose length is determined by the size of the channel buffer. The data must be sent in packets because the receive interrupt cannot indicate that the buffer is partially full and the transmit interrupt cannot indicate that the buffer is partially empty.

As mentioned previously, a node must have a transmitting and a receiving component for each channel, so that it can both send and receive messages. If the transmitting component and the receiving component of the channel are completely separate, each node connected by a channel can write into the other's channel buffer without interference. Such a channel is known as *full-duplex* since both sides can transmit independently. However, two sets of wires are needed to connect a full-duplex channel since the two sides of the channel are independent. Fewer wires are needed to connect a channel if a *half-duplex* circuit is used. In a half-duplex circuit the same wires are used by both sides of the channel, so only one of the nodes can be transmitting at a time. In the context of the crystalline communication system, using a half-duplex channel does not restrict communication, since in the crystalline system it is required that a write on one side of the channel be complemented by a read on the other.

In general, each node has several such communication channels, each consisting of a channel buffer and receive and transmit interrupt lines. The processor must have a means of addressing which of the channels it wants to access, and specifying whether it wants to transmit or receive. When a packet is read from a channel, the channel is first selected for reading. When the processor attempts to read the packet, only the selected channel sends data to the processor. Likewise, when a packet is to be written to a channel, the channel is first selected for transmitting, so the packet is transmitted by only the selected channel.

Clearly, having only one channel selected for reading is essential because otherwise several channels could try to send different packets to the processor. However, allowing several channels to be selected for transmitting at the same time is a useful feature. No interference can occur as it could if several channels were selected for reading, since the identical packet is being transmitted simultaneously on all selected channels. When we discussed matrix algorithms in Chap. 10, we saw an instance in which being able to write the same packet to several channels at once is desirable. In Sec. 14-5, we implement a broadcast communication routine similar to that introduced in Chap. 4, which writes the same packet to several channels at once. One additional generalization that will prove useful is to allow a packet to be transmitted on selected channels as it is being read from a different channel. We simply note here that allowing simultaneous transmits and receives does not substantially increase the complexity of the nodes' hardware.

While having the ability to perform simultaneous transmits and receives on several channels is a desirable feature, not all concurrent processors have this ability. Even if the processors only allow single channels to transmit or receive at once, the discussion in the following sections will still be useful. However, the implementations of the basic communication routines will be slightly more complicated, since they will have to loop over the indicated channels to simulate the simultaneous channel operations. The basic communication routines will then have the same functionality as those implemented with channels that allow simultaneous transmits and receives. The only difference to keep in mind is that the broadcast algorithm presented in Sec. 14-5 will not always be optimal.

An important issue in the design of the channel that we have overlooked is the size of the channel buffer. Since only full packets can be sent by the channel, if the packet size is much larger than a message, time will be wasted padding the buffer and sending more data on the channel than necessary. However, if the buffer is too small, the overhead of polling the channel is proportionally greater, and the maximum data transfer rate of the channel is reduced.

It has been found in practice that the software overhead associated with polling the channel and transferring data from memory to the channel is substantially greater than the time the channel hardware takes to transfer the data across the channel. Thus, sending a moderate amount of unnecessary data on the channel is not very important compared with performing extra software operations. If data can be transferred into and out of the channel buffer through a direct memory access (DMA) circuit, the major cost becomes that of testing the status of the channel and initializing the DMA controller. In such a system, the packet size can be quite large before it becomes a dominating factor. The Mark III hypercube at Caltech, which has a DMA controller connecting the node memory and channel hardware, uses a channel buffer of 64 bytes. Our present estimates indicate that the buffers could be considerably larger without substantially slowing the transmission of short messages.

14-3 Basic Crystalline Routines

Having defined a specific hardware implementation of the communication channels, we are ready to proceed with the implementation of the CrOS III crystalline communication system. The implementation that we consider will reflect many of the features of the virtual concurrent processor presented in Chap. 4. However, several new features will be added, since the system we describe is meant to be a real system that gives good performance on a real concurrent processor. In addition, we will pay attention to details that were ignored in Chap. 4, such as the detection of communication errors.

Another difference from the discussion of the virtual concurrent processor involves restrictions on the interconnection topology. In the case of the virtual concurrent processor the communication channels are numbered by the processor number of the node on the other side of the channel. Thus, communication is said to be *node-addressed*. In our CrOS III crystalline communication system the basic routines *cread* and *cwrite* implement communication only between nodes directly connected by a communication channel. Since we are not assuming a fully interconnected topology, node-addressed communication is no longer desirable. Instead, we simply number the channels with consecutive numbers starting at 0. This type of communication system is said to be *channel-addressed*.

One of the features we add here to *cwrite* is the ability to send a message to several channels simultaneously, instead of only one channel. The channels on which the message is to be sent can be efficiently specified by a bit field. A bit field is a data object whose individual binary digits represent quantities that can assume only two states. Thus, a bit field consisting of one bit for each channel can specify the channels on which a message is to be sent. The bits corresponding to the desired channels are set while the rest are cleared. The bit field specifying the desired channels is known as a *channel mask*, which replaces the channel number as an argument to *cwrite* in the current implementation. Thus, *cwrite* is defined with the calling syntax given in Code 14-1.

```
int cwrite(buffer, chan, nbytes)
char *buffer;          /* pointer to buffer */
unsigned int chan;     /* channel mask */
int nbytes;            /* number of bytes to transmit */
```

Code 14-1 The Routine *cwrite*

The channel mask, *chan*, is an unsigned integer since a bit field has no sign associated with it. We define the following special cases for the arguments of *cwrite*. If the channel mask is 0, indicating the message is to be sent on no channels, the call to *cwrite* is ignored and it should not be complemented by a *cread* on the other side of the channel. However, if the channel mask is nonzero and the byte count is 0, the call to *cwrite* must still be complemented by a call to *cread* since a message whose length is 0 is sent to the destination node. Sending messages of length 0 is sometimes useful if some nodes have nothing to write, since all nodes typically read and write together when crystalline communications are used.

The data sent by *cwrite* consist of a header that specifies the length of the message, the message itself, and a trailer that consists of the checksum of the header and the data. A header is necessary so that the corresponding *cread* on the other side of the channel can determine the length of the message. The checksum is useful because it allows the complimentary *cread* routine to detect communication errors when the data are read. While *cwrite* can easily calculate the checksum in software, generating the checksum in the channel hardware is relatively simple and allows a faster implementation of both *cwrite* and *cread*. If the hardware calculates the checksum, *cwrite* first writes the message except for the checksum and then instructs the channel hardware to append the checksum. Since at the user level, the length of the message is specified in terms of bytes rather than packets, and a header and trailer are added to the message, the number of bytes that *cwrite* transmits may not be a whole number of packets. However, at the system level the channel requires that data be transmitted only as whole packets, so if the data does not fill the last packet in the message, *cwrite* must pad it with additional bytes to fill the packet.

Having discussed the format of data to be sent by *cwrite*, we now describe how *cwrite* interacts with the channel hardware in order to send the packets containing the data. The process of sending packets on the selected channels consists of two basic steps. First, *cwrite* writes one packet, which the channel hardware simultaneously transmits on each of the channels indicated by the channel mask *chan*. After writing the packet, *cwrite* polls the transmit interrupt line for each of the indicated channels until all the channel buffers are empty. The length of time that *cwrite* spends polling the interrupt lines is indefinite, leading to the possibility of deadlock if the destination node never calls *cread* to empty its channel buffer by reading its contents.

After determining that the buffers of the selected channels are empty, *cwrite* repeats the cycle of sending a packet and polling the transmit interrupt lines until all the data are transmitted; *cwrite* will not return until the whole message has been transmitted and read by the destination node. Unless an error occurs, *cwrite* returns the number of bytes in the message. Communication errors cannot be detected by *cwrite* since it receives no acknowledgement from the receiving node, but other types of errors may occur. If the buffer refers to data residing outside of the user's data space and the node has memory-management facilities, *cwrite* should indicate the error. The channel mask is invalid if it specifies nonexistent channels, and the number of bytes in the message could be too large for the system to handle.

The routine *cwrite* indicates an error condition by returning −1 and identifies the specific type of error by setting the external integer *errno*. All the routines in CrOS III use the convention of returning −1 to indicate an error and identifying the type of error by setting *errno*. Since *errno* is not reset after each error, it should only be examined after an error occurs, as indicated by a return value of −1.

In order to incorporate the enhancements in the channel hardware that we discussed in the previous section, we add an additional argument to the version of *cread* discussed in Chap. 4. The new argument is a channel mask indicating the channels on which the message is to be forwarded as it is being read from the incoming channel buffer. To avoid problems with deadlock, the message must not be forwarded to the channel from which it is being read. In addition, the incoming channel is also specified as a channel mask, so that the channels are always labeled the same way. Thus, the capability of the channel hardware to read a message and forward it in one operation is reflected in CrOS III. We note that allowing *cread* to forward messages as it is reading them requires relaxing the requirement that *cread* always be complemented by *cwrite*. A call to *cread* may now also be complemented by another call to *cread* that forwards the message. Of course, *cwrite* must still be called at the source node since *cread* cannot originate a message. The usage of *cread* is defined in Code 14-2.

```
int cread(buffer, inchan, outchan, nbytes)
char *buffer;                 /* pointer to buffer */
unsigned int inchan;          /* mask of incoming channel */
unsigned int outchan;         /* mask of forwarding channels */
int nbytes;                   /* maximum number of bytes to read */
```

Code 14-2 The Routine *cread*

The routine *cread* performs a sequence of operations complementary to those performed by *cwrite*. In order to read a packet, *cread* first polls the receive interrupt line of the channel specified by *inchan* until its channel buffer is full. As with *cwrite*, the length of time that *cread* spends polling the interrupt line is indefinite, leading to the possibility that *cread* will never return if the source node does not fill the buffer by sending a packet. When the incoming channel is ready, a packet is read from the channel buffer of the channel specified by *inchan*. As the packet is being read, the channel hardware simultaneously transmits the packet on any channels indicated by *outchan*. The transmit interrupt lines of any forwarding channels are then polled until all of their channel buffers are empty as in *cwrite*.

The number of bytes and, hence, the number of packets to be read by *cread* is determined by the message length, which is prepended to the message sent by *cwrite*. After reading the first packet of the message, *cread* knows how many additional packets it must read. The header containing the message length is kept by *cread* and the remaining bytes of the first packet are stored in *buffer*. The argument *nbytes* specifies the maximum number of bytes that *cread* will store in memory. If the message length exceeds the maximum, *cread* truncates the message and returns −1 to indicate the error. In addition, the number of bytes in the untruncated message is saved in the external variable *errcnt*. In any case, the whole message is always read from the incoming channel and transmitted on any forwarding channels so that the complementary call to *cwrite* can finish sending the whole message and each of the receiving nodes can always receive the whole message.

When *cread* receives the last packet in the message, it obtains the checksum appended to the data by *cwrite*. Any additional bytes following the checksum that were used to fill the last packet are discarded, though they must be read from the channel buffer in order to empty the buffer, allowing the next transmission to occur. By keeping its own checksum of the data in the message, *cread* can compare the two checksums to determine whether any communication errors occurred. If the checksums match, no errors occurred, but if they are different, *cread* returns −1 to indicate the error. The appropriate value of *errno* is set to identify the communication error. Thus, even though the transmitting node cannot detect the communication error, the error can be detected before the data are used in subsequent computations. Since the transmitting node does not know an error occurred, it cannot simply retransmit the data without defining a higher-level protocol. However, in the present context, the error rate on the channels can usually be made low enough that error correction is not an important need. In addition to the errors just described, *cread* can report errors in any of its arguments, as was the case with *cwrite*. In particular, *cread* reports an error if the channel mask *inchan* indicates more than one channel.

In some cases, an application program may want to forward the incoming message without keeping a copy in local memory. If *buffer* has the special value defined by the macro NULLPTR, the data is only written to the channels indicated by *outchan*. In addition, we define several other special cases for the arguments of *cread*. If *outchan* is 0, the message is read into memory without forwarding on any channels. If *inchan* is 0, the call to *cread* is ignored, and it should not be be complemented by a *cwrite* on the other side of the channel. However, if *inchan* is not 0, and the byte count is 0, a call to *cwrite* must still complement the call to *cread*, even though *cread* will not write any bytes into memory.

We are now ready to examine the synchronizing effects of the crystalline routines *cwrite* and *cread* in more detail than in Sec. 4-3. In particular, we want to justify our decision to prevent *cwrite* from returning until the destination node calls *cread*. While the implementation of *cwrite* would be more analogous to that of *cread* if it first polled the channel status and then transmitted a packet, such an implementation leads to an undesirable feature in the synchronizing condition that *cwrite* imposes. We illustrate the problem by considering the effect of writing a message that is short enough to be sent in a single packet. If *cwrite* polled the channel status before sending the message, it could return before the destination node called *cread*, since the message is sent in a single packet. However, if the message required more than one packet to be sent, *cwrite* could not return until the destination node called *cread*, since the second packet could not be sent until the first was read. Thus, the synchronizing condition imposed by *cwrite* would depend on the message length and on the size of the channel buffer.

A more severe problem than the dependence of the synchronizing conditions on the size of the channel buffer, is that the response of *cwrite* to a programming error also depends on the size of the channel buffer. To illustrate the problem, we consider a programming error in which two nodes write to each other at the same time. Such a situation is an obvious error since we have stated that a call to *cwrite* must be complemented by a call to *cread* in the destination node. If both nodes attempt to write messages that require more than one packet to send, deadlock occurs after they both write their first packet, since neither node can call *cread* to read the incoming message until it has finished writing its message. However, if both nodes wrote a single packet message, deadlock would not occur because each node could write the single packet into the channel buffer without waiting for the destination node to call *cread*. Then after calling *cwrite*, both nodes could call *cread* to read the messages. Thus, the effect of making a programming error would depend on the length of the message and the size of the channel buffer. Such a situation is a serious problem because simply changing the length of a message or moving the program to a concurrent processor with a different packet size could cause a working program to break, or conversely, cause a formally incorrect program to work.

A preferable choice is to ensure that *cwrite* always causes deadlock when it is used incorrectly, regardless of the message length or the packet size. By polling the status of the channel buffer after sending a packet, rather than before, we guarantee that *cwrite* can never return before the destination node calls its complementary *cread*. The channel status does not need to be tested before writing a packet since *cwrite* always leaves the channel ready for the next packet to be written. With such an implementation of *cwrite*, the synchronizing condition that it imposes is exactly analogous to that of *cread*: neither routine can ever return until its complement is called.

Since we are introducing a crystalline communication system that is meant to provide communication facilities for real application programs, we expand our list of basic routines to include three additional routines. Two of the routines, *vwrite* and *vread*, are closely related to *cwrite* and *cread* but are more flexible in the types of data that they can handle. While *cwrite* and *cread* can only write and read contiguous blocks of memory, *vwrite* and *vread* write and read vectors whose elements are regularly spaced in memory. The ability to write such vectors is very useful in certain problems in which the data to be communicated are not contiguous. A simple example is sending the first row of a matrix when the matrix is stored by columns. Without the ability to send vectors, the user would have to first gather the data into a contiguous block and then use *cwrite* to transmit the data, a process that is cumbersome and inefficient.

Instead of accepting only the total number of bytes to transmit as *cwrite* does, *vwrite* requires as input the size of the data items, the separation between data items, and the total number of such items. The usage of *vwrite* is defined in Code 14-3.

```
int vwrite(buffer, chan, size, offset, nitems)
char *buffer;              /* pointer to buffer */
unsigned int chan;         /* channel mask */
int size;                  /* size of data items in bytes */
int offset;                /* offset of data items in bytes */
int nitems;                /* number of data items to transmit */
```

Code 14-3 The Routine *vwrite*

Any vector whose elements are regularly spaced can be specified as an argument. As with *cwrite*, a call to *vwrite* must be complemented by a call to *vread* in the destination node. The implementation of *vwrite* is identical to that of *cwrite*, except that when it writes packets to the channel, it writes *size* bytes, increments the memory pointer by *offset* bytes, and writes another *size* bytes, until the packet is full. If the packet becomes full before all *size* bytes are written, *vwrite* finishes writing the data item in the next packet. We note that *offset* can be negative so that data objects can be sent in reverse order from *buffer*. Another distinction of *vwrite* is that the value of *nitems* is used as the message header instead of the byte count as in the case of *cwrite*. The polling of the channels and the resulting synchronizing condition that *vwrite* imposes is identical to that of *cwrite*. A checksum is also sent with the message in the same way as in *cwrite* and the error conditions that *vwrite* can report are similar.

The routine *vread* incorporates the same conventions in its arguments as *vwrite*. The argument *nbytes* in *cread* is replaced by the three arguments, *size*, *offset*, and *nitems*.

The new arguments have the same meaning as in *vwrite*, except that *nitems* is the maximum number of data items that *vread* will read. The actual number of data items read is determined by the number sent by *vwrite* as indicated in the message header. The usage of *vread* is defined in Code 14-4.

```
int vread(buffer, inchan, outchan, size, offset, nitems)
char *buffer;                   /* pointer to buffer */
unsigned int inchan;            /* mask of incoming channel */
unsigned int outchan;           /* mask of forwarding channels */
int size;                       /* size of data items in bytes */
int offset;                     /* offset of data items in bytes */
int nitems;                     /* maximum number of items to read */
```

Code 14-4 The Routine *vread*

The implementation of *vread* is again identical to that of *cread*, except that the data items are not written into memory in a contiguous block. Instead, the first item is written at the start of *buffer*, the second item is written at byte number *offset* of *buffer*, and so on. The procedure continues until either all the data items in the message have been read from the channel and stored in memory, or the maximum number of data items specified by *nitems* has been reached. The routine *vread* and its complementary *vwrite* must agree on the size of the data items, but they do not have to use the same value of *offset*. A communication error can be detected by *vread* by comparing the checksum it calculates with the one that *vwrite* appended to the message. The errors that *vread* can report are similar to those associated with *cread*.

The final routine that we introduce in this section is *rdstat*, which provides information about the status of the channels. Since *cwrite* and *vwrite* always leave a channel ready to write another packet, checking the transmit interrupt lines is pointless. However, checking whether a message is ready to be received may be useful in some cases. For instance, an application may increment a counter while waiting for a message to arrive in order to measure the amount of time it had to wait. By calling *rdstat*, the application can determine when the message arrives so it can stop incrementing the counter and call *cread* or *vread* to read the message.

```
int rdstat(chan)
unsigned int chan;              /* mask of channels to check */
```

Code 14-5 The Routine *rdstat*

The routine *rdstat*, defined in Code 14-5, tests the status of the channels indicated by the channel mask *chan*. If messages are ready to be received on all of the indicated channels, *rdstat* returns 1. If the channel mask is invalid because it specifies a nonexistent channel, *rdstat* returns −1 to flag the error. Otherwise, it returns 0.

14-4 The Hypercube Interconnection Topology

In the previous section we discussed the implementation of the basic crystalline communication routines without explicit reference to the interconnection topology of the concurrent processor. However, before we continue with the discussion of implementing the collective communication routines, we must select an interconnection topology. Without a specific topology we cannot describe algorithms that implement the collective routines. The topology we select should be sufficiently general to be useful on a rich variety of problems, yet practical enough that a real concurrent processor can be built with that topology.

First, we shall briefly examine the fully interconnected topology that we assumed for our virtual concurrent processor in Chap. 4. Having all pairs of nodes directly connected by a communication channel is clearly the most general interconnection scheme, which is why it was adopted for the virtual concurrent processor. However, building a real machine with so many connections is completely impractical unless the size of the machine is limited to relatively few nodes. If the ensemble consists of N nodes, each node must have $N-1$ communication channels so it can communicate with all the other nodes in the system. The total number of channels in the ensemble is then $N(N-1)/2$. The number of channels required per node and the total number of channels, which are usually connected by some type of backplane, increases so rapidly with the number of nodes that building a large system using the fully interconnected topology is out of the question.

In Chap. 9, we saw that only a ring topology is required for problems with long-range interactions. For an ensemble to be connected as a ring, each node needs two communication channels, regardless of the total number of nodes in the ensemble. Since the number of channels per node is fixed, a very large system can be connected as a ring. The ability to scale a concurrent processor architecture easily to larger systems is very desirable since this allows application programs to be written in a manner which is independent of ensemble size. However, the ring topology has a serious drawback because the number of channels is so restricted. Efficiently programming a problem that requires a richer interconnection topology than the ring may not be possible on such machines. Many problems require that data be sent between nodes that are not directly connected by a communication channel, and the maximum distance between nodes grows rapidly in a ring topology. In contrast to the fully interconnected topology in which all nodes are directly connected, the maximum distance between nodes in the ring is $N/2$. Such a rapid growth in the maximum distance between nodes motivates us to consider other connection topologies.

By examining the extremes of the fully interconnected topology and the ring topology, we can see the trade-offs involved in selecting an interconnection topology for a real machine. An ensemble with few channels per node, such as in the ring case, is easily built and scales easily as the size of the ensemble grows, but the maximum distance between nodes grows rapidly, restricting its usefulness. On the other hand, a machine with many channels per node, such as one using the fully interconnected topology, is very general since all nodes are directly connected by a communication channel, but it is

not practical for a large system since the number of channels required becomes prohibitive with increasing ensemble size.

Keeping these trade-offs in mind, we consider the communication requirements of
some of the algorithms presented in previous chapters. Several of the applications, such
as the matrix problems described in Chap. 10, require only a two-dimensional grid connection. An ensemble with such an interconnection topology can easily be built since the
number of channels per node is fixed, as it is in the ring topology. A two-dimensional
grid connection with periodic boundaries requires four channels per node, regardless of
the total number of nodes in the ensemble. Since the number of channels per node is not
affected by the system size, the two-dimensional grid can be used to build large systems.
The maximum distance between nodes in a square grid with periodic boundaries, i.e., a
torus, is $\sqrt{N}$, where N is the total number of nodes in the ensemble. Thus, we see that
the two-dimensional grid topology requires twice as many channels per node as the ring
topology but is more flexible because more nodes are directly connected by a channel,
and the maximum distance between nodes grows more slowly as the size of the ensemble
is increased.

Another important feature of the two-dimensional grid connection is that the ring
topology is contained within the grid. By ignoring certain communication channels, a
ring topology can be obtained for applications that require only a ring connection. The
results for the two-dimensional grid can be generalized to any number of dimensions.
The number of channels required for a d-dimensional grid is $2d$ and is independent of N,
the number of nodes in the ensemble. The maximum distance between nodes in a d-
dimensional grid with periodic boundaries is $N^{1/d}$. All grid connections scale nicely with
the ensemble size, though the nodes become more complicated as the dimensionality of
the grid increases since the number of communication channels per node also increases.
Another desirable feature of grid connections is that grids of each lower dimensionality
are contained within the topology.

Though grid topologies are convenient for solving many problems, a grid whose
dimensionality is fixed is not always adequate. Consider the case of the Fast Fourier
Transform. The algorithm given in Chap. 11 requires that the dimensionality of the grid
increase as the number of nodes in the ensemble increases. An interconnection structure
whose dimensionality depends on the number of nodes is the hypercube interconnection
topology. The hypercube topology can easily be described inductively. A zero-
dimensional hypercube, a 0-cube for short, consists of a single node with no communication channels, i.e., a standard sequential computer. A 1-cube is constructed from two 0-
cubes by connecting them with a single communication channel. A 2-cube is constructed
from two 1-cubes by connecting their corresponding nodes with an additional channel,
forming a square with the nodes at the vertices and the communication channels on the
edges. In general, a d-cube is constructed by connecting the corresponding nodes of two
$(d-1)$-cubes with an additional channel.

The number of nodes in a hypercube is $N = 2^d$, and the number of communication
channels per node is d. Thus, we see that the number of channels required per node
increases as the size of the ensemble increases, unlike the fixed-dimensional grid

topologies. In terms of N, the number of channels is $\log_2 N$. Although the number of channels per node increases with N, the increase is slow enough that comparatively large ensembles are practical. The maximum distance between nodes of a hypercube grows more slowly with increasing N than any fixed-dimensional grid; the maximum distance is $\log_2 N$. As in the case of the fixed-dimensional grid, the hypercube contains grids of each lower dimensionality.

By now the direction of our discussion should be apparent. The hypercube is adequate for all the applications we have discussed so far, yet it is practical for fairly large ensembles. A balance between the number of channels per node and the maximum distance between nodes is achieved, since both increase logarithmically with the total number of nodes in the ensemble. In order to discuss the implementation of the crystalline communication system in concrete terms, we have chosen to use the hypercube interconnection topology in the remainder of the chapter. While much of the discussion will be specific to the hypercube, many of the general ideas can be applied to other topologies.

Before resuming discussion of the implementation of the crystalline communication system, we need a specific numbering of the nodes and channels in the hypercube. A d-dimensional hypercube consists of 2^d nodes, each of which is connected to one other node in each dimension. Thus each node requires d channels. The processor number of a node is conveniently chosen to be a d-bit binary number where the ith bit of the processor number represents the coordinate of the node in the ith dimension of the hypercube. This immediately suggests a convenient convention for the local numbering of channels connected to a given node, since any two neighboring nodes in the hypercube have processor numbers that differ in exactly one bit position. Thus, in a 3-cube, channels 0, 1, and 2 connect node 0 to nodes 1, 2, and 4, respectively. Fig. 14-1 illustrates this numbering scheme for a hypercube of dimensionality 3.

The important point here is that all nodes connected by a communication channel differ by a single bit in their processor numbers. The number of bits that differ between the processor numbers of two nodes gives the "distance" between the nodes. In programming examples using the hypercube topology, we will assume that in addition to the variables *procnum* and *nproc*, which contain the processor number and the total number of nodes, respectively, the variable *doc* (dimension of cube) will contain the hypercube dimension.

Because of the symmetry of the hypercube, any node could be assigned the processor number 0 arbitrarily, using the hypercube topology and the numbering scheme to determine the remaining processor numbers. However, we do have one asymmetry in the concurrent processor, namely the control process. Until now, we have said nothing about where the control process resides. In order to facilitate the discussion of the collective routines involving the control process, we now assign the control process to its own processing element, which is distinct from the nodes composing the hypercube. We allow only one of the nodes in the hypercube to communicate directly with the control processor through a communication channel that is identical to those connecting the nodes in the ensemble. The node connected to the control processor will be assigned a

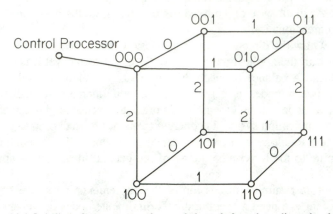

Figure 14-1 Labeling of processor numbers and channels for a three-dimensional hypercube.

processor number of 0. A variable *cpmask* is defined which contains a channel mask to specify the channel connecting node 0 and the control processor. Of course, the number of the channel connecting node 0 and the control processor must be at least as large as the largest available hypercube dimension. In the nodes other than 0, *cpmask* contains 0 so that any attempted communication with the control processor is ignored. The variable *cpmask* will be used in Sec. 14-6, which describes the collective routines implementing communications between the nodes and the control process.

14-5 Collective Communication Routines

Having decided to restrict our discussion to a concurrent processor with a hypercube interconnection topology, we see more clearly the second reason given in Chap. 4 for using collective communication routines. In addition to providing a conceptual grouping to guide our thinking, the collective routines allow machine dependencies in their implementation to be hidden from the application program. In this section we will examine implementations on a hypercube of the collective routines introduced in Sec. 4–4, using the basic communication routines described in Sec. 14-3. In addition, we introduce two new routines in this section that are part of CrOS III. Chapters 21 and 22 have other useful communication utilities which we consider as part of a user library rather than the basic CrOS III system.

14-5.1 cshift

The first collective routine we will implement is the simplest one, *cshift*. The purpose of *cshift* is to allow a group of nodes to both write and read messages among themselves without the application program specifying which nodes write first and which nodes read first. For instance, a pair of nodes can exchange messages, and a group of nodes can pass messages one step around a ring using *cshift*. The essential feature is that *cshift* is complemented on the other side of a channel by itself, rather than by a different routine. Since all the nodes in applications for which the crystalline communication routines are useful typically both read and write together, using *cshift* instead of *cwrite* and *cread* makes programming such applications much easier. In fact, *cshift* and the other collective communication routines we discuss in this section should eliminate the need to explicitly use *cwrite* and *cread* in many application programs.

Stating the purpose of *cshift* makes most of its implementation obvious. It must call both *cwrite* and *cread*, but the order in which it calls them must be different for different nodes. Since the only available means of distinguishing the nodes is their processor numbers, the order of reading and writing must be based on only a node's processor number and the hypercube topology.

As discussed above, an important feature of the scheme that we use for assigning processor numbers to the nodes of the hypercube is that nodes connected by a communication channel differ by a single bit in their processor numbers. Thus, nodes with an even number of one bits in their processor numbers are only connected to nodes with an odd number of one bits in their processor numbers, and vice versa. Thus, we can use the number of one bits in a node's processor number to determine whether the node reads or writes first in *cshift*.

Since a node's processor number does not change, we can calculate the number of one bits in an initialization routine to avoid recalculating it every time *cshift* is called. Instead of storing the number of one bits, we should just store a flag indicating whether the number of one bits is even. Let us assume that the initialization has been performed and the result stored in the variable *iseven*. If the number of one bits in a node's processor number is even, then *iseven* contains 1; otherwise, it contains 0.

Given the initialized variable *iseven*, the implementation of *cshift* is almost trivial, and is given in Code 14-6. The implementation shows that we have changed two of the arguments of *cshift* from the calling sequence of *vm_shift* introduced in Sec. 4-4. Instead of using the channel number, we specify the channels on which the outgoing data are to be written with the channel mask *outchan*. Likewise, the channel from which the message is to be read is indicated by a channel mask for consistency with the way the output channels are specified. The value returned by *cshift* is the number of bytes read unless an error occurs, in which case −1 is returned.

```
extern int iseven;
int cshift(inbuf, inchan, inbytes, outbuf, outchan, outbytes)
char *inbuf;              /* pointer to buffer for incoming data */
unsigned int inchan;      /* mask of channel to read */
int inbytes;              /* maximum number of bytes to read */
char *outbuf;             /* pointer to buffer for outgoing data */
unsigned int outchan;     /* mask of channels to write */
int outbytes;             /* number of bytes to write */
{
      int rstatus, wstatus;
      if(iseven) {
            wstatus = cwrite(outbuf, outchan, outbytes);
            rstatus = cread(inbuf, inchan, 0, inbytes);
      }
      else {
            rstatus = cread(inbuf, inchan, 0, inbytes);
            wstatus = cwrite(outbuf, outchan, outbytes);
      }
      if(wstatus == -1) return(wstatus);
      else return(rstatus);
}
```

Code 14-6 The Routine *cshift*

In the current implementation of *cshift*, the buffers provided by the application for the incoming and outgoing messages must not overlap. Otherwise, *cshift* corrupts the outgoing data in the nodes in which it calls *cread* before calling *cwrite*. However, in many applications having the incoming data overwrite the outgoing data is desirable, since the outgoing data are no longer needed after being transmitted. Thus, a useful enhancement to *cshift* as presented here would allow *outbuf* and *inbuf* to be identical. Such an enhancement could be implemented in several ways. The most obvious implementation involves copying the contents of *outbuf* into a temporary buffer in those nodes where *cread* is called first. After calling *cread*, *cshift* calls *cwrite* to transmit the data in the temporary buffer. In order to avoid problems with the availability of a temporary buffer of adequate size, *cshift* could declare a buffer of some reasonable size and transfer the message in pieces no larger than the temporary buffer.

If the communication channels of a particular machine make use of full-duplex communication, the implementation could use the channel buffers as the temporary buffer by alternating between writing a single packet into the channel buffer and then reading an incoming packet. Of course, *cshift* would directly access the communication channels in such an implementation, rather than using *cwrite* and *cread*. Using the channel buffer as the temporary buffer is faster than copying the outgoing message into a buffer in memory, which involves copying the message and additional time. However, such an implementation may not be optimal in a concurrent processor with half-duplex communication channels, because both sides of the channel cannot write simultaneously in all cases. To prevent problems arising from both sides of a channel attempting to write simultaneously, a node must test to determine whether the node on the other side of the channel is writing a packet before writing its own packet. Such a test slows the data transfer rate, and is not needed in an implementation that requires writes on a channel to be complemented by reads, such as *cwrite* and *cread*. Thus, we see that when *inbuf* and *outbuf* are the same in *cshift*, the communication speed depends on the details of the hardware implementation of the channels. In order to obtain maximum communication speed on any system, *inbuf* and *outbuf* should refer to distinct regions of application memory.

Several additional features are built into the standard CrOS III definition of *cshift* that are not included in the simplified definition of Code 14-6. In addition to allowing *inbuf* and *outbuf* to be identical, the special cases already discussed for *cwrite* and *cread* are supported, such as the suppression of the read or write when the channel mask is 0. One additional special case is provided to allow for easier programming of applications that use periodic boundaries. An important feature of a good implementation of a hypercube application is that a specific dimensionality of the hypercube not be programmed into the implementation. If the algorithm uses a two-dimensional grid topology and requires that each node writes a message to its left neighbor and reads a message from its right neighbor, periodic boundaries do not cause any problems for *cshift*. However, if the application is run with only one node in the grid direction in which the communication occurs, *cshift* no longer works because the node has no neighbors with which to trade messages, so both *inchan* and *outchan* are 0. The application will still work in such a situation if the contents of *outbuf* are copied to *inbuf*, as if the node had sent a message to itself. Since calling *cshift* with both *inchan* and *outchan* set to 0 has no other meaning, no ambiguity arises from adding such a copying feature to *cshift*. In particular, if non-periodic boundaries were used, *cshift* might also be called with *inchan* and *outchan* set to 0 to avoid unnecessary conditionals in the application program. However, in such a case the data in *inbuf* is ignored anyway, since the application would not try to use data from outside the boundary of the decomposition.

14-5.2 vshift

One of the new routines we introduce in this section is the collective communication routine, *vshift*, which is similar to *cshift* except that it uses *vwrite* and *vread* instead of *cwrite* and *cread* in its implementation. All the comments on the use of *cshift* and its special features apply to *vshift*, except that *vshift* will work correctly for identical values of *inbuf* and *outbuf* only if *insize* and *outsize* and *inoffset* and *outoffset* are also identical. If all three pairs of arguments are not identical, the special feature does not apply and errors may result. Since the implementations of *cshift* and *vshift* are so similar, we will not repeat the previous discussion. As in *vwrite* and *vread*, the byte counts are replaced with the size of the data items, their offset from each other, and their number. The calling syntax is given in Code 14-7.

```
int vshift(inbuf, inchan, insize, inoffset, initems, outbuf, outchan, outsize, outoffset, outitems)
char *inbuf;                            /* pointer to buffer for incoming data */
unsigned int inchan;                    /* mask of channel to read */
int insize;                             /* size of incoming data items */
int inoffset;                           /* offset of incoming data items */
int initems;                            /* maximum number of items to read */
char *outbuf;                           /* pointer to buffer for outgoing data */
unsigned int outchan;                   /* mask of channels to write */
int outsize;                            /* size of outgoing data items */
int outoffset;                          /* offset of outgoing data items */
int outitems;                           /* number of items to write */
```

Code 14-7 The Routine *vshift*

14-5.3 broadcast

The next collective communication routine we examine is *broadcast*. Instead of implementing a version of *broadcast* that is as general as the one described in Sec. 4-4, we impose a restriction on which nodes can be included in a broadcast. Since specifying a list of all nodes involved in the broadcast is rather cumbersome, we restrict broadcasts to *subcubes* within the hypercube topology. A subcube is a hypercube whose dimensionality is less than or equal to the dimensionality of the full hypercube being used by the application. An important feature of subcubes is that when the hypercube is mapped onto decomposition topologies using the specific *gridmap* routines that we discuss in Sec. 14-7, all of the nodes along a dimension of the topology comprise a subcube. Thus, *broadcast* is useful in matrix algorithms for sending a submatrix from one node to all other nodes along a row of the matrix as described in Chap. 10. Since a subset of the available channels span any subcube, a node can uniquely specify a subcube by indicating the desired subset of channels. A channel mask is an efficient means of specifying the subset of channels involved in the broadcast.

All nodes involved in the subcube broadcast must specify the same subset of channels and the same source node. The source node then writes the message in its buffer on the indicated channels. Since all the nodes in the subcube are not connected to the source node by a communication channel, some of the nodes must retransmit the message received from the source node. The broadcast algorithm is a tree algorithm that results in each node in the subcube receiving a single copy of the message sent by the source node.

Before treating the more general case, we will examine the algorithm for broadcasting to a hypercube when the source node is node 0. The procedure for broadcasting to a 0-cube is trivial since node 0 is the only node in the system. The situation is barely more complicated for a 1-cube since the only possibility is for node 0 to send the message to node 1. The procedure for broadcasting to a 2-cube is similar to that for a 1-cube since a 2-cube consists of two 1-cubes whose corresponding nodes are connected by an additional communication channel. Node 2 corresponds to node 0 and node 3 corresponds to node 1. Thus, node 2 sends the message to node 3 and node 0 sends the message to node 1. Since node 2 is connected to node 0, node 0 can send the message to node 2.

The broadcast algorithm continues by repeating the same procedure for each higher dimension. The broadcast tree of a d-cube contains broadcast trees for two $(d-1)$-cubes with node 0 sending the message on the one additional channel connecting it to the second $(d-1)$-cube. The broadcast tree is illustrated in Fig. 14-2 for a 4-cube.

Broadcast Tree for 4-cube

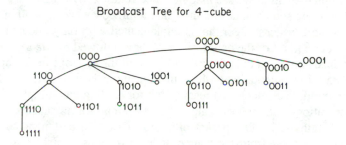

Figure 14-2 *broadcast* tree for a four-dimensional hypercube.

Having described the broadcast tree, we must now design an algorithm that allows each node in the tree to determine on which channel to read and on which channels, if any, to retransmit the message. As with *cshift*, the determination can be based on a knowledge only of the hypercube topology and the node's processor number. The channel on which to receive the broadcast message will be indicated by the channel mask *rchan*, and the channels on which to retransmit the message will be indicated by the channel mask *wchan*. By examining Fig. 14-2, we see that *rchan* consists of only the rightmost one bit in the node's processor number, and *wchan* is the mask of all channel numbers less than *rchan*. In the special case of the source node (node 0), *rchan* is not used and *wchan* contains all the channels in the hypercube.

Now we are ready to generalize the algorithm for broadcasting from node 0 to a full hypercube to allow it to broadcast to a subcube using any node as the source node. The method of generalizing the previous algorithm consists of one transformation of each node's processor number, and an additional condition for determining *rchan* and *wchan*. The transformation consists of combining the node's processor number and the source node's processor number with the exclusive-OR operation. The exclusive-OR operation leaves a one bit in the bit locations where the two processor numbers differ and a zero bit where they are identical. The effect of the exclusive-OR operation is to temporarily renumber the nodes of the subcube so that the source node becomes node 0. Thus, we can use the previous algorithm, which specifies how to broadcast from node 0, to broadcast to the whole hypercube using any node as the source node.

In order to restrict the broadcast to a subcube, we impose the additional condition that only those channels spanning the subcube are to be used in determining *rchan* and *wchan*. With the additional condition, *rchan* specifies the channel corresponding to the rightmost one bit in the transformed processor number that is also one of the channels spanning the subcube. Likewise, *wchan* is the mask of all channel numbers less than *rchan* that are also contained in the mask of channels spanning the subcube. For the special case of the source node, *wchan* is the same as the mask of channels spanning the subcube.

We have now taken the algorithm for broadcasting from node 0 to the whole hypercube and generalized it so that any node can broadcast a message to any subcube. We present the routine that implements the general broadcast algorithm in Code 14-8.

From this implementation we see that the value returned by *broadcast* is the value returned by *cwrite* in the source node and the value returned by *cread* in all other nodes. We also note that the broadcast algorithm is implemented with only one call to a basic communication routine in all of the nodes, since we have allowed *cwrite* to write to multiple channels at once and *cread* to both read and forward the message in one operation.

If the hardware implementation of the communications is as described in Sec. 14-2, so that writing on multiple channels and reading and forwarding on multiple channels are actually single operations, the broadcast algorithm is optimal for all subcube dimensions and all message lengths. The first packet of a broadcast to a d-dimensional subcube arrives at the nodes farthest from the source node in d steps, which is the minimum number of steps possible with the hypercube topology. Each additional packet in the message takes one unit of time since each node in the broadcast tree forwards it in one operation. Thus, the algorithm must be optimal since each packet cannot require less than a single operation.

However, if the channels were implemented so that each reading and writing operation was done separately, the broadcast algorithm would not be optimal for all subcube dimensions and all message lengths. In broadcasting to a d-dimensional subcube, the source node would always need d operations to transmit a packet, since it has d channels on which it must write the packet. If the message were broadcast in a chain with the source node at the middle of the chain, only two operations would be needed to broadcast each packet. While the first packet would take longer to arrive at the furthest nodes when $d > 2$, if the message were many packets long, the smaller number of steps per packet would make the chain broadcast a better algorithm. This type of broadcast was called a *pipe* in Sec. 10-3.2, and will be elaborated on in Sec. 20-4 as the better *split_pipe*. Thus, we see that properly designed channel hardware makes optimal subcube broadcasts easier to obtain. A more detailed discussion of broadcast algorithms for hypercubes whose nodes cannot write to multiple channels and read and forward in a single operation is given in [Johnson 85], [Ho 86a], and [Fox 86b]. This topic will be discussed further in Sec. 21-4.1.

```
int broadcast(buf, src, chan, nbytes)
char *buf;                    /* pointer to data buffer */
int src;                      /* source processor number */
unsigned int chan;            /* mask of channels spanning subcube */
int nbytes;                   /* number of bytes */
{
    int i, proc, bit, rchan, wchan, status;
    proc = procnum ^ src;     /* transformed processor number */
    if(proc == 0) {           /* if source node ... */
        status = cwrite(buf, chan, nbytes);
        return(status);
    }
    wchan = 0;                /* otherwise, not source node ... */
    bit = 1;
    for(i = 0; i < doc; ++i) {    /* generate rchan and wchan */
        if((chan & bit) != 0) {
            if((proc & bit) != 0) {
                rchan = bit;
                break;
            }
            else wchan |= bit;
        }
        bit = bit << 1;
    }
    status = cread(buf, rchan, wchan, nbytes);
    return(status);
}
```

Code 14-8 The Routine *broadcast*

14-5.4 combine

The fourth collective communication routine that we will implement in this section is *combine*. Unlike *vshift* and *broadcast*, we will use exactly the same arguments for *combine* as we used in Sec. 4-4. In contrast to *broadcast*, *combine* will be implemented with a different type of tree algorithm. In fact, the tree that is utilized by the *combine* algorithm is actually a collection of binary trees with each node in the hypercube at the top of one of the trees. Fig. 14-3 illustrates the collection of binary trees.

Each node starts with a block of data items that are to be combined with the similar blocks from all other nodes. First, all nodes exchange their blocks across channel 0. Each node then uses the combining function provided by the application program to combine the items in their original block with those in the block received on channel 0. Next, all nodes exchange their partial results from the first step across channel 1. The blocks received on channel 1 are then combined with the current partial result to give a new partial result. The process of exchanging current partial results and combining the two partial results to obtain a new partial result is repeated for each channel in the hypercube. The resulting block is the combination of the original blocks from each of the nodes. This communication strategy is generalized to the method of *ordered cube geodesics* in Chap. 21. The example implementation of *combine* is given in Code 14-9.

Combine Tree for 3 dimensional hypercube

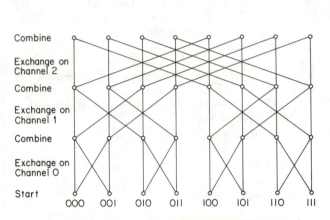

Figure 14-3 *combine* tree for a three-dimensional hypercube.

```
int combine(buf, func, size, nitems)
char *buf;                          /* pointer to data buffer */
int (*func)();                      /* pointer to the combining function */
int size;                           /* size of data items being combined */
int nitems;                         /* number of data items to combine */
{
        int i, j, temp[BIG], status, error;
        if(size > BIG) return(-1);
        error = 0;
        for(i = 0; i < doc; ++i) {
                status = cshift(temp, 1<<i, BIG, buf, 1<<i, size*nitems);
                if(status == -1) error = -1;
                for(j = 0; j < nitems*size; j += size)
                        if((*func)(buf + j, temp + j, size) == -1) error = -1;
        }
        if(error == -1) return(error);
        else return(status);
}
```

Code 14-9 The Routine *combine*

In this implementation, a temporary buffer is used to store the block of data items obtained from *cshift*. We have avoided the issue of how large the temporary buffer should be by defining its size with the macro BIG. In a more sophisticated application, all *nitems* would not need to fit into the temporary buffer since each item could be exchanged separately and combined, rather than exchanging all the items together. Still, the problem remains that at least one of the data items must be buffered temporarily, and the data items might be very large. One way of dealing with the problem is to have *combine* return -1 to indicate an error if *size* is larger than its temporary buffer, as we have done.

The combining function, *func*, has three arguments because in some cases allowing a single combining function to operate on variable-sized data objects may be useful. A generalized combining function could then obviate the need for having distinct functions for every instance of a general group of functions that operate on different sizes of data objects. For instance, the combining function could implement a bitwise OR of the two data items. If the combining function handles only single byte objects, *combine* must call *func* once for every byte to be combined. Although such a method works, it is slow because of the large number of calls to *func*. A more efficient implementation would use a combining function that would perform the bitwise OR of two data objects that are *size* bytes in length, so that *func* would only need to be called once. In any case, the combining function can always ignore the third argument, so the increased flexibility costs very little, even if it is not used.

The algorithm for combining the blocks of data items from each node is redundant since each node calculates the same result. However, the result for a single data item is still calculated in a minimum number of steps, since all of the redundant calculations are performed in parallel. The number of steps needed to combine the blocks of data items from all the nodes in a d-dimensional hypercube is d, which is the same as the maximum distance between nodes in the hypercube measured in communication steps. However, if the number of data objects being combined is large, the algorithm used in *combine* may not be optimal. Allowing different nodes to combine different objects and then distribute the results at the end of the calculation may be faster. A more sophisticated combining algorithm that distributes the calculation and collects the resulting combined items will be discussed in Chap. 19.

14-5.5 concat

The last collective communication routine that we present in this section uses an algorithm that is similar to *combine*. The routine *concat* broadcasts blocks of data from each of the nodes to each of the other nodes in $N-1$ steps, where N is the number of nodes. The algorithm uses the same set of binary trees illustrated in Fig. 14-3, except that a concatenation replaces each combining operation.

Each node starts with a block of data that is to be broadcast to each of the other nodes. First, all nodes copy the block of data into the buffer that will contain a block from each of the nodes in order of processor numbers. The buffer contains *nproc* blocks of size *maxsz* bytes, since *maxsz* is the maximum size of any data block. After copying its own block into the buffer, each node writes its block on channel 0 and reads a similar block from channel 0, storing the block in the appropriate location in the buffer. Next, each node exchanges the two blocks in its buffer with those of the node connected by channel 1. The process repeats for each of the *doc* channels in the hypercube, with twice as many blocks being exchanged in each successive step. When the process is complete, the buffer in each of the nodes contains blocks of data from each of the nodes. Since twice as many blocks of data are exchanged on each successive channel, a total of $N-1$ blocks of data must be exchanged by each node.

```
int concat (fromptr, nbytes, toptr, maxsz, szarray)
char *fromptr;      /* pointer to data block */
int nbytes;         /* number of bytes in data block */
char *toptr;        /* pointer to buffer for all blocks */
int maxsz;          /* maximum size of any block */
int *szarray;       /* pointer to array of block sizes */
{
        int i, j, send, recv, chan, status;
        char *in, *out;

        for (i=0;i<nbytes;++i) toptr[procnum*maxsz+i]=fromptr[i];
        szarray [procnum]=nbytes;
        status = 0;

        for (i=0; i < doc; ++i){
                chan = 1<<i;
                send = procnum/chan;
                for (j = send; j < (send + chan); ++j){
                        recv = j^chan;
                        in = toptr + (recv*maxsz);
                        out = toptr + (j*maxsz);
                        szarray [recv] = cshift (in,chan,maxsz,out,chan,szarray[j]);
                        if (szarray[recv]==-1) status= -1;
                }
        }
        if (status ==0) status=nproc;
        return (status);
}
```

Code 14-10 The Routine *concat*

The array, *szarray*, contains the length of each block of data since a node may send a block that is smaller than *maxsz*. However, the buffer containing the concatenated blocks is indexed as if all of the blocks contained *maxsz* bytes. The routine *concat* calls *cshift* once for each block it receives, giving a total of $N-1$ calls. Since $N-1$ blocks must be received by each node in order to receive a block from every other node, and the communication occurs concurrently in all of the nodes, *concat* is the optimal method of broadcasting blocks of data from every node to each of the other nodes.

We should note that for reasons of history and simplicity we have presented definitions of *broadcast*, *combine*, and *concat* that apply to a full hypercube. Each of these utilities has a natural implementation on a subcube of the full computer and this useful extension will be given in the Software Supplement - Vol. 2 of this book.

14-5.6 cparam

Another new routine we introduce in this section is *cparam*, which returns various constants and parameters of the hypercube to the application program. Although *cparam* is not a collective communication routine, it is introduced in this section because it supplies important information about the node environment, some of which is specific to the hypercube topology. These constants and parameters are actually declared in the file *cros.h*, which must be included at the start of each application program. Although these quantities could be made available to the application program as initialized external variables, such a method is undesirable in a real operating system, since it makes the system too vulnerable to errors in the application program. In CrOS III, we do not allow the application program to have direct access to the system's copy of the parameters, so that an error in the application program cannot easily corrupt the system's parameters. Instead, the routine *cparam* takes a pointer to the structure *cubenv* as an argument, and copies the parameters defining the current node environment into the structure. Code 14-11 defines the contents of this structure.

```
struct cubenv {
      int doc;
      int procnum;
      int nproc;
      int cpmask;
      int cubemask;
};
cparam(env)
struct cubenv *env;                    /* pointer to structure to contain environment */
```

Code 14-11 The Structure *cubenv* as Used by the Routine *cparam*

KCPARA, the FORTRAN equivalent of *cparam*, supplies the values of *doc, procnum, nproc, cpmask*, and *cubemask* to the application program in an integer array.

14-6 Communications between Nodes and Control Process

In this section we shall examine implementations of the collective communication routines that provide communication between the nodes and the control process. As we mentioned in Sec. 14-4, we shall assume that the control process resides in a special processing element, the control processor, which is connected only to node 0 by a communication channel. We further assume that the control processor can use *cwrite* and *cread* in the same way as the nodes to access its communication channel. The channel mask *cubemask* contains the channel mask of its communication channel, which connects it to node 0. In node 0 *cpmask* is the mask of the channel that connects it to the control processor. In nodes other than node 0, *cpmask* is set equal to 0.

As in Sec. 4-5, we continue to require that all the nodes communicate with the control process collectively. A pair of complementary routines implements each mode of communication between the control process and the ensemble. Each of the nodes in the hypercube calls one of the routines while the control process calls the other. Although all of the nodes do not have to call their respective routines strictly simultaneously, they must issue the calls before calling any other communication routine. This is the loose synchronization condition discussed in earlier chapters. By requiring all the nodes to call the routines in loose synchronization, the details of how messages are routed between the control processor and the nodes are hidden from the application programmer.

14-6.1 fcread, fcwrite

Two of the routines that we discuss in this section require access to a file system so that they can transfer more data than will fit in the memory of the control processor. Since we do not have a full operating system in the conventional sense for the ensemble nodes, we have not assumed that the nodes have direct access to any kind of file system. Thus, we will provide the nodes with access to an operating system with a file system only through the control process.

We introduce two routines that provide an interface between the file system of the control processor and its communication channel to node 0. The routines, *fcread* and *fcwrite*, are analogous to *cread* and *cwrite*, except that they use the file system of the control processor instead of application memory. That is, *fcread* reads data from the communication channel and writes them to the file system, while *fcwrite* performs the inverse operation. The routines are defined in Code 14-12.

```
int fcread (fd, chan, nbytes)
int fd;                 /* file descriptor */
unsigned int chan;      /* mask of incoming channel */
int nbytes;             /* maximum number of bytes to read */

int fcwrite (fd, chan, nbytes)
int fd;                 /* file descriptor */
unsigned int chan;      /* mask of outgoing channels */
int nybtes;             /* number of bytes to transmit on channel */
```

Code 14-12 The Routines *fcread* and *fcwrite*

For convenience, we assume that open files in the control processor's file system can be identified by an integer "file descriptor". In a UNIX system, for example, a file descriptor is returned by a successful call to *open, creat, dup,* or *pipe*.

14-6.2 setup

Both of the modes of communication between the control process and the ensemble that were introduced in Sec. 4-5 will be implemented using the same type of broadcast tree as described in the previous section. The only difference is that node 0 communicates with the control process, rather than acting as the source. Since the broadcast tree depends only on the hypercube dimension, the quantities corresponding to *rchan* and *wchan* can be calculated as part of the initialization of each node and stored in external variables. The routine *setup* (Code 14-13) illustrates the initialization of the node variables needed to implement communications between the control process and the hypercube.

In *setup*, the variable *tocp* is defined as the channel mask of the channel which gets messages closer to the control process in the broadcast tree. The variable *brchan* is the channel mask specifying those channels on which messages from the control process are to be forwarded. The dimension of the subcube to which each node must forward messages from the control process is stored in *subdoc*. The algorithm for determining the variables is essentially the same as that used in *broadcast* to determine *rchan* and *wchan*. As before, node 0 is treated as a special case.

```
extern int subdoc, tocp, brchan;
setup()
{
    int i, bit;
    if(procnum == 0) {              /* if node 0 ... */
        subdoc = doc;
        tocp = cpmask;
        brchan = nproc-1;
        return;
    }
    brchan = 0;
    bit = 1;                        /* if not node 0 ... */
    for(i = 0; i < doc; ++i) {
        if((procnum & bit) != 0) {
            subdoc = i;
            tocp = bit;
            break;
        }
        else brchan |=bit;
        bit = bit << 1;
    }
}
```

Code 14-13 The Routine *setup*

14-6.3 bcastcp, bcastelt

Having initialized variables containing the channel numbers and masks that will be needed for the routines implementing communications between the control process and the nodes, we can proceed to describe the routines that implement the four modes of communication. The first such routines we will examine are *bcastelt* and *bcastcp* (Code 14-14).

As we clearly see, the implementations of *bcastelt* and *bcastcp* are very simple once we have initialized the necessary channel masks. Essentially all that is involved is calling *cwrite* and *cread* with the correct arguments. Since we are using the same broadcast algorithm as presented in the previous section, the same comments about the optimality of the algorithm apply.

```
extern int tocp, brchan;
int bcastelt(buf, nbytes)      /* called by nodes */
char *buf;                     /* pointer to buffer for incoming data */
int nbytes;                    /* maximum amount of data to read */
{
      int status;

      status = cread(buf, tocp, brchan, nbytes);
      return(status);
}

int bcastcp(buf, nbytes)       /* called by control process */
char *buf;                     /* pointer to data to broadcast */
int nbytes;                    /* amount of data to broadcast */
{
      int status;

      status = cwrite(buf, cubemask, nbytes);
      return(status);
}
```

Code 14-14 The Routines *bcastelt* and *bcastcp*

14-6.4 floadcp, mloadcp, loadelt

The second mode of communication from the control process to the nodes is implemented by the routines *loadelt* and *loadcp*. A broadcast algorithm similar to the one described in Sec. 14-5.3 is used, except that it is modified slightly so that separate messages arrive at each node. A problem that arises when using the *load* routines is that they are designed so that they may be used to reload large ensembles of data from suspended computations. Since the nodes and the control processor presumably have comparable amounts of memory, the control processor cannot in general accommodate, in memory, the large "checkpoint" buffers for all of the nodes in a large ensemble. However, the problem is rather artificial since the control processor would normally load such buffers directly from its file system. Thus, we avoid the problem by defining two *load* routines that can be run in the control processor, one that reads the buffers from memory, *mloadcp*, and one that reads the buffers directly from the control processor's file system, *floadcp*. The three loading routines are given in Codes 14-15, 14-16, and 14-17.

```
extern int tocp, subdoc;
int loadelt(buf, nbytes)        /* called by nodes */
char *buf;                      /* pointer to buffer for incoming data */
int nbytes;                     /* maximum amount of data to read */
{
        int i, j, n, status;

        status = cread(buf, tocp, 0, nbytes);
        n = 1;
        for(i = 0; i < subdoc; ++i) {
                for(j = 0; j < n; ++j) cread(NULLPTR, tocp, n, nbytes);
                n = n << 1;
        }
        return(status);
}
```

Code 14-15 The Routine *loadelt*

```
int mloadcp(buffer, bufmap)     /* called by control process */
char *buffer;                   /* pointer to data to write */
int *bufmap;                    /* number of bytes of data for each node */
{
        int i, status, error;
        char *ptr;

        if (bufmap[0] != nproc) return (-1);
        ptr = buffer;
        error = 0;
        for(i = 0; i < nproc; ++i) {
                if (cwrite (ptr, cubemask, bufmap [i+1]) == -1) error = -1;
                ptr += bufmap[i+1];
        }
        if(error == -1) return(error);
        else return(nproc);
}
```

Code 14-16 The Routine *mloadcp*

```
int floadcp(fd, bufmap)        /* called by control process */
int fd;                        /* file descriptor */
int *bufmap;                   /* number of bytes of data for each node */
{
        int i, error;
        if (bufmap [0] ! = nproc ) return (-1);
        error = 0;
        for(i = 0; i < nproc; ++i) {
                if (fcwrite (fd, cubemask, bufmap [i + 1]) == -1) error = -1;
        }
        if(error == -1) return(error);
        else return(nproc);
}
```

Code 14-17 The Routine *floadcp*

The modification incorporated in the broadcast algorithm in *loadelt* is designed to send as many separate messages on each channel as there are nodes connected through that channel. Referring back to Fig. 14-2, which illustrates the broadcast tree, we see that the number is 2^{chan}, where *chan* is the channel number. Interestingly, 2^{chan} is also the mask for channel *chan*. The value of *nbytes* in the second call to *cread* is irrelevant since the whole message will always be forwarded.

The routine *mloadcp* uses the information contained in the array *bufmap* to direct separate blocks of data from the array *buffer* to each of the nodes. First, *mloadcp* checks that the number of nodes indicated by the first element of *bufmap* agrees with *nproc*, the total number of active nodes. If the number of nodes indicated in *bufmap* is correct, *mloadcp* obtains the length of the first block of data from *bufmap*. It transmits the block of data using *cwrite* and increments the pointer to *buffer* appropriately. The process then repeats until *mloadcp* has sent a block of data to each of the nodes. If any type of error occurred while transmitting the blocks, *mloadcp* returns −1 to indicate the error. Otherwise, it returns the number of data blocks that it sent.

The routine *floadcp* is nearly identical to *mloadcp* except that the data blocks are taken from the file specified by the file descriptor *fd* using the routine *fcwrite*. However, *bufmap* resides in memory as in the case of *mloadcp*. Thus, in order to use *floadcp* to restore a "dump" of the ensemble from the file system the contents of *bufmap* must be read from the file system separately.

14-6.5 fdumpcp, mdumpcp, dumpelt

The same problem with buffering occurs in the *dump* routines, which allow each of the nodes to send a separate message to the control process. One possible use of the *dump* routines is, as alluded to above, to "checkpoint" a long-running program. If all of the nodes tried to send the control process a long message, the control process might not be able to buffer all of the messages at once. Thus, we also need two versions of the control process routine, *mdumpcp* and *fdumpcp*, which store the messages in memory and in the file system, respectively. The implementations of the *dump* routines is almost the same as for the *load* routines, except that the direction of data flow is reversed. Codes 14-18, 14-19, and 14-20 contain implementations of these routines.

```
extern int tocp, subdoc;
int dumpelt(buf, nbytes)        /* called by nodes */
char *buf;                      /* pointer to data to write */
int nbytes;                     /* amount of data to write */
{
        int i, j, n, status;

        status = cwrite(buf, tocp, nbytes);
        n = 1;
        for(i = 0; i < subdoc; ++i) {
                for(j = 0; j < n; ++j) cread(NULLPTR, n, tocp, nbytes);
                n = n << 1;
        }
        return(status);
}
```

Code 14-18 The Routine *dumpelt*

```
int fdumpcp(fd, nbytes, bufmap)     /* called by control process */
int fd;                             /* file descriptor */
int nbytes;                         /* maximum amount of data to read per node */
int *bufmap;                        /* actual number of bytes read from each note */
{
        int i, error;

        bufmap [0] = nproc;
        error = 0;
        for(i = 0; i < nproc; ++i) {
                bufmap [i+1] = fcread (fd, cubemask, nbytes);
                if (bufmap [i+1] == -1) error = -1;
        }
        if(error == -1) return(error);
        else return(nproc);
}
```

Code 14-19 The Routine *fdumpcp*

We see here that *dumpelt* is identical to *loadelt*, except that one of the calls to *cread* has been changed to a call to *cwrite*, and the direction of data flow through the other *cread* has been reversed. Both *mdumpcp* and *fdumpcp* are similar to the corresponding *load* routines, except that the direction of data flow is reversed. The error response could

```
int mdumpcp(buffer, nbytes, bufmap)  /* called by control process */
char *buffer;                        /* pointer to buffer for incoming data */
int nbytes;                          /* maximum amount of data to read per node */
int *bufmap;                         /* actual number of bytes read from each node */
{
     int i, error;
     char *ptr;

     bufmap [0] = nproc;
     ptr = buffer;
     error = 0;
     for(i = 0; i < nproc; ++i) {
          bufmap [i+1] = cread (ptr, cubemask, 0, nbytes);
          if (bufmap [i+1] == -1) {
               error = -1;
               ptr += nbytes;
          }
          else ptr += bufmap [i+1];
     }
     if(error == -1) return(error);
     else return(nproc);
}
```

Code 14-20 The Routine *mdumpcp*

be made somewhat more sophisticated in a real implementation of the *dump* routines, as it should be with all the implementations in this chapter. When creating a checkpoint for the ensemble with *fdumpcp*, the contents of *bufmap* must be written to a file, since *floadcp* requires both the data blocks and the format information in *bufmap*.

14-6.6 combcp, combelt

The last of the collective communication routines we will discuss in this section are *combelt* and *combcp*. Since the control process will receive only one block of data from the ensemble as a whole, the ability to write the data directly to the control processor's file system is not needed. The control process does not contribute a block of data to the combining routine, so it only has to read the result from node 0. Thus, we can easily implement *combelt* using *combine*. We note that *cwrite* is called by every node in *combelt*, but node 0 is the only node that actually writes the block of data items, since only node 0 has a nonzero value of *cpmask*. The routines *combelt* and *combcp* are given in Codes 14-21 and 14-22 respectively.

```
int combelt(buf, func, size, nitems)    /* called by nodes */
char *buf;                              /* pointer data buffer */
int (*func)();                          /* pointer to the combining function */
int size;                               /* size of data items being combined */
int nitems;                             /* number of data items to combine */
{
        int status, error;

        error = 0;
        status = combine(buf, func, size, nitems);
        if(status == -1) error = -1;
        if(cwrite(buf, cpmask, size*nitems) == -1) error = -1;
        if(error == -1) return(error);
        else return(status);
}
```

Code 14-21 The Routine *combelt*

```
int combcp(buf, size, nitems)    /* called by control process */
char *buf;                       /* pointer to data to broadcast */
int size;                        /* size of data items being combined */
int nitems;                      /* maximum number of data items to read */
{
        int status;

        status = cread(buf, cubemask, 0, size*nitems);
        return(status);
}
```

Code 14-22 The Routine *combcp*

14-6.7 cubeld

So far we have not described how a program is loaded into the nodes and executed. We now introduce an additional family of routines that are called in the control processor to load a program into each node of the ensemble. The difference between the various possible *cubeld* routines involves the issue of how the argument list is passed to the node programs. We describe only one of the routines, *cubeldl*, in this section, and defer a discussion of the remaining variations until Appendix E. The routine *cubeldl* is defined in Code 14-23.

```
int cubeldl (doc, name, arg0, arg1,..., argN, NULLPTR)
int doc;                        /* dimension of cube */
char *name;                     /* name of file containing program */
char *arg0, *arg1, ...,*argN    /* Argument list */
```

Code 14-23 The Routine *cubeldl*

The specified value of *doc* must be less than or equal to the maximum hypercube dimension as fixed by the actual machine. The second argument to *cubeldl*, *name*, gives the name of the file containing the program to be run in each node. We note that the *cubeld* routines load the same program into every node, although more general versions could allow different programs to be loaded into the argument list for *main* in each of the nodes. The list of arguments passed to each node is terminated by the final argument to *cubeldl*, which must be NULLPTR.

14-7 Mapping of Nodes onto Decomposition Topology

In Sec. 4-6, we introduced a specific instance of a class of functions that map the nodes of the concurrent processor onto the decomposition topology of an application. The particular mapping we introduced, *gridmap*, is limited to decomposition topologies that are Cartesian grids. As we anticipated in Sec. 4-6, not all possible mappings of nodes onto the decomposition topology of an application are equally efficient. In fact, since the hypercube interconnection does not allow direct communication between all pairs of nodes, the mapping of nodes onto the decomposition topology must be done carefully, so that a communication channel connects (as well as possible) adjacent regions of the decomposition topology.

In Sec. 14-4, we mentioned that the hypercube topology also contains grids of lower dimensionality than that of the hypercube. Thus, we restrict our implementation of *gridmap* to mapping grids onto the nodes of the hypercube. In the interest of simplicity, we imposed an additional condition on *gridmap*: that the number of nodes in any dimension of the mapping be a power of two. This additional condition is not strictly necessary, but it simplifies the algorithm and ensures that periodic boundaries can always be provided by a communication channel connecting nodes on opposite edges of the grid.

Grids cannot be mapped onto the hypercube by means of a decimal ordering of the nodes, since in that case, consecutively numbered nodes would not, in general, be linked by a communication channel. In discussing the mapping algorithm, we return to a property of the numbering scheme we used for labeling the nodes of the hypercube, and examine it in more depth. The important property to which we refer is that the processor numbers of adjacent nodes, those directly linked by a communication channel, differ in their binary representation by a single bit. A numbering scheme in which only a single bit differs between successive numbers is known as a binary *Gray Code* [Gilbert 58]. While many Gray Codes are possible for a given number of bits, one particular Gray Code is generally regarded as *the* Gray Code because of its ease of computation.

The d-bit Gray Code can be generated recursively by first prepending a 0 bit to the $(d-1)$-bit Gray Code and then prepending a 1 to the same $(d-1)$-bit Gray Code written in reverse order. Let us start with the trivial 1-bit Gray Code: 0, 1. We can easily generate the 2-bit Gray Code, which is written in binary: 00, 01, 11, 10. Applying the generating rule again, we obtain the 3-bit Gray Code: 000, 001, 011, 010, 110, 111, 101, 100. Notice that the first and last numbers in the Gray Code always differ in their highest bits. The availability of periodic boundaries is due to the first and last number always differing by a single bit. Algorithms exist that rapidly convert between a Gray Code and its corresponding binary value, and these will be utilized in the actual implementation.

By now the direction in which we are proceeding should be clear. The processor numbers of the nodes form a Gray Code, and the mapping procedure requires a conversion of the Gray Codes into coordinates on a grid of some specified dimensionality. To illustrate, we examine the case of the mapping of all the nodes in a 3-cube onto a ring. The 3-bit Gray Code gives the processor number of the node at each position in the ring. Starting with the coordinate 0 we have the following sequence of nodes: 0, 1, 3, 2, 6, 7, 5, 4, which map onto the coordinates 0 through 7 of the ring. Since the nodes whose coordinates are 0 and 7 differ by a single bit, a ring is formed.

For grids of higher dimensionality than a ring, the same procedure is applied, but first the bits of the nodes' processor numbers are divided between the dimensions of the desired grid. The processor numbers of a d-dimensional hypercube contain d bits. Thus, a two-dimensional grid can be formed by assigning m bits to the x-dimension and n bits to the y-dimension in such a manner that $m + n = d$. Dividing the bits of the processor numbers into groups for each dimension of the grid guarantees that the number of nodes in each dimension is a power of two. Once the bits of a node's processor number are so divided, the groups are independently mapped to a coordinate, yielding a coordinate for each dimension of the grid. The mapping uniquely assigns each node to a position in the grid. Fig. 14-4 illustrates the assignment of nodes in a 3-cube to a two-dimensional grid with 4 nodes in the x-dimension and 2 nodes in the y-dimension.

By grouping the bits comprising each node's processor number according to the number of nodes in each dimension of the grid and converting the groups of bits into coordinates, a map is created which assigns each node to a position in the grid. Adjacent nodes in the grid are guaranteed to be connected by a communication channel due to the properties of the Gray Code. The only remaining problem is that of determining the numbers of the channels connecting a particular node to its neighbors in the grid. Finding these channel numbers is an easy task once the grid assignment of nodes is known. By performing an exclusive-OR operation of the bits of the node's processor number with those of a neighbor's processor number, the channel mask of the connecting channel is obtained. The numbers of the channels connecting adjacent regions of the two-dimensional grid in Fig. 14-4 are indicated.

We present the implementation of *gridmap* beginning with a pair of routines that convert between Gray Codes and binary *procnum* representation. Both routines will be used to implement the functionality of *gridmap*.

Mapping of a 3-cube onto a 2D grid

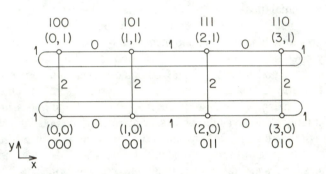

Figure 14-4 Mapping of a three-dimensional hypercube onto a two-dimensional grid.

```
static unsigned int mask[16] = {  0x0001, 0x0002, 0x0004, 0x0008,
                                  0x0010, 0x0020, 0x0040, 0x0080,
                                  0x0100, 0x0200, 0x0400, 0x0800,
                                  0x1000, 0x2000, 0x4000, 0x8000 };


unsigned int graytobin(g)
unsigned int g;
{
     int i, n;

     n = mask[15] & g;
     for(i = 14; i >= 0; --i) n += (mask[i] & g) ^ ((mask[i + 1] & n) >> 1);
     return(n);
}
```

Code 14-24 The Routine *graytobin*

We begin by initializing a static integer array with a mask for each of the bits in a 16-bit integer. The values of the masks are given as hexadecimal numbers so that the bit position of each mask is easily seen. The routine *graytobin* (Code 14-24) takes a Gray Code as its argument and converts it to a cardinal number. The Gray Code is restricted to a 15-bit value since 16-bit integers are used in the conversion and one extra bit is required. The routine *bintogray* (Code 14-25) takes a cardinal number as its argument and converts it to a Gray Code. The correctness of the algorithms for performing the conversions is easily verified by applying them to test cases.

```
unsigned int bintogray(n)
unsigned int n;
{
    int temp;

    temp = n << 1;
    return((temp ^ n) >> 1);
}
```

Code 14-25 The Routine *bintogray*

Another utility that we will use in the routines that implement *gridmap* is *log2* (Code 14-26), which returns the logarithm to the base 2 of its argument. If its argument is not a power of 2, a value of -1 is returned to indicate the error.

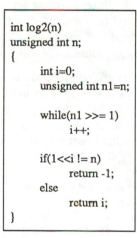

```
int log2(n)
unsigned int n;
{
    int i=0;
    unsigned int n1=n;

    while(n1 >>= 1)
        i++;

    if(1<<i != n)
        return -1;
    else
        return i;
}
```

Code 14-26 The Routine *log2*

The first of the *gridmap* routines is *gridinit* (Code 14-27), which is simply an initialization routine for the other three routines comprising *gridmap*. The routine *gridinit* takes as input the dimension of the decomposition topology and an array of integers containing the number of nodes in each dimension. If the requested mapping is not possible, *gridinit* returns -1; otherwise, 0 is returned.

In addition to saving a copy of *dim* and the array *num*, two data arrays and a mask that are used by the other *gridmap* routines are initialized by *gridinit*. Several checks are also made to determine whether the requested mapping is possible. First, the dimensionality of the requested topology must not be larger than the maximum specified by the macro MAXDIM, since that is the size of the various static arrays used by the *gridmap* routines. As mentioned previously, the number of nodes in each dimension is required to be a power of two in our implementation of *gridmap*, although a more sophisticated implementation might have no such restriction. The special case, in which there is only one node in a dimension of the decomposition topology, is handled correctly by the *gridmap* routines. Finally, the total number of nodes required by the requested topology must not exceed the number of nodes in the ensemble.

The arrays *goffset* and *gmask* contain information that allows the bits of a processor number to be easily grouped according to the number of bits assigned to each dimension of the topology. The groups can then be converted into coordinates using *graytobin*. The array *goffset* contains the position of the first bit assigned to the ith dimension of the topology, and *gmask* contains a bit mask whose width is the number of bits assigned to the ith dimension. The procedure for obtaining the subset of bits of a processor number corresponding to a dimension of the topology consists of shifting the processor number by *goffset* bits to the right, and performing the bitwise AND of the resulting number and *gmask*.

The mask *grem* is a mask of any bits of a processor number that are not needed in the requested topology. It allows the other *gridmap* routines to ensure that only one node is assigned to a set of grid coordinates. Since having any unused bits in the processor number means that at least half the nodes are not being used, the situation should not arise often, but the *gridmap* routines will still work correctly.

The *gridmap* routine *gridcoord* (Code 14-28) uses the algorithm for breaking a processor number into groups of bits, in order to convert the processor number into the coordinates of the node in the requested topology. It takes two arguments, a processor number and a pointer to an integer array in which the coordinates of the node will be stored. If the indicated node is not part of the topology, or *gridinit* has not been called, −1 is returned. Otherwise, 0 is returned.

```
int gridcoord(proc, coord)
int proc;
int *coord;
{
        int i, temp;

        if(ginit == 0) return(-1);
        if((proc & grem) != 0) return(-1);
        for(i = 0; i < gdim; ++i) {
                temp = (proc >> goffset[i]) & gmask[i];
                coord[i] = graytobin(temp);
        }
        return(0);
}
```

Code 14-28 The Routine *gridcoord*

```
static int ginit = 0;                    /* indicates whether gridinit called */
static int gdim;                         /* keep a copy of dim */
static int gnum[MAXDIM];                 /* keep a copy of array num */
static unsigned int goffset[MAXDIM];     /* offset of first bit in procnum */
static unsigned int gmask[MAXDIM];       /* mask of bits for each dimension */
static unsigned int grem;                /* mask of bits not used in topology */


int gridinit(dim, num)
int dim;                                 /* dimension of decomposition topology */
int *num;                                /* number of nodes in each dimension */
{
    int i, n, offset;

    ginit = 1;                           /* indicate that gridinit called */
    n = 1;                               /* keep count of total nodes used */
    offset = 0;
    if(dim > MAXDIM) return(-1);         /* check if dim is too large */
    gdim = dim;                          /* save dim */
    for(i = 0; i < dim; ++i) {
        if(log2(num[i]) == -1)           /* is number of nodes a power of 2 ? */
            return(-1);
        goffset[i] = offset;             /* save current offset */
        offset += log2(num[i]);          /* increment offset by # bits in dim i */
        gmask[i] = num[i] - 1;           /* mask of bits needed by dimension i */
        gnum[i] = num[i];                /* save number of nodes in dimension i */
        n *= num[i];                     /* update total number of node used */
    }
    if(n > nproc) return(-1);            /* check that enough nodes are available */
    grem = ((1 << (doc - offset)) - 1) << offset; /* mask of bits not used */
    return(0);                           /* no error - return 0 */
}
```

Code 14-27 The Routine *gridinit*

The *gridmap* routine *gridproc* (Code 14-29) performs the inverse of the mapping performed by *gridcoord*. Given an integer array containing the grid coordinates of the desired node, *gridproc* returns the node's processor number, unless the specified coordinates are outside the range of the grid or *gridinit* has not been called, in which case a value of −1 is returned. After checking the bounds on each of the coordinates, *gridproc* calls *bintogray* to convert the coordinate into its Gray Code. The resulting Gray Code is then shifted to the left by *goffset* bits to its correct position in the processor number. The processor number is then assembled by using a bitwise OR operation to combine the pieces obtained from the individual coordinates.

```
int gridproc(coord)
int *coord;
{
        int i, proc;

        if(ginit == 0) return(-1);
        proc = 0;
        for(i = 0; i < gdim; ++i) {
                if(coord[i] > gnum[i]) return(-1);
                if(coord[i] < 0) return(-1);
                proc |= bintogray(coord[i]) << goffset[i];
        }
        return(proc);
}
```

Code 14-29 The Routine *gridproc*

We now introduce one additional *gridmap* routine that was not discussed in Sec. 4-6. The routine *gridchan* (Code 14-30) takes a processor number, a grid dimension and a direction, and returns the channel mask of the channel connecting the specified node to its neighbor in the indicated direction. Thus, an application can use *gridchan* to determine the mask of the channel on which to send a message, so that it arrives at the neighboring node in any of the particular decomposition grid directions.

```
int gridchan(proc, dim, dir)
int proc;
int dim;
int dir;
{
        int temp, coord[MAXDIM];

        if(ginit == 0) return(-1);
        if((dir != 1) && (dir != -1)) return(-1);
        if((dim < 0) || (dim > gdim)) return(-1);
        if(gridcoord(proc, coord) == -1) return(-1);
        coord[dim] += dir;
        if(coord[dim] < 0) coord[dim] = gnum[dim] - 1;
        if(coord[dim] >= gnum[dim]) coord[dim] = 0;
        if((temp = gridproc(coord)) == -1) return(-1);
        return(proc ^ temp);
}
```

Code 14-30 The Routine *gridchan*

Checks on the arguments are performed to ensure that the channel requested actually exists. The argument *dir* must be either +1 or −1 to indicate that the *dim* coordinate increases or decreases by 1. If *dim* is not one of the dimensions of the grid, *gridchan* returns −1 to indicate the error. The algorithm begins by obtaining the coordinates of *proc* by using *gridcoord* and adding *dir* to the coordinate in the *dim* dimension of the grid. Periodic boundaries are handled by testing to determine whether the resulting coordinate is out of range and, if so, making the necessary adjustment. The routine *gridproc* is then used to convert the modified coordinates into a processor number. The mask of the connecting channel is obtained by performing an exclusive-OR of the two processor numbers.

It should be emphasized that *gridchan* always assumes periodic boundaries when it calculates the channel mask specified by its arguments, even though some applications do not involve periodic boundaries. In those applications, the coordinate in the appropriate dimension should be tested to determine whether it is at one of the edges before calling *gridchan*. If the node is at the edge of one of its nonperiodic boundaries, it can simply use a channel mask of 0 for any communications that would go across the edge. We also note that if *gridchan* is called along a dimension containing only one node, the periodic boundaries apply and it correctly returns a channel mask of 0.

The implementations of all the *gridmap* routines given here are not necessarily as fast as they could be. In a real system, several additional data arrays could be initialized by *gridinit* so that the other *gridmap* routines could obtain their results by reading the appropriate data array instead of calculating the result each time. However, the implementations were meant to clearly illustrate the underlying methods, and a more sophisticated implementation would not have served our present purposes.

14-8 A More General Communication System

The only type of internode communications that has been discussed in any detail so far in this book is crystalline communications. In Chap. 4 we defined the features that characterize a crystalline communication system. Its essential feature is that its routines poll the communication channels indefinitely while waiting for them to become ready for transmitting or receiving. As a result of polling the channels indefinitely, the crystalline communication routines impose a synchronizing condition that forces the nodes to execute their programs in a loose lockstep as discussed in Sec. 4-3. Due to the synchronization imposed by the crystalline communications, they are most useful in applications whose communications can be expected by the participating nodes, and whose computational loads are well balanced. In addition, any message-forwarding must be done explicitly, as in the routines that implement communication between the nodes and the control process, requiring that intermediate nodes also "know" in advance about the intended communication. In Sec. 22-2 the *crystal_router* algorithm will be described. This algorithm provides for automatic forwarding of messages within a crystalline communications system, and shows that loose synchronization, and not forwarding, is the essential restriction of this environment.

Clearly, crystalline communication systems such as CrOS III are not suitable for all applications, although we have shown their usefulness in a rich variety of problems. We shall now briefly examine a more general method of providing internode communication. However, a detailed discussion of the method is outside the scope of this volume.

The essential defining feature of crystalline communications, polling the channels to determine whether they are ready for transmitting or receiving, is also its fundamental limitation. Another method for a processor to obtain the status information from its channels is to allow the channel interrupt lines to interrupt its main process. Thus, instead of polling the receive interrupt line of a channel to determine whether a packet can be read from the channel buffer, the processor is interrupted when a packet arrives in the buffer. When the interrupt occurs, the processor stops its current task and executes an *interrupt handler*. The interrupt handler then reads the packet and stores it in some special location. When the interrupt handler is finished, the processor resumes execution of the task that was interrupted.

In the same way, the processor can be interrupted when a channel is ready for a packet to be written. The interrupt handler for a transmit operation then writes the next packet in the message currently being sent. However, if no messages are ready to be sent, the processor should disable the channel's transmit interrupt to prevent continual interruption by the channel. When a transmit interrupt line is disabled, it does not interrupt the processor even though the channel is ready to send a packet. Thus, a channel's transmit interrupt must be enabled when the next message is ready to be sent.

A communication system that allows the processor to be interrupted, rather than polling the interrupt lines, is known as an *interrupt-driven* communication system. Since packets are read from the channels when they arrive instead of when *cread* is called, the messages do not need to be anticipated by the application program of the destination node, as in the case of crystalline communications. If the message header contains the processor number of its destination in addition to the message's length, the message can be forwarded toward its destination by an intermediate node. Since the interrupt handlers that actually read and write packets can also forward the messages, message forwarding can be done in a manner transparent to the application programmer.

The synchronization imposed on an application by a crystalline communication system is not present when an interrupt-driven communication scheme is used. Thus, applications are freed to an extent from the constraint that the loads be well balanced between every communication step. However, the requirement that the computational loads be balanced in a good concurrent algorithm is not removed, but only somewhat relaxed. The total computational load should be balanced even when an interrupt-driven communication system is used, but it does not need to be balanced between every communication step in the algorithm.

Another seeming advantage of an interrupt-driven communication system is that its user interface can be made more independent of the concurrent processor on which it is running. The interconnection topology of the ensemble is less important than with the CrOS III communication system, since the interrupt-driven system can automatically route messages between any nodes in the ensemble transparently to the application program. Further, messages will be sent more quickly to nodes that are closer together, so the interconnection topology still has an important effect on the performance of the communication system. In Sec. 22-5, we will define the virtual machine loosely synchronous communication system and show it can be implemented either in terms of a crystalline or an asynchronous communication system. In the case of the hypercube, we use the *crystal_router* built on top of CrOS III. This illustrates that the essential advantage of an asynchronous system lies in its application to problems that are outside the loosely synchronous class, and not for its utility in irregular loosely synchronous problems. In other words, asynchronous communication systems are needed for temporally irregular problems; they are applicable to but not needed for spatial irregularity. Note that temporal irregularity occurs not only in problems such as event-driven simulations, but also in system functions like debuggers which require the computer to interact with a highly unpredictable user.

Unfortunately, the many advantages of an interrupt-driven communication do not come without a cost. While an interrupt-driven system has more capabilities than a crystalline system, it is correspondingly more complicated. One effect of its additional complexity is that an interrupt-driven system is generally slower than a crystalline system. If the crystalline system is incapable of providing the communication facilities required by an application, an interrupt-driven system may be the only choice. However, problems that can be programmed with crystalline communications normally should be, since they will almost certainly run faster. In addition to providing slower communication, an interrupt-driven communication system is substantially more difficult to design than a crystalline system. Fortunately, the substantial body of literature on computer networking provides a useful starting point for the design of an interrupt-driven communication system.

14-9 Comments on Shared-Memory Machines

Throughout this chapter we have considered communication channels that are implemented separately in each node's hardware. However, some concurrent processors are designed as shared-memory machines, either by actually connecting several processing elements to a common block of memory, or by building a switch in hardware that allows each of the nodes to access any of several blocks of common memory. Throughout this book we have described domain decomposition as the essential idea behind concurrent computation. Although this probably underlies most effective uses of all concurrent processors, it is necessary to explicitly partition the data domain only for distributed memory machines, such as the hypercube. Shared-memory concurrent processors allow more general, and possibly more convenient, programming techniques where the data domain is shared in a single large memory and never needs to be explicitly decomposed. However, one can use domain decomposition and the associated message-passing communication environment on such machines, and this may well lead to their best performance. In particular shared-memory concurrent processors with large local caches are naturally programmed by domain decomposition [Fox 87]. Indeed, the use of caches on sequential machines is optimized by domain decomposition. So although we realize that this is not the only method of using shared memory, we describe below how to implement a crystalline environment on such machines.

A communication channel that can easily be implemented using shared-memory consists of a channel buffer and a pair of indices keyed to this channel buffer. One of the indices specifies the next location in the buffer to be written by the transmitting node, and the other indicates the next location to be read by the receiving node. In such an implementation, no memory conflicts occur since only the transmitting node modifies the channel buffer and the transmit index, while only the receiving node modifies the receiving index. Of course, the transmitting node must be able to read the receiving index, and the receiving node must be able to read the channel buffer and the transmitting index. The two indices provide the same type of information as the interrupt lines of the communication channels implemented in hardware, but they are more flexible. In particular, a message does not need to be transmitted as a string of packets in the shared-memory implementation of the channels.

We can implement *cwrite* and *cread* easily using the shared-memory communication channels, so that they impose the same synchronizing conditions as discussed in Sec. 4-3 and 14-3. The channel buffer is a data structure known as a circular buffer which is empty when the transmit and receive indices are identical, and full when the transmit index is one less than the receive index. In order to transmit a message, *cwrite* first writes a block of data whose size is one less than the size of the channel buffer into the channel buffer, and makes the transmit index one less than the receive index. It cannot write any more data into the buffer until *cread* has been called in the receiving node. To determine whether *cread* has read any of the data in the buffer, *cwrite* compares the two indices. If any data have been read by *cread*, *cwrite* can write additional data into the buffer and adjust the transmit index accordingly. After writing the whole message, *cwrite* continues to compare the two indices until they are identical, indicating that *cread* has finished in the receiving node, and then *cwrite* returns.

The routine *cread* is implemented in a similar way. It first compares the two channel indices to determine if the transmitting node has written any data. When the channel buffer contains data, *cread* reads the amount indicated by the difference of the indices and adjusts the receive index accordingly. As in the version of *cread* implemented on the hardware communication channels, *cread* obtains the length of the message from the header that *cwrite* has prepended to the contents of the message. It then continues to compare the channel indices, read data from the channel, and adjust the receive index until it has read the whole message. After reading the last of the message and adjusting the receive index, the two channel indices are again identical, indicating that the channel buffer is empty.

The other basic communication routines, such as *vwrite* and *vread*, can be implemented in a similar way. Since the collective communication routines in CrOS III can be implemented using the basic communication routines, the example implementations in Sec. 14-5 and 14-6 can be applied to the shared-memory version of CrOS III. However, restricting the shared-memory implementation to reflect a hypercube interconnection topology would be a serious waste of the shared-memory resources. Since a full-duplex channel connecting two nodes requires only two channel buffers and two pairs of channel indices, a channel can easily be established between every pair of nodes unless the amount of shared-memory is severely limited. Thus, the shared-memory implementation of crystalline communications could closely resemble the virtual concurrent processor described in Chap. 4.

Still, an implementation of the message-passing environment we have described falls far short of the possibilities allowed by a shared-memory machine. In particular, broadcasts could be implemented directly by some scheme that reserves a block of memory for global messages, rather than by writing the same message into several channel buffers. In addition, by transferring pointers to blocks of memory, rather than the blocks themselves, the crystalline communication routines could be made faster. Simply transferring pointers would not always be desirable, but it could greatly reduce the amount of time spent communicating when it was appropriate, especially when large messages were involved. However, when making comparisons between shared-memory architectures and message-passing architectures, we must remember that using shared-memory facilities to implement a message-passing system imposes restrictions on the access of the shared-memory and, therefore, is not necessarily the best way to program such machines.

15

CUBIX - Implementation Issues

15-1 Introduction

In Chap. 6 we introduced the CUBIX system for concealing the details of the control processor from programs running in the parallel processor. In the intervening chapters, and in the corresponding sections of the Software Supplement, we have made extensive use of CUBIX's I/O facilities. In this chapter we give a more detailed specification of CUBIX than the overview in Chap. 6, and we describe an implementation of CUBIX using the CrOS III library of Chap. 14.

15-2 Specification of CUBIX

CUBIX is a software system designed to simplify the programming of distributed computers. It consists of two parts: a universal program which runs in the control processor and remains unchanged from one application to the next, and a library of subroutines which may be linked with the node program. These subroutines interact with the universal control processor program to provide operating system services to programs running in the nodes of the concurrent processor. As discussed in Chap. 6, use of CUBIX results in programs which are easier to debug and maintain, and are more portable. Parallel CUBIX programs may often be ported to sequential machines with little or no effort. CUBIX incurs little or no speed performance penalty, but does require memory for additional code which must be present in every processor of the distributed machine.

15-2.1 System Calls

If CUBIX is to make the control processor's operating system available to the concurrent processor, its specification must depend on the control processor and its operating system. The basic ideas remain unchanged under different operating systems, but in order to avoid vague generalities, we specialize in this chapter to a discussion of control processors running the UNIX operating system. UNIX is attractive because of its popularity as well as the economy of its design. For example, the UNIX System V Programmer Reference Manual [AT&T 84] lists 58 system calls which comprise the totality of all services a node process may request from the operating system.

The UNIX system calls are defined in terms of their interface to C programs, so by specializing to UNIX, we are automatically biased toward the C programming language. Other languages may be accommodated by defining an appropriate set of bridges to the C system calls.

A CUBIX program running in the concurrent processor interacts with the control processor's operating system by using the same system calls and calling sequences that would appear in a sequential program running on the control processor. The system calls available on a host running UNIX System V are listed in Table 15-1.

access	close	getuid	msgctl	plock*	setpgrp	stime	uname
acct	creat	ioctl	msgget	profil*	setuid	sync	unlink
alarm	dup	kill	msgop	ptrace*	shmctl*	time	ustat
brk,sbrk*	exec	link	nice	read	shmget*	times	utime
chdir	exit,_exit	lseek	open	semctl	shmop*	ulimit	wait
chmod	fcntl	mknod	pause	semget	signal*	umask	write
chown	fork*	mount	pipe	semop	stat	umount	
chroot	getpid						

Table 15-1 List of UNIX System V Calls
Those marked with an asterisk are not available in CUBIX.

The system calls in Table 15-1 behave in the node processors exactly as if they were executed directly on the control processor. Their exact specifications may be found in the UNIX System V Programmer Reference Manual, or the equivalent manual if the control processor has a different operating system. Erroneous calls are treated in the usual way by returning an impossible value and setting the value of *errno* to indicate the type of error. There are two important restrictions:

1- System calls must be made loosely synchronously in all processors.
2- All processors must provide the same arguments to the system call. In the case of arguments which are pointers, the pointers may be different, but they must point to identical data.

Since all nodes request the same thing, only one call is made on the control processor, and only one value is returned to all the nodes. It is important to realize that the nodes do not attempt to internally emulate the control processor's operating system. In all cases, the arguments passed to the system call in the nodes are transmitted to the control processor, where the system call is executed. Result codes and returned data are collected by the universal program in the control processor and sent back to the nodes.

The system calls marked with an asterisk in Table 15-1 may not be invoked via CUBIX because they don't make sense within the CUBIX model. The disallowed system calls would change the run-time environment of the control process in a way that is not useful when the control process is a universal application-independent program. For example, *sbrk* would allocate system memory to the control process. This memory would not be accessible to the nodes of the parallel machine, as might be expected. Furthermore, once allocated, the control process would not make use of the new memory.

In addition to the system calls defined by the control processor's operating system, CUBIX provides two more, *mread* and *mwrite*, which facilitate I/O operations when different nodes read or write distinct data. They are called like *read* and *write* as shown in Code 15-1.

```
int mread(fd, ptr, cnt)
int fd;
char *ptr;
int cnt;


int mwrite(fd, ptr, cnt)
int fd;
char *ptr;
int cnt;
```

Code 15-1 Specification of *mread* and *mwrite*

The system call *mread* causes cnt_0 bytes to be read from the file identified by the file descriptor, *fd*, into the memory of processor 0 starting at ptr_0. The next cnt_1 bytes are read from the file into the memory of processor 1 starting at ptr_1, etc. Subscripts refer to the value of the argument in the corresponding processor. The call *mwrite* behaves like *mread*, except that data is copied from the memory of the various processors to the file. Both *mread* and *mwrite* must be called loosely synchronously, and the file descriptor argument must be the same in all processors, but the number of bytes read or written and the actual data sent may be different in each.

These calls allow for distinct data to be read or written by each node, and they return different values to each node, corresponding to the number of bytes actually read or written. For example, if the file descriptor, *fd*, refers to a file with 17 remaining bytes, and the following statement is executed loosely synchronously in all processors:

howmany = mread(fd, ptr, 7)

the variable *howmany* will take on the value 7 in nodes 0 and 1, the value 3 in node 2, and the value 0 in nodes 3 and higher.

15-2.2 The Standard I/O Library in CUBIX

In the previous section we described the low level interface between node programs and the control processor's operating system. Usually, however, programmers do not use these primitive system calls directly. High-level languages provide standard ways of performing the most common I/O tasks, allowing the programmer the option of remaining ignorant about the underlying operating system. Different languages treat I/O in very different ways, with important implications about how effectively they can incorporate CUBIX.

In C, I/O capabilities are not defined as part of the language. Instead, a standard library of subroutines is provided which performs common tasks reasonably uniformly and efficiently. Any programmer or installation is free to rewrite or modify the library to change the behavior of the various routines. Thus, we can easily extend the Standard I/O Library, which is often written in C, to include routines appropriate for concurrent programming.

Conversely, in FORTRAN, I/O is explicitly part of the language. FORTRAN CUBIX, as specified in Appendix C, requires the extension of the I/O system familiar to FORTRAN programmers and compiler-dependent modifications to the FORTRAN run-time libraries. This is difficult to implement, and because of the compiler dependence, is less portable than the C version of CUBIX. Thus, we again specialize to C, at the expense of language independence, and discuss only the C implementation of CUBIX.

There are two principal forms of Standard I/O allowed in CUBIX, which we denote as *singular* and *multiple*. Singular Standard I/O is similar to system calls described in the previous section. It requires loose synchronization and identical arguments, and its usage is identical to that in a sequential implementation. It is useful for obtaining or reporting global data. Multiple Standard I/O resembles the use of *mread* and *mwrite*. In multiple I/O, distinct data is read or written by each node. Multiple I/O is not bound by the rule of identical arguments, and in the case of output, loose synchronization is not necessary either.

In the CUBIX version of the Standard I/O Library, the attribute of multiplicity, i.e., either singular or multiple, is associated with each open stream (FILE pointer). All streams, including *stdin, stdout,* and *stderr* are initially opened in the singular state. The new functions *fmulti* and *fsingl* change their argument's multiplicity. The function *ismulti* returns a nonzero value if its argument is in multiple mode, and zero otherwise. These three functions are defined in Code (15-2).

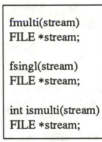

```
fmulti(stream)
FILE *stream;

fsingl(stream)
FILE *stream;

int ismulti(stream)
FILE *stream;
```

Code 15-2 Specification of *fmulti, fsingl* and *ismulti*

In contrast to the situation with system calls, the nodes execute the code for the Standard I/O Library routines. The control processor only plays a part if a system routine from Table 15-1 is called by the library routine.

```
fmulti(stdin);
scanf("%d", &i);
scanf("%d", &j);
```

Code 15-3 Example of Multi Mode Input

Use of multiple streams does require some explanation beyond a reference to sequential usage. Input streams in multiple mode behave in a reasonable fashion. Data is read by processors in order of increasing *procnum*; each processor begins immediately after the point where the previous one finished. Each call is completed in all processors before the next begins. Thus, if Code 15-3 were provided with the input:

$$0\ 1\ 2\ 3\ 4\ 5\ 6\ 7$$

the following variable bindings would result on a four-processor system:

$$i_0 = 0, \quad j_0 = 4$$
$$i_1 = 1, \quad j_1 = 5$$
$$i_2 = 2, \quad j_2 = 6$$
$$i_3 = 3, \quad j_3 = 7$$

where subscripts refer to the different values of the variables in the different processors. Input functions must be called loosely synchronously, even if their stream argument is in multiple mode. The stream argument must be identical in all processors, although the other arguments need not be.

The function *ungetc* presents a problem for multiple input. It is only possible to replace one character on the input stream, even if the stream is in multiple mode. Thus, *ungetc* replaces the last character read by the last processor, regardless of the multiplicity of its stream argument. In practice, this is not a serious limitation. Both of *ungetc*'s arguments must be identical in all nodes.

Since output is buffered, it is possible to perform multiple output completely asynchronously (at least to the extent of putting the data into the buffer). Thus, *putc*, *putchar*, *printf*, *fwrite*, etc., may be executed completely asynchronously on multiple streams. Code 15-4 demonstrates a simple error-reporting mechanism which makes use of this feature. Even if the error condition occurs in only one processor, the call to *fmulti* places *stderr* in a state capable of handling such a situation. Of course, *fmulti* may be called at any time prior to the *fprintf*, and it need only be called once, allowing for numerous *fprintfs*, *putcs*, etc.

```
fmulti(stderr);                    /* must be loosely synchronous*/
    ...
if(error_condition){               /* not necessarily loosely synchronously */
    fprintf(stderr, message);
}
    ...
fflush(stderr);                    /* must be loosely synchronously */
```

Code 15-4 Example of Error Reporting Using *fmulti*

The example also includes a call to *fflush* which is not necessary when using singular output. Multiple output buffers are never flushed automatically. This has three important consequences:

1) The user *MUST* call *fsingl*, *fmulti*, *fflush*, *fclose* or *exit* to see anything written to a multiple output stream. These functions must be called loosely synchronously, even if the named output stream is in multiple mode.

2)   In order to avoid errors, the user must be certain to call *fflush* frequently enough to insure that the buffer does not overflow. Failure to obey this rule will result in the loss of data.

3)   At the time that *fsingl, fmulti, fflush, fclose,* or *exit* is called, the buffers are flushed to the output device in order of increasing *procnum*. This fact may be used to control the interleaving of the output from different nodes, as was demonstrated in Code 6-2.

Buffers are normally BUFSIZ bytes in length, and are allocated automatically by the system. BUFSIZ is a constant defined in the header file *stdio.h*, and is normally between 512 and 4096. The function *setbuffer* which is defined in Code 15-5 may be used to specify a new buffer of arbitrary size. It is similar to the function *setvbuf*, which is defined in [ANSI 87], except that it does not change the buffering policy associated with the given stream. Normally, *buf* is obtained by calling *malloc*, or by declaration as an external array. *Setbuffer* is useful for providing CUBIX with large user-allocated buffers which will not overflow at inopportune times.

```
setbuffer(stream, buf, sz)
FILE *stream;
char *buf;
int sz;
```

Code 15-5 Specification of *setbuffer*

The Standard I/O Library provides for unbuffered output streams in which a read/write system call is generated for each byte of I/O. The stream *stderr* is unbuffered by default, and *stdout* is unbuffered if it is connected to an interactive terminal. Normally buffered streams may be forced into an unbuffered state by use of the routines *setbuf* or *setvbuf*. Unbuffered streams are supported by CUBIX with the following provision: when an unbuffered stream is converted to multiple mode, it becomes a buffered stream with an automatically allocated buffer of the default size, BUFSIZ. Multiple streams revert to their unbuffered behavior upon calling *fsingl*, if they obtain their buffer by this mechanism. Thus, although *stderr* is normally unbuffered, *fmulti*(*stderr*) will work correctly, and automatically provide a buffer of BUFSIZ bytes. A subsequent execution of *fsingl*(*stderr*) will cause it to revert to its unbuffered state.

15-3 Implementation

The implementation of CUBIX is divided roughly into two parts. First, we describe a universal control processor program and a control processor/node protocol that provides the concurrent program access to all of the control processor's operating system. We must arrange that the concurrent program can make the system calls in Table 15–1. We also introduce the two new routines *mread* and *mwrite* at this level.

Second, we must implement the C Standard I/O Library in terms of the system routines just mentioned. Fortunately, the bulk of the work has already been done, because the C Standard I/O Library has, presumably, already been implemented in terms of the operating system primitives. Of course we must modify the sequential implementation so it distinguishes between multiple and singular I/O, and uses *mread* and *mwrite* when appropriate. We will restrict our attention to the extensions.

15-3.1 Implementation of System Calls

The first step in the implementation of CUBIX is to get the system started. Code 15-6 is an outline of the general approach. A CUBIX process is begun on the control processor by running the main program of Code 15-6 with command line arguments indicating the desired cube dimensionality, the file to be loaded into the cube, and arguments to be passed to the cube program. After parsing the command line, the program of Code 15-6 calls *cubeldve* which starts the application's *main* routine in the cube, and passes the arguments requested on the command line along with the environment of the control process.

The control processor now effectively gives up control and enters a loop which serves requests from the nodes. The loop terminates when the nodes request the *exit* system call, which terminates the control program.

```
#define FOREVER 1
extern char **environ;
/* the following are set by parse, based on the command line argc,argv */
int cubedim;
char **cubeargv;

main(argc, argv)
int argc;
char **argv;
{

    parse(argc, argv);
    cubeldve(cubedim, cubeargv, environ);

    while(FOREVER) serve_request();
    /* serve_request() will call exit or _exit */
}
```

Code 15-6   Main Routine for Universal Control Processor Program

The subroutine *serve_request* reads one request from the concurrent processor, identifies what system service is being requested, performs that service and provides appropriate data, and return codes to the concurrent process. Such a routine is a standard programming exercise and can be written in many ways. A very elegant technique uses an array of pointers to functions, each of which is responsible for collecting and disseminating the data for one of the system calls. An outline is given in Code 15-7.

```
#include <cros.h>

extern int Xaccess();
extern int Xcreat();
 ...
int (*functbl)()[] = {
  Xaccess,          /*funcnum = 0 */
  Xcreat,           /*funcnum = 1 */
  ...
} ;

serve_request()
{
  int funcnum;
  struct cubenv ce;

  cparam(&ce);
  cread(&funcnum, ce.cubemask, 0, sizeof(int));
  (*functbl[funcnum])();
}
```

Code 15-7 Control Processor Subroutine *serve_request*

The various functions in the table are responsible for obtaining their arguments from the nodes and returning their results. Node programs will identify the control process program to execute by providing *serve_request* with the appropriate index into the array *functbl*. A header file, e.g., *funcnums.h*, can be used to consolidate this information.

```
#define ACCESS 0
#define CREAT 1
...
```

Code 15-8 The Header File funcnums.h

An implementation of the system call *creat* is shown in Codes 15-9 and 15-10.

All of the routines listed in Table 15-1 can be implemented according to the template of Codes 15-9 and 15-10. The two new routines *mread* and *mwrite* are more complicated because each node must communicate with the control processor to either read or write distinct data. The CrOS III routines *fdumpcp*, *mdumpcp*, *dumpelt*, *floadcp*, *mloadcp*, and *loadelt* are useful in implementing *mread* and *mwrite*. An implementation of *mwrite* is shown in Codes 15-11 and 15-12.

```
#include <errno.h>
#include <cros.h>

#define MAXLEN 256 /* maximum path length we can handle */

Xcreat()
{
    int len, nread;
    char name[MAXLEN];
    struct {
        int fd;
        int errno;
    } reply;
    struct cubenv ce;

    cparam(&ce);
    len = cread(name, ce.cubemask, 0, MAXLEN);
    nread = cread(&mode, ce.cubemask, 0, sizeof(int));
    if(len >= 0 && nread == sizeof(int)){
        reply.fd = creat(name, mode);
        if(reply.fd < 0)
            reply.errno = errno;
    }else{
        reply.fd = -1;
        reply.errno = EBAD;
    }
    bcastcp(&reply, sizeof(reply));
}
```

Code 15-9 Implementation of *creat* in Control Processor

15-3.2 Implementation of the C Standard I/O Library

The C standard I/O library is a collection of routines designed to provide the C programmer with a fast, portable, and reliable input/output facility. The library itself is, of course, operating-system dependent, but the interface seen by the C program is not. Thus, programs written using the standard I/O library are potentially operating-system independent. In practice, the vast majority of C programs use the standard I/O library, so it is of the utmost importance to implement it efficiently.

In this section, we are interested in the implementation of the library, and especially how it can be modified to handle the extensions of Sec. 15-2.2. Rather than embarking on a detailed exploration of the issues involved in a sequential implementation of the library, we will assume that the reader already has such an implementation. If the sequential library has a clear and simple design, only a very small amount of code will have to be changed to support the parallel CUBIX extensions.

```
#include "funcnums.h"
#include <cros.h>

extern int errno;

int creat(name, mode)
/* node version of creat.*/
char *name;
int mode;
{
    int funcnum = CREAT;   /* CREAT defined in funcnums.h */
    struct {
        int fd;
        int errno;
    }reply;
    struct cubenv ce;

    cparam(&ce);
    cwrite(&funcnum, ce.cpmask, sizeof(funcnum));
    cwrite(name, ce.cpmask, strlen(name)+1);
    cwrite(&mode, ce.cpmask,sizeof(int));
    bcastelt(&reply, sizeof(reply));
    if(reply.fd < 0)
        errno = reply.errno;
    return reply.fd;
}
```

Code 15-10 Implementation of *creat* for Nodes

It is reasonable to assume that the sequential library makes use of system calls in only a few places, i.e., in a handful of common subroutines used by all the functions accessible to the user. Typically, the *write* system call is made only within *fflush* and a common routine _*flsbuf*, which is called by the *putc* macro. Similarly, the *read* system call is made only within _*filbuf*, which is called by the *getc* macro. Hopefully, the only routines needing non-trivial modifications will be _*flsbuf*, *fflush*, and _*filbuf*. Of course, we will also need to write *fmulti*, *fsingl*, and *ismulti* from scratch.

The first thing we must add is a way to distinguish between multiple and singular streams. All that is required is that a single bit in the stream structure be reserved for this purpose. The structure (in UNIX implementations) already has a field called _*flag*, which is treated as a bit-field and stores information such as whether the file has been opened for reading or writing, whether I/O is to be buffered, whether any errors have occurred accessing this stream, etc. Adding a new bit-field to _*flag* is trivial. For example, *ismulti* can be implemented by placing Code 15-13 in *stdio.h*.

The functions *fmulti* and *fsingl* are not as simple. Complications arise because of the need to allocate a new buffer when an unbuffered singular stream is switched into

```
#include <cros.h>
#define MAXPROCS 256    /* maximum number of processors in cube */
#define HUGEINT 0x7fff  /* a large integer, for 16-bit machines */

Xmwrite()
{
    int fd, i;
    int nload, ndump;
    int szarray[MAXPROCS+1];
    int array_of_intsz[MAXPROCS+1];
    struct{
        int ret;
        int errno;
    } reply;
    struct cubenv ce;

    cparam(&ce);
    cread(&fd, ce.cpmask, 0, sizeof(fd));

    ndump = fdumpcp(fd, HUGEINT, szarray);

    array_of_intsz[0] = ce.nproc;
    for(i=1; i<=ce.nproc; i++)
        array_of_intsz[i] = sizeof(int);

    nload = mloadcp(&szarray[1], array_of_intsz);
    if(nload < 0 || ndump < 0){
        reply.ret = -1;
        reply.errno = errno;
    }else{
        reply.ret = 0;
    }
    bcastcp(&reply, sizeof(reply));
}
```

Code 15-11 Control Processor Implementation of *mwrite*

multiple mode. Correctly programming this feature requires careful study of how and when buffers are allocated and freed in the sequential implementation. It is necessary to add additional bit-fields to *flag* to record the ownership and status of such buffers.

The only difference between multiple and singular output streams is manifested when the buffers are flushed. With the *mwrite* and *write* system calls, this difference is trivial to include. If the stream is multiple, then call *mwrite*; otherwise, call *write*. A small additional complication is that *fflush* does not necessarily call *write* at all if there is nothing to be written. This is a perfectly acceptable timesaving measure for singular files, because all processors are guaranteed to have nothing to write if any one of them has nothing to write. Unfortunately, it is not acceptable for multiple files, because even if

```
#include "funcnums.h"
#include <cros.h>

extern int errno;

int mwrite(fd,ptr,cnt)
int fd;
char *ptr;
int cnt;
{
    int funcnum=MWRITE;
    struct{
        int ret;
        int errno;
    } reply;
    struct cubenv ce;

    cparam(&ce);
    cwrite(&funcnum, ce.cpmask, sizeof(int));
    cwrite(&fd, ce.cpmask, sizeof(int));

    dumpelt(ptr, cnt);

    loadelt(&cnt, sizeof(int));
    bcastelt(&reply, sizeof(reply));

    if(reply.ret != 0)
        errno = reply.errno;
    return(cnt);
}
```

Code 15-12 Implementation of *mwrite* for Nodes

```
#define _IOMULTI (1<< a bit location not used elsewhere in _flag)
#define ismulti(p) (((p)-> _flag) & _IOMULTI)
```

Code 15-13 Definitions in stdio.h to Implement *ismulti*

one processor has nothing to write, other processors might still wish to write a nonzero number of bytes. In order to satisfy loose synchronization, the processor with nothing to write must also call *mwrite* , with *cnt* set to 0.

15-3.3 Standard Input Functions

Input streams are significantly more difficult than output streams. The difficulty arises because multiple input involves global behavior. What is read in one processor depends in detail on what has been read already by lower-numbered processors. Nevertheless, we would like to use as much code as possible from a sequential implementation of the Standard I/O Library. We can use most of the Standard I/O Library input routines, with little modification, if we add a subroutine to the beginning of each one which waits for all the processors with lower processor numbers to finish reading their input. When they are done, we adjust the stream's internal pointers in the next processor so that the next byte read from the stream is correct. Code 15-14 shows how we propose to change the function *fscanf* so it performs properly with multiple streams. Within the function *fscanf* the macro *getc* should behave exactly as in the sequential library. This is in contrast to its behavior in an application program, which depends on the multiplicity of its argument. To accomplish this, we define the symbol _LIBRARY in the code for *fscanf* and all other library routines, and make the change to *stdio.h* indicated by Code 15-15. The function *mgetc*, referred to by the *getc* macro in Code 15-15 is shown in Code 15-16. The constants _DONE and _REFILL, and the structure *cmd_struct* will be used shortly.

```
#define _LIBRARY
#include <stdio.h>

fscanf(stream, fmt, arg1)
FILE *stream;
char *fmt;
int arg1;
{
   if(ismulti(stream))
      wait(stream);

   code identical to the sequential version

   if(ismulti(stream))
      release(stream);
   return( value from sequential code );
}
```

Code 15-14 Implementation of CUBIX *scanf*

The function *wait*, shown in Code 15-17, consists of a loop which terminates when each of the processors with processor number lower than *procnum* has executed a call to *release*. During execution of this loop, one of the lower-numbered processors might exhaust the buffer associated with the stream and call *_filbuf* to refill it. Since *_filbuf* calls *read*, a system call in Table 15-1 to fill the buffer, we must arrange that all of the other processors also call *read*, or we would violate the rule of loose synchronization.

```
#ifndef _LIBRARY
#define getc(p)   (ismulti(p)) ? _mgetc(p) : usual definition
#else
#define getc(p)   usual definition
#endif

struct cmd_str{
    int type;
    int newposition;
};
#define _REFILL 1
#define _DONE 2
```

Code 15-15   Code added to *stdio.h* to Facilitate Multiple Input

```
#define _LIBRARY
#include <stdio.h>

int _mgetc(stream)
FILE *stream;
{
    int c;

    wait(stream);
    c = getc(stream);
    release(stream);
    return(c);
}
```

Code 15-16 Implementation of Multimode *getc*

This is the purpose of the *broadcast* and the conditional call to *refill* in the **do-while** loop in *wait*. After releasing control to higher-numbered processors, the function *release*, shown in Code 15-18, waits for the rest of the processors to call *release*, calling *refill*, in Code 15-19, whenever necessary. When the last processor has announced completion, *release* repositions the stream so all processors agree on the next character to be read. The function *_filbuf* is outlined in Code 15-20. In several places, the code is strongly dependent on the details of the implementation of the Standard I/O Library. In these places, we simply indicate in italics what should be done. With these routines and an implementation of the Standard I/O routines, multiple standard input is accomplished. All of the input routines can be implemented by analogy with the template for *fscanf* in Code 15-14.

The use of *wait* and *release* minimizes the modifications necessary to convert a sequential Standard I/O Library into a concurrent one, but it does so at the expense of speed. All the data is copied into all of the processors by *refill*, even though only one processor intends to use the data. In the case of *scanf* this is probably of little consequence because the computation required to unformat each byte of input data is substantial. The performance of other functions, e.g., *fread*, can be severely degraded, however. An alternative to the use of *wait* and *release* is to use *mread* whenever the number of bytes to be read is known in advance, i.e., in *fread*, *getw*, and *getc*. The use of *wait* and *release* are still necessary for library routines which read an amount of data that depends on the data itself, e.g., *scanf* and *gets*.

```
#include <cros.h>
#include <stdio.h>

wait(stream)
FILE *stream;
{
    struct cmd_str cmd;
    int mask;
    struct cubenv ce;
    cparam(&ce);
    mask = ce.nproc - 1;   /* broadcast on all channels */
    for(source=0; source<ce.procnum; source++){
        do{
            broadcast(&cmd, source, mask, sizeof(cmd));
            if(cmd.type == _REFILL)   refill(stream);
        }while(cmd.type != _DONE);
    }
    reposition the read pointer in the stream to cmd.newposition.
}
```

Code 15-17 Implementation of *wait*

```
#include <cros.h>
#include <stdio.h>
release(stream)
FILE *stream;
{
    struct cmd_str cmd;
    int mask, source;
    struct cubenv ce;
    cmd.type = _DONE;
    cmd.newposition = the correct position for the next call to getc
    cparam(&ce)
    mask = ce.nproc - 1;
    broadcast(&cmd, ce.procnum, mask, sizeof(cmd));
    for(source=ce.procnum+1; source<ce.nproc; source++){
        do{
            broadcast(&cmd, source, mask, sizeof(cmd));
            if(cmd.type == _REFILL)   refill(stream);
        }while(cmd.type != _DONE);
    }
    reposition the read pointer in the stream to cmd.newposition.
}
```

Code 15-18 Implementation of *release*

```
refill(stream)
FILE *stream;
{
    issue a call to read which fills the buffer associated with stream.
}
```

Code 15-19 Implementation of *refill*

```
_filbuf(stream)
FILE *stream;
{
    identical to the Standard I/O _filbuf, except calls to read are preceded by:
    {
        struct cmd_str cmd;
        struct cubenv ce;
        unsigned int mask;

        cparam(&ce);
        cmd.type = _REFILL;
        mask = ce.nproc - 1;
        broadcast(&cmd, ce.procnum, mask, sizeof(cmd)); /* src is this processor */
    }
    read(data into buffer associated with stream);
}
```

Code 15-20 Implementation of *_filbuf*

15-4 Conclusion

It is not difficult to implement a universal server process to run in the control processor of a concurrent computer which transparently provides system services to the nodes. Once this is done, libraries that provide a standard interface to the operating system can be executed in the nodes. The resulting environment is easy to use, familiar to the experienced programmer, and a significant improvement over the control processor/node environment described in Chap. 14.

16

Particle Dynamics: Problems with a Slightly Irregular Communication Structure

16-1 Introduction

The problems discussed so far have involved predictable overhead, in the sense that the programmer could determine *a priori* when and how much interprocessor communication would be necessary. We have further seen that the class of predictable problems is surprisingly rich. Nevertheless, there are many problems in which the interprocessor communication is not so easily predicted. We shall refer to the simplest class of nonpredictable problems as *need-predictable*. In need-predictable problems, the need for communication is predictable at compile time, but the details, such as exactly which data will be transferred, are not known until run time. This case stands in contrast to fully unpredictable problems in which even the necessity of communication is not known beforehand.

16-2 Position Updates: A Simple Example

A simple example of a need-predictable problem is the position update phase of an N–body particle dynamics simulation. Suppose that the positions and velocities of the particles are known at some time and the positions are to be obtained at some later time. In general, we can relate the updated position, $\vec{x}_{new}$, to the previous position, $\vec{x}_{old}$ by Eq. (16–1):

$$\vec{x}_{new} = \vec{x}_{old} + \vec{\Delta}(\vec{x}, \vec{v}, \cdots)$$

(16-1)

Usually, $|\vec{\Delta}|$ is small in comparison with other relevant length scales (in the simplest case, $\vec{\Delta} = \vec{v}\, dt$, with dt a small time step), so the particles don't move very much in each time interval. Now, let us suppose that a spatial decomposition has been adopted in which each processor controls a fixed region of space, and all the data connected with particles in that region are stored in the corresponding processor's memory. Note that this is not necessarily a good decomposition for all types of dynamical simulations (see, for example, Chap. 9 on long-range interactions).

In order to maintain the decomposition after the position update, some particles will have to move between processors. The precise identities of the movers is not known until run time. Nevertheless, the programmer knows that some communication must be done after each update, even if it is only to say, "I have no particle to be moved." Thus, the need for communication is predictable.

Before discussing the position update problem in the context of CrOS III, we may see how it is solved with a more general operating system. For this particular problem, the general operating system utilities, such as message queuing and routing, make the problem somewhat easier to program. As mentioned in Chap. 14, these utilities are costly in terms of performance, however, so it is important to ask whether CrOS III (crystalline communications) can be used instead. The pseudocode fragment in Code 16-1 shows how one might update particle positions using a general operating system which automatically routes and queues messages for subsequent processing.

```
proc_begin update_particles ( update particle data )
declare_buf new_part ( storage for incoming particle )
    for_begin ( each particle, p )
            [update particle data for p]
            if_begin ( p is no longer in this processor ) then
                    [remove p from local data structures]
                    [send p to the correct processor]
            if_end
    for_end
    [send an end of transmission message to all possible destination processors]
    for_begin ( all possible source processors, src ) then
            [receive a new particle into buffer new_part]
            while_begin ( src has not signalled end of transmission ) then
                    [insert new_part into local data structures]
                    [receive a new particle into buffer new_part]
            while_end
    for_end
proc_end
```

Code 16-1 Updating Particles on an Advanced Operating System

Code 16-1 contains perhaps the most straightforward solution of the problem as seen from the programmer's point of view, and we present it here as a point of departure for the rest of the discussion in this chapter. The algorithm could be improved in several ways. However, it is not our intention here to develop techniques for using general operating systems. Message forwarding and queuing are handled entirely by the operating system. The program is divided very clearly into two phases:

1)   an *update/scan* phase in which particle positions are updated, and those which need to be moved are extracted from the local data structures and forwarded via the operating system

2)   a *receive/cleanup* phase in which incoming messages are interpreted and incoming particles are placed in local data structures.

Unfortunately, simplicity has its price: general operating systems are slow because they must handle general message routing and queuing operations. For a need-predictable problem, the power of a general operating system is wasted. In the following section, we solve the same position update problem using the substantially faster

CrOS III polled communication scheme.

16-2.1 A Polled Algorithm

For concreteness, we will restrict the problem under consideration to two dimensions; the generalization to three or more dimensions is not difficult. We will also assume that $|\vec{\Delta}|$ is always smaller than the smallest linear dimension of any processor's region. Thus, a particle can never jump completely over a processor in a single step. This assumption is not necessary for the correctness of the algorithm that uses automatic routing and queuing, but relaxing the condition would substantially complicate the crystalline program. With this restriction, communication is only necessary between nearest neighbors in a rectangular two-dimensional grid. Of course, diagonal moves are also possible, and we must either provide diagonal communication paths in hardware or route particles around corners in software. We elect to route particles in software because the hypercube topology, commonly available in hardware, contains the Cartesian links, but not the diagonal links.

The overall approach is similar to that taken earlier with the advanced operating system. The problem is divided into an update/scan phase and a receive/cleanup phase. An important difference is that we don't simply give the particles to the operating system during the update/scan phase, and rely on the system to manage sufficient queue space and the like. Instead, we transfer the items from the local list to one of several export queues. We will have one export queue for each communication channel, for a total of four in the two-dimensional problem. The application process manages the queues, and communication is only done at predetermined times, when both sides of the channel expect it. The algorithm is given in Code 16-2.

This algorithm is incomplete, however. The routing strategy necessary for moving particles around corners is hinted at, but not described. Forwarding is accomplished by conditionally placing incoming particles (those from the import queue) into a new export queue. This operation is in error, however, if the new queue corresponds to a direction in which communication is already complete. We must design the algorithm to make sure that this never happens. Codes 16-3 and 16-4 illustrate a correct routing strategy.

We may consider a particular case to see how this algorithm guarantees that particles will be forwarded properly. In Fig. 16-1, the position of particle p has changed so that it must move from processor P_1 to processor P_3, which is up and to the left from its initial location. We could move it there in two ways: up first and then left, or left first and then up. Since the constant LEFT, whose value is 1, is less than the constant UP, whose value is 2, loop 1 will export particles to the left before they are exported up. Thus, it is imperative that p be placed on the left export queue first. This is guaranteed by loop 2 in *next_dir*, which tests for export to the left before it tests for export up. Correctness is guaranteed for all directions because loop 1 and loop 2 cycle through the directions in exactly the same way. If a particle must go around a corner, it is always placed in the queue which will be exported first.

To see how routing works, let's follow particle p after it is exported to the left. Based on the assumption that $|\vec{\Delta}|$ is small, we can be sure that p is now in the correct

```
proc_begin update_particles ( update particle data )
declare_buf export ( four buffers for storing outgoing particles )
declare_buf import ( four buffers for storing incoming particles )
      for_begin ( each particle, p )
            [update particle data for p]
            if_begin ( p is no longer in this processor ) then
                  [remove p from the local list of particles]
                  [identify first direction, dir, in which p must move]
                  [place data for p in buffer export[dir]]
            if_end
      for_end
      for_begin ( each direction, dir )
            [write buffer export[dir] to neighboring processor in direction dir,
                  while receiving incoming particles into buffer import[dir]]
            for_begin ( each particle, p, in import[dir] )
                  if_begin ( p belongs to this processor ) then
                        [copy p to the local list]
                  else
                        [identify next direction in which p must move, nextdir]
                        [copy p to export[nextdir]]
                  if_end
            for_end
      for_end
proc_end
```

Code 16-2 Outline of Particle Update Procedure Using a Crystalline Operating System

column of processors, and that it does not need to move farther left. Thus, when *next_dir* is called and *p* is in the import queue of processor P_2 in Fig. 16–1, UP is the first direction for which *test_export* returns TRUE. So *p* is placed in the up export queue, and in the next iteration of loop 1, in Code 16–4, it makes its way to its final destination.

16-3 Potential Energies with a Short-Range Interaction: A More Complicated Example

In the previous section, we saw how irregular short-range communication could be handled with CrOS III. We chose a very simple problem to illustrate the salient points of message forwarding. In this section, a more demanding example is considered. We compute the potential energy of interaction of a collection of particles which interact via a short-range potential, such as the Lennard-Jones potential:

$$U(r) = \frac{U_0}{4}\left[\left[\frac{\sigma}{r}\right]^{12} - \left[\frac{\sigma}{r}\right]^6\right] \tag{16-2}$$

This particular interaction is a semiempirical representation of the force between neutral noble gas atoms. The interatomic forces are attractive at large distances due to dipole fluctuations (see for example [Kittel 76]), and are strongly repulsive at short

```
proc_begin update_particles ( update particle data )
declare_buf export ( storage for outgoing particles )
declare_buf import ( storage for incoming particles )
        [let RIGHT = 0]
        [let LEFT   = 1]
        [let DOWN = 2]
        [let UP      = 3]
        [let STAY_HERE = -1]
        for_begin ( each particle, p )
                [update particle data for p ]
                proc_call next_dir ( check if p must move by returning next )
                if_begin ( next ≠ STAY_HERE ) then
                        [remove p from the local list of particles]
                        [place data for p in buffer export[next]]
                if_end
        for_end
        for_begin ( each direction, dir = 0 to 3 ) /* LOOP 1 */
                [write buffer export[dir] to neighboring processor in direction dir, while
                receiving incoming particles into buffer import[dir]]
                for_begin ( each particle, p, in import[dir] )
                        proc_call next_dir ( find next direction, next, in which p must move )
                        if_begin ( next = STAY_HERE ) then
                                [copy p to the local list]
                        else
                                [copy p to export[next]]
                        if_end
                for_end
        for_end
proc_end
```

Code 16-3 Detailed Code for Updating Particle Positions Using a Crystalline Operating System

distances due to the "hard core" electrostatic and exchange interactions. The Lennard-Jones potential is short ranged because it falls off sufficiently rapidly with increasing r that to a good approximation

$$U(r) \approx 0 \text{ for } r > 3\sigma \qquad (16\text{-}3)$$

In this example 3σ is the *cutoff* length or the separation beyond which pairwise interactions are considered negligible. It is the existence of such a cutoff that characterizes short-range problems. We can justify the introduction of a cutoff by imagining particles distributed uniformly in space with density ρ. The average number of particles in a shell of thickness dr, a distance of r from the origin is:

$$dN = 4\pi r^2 dr \, \rho \qquad (16\text{-}4)$$

and their cumulative affect on the potential energy of a particle at the origin is:

```
proc_begin next_dir ( find next direction, next, in which particle p must move )
      for_begin ( each direction, dir = 0 to 3 )    /* LOOP 2 */
             proc_call test_export ( return test = TRUE if p needs to go in direction dir )
             if_begin ( test = TRUE ) then
                    [next = dir]
                    [return]
             if_end
      for_end
      [next = STAY_HERE]
      [return]
proc_end

proc_begin test_export ( return test = TRUE if p needs to go in direction dir )
      if_begin ( p needs to go past boundary orthogonal to dir ) then
             [test = TRUE]
      else
             [test = FALSE]
      if_end
proc_end
```

Code 16-4 Procedures to Find the Next Direction to Send a Particle

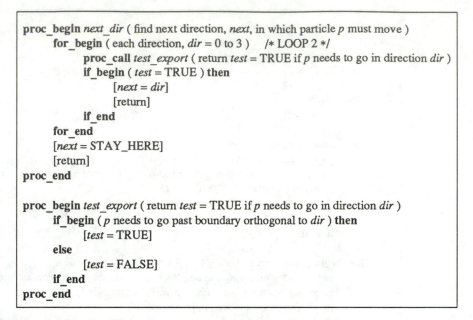

Five Steps (a), (b), (c), (d), (e)

in TRANSIT of p from P_1 to P_3

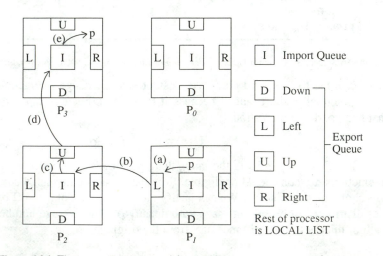

Figure 16-1 The route taken by a particle, p, which is required to move from processor P_1 to P_3, a diagonal connection. The steps in the route are: (a) from local list in P_1 to LEFT export queue in P_1, (b) from LEFT export queue in P_1 to the import queue of P_2, (c) from the import queue in P_2 to the UP export queue of P_2, (d) from the UP export queue in P_2 to the import queue in P_3, (e) from the import queue of P_3 to the local list in P_3.

$$dU = U(r)dN = 4\pi r^2 \rho \frac{U_o}{4}\left[\left[\frac{\sigma}{r}\right]^{12} - \left[\frac{\sigma}{r}\right]^{6}\right]dr \qquad (16\text{-}5)$$

For large r, i.e., $r >> \sigma$, we find that:

$$dU \approx U_o\left[\pi\rho\sigma^3\right]\left[\frac{r}{\sigma}\right]^{-4}d\left[\frac{r}{\sigma}\right] \qquad (16\text{-}6)$$

so the contribution from shells of increasing radii is a rapidly decreasing function of r/σ. If we are interested in the potential energy of a particle at the origin, we introduce a negligible error by restricting our attention to shells smaller than a fixed cutoff, for example $r < 3\sigma$.

Short-range forces appear on a more macroscopic scale in granular flow problems [Werner 85]. In such problems, irregularly shaped objects which are touching interact via friction and elastic deformation. There is no interaction at all between particles which are not touching. The interaction is short-range, with a cutoff given by the diameter of the largest particle, but it can be extremely complicated over that range.

Finally, short-range forces play a role in "Particle-Particle Particle-Mesh" N-body calculations, where they are used as a correction to a long-range force computed by other methods [Hockney 81a]. The Lennard-Jones potential treated in this chapter is intended as an illustrative example. More complicated interactions can be treated in much the same way.

16-3.1 The Sequential Problem: Cells and Linked Lists

Before further considering local particle dynamics problems in parallel, it is important to understand the problem in a sequential context. An important characteristic of the algorithm is how well it takes advantage of the locality of the interaction. Clearly, one could solve these problems by the methods discussed in Chap. 9 (Long-Range Interactions), but at the expense of a huge amount of wasted computation. The techniques of Chap. 9 explicitly compute the interaction between each pair of particles. Since the number of pairs grows as the square of the number of particles, these methods quickly become impractical as the number of particles increases. Thus, the methods of Chap. 9 are inappropriate for short-range problems.

One approach might be to abandon the computation of the potential when the separation is found to be greater than *cutoff* in length. However, computing the separations for each pair is still too much work because the computation of the separation must be performed for each pair of particles. What is needed is a means to quickly identify the neighbors of a particle i.e., those within the cutoff. To be useful, the time spent identifying neighbors of a given particle should be proportional to the number of neighbors rather than to the total number of particles.

A simple way to identify neighbors is to presort the particles into cells of linear size equal to the *cutoff* length. Then the search for particles near a given particle can be restricted to those cells adjacent to the cell in which the given particle is found. This technique, known as *geometric hashing,* is illustrated in Fig. 16–2.

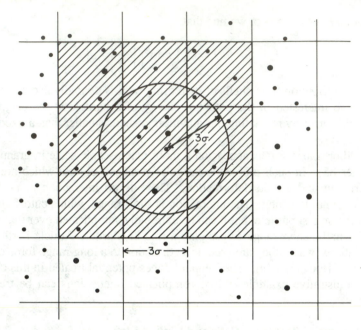

PARTICLES • IN A TWO DIMENSIONAL DECOMPOSITION
INTO CELLS OF SIDE 3σ

Figure 16-2 To find all particles within 3σ for particle p, it is necessary to search only in the shaded cells. Note that the cells are chosen to have linear size equal to the 3σ.

We are interested in finding all the neighbors of particle p. The particles of interest are those within the cutoff indicated by the circle. Obviously, it is only necessary to search within the nearby shaded cells. The interaction does not extend into any other cells, and we would be wasting our time by computing the separation between p and particles anywhere else. In Fig. 16-2, the savings realized by limiting our search is not especially great. We have managed to avoid searching about half of the cells. Fig. 16-2, however, might represent only a tiny part of a much larger problem such as that shown in Fig. 16-3. Searching only the particles within the shaded area there represents a huge savings over the full $O(N^2)$ search.

16-3.2 Linked Lists

Now consider the operations we will need to perform on the cells in our simulation. Firstly, and most importantly, given a cell, we must be able to quickly find all the particles contained within it. Secondly, we must be able to fill the cells in a reasonable time. It must be possible to insert a new particle into a cell so that the time required to generate the entire cell structure is proportional to the number of particles. Thirdly, cells must be

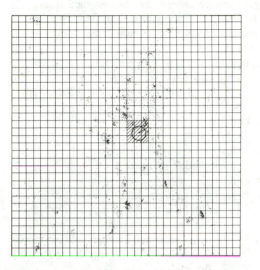

Figure 16-3 A larger scale version of Fig. 16-2 which shows that by searching only the nine shaded cells, we can immediately eliminate about 99% of the particles from those that could interact with our chosen particle.

capable of holding different numbers of particles. This suggests that simple arrays cannot be used for the cells because an array cannot grow dynamically as a cell becomes full. If we made all the arrays big enough to hold the maximum number of particles, we would waste a tremendous amount of memory, since most of the arrays would be almost empty. A simple data structure which meets the requirements is a *linked list*. In a simple implementation, a linked list consists of a collection of items. Each item consists of a pointer to the contents of that item (the particle) as well as a pointer to the next item. Linked lists require a fixed additional amount of memory per particle (the space for the pointers) and, therefore, are not too costly. A detailed discussion of linked lists at this point would take us rather far afield, so the interested reader is referred to any standard treatise on algorithms and data structures, e.g., [Knuth 73c].

16-3.3 A Sequential Implementation

We are now ready to present a sequential algorithm to compute the potential energy of a collection of particles interacting through a short-range potential. This algorithm is outlined in Codes 16-5 and 16-6.

The program in Code 16-5 is quite simple. First, the array of cells is initialized. Next, the list of particles is scanned and the individual particles are inserted into the appropriate cells. Once the particles are sorted into cells, it is possible to find the neighbors of a particle by searching only its own cell and neighboring cells. This is the purpose of the procedure, *interact*, illustrated in Code 16-6, which computes the interaction between a particle and all particles in neighboring cells. In order to count each pair only

```
proc_begin compute_energy ( evaluate interaction energy, U )
declare_int ncells_x ( number of cells in the x direction )
declare_int ncells_y ( number of cells in the y direction )
      [initialize U = 0]
      for_begin ( i = 0 to (ncells_x + 1))
            for_begin ( j = 0 to (ncells_y + 1) )
                  [initialize a linked list for cell number (i,j)]
            for_end
      for_end
      for_begin ( each particle, p )
            [find out which cell particle p is in]
            [insert particle in list for this cell]
      for_end
      for_begin ( i = 1 to ncells_x )
            for_begin ( j = 1 to ncells_y )
                  for_begin ( each particle, P, in the list for this cell )
                        proc_call interact ( add contribution of interaction
                                          energy due to P to U )
                  for_end
            for_end
      for_end
proc_end
```

Code 16-5 Sequential Evaluation of the Potential Energy Using Linked Lists

once, it computes the interaction between particles p_1 and p_2 only if the x-coordinate of p_1 is greater than or equal to that of p_2. If the x-coordinates are identical, it computes the potential only if the y-coordinate of p_1 is greater than that of p_2. This method is completely robust, and any other unambiguous criterion would be equally acceptable. The particular test we have adopted here has the advantageous property that a particle will never interact with itself. Such a self-interaction would have disastrous consequences in the computation of energies which contain terms varying as $1/r^{12}$.

We have simplified the code in *interact*, at the cost of some memory expenditure, by introducing a guard layer of empty cells at the edge of our simulation. In a sequential program, this guard layer is always empty and serves no purpose other than to provide a uniform neighborhood for all the internal cells. In the parallel version of the program, however, it will be used to store data received from neighboring processors, so that the neighborhood of a cell on the edge of one processor is consistent with the state of cells in neighboring processors.

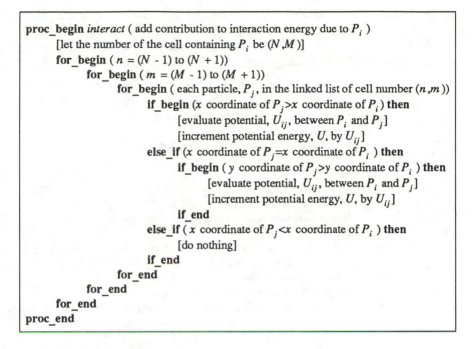

```
proc_begin interact ( add contribution to interaction energy due to P_i )
      [let the number of the cell containing P_i be (N,M)]
      for_begin ( n = (N - 1) to (N + 1))
            for_begin ( m = (M - 1) to (M + 1))
                  for_begin ( each particle, P_j, in the linked list of cell number (n,m))
                        if_begin (x coordinate of P_j > x coordinate of P_i) then
                              [evaluate potential, U_ij, between P_i and P_j]
                              [increment potential energy, U, by U_ij]
                        else_if (x coordinate of P_j = x coordinate of P_i ) then
                              if_begin ( y coordinate of P_j > y coordinate of P_i ) then
                                    [evaluate potential, U_ij, between P_i and P_j]
                                    [increment potential energy, U, by U_ij]
                              if_end
                        else_if ( x coordinate of P_j < x coordinate of P_i ) then
                              [do nothing]
                        if_end
                  for_end
            for_end
      for_end
proc_end
```

Code 16-6 Routine for Finding the Contribution of a Single Particle to the Interaction Energy

16-3.4 Parallel Decomposition

The parallel decomposition of local dynamics problems is very similar to that of local finite difference and finite element problems (Chaps. 7 and 8). Such problems are decomposed spatially, so that each processor controls either an equal volume of space or an equal number of degrees of freedom. The update algorithm then follows the general scheme:

(1) exchange degrees of freedom near edges with neighbors.
(2) compute exactly as in the sequential case, using the boundary conditions obtained from neighbors.

The same approach works for local dynamics problems. Again, the processors are assigned to equally sized regions of space. The degrees of freedom are now the positions of the particles. The particles in cells on the edges of a processor's region will interact with particles in neighboring processors, and it will be necessary to communicate relevant information about them to all processors which might be affected. This communication is analogous to the exchange of boundary degrees of freedom in finite difference problems. An important difference is that the number of particles near the edges is not known in advance, so that communication is only need-predictable. In fact, the number of such particles and even their location in memory will vary from processor to processor, as well as from one boundary to another within the same processor. Thus, the algorithm that exchanges particles across boundaries can no longer simply call *vm_shift*.

The parallel decomposition divides the cells evenly among the processors and initializes the guard layer in each processor. We will assume that there is available sufficient memory to store all of the additional particles contained in the guard layer. The algorithm for computing the short-range potential energy is given in Code 16-7.

```
proc_begin compute_energy ( evaluate the contribution, U, to the interaction energy
                            arising from this processor )
      [initialize U = 0]
      for_begin ( each cell in this processor and the guard ring cells )
            [initialize a linked list for this cell]
      for_end
      for_begin ( each particle, p, in this processor )
            [find out which cell particle p is in]
            [insert particle into list for this cell]
      for_end
      proc_call bound_exchg ( exchange boundary cell data with neighboring processors,
                              store incoming data in appropriate guard ring cells )
      for_begin ( each cell resident in this processor )
            for_begin ( each particle, P_i, in the list for this cell)
                  proc_call interact ( add contribution to interaction energy due to P_i )
            for_end
      for_end
      proc_call vm_combine ( compute sum of partial energies, U,
                                      accumulated in each processor)
proc_end
```

Code 16-7 Concurrent Code to Evaluate Interaction Energy

The principal difference between the sequential program of Codes 16-5 and 16-6 and the parallel program of Code 16-7 is the use of the procedure *bound_exchg*. In the parallel case, the guard layer in each processor is initialized by *bound_exchg* which exchanges the information about particles near processor boundaries.

Another addition in the parallel program is the use of the procedure *vm_combine*. As discussed in Sec. 4-4, *vm_combine* globally merges quantities across the ensemble, according to a specified combining function. In this case, the function, would perform floating-point addition. Thus, after the call to *vm_combine*, the energy, U, is the sum of all the partial energies computed concurrently in the processors.

16-3.5 Communication Routines

The subroutine *bound_exchg* is used to exchange all relevant information about particles in boundary cells. The communication arrangement is shown in Fig. 16-4. The guard strip on each boundary is filled with the contents of the true edge of its neighbors. This problem requires diagonal communication, after the manner of Sec. 16-2. As in that treatment, the diagonal moves will be composed of two orthogonal transfers, adding almost nothing to the complexity of the code. The main business of *bound_exchg* is to deal with each cell on each boundary in turn. The subroutine *bound_exchg* is outlined in Code 16-8.

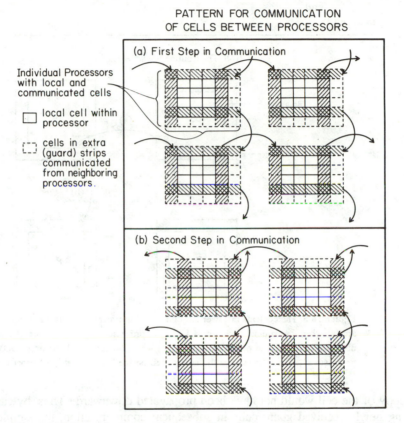

PATTERN FOR COMMUNICATION
OF CELLS BETWEEN PROCESSORS

(a) First Step in Communication

Individual Processors with local and communicated cells

□ local cell within processor

┌──┐
└──┘ cells in extra (guard) strips communicated from neighboring processors.

(b) Second Step in Communication

Figure 16-4 Rows of cells are moved vertically and columns of cells are moved horizontally so that the extra (dotted) strip of cells on the boundary of each processor is filled with particles from neighboring processors. In (a) the downward moving cells are highlighted with \\\ and the rightward moving cells with ///. In (b) the upward moving cells are highlighted with \\\ and the leftward moving cells with ///.

Figure 16-5 shows schematically which cells are communicated when *edge_exchange* is called for each of the four directions. To see how particles traverse the corners, consider the lower-left cell in the upper-right processor. In Fig. 16-5(a) it moves leftward into the guard layer of its neighbor. In Fig. 16-5(b), both the original cell and its copy are transmitted down, so that copies of the cell now appear in the guard layers of each of the three neighboring processors.

Forwarding around corners follows from the fact that the strips of cells communicated in Fig. 16-5 extend into the guard layer at both ends. Otherwise, in step (b) the

```
proc_begin bound_exchg ( exchange boundary cell data with neighboring processors )
        for_begin ( each of the cardinal directions, d )
                proc_call edge_exchange ( send data in appropriate strip of boundary cells to
                        processor in direction d, store incoming data in opposing guard cell strip )
        for_end
proc_end
```

Code 16-8 The Routine *bound_exchg*

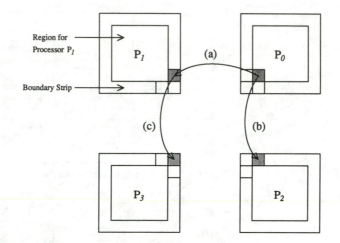

Figure 16-5 The contents of lower left corner cell in processor P_0 is transmitted across: arc (a) when the cardinal direction is LEFT, in processor P_0, arc (b) when the cardinal direction is DOWN, in processor P_0, arc (c) when the cardinal direction is DOWN, in processor P_1. Thus, it reaches the correct cell on the boundary strip of processors P_1, P_2, and P_3.

copy of the cell would not have been propagated downward. Thus, by carefully including newly received guard cells in subsequent communication, the simple algorithm of Code 16-8 correctly transfers cells around corners. The algorithm of Code 16-8 is a special case of a general purpose algorithm for long-distance communication in the hypercube, the *crystal_router*, which will be discussed in Chap. 22. In the general case, the loop over directions is not limited to the cardinal directions of a two-dimensional simulation, but rather includes all possible directions in the hypercube's hardware topology. As with Code 16-3, and implicitly in Code 16-8, incoming data is copied to an outgoing buffer, as well as local memory, according to whether it should be kept, kept and forwarded, or simply forwarded.

The procedure *edge_exchange* is not a simple application of *vm_shift* because the cells which it must exchange do not reside in contiguous or regularly spaced memory locations. *Edge_exchange*, in Code 16-9 is implemented with an auxiliary buffer to hold particles scheduled for export, and/or insertion into cells.

```
proc_begin edge_exchange ( send boundary cell data to processor in direction d,
                store incoming data in guard ring cells opposite )
declare_buf part_buf ( storage for particle data exchanged between processors )
declare_buf num_buf ( integer array, element i contains the number of particles
                in the i^{th} cell part_buf )
    for_begin ( each cell, c, on edge facing direction d )
        for_begin ( each particle, p, in cell c )
                [copy particle p to next position in part_buf]
        for_end
        [store number of particles in cell c in next element of num_buf]
    for_end
    [send part_buf to processor in direction d; receive incoming data
                and store in part_buf]
    [send num_buf to processor in direction d; receive incoming data
                and store in num_buf]
    for_begin ( each cell, c_i, in the guard layer opposite direction d )
        for_begin ( each of the next num_buf[i] particles, p, in part_buf]
                [insert p into cell c_i]
        for_end
    for_end
proc_end
```

Code 16-9 The Routine *edge_exchange*

16-4 Fully Unpredictable Problems

A significant class of scientific and engineering problems are need-predictable, and crystalline style "operating systems" are appropriate in such cases. Nevertheless, fully unpredictable problems are also important, and we will comment briefly on them here. Fully unpredictable problems could, in principle, be treated with crystalline communications also. It would be necessary in such a case to poll sufficiently often to be sure that whenever something "interesting" has occurred in another processor, it would not take long to learn about it. Interrupt-driven operating systems become useful when the time spent in fruitless polling becomes prohibitive. This is the case, for example, in certain types of Monte Carlo simulations, in which an interesting change in state in a neighboring processor is a relatively improbable occurrence [Johnson 86]. The only way to guard against such an occurrence in a crystalline environment, however, requires that each processor frequently poll all of its neighbors. This is usually a waste of time, since by the nature of the problem interesting state changes happen only rarely. Thus, the communication overhead due to polling is unacceptable.

In contrast, an interrupt-based operating system can be used to eliminate the polling overhead. A processor can determine whether any of its neighbors have sustained any interesting state changes simply by asking whether any messages are waiting in a mailbox. The result is the elimination of a large number of null or empty messages.

16-5 Conclusion

We have analyzed two types of need-predictable problems, position updates and short-range interactions. In both cases, the fact that the amount of communication could not be determined until run time presented no serious problems. We also found that communication between diagonally connected processors could be naturally achieved without direct connections. Forwarding around corners is accomplished by routing incoming data from one direction to the queue waiting to go out in another direction. It is important to stress that this is done completely within the crystalline environment. There is no inherent need for complicated message routing to be performed by an operating system or by higher-level system subroutines.

17

WaTor–An Irregular
Distributed Simulation Problem

17-1 Introduction

This chapter describes a model problem which exhibits many features of more advanced applications on a parallel computer. The algorithm is WaTor [Dewdney 84]: a simple Monte Carlo dynamical simulation in which idealized fish and sharks live, move randomly, breed, and eat one another in a two-dimensional periodic ocean. The name WaTor derives from the toroidal topology of the imaginary watery planet. Although the algorithm may not be relevant to realistic biological population dynamics studies, the program is intriguing and provides a rich learning environment for the parallel programmer. It serves to illustrate many crucial ideas in dynamic time-and event-driven simulation. Our goal in the present discussion is to achieve an efficient optimal implementation on the concurrent machine. Our approach to concurrent decomposition will require the simulation objects to be organized in machine memory as doubly linked lists. This structure, in turn, implies that the order in which the fish and sharks are updated is not predetermined, and that contention between processors attempting to make mutually conflicting moves must be an issue. The contention problem can be handled by the roll-back strategy. Simply stated, rollback involves taking update steps normally under the assumption that contention events occur relatively rarely. In the event of a conflict, the simulation is backed up in a such a manner as to undo the erroneous step.

In addition to rollback, this algorithm displays another characteristic of many advanced applications: the computational load can be imbalanced because the computational graph (and hence the load in each processor) is changing with time. In this example, the load imbalance comes about naturally because of the dynamics of the problem: the fish and sharks tend to aggregate in schools as they breed, move, and eat each other. If we perform a simple rectangular subdomain decomposition of the space (the ocean), some processors may contain very few if any fish and therefore will fall idle. Two methods for counteracting this dynamical load imbalance will be described.

In a more abstract vein, WaTor can be thought of as a two-dimensional cellular automaton [Wolfram 86]. By giving each fish and shark a "time to update" parameter during which time the update routine becomes inactive or sleeps, WaTor can be made to behave in a highly inhomogeneous fashion. This gives the simulation some of the characteristics of a wargame simulation, although involving only short-range interactions.

We will begin the discussion of WaTor by specifying the dynamical rules governing the moves of sharks and fish during the simulation. After briefly describing a simple-minded approach to coding this problem, we will proceed to examine the superior linked list method. The resultant concurrent application (making use of the CUBIX I/O system) will turn out to be fully portable between concurrent and single-processor computers. We will conclude with an examination of the rollback method and a discussion of load balancing techniques.

17-2 Dynamical Rules

The dynamics of WaTor consist of the rules to which the fish and sharks adhere as they move about. The underlying space of the simulation is taken to be a two-dimensional ocean with the periodic boundary conditions of a torus. The domain is discrete in that fish and sharks are allowed to live only on points of a mesh. The simulation input data consist of five numbers: *nfish* and *nshark*, the numbers of fish and sharks at the start of the simulation; *fbreed* and *sbreed*, the ages at which they breed; and finally, *starve*, the length of time a shark can survive without eating a fish. Here, time refers to the number of iterations the simulation has undergone, so that the simulation is temporally as well as spatially discrete.

The fish move in a simple way. Each fish examines its four nearest-neighbor locations. If empty locations are found, the fish is moved into one of these sites at random, making use of the *prand* routine described in Chap. 12. If no empty locations are discovered, the fish remains where it is. In either case, the age of the fish in incremented. In addition, if the age has reached *fbreed* and the fish has actually moved, a new fish of age 0 is placed at the old location.

Sharks are similar to fish, except they are hungry (presumably, the fish are eating universally abundant plankton). This means that sharks look for fish at their four neighboring positions. If any are found, the shark picks one at random, eats it, and resets its starve parameter to zero. If no fish are nearby, the shark resorts to moving at random, just as the fish do. Again, the shark breeds if its age has reached *sbreed*. If a shark goes for *starve* time units without eating, it dies.

17-3 The Software and Algorithm

17-3.1 The Sequential Code

Before delving into the parallel program, let us first discuss what constitutes an intelligent algorithm for the simulation of this dynamical system. A very simple programming strategy is immediately apparent whose parallel extension is quite straightforward. However, we shall see that this simple method can be significantly slower than a clever alternative, which will be the ultimate goal of our present discussion.

The simple method involves storage of all relevant information at the ocean sites (the mesh locations). One could imagine a few two-dimensional arrays: $ocean_{x,y}$, $age_{x,y}$, and $starve_{x,y}$. A fish at location 17,26 could be represented by a "1" in $ocean_{17,26}$, a shark by a "2," an empty spot by "0." The update step would then simply require a doubly nested set of loops which run over all locations.

The parallel extension of this method is straightforward. By analogy with the Laplace equation solver of Chap. 7, the ocean array is divided among the processors via the usual rectangular domain decomposition. The standard statement, "the parallel code is like the sequential code, but with special boundary conditions," again applies. The processors update their subdomains and communicate when necessary. Since the ocean consists of a regular homogeneous mesh, the problem of preventing processor contention is simply handled in the same manner that we accommodated nonsimultaneous relaxation in Chap. 7. An example of contention in the present context would be two processors trying to move fish to the same ocean location, resulting in an unforeseen collision. With our simple decomposition scheme, a four-color update ordering strategy, such as that discussed in Sec. 7-6, or the segregation of edge points would suffice to forestall any such contention problems.

The drawback of the simple method is that the time to perform an update scales with the size of the ocean. In this approach, the program can spend significant time looping through empty regions of the ocean, doing nothing useful. The standard approach to overcoming this inefficiency is to store the fish and sharks as linked lists. This approach allows the program to step through the active objects, concentrating on useful work only. The result is that the time to update now scales with the number of fish. If there is a mass die-off of fish, the program will run proportionately more rapidly until the population again increases.

Although the simple method has such a straightforward parallel extension, it will be abandoned here in favor of the richer problem of devising a parallel version of the linked-list approach.

17-3.2 Parallel Implementation

We begin by defining the data structures that are central to the linked-list approach. The attributes of a fish or shark are stored in a structure denoted *fishy* in Code 17-1.

```
declare_struct fishy {
        declare_int type; (fish or shark)
        declare_int age;
        declare_int starve; (applies only to sharks)
        declare_int locx; (x-coordinate)
        declare_int locy; (y-coordinate)
        declare_int nupdate; (update number)
        declare_buf pnext; (pointer to next item in list)
        declare_buf pprev; (pointer to previous item in list)
                };
```

Code 17-1   Fish/Shark Data Structure

The *type* member tells whether this is a fish or shark; members *age* and *starve* are the storage locations for the age and starvation factor of the fish; and *locx* and *locy* give the location of the fish in the ocean. Finally, *pnext* and *pprev* are pointers to the next and previous fish in the (doubly) linked list.

The other important data structure is that which defines the ocean mesh. Though the update loop of the program will run only through the actual fish, some sort of mesh is still needed. This facilitates the search for neighboring fish. In order to find out where a given fish can legally move, the *ocean* structure is queried for the existence of fish or sharks nearby. In the event of a positive result, *ocean* also contains a pointer to the fish or shark in question so that further queries may be addressed. For each location in the ocean, we have the structure defined in Code 17-2.

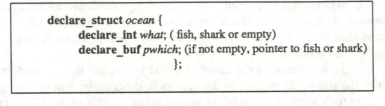

```
declare_struct ocean {
    declare_int what; ( fish, shark or empty)
    declare_buf pwhich; (if not empty, pointer to fish or shark)
};
```

Code 17-2 The Ocean Domain Data Structure

The parallel WaTor algorithm employs the familiar rectangular subdomain decomposition for the ocean, assigning to each node of the concurrent processor a subdomain of *ocean* and an independently linked list of fish (one which incorporates no links crossing processor boundaries). This decomposition is illustrated in Fig. 17-1.

The heart of WaTor is the update routine, called *move_fish*. It runs through the linked lists and attempts to move/breed each member of the list. The basic outline of the routine is given in Fig. 17-2. In order to update all the fish in its region, each node must know the contents of neighboring boundary strips of the *ocean* mesh. As a result, the first step, shown in Fig. 17-2(a), involves the interprocessor exchange of these strips of *ocean*. This array includes an extra set of sites all around the subdomain so as to be able to store the boundary strips. This closely parallels the guard ring approach to the Laplace equation decomposition in Chap. 7. This first stage is accomplished by the subroutine *send_bound* which, in turn, calls the CrOS III routine *vshift* to do the communication.

In Fig. 17-2(b), *move_fish* processes the linked lists and performs updates for every fish and shark in the region. A point to which we will return later is that fish and sharks are updated separately. By this we mean that first all the fish in the region are updated with the sharks held fixed. Then the sharks are moved, holding the fish fixed. Update order is not included as part of the canonical WaTor dynamical rules, so we shall neglect the possible influence of this special choice of update ordering. Different choices of update order will be discussed later.

As the fish are moved, those which decide to leave the processor subdomain are not immediately communicated, but are instead removed from the linked lists and stored in a separate buffer. They are communicated at the end of the update step. The routine *return_bound* performs the communication (calling the CrOS III routine *cshift*) and is sketched in Fig. 17-2(c). In addition to the actual communication, *return_bound* also handles the task of receiving the fish and inserting them into the appropriate linked lists of the destination node. It also detects contentions and rebuffers these fish.

Typical WaTor Configuration

(a)   Fish (dots) and Sharks (◇)

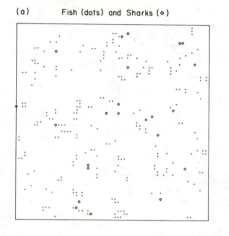

(b)   Linked lists after Decomposition

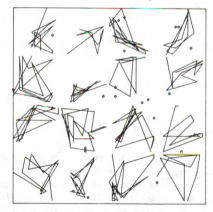

Figure 17-1 A typical WaTor configuration: (a) WaTor, on a 128 x 128 ocean. Fish are represented by dots, sharks by diamonds, (b) The problem decomposed onto a 4 x 4 mesh of nodes with the fish linked lists drawn. No links cross any processor boundaries.

The final phase of *move_fish* is a call to the routine named *resolve*, which is illustrated in Fig. 17-2(d). This routine sends back those fish which encountered collisions and attempts to move the fish in a different direction. Contention resolution will be discussed in more detail below. The pseudocode outline of *move_fish* is given in Code 17-3.

The routine *send_bound* simply consists of four calls to the CrOS communication routines in order to transfer the boundary strips of the *ocean* mesh. The structure of *update_fish* is defined by the implemented dynamical rules outlined previously, with the

Steps in WaTor Algorithm

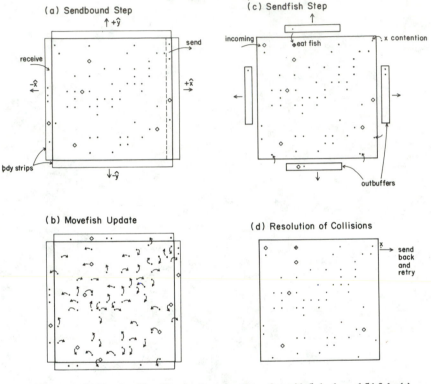

Figure 17-2 WaTor algorithm illustrated on a configuration with 5 sharks and 54 fish: (a) The *sendbound* step: a single node is shown. The *vshift* of $+\hat{x}$ is actually shown. Each node sends out its own $+\hat{x}$ strip of *ocean* and then turns around and receives the corresponding data into the extra padding of *ocean*. (b) *Movefish* updates everyone in its subdomain, (c) *Sendfish* sends and receives buffers, inserts incoming fish, (d) *Resolve* any collisions by picking one fish to go back and try again.

few modifications necessary for the parallel case. While the details of the algorithm may be obtained from a detailed inspection of the Software Supplement, we will roughly outline the workings here.

When a shark eats a fish, the first thing that happens is that the fish is removed from its linked list by the routine *remfish*. If the fish is in a boundary strip, and is therefore actually stored in a neighboring processor, this is unnecessary. For this reason, before actually calling *remfish*, we test to determine whether or not the fish is in the boundary strip. If not, only then is the fish removed. In either case, the shark moves to the new location. This movement, done by the routine *movf*, tests to determine if the fish or shark is leaving (that is, if it has entered a boundary strip). If the fish or shark is leaving, it is removed from the linked list and buffered in an array of *fishy* structures, *fbuff* . The actual communication to neighboring processing nodes is done by *return_bound*.

```
proc_begin move_fish ( perform an update cycle )
    for_begin ( each cell )
        proc_call send_bound ( exchange boundary fish with other processors )
        proc_call update_fish ( update the fish in this cell )
        proc_call return_bound ( return updated boundary fish to their home processor )
        proc_call resolve ( resolve contention conflicts )
    for_end
proc_end
```

Code 17-3 The WaTor Update Cycle

If a shark is eating an out-of-processor fish, the actual eating of the fish (that is, the *remfish* of it) will occur within the *return_bound* call in the neighboring processor. In this case, the shark is sent to its destination, the fish to be eaten is removed by *remfish*, and the shark is inserted by *addfish*.

So far, the program has been explained mainly in reference to the parallel machine. The code, however, continues to work on a sequential machine as long as the appropriate I/O subroutine library routines are defined. In the limit of a single-processor machine, *doc*, *procnum*, and other members of the *cubenv* structure (Sec. 14-5.6) are still defined. These variables simply assume the appropriate values for a single processor: $doc = 0$, $procnum = 0$, etc. The *gridmap* routines still work, although trivially. The communication routines, though not sending information to another processor, are not entirely trivial in the sequential case. This is because they still must perform memory-to-memory copies from one strip of *ocean* to another, as shown in Fig. 17-3. If we assume the existence of a dummy sequential CrOS / CUBIX library, the very same code is applicable to both parallel and sequential machines. This code, when executed on the sequential computer, will not run at quite the optimal speed for the sequential machine. This is due to the fact that we are spending part of our time doing the memory-to-memory copies. These operations need not be done on the sequential machine and therefore waste time. However, it is also clear that the wasted work is a surface effect and for large problems will be negligible. In fact, this asymptotic "immunity" holds for exactly the same reasons that the algorithm is efficient on the MIMD machine in the first place (see also Sec. 3-5 and the discussion of communication in other chapters). In general, we may well conjecture that for any algorithm which is reasonably efficient on the parallel computer, it will also be reasonable to run the same code on a sequential machine with a dummy library of concurrent utility routines.

A certain degree of code portability has been arrived at in this example. It is of more than passing interest to be able to run an application on various machines, some of which may have superior debuggers, output devices, discount prices, and so on. Clearly, we can make no claim to have solved the classic supercompiler problem, in which the ideal is to obtain a parallel application transparently, starting from a sequential program.

Rather we have found that one correct way to write code is to do so with the parallel machine in mind, retaining the option to run on different types of machines (e.g., sequential computers, multiprocessor, shared-memory machines) through the use of simple dummy routines.

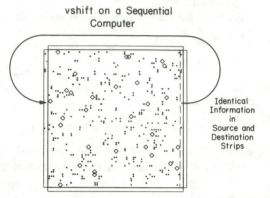

Figure 17-3 *vshift* on sequential computer. The *vshift* of the $+\hat{x}$ strip is shown. On the sequential machine, *vshift* does a memory- to-memory copy.

It is tempting to make the strong assertion that some sort of parallel language / operating system / subroutine library standard needs to be established. Once this is done, codes are written according to this standard and run on all machines of MIMD architecture. We have attempted a modest start in this direction with our standard CrOS / CUBIX communication system.

17-4 The Resolution of Collisions and Conflict

17-4.1 A Simple Technique

Occasionally during the simulation, conflicts or collisions such as that shown in Fig. 17-4(a) will occur. The problem occurs along processor boundaries: since the boundary strips are communicated only at the beginning of an update sweep, the information contained in them becomes out of date. As shown in the diagram, a fish from each processor has spotted the same empty place in the ocean and both have attempted to occupy it. Three-fish collisions, shown in Fig. 17-4(b), can also occur.

A simple fix for the case of a collision may be incorporated in WaTor. The fish which has crossed the processor boundary and now has no place to go is simply returned back to the processor from which it came. Once returned, an attempt is made to reinsert the fish in the spot from which it came. This will usually be possible, although a double-conflict situation such as that shown in Fig. 17-5 can occur. In the current implementation, if the reinsertion is permitted, it is performed. Otherwise, the fish in question is simply thrown away.

This simple version of rollback is not rigorously correct. Due to the collisions and the consequent return of the fish (or shark), they will have a slightly more difficult time

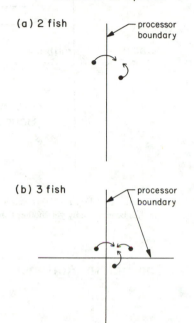

Conflicts in Update

(a) 2 fish

(b) 3 fish

Figure 17-4 (a) A two fish conflict. Both fish are moving to the same empty location. (b) A three fish conflict.

crossing over processor boundaries than in making nonboundary moves. In effect, the ocean contains lines (corresponding to the processor boundaries) which exert on fish and sharks a slight repulsive force which tends to keep them in their current subdomain. A more correct rollback code must keep track of the old locations of the fish, so that the multiple rollback drawn in Fig. 17-6 can be performed. Correct rollback involves undoing the simulation in an unbiased manner sufficiently far back so that the update may be retried. It is important to note that rollback for this time-driven simulation can retreat only a limited amount. It is possible (though very unlikely) to encounter the need to rollback all the fish in the ocean. This is the largest possible rollback however, since the rollback doesn't extend back into previous time steps as is more generally the case for event-driven simulations [Jefferson 85].

17-4.2 Alternative Update Strategies

We have seen that our insistence on writing an efficient, linked-list-based code has led to the somewhat difficult problem of rollback. In the present context, this provides us with an interesting new problem in parallel programming. Our primary motivation has not been to solve the WaTor problem per se, but rather to illustrate the issues common to

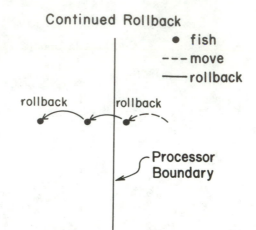

Figure 17-5 The frustrated fish of Fig. 17-4(a) is sent back to its original processor, only to discover that its spot has been taken by yet another fish.

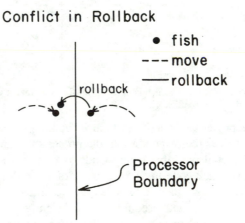

Figure 17-6 The correct thing to do is to continue rolling back until everyone has a place to go.

other important applications. Before pressing on, however, we should mention other possible ways of writing the code.

The first alternative has already been mentioned in the introduction. In this approach, we abandon the linked lists and store all information in the ocean structure. The program proceeds by looping through this array. In this strategy, the program can be so structured that processors avoid fish collision contention problems. Each node may first update all of its nonboundary domain. Then, all nodes concurrently update their left-hand boundary strips. The processors are kept synchronized by the CrOS communication routines. They then proceed to the right-hand, the top, and the bottom boundaries. No contention can occur since the processors are always operating on boundary cells well removed from those currently being updated in any other processor.

A second technique involves keeping the linked-list nature of the current program, but locking the neighboring ocean sites of each fish currently undergoing update. Once the fish is moved, the neighboring sites are unlocked. To be more explicit, consider a node attempting to update a particular fish. Before actually doing anything, flags are set at the neighboring ocean sites which have the meaning: "do not move anything into these sites– they are already under consideration." In general, messages will need to be sent to other nodes to request the current contents and to lock up these neighboring ocean sites. Since this message traffic will be random in nature, it must proceed within an asynchronous communications system. If a processor encounters previously locked sites, it notes the fact and moves on to the next fish in the linked list. These failures are later tried again until they are successfully updated. In this way, the processors are able to randomly update their fish. When they bump into one another, only one updates, while the other tries somewhere else.

Finally, a third alternative approach to writing the WaTor simulation without having to resort to rollback avoids contention through checkerboard ordering. We again keep the linked-list nature of the program, but, as shown in Fig. 17-7, we further subdivide the domain of each processor into four smaller domains. Each of these subdomains is associated with its own linked-list and the processors start by all updating their lower left-hand subdomains. Communications then occur, having the effect of synchronizing the processors. All processors next proceed to their lower right-hand subdomains and update these regions, and so on. In this way, the updated cells are segregated so that communicated *ocean* members never become out of date. Thus it is always safe to use a boundary site without concern for changes being made by another processor.

17-5 Load Imbalance and Its Resolution

17-5.1 Load Imbalance in WaTor

Figure 17-8 shows some typical WaTor fish/shark configurations. A clear effect is the tendency of the fish to form large schools with the sharks eating around the edges of these areas. The asymptotic configurations typically bear little resemblance to the random starting configuration. The system develops a coherent structure. This structure results in a performance impact, since with the simple rectangular decomposition so far described, the work load within different processor regions may vary widely. Processing nodes which happen to be responsible for domains containing few fish or sharks will have little to do. They will update their fish and then call the communication routines within *return_bound*. At this point, they will wait until the neighboring nodes catch up to them. We cannot relax the waiting condition. Otherwise, some processors could get far ahead of others (in terms of simulation time) and very costly rollbacks would become necessary.

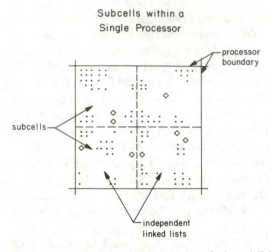

Figure 17-7 A single processor's subdomain which has been further subdivided into four smaller subcells. The fish and sharks in each subcell are stored in their own linked list; i.e., the processor has four sets of linked lists.

We here encounter an issue of fundamental importance for parallel computing: the case of a dynamically changing, fluctuating load and the problem of keeping the performance of the parallel computer high throughout such a computation. The problem is dynamical because the computational graph is continually changing with simulation time. Fish are eaten and sharks starve; the schools change shape and move about. If we resort to a more general decomposition than the simple rectangular case, (for instance, a decomposition like that shown in Fig. 17-9), a significant imbalance can quickly ensue after a few time steps. We touched upon the problem of load balancing earlier in this volume, but the present problem offers the best context for a more extensive discussion and treatment of the possible solutions.

It has been found [Fox 86a] that the problem of finding decompositions can be fruitfully recast in the form of an equivalent physical system. This is done by identifying a Hamiltonian or energy function which somehow parameterizes the properties of a desirable decomposition. Another name for this Hamiltonian is the objective function which was introduced in Chap. 13. A low-energy decomposition will be a good decomposition. In other words, a decomposition with a well-balanced load and relatively low communication overhead cost would correspond to a minimal Hamiltonian. The problem of decomposition now becomes that of finding a ground state (configuration of lowest energy) solution for the Hamiltonian.

Before proposing a specific Hamiltonian, let us abstract a bit from the case of WaTor. Consider the fundamental computational objects or elements as particles which are free to move about in the space of the concurrent processor. These computational objects are, in the case of WaTor, individual fish or sharks. In a more general setting, the

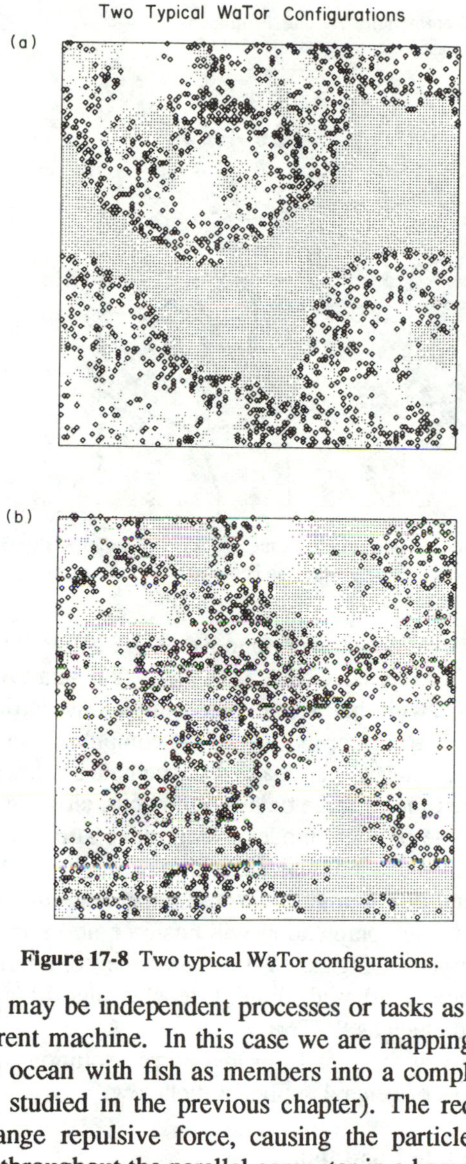

Two Typical WaTor Configurations

(a)

(b)

Figure 17-8 Two typical WaTor configurations.

objects may be independent processes or tasks as viewed by the operating system of the concurrent machine. In this case we are mapping the complex system consisting of the WaTor ocean with fish as members into a complex system of interacting particles (the system studied in the previous chapter). The requirement of load balancing acts as a short-range repulsive force, causing the particles, and therefore the computation, to spread throughout the parallel computer in a homogeneous, balanced manner. The situation is somewhat similar to a gas or fluid filling up a container. This particular analogy, however, is not precise. In a perfect gas, the repulsive pressure which fills the container is due to the random microscopic motion (velocity) of the particles, rather than to any actual repulsive force between them. In the case at hand, we do not want the particles (fish or processes) to retain a memory of velocity. Instead, we want them to move slowly

Approximately Load Balanced
Domain Decomposition

Figure 17-9 A more general decomposition of the WaTor configuration shown in Fig. 17-8. This decomposition was drawn by hand and is meant to be approximately load balanced.

so that they stay put in processors unless forced to move on. A better analogy, therefore, is that of particles interacting via a repulsive force with the system at a low temperature.

The requirement in conflict with that of load balancing is interparticle communications. The various elements (e.g., neighboring fish) of the computation need to communicate with one another. If the particles are far apart (distance being defined as the number of communication steps between them) large delays will occur, slowing down the computation. We therefore add to the physical model a long-range attractive force between those pairs of particles which need to communicate with one another. This force will be made proportional to the amount of communication traffic between the particles, so that heavily communicating parts of the computation will coalesce and remain close to one another in the concurrent computer. Figure 17-10 shows the communication requirements for partial differential equation-based, finite difference algorithms as well as for irregular short-range simulations such as WaTor.

There are many different ways to search for low-energy solutions to Hamiltonians. We will describe two approaches of general applicability below.

17-5.2 Simulated Annealing Approach to Load Balancing

The method of simulated annealing [Kirkpatrick 83] has already been discussed within the context of the traveling salesman problem in Chap. 13. Here we will describe how an annealing Monte Carlo method can be used to find and adapt decompositions for irregular problems such as that posed by WaTor. This section describes a reasonable choice of the objective function (or Hamiltonian) for the annealing and mentions some

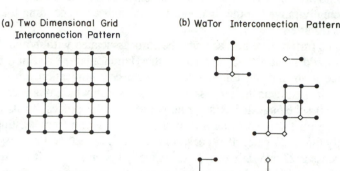

Interconnection becomes Communication
when links cross processor boundaries

Figure 17-10 (a) The communication requirements for a two-dimensional partial differential equation-based problem. The dots represent degrees of freedom located at the grid sites. They interact in a nearest neighbor fashion and this is represented by the connecting lines. These lines form the "communication pattern" of the algorithm. (b) The communication pattern for WaTor.

additional issues pertinent to dynamical cases such as WaTor.

The technique has an obvious motivation in at least one sense. We are seeking more general decompositions than the simple rectangular case, allowing the decomposition to dynamically adapt to the simulation by following the schools of fish as they develop. The crux then becomes: "How do we effectively and rapidly readapt the decomposition?" Simulated annealing provides a powerful general answer to this question. This point conceded, we are forced to ask, "Can we anneal rapidly enough to be able to closely track the computation?" Remember, the annealing steals computational cycles away from the principal computation task of interest.

Consider some general irregular problem executing on the MIMD parallel machine with decomposition of the general type shown in Fig. 17-9. The Monte Carlo annealing procedure starts by quantifying the current effectiveness of the decomposition. If serious load imbalances or unnecessarily long-distance communications are in evidence, the system suspends the computation and proceeds to anneal the decomposition. This is accomplished by the Metropolis method [Metropolis 53]. Trial moves are offered which are unconditionally accepted if they lower the energy. If the energy is raised (i.e., heading toward an even worse decomposition) the move is rejected except for a fraction of the attempted moves. The probability of any such move's acceptance decreases exponentially with the magnitude of the energy increase. It is important to note that it may be relatively expensive to actually move the fundamental particles or processes between processors. A significant improvement, therefore, involves moving tokens of the processes which consist of small data packets sufficient to describe the essential features of the process. The annealing proceeds for some length of time, with the aim of substantially improving the decomposition. At the conclusion of annealing, the processes are actually moved to the final locations of their corresponding tokens and the computation is restarted.

To further take into account the costs associated with moving processes, it is advisable to add a third type of force to the Hamiltonian in addition to the repulsive load-balance term and the long-range attractive communication term. This third term is a force which attracts the process to the processor in which it is currently residing. We can picture it schematically as a spring connecting the process to its current location. The rationale for this kind of term is to prevent the system from wasting time making moves of only marginal gain. If it doesn't matter much whether a process is in processor 21 or in processor 22 one step away, it is generally better to leave it where it is.

In the simulated annealing approach, the annealing algorithm acts analogously to a physical heat bath, with the task of keeping the computation "cool." It is important to note that the annealing procedure can accomplish only so much. If annealing is allowed to continue for a very long time (attempting to reach the optimal solution) the cost is too many computational cycles stolen away from the actual calculation. This realization suggests the importance of the concept of temperature in the annealing computation. Given a specific algorithm, the annealing procedure can keep the computation only so cool. The minimum achievable temperature is characteristic of the underlying algorithm and is independent of the parameters of the computer used. More detailed discussions of simulated annealing as applied to the problem of decomposition can be found in [Fox 85a, 86a, 86g] and as applied to the finite element method in [Flower 86].

17-5.3 The Scattered Decomposition Approach to Load Balancing

The scattered decomposition is an effective solution strategy for the decomposition problem posed by the large class of irregular problems of which WaTor is an example. The scattered decomposition has also been successfully applied to the parallel solution of irregular finite element problems [Morison 86].

The concept is illustrated in Fig. 17-11. As in the usual rectangular decomposition, we map the parallel machine onto a two-dimensional mesh. Instead of simply superposing this mesh on the ocean of WaTor, however, we subdivide the ocean into many rectangular regions and subsequently distribute these subregions or templates among the processors of the concurrent machine. Each processing node ends up being responsible for many small mutually disjoint regions, which we will refer to as granules. Figure 17-12 shows, for example, the granules for which processor 0 would be responsible in a typical scattered decomposition.

The scattered decomposition accomplishes load balancing for all but the most improbable of possible WaTor configurations. Neglecting any conspiratorial arrangement of fish, each processor has a piece of the action across the entire space of the problem. In essentially any simulation run, each processor will end up with roughly the same work load. This spatial averaging approach to load balancing works best as the granule size decreases, although the communication overhead increases in this limit.

Scattered Decomposition for 16 Processors

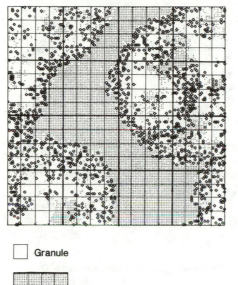

☐ Granule

Template

Figure 17-11 The scattered decomposition. Shown is a 4 × 4 array of processors over-
laid over the problem 16 times. That is, there is a 4 × 4 array of templates, each of which
consists of a 4 × 4 set of granules.

Another appealing feature of the scattered decomposition is that the required communication pattern between the nodes retains a regular rectangular topology. Since this
regular topology is often directly reflected in the machine hardware and the associated
low-level message-passing system (e.g., CrOS III), communications will generally be
fast in this method. On the other hand, as mentioned above, small granule sizes yield a
greater communication perimeter relative to the contained area of useful work (i.e., the
surface-to-volume ratio is increased). As a result, it is not immediately clear whether
scattered decomposition leads to higher or lower absolute communication overhead costs.
The answer to this question is dependent upon the choices of both machine and algorithm.

There remains one important point to be discussed with regard to coding of the
scattered decomposition algorithm. A blunder in programming technique can actually
prevent an algorithm which employs the scattered decomposition from achieving load
balance. Care must be taken not to impose excessive synchronization conditions during
update of a template. If communication-imposed synchronization occurs after each
granule of the template, the program is self-defeating, in that at any given time different

Role of Processor O in Scattered Decomposition

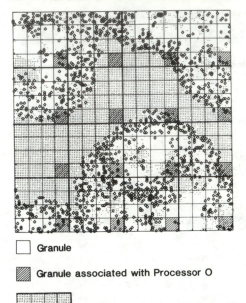

☐ Granule

▨ Granule associated with Processor O

Template

Figure 17-12 The granules for which processor 0 is responsible.

processors may be working on granules with very different loads. In fact, the result will be a worse load imbalance than without the scattered decomposition! In order to correctly achieve load balancing, we need to allow processors to move immediately to the next granule without waiting, so that the load balance is averaged over the whole problem. The processors run free without communication until reaching the last template. As a result, the communications between all of the granules throughout the ocean must be buffered and stored as the processors sweep through the ocean, and only at the very end of an update cycle are the communications actually performed.

Throughout this book, we have emphasized the need for MIMD hardware; we must be careful not to shoot ourselves in the foot on the software level by mistakenly coding in a manner more appropriate to SIMD machines!

As described so far, the scattered decomposition algorithm still must deal with the contention problem. One solution is rollback. Another, possibly simpler solution is to have processors skip over some of the templates. The update now proceeds as a sequence of "mini-cycles". As an example, in the first mini-cycle, processor 0 would update its granule in template 0,8, etc., processor 1 would update its granule in template 1,9, and so on. The pattern is chosen so as to load balance and keep the processors far apart during any mini-cycle. As we proceed through the mini-cycles, the patterns change and are chosen so as to eventually update all the granules.

It seems that we have hit upon the solution to all of our load balance/conflict problems. By virtue of the scattered decomposition, the computation is well load balanced and a straightforward method for resolving the conflict problem fits easily within this approach. In any practical application, however, the problem-dependent and machine-dependent factors influencing the solution of irregular problems may tilt the balance in favor of one or another of the alternative approaches.

18

Sorting on the Hypercube

18-1 Introduction

This chapter discusses sorting: the arrangement of data, which may consist of any of a variety of symbolic or numerical objects, into some set sequential order. With this generalized concept of order, we are not restricted to sorting only numerical values. In general, any data that can be keyed to values through some function are appropriate. This chapter is based upon work by Felten, Karlin, and Otto [Felten 85a]. The ideas presented here are appropriate for MIMD machines and are somewhat specific to hypercubes. Similar work appears in [Wagar 86]. Parallel sorting is discussed in other contexts, in [Akl 85, Batcher 68, Baudet 78, Johnson 84, Li 86, Thompson 77].

Sorting is an algorithm of fundamental importance because it occupies a central part of many computational applications. To give just one example, we might consider a hypothetical symbolic manipulation program running on a concurrent machine. Having arrived at a complex set of algebraic expressions the program may be faced with the task of simplifying them to obtain a reduced result. This is done by expanding out all functions, combining expressions over common denominators, and so on. The process expands the original expression into many terms (perhaps hundreds of thousands), rapidly using up processors and memory throughout the parallel machine until, finally, only atomic expressions remain (for example, polynomials). The simplification is now a relatively straightforward process: like terms need only to be brought together, and their coefficients combined. This is where the parallel sorting algorithm enters. Sorting is also useful for load balancing parallel algorithms. In [Gottschalk 87] a parallel sort is employed to automatically decompose a missile tracking problem. Section 22-3 illustrates a recursive bisection decomposer which is closely related to the parallel quicksort discussed in this chapter.

It is not immediately clear how to define the canonical form for "sorted" data when dealing with a distributed-memory parallel computer. Should the resulting sorted list wind up in one of the processing nodes of the machine, or should the list remain distributed? The answer to this question depends somewhat upon the specific purpose for which the sort is intended. For the purposes of this chapter, we will be motivated by examples such as the above (load balancing, symbolic manipulation) and as a result, we will require that the sorted list remain distributed throughout the machine. In this way, it can easily form the input for further concurrent processing. Further pursuing the example of symbolic manipulation, consider the following: if the user, having simplified the expression down to some collection of relatively few terms, now desires the derivative of the expression, each processing node is able to compute the derivative of its part without preliminary manipulation.

In this discussion, we will suppose that the list to be sorted initially resides in a distributed fashion in the parallel computer. The data items will be taken to be positive integers and the key will consist simply of their respective numeric values. We will require that at the end of the sorting, the data residing in each node are sorted internally and that these sublists are also sorted globally across the machine in some way. The natural way to specify this global order is to map the concurrent processor into a one-dimensional periodic array or ring via the *gridmap* utility discussed in Chaps. 4 and 14. The nodes along the ring are labeled by ring position, or *ringpos*. Global order is now defined by relative values of *ringpos*. Items in the node with *ringpos*=0 precede items in the node with *ringpos*=1, which in turn precede the items in the node with *ringpos*=2, and so on.

For some simple types of sorting strategies, such as bubblesort, a ring topology for the parallel computer would be sufficient. However, many faster sorting methods will turn out to require a much higher connectivity or dimension (actually, in the sense of Sec. 3-5, *infinite* system dimension) and we will assume that our parallel machine has a connectivity at least as rich as that of the hypercube. This is not to say that other types of connectivity (e.g., perfect shuffle) are not also attractive for sorting. Since we will see that the hypercube does a good job as compared with the best sequential algorithms, Shellsort and quicksort, no compelling argument for other connectivities is immediately obvious.

The first algorithm we will present, Batcher's bitonic sort, does not leave the list in the desired one-dimensional *ringpos* order, but instead, the list ends up sorted according to the binary labeling scheme of the hypercube, (i.e., *procnum*). Consecutive items may not even be near one another in the machine, but for many applications this presents no problem. Some applications of sorting simply require that one know where the items are, not that they be nearby.

Three algorithms for sorting will be covered: In addition to Batcher's bitonic sorter [Batcher 68; Knuth 73a, pp. 232-33; Nassimi 79], we consider Shellsort and quicksort [Knuth 73a, pp. 379-81]. As discussed in Sec. 3-6, there are two ways of measuring the quality of a concurrent algorithm: "speed at any cost," or "speed per unit cost." It is interesting that the sorting algorithms to be discussed here illustrate these different criteria rather well. The bitonic sorter turns out to be the speed at any cost champion of the algorithms; if one fixes the list size and allows the hypercube to grow without bound (i.e., work on small lists) this algorithm is fastest. On the other hand, bitonic is very inefficient. For efficient algorithms, or equivalently, algorithms which run much faster on large lists, (holding the machine size fixed and allowing the list to grow) one needs to turn to Shellsort and quicksort.

Before plunging into the first method, it should be pointed out that the subject of sorting is an extremely diverse one and we have chosen to address only a small fraction of the known methods. We have concentrated on the best general-purpose algorithms, so that no special properties of the sorted list are exploited. If the list to be sorted has special properties, such as a known distribution range (e.g., random numbers with a flat distribution between 0 and 1) or high degeneracy (many redundant items, e.g., text files), then other strategies can be faster than Shellsort and quicksort. In the case of known data distribution, a bucketsort strategy (e.g., radix sort) is best, while the case of high degeneracy is best handled by the distribution counting method [Knuth 73a, pp. 379-81]. We will comment on these methods at the end of the chapter and these form useful extensions for the interested reader to pursue.

18-2 The Merge Strategy

In the merging strategy to be used in all our sorting algorithms, the first step is for each processor to sort its own sublist using some fast algorithm, which we will assume to be quicksort. Quicksort will be discussed later; for now let us just mention that an optimal choice is obtained through a combined quicksort/insertion sort and is described in detail as Algorithm Q by Knuth [Knuth 73a, pp. 118-19]. Once the local (processor) sort is complete, it must be decided how to merge all of the sorted lists in order to form one globally sorted list. This is done in a series of compare-exchange steps. In each step, two neighboring nodes exchange items so that each node ends up with a sorted list and all of the items in one node are greater than all of the items in the other. Thus, two sorted lists of m items each are merged into a sorted list of $2m$ items (stored collectively in the memory of the two nodes).

18-3 The Compare-Exchange Routine

The concept of the compare-exchange process between two processors is fairly simple, though we will see that what actually goes on between the processors becomes slightly tricky. The idea is illustrated in Fig. 18-1. The start is shown in Fig. 18-1(a). We have two processors which have each sorted their internal lists of five numbers. We wish to merge so that the processor on the right ends up with the high half of the collective list, the one on the left ends up with the low half. The high processor will begin by sending its *lowest* number over to the empty buffer in the low processor (the empty box), offering to give this number over. The low processor will do the reverse, resulting in the situation shown in Fig. 18-1(b).

The low processor now has what it needs to begin constructing the new list-it knows its own lowest member, and it has the other processor's lowest member also. The 7 and 10 are compared and it is decided that the new list should begin with the 7. The new list is constructed in a currently free section of memory and this is shown in Fig. 18-1(c). The high processor has done likewise, except that it works from the bottom up and has not yet used the offered number residing in the communications buffer. It will use it on the next cycle however, when the next pair of numbers are exchanged, leading to Fig. 18-1(d). The process continues, Figs. 18-1(e)-(g), until the process terminates when the size of the new lists are the same as the old.

Note that the new lists are constructed by actually copying the items from one memory location to another. If the items to be sorted were large data structures of many bits, we would, instead, deal with pointers to the objects and not the objects themselves. The objects would never move; lists of pointers would be manipulated.

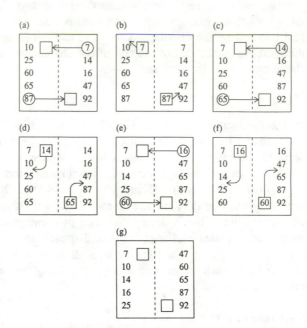

Figure 18-1 Compare-exchange step between nodes. This figure illustrates a simple compare-exchange between two connected nodes. Each processor contains a sorted list of five items and the goal of the compare-exchange process is to put the largest five items in the right-hand processor and the smallest five items on the left. In (a), each processor sends an "unwanted" item to a register in the other processor. The right-hand processor, which is collecting the large items, sends its smallest item, and the left-hand processor sends its largest. In (b), each processor inserts its new item into the list. One item is pushed "off the end" of each list, but that item is already residing safely in the other processor. This two-step process is repeated twice more (c, d, e, and f). After (f), the items are all in the correct final position, but the processors don't realize it yet. When the next exchange of items takes place, in step (g), neither processor will want the received item, so the compare-exchange process will be terminated.

In our description of the compare-exchange process, we were a bit sloppy in specifying when the items were actually transferred. The point is that, in a fast-polled communication environment, communications do not occur until both processors agree that more items need to be transferred. This, in turn, means that sometimes one processor will wait while the other catches up, giving rise to load imbalance. In the above example, this occurs at the step of Fig. 18-1(c): the low processor has emptied its buffer and would like the next item to be transferred, while the high processor is still busy. To avoid this, the actual implementation should transfer many items at once, reducing the frequency of such occurrences. This is also a good approach because in almost any hardware implementation, communications are cheaper (per bit) if many bits are sent in one large burst, than if sent as separate smaller messages.

We next examine the implementation. The reader more interested in concepts than implementation details may wish to skip to the next section. Here, we will present the compare-exchange code and show how it works for the above example. This description is instructive in that it shows that relatively simple code can exhibit rather complex behavior and that one must think carefully about what is going on in the parallel machine in order to obtain a fast, efficient implementation.

The routine *cmp_ex_hi* is called by a node which performs a compare-exchange step with a neighboring node, keeping the high part of the merged list. Similarly, *cmp_ex_low* is what the node on the other side runs so that it keeps the low half of the merged list. Note that, in keeping with polled communication, if a given node calls *cmp_ex_hi*, its corresponding neighbor must call *cmp_ex_low* concurrently.

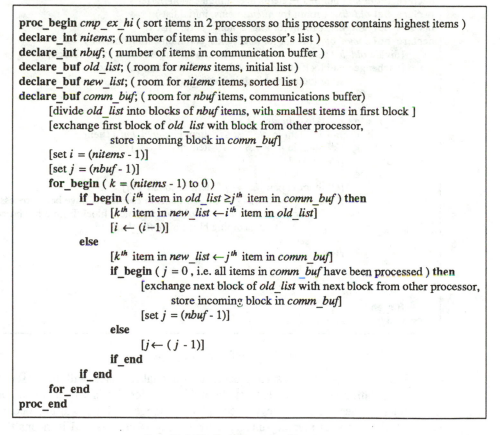

```
proc_begin cmp_ex_hi ( sort items in 2 processors so this processor contains highest items )
declare_int nitems; ( number of items in this processor's list )
declare_int nbuf; ( number of items in communication buffer )
declare_buf old_list; ( room for nitems items, initial list )
declare_buf new_list; ( room for nitems items, sorted list )
declare_buf comm_buf; ( room for nbuf items, communications buffer)
        [divide old_list into blocks of nbuf items, with smallest items in first block ]
        [exchange first block of old_list with block from other processor,
                    store incoming block in comm_buf]
        [set i = (nitems - 1)]
        [set j = (nbuf - 1)]
        for_begin ( k = (nitems - 1) to 0 )
            if_begin ( i^th item in old_list ≥ j^th item in comm_buf ) then
                [k^th item in new_list ← i^th item in old_list]
                [i ← (i−1)]
            else
                [k^th item in new_list ← j^th item in comm_buf]
                if_begin ( j = 0 , i.e. all items in comm_buf have been processed ) then
                    [exchange next block of old_list with next block from other processor,
                            store incoming block in comm_buf]
                    [set j = (nbuf - 1)]
                else
                    [j ← ( j - 1)]
                if_end
            if_end
        for_end
proc_end
```

Code 18-1 The Routine *cmp_ex_hi*

These routines are outlined in Code 18-1 and 18-2 respectively, while their operation, for the example of Fig. 18-1, is illustrated in Fig. 18-2. The illustration is for the case of a buffer holding two items. The indices *i* and *j* are employed in this illustration to show in detail how load imbalance occurs for this particular choice of buffer size. By the time step (d) has been reached, the low processor has emptied its buffer. The processor will have to wait at the exchange step within the k loop of *cmp_ex_low*. This waiting occurs because of the nature of polled communications: the low processor tries to exchange items, but the high processor has not yet reached the corresponding exchange, so the low processor must stand idle. The high processor continues processing through step (e), when it finally empties its buffer. It now reaches the exchange step and the items are communicated. The entire process stops when each processor has gone through the k loop *nitems* times; this means that *nitems* items have been assigned to the new list.

```
proc_begin cmp_ex_low ( sort items in 2 processors so this processor contains lowest items )
declare_int nitems; ( number of items in this processor's list )
declare_int nbuf; ( number of items in communication buffer )
declare_buf old_list; ( room for nitems items, initial list )
declare_buf new_list; ( room for nitems items, sorted list )
declare_buf comm_buf; ( room for nbuf items, communications buffer )
        [divide old_list into blocks of nbuf items, with largest items in first block]
        [exchange first block of old_list with block from other processor,
                        store incoming block in comm_buf]
     [set i = 0]
     [set j = 0]
     for_begin ( k = 0 to (nitems - 1) )
             if_begin ( i^th item in old_list ≤ j^th item in comm_buf ) then
                     [k^th item in new_list ← i^th item in old_list ]
                     [i ← (i + 1)]
             else
                     [k^th item in new_list ← j^th item in comm_buf]
                     if_begin ( j = ( nbuf - 1), i.e., all items in comm_buf have been processed ) then
                             [exchange next block of old_list with next block from other processor,
                                     store incoming block in comm_buf]
                             [set j = 0]
                     else
                             [j ← (j + 1) ]
                     if_end
             if_end
     for_end
proc_end
```

Code 18-2 The Routine *cmp_ex_low*

The number of times such processor idling takes place will be lessened if we increase the buffer size. In the extreme limit, if the buffer size is set equal to *nitems*, only one exchange need take place per compare-exchange and no waiting occurs. This approach, however, is memory-intensive for sorting large lists and it means that many items (on average, half of them) are transferred unnecessarily.

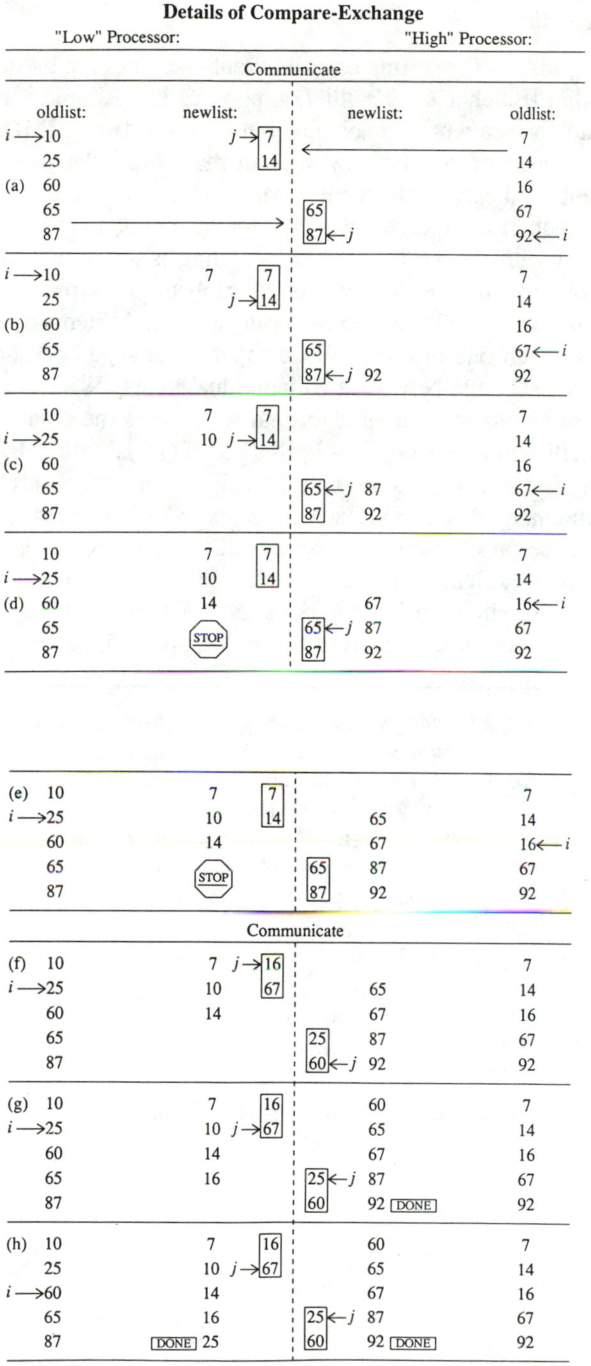

Details of Compare-Exchange

"Low" Processor: "High" Processor:

Communicate

oldlist:	newlist:		newlist:	oldlist:
i —>10	j→ [7]	←		7
25	[14]			14
(a) 60				16
65		—————————>	[65]	67
87			[87]←j	92←i

i —>10	7 [7]			7
25	j→[14]			14
(b) 60				16
65			[65]	67←i
87			[87]←j 92	92

10	7 [7]			7
i —>25	10 j→[14]			14
(c) 60				16
65			[65]←j 87	67←i
87			[87] 92	92

10	7 [7]			7
i —>25	10 [14]			14
(d) 60	14		67	16←i
65	(STOP)		[65]←j 87	67
87			[87] 92	92

(e) 10	7 [7]			7
i —>25	10 [14]		65	14
60	14		67	16←i
65	(STOP)		[65] 87	67
87			[87] 92	92

Communicate

(f) 10	7 j→[16]			7
i —>25	10 [67]		65	14
60	14		67	16
65			[25] 87	67
87			[60]←j 92	92

(g) 10	7 [16]		60	7
i —>25	10 j→[67]		65	14
60	14		67	16
65	16		[25]←j 87	67
87			[60] 92 [DONE]	92

(h) 10	7 [16]		60	7
25	10 j→[67]		65	14
i —>60	14		67	16
65	16		[25]←j 87	67
87	[DONE] 25		[60] 92 [DONE]	92

Figure 18-2 The time steps in the implementation of the compare exchange algorithm for two lists of 5 numbers to be sorted so that the low 5 end up in the left and the high 5 end up in the right processor. The numbers start in the array old and end in new.

18-4 The Bitonic Algorithm

Many algorithms for sorting on concurrent machines are based on Batcher's bitonic sorting algorithm [Batcher 68; Knuth 73a, pp. 232-33]. Bitonic sort is not a particularly good algorithm for sequential machines, but it is good for SIMD machines because it allows a high degree of concurrency without requiring independent flow control in the nodes. As mentioned earlier, the method sorts the list into ascending *procnum* order.

The first step in the merge strategy is for each node to internally sort via quicksort. One is then left with the problem of constructing a series of compare-exchange steps which will correctly merge $N = 2^d$ sorted sublists. This problem is completely iso-morphic with the sequential problem of sorting a list of 2^d items by pairwise comparisons between items. Each one of our sublist compare-exchange operations is equivalent to a simple compare-exchange between two individual items. We can construct a concurrent algorithm based on any sequential algorithm which uses the comparison strategy. In the algorithm specification of Code 18-3, *cmp_ex_hi*(j) is called by a node which is to undergo a compare-exchange step with the neighboring node on channel j, keeping the high part of the merged list. Similarly, *cmp_ex_low*(j) applies to a compare-exchange step with the node on channel j, with the calling processor keeping the low part. This pattern of compare-exchanges is shown in Fig. 18-3 for the $d=3$ case. It is not intuitively obvious why the bitonic algorithm works at all. We merely give the $d = 3$ example and appeal to the references to give a proof that it does, indeed, sort.

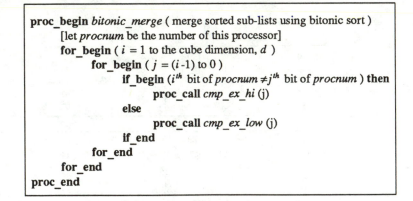

```
proc_begin bitonic_merge ( merge sorted sub-lists using bitonic sort )
     [let procnum be the number of this processor]
     for_begin ( i = 1 to the cube dimension, d )
          for_begin ( j = (i -1) to 0 )
               if_begin (i^th bit of procnum ≠ j^th bit of procnum ) then
                    proc_call cmp_ex_hi (j)
               else
                    proc_call cmp_ex_low (j)
               if_end
          for_end
     for_end
proc_end
```

Code 18-3 Routine for Performing Bitonic Merge

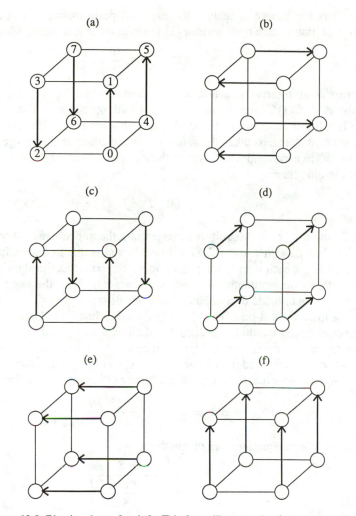

Figure 18-3 Bitonic scheme for $d=3$. This figure illustrates the six compare-exchange steps of the bitonic algorithm for $d=3$. Each diagram illustrates four compare-exchange processes which happen simultaneously. A boldface arrow represents a compare-exchange between two processors. The largest items go the the processor at the point of the arrow, and the smallest items to the one at the base of the arrow.

18-5 Comments on the Efficiency of the Bitonic Algorithm

It is fairly easy to analyze the expected performance of this algorithm. If we are sorting M items, each node sorts $M/2^d$ items in the initial phase, taking time

$$t_s(M,d) = \tau \frac{M}{2^d} \ln(\frac{M}{2^d}) \qquad (18\text{-}1)$$

where τ is an implementation-dependent time constant. In the merging phase, each node performs $d(d+1)/2$ *cmp_ex_low* or *cmp_ex_hi* operations. The time required by each step is a linear function of the number of items per node. However, we cannot assume that each of the steps takes the same amount of time; as the merge phase proceeds, the list begins to assume global order, so the steps should require less time. We write for the total merging time:

$$t_m(M,d) = f(d)\tau \frac{M}{2^d} \qquad (18\text{-}2)$$

The function $f(d)$ is difficult to derive from a theoretical basis. We expect it to be proportional to d^α with $1 < \alpha < 2$. The lower bound is due to the minimum communication required to get each item to the proper node. Suppose that the algorithm is such that each item follows the optimum (shortest) path in going from the node in which it initially resided, to its ultimate destination. Since this distance grows linearly with d on a hypercube, a lower bound on α is unity. On the other hand, the bitonic algorithm involves a number of cycles quadratic in d, so that if all *cmp_ex_hi* and *cmp_ex_low* steps took the same amount of time, α would be 2. Since these comparisons actually become faster as the list becomes ordered, this value represents an upper bound on α.

We can now derive an expression for the efficiency. By definition, we have

$$\varepsilon = \frac{1}{2^d} \frac{t_s(M,0)}{t_s(M,d) + t_m(M,d)} \qquad (18\text{-}3)$$

Using the above equations, we obtain the result

$$\varepsilon = \frac{1}{1 + \dfrac{f(d) - d}{\ln M}} \qquad (18\text{-}4)$$

If we fix d and let M become arbitrarily large, the efficiency approaches 1. However, the approach to this limit is very slow due to the logarithmic dependence. If we increase d with M fixed, the efficiency goes to zero. We do not know $f(d)$ a priori, so actual timings must be employed to evaluate it.

Before presenting the performance measurements of the bitonic algorithm, it will be useful to explain the derivation of the efficiency measurements. The most robust method is to directly measure the speedup, S, by comparing the hypercube timing with the same sorting procedure running on a single processor of the hypercube, and then using the formalism described in Sec. 3-5 to find ε. This was followed in the current examples, except for the larger sorts that would not fit within the memory (256 kbytes on the Caltech/JPL Mark II) of a single node. To circumvent this problem, single processor times were extrapolated via the theoretical functional form for sequential quicksort, $M \ln M$. This extrapolation is shown in Fig. 18-4. As seen from this figure, the fit to the theoretical form is rather good, so we can, with confidence, use this fit to extrapolate and give single-node times for large lists.

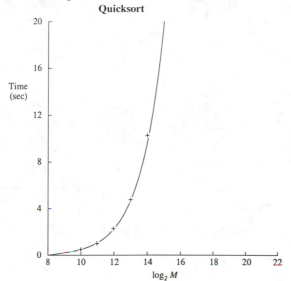

Figure 18-4 The quicksort timing data for a single processor. Also shown is the $M \ln M$ fit.

Table 18-1 shows the actual times and efficiencies for our implementation of the bitonic algorithm. Results are shown for sorting lists of sizes (M) 1k to 2048k items on hypercubes with dimensions, d, ranging from 1 (two nodes) to 7 (128 nodes). The same information is also shown, graphically, in Fig. 18-5. The efficiency data are fit fairly well by the functional form suggested above, with $\alpha \approx 1.9$.

Clearly, the efficiencies fall off rapidly with increasing d. From the standpoint of cost effectiveness, this algorithm is a failure. On the other hand, a glance at Table 18-1 shows that for fixed size lists and increasing machine size, the execution times continue to decrease. Even for the very small 1024-item list, the 7-cube still outperforms the 6-cube: the classic rollover point (times actually increasing as machine size is increased) is not reached until there are just a few items per processing node. So, from the speed at any cost point of view, the algorithm is a success. We attribute the inefficiency of the bitonic algorithm partly to communication overhead and some load imbalance during the compare-exchanges, but mostly to nonoptimality of the algorithm itself. Remember, in our definition of efficiency we are comparing the parallel bitonic algorithm to the best available sequential algorithm-in this case, quicksort. In bitonic, the number of cycles grows quadratically with d. This suggests that the efficiency can be improved greatly by using a parallel algorithm that sorts in fewer operations without sacrificing concurrency.

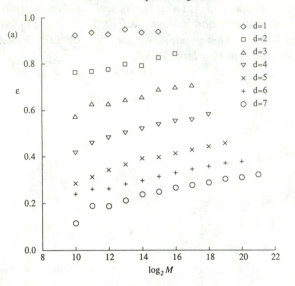

Figure 18-5(a) The efficiency of the bitonic algorithm versus list size for various size cubes.

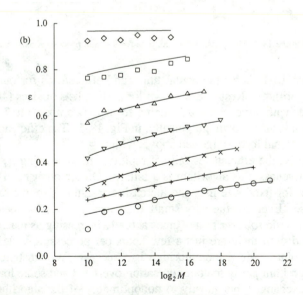

Figure 18-5(b) Same as Fig. 18-5, but with the fit to Eq. (18-4) shown.

Execution times (sec)

Total List Size*	1k	2	4	8	16	32	64	128	256	512	1024	2048k
d												
1	.25	.54	1.19	2.52	5.50	11.72						
2	.15	.33	.71	1.49	3.24	6.66	13.92					
3	.10	.20	.44	.92	1.95	3.98	8.41	17.56				
4	.07	.14	.29	.60	1.26	2.60	5.39	11.31	23.11			
5	.05	.10	.20	.40	.82	1.71	3.50	7.15	14.80	30.34		
6	.03	.06	.13	.26	.53	1.08	2.20	4.48	9.15	18.74	38.26	
7	.03	.04	.09	.17	.33	.67	1.35	2.77	5.60	11.37	23.22	47.00

Efficiency ε

Total List Size*	1k	2	4	8	16	32	64	128	256	512	1024	2048k
d												
1	.92	.94	.93	.95	.94	.94						
2	.77	.77	.78	.80	.80	.83	.85					
3	.58	.63	.63	.65	.66	.69	.70	.71				
4	.41	.45	.48	.50	.51	.53	.55	.55	.57			
5	.29	.32	.35	.37	.39	.40	.42	.44	.45	.46		
6	.24	.26	.27	.29	.30	.32	.34	.35	.36	.37	.39	
7	.12	.20	.19	.22	.24	.26	.27	.28	.30	.31	.32	.33

*   In units of 1k = 1024 items. Divide by 2^d for items per processor.

Table 18-1: Bitonic Sort

18-6 Shellsort/Diminishing Increment Algorithm

This algorithm again follows the merge strategy and is motivated by the fact that d compare-exchanges in d different directions of the hypercube result in a list with an almost sorted order. Global order is defined via *ringpos*, that is, the list will end up sorted on the embedded ring in the hypercube. After the d compare-exchanges, the algorithm switches to a simple mopping-up stage which is specially designed for almost sorted lists. This stage is optimized for moving relatively few items quickly through the machine and amounts to a parallel bubblesort or bucket brigade algorithm. Each node passes its largest items upward along the line and its smallest items downward. After each stage of this process, an efficient hypercube broadcast is done which decides whether any items remain to be propagated along the ring.

Note that the mop-up algorithm takes advantage of the MIMD nature of the machine and that this characteristic is central to its speed-only the few items which need to be moved are examined and processed. The bitonic algorithm, on the other hand, is natural for a SIMD machine. It involves much extra work in order to be able to handle the worst case, which rarely occurs.

We will refer to this algorithm as Shellsort [Shell 59; Knuth 73a, pp. 84-5, 102-5] or a diminishing increment sorting algorithm. This is not because it is a strict concurrent implementation of the sequential namesake, but because the algorithms are similar in spirit. The important feature of Shellsort is that in early stages of the sorting process, items take very large jumps through the list, reaching their final destinations in few steps. As shown in Fig. 18-6, this is exactly what occurs in the concurrent algorithm, and, as we shall see below, is responsible for its speed.

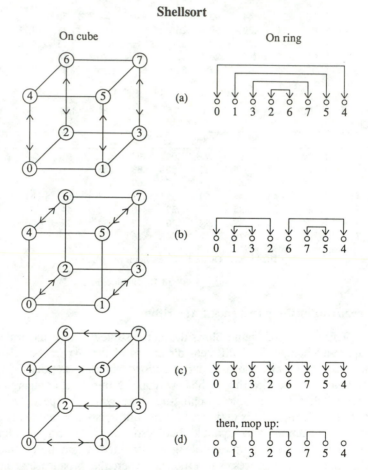

Shellsort

Figure 18-6 The parallel Shellsort on a $d=3$ hypercube. The left side shows what the algorithm looks like on the cube, the right shows the same when the cube is regarded as a ring.

The complete algorithm is outlined in Code 18-4. The **for** loop comprises the actual Shellsort process; the **while** is the mopping-up operation.

```
proc_begin shell_merge ( merge sorted sublists using Shellsort )
declare_int d ; ( the dimension of the hypercube )
declare_int ring_pos; ( position in ring of processors )
    for_begin ( i = (d-1) to 0 )
        if_begin (i^{th} bit of ring_pos is 1 ) then
            proc_call cmp_ex_hi (i )
        else
            proc_call cmp_ex_low (i )
        if_end
    for_end
    [let done be FALSE]
    while_begin ( done is FALSE ) then
        if_begin ( 0^{th} bit of ring_pos is 1 ) then
            proc_call cmp_ex_hi ( do compare-exchange with the previous processor
                    in ring, keeping highest items in this processor )
            proc_call cmp_ex_low ( do compare-exchange with the next processor
                    in ring, keeping lowest items in this processor )
        else
            proc_call cmp_ex_low ( do compare-exchange with the next processor
                    in ring, keeping lowest items in this processor )
            proc_call cmp_ex_hi ( do compare-exchange with the previous processor
                    in ring, keeping highest items in this processor )

        if_end
        if_begin ( received items need to be passed further ) then
            [broadcast FALSE to all processors]
        else
            [broadcast TRUE to all processors]
        if_end
        if_begin ( all processors broadcast TRUE ) then
            [set done = TRUE]
        if_end
    while_end
proc_end
```

Code 18-4 Routine for Performing Shellsort Merge

18-7 Performance of Shellsort

We have not tried to predict the Shellsort efficiency theoretically, though this could certainly be done for both the average and worst cases. The algorithm was implemented and timed with the same starting problem used for the bitonic algorithm. The results appear in Table 18-2 and are also plotted in Fig. 18-7.

This algorithm is much more efficient than the bitonic algorithm, and seems to offer the prospect of reasonable efficiency at large d. The inefficiency is the result of both communication overhead and algorithmic nonoptimality relative to quicksort.

Execution times (sec)

Total List Size	1k	2	4	8	16	32	64	128	256	512	1024	2048k
d												
1	.25	.54	1.20	2.52	5.51	11.73						
2	.15	.31	.68	1.43	3.13	6.40	13.44					
3	.07	.16	.36	.76	1.62	3.30	7.03	14.96				
4	.04	.09	.19	.40	.85	1.82	3.70	7.91	16.66			
5	.05	.07	.11	.23	.44	.91	1.93	4.01	8.47	17.51		
6	.07	.08	.09	.16	.27	.52	1.05	2.12	4.36	9.15	18.81	
7	.21	.16	.16	.17	.23	.37	.67	1.30	2.44	5.23	10.22	21.03

Efficiency ε

	1k	2	4	8	16	32	64	128	256	512	1024	2048k
1	.92	.94	.92	.95	.94	.94						
2	.77	.82	.81	.84	.82	.86	.88					
3	.82	.79	.77	.79	.80	.84	.84	.84				
4	.72	.70	.73	.75	.76	.76	.80	.79	.80			
5	.29	.45	.63	.65	.73	.76	.76	.78	.78	.80		
6	.10	.20	.38	.47	.60	.66	.70	.74	.76	.77	.78	
7	.02	.05	.11	.22	.35	.47	.55	.60	.68	.67	.72	.74

Table 18-2: Shellsort

The worst case mop-up phase may be summarized as follows. Suppose we seek to sort M items on a d-dimensional hypercube, so that there are $n = M/2^d$ items per node. Now, if more than n of the largest (or smallest) $2n$ items happen to occupy a particular pair of nodes in the first compare-exchange step, then some of the items will be put in the wrong plane of the hypercube in this first step. The subsequent $d-1$ stages will just rearrange the items in each $(d-1)$-dimensional subcube, but these wrong way items will stay in the wrong half of the hypercube. Consequently, in the mop-up phase, these items must travel a long distance to reach the top (or bottom) of the list, requiring $2^{d-1}-1$ steps. The probability that such a collision of items will occur, for random initial lists, is given by:

$$P_{collision} \approx (\frac{1}{2^{d-1}})^{n-1} \frac{(2n)!}{n!\,n!} \qquad (18\text{-}5)$$

This probability rapidly becomes negligibly small as n increases.

In the other hypercube applications presented in this book, it is a general rule that algorithms become more efficient as the grain size, n, grows. That is also true here, but a qualitatively different effect has entered the picture. The probability of hitting a "bad" case decreases with increasing grain size. For the random lists which were run in the examples, the mop-up step was separately timed. The mop-up time, not surprisingly, increases with increasing d, but even for $d=7$ is only 10% to 20% of the total time for the larger lists. For the small lists on the $d=7$ cube, the mop-up time dominates.

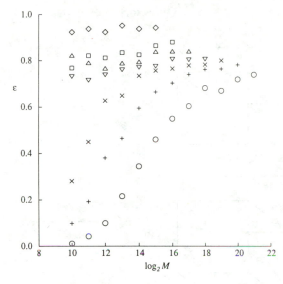
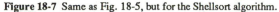

"Shellsort" vs Sequential Quicksort

Figure 18-7 Same as Fig. 18-5, but for the Shellsort algorithm.

18-8 Quicksort/Samplesort Algorithm

The classic quicksort technique is a divide-and-conquer sorting method [Hoare 62; Knuth 73a, pp. 118-23]. As such it would seem to be amenable to a concurrent implementation, and with a slight modification (actually, an improvement of the standard algorithm) this turns out to be the case.

The standard algorithm begins by picking some item from the list and using this as the splitting key. A loop is entered which takes the splitting key and finds the point in the list where this item will ultimately end up once the sort is completed. This is the first splitting point. While this is being done, all items in the list which are less than the splitting key are placed on the low side of the splitting point, all higher items are placed to the high side of the splitting point. This completes the first divide. The list has now been broken into two independent lists, each of which still needs to be sorted. Now the algorithm is repeated recursively, splitting each of the two sublists, and so on, until the sort is complete.

The essential idea of the concurrent (hypercube) quicksort is the same. The first splitting key is chosen (a global step to be described below) and then the entire list is split, in parallel, between two subcubes of the hypercube. All items higher than the splitting key are sent in one direction in the hypercube, and all items less than the key are sent the other way. The procedure is then called recursively, splitting each of the subcubes' lists further. As in Shellsort, the ring-based labeling of the hypercube is used to define global order. Once d splits occur, there remain no further interprocessor splits to do, and the algorithm continues by switching to the internal quicksort mentioned earlier. An illustration of this algorithm is given in Fig. 18-8.

Quicksort

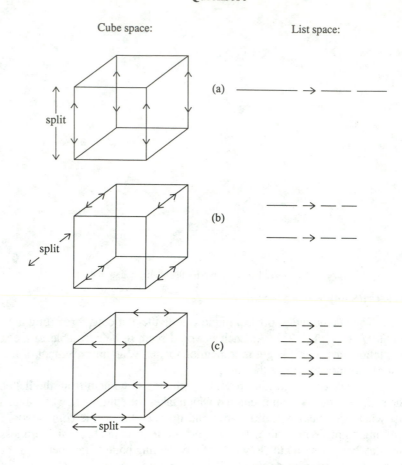

(d)   then, internal quicksort.

Figure 18-8 An illustration of the parallel quicksort.

So far, we have described the standard quicksort. For quicksort to perform well, even on sequential machines, it is essential that the splitting keys be chosen so that the splitting points land somewhere near the median of the list. If this isn't true, quicksort may behave rather poorly, the usual example being the quadratic time that standard quicksort takes on almost-sorted lists. To counteract this, it is a good idea to choose the splitting keys with some care, so as to make evenhanded splits of the list.

This point becomes much more important on the concurrent computer. In this case, if the splits are done haphazardly, not only will an excessive number of operations be necessary, but large load imbalances will also occur. If half of the hypercube has a sub-list three times as long as the other half, much idle time will be incurred. Therefore, in the concurrent algorithm, the splitting keys are chosen with some care. The present version of the concurrent algorithm randomly samples a subset of the entire list (giving an estimate of the true distribution of the list) and then picks splitting keys based upon this sample. To save time, all 2^d-1 splitting keys are found at once. This modified quicksort should perhaps be called a parallel samplesort and contains the following steps:

(1)   each processor picks sample of l items at random.
(2)   sort the sample of $l\,2^d$ items using the Shellsort algorithm.
(3)   choose splitting keys as if this was entire list.
(4)   broadcast splitting keys so that all nodes know all splitting keys.
(5)   perform the splits in the d directions of the hypercube.
(6)   each node quicksorts its sublist.

Correct choice of the sample size, l, is important. A large value of l increases the time spent sorting the sample, but tends to reduce the load imbalance in the splitting phase. Experimentation with various values of l has shown that the best value depends on the number of items per processor. Times and efficiencies for the parallel quicksort are shown in Table 18-3. The efficiencies are also plotted in Fig. 18-9. The times shown are for fairly good choices of the sample size, l. The first part of Table 18-4 shows the choices for l (in terms of number of items per node sampled) which correspond to the runs of Table 18-3.

Execution times (sec)

Total List Size	1k	2	4	8	16	32	64	128	256	512	1024	2048k
d												
1	.27	.60	1.18	2.51	5.24	11.37						
2	.18	.34	.71	1.41	2.93	6.10	12.71					
3	.12	.20	.43	.83	1.59	3.32	6.69	13.25				
4	.09	.13	.24	.44	.96	1.83	3.80	7.46	15.64			
5	.06	.09	.15	.28	.51	1.02	2.02	3.94	8.26	19.45		
6	.08	.11	.13	.20	.34	.61	1.11	2.12	4.26	10.11	25.87	
7	.20	.16	.18	.20	.24	.45	.76	1.29	2.38	5.59	13.66	37.91

Efficiency ε

	1k	2	4	8	16	32	64	128	256	512	1024	2048k
1	.85	.84	.94	.95	.98	.97						
2	.64	.75	.78	.85	.88	.91	.93					
3	.48	.63	.64	.72	.81	.83	.88	.95				
4	.32	.49	.58	.68	.67	.76	.78	.84	.85			
5	.24	.35	.46	.53	.63	.68	.73	.80	.80	.72		
6	.09	.14	.27	.37	.47	.57	.66	.74	.78	.69	.57	
7	.02	.05	.10	.19	.34	.38	.49	.61	.70	.63	.54	.41

Table 18-3: Quicksort

There are two main causes of inefficiency in this algorithm. The first is a result of the time wasted sorting the sample. The second is due to load imbalance in the

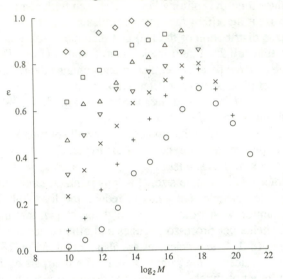

Figure 18-9 Efficiency data for the parallel quicksort described in the text.

splitting/sorting phase, as a result of uneven distribution of items among the processors. By varying the sample size l, we achieve a trade-off between these two sources of inefficiency.

The second part of Table 18-4 conveys some information about the amount of load imbalance for each run. As an algorithm becomes load imbalanced, the efficiency is degraded by the ratio of average processor sort time to the maximum of all processor times. This relation holds as long as the sum of all processor times remains a constant with varying configurations. In other words, it holds as long as the computation time of a node depends linearly on the number of items in the node. This isn't precisely correct in our case (the dependence includes logarithmic factors) but the balance factor, average/maximum, is still generally indicative of the amount of load imbalance. This factor is determined in the examples by employing timing routines independently in each node, yielding a timing profile of the concurrent machine.

The striking feature of the quicksort results, in comparison to those of Shellsort, is that while the parallel quicksort does surpass the latter for a large range of list and hypercube sizes, for the largest lists on the largest cubes, it exhibits a sharp rolloff in performance. This behavior is a direct consequence of the statistical nature of the sampling procedure for estimating the medians of the list. Because the method is statistical, the estimated median converges to the true value only as $1/\sqrt{l}$. This is reasonably effective for the smaller lists, and does the job well enough so that the performance surpasses that of Shellsort. For the largest lists on the largest cubes, however, precise load balancing becomes critical and the algorithm rapidly succumbs to imbalance. It is clear that a more

Sample size per node

Total List Size	1k	2	4	8	16	32	64	128	256	512	1024	2048k
d												
1	50	100	100	100	100	400						
2	50	50	100	100	100	100	200					
3	50	50	100	100	100	200	200	400				
4	40	40	50	50	100	200	400	200	400			
5	10	20	20	20	20	100	200	200	200	400		
6	10	20	20	20	50	50	100	100	100	400	400	
7	20	20	20	20	100	100	100	100	100	200	200	400

Balance: average/maximum

	1k	2	4	8	16	32	64	128	256	512	1024	2048k
1	.94	.95	.98	.97	.99	.99						
2	.88	.90	.93	.93	.92	.94	.95					
3	.91	.91	.91	.89	.91	.92	.93	.98				
4	.90	.91	.88	.88	.85	.93	.94	.90	.91			
5	.80	.88	.83	.76	.78	.88	.92	.91	.89	.91		
6	.99	.95	.93	.88	.87	.86	.90	.89	.89	.93	.92	
7	.99	.98	.94	.89	.85	.77	.89	.88	.88	.87	.89	.92

Table 18-4: Quicksort

robust approach to the determination of list medians is required.

A possible approach to this problem is outlined below. A deterministic method of finding the median is inspired by the sequential algorithm for finding the median of a list by using a divide-and-conquer process. The search for the median begins by guessing at a value for the median item and broadcasting this guess to all nodes. Then, each node splits its own sublist into those items greater than and those less than this guessed value. Having divided the data into two global sublists (which are not, however, physically divided in the hypercube), it is determined (by the sizes of the sublists) in which sublist the median lies. This sublist is then divided again (in parallel, on each node) and the process continues recursively until the true median is approached. This median then forms the splitting key for the quicksort algorithm. It may prove that a parallel quicksort coupled with the deterministic median finder outlined above will be the most efficient general purpose parallel sorting technique.

Before closing this section, it may be noted that there exists another way of thinking about the parallel quicksort algorithm. It can, in fact, be regarded as a bucketsort, in which each processor of the hypercube comprises one bucket. In the sampling phase, one attempts to determine reasonable choices for the limits (or sizes) of the 2^d buckets so that approximately equal numbers of items will end up in each bucket. The splitting process can then be thought of as an optimal routing scheme on the hypercube which brings each item to its correct bucket. So, our version of quicksort is also a bucketsort in which the bucket limits are chosen dynamically to match the properties of the particular input list.

18-9 Concluding Remarks

There seem to be several reasonable algorithms for sorting on a hypercube. Batcher's bitonic method is the leader of the low-efficiency, speed at any cost algorithms and it is the best method for small lists (measured relative to the machine size). The Shellsort- and quicksort-inspired algorithms, on the other hand, can give close to linear speedups for large lists. An important enhancement of the quicksort approach is the incorporation of a deterministic algorithm for finding the splitting points.

It is interesting to note that the two most efficient algorithms utilize the MIMD nature of the hypercube. As in sequential sorting, good algorithms make dynamical adjustments during execution. On a SIMD machine, one would be stuck with something like the bitonic algorithm, sacrificing a great deal of possible speed.

Quicksort is a very natural algorithm for the hypercube. The first d divide-and-conquer splits correspond nicely with the d dimensions of the hypercube. In addition, each datum arrives at its ultimate destination along a cube geodesic, that is, along a shortest path. The communication pattern of quicksort on a hypercube is the same as that of the *crystal_router*, an important communication utility to be discussed in Chap. 22.

This chapter has concentrated on sorting lists of unknown data distribution and low degeneracy (few identical items). Other cases require specialized algorithms. When the input data distribution is known, bucketsort (with small buckets) is most efficient on a sequential machine. A simple generalization of the quicksort (remember, it can be thought of as a bucketsort) to many buckets per processor would handle this case. One would simply replace the sequential quicksort phase with a sequential bucketsort in each processor.

The high degeneracy case is handled best by an algorithm which simply counts the number of items of each type. In this case, we could perform the same counting within each node, and then use an efficient global sum algorithm to add up the total result.

19

Scalar Products:
Mapping the Hypercube into a Tree

19-1 Introduction

Since the topological structures of many interesting algorithms can be represented by various types of trees, we will investigate the mapping of trees onto a hypercube in this chapter. Among the applications that use tree algorithms are computer chess, symbolic manipulation, and more general artificial intelligence applications, such as expert systems. Although a single tree, such as the binary tree shown in Fig. 19-1, maps naturally onto a hypercube, significant load imbalance occurs in this decomposition. Rather surprisingly, we will see that a collection of many trees maps onto a hypercube both naturally and efficiently. Many trees arise in a concurrent tree-based algorithm in which the number of "leaves" is greater than the number of nodes in the concurrent processor. If a tree algorithm with a topology as shown in Fig. 19-1 is to be run concurrently on eight nodes, it could be decomposed as illustrated by the dashed line. Each of the eight nodes could be placed at the top of one of the eight trees below the dashed line. Since relatively little of the tree is above the dashed line, most of the computation occurs below the dashed line and can be run concurrently.

A Binary Tree Topology

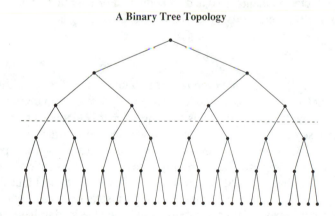

Figure 19-1 A binary tree with 32 terminal nodes discussed in Sec. 19-1.

The artificial intelligence applications mentioned above are quite complicated, so that in general they would require a sophisticated operating system capable of maintaining load balance dynamically. Since such a system is beyond the scope of this book, we will examine a much simpler application that uses a fixed tree. As will be explained in

Chap. 21, many matrix algorithms involve the calculation of several global scalar products as a subcomponent. Examples include matrix-vector multiplication and the determination of the eigenvalues of full matrices. In this chapter we examine a method of calculating multiple scalar products concurrently on a hypercube. In Chap. 21 we will generalize the *addvec* algorithm described here in the routines *fold* and *expand*, and will argue that these represent a class of distinct and interesting communication algorithms. We will show in Chap. 22 how they generalize to the *crystal_accumulator* and are very important in some circuit simulations [Furmanski 87b].

The scalar product of two vectors, A and B, each of which contains Q elements is given by:

$$R = \sum_{i=1}^{Q} A_i B_i \tag{19-1}$$

where R is the resulting scalar product. We see that calculating a scalar product involves multiplying the corresponding elements of the two vectors A and B and adding the products to obtain a single value. On a sequential computer, several scalar products are calculated by simply computing each one in succession. However, on a concurrent processor we would like an algorithm that distributes the computation among the nodes so that many scalar products can be generated in parallel. We will assume that each of the vectors being multiplied is distributed evenly among the nodes with a contiguous subset of both vectors' elements in each node. Such a distribution of the vectors is natural and recalls the treatment of Chap. 8 as well as the example matrix algorithms to be found in Chap. 21.

We first examine the calculation of a single scalar product on a concurrent processor consisting of N nodes. We rewrite the vectors A and B as matrices in which column j contains the vector elements assigned to node j. For simplicity we will assume that each node has $q = Q/N$ elements. We then rewrite Eq. (19-1) as

$$R = \sum_{j=1}^{N} \sum_{i=1}^{q} A_{ij} B_{ij} \tag{19-2}$$

From Eq. (19-2) we see that each node can multiply its pairs of matrix elements A_{ij} and B_{ij} in parallel with all the other nodes. The multiplication step involves no communication since each node already contains the pairs of matrix elements to be multiplied. In Eq. (19-2) the resulting products are added in two steps in contrast to Eq. (19-1), which has only one addition step. The summation over the index i adds the products within each node and runs completely concurrently since no communication is required. The summation over the index j adds the results from each node to obtain the final result. Since the second addition step combines the partial results from each node, communication is required and for a single scalar product has inevitable load imbalance.

We now discuss the calculation of multiple scalar products on a concurrent processor. We start by generalizing Eq. (19-2) to the case of many scalar products by adding another index, k, which labels each of the P scalar products:

$$R_k = \sum_{j=1}^{N} \sum_{i=1}^{q} A_{ijk} B_{ijk} \tag{19-3}$$

Calculating P scalar products is very similar to calculating a single scalar product. As before, both the multiplication step and the summation over the index i for each of the scalar products requires no communication and so runs completely concurrently. Labeling the partial results from each node as r_{jk} and rewriting Eq. (19-3) gives:

$$R_k = \sum_{j=1}^{N} r_{jk} \qquad\qquad (19\text{-}4)$$

which is the formula for adding the vectors formed by the rows of the matrix r_{jk}, which has N rows and P columns. Thus, we can think of the P scalar products as forming a vector, R_k, which is the sum of the vectors r_k containing the P partial results from each of the N nodes. Accordingly, the algorithm that we will study in this chapter adds a vector from each of the nodes and then distributes the resulting vector to all of the nodes.

In Sec. 4-4, we introduced the routine *vm_combine* that takes a block of data items from each node and combines them into a single block using a combining function specified as an argument. By using a combining function that returns the sum of its two arguments, we can form the sum of each node's vectors. However, the routine presented in Sec. 14-5 that implements *combine* on a hypercube uses a tree algorithm that calculates the same result in each node. When a large number of data items are to be combined, a more efficient algorithm would calculate separate results in each node and then distribute the results to all of the nodes. By distributing the calculation among the nodes, many separate results can be calculated concurrently instead of performing the same calculation in each node. When the calculation is finished, the separate results must be collected so that each node contains all of the results.

The routine we describe in this chapter is more specific than *combine* because it only calculates the sum of a vector from each of the nodes. The vector is an array of floating-point values and is the same length in each of the nodes. After discussing the implementation of the routine *addvec*, which adds the vectors, we will analyze its efficiency and compare it with *combine*. Although we only examine the specific routine *addvec*, the underlying algorithm can be easily generalized to provide an alternate implementation of *combine* that would be faster for other tasks that involve combining many data items.

19-2 Description of Algorithm

As we mentioned in the previous section, the algorithm we will use to implement *addvec* is similar to that used by *combine* but without its redundancy of computation. As with the algorithm used to implement *combine* in Sec. 14-5, we will map the hypercube onto a collection of binary trees with each node at the top of a different tree, but in the *addvec* algorithm each tree calculates separate results. The method we will describe was developed by Furmanski following a remark by Fox [Fox 86b, Cisneros 85].

The essential feature of the algorithm is that the communication of partial results is correctly interleaved so that the computation and communication loads are balanced optimally. Since we do not want to impose any conditions on the number of elements in the vectors being added, the algorithm should disperse the computation as evenly as possible even when the number of elements in the vectors is not a multiple of the number of nodes. In addition, the results must also be distributed to all nodes efficiently at the end of the calculation so that each node contains the complete result.

We begin the description of the algorithm by considering the case of a 1-cube (two nodes) in which both nodes contain a vector consisting of two elements that we label a and b to avoid confusion. Instead of exchanging both elements, as was done in *combine*, node 0 sends element b to node 1, while node 1 sends element a to node 0. After both nodes add their pair of corresponding elements, each contains one of the two results. The two trees that comprise the algorithm are illustrated in Fig. 19-2. It is evident that each node is at the top of one of the trees. The individual results are then distributed by going back down the trees, with node 0 sending the result for element a to node 1, and node 1 sending the result for element b to node 0. When the bottoms of both trees are reached after the results are exchanged, both nodes contain the sum of the two original vectors.

Addvec Algorithm on a 1-cube

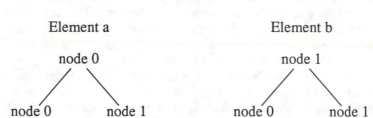

Element a   Element b

node 0   node 1

node 0   node 1   node 0   node 1

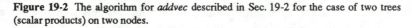

Figure 19-2 The algorithm for *addvec* described in Sec. 19-2 for the case of two trees (scalar products) on two nodes.

The algorithm is easily generalized to vectors containing P elements by first grouping the elements into blocks containing two elements. If P is odd, the last block will have a missing element which will not cause any problem. For each block of two elements the previous procedure is repeated, except that all the necessary exchanges for all the blocks are performed together. Each node then calculates the result for one of the elements in each block and exchanges its results with the other node. If one of the blocks contains a missing element, the steps involving the missing element are skipped. Thus, both nodes contain the complete result of adding the two vectors of P elements, but each did only half the number of additions that would have been required by the implementation of *combine* in Sec. 14-5. We recall that *combine* exchanges all of the elements in the vector once, rather than half of the elements twice as in the current algorithm, so both algorithms require the same total number of elements to be exchanged.

We can easily extend this algorithm to implement *addvec* on hypercubes with more than two nodes. From the description of the algorithm on a 1-cube, we see that applying the algorithm to a block of N elements, where N is the number of nodes, fully defines the algorithm since the generalization to several such blocks is straightforward. If the vector does not contain enough elements to completely fill the last block, the steps involving the missing elements are merely ignored. Thus, we will outline the extension of the algorithm to a 2-cube (where $N = 4$) by only considering vectors that contain four elements.

As in the previous case, the nodes will be mapped onto a collection of binary trees with one tree per element of the vectors being added, and a different node at the top of every tree. The four resulting trees are shown in Fig. 19-3, in which the nodes are labelled with their binary processor numbers. As before, the algorithm traverses each of the trees twice, once from bottom to top to calculate the result for each element, and again from top to bottom to distribute each of the results to all of the nodes. The first step in the algorithm is similar to the previous case: node 0 sends elements b and d to node 1, which in turn sends elements a and c to node 0. After adding their pairs of corresponding elements, node 0 contains partial results for elements.nr 99 10 a and c while node 1 contains partial results for elements b and d. Nodes 2 and 3 perform the same first step as if node 2 were node 0 and node 3 were node 1. In fact, if we use only the lowest bit of the processor numbers to label the nodes, the numbering is identical to that in a 1-cube in which the processor numbers only have one relevant bit. We also note that in the first step all communication occurs across channel 0.

The second step consists of node 0 sending its partial result for element c to node 2, while node 2 sends its partial result for element a to node 0. Nodes 1 and 3 perform a similar exchange involving elements b and d. Each node again sums its pair of corresponding elements, so that each of the nodes contains the result for one of the four elements. In the second step we note that both exchanges use channel 1 and involve half as many elements being exchanged and half as many additions as in the first step. After the second step, the algorithm is at the top of each of the trees in Fig. 19-3.

We now travel back down each of the trees in order to distribute the result for each of the elements to all the nodes. In the first step, which involves exchanging elements across channel 1, node 0 sends its result for element a to node 2, while node 2 sends its result for element c to node 0. Nodes 1 and 3 perform a similar exchange of elements b and d. Next, the results are exchanged across channel 0, as in the algorithm for a 1-cube, with node 0 sending elements a and c to node 1, while node 1 sends elements b and d to node 0. Nodes 2 and 3 perform a similar exchange. The algorithm is again at the bottom of the trees in Fig. 19-3, where it started, and all four nodes contain the result for each of the four elements.

We now generalize the algorithm used in *addvec* to a v-cube with $N = 2^v$. As in the previous two examples, the basic algorithm operates on blocks of N elements and maps the hypercube onto N binary trees, placing each node at the top of one of the trees. The trees are traversed from bottom to top to calculate the result for each element and then from top to bottom to distribute each result to every node. The number of steps in both directions is v and the number of the channel on which the exchanges occur conveniently labels each step, where channel 0 corresponds to the bottom of the trees and channel v−1 to the top.

Addvec Trees on a 2-cube

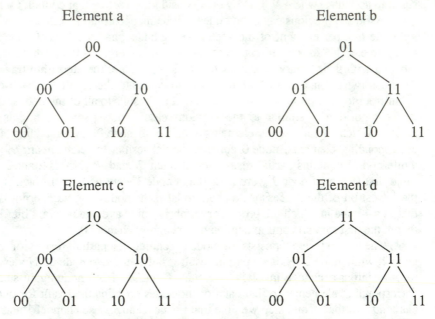

Figure 19-3 The algorithm for *addvec* described in Sec. 19-2 for the case of four trees
(scalar products) on four nodes.

We begin a typical step c by grouping the N elements into blocks containing 2^{c+1}
elements. Every node exchanges a single element from each group with the node across
channel c. The element from each group that is received is labeled by the rightmost $c+1$
bits of the node's processor number, while the element that is transmitted is labeled by
the same $c+1$ bits of the destination node's processor number. The elements in each
group are numbered from 0 to $(2^{c+1}-1)$. Figure 19-3 illustrates the pattern of exchanges
by conveniently labeling the processor numbers in binary. In the first part of the algorithm, when the trees are being traversed from bottom to top, the received element for
each block is added to the corresponding element in the block. Since each step involves
half as many blocks as the previous step, each step involves half as many additions and
requires half as many elements to be exchanged as the previous step. In the second part
of the algorithm, where the order of the steps is reversed, each step involves exchanging
twice as many elements as the previous step. However, the steps in the second part of the
algorithm require no additions since the received values are the results for each element,
and so are simply stored in their appropriate locations.

19-3 Implementation of Algorithm

We will now examine the actual implementation of the routine *addvec*, which adds up N contributions to P vectors and returns the P results to all N of the nodes. Even though the algorithm is rather complicated, its implementation is relatively simple because the sequence of exchanges and additions is so regular and fits the hypercube topology perfectly. As we noted in the previous section, the number of elements in a block is different for each step in the procedure, so the subset of elements being exchanged is different in every step. Since the elements to be exchanged cannot be conveniently gathered into a contiguous block at the beginning of the routine, we have a good example of a case in which the communication routines that transmit and receive vectors are useful. As usual, the nodes will always be transmitting and receiving together, so we use *vshift* in the implementation of *addvec*.

```
proc_begin addvec ( add vector, V, of length P over hypercube )
declare_buf T; ( same length as V, for storing data received from other nodes ]
declare_int S; ( the number of elements sent )
declare_int R; ( the number of elements received )
    for_begin ( each dimension, c, from 0 to (doc −1) )
            [ divide V and T into blocks of length b=2^{c+1} ]
            [ r_0 = the lowest c+1 bits of procnum ]
            [ s_0 = r_0 with bit number c flipped ]
            [ R = number of blocks having an element at position r_0 ]
            [ S = number of blocks having an element at position s_0 ]
            proc_call vshift ( send S elements on channel c, one from position s_0 of each block
                of V; receive R elements on channel c, and store in T at position r_0 in each block )
            [ add to the element at position r_0 of each block of V the
                    corresponding element in T ]
    for_end
    for_begin ( each dimension c, from (doc −1) to 0 )
            [ divide V and T into blocks of length b=2^{c+1} ]
            [ s_0 = the lowest c+1 bits of procnum ]
            [ r_0 = s_0 with bit number c flipped ]
            [ R = number of blocks having an element at position r_0 ]
            [ S = number of blocks having an element at position s_0 ]
            proc_call vshift ( send S elements on channel c, one from position s_0 of each block
                of V; receive R elements on channel c, and store in V at position r_0 in each block )
    for_end
proc_end
```

Code 19-1 The addvec Algorithm in Pseudocode

In order to use *vshift* we must specify the location of the first element to be sent, the size of the elements, the separation between elements that we want to send, and the total number of elements to be sent. In addition, the same information must be provided for the elements to be received by *vshift*. The size of each of the elements is given by *sizeof(float)*, which returns the number of bytes in a variable defined to be a *float*. The offset between both the elements to be sent and those to be received is *sizeof(float)* times

```
int addvec(buf,tmp,P)
float buf[],tmp[];
int P;
{
    int c,j,error,mask,chan,size,block,offset,recv,send,recvn,sendn;
    error = 0;
    mask = chan = 1;
    size = sizeof(float);
    block = 2;
    offset = size<<1;
    for(c=0;c<doc;++c){
        recv  = procnum&mask;
        send  = recv^chan;
        recvn = (P+mask-recv)>>(c+1);
        sendn = (P+mask-send)>>(c+1);
        if( vshift(tmp+recv,chan,size,offset,recvn,
                buf+send,chan,size,offset,sendn) == -1 ) error= -1;
        for(j=recv;j<P; j += block) buf[j] += tmp[j];
        chan   = chan<<1;
        mask   = mask|chan;
        block  = block<<1;
        offset = offset<<1;
    }
    chan   = 1<<(doc-1);
    mask   = nproc-1;
    offset = size<<doc;
    block  = 1<<doc;
    for(c=(doc-1);c>=0;--c){
        send  = procnum&mask;
        recv  = send^chan;
        sendn = (P+mask-send)>>(c+1);
        recvn = (P+mask-recv)>>(c+1);
        if( vshift(buf+recv,chan,size,offset,recvn,
                buf+send,chan,size,offset,sendn) == -1 ) error= -1;
        mask   = mask&(~chan);
        chan   = chan>>1;
        block  = block>>1;
        offset = offset>>1;
    }
}
```

Code 19-2 The addvec Algorithm in C

After exchanging the appropriate vector elements, the corresponding pairs of elements are added and then the various parameters are adjusted for the next step in the algorithm. When the exchange of elements and addition of the corresponding pairs has been repeated for all the channels in the hypercube, the algorithm is at the top of each of the N trees. As discussed in the previous section, each of the nodes now contains the result for the element whose index within each of the blocks of N elements is given by the node's processor number.

The second part of the algorithm involves traversing the trees from top to bottom in order to distribute the results obtained in the first part. Thus, the order of the channels is reversed and the elements to be transmitted and received are interchanged. The various parameters, such as *chan*, *mask*, and *offset*, are the same for each step as in the first part of the algorithm, but they are generated in reverse order. When the second series of calls to *vshift* is complete, *buf* contains the result of summing the original vectors from all of the nodes.

In Chap. 21 we will consider a further generalization of the first step. This calculation of scalar products will be encountered in the routine *fold*. The second step, the distribution of results, will be found in the routine *expand* in the library of generalized communication utilities of Chap. 21. As explained there, *expand* is closely related to *concat* introduced in Chap. 14.

19-4 Efficiency Analysis

Having described the algorithm for adding vectors from each of the nodes and its implementation, we are now ready to examine the concurrent efficiency of the algorithm. Regarding the routine *addvec* as only a part of the overall algorithm we have developed to calculate scalar products concurrently, we should properly calculate the efficiency of the total concurrent scalar product algorithm, rather than analyzing *addvec* in isolation. As usual, we assume that all floating-point operations require a characteristic time of t_{calc} and that all communication operations, such as exchanging a floating-point value with a neighboring node, involve a characteristic time of t_{comm}. The efficiency of the concurrent algorithm follows from Eq. (5-5):

$$\varepsilon = \frac{T_1(P,Q)}{N\,T_N(P,Q)} \tag{19-5}$$

where $T_1(P,Q)$ is the time taken by the sequential algorithm, $T_N(P,Q)$ is the time taken by the parallel algorithm, and N is the number of nodes in the concurrent processor.

In order to calculate T_1, we count the number of floating-point operations required to calculate the P scalar products and multiply that quantity by t_{calc}. From Eq. (19-1) we see that calculating each scalar product requires Q multiplications and $Q-1$ additions. Thus, the total number of floating-point operations required to calculate P scalar products is

$$n_{calc} = P\,(2Q - 1) \tag{19-6}$$

and total amount of time taken by the sequential computer is

$$T_1 = n_{calc}\, t_{calc} = P\,(2Q - 1)\, t_{calc} \tag{19-7}$$

In order to calculate T_N, we break the concurrent scalar product algorithm into two components. The first component involves all of the computation that is performed without need for communication, while the second component involves the summing of partial results from each node via *addvec* to give the final result. We will denote the time taken by the first component as T_a and the time taken by the second component as T_b.

Q is not restricted to be a multiple of N in this analysis, so the amount of computation required by the first component of the algorithm is not necessarily the same in every node. While the average number of multiplications per node for each scalar product is Q/N, the maximum number is $\lceil Q/N \rceil$, where $\lceil x \rceil$ is the integer part (ceiling) of x rounded to the next higher integer. Since the communication between nodes in *addvec* will force the nodes that perform less computation to wait for those that perform more, load imbalance occurs when Q is not an exact multiple of N. To account for the load imbalance, we must use the maximum number of multiplications per node when we calculate the efficiency. Accordingly, the maximum number of multiplications per node for each scalar product is $\lceil Q/N \rceil$ and the maximum number of additions is $\lceil Q/N \rceil - 1$, so the total time for the P products is:

$$T_a = P \, [2\lceil \frac{Q}{N} \rceil - 1] \, t_{calc} \tag{19-8}$$

We now examine the amount of time taken by *addvec* to sum the vector containing the P partial results from each node as given in Eq. (19-4). As discussed in Sec. 19-2 and 19-3, the first part of the algorithm consists of $\log_2 N$ steps, one for each dimension of the hypercube. In the first step half of the elements from each node's vector are exchanged with the node connected by channel 0 and the resulting pairs are summed by each node. For each of the channels in the hypercube, *addvec* performs the same type of exchange and addition using half as many elements as in the previous step. When the first part of the algorithm is complete, the resulting scalar products are distributed to each of the nodes in the second part of the algorithm. The second part of the algorithm, which involves another $\log_2 N$ steps, uses the same amount of communication as the first part but involves no computation.

The number of floating-point additions in *addvec* is given by:

$$n_{calc} = \sum_{i=1}^{\log N} \lceil 2^{-i} P \rceil \tag{19-9}$$

where we have used the ceiling function $\lceil x \rceil$ to account for the effect of any load imbalance at each step. The load balance of each step must be considered separately because each step involves communication calls which resynchronize the nodes. The number of elements that are exchanged is twice n_{calc} since the second part of *addvec* requires no floating-point additions. As a result, the total amount of time taken by *addvec* is given by:

$$T_b = (t_{calc} + 2t_{comm}) \sum_{i=1}^{\log N} \lceil 2^{-i} P \rceil \tag{19-10}$$

Adding the two contributions from Eqs. (19-8) and (19-10) gives the total time for the calculation of the scalar products on the concurrent processor:

$$T_N = P \ [2 \lceil \frac{Q}{N} \rceil - 1] \, t_{calc} + (t_{calc} + 2t_{comm}) \sum_{i=1}^{\log N} \lceil 2^{-i} \, P \rceil \qquad (19\text{-}11)$$

Using Eq. (19-5), the efficiency of the concurrent algorithm is predicted to be:

$$\varepsilon = \frac{P \ (2Q - 1) \, t_{calc}}{NP \ [2 \lceil \frac{Q}{N} \rceil - 1] t_{calc} + N \, (t_{calc} + 2t_{comm}) \sum_{i=1}^{\log N} \lceil 2^{-i} \, P \rceil} \qquad (19\text{-}12)$$

Although Eq. (19-12) is quite complicated and cannot easily be simplified due to the integer ceiling function $\lceil x \rceil$ used to account for load imbalance, we can simplify it considerably if we assume that the loads *are* balanced. In particular, we consider the case in which Q and P are multiples of N. In this case,

$$\frac{1}{\varepsilon} = 1 + \frac{2(N - 1)}{2Q - 1} \frac{t_{comm}}{t_{calc}} \qquad (19\text{-}13)$$

As expected, the efficiency given by Eq. (19-13) is independent of the number of scalar products. When both Q and P are multiples of N, the problem is already completely balanced, so that increasing P yields no further improvement in the efficiency. If $t_{comm} \approx 2t_{calc}$ and N is reasonably large, the efficiency is about 30% when each node contains only one element from each vector (i.e., $Q = N$) and increases as the number of elements per node increases. With only ten elements from each vector per node, i.e., $Q = 10N$, the efficiency rises to about 80%. Thus, the concurrent scalar product algorithm yields good efficiency, even when each node contains only a comparatively small number of vector elements.

It is desirable, however, not to impose any restrictions on P, such as requiring it to be a multiple of N in order to obtain an efficient algorithm. Therefore, we next examine the efficiency when P is *not* a multiple of N. Using $t_{comm} = 2t_{calc}$ and $N = 32$, we have plotted the efficiency given by Eq. (19-12) for several values of Q as a function of P in Fig. 19-4. Since $N = 32$, the maximum efficiency is obtained at $P = 32$ and $P = 64$. The efficiency of the scalar product algorithm rapidly approaches the upper bound, and this limiting value increases with Q. The jumps in the plots illustrate the sensitivity of the efficiency to the load balance of the algorithm, but also show that the sensitivity declines as P increases. Thus, even in the arbitrary case given by Eq. (19-12) and illustrated in Fig. 19-4, the scalar product algorithm implemented with *addvec* yields good performance. Figure 19-5 illustrates the insensitivity of these results to the value of P. $T_N(P,Q)$ is plotted as a function of P for the fixed values $N=Q=16$. These measured timings were obtained on the Caltech Mark II hypercube using an optimized assembly code version of *addvec* for which $t_{comm}/t_{calc} = 1.5$ in 64-bit arithmetic. The results fit an essentially straight line with only minor dips at the special (optimal) points where $P=16$, 32, 48 (multiples of N). This graph also breaks down the timings by component, as defined at the end of Sec. 19-3.

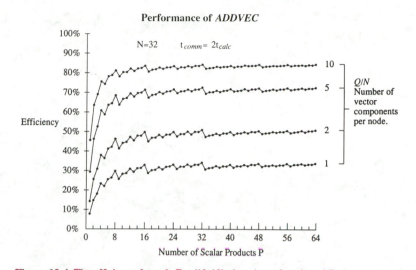

Figure 19-4 The efficiency formula Eq. (19-12) plotted as a function of P, the number of scalar products, for various values of Q, the number of terms in each scalar product. The number of nodes N is fixed at 32.

We now calculate the efficiency that would have been obtained using the implementation of *combine* in Sec. 14-5 in place of *addvec*. Each node separately calculates all of the P scalar products in *combine*, so that all nodes perform $P \log_2 N$ floating-point additions (the combining algorithm takes $\log_2 N$ steps to sum each scalar product). In addition, all P partial results from each node are exchanged across each of the $\log_2 N$ channels in the hypercube, so that the total number of elements exchanged by each node is also $P \log_2 N$. Thus, the total amount of time taken by *combine* is

$$T_b = P \log_2 N \, (t_{calc} + t_{comm}) \qquad (19\text{-}14)$$

For simplicity, we will assume that Q is a multiple of N and use Eqs. (19-5), (19-7), and (19-8) to obtain the efficiency:

$$\varepsilon = \frac{(2Q - 1)\, t_{calc}}{(2Q - N)\, t_{calc} + N \log_2 N \, (t_{calc} + t_{comm})} \qquad (19\text{-}15)$$

It is apparent from Eq. (19-15) that when *combine* is used in place of *addvec* the efficiency is independent of P, regardless of whether P is a multiple of N. For $N \gg 1$, the simplified expression is obtained:

$$\frac{1}{\varepsilon} \approx 1 + \frac{\log_2 N - 1}{2q} + \frac{\log_2 N}{2q} \frac{t_{comm}}{t_{calc}}, \qquad (19\text{-}16)$$

where $q = Q/N$. Noteworthy is the appearance of a factor of $\log_2 N$ in both the calculation and communication loads of *combine*, in contrast with Eq. (19-13). While the

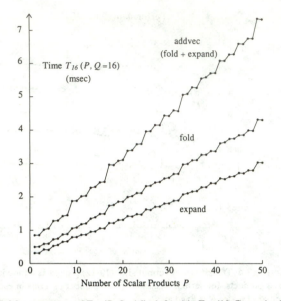

Figure 19-5 Measurements of $T_{16}(P,Q=16)$, defined in Eq. (19-5), on the Caltech Mark II hypercube [Fox 86b].

logarithm in Eq. (19-16) is not surprising since it is related to the number of levels in the binary trees, its absence from Eq. (19-13) is interesting and is due to the number of operations being reduced by half in each level of the binary trees of *addvec*. In fact, even in Eq. (19-12), where P is not necessarily a multiple of N, the logarithmic factor does not enter.

20

Matrix Algorithms II:
Banded Matrix LU Decomposition

20-1 Introduction

In Chap. 10 we showed how concurrent computers, and the hypercube in particular, can be used effectively for matrix multiplication. Although multiplication is the simplest, it is not the most important matrix algorithm. Furthermore, it is this simplicity that makes the decomposition easier and the concurrent performance better than may be the case for other matrix problems. However, as stated in Chap. 10, we believe that concurrent computers like the hypercube can perform reasonably well on essentially all matrix problems. In the present chapter, we will illustrate this point by discussing in detail the solution of linear systems of equations, represented in matrix notation by:

$$A\underline{x} = \underline{b} \tag{20-1}$$

We will examine the LU decomposition method for obtaining the solution $\underline{x}$. This approach does not produce the inverse of the matrix A, which is a more costly computation. In Chap. 21 we will generalize the results of Chaps. 10 and 20 and discuss other key matrix algorithms more quantitatively.

The numerical solution of Eq. (20-1) on any computer depends crucially on the structure of A. We will choose the case in which A is banded, as illustrated in Fig. 20-1, with the nonzero elements of A clustered about the diagonal. Such matrices are characterized by the values M and w, the matrix order and bandwidth, respectively. Here we will consider the case:

$$M \gg w \gg 1 \tag{20-2}$$

This is an important parameter range, as the solution of many partial differential equations as discussed in Chaps. 7 and 8 can be formulated as the solution of Eq. (20-1) with parameters satisfying (20-2). For instance, if we consider the finite difference matrix for a $N_x \times N_y$ grid in two dimensions, then:

$$M = N_x N_y \; ; \; w \sim 2 \min(N_x, N_y) \tag{20-3}$$

As both N_x and N_y are large in problems of practical importance, the inequalities (20-2) are satisfied.

We have chosen this example because it illustrates the handling of both linear equation solving and banded matrices on concurrent processors. In the next section, we discuss conventional sequential algorithms by way of introduction to Sec. 20-3, in which we discuss the concurrent decomposition. This discussion is extended in Sec. 20-4 to a

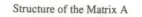

(a) Full Matrix

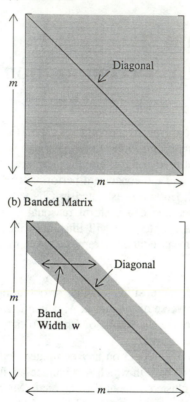

Shaded area contains
all nonzero matrix
elements.
Unshaded area
corresponds to
zero matrix elements.

(b) Banded Matrix

Figure 20-1 Comparison of zero structure of (a) Full and (b) Banded Matrix A in Eq. (20-1).

concurrent algorithm for LU decomposition along with performance analyses and measurements from the implementation on Caltech hypercubes. In Sec. 20-5 we extend the algorithm to include pivoting. In Sec. 20-6 we complete the treatment of equation solving by presenting the forward reduction and backsubstitution steps. These are also accompanied by experimental performance measurements. In the final sections concerned with systems of equations (Sec. 20-7 and 20-8), we discuss various "end effects" and then summarize the lessons from the previous sections.

The discussion of the concurrent LU decomposition algorithm is based on work by T. Aldcroft, A. Cisneros, W. Furmanski, D. Walker, and G. Fox [Aldcroft 87]. Similar issues are discussed in [Chan 86, Chu 87, Geist 86, Geist 87, O'Neil 87, Utku 86] with particular attention to the BBN Butterfly and INTEL iPSC implementations.

20-2 The Sequential Algorithm

20-2.1 Overview

In general, we will seek to solve Eq. (20-1) for a number n_b of distinct right hand sides $\underline{b}$. The n_b solutions $\underline{x}$ may be regarded as the columns of a rectangular solution matrix X. We can write the generalized problem in the form:

$$AX = B \qquad (20\text{-}4)$$

where X and B are each $M \times n_b$ matrices. Our approach [Martin 67] involves three stages which are described below:

Stage I: LU Decomposition:

Factorize the coefficient matrix according to

$$A = LU \qquad (20\text{-}5a)$$

where L is a lower triangular matrix and U is upper triangular. As we will see, L and U share a band structure similar to that of A. Equation (20-5a) is a unique factorization if we restrict L to have unit diagonal elements. Other choices are possible, as in Cholesky's method in which L and U have equal valued diagonal matrix elements. The factorization (20-5a) is useful because it is essentially trivial to invert L and U.

Stage II: Forward Reduction

Stepping through the succession of right-hand sides in B, we next make the replacement of B by B_{FR} where:

$$B_{FR} = L^{-1}B \qquad (20\text{-}5b)$$

Stage III: Backsubstitution

Finally, the solution vectors comprising X are obtained through:

$$X = U^{-1}B_{FR} \qquad (20\text{-}5c)$$

Following this cursory outline of the basic method, we will now proceed to detail the standard sequential algorithm, which is actually a modification of the Gaussian elimination method for inversion of general matrices. We begin by noting that it is convenient and natural to store L and U in exactly the same space used by A. L overlaps the lower triangular part of A, and U occupies the remaining space. The diagonal elements of U replace those of A, and there is no need to explicitly store the unit diagonal of L. Similarly, B, B_{FR}, and X can make use of the same memory locations. Thus the algorithm amounts to a modification of the original A into L and U, while B is successively transformed to obtain B_{FR} and finally the solution X.

20-2.2 LU Decomposition

The sequential algorithm for LU decomposition involves M steps where step k, $(k=0, \ldots, M-1)$, is illustrated in Fig. 20-2. This step involves an $m \times m$ square "window" of the matrix A, where the bandwidth is given by $w = 2m-1$. Elements of A above the window have already undergone factorization. At the kth step, we subtract a multiple of the first row of the window, which is the kth row of the original matrix A, from the $m-1$ following rows. In Gaussian elimination, this corresponds to the familiar strategy of zeroing the coefficients of x_k in all but the first row. Notationally this procedure is expressed as follows:

Find the kth column of L with elements given by:

$$L_{kk} = 1$$

$$L_{k+i,k} = A_{kk}^{-1} A_{k+i,k} \quad 1 \le i < m \tag{20-6}$$

Find the kth row of U with elements given by:

$$U_{k,k+j} = A_{k,k+j} \quad 0 \le j < m \tag{20-7}$$

Modify elements of A inside the window but not in the first row or column by:

$$A_{k+i,k+j} = A_{k+i,k+j} - L_{k+i,k} U_{k,k+j} \quad 0 < i < m,\ 0 < j < m \tag{20-8}$$

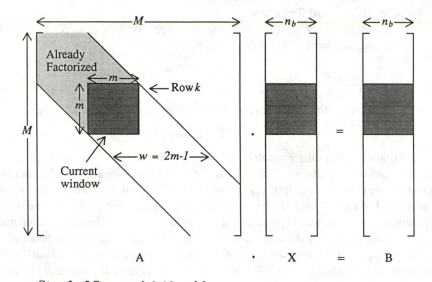

Step k of Sequential Algorithm

Dark Shaded Areas are Active

Figure 20-2 Step k of sequential algorithm showing current window.

20-2.3 Forward Reduction

We may choose to obtain the modification $B \leftarrow B_{FR}$ simultaneously with the formation of L and U. However, for clarity we choose here to complete the factorization first, and then apply the following algorithm. Forward reduction consists of M steps labeled by first row k as above. At step k, we modify elements of B according to:

$$B_{k+i,j} = B_{k+i,j} - B_{k,j} L_{k+i,k} \quad 1 \leq i < m, \ 0 \leq j < n_b \qquad (20\text{-}9)$$

20-2.4 Backsubstitution

The backsubstitution step works from the last row to the first. We label the M steps by k, an index which now runs from $M-1$ to 0. The algorithm now proceeds with the steps:

$$X_{k,j} = B_{k,j} U_{kk}^{-1} \quad 0 \leq j < n_b, \ 1 \leq i < m \qquad (20\text{-}10)$$

$$B_{k-i,j} = B_{k-i,j} - X_{k,j} U_{k-i,k}$$

20-3 Concurrent Decomposition

In Chap. 10 we showed that a simple square subblock decomposition was optimal. As shown in Fig. 20-3(a), this presents two serious difficulties for the problem at hand. Firstly, many of the processors are wasted, by operating on zeros outside the band. Secondly, each of the steps of the algorithms in Eqs. (20-6) to (20-10) involve only a limited number of the processors. Clearly we need to ensure that each of the windows involve all processors in as load-balanced a fashion as possible. This is achieved with the scattered square decomposition illustrated in Fig. 20-3(b) [Fox 84d]. Adjacent matrix elements are assigned to different processors. We shall assume for the present discussion that the number of processors N is a perfect square. For the hypercube topology this restricts us to consideration of cubes of even dimension. We impose a periodic template over the matrix as shown in Fig. 20-3(c). In this, and all subsequent figures in this chapter, the value associated with a given cell of the template indicates the processor in which the corresponding matrix element is to be stored. The labeling of processors corresponds to that appropriate for a row-ordered, two-dimensional mesh topology, and is not the same as the *procnum* labeling scheme for hypercubes described in Sec. 14-7.

We note that the *scattered square* decomposition would in fact have been as good as the *local square* decomposition in the application of Chap. 10. The locality property of contiguous decompositions is not particularly important in matrix multiplication problems. We previously employed the scattered decomposition in the discussion of Chap. 17 and the utility of this approach has been further demonstrated for irregular geometry finite element problems [Morison 86]. We will assume here that the topology of our concurrent processor includes the periodic two-dimensional mesh connectivity. A straightforward modification of the scattered square decomposition is required for other topologies. In the case of a one-dimensional machine topology, a scattered ring decomposition would be a viable approach.

Two Decompositions of a 16 by 16 Matrix

Onto a 16 Node Concurrent Computer

(a) Local Square   (b) Scattered Square

(a) Local Square															
0	0	0	0	1	1	1	1	2	2	2	2	3	3	3	3
0	0	0	0	1	1	1	1	2	2	2	2	3	3	3	3
0	0	0	0	1	1	1	1	2	2	2	2	3	3	3	3
0	0	0	0	1	1	1	1	2	2	2	2	3	3	3	3
4	4	4	4	5	5	5	5	6	6	6	6	7	7	7	7
4	4	4	4	5	5	5	5	6	6	6	6	7	7	7	7
4	4	4	4	5	5	5	5	6	6	6	6	7	7	7	7
4	4	4	4	5	5	5	5	6	6	6	6	7	7	7	7
8	8	8	8	9	9	9	9	10	10	10	10	11	11	11	11
8	8	8	8	9	9	9	9	10	10	10	10	11	11	11	11
8	8	8	8	9	9	9	9	10	10	10	10	11	11	11	11
8	8	8	8	9	9	9	9	10	10	10	10	11	11	11	11
12	12	12	12	13	13	13	13	14	14	14	14	15	15	15	15
12	12	12	12	13	13	13	13	14	14	14	14	15	15	15	15
12	12	12	12	13	13	13	13	14	14	14	14	15	15	15	15
12	12	12	12	13	13	13	13	14	14	14	14	15	15	15	15

(b) Scattered Square															
0	1	2	3	0	1	2	3	0	1	2	3	0	1	2	3
4	5	6	7	4	5	6	7	4	5	6	7	4	5	6	7
8	9	10	11	8	9	10	11	8	9	10	11	8	9	10	11
12	13	14	15	12	13	14	15	12	13	14	15	12	13	14	15
0	1	2	3	0	1	2	3	0	1	2	3	0	1	2	3
4	5	6	7	4	5	6	7	4	5	6	7	4	5	6	7
8	9	10	11	8	9	10	11	8	9	10	11	8	9	10	11
12	13	14	15	12	13	14	15	12	13	14	15	12	13	14	15
0	1	2	3	0	1	2	3	0	1	2	3	0	1	2	3
4	5	6	7	4	5	6	7	4	5	6	7	4	5	6	7
8	9	10	11	8	9	10	11	8	9	10	11	8	9	10	11
12	13	14	15	12	13	14	15	12	13	14	15	12	13	14	15
0	1	2	3	0	1	2	3	0	1	2	3	0	1	2	3
4	5	6	7	4	5	6	7	4	5	6	7	4	5	6	7
8	9	10	11	8	9	10	11	8	9	10	11	8	9	10	11
12	13	14	15	12	13	14	15	12	13	14	15	12	13	14	15

Each cell is a matrix element.
The Number in each cell is the node in which
this element is stored.
The nodes are numbered 0...15.

Figure 20-3 Comparison of (a) *local square* and (b) *scattered square* decompositions of a 16 × 16 matrix onto a 16-node concurrent processor. Each cell represents a matrix element and the number in the cell indicates the node in which this element is stored.

We note that the existence of the matrix band structure does not alter the applicability of the scattered decomposition. The same decomposition template is used whatever the band size. Similarly, we may define the scattered decompositions for the matrices X and B. The resultant decomposition for a sample problem is shown in Fig. 20-4.

20-4 Concurrent LU Algorithm

We now consider the concurrent implementation of the basic LU decomposition of Eqs. (20-6, 7, 8). We consider the kth step illustrated in Fig. 20-5. This figure shows the current window for the parameter value $m=12$. We now introduce the quantity:

$$\hat{m} = m/\sqrt{N} \qquad\qquad (20\text{-}11)$$

(c) Scattered Decomposition Templates

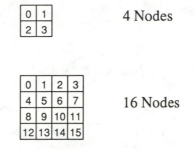

Figure 20-3(c) Shows the basic template whose periodic placement leads to the scattered decomposition.

Each processor holds $n = \hat{m}^2$ matrix elements. These elements do not comprise a contiguous $\hat{m}$ by $\hat{m}$ submatrix, but are rather scattered uniformly throughout the window. This illustration brings out a useful feature of the scattered decomposition. By comparing the windows for steps k and $k+1$, we see that row k and column k are active at step k but not afterward. The processors assigned to these now inactive elements obtain a compensating amount of new work (from row $k+m$, column $k+m$) in the form of the new matrix elements introduced at the next step. This illustrates the importance of the periodic property of this decomposition scheme.

The algorithm of Eqs. (20-6), (20-7) and (20-8) consists of five stages in its concurrent implementation. These are illustrated in Fig. 20-6 and are described here:

a)   Invert coefficient A_{kk} in the processor at the top left of the current window. In the examples of Figs. 20-5 and 20-6 this is taken to be processor 0.

b)   The elements $A_{k,k+j}$ $(0 \le j < m)$ are now the appropriate elements of the kth row of U with the diagonal element inverted as needed below and in the backsubstitution algorithm. Broadcast this row downward with the *pipe* utility that was described in Sec. 10-3.2.

c)   We can now form the multipliers of Eq. (20-6). This only involves the first "column of processors." These are processors 0, 4, 8, and 12 in the example of Fig. 20–6(c). The other processors are idle at this time.

d)   Transmit these multipliers from the first column of processors to their row neighbors. After this stage, all processors in the same row of a template (such as that of Fig. 20–3(d)) contain identical subsets of the multipliers $L_{k+i,k}$ $(0 < i < m)$.

e)   Modify the matrix elements of A in the window according to Eq. (20-8). All information necessary to do this for a given matrix element is contained within the processor holding that element.

Before examining this algorithm in further detail, let us mention some interesting points. We first note that in steps (a) and (c) serious load imbalance occurs. In fact, in stage (a) only one processor is doing any work. As there is but one floating-point calculation $(A_{kk} \rightarrow A_{kk}^{-1})$, this is a somewhat trivial example of a sequential bottleneck. We can attribute the load imbalance to the lack of available work. This is an example of

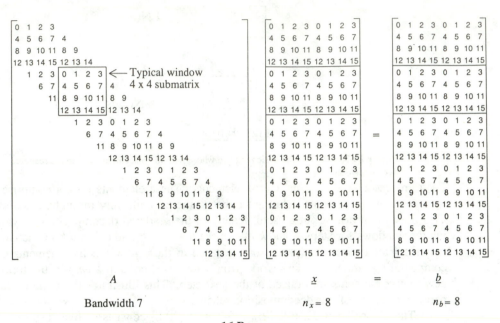

16 Processors

Figure 20-4 A banded matrix equation $AX = B$ corresponding to the matrix order $M=20$, bandwidth $w=7$, submatrix size $m=4$ and $n_x = n_b = 8$ equations. We show the *Scattered Square* decomposition onto a 16 node concurrent processor. Each cell represents a matrix element and the numbers in the cell indicates the node in which this element is stored.

Amdahl's law introduced in Sec. 3-6 which states that the concurrency attainable in an algorithm is limited by the sequential parts of the problem [Amdahl 67]. Fortunately, Amdahl's law does not pose a serious problem in this case, and it is worth understanding why that is the case both here and quite generally for coarse-grained algorithms. This gives a specific example of the general analysis in Sec. 3-6.

In Table 20-1, we analyze the three stages of LU decomposition. Stage (a) is very inefficient but this becomes irrelevant when we compare the net concurrent time of the dominant stage (e). Stage (c) is more efficient than (a) but in fact contributes rather more to the net inefficiency given in the last column of Table 20-1. The lesson in this discussion is that so-called sequential bottlenecks correspond to the stages of the calculation involving very few degrees of freedom. These particular steps are implemented poorly from a concurrency standpoint but are unimportant because the concurrent stages require

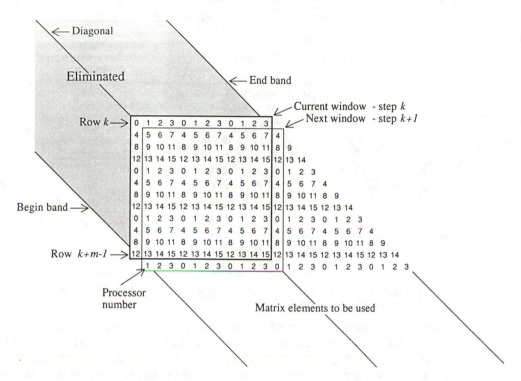

Figure 20-5 Scattered decomposition of a banded matrix of full bandwidth 23 onto 16 processors. We show the window at step k of the LU decomposition.

times of order n, where $n = \hat{m}^2$ is the grain size of the dominant part of the calculation. Sequential components tend to contribute terms proportional to $1/n$ to the inefficiency, and these terms are usually small.

A second general remark may be made with regard to comparison of the communication in this algorithm with that in the algorithm of Chap. 10. In the present case, it is necessary only to broadcast rows and columns, in strong resemblance to the row broadcast strategy of Chap. 10. On the other hand, we find here nothing analogous to the simple rolling shift of the matrix B discussed in Sec. 10-3.1. The broadcast algorithm is central to the discussion in this chapter because we are only transmitting single rows or

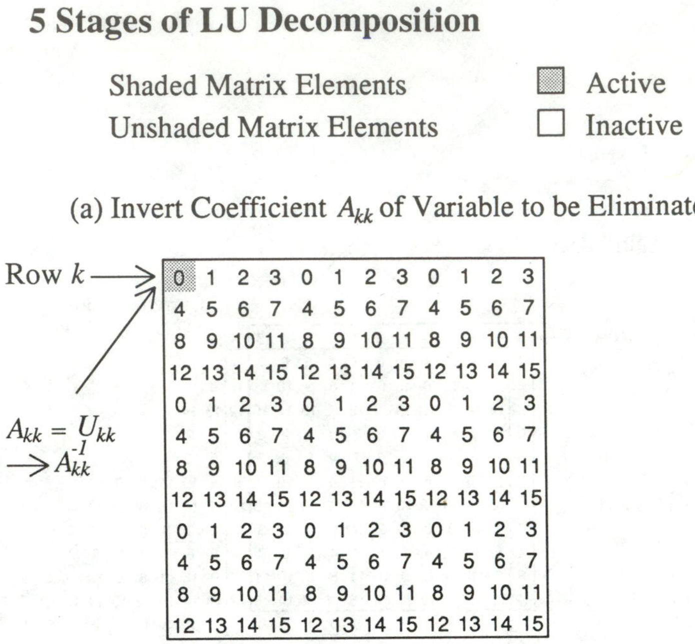

5 Stages of LU Decomposition

Shaded Matrix Elements   ▨ Active

Unshaded Matrix Elements   ☐ Inactive

(a) Invert Coefficient A_{kk} of Variable to be Eliminated

Row k ⟶

$A_{kk} = U_{kk}$
$\longrightarrow A_{kk}^{-1}$

0	1	2	3	0	1	2	3	0	1	2	3
4	5	6	7	4	5	6	7	4	5	6	7
8	9	10	11	8	9	10	11	8	9	10	11
12	13	14	15	12	13	14	15	12	13	14	15
0	1	2	3	0	1	2	3	0	1	2	3
4	5	6	7	4	5	6	7	4	5	6	7
8	9	10	11	8	9	10	11	8	9	10	11
12	13	14	15	12	13	14	15	12	13	14	15
0	1	2	3	0	1	2	3	0	1	2	3
4	5	6	7	4	5	6	7	4	5	6	7
8	9	10	11	8	9	10	11	8	9	10	11
12	13	14	15	12	13	14	15	12	13	14	15

Figure 20-6(a) The first of five stages involved in step k of LU decomposition. Active matrix elements are shaded.

columns with a message length of $\hat{m} = \sqrt{n}$, as opposed to the message lengths of $\hat{m}^2 = n$ in Chap. 10. As a result, the startup time given in Eq. (10-3) is proportionately more important in the Eqs. (20-12) and (20-13) below. In addition to this machine-independent performance impact, the employment of shorter messages contributes more to overhead on machines which incur significant fixed costs for message initiation.

A third comparison between the present algorithm and that of Chap. 10 is that both involve approximately equal amounts of communication among the matrix rows and columns. Thus the square subblock (albeit scattered rather than local) decomposition remains preferable to rectangular decompositions. In particular, pure row or column decompositions are distinctly inferior. The analysis relevant to this point follows by analogy with that in Sec. 10-4 for multiplication and need not be repeated here.

We next analyze the performance of the LU algorithm discussed above. Up to this point we have only considered the cases in which $\sqrt{N}$ is an exact divisor of the window order m. However, as we have seen previously in Chap. 10, significant performance degradation results in the case that m is not exactly divisible by $\sqrt{N}$. The working matrices (the window in A and active parts of B and X) must be padded with zeros in order to provide each processor node with a square submatrix. The worst case occurs when m exceeds an exact multiple of $\sqrt{N}$ by one. In this case, $\hat{m}$ assumes the value $[m/\sqrt{N}]$, where the square-bracketed quantity is truncated to the integer part. The

(b) Transmit Top Rows Downwards

0	1	2	3	0	1	2	3	0	1	2	3
4	5	6	7	4	5	6	7	4	5	6	7
8	9	10	11	8	9	10	11	8	9	10	11
12	13	14	15	12	13	14	15	12	13	14	15
0	1	2	3	0	1	2	3	0	1	2	3
4	5	6	7	4	5	6	7	4	5	6	7
8	9	10	11	8	9	10	11	8	9	10	11
12	13	14	15	12	13	14	15	12	13	14	15
0	1	2	3	0	1	2	3	0	1	2	3
4	5	6	7	4	5	6	7	4	5	6	7
8	9	10	11	8	9	10	11	8	9	10	11
12	13	14	15	12	13	14	15	12	13	14	15

Processors   0 4 8 12   now contain
1 5 9 13   same subset
2 6 10 14   of top row
3 7 11 15

Figure 20-6(b) The second of five stages involved in step k of LU decomposition. Active matrix elements are shaded.

(c) Calculate Multipliers in First Column

0	1	2	3	0	1	2	3	0	1	2	3
4	5	6	7	4	5	6	7	4	5	6	7
8	9	10	11	8	9	10	11	8	9	10	11
12	13	14	15	12	13	14	15	12	13	14	15
0	1	2	3	0	1	2	3	0	1	2	3
4	5	6	7	4	5	6	7	4	5	6	7
8	9	10	11	8	9	10	11	8	9	10	11
12	13	14	15	12	13	14	15	12	13	14	15
0	1	2	3	0	1	2	3	0	1	2	3
4	5	6	7	4	5	6	7	4	5	6	7
8	9	10	11	8	9	10	11	8	9	10	11
12	13	14	15	12	13	14	15	12	13	14	15

Multipliers

$$L_{k+i,\,k} = A_{ik} A_{kk}$$

Figure 20-6(c) The third of five stages involved in step k of LU decomposition. Active matrix elements are shaded.

(d) Transmit Multipliers From First Column

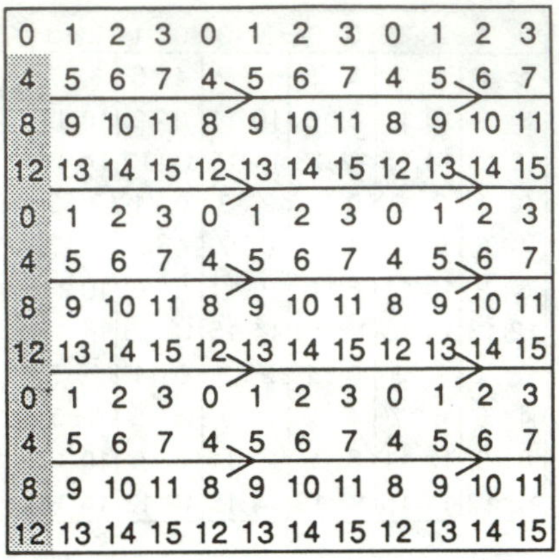

0	1	2	3	0	1	2	3	0	1	2	3
4	5	6	7	4	5	6	7	4	5	6	7
8	9	10	11	8	9	10	11	8	9	10	11
12	13	14	15	12	13	14	15	12	13	14	15
0	1	2	3	0	1	2	3	0	1	2	3
4	5	6	7	4	5	6	7	4	5	6	7
8	9	10	11	8	9	10	11	8	9	10	11
12	13	14	15	12	13	14	15	12	13	14	15
0	1	2	3	0	1	2	3	0	1	2	3
4	5	6	7	4	5	6	7	4	5	6	7
8	9	10	11	8	9	10	11	8	9	10	11
12	13	14	15	12	13	14	15	12	13	14	15

Processors   0   1   2   3   now contain
              4   5   6   7   same subset
              8   9   10   11   of multipliers (first column)
              12   13   14   15

Figure 20-6(d) The fourth of five stages involved in step k of LU decomposition. Active matrix elements are shaded.

padded decomposition now assigns matrices of size $(\hat{m}+1) \times (\hat{m}+1)$ to each node. This procedure is illustrated in Fig. 20-7 for a simple example. In Table 20-2 the sequential and concurrent theoretical execution times are listed for the five stages of concurrent LU decomposition. The results are tabulated separately for the best case ($m = \hat{m}\sqrt{N}$) and worst case ($m = \hat{m}\sqrt{N} + 1$) decompositions described above.

We may now proceed to derive the net overhead and concurrent efficiencies, following the definitions established in Chap. 5. Actually, the true algorithm is somewhat more complicated than the simple model used to derive Table 20-2 and may not be fully represented. With this in mind, we begin by noting that the timings obtained for stages (b) and (d) apply to the Caltech/JPL Mark II hypercubes which incorporate no hardware assist for broadcast operations. The already quoted formulae apply to the communication algorithm given in Code 10-3. This is the algorithm also used in the hypercube timings of the current chapter. It is possible however, to devise a better algorithm for the same hardware environment, which we will refer to as the *split pipe*. The initiating node in the scheme sends information in both directions (e.g., "up" and "down" in stage (b), with the "up" direction wrapped periodically to the bottom of the window). This enhancement approximately halves the startup time previously given by $(\sqrt{N} - 2)t_{comm}$. Example pseudocode illustrating this method is given in Code 20-1.

(e) Correct Remaining Matrix Elements

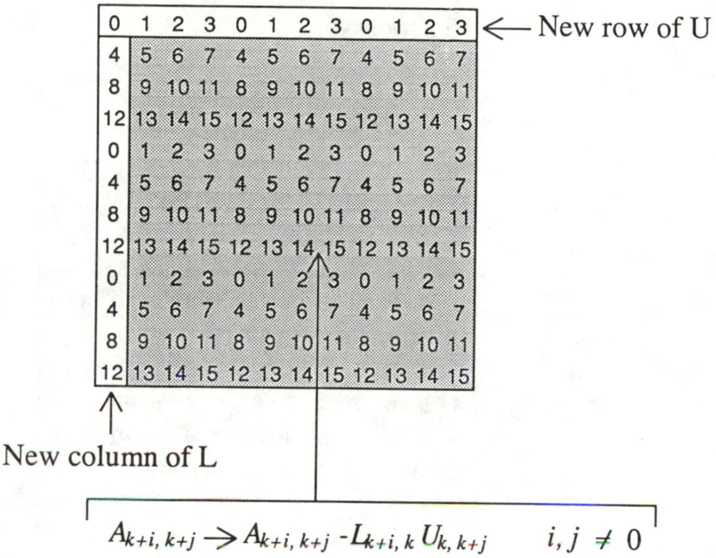
New row of U
New column of L
$A_{k+i,\,k+j} \rightarrow A_{k+i,\,k+j} - L_{k+i,\,k}\, U_{k,\,k+j} \qquad i, j \neq 0$

Figure 20-6(e) The fifth of five stages involved in step k of LU decomposition. Active matrix elements are shaded.

Stage	Time in units of t_{calc}		Local	Contribution to Total
	Sequential	Concurrent	Efficiency	Concurrent Overhead $1/\varepsilon - 1$
(a) Invert A_{kk}	$0(1)$	$0(1)$	$0(1/N)$	$0(1/\hat{m}^2)$
(c) Form Multipliers	$\hat{m}\sqrt{N} - 1$	$\hat{m}$	$0(1/\sqrt{N})$	$0(1/\hat{m})$
(e) Update Matrix	$(\hat{m}\sqrt{N} - 1)^2$	$\hat{m}^2$	$1 - 0(1/\hat{m}\sqrt{N})$	$0(1/\hat{m}\sqrt{N})$

Table 20-1 Utilization of Hypercube for Three Stages of LU Decomposition

In Table 20-2, we have assumed that the times required for multiplications and additions are both equal to t_{calc}. Floating-point scalar inversion is assumed to take a time t_{inv}, although this term is irrelevant to the asymptotic form of the concurrent overhead.

Returning to the simple predictions of Table 20-2, we may derive the theoretical overhead relations:

$$f_{LU}(\text{best case}) = \frac{1.5}{\hat{m}\sqrt{N}} + \frac{0.5}{\hat{m}} + \frac{\tau}{\hat{m}}\left[1 + \frac{(\sqrt{N} - 2)}{\hat{m}}\right] \tag{20-12}$$

$$f_{LU}\ (\text{worst case}) = \frac{-0.5}{\hat{m}\sqrt{N}} + \frac{2.5}{\hat{m}} + \frac{\tau}{\hat{m}}\left[1 + \frac{(\sqrt{N} - 1)}{\hat{m}}\right] \tag{20-13}$$

Effect of Imbalanced Decomposition

Full Bandwidth 25

16 Processors

```
0  1  2  3  0  1  2  3  0  1  2  3  0
4  5  6  7  4  5  6  7  4  5  6  7  4
8  9 10 11  8  9 10 11  8  9 10 11  8
12 13 14 15 12 13 14 15 12 13 14 15 12
0  1  2  3  0  1  2  3  0  1  2  3  0
4  5  6  7  4  5  6  7  4  5  6  7  4
8  9 10 11  8  9 10 11  8  9 10 11  8
12 13 14 15 12 13 14 15 12 13 14 15 12
0  1  2  3  0  1  2  3  0  1  2  3  0
4  5  6  7  4  5  6  7  4  5  6  7  4
8  9 10 11  8  9 10 11  8  9 10 11  8
12 13 14 15 12 13 14 15 12 13 14 15 12
0  1  2  3  0  1  2  3  0  1  2  3  0
```

13 x 13 window

Processor	0	16 elements
	1, 2, 3, 4, 8, 12	12 elements
Remaining processors		9 elements

Figure 20-7 An example of an imbalanced decomposition. We show the 13×13 window corresponding to a matrix of bandwidth 25. We shade the matrix elements which give processors 0, 1, 2, 3 additional work.

These formulae have ignored the nonasymptotic contribution, but more importantly, they have ignored some issues related to concrete implementation. As an example, stages (c) and (d) for the case of the Caltech machines are almost completely overlapped (concurrent). In addition, there enters significant software overhead of the type discussed in Sec. 10-5.1. This effect will alter the effective value of t_{comm} and call into question the assumption $t_{start} = t_{comm}$ used in Eq. (10-3) to obtain Table 20-2. As a result of these departures from ideality, we can at best expect Eqs. (20-12) and (20-13) to provide an indicative, qualitative description of the measurements.

Figure 20-8 presents the measurements on the Caltech/JPL Mark II hypercube in comparison with the above theoretical predictions. From this plot we derive the ratio:

$$\tau = \frac{t_{comm}}{t_{calc}} = 4.7 \qquad (20\text{-}14)$$

Stage	Best Case $m = \hat{m}\sqrt{N}$		Worst Case $m = \hat{m}\sqrt{N} + 1$	
	Time		Time	
	Sequential	Concurrent	Sequential	Concurrent
(a) Invert A_{kk}	t_{inv}	t_{inv}	t_{inv}	t_{inv}
(b) Pipe First Row Downward	0	$\left[\hat{m} + (\sqrt{N}-2)\right] t_{comm}$	0	$\left[\hat{m} + 1 + (\sqrt{N}-2)\right] t_{comm}$
(c) Form Multipliers	$(\hat{m}\sqrt{N}-1)t_{calc}$	$\hat{m}t_{calc}$	$\hat{m}\sqrt{N}\, t_{calc}$	$(\hat{m}+1)t_{calc}$
(d) Pipe Multipliers Across	0	$\left[\hat{m} + (\sqrt{N}-2)\right] t_{comm}$	0	$\left[\hat{m} + 1 + (\sqrt{N}-2)\right] t_{comm}$
(e) Correct Matrix	$2(\hat{m}\sqrt{N}-1)^2 t_{calc}$	$2\hat{m}^2 t_{calc}$	$2\hat{m}^2 N t_{calc}$	$2(\hat{m}+1)^2 t_{calc}$

Table 20-2: Estimated Times for Stages in LU Decomposition

```
proc_begin split_pipe ( send buffer around ring using split pipe )
    [ let nring be number of processors in the ring ]
    [ let ringpos be the number of steps around ring from source processor ]
    if_begin ( ringpos = 0, i.e., this processor is the source processor ) then
        [ send buffer to processors in the clockwise and anticlockwise directions ]
    else_if ( ringpos = nring/2, i.e., this processor is opposite source processor ) then
        [ receive buffer from processor in the clockwise direction ]
    else_if ( ringpos = nring /2 - 1 ) then
        [ receive buffer from processor in the anticlockwise direction]
    else_if ( ringpos < nring/2 ) then
        [ receive buffer from processor in the anticlockwise direction and
            forward to processor in the clockwise direction ]
    else_if ( ringpos > nring/2 ) then
        [ receive buffer from processor in the clockwise direction and
            forward to processor in the anticlockwise direction ]
    if_end
proc_end
```

Code 20-1 The *split_pipe* Sub-cube Broadcast Algorithm

This is larger than the value obtained for matrix multiplication in Eq. (10-19) for two main reasons. First 32-bit numbers are used in Chap. 10 and 64-bit numbers are used here: t_{comm} (32-bit) = 0.5 t_{comm} (64-bit), whereas the 8087 chip used on the Mark II hypercube performs single and double precision calculations in roughly comparable times. This accounts for a factor of two in the discrepancy with Chap. 10. The second cause of additional overhead is the nonoptimal implementation of the CrOS III routine *vshift* on the Mark II hypercube. The scattered decomposition leads naturally to the use of *vshift* to transfer rows and columns of the matrices. However, *vshift* on the Mark II hypercube is implemented in terms of *cshift* so that two additional memory-to-memory copies are necessary. In an efficient implementation this copying can be avoided on hypercubes like the Mark II where messages are packetized. The routine *vshift* will always be inefficient if the hardware is optimized for DMA (direct memory transfers) from contiguous memory to the communication system. An implementation of these algorithms without using the scattered decomposition and so with efficient communication had $\tau = t_{comm}/t_{calc} = 2.7$. We can expect an optimal version of *vshift* to give a τ value similar to this.

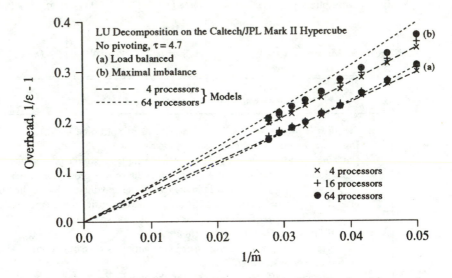

Figure 20-8 Measurements of the concurrent overhead $1/\varepsilon -1$ as a function of the natural parameter $\sqrt{N}/m$ for LU decomposition with no pivoting. We show results from the Caltech/JPL Mark II hypercube for 4, 16 and 64 node machines. The results (a) correspond to the balanced case where m is an exact multiple of $\sqrt{N}$. (b) corresponds to m values that are 1 more than such exact multiples. General values of m lie between these extreme cases. We also show the expectations for (a) and (b) coming from the model Eq. (20-12, 13) for the parameter value $t_{comm}/t_{calc} = 4.7$

It is apparent from Fig. 20-8 that the model agrees quite nicely with the measurements. The overhead is proportional to $1/\hat{m}$ and the model adequately describes the difference between the best and the worst case efficiencies (i.e., the effect of the load imbalance when $\sqrt{N}$ does not divide m exactly). A fortuitous cancellation occurs between the $1.5/\hat{m}\sqrt{N}$ and $\tau(\sqrt{N}-2)/\hat{m}^2$ terms in Eq. (20-12), so that the best case efficiency shows little dependence on N when plotted as a function of $\hat{m}$ This cancellation does not occur for Eq. (20-13), and the divergence of the $N = 4$ and $N = 64$ measurements is a direct consequence of the pipe startup term being proportional to $(\sqrt{N}-2)$.

In practical applications, we might expect that a typical value of m lies between the best- and worst-case results, and quite good performance is obtained in this intermediate case. For the case of a 20×20 matrix in each node, the concurrent overhead is about 35% on a 64-node hypercube.

As long as $\hat{m} = \sqrt{n}$ is large compared with $(\sqrt{N} - 2)$, the inefficiency follows the expected relation:

$$f = \frac{1}{\varepsilon} - 1 \sim \frac{\text{constant}}{n^{1/2}} \tag{20-15}$$

corresponding in the language of Chap. 3 to a system of system dimension $d_S = 2$. This is a general result; all full and banded matrix algorithms have dimension 2. This is an interesting result because matrices have no metric associated with them. It would appear that the system dimension d_S can reflect the dimension of the world being decomposed rather than some local property of a metric space where $1/n^{1/d_S}$ is a natural formula for the generalized surface to volume ratio.

Both matrix multiplication and LU decomposition have dimension 2, corresponding to an overhead proportional to $1/n^{1/2}$, with n equal to the grain size. In multiplication, we find a basic calculational cost proportional to $n^{3/2}$ and communication costs linear in n. In LU decomposition, calculation is proportional to n and communication varies as $\sqrt{n}$. The ratio of the communication to calculation costs has the same $(1/\sqrt{n})$ dependence in each case, corresponding to the same system dimension. It is interesting that this uniformity occurs even though the calculational complexity has a quite different dependence on grain size in the two cases.

20-5 Pivoting in the Concurrent LU Decomposition

The algorithm described in Sec. 20-2 and 20-4 is appropriate when the diagonal elements A_{kk} are dominant. This is often the case, but in general, attention must be given to numerical instability resulting from the division by A_{kk} if its value is small or vanishing. This problem is handled by means of a pivoting rearrangement of rows and columns in order to obtain a larger element in the top corner of the window. We consider here the case of partial pivoting in which we search the first column in the window for the maximum entry $A_{k+i, k}(0 \le i < m)$. If this maximum corresponds to row number $k + i_{\max}$ then the rows corresponding to $i = 0$ and $i = i_{\max}$ are swapped. Then the algorithm proceeds according to the description of Sec. 20-2. There arises one obvious complication in that the resultant matrix within the window is no longer square. As shown in Fig. 20-9, the window could be as big as m rows and $2m - 2$ columns before this step. The number of columns depends on the details of pivoting in the previous $m - 1$ steps. Pivoting at step k may or may not increase the window size. The A matrix window is at most m by $2m - 1$ in size after the pivoting at step k. This possible increase in window size affects the speed of the algorithm but does not alter in any essential way the steps outlined earlier in Section 20-2.

The variable size of the window encountered here is handled naturally within the context of the earlier scattered decomposition. This decomposition ensures that the loads of different processors differ by at most one column. This illustrates the general utility of this simple decomposition approach. While originally motivated by the need to cope with the banded matrix structure, it represents a powerful method of dealing with other sources of imbalance. Despite the generality of this approach, we have simplified matters in the present example by assuming a constant window size of m by $2m$ at all steps. This restriction simplifies both the sequential and concurrent algorithms. All columns beyond the end of the significant window are assumed to be padded with zeros. This simplification was used in the example runs whose measured performance values are given in Fig. 20-11.

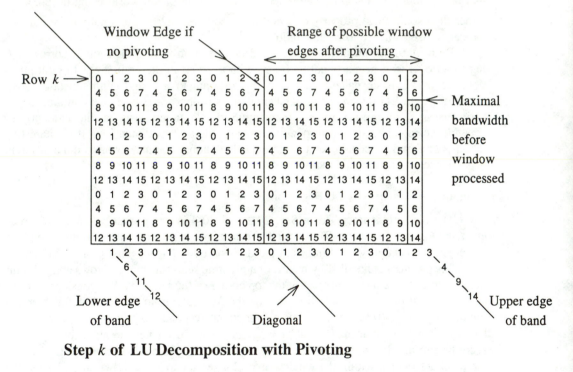

Step k of LU Decomposition with Pivoting

Original Bandwidth 23
16 Processors

Figure 20-9 The window in the matrix A at step k of LU decomposition when partial pivoting is used. The example matrix has the same parameters as that in Fig. 20-5.

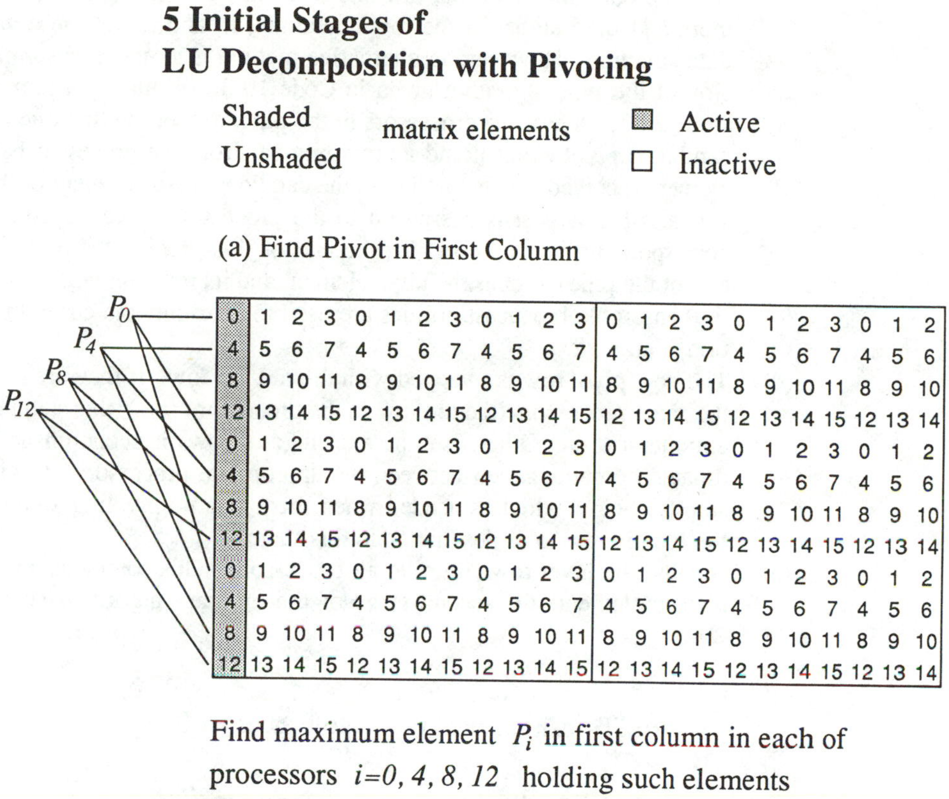

5 Initial Stages of LU Decomposition with Pivoting

Shaded   matrix elements   ▨ Active

Unshaded   ☐ Inactive

(a) Find Pivot in First Column

P_0 P_4 P_8 P_{12}

0	1 2 3 0 1 2 3 0 1 2 3	0 1 2 3 0 1 2 3 0 1 2
4	5 6 7 4 5 6 7 4 5 6 7	4 5 6 7 4 5 6 7 4 5 6
8	9 10 11 8 9 10 11 8 9 10 11	8 9 10 11 8 9 10 11 8 9 10
12	13 14 15 12 13 14 15 12 13 14 15	12 13 14 15 12 13 14 15 12 13 14
0	1 2 3 0 1 2 3 0 1 2 3	0 1 2 3 0 1 2 3 0 1 2
4	5 6 7 4 5 6 7 4 5 6 7	4 5 6 7 4 5 6 7 4 5 6
8	9 10 11 8 9 10 11 8 9 10 11	8 9 10 11 8 9 10 11 8 9 10
12	13 14 15 12 13 14 15 12 13 14 15	12 13 14 15 12 13 14 15 12 13 14
0	1 2 3 0 1 2 3 0 1 2 3	0 1 2 3 0 1 2 3 0 1 2
4	5 6 7 4 5 6 7 4 5 6 7	4 5 6 7 4 5 6 7 4 5 6
8	9 10 11 8 9 10 11 8 9 10 11	8 9 10 11 8 9 10 11 8 9 10
12	13 14 15 12 13 14 15 12 13 14 15	12 13 14 15 12 13 14 15 12 13 14

Find maximum element P_i in first column in each of processors $i=0, 4, 8, 12$ holding such elements

Figure 20-10(a) The first of five initial stages in the pivoting algorithm for the kth step of the decomposition. These are followed by the stages in Fig. 20-6 just as in the case with no pivoting.

The concurrent pivoting algorithm incorporates five additional steps. These supplementary implementation steps are illustrated in Fig. 20-10 and are described as follows:

(a) Each processor containing elements of the first column determines the local maximum of $|A_{k+i,k}|$ for those elements in the node. This step only involves $\sqrt{N}$ nodes. The other processors are idle.

(b) Next, determine the global maximum over these $\sqrt{N}$ local pivot candidates. At first glance it might seem appropriate to use the *combine* collective routine which was introduced in Chaps. 4 and 14. In this case, we would apply *combine* not over the full hypercube but over the nodes containing elements in the first column of the window. These nodes make up a subcube. The pseudocode for performing a general *subcube combine* is given in Code 20-2. For historical reasons subcube combine is not part of the basic CrOS III library, but it is given as a utility in the Software Supplement, Vol. 2 of this text. The subcube combine algorithm in Code 20-2 may be used to find the pivot element and the number of the row containing it, and return these values in a data structure. However, an alternative method is to use a "customized" version of the pipe algorithm given in Code 10-3. In this algorithm, shown in Code 20-3, each of the processors in the pipe, except the first one, receives a candidate pivot element and its row number from the processor below. The element received is compared with the candidate pivot element of the processor, and the largest is passed on to the processor above, together with the corresponding row number. At the end of this process the processor at the end of the pipe contains the pivot element and its row number.

(c)   Full ensemble broadcast utilities are used to distribute the current pivot location to all nodes.

(d)   The new pivot row is swapped with the old top row. If they are contained in the same processors (the top row in the processor array), this step involves no communication. Otherwise, the exchange of rows is accomplished by coordinated communication between the appropriate processors. In view of the step (e) below which is needed when there was no pivoting, one only sends the old top row to its destination in this stage.

(e)   Finally, the pivot row is sent to all processors. This completes the swap and also implements the second stage of the ordinary algorithm shown in Fig. 20-6.

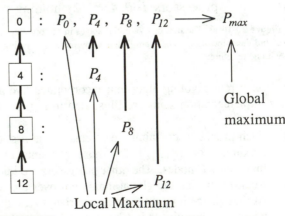

(b) Transmit Local Pivots to Processor 0

Figure 20-10(b) The second of five initial stages in the pivoting algorithm for the kth step of the decomposition. These are followed by the stages in Fig. 20-6 just as in the case with no pivoting.

(c) Broadcast Pivot Information
To All Processors

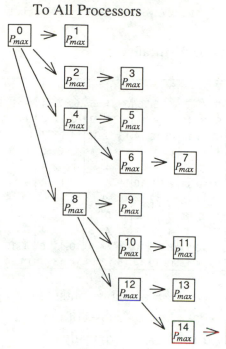

Figure 20-10(c) The third of five initial stages in the pivoting algorithm for the kth step of the decomposition. These are followed by the stages in Fig. 20-6 just as in the case with no pivoting.

(d) Send Old Top Row to Position of Pivot Row

Band edge at least here

0	1	2	3	0	1	2	3	0	1	2	3	0	1	2	3	0	1	2	3	0	1
4	5	6	7	4	5	6	7	4	5	6	7	4	5	6	7	4	5	6	7	4	5
8	9	10	11	8	9	10	11	8	9	10	11	8	9	10	11	8	9	10	11	8	9
12	13	14	15	12	13	14	15	12	13	14	15	12	13	14	15	12	13	14	15	12	13
0	1	2	3	0	1	2	3	0	1	2	3	0	1	2	3	0	1	2	3	0	1
4	5	6	7	4	5	6	7	4	5	6	7	4	5	6	7	4	5	6	7	4	5
8	9	10	11	8	9	10	11	8	9	10	11	8	9	10	11	8	9	10	11	8	9
12	13	14	15	12	13	14	15	12	13	14	15	12	13	14	15	12	13	14	15	12	13
0	1	2	3	0	1	2	3	0	1	2	3	0	1	2	3	0	1	2	3	0	1
4	5	6	7	4	5	6	7	4	5	6	7	4	5	6	7	4	5	6	7	4	5
8	9	10	11	8	9	10	11	8	9	10	11	8	9	10	11	8	9	10	11	8	9
12	13	14	15	12	13	14	15	12	13	14	15	12	13	14	15	12	13	14	15	12	13

← Pivot position

Processors 12, 13, 14, 15 now contain the same subsets

of top row as processors 0, 1, 2, 3 respectively.

Figure 20-10(d) The fourth of five initial stages in the pivoting algorithm for the kth step of the decomposition. These are followed by the stages in Fig. 20-6 just as in the case with no pivoting.

(e) Send Pivot Row Vertically

```
 0  1  2  3  0  1  2  3  0  1  2  3  0  1  2  3  0  1  2  3  0  1
 4  5  6  7  4  5  6  7  4  5  6  7  4  5  6  7  4  5  6  7  4  5
 8  9 10 11  8  9 10 11  8  9 10 11  8  9 10 11  8  9 10 11  8  9
12 13 14 15 12 13 14 15 12 13 14 15 12 13 14 15 12 13 14 15 12 13
 0  1  2  3  0  1  2  3  0  1  2  3  0  1  2  3  0  1  2  3  0  1
 4  5  6  7  4  5  6  7  4  5  6  7  4  5  6  7  4  5  6  7  4  5
 8  9 10 11  8  9 10 11  8  9 10 11  8  9 10 11  8  9 10 11  8  9
12 13 14 15 12 13 14 15 12 13 14 15 12 13 14 15 12 13 14 15 12 13  <—
 0  1  2  3  0  1  2  3  0  1  2  3  0  1  2  3  0  1  2  3  0  1
 4  5  6  7  4  5  6  7  4  5  6  7  4  5  6  7  4  5  6  7  4  5
 8  9 10 11  8  9 10 11  8  9 10 11  8  9 10 11  8  9 10 11  8  9
12 13 14 15 12 13 14 15 12 13 14 15 12 13 14 15 12 13 14 15 12 13
```

Processors   0 4 8 12   now contain same
            1 5 9 13   subset of row ————
            2 6 1014   originally in
            3 7 1115   12, 13, 14, 15 only.

Figure 20-10(e) The fifth of five initial stages in the pivoting algorithm for the kth step of the decomposition. These are followed by the stages in Fig. 20-6 just as in the case with no pivoting.

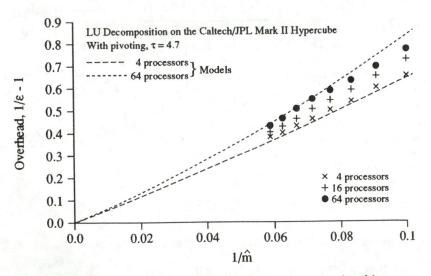

Figure 20-11 Measurements of the concurrent overhead $1/\varepsilon - 1$ as a function of the natural parameter $\sqrt{N}/m$ for LU decomposition with pivoting. We show results for the Caltech-JPL Mark II hypercube for 4, 16 and 64 node machines. We show the expected dependence of $1/\varepsilon - 1$ on $\sqrt{N}/m$ from the model of Table (20-3) for the parameter value $t_{comm}/t_{calc} = 4.7$. We note that as described in the text both the concurrent and sequential algorithms have been simplified and are nonoptimal.

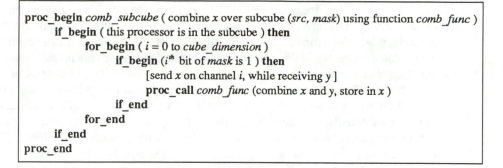

proc_begin *comb_subcube* (combine *x* over subcube (*src, mask*) using function *comb_func*)
    if_begin (this processor is in the subcube) **then**
        for_begin (*i* = 0 to *cube_dimension*)
            if_begin (*i*th bit of *mask* is 1) **then**
                [send *x* on channel *i*, while receiving *y*]
                proc_call *comb_func* (combine *x* and *y*, store in *x*)
            if_end
        for_end
    if_end
proc_end

Code 20-2 Pseudocode for General Combine Over a Subcube of the Hypercube

proc_begin *find_pivot* (find pivot row, *p_row*, and pivot element, *pivot*)
    if_begin (this processor has elements in first column of window) **then**
        [find maximum element, *max_el*, in first column for this processor]
        [store row number of maximum element in *max_row*]
    if_end
    if_begin (this processor contains the element in the last row of first column
                      of the window) **then**
        [send *max_el* and *max_row* to processor above]
    else_if (this processor contains the element in the first row of the first column) **then**
        [receive *cand_el* and *cand_row* from processor below]
        if_begin (*max_el* > *cand_el*] **then**
            [*pivot* ← *max_el*]
            [*p_row* ← *max_row*]
        else
            [*pivot* ← *cand_el*]
            [*p_row* ← *cand_row*]
        if_end
    else_if (this processor contains elements in the first column of the window) **then**
        [receive *cand_el* and *cand_row* from processor below]
        if_begin (*max_el* > *cand_el*) **then**
            [*cand_el* ← *max_el*]
            [*cand-row* ← *max_row*]
        if_end
        [send *cand_el* and *cand_row* to processor above]
    if_end
    [broadcast *p_row* from processor containing element in first row
                and column of window to all other processors]
proc_end

Code 20-3 Determination of the Pivot Element and Row

These pivoting steps are followed by those of the nonpivoting algorithm with the obvious changes required by the increased number of columns. It is apparent that while pivoting is an almost trivial operation on a sequential machine, it can require a fairly complicated algorithm in the concurrent implementation. The concurrent implementation is in this case significantly less transparent than the sequential equivalent. One approach described in Chap. 21 is that taken in Fox and Furmanski [Fox 86b] to build a library of general purpose concurrent matrix subroutines. A single such set of routines can be used to tackle essentially all matrix problems. By way of a general remark, we have found that matrix problems are in many ways the hardest for concurrent machines. The algorithms are so involved that although high speedup is possible, the software implementation overhead cost is relatively greater than for the other problems discussed in this volume.

Stage	Time	
	Sequential	Concurrent
(a) Find Pivot	$\hat{m}\sqrt{N}\ t_{calc}$	$\hat{m}t_{calc}$
(b) Transmit to Corner Node	0	$2(\sqrt{N}-1)t_{comm}$
(c) Inform All Nodes of Pivot Parameter	0	$2\log_2 N\ t_{comm}$
(d) Send Top Row in Window to Position of Pivot Row	0	$\dfrac{(\sqrt{N}-1)}{\sqrt{N}}\left[2\hat{m}+\dfrac{1}{4}\dfrac{(\sqrt{N}-2)^2}{\sqrt{N}-1}\right]t_{comm}$
(e) Send Pivot Row Everywhere	0	$\left[2\hat{m}+(\sqrt{N}-2)\right]t_{comm}$
(f) Invert a_{kk}	t_{inv}	t_{inv}
(g) Form Multipliers	$(\hat{m}\sqrt{N}-1)\ t_{calc}$	$\hat{m}t_{calc}$
(h) Pipe Multipliers Across	0	$\left[\hat{m}+(\sqrt{N}-2)\right]t_{comm}$
(i) Correct Matrix	$2(\hat{m}\sqrt{N}-1)(2\hat{m}\sqrt{N}-1)$ t_{calc}	$4\hat{m}^2\ t_{calc}$

Table 20-3 Estimated Times for Stages in LU Decomposition with Pivoting

In Table 20-3, we detail the simple model describing the performance of the concurrent pivoting algorithm. We will only discuss the "best-case" scenario, when m is an exact multiple of $\sqrt{N}$. The entry (d) is this table corresponds to a simple algorithm where the top row is sent by the shortest pipe between the source and destination nodes. In Chap. 21 we will formalize this utility as *transfer* and discuss optimal algorithms.

This table contains more steps than Table 20-2 but the two share essentially the same structure. In Fig. 20-11 we compare measured concurrent overheads, $1/\varepsilon-1$, with the estimate obtained from Table 20-3 using the same parameter value $t_{comm}/t_{calc} = 4.7$ as in Sec. 20-4. There is now a more evident separation between the $N = 4$ and 64 measurements due to the increased importance of the subasymptotic $(\sqrt{N}-2)/\hat{m}^2$ and $\log_2 N/\hat{m}^2$ terms in $1/\varepsilon-1$.

20-6 Forward Reduction and Backsubstitution

We now turn to the use of the factored form $A=LU$ to complete the solution of $A\underline{x}=\underline{b}$ or more generally $AX=B$. This task involves forward reduction $\underline{b}\leftarrow L^{-1}\underline{b}$, followed by backsubstitution $\underline{x}\leftarrow U^{-1}\underline{b}$, as described for the sequential case in Sec. 20-2. In the case of a single right-hand side, the discussion is largely academic, since the costs associated with this final phase are small (by a factor m) compared with those for LU decomposition. An optimized decomposition for the single right-hand side problem uses techniques discussed by Fox and Furmanski [Fox 86b] and discussed in Sec. 21-3.4. Instead, we will here suppose that Eq. (20-4) is to be solved for n_b right-hand sides, and further that n_b is large compared with $\sqrt{N}$.

Forward reduction is illustrated in Figs. 20-12 and 20-13 and consists of three stages in the concurrent implementation of Eq. (20-9). The theoretical times are tabulated in Table 20-4 but we will not discuss them in great detail because they follow by analogy from the steps discussed in Sec. 20-4.

In Table 20-4, we draw an analogy to Eq. (20-11) in making the definition:

$$\hat{n}_b = n_b/\sqrt{N} \tag{20-16}$$

We obtain the predicted concurrent overhead given by

$$f = 1/\varepsilon - 1 = \frac{1}{\hat{m}\sqrt{N}} + \frac{\tau}{2}\left[\frac{1}{\hat{m}} + \frac{1}{\hat{n}_b} + \frac{2(\sqrt{N}-2)}{\hat{m}\hat{n}_b}\right] \tag{20-17}$$

We have assumed here that $\sqrt{N}$ divides m and n_b exactly. The modifications required to accommodate other problem sizes follow the treatment given in Sec. 20-4.

Equation (20-17) is compared with measured performance on the Mark II hypercube in Fig. 20-14. The measured and theoretical overhead values are plotted as functions of $1/\hat{n}_b$ at fixed $\hat{m}$. It is noteworthy that the overhead does not vanish as $\hat{n}_b \rightarrow \infty$ because of the presence of terms proportional to $1/\hat{m}$ in Eq. (20-17).

Backsubstitution is implemented in a fashion similar to forward reduction and is illustrated in Figs. 20-15 and 20-16. The expected performance of this algorithm is given in Table 20-5.

Step k of Forward Reduction
Form of Matrix L

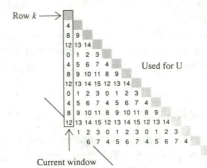

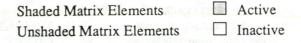

Figure 20-12 The form of the lower triangular matrix L and its window at step k of forward reduction.

3 Stages of Forward Reduction

Shaded Matrix Elements   ▨ Active

Unshaded Matrix Elements   ☐ Inactive

(a) Transmit L Window Horizontally to Right

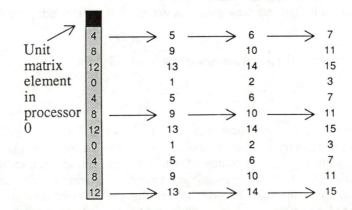

Figure 20-13(a) The first of three stages involved in step k of forward reduction. We show this for the same size of matrix A as in Fig. 20-5 and a total $n_b = 8$ right hand sides b.

(b) Transmit Top Row in $\underline{b}$ Window Downwards

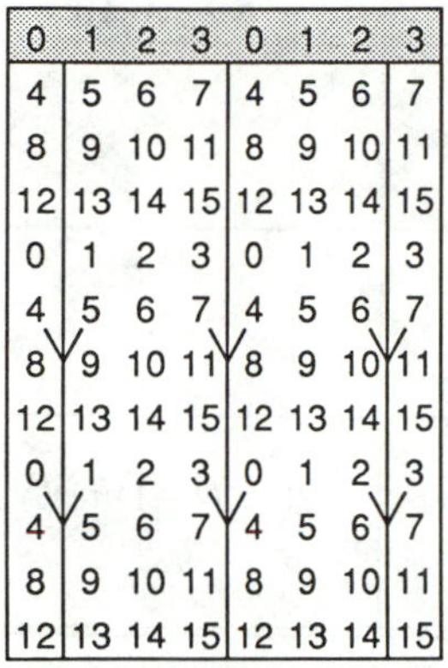

0 1 2 3 0 1 2 3
4 5 6 7 4 5 6 7
8 9 10 11 8 9 10 11
12 13 14 15 12 13 14 15
0 1 2 3 0 1 2 3
4 5 6 7 4 5 6 7
8 9 10 11 8 9 10 11
12 13 14 15 12 13 14 15
0 1 2 3 0 1 2 3
4 5 6 7 4 5 6 7
8 9 10 11 8 9 10 11
12 13 14 15 12 13 14 15

Processors	0	4	8	12	now contain same
	1	5	9	13	subset of top row
	2	6	10	14	of current
	3	7	11	15	$\underline{b}$ window

Figure 20-13(b) The second of three stages involved in step *k* of forward reduction. We show this for the same size of matrix *A* as in Fig. 20-5 and a total $n_b = 8$ right hand sides *b*.

(c) Correct Elements of $\underline{b}$ in Window

j
k
i
0 1 2 3 0 1 2 3
4 5 6 7 4 5 6 7
8 9 10 11 8 9 10 11
12 13 14 15 12 13 14 15
0 1 2 3 0 1 2 3
4 5 6 7 4 5 6 7
8 9 10 11 8 9 10 11
12 13 14 15 12 13 14 15
0 1 2 3 0 1 2 3
4 5 6 7 4 5 6 7
8 9 10 11 8 9 10 11
12 13 14 15 12 13 14 15

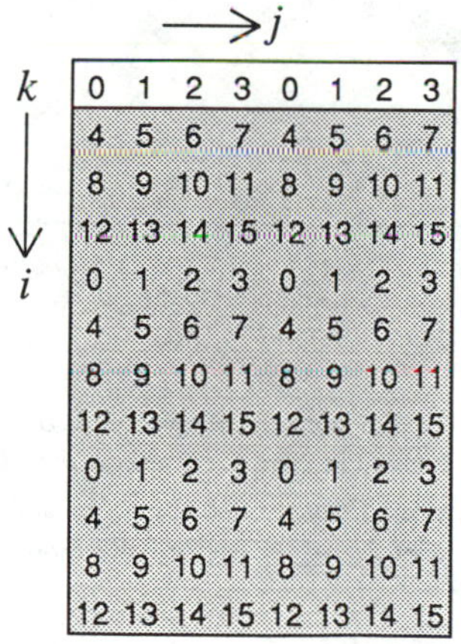

$$B_{ij} \rightarrow B_{ij} - B_{kj} L_{ik}$$
$$i = k+1 \text{ to } k+m-1$$
$$j = k \text{ to } k+m-1$$

Figure 20-13(c) The third of three stages involved in step *k* of forward reduction. We show this for the same size of matrix *A* as in Fig. 20-5 and a total $n_b = 8$ right hand sides *b*.

Stage	Time	
	Sequential	Concurrent
(a) Transmit Active Column of L to Right	0	$\left[\hat{m} + (\sqrt{N} - 2)\right] t_{comm}$
(b) Transmit Top Row in B Window Downward	0	$\left[\hat{n}_b + (\sqrt{N} - 2)\right] t_{comm}$
(c) Correct Elements of B in Window	$2(\hat{m}\sqrt{N} - 1)\hat{n}_b \sqrt{N}$ t_{calc}	$2\hat{m}\hat{n}_b \, t_{calc}$

Table 20-4 Performance of the Concurrent Forward Reduction Algorithm

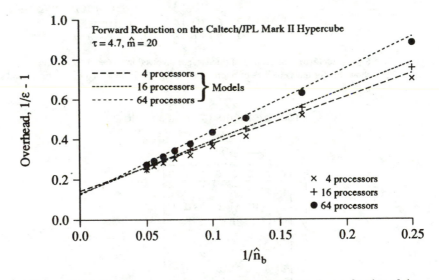

Figure 20-14 Measurements of the concurrent overhead $1/\varepsilon - 1$ as a function of the parameter $\sqrt{N}/n_b$ for forward reduction. The parameter $m/\sqrt{N}$ is fixed at 20. We show results from the Caltech/JPL Mark II hypercube for 4, 16 and 64 node machines. We show the expected dependence of $1/\varepsilon - 1$ of $\sqrt{N}/n_b$ the model of Eq. (20-17) for the parameter value $t_{comm}/t_{calc} = 4.7$.

Step *k* of Backward Substitution

Form of Matrix U

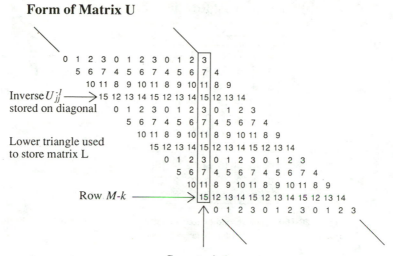

Inverse U_{jj}^{-1} ——→ stored on diagonal

Lower triangle used to store matrix L

Row *M-k* ——→

Current window

Figure 20-15 The form of the upper triangular matrix U and its window at step k of backsubstitution.

4 Stages of Backward Substitution

Shaded Matrix Elements   ▨ Active

Unshaded Matrix Elements   ☐ Inactive

(a) Transmit U Window Horizontally to Left

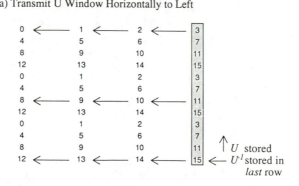

U stored

U^{-1} stored in *last* row

Figure 20-16(a) The first of four stages involved in step k of backsubstitution. The example problem has the same parameters as in Fig. 20-13.

(b) Solve for Last Row in Window

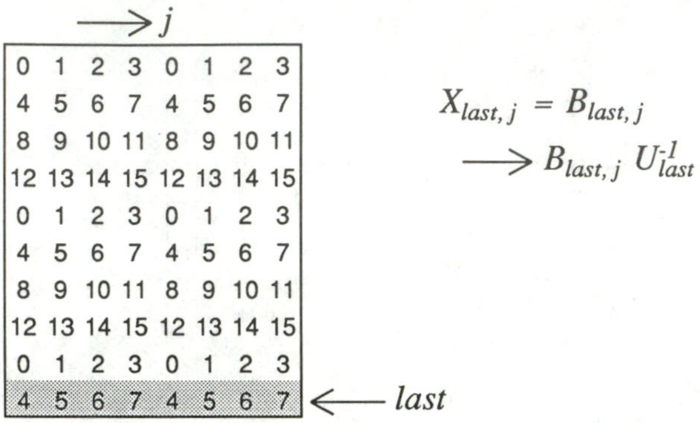

$$\longrightarrow j$$

0	1	2	3	0	1	2	3
4	5	6	7	4	5	6	7
8	9	10	11	8	9	10	11
12	13	14	15	12	13	14	15
0	1	2	3	0	1	2	3
4	5	6	7	4	5	6	7
8	9	10	11	8	9	10	11
12	13	14	15	12	13	14	15
0	1	2	3	0	1	2	3
4	5	6	7	4	5	6	7

$X_{last,j} = B_{last,j}$

$\longrightarrow B_{last,j}\, U_{last}^{-1}$

$\longleftarrow last$

Figure 20-16(b) The second of four stages involved in step k of backsubstitution. The example problem has the same parameters as in Fig. 20-13.

(c) Transmit Last Row in Window Upwards

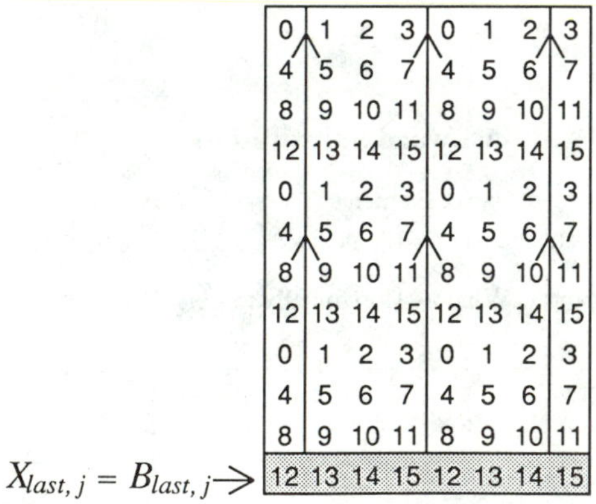

0	1	2	3	0	1	2	3
4	5	6	7	4	5	6	7
8	9	10	11	8	9	10	11
12	13	14	15	12	13	14	15
0	1	2	3	0	1	2	3
4	5	6	7	4	5	6	7
8	9	10	11	8	9	10	11
12	13	14	15	12	13	14	15
0	1	2	3	0	1	2	3
4	5	6	7	4	5	6	7
8	9	10	11	8	9	10	11
12	13	14	15	12	13	14	15

$X_{last,j} = B_{last,j} \longrightarrow$

Figure 20-16(c) The third of four stages involved in step k of backsubstitution. The example problem has the same parameters as in Fig. 20-13.

(d) Correct Elements of $\underline{b}$ in Window

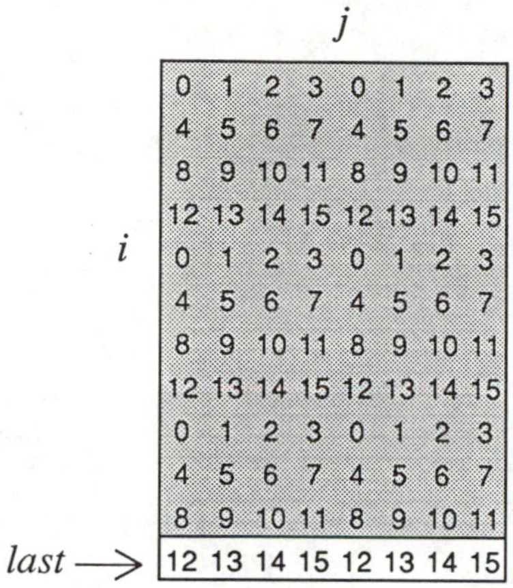

$$j$$

$B_{ij} = B_{ij} - U_{ij}X_{last,j}$

all j

$i < last$

Figure 20-16(d) The last of four stages involved in step k of backsubstitution. The example problem has the same parameters as in Fig. 20-13.

Stage	Time	
	Sequential	Concurrent
(a) Transmit Active Column of U to Left	0	$\left[\hat{m} + (\sqrt{N} - 2)\right] t_{comm}$
(b) Solve for X in Last Row of B, X Windows	$\hat{n}_b \sqrt{N} t_{calc}$	$\hat{n}_b t_{calc}$
(c) Transmit New Solution Upwards	0	$\left[\hat{n}_b + (\sqrt{N} - 2)\right] t_{comm}$
(d) Correct Remaining Window Elements	$2(\hat{m}\sqrt{N} - 1)\hat{n}_b \sqrt{N} \ t_{calc}$	$2\hat{m}\hat{n}_b t_{calc}$

Table 20-5 Performance of the Concurrent Backsubstitution Algorithm

the number of elements in the block. This is just 2^{c+1}, where c is the current channel number. The index of the first element to be received is obtained by extracting the right-most $c+1$ bits of *procnum*, which we will recall is the node's processor number. The index of the first element to be transmitted is obtained from the exclusive-OR of the channel mask of channel c and the index of the first element to be received. The number of elements to be received is the number of blocks containing the element labeled by the receive index. Since the number of elements to be transmitted can differ from the number to be received by one if the last block is not full, the number of elements to be transmitted must be calculated separately.

The arguments of *addvec* consist of *buf*, a pointer to the array containing the vector to be added to the vectors of the other nodes, *tmp*, a pointer to a scratch buffer that is at least as large as the vector, and P, the number of elements in the vector. The scratch buffer is needed to hold the vector elements received from other nodes until they are combined with the partial results. The routine *addvec* makes the resultant vector available by overwriting the contents of *buf*. In addition, *addvec* returns a value of -1 if *vshift* returns an error. Otherwise, it returns a value of 0. The routine *addvec* is outlined in pseudocode in Code 19-1, and in the C language in Code 19-2.

Although Code 19-2 contains quite a few lines of code, most are involved with housekeeping the various sizes and indices. The variable *mask* contains a mask for the bits of *procnum* that are used in each iteration of the loop. Thus, *mask* is one less than the number of elements in the current block, which is stored in *block*. The variable *chan* is the channel mask of the channel being used in the current iteration of the loop, which is also the highest bit in *mask*. The variable *size* contains the size in bytes of the floating-point variables and *offset* is *size* times the number of elements in the current block. After each iteration of the loop, *chan* is shifted to the next higher channel, one more bit is included in *mask*, and *block* and *offset* are multiplied by two. The bitwise left shift operator is used in the C implementation because it is normally faster than multiplying by two and it gives the same result.

The index of the first vector element to be received, which is stored in *recv*, is obtained by using only the bits in *procnum* indicated by *mask*. The index of the first vector element to be transmitted to the node across channel c, whose channel mask is *chan*, is obtained from the exclusive-OR of *recv* and *chan*, and is stored in *send*. The variables *recvn* and *sendn* contain the numbers of elements to be received and transmitted, respectively. The correctness of the formulas for obtaining *recvn* and *sendn* are easily verified by applying them to test cases.

The actual exchange of vector elements is accomplished through the call to *vshift* with the various arguments that have already been discussed. The incoming elements are placed in a scratch buffer because the original buffer may not have enough room for them. Even if we were to overwrite the outgoing elements with the incoming elements, we would not be guaranteed sufficient room, since the number of elements received may be one more than the number transmitted. Since we do not want to impose any restrictions on P, the number of elements in the vectors, we simply require that the application program must furnish a suitable scratch buffer.

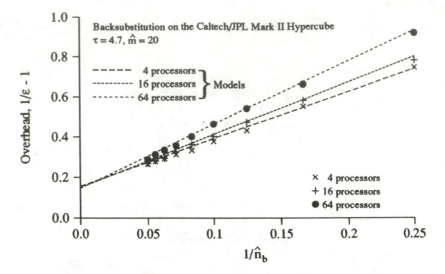

Figure 20-17 Measurements of the concurrent overhead $1/\varepsilon - 1$ as a function of the parameter $\sqrt{N}/n_b$ for back substitution. The parameter $m/\sqrt{N}$ is fixed at 20. We show results from the Caltech-JPL Mark II hypercube for 4, 16 and 64 node machines. We show the expected dependence of $1/\varepsilon - 1$ on $\sqrt{N}/n_b$ for the model of Eq. (20-18) with the parameter value $t_{comm}/t_{calc} = 4.7$.

The inefficiency overhead associated with backsubstitution assumes the form:

$$f = 1/\varepsilon - 1 = \frac{0.5}{\hat{m}\sqrt{N}} + \frac{0.5}{\hat{m}} + \frac{\tau}{2}\left[\frac{1}{\hat{m}} + \frac{1}{\hat{n}_b} + \frac{2(\sqrt{N}-2)}{\hat{m}\hat{n}_b}\right] \qquad (20\text{-}18)$$

which is compared with the measured performance in Fig. 20-17. The derivation of Eq. (20-18) neglects the mutual concurrency of communication and calculation which has the effect of nullifying the $0.5/\hat{m}$ term in Eq. (20-18). In this case, backsubstitution and forward reduction have identical predicted efficiencies. It should be noted that Eqs. (20–17) and (20–18) display the same $1/\hat{m}$ behavior (proportional to $1/\sqrt{n}$) obtained in Eqs. (20–12) and (20–13) for LU decomposition.

Both forward reduction and backward substitution show excellent agreement in Figs. 20-14 and 20-17 between the measured efficiencies and the model Eqs. (20-17) and (20-18). We use the same value of $\tau = t_{comm}/t_{calc} = 4.7$ as given in Eq. (20-14).

20-7 End Effects

Referring to the earlier Figs. 20-1 through 4, it may be seen that all the foregoing discussion of this chapter applies to the situation in which the window is not near the beginning or the end of the matrix bands. At the beginning steps $k < m$ or at the end $k > M - m$, the algorithm of Sec. 20-2, 4, 5, 6 is modified in correspondence with the reduced size of the matrix. This raises load-balancing issues as illustrated in Fig. 20-18. However, just as in the other situations involving potential load-balance problems, the scattered decomposition is effective. As shown in Fig. 20-18, the matrix fluctuates around exact balance but the number of rows and columns in individual nodes differs by at most one. As before, this imbalance leads to inefficiencies of order $1/\hat{m}$ for the relevant steps, but for the total problem it becomes unimportant because it only arises in those steps at the beginning and end of the band. As a result, the contribution to overhead from end effects is given approximately by:

$$f_{\text{end effects}} = O\left[\frac{m}{M}\frac{1}{\hat{m}}\right] = O\left[\frac{\sqrt{N}}{M}\right] \qquad (20\text{-}19)$$

The same load-imbalance issues arise in LU decomposition for full matrices but in the latter case it is even more important because the effect is not reduced by the factor m/M.

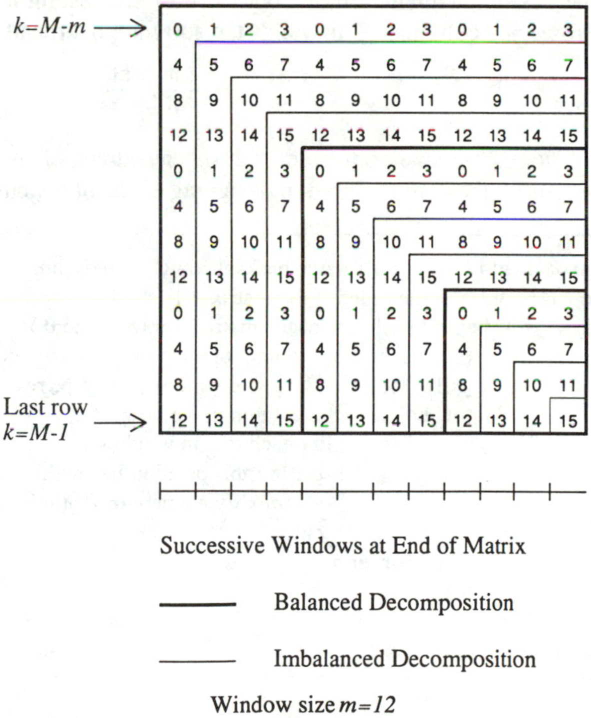

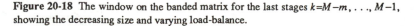

Successive Windows at End of Matrix

——————   Balanced Decomposition

——————   Imbalanced Decomposition

Window size $m=12$

Figure 20-18 The window on the banded matrix for the last stages $k=M-m, \ldots, M-1$, showing the decreasing size and varying load-balance.

At this point we can profitably return to the discussion of software overhead initially given in Chap. 10. In Code 20-4 we illustrate three implementations of the back-substitution step which incorporate the necessary tests to cope with the end effects.

Consider step (d) in Table 20-5, in which the elements of B in the current window are modified. In the naive implementation of Code 20-4(a), the tests for end effects are contained in the inner loop over rows and columns of B. This leads to a contribution to inefficiency overhead that does not vanish as $\hat{m}$ and $\hat{n}_b$ become large. In this case:

$$f_{\text{software}} \rightarrow \text{a nonzero constant as } \hat{m}, \hat{n}_b \rightarrow \infty \qquad (20\text{-}20)$$

In the better implementation of Code 20-4(b), the tests are moved outside the inner loop over rows of B. In this case we obtain:

$$f_{\text{software}} = \frac{\text{constant}}{\hat{m}} \qquad (20\text{-}21)$$

As discussed in Chap. 10, this overhead has the same dependence on problem size as those due to communication and load imbalance. It is therefore difficult to distinguish these effects in an analysis of performance measurements.

In the best implementation of Code 20-4(c), the testing is moved outside the loops over both rows and columns. This yields the software overhead dependence:

$$f_{\text{software}} = \frac{\text{constant}}{\hat{m}\hat{n}_b} \qquad (20\text{-}22)$$

which is of negligible size compared with other sources of inefficiency. The foregoing discussion typifies the care required in designing efficient concurrent matrix algorithms.

```
proc_begin back_sub1 ( naive backsubstitution algorithm )
declare_int n ; ( the order of the matrix A )
     for_begin ( each row of the matrix, k = (n - 1) to 0 )
          [pipe right-most column of window across window]
          [solve for x in last row of window, and pipe result up across window]
          for_begin ( each column in window)
               for_begin ( each row in window )
                    if_begin ( this position lies within matrix B ) then
                         [modify element of B at this position in window]
                    if_end
               for_end
          for_end
     for_end
proc_end
```

Code 20-4(a) Naive Backsubstitution Algorithm

```
proc_begin back_sub2 ( a better backsubstitution algorithm )
declare_int n ; ( the order of the matrix A )
      for_begin ( each row of the matrix, k = (n - 1) to 0 )
            [pipe right-most column of window across window]
            [solve for x in last row of window, and pipe result up across window]
            for_begin ( each column in window )
                  [evaluate number of smallest row, r_min, in window which still lies within B ]
                  for_begin ( each row in window, starting at r_min )
                        [modify element of B at this position in window]
                  for_end
            for_end
      for_end
proc_end
```

Code 20-4(b) A Better Backsubstitution Algorithm

```
proc_begin back_sub3 ( best backsubstitution algorithm )
declare_int n ; ( the order of the matrix A )
      for_begin ( each row of the matrix, k = (n - 1) to 0 )
            [pipe right-most column of window across window]
            [solve for x in last row of window, and pipe result up across window]
            [evaluate number of smallest row, r_min, in window which still lies within B ]
            for_begin ( each column in window )
                  for_begin ( each row in window, starting at r_min )
                        [modify element of B at this position in window]
                  for_end
            for_end
      for_end
proc_end
```

Code 20-4(c) The Best Backsubstitution Algorithm

20-8 Conclusions

We have demonstrated the manner in which the techniques introduced in Chap. 10 may be generalized to a more complicated matrix algorithm involving matrices of non-trivial structure. Among the key issues identified as important in making the transition from matrix multiplication to the richer problems are the following:

(i)   The importance of the scattered decomposition in reducing load imbalance.
(ii) The use of the square subblock decomposition.

(iii)   The increased importance of short messages with the corresponding greater demand on both the hardware for message transmission and the algorithm used for the pipe.

(iv)   Communication inefficiency retains the dependence on $1/\sqrt{n}$ as in matrix multiplication.

(v)   The presence of components of the calculation for which many nodes are idle is irrelevant in a correctly designed algorithm. This conclusion represents an illustration of the irrelevance of Amdahl's law for large grain size machines applied to this class of decompositions.

(vi)   Concurrent implementation of matrix algorithms requires great care. We have found that this class of problems leads to greater ratio of implementation time on concurrent versus sequential machines than for most other algorithms.

21

Communication Strategies and General Matrix Algorithms

21-1 Introduction

This chapter generalizes and builds upon the methods introduced in Chaps. 19 and 20. In this chapter, we present a set of communication utilities that use algorithms similar to *addvec* (Chap. 19). Where appropriate, we illustrate these algorithms by applying them to matrix problems. In particular, Sec. 21-3.4 contains an extensive treatment of matrix-vector multiplication. A summary of the issues involved in the performance of matrix algorithms on the hypercube is given in Sec. 21-5.

It should be emphasized that these advanced algorithms are nearly all hypercube-specific and are not immediately applicable to machines of lower connectivity. This restriction stands in contrast with the discussion of Chaps. 10 and 20, in which a two-dimensional mesh topology was adequate. Also noteworthy is the fact that the utilities developed in this chapter are equally applicable to a full hypercube and to any subcube of lower dimensionality contained within the ensemble. For clarity we will present only the full hypercube versions of each algorithm.

21-2 Cube Geodesics

The problem of multiple scalar products discussed in Chap. 19 was solved by the introduction of the routine *addvec*. We note that Chap. 19 made use of a rather general communication strategy which we will call the *method of ordered cube geodesics*. In fact this strategy is also used in Chap. 18 for the parallel shellsort. This general approach will apply to several other interesting utilities. Consider the task of sending a message between any two nodes n_1 and n_2 of the hypercube. In the case of *addvec*, we accumulated the product, altering the message during transmission. However, in the utilities discussed in the present chapter, we will primarily concern ourselves with algorithms which leave the message untouched after transmission.

A shortest path between n_1 and n_2 is a *geodesic*, and if n_1 and n_2 are h hops apart then there are $h!$ geodesics in the hypercube connecting them. This point is illustrated in Fig. 21-1. In Chap. 19 all the messages traveled along geodesics. Now consider a general problem in which a collection of J messages, labeled by the index j, are to be sent concurrently from $n_1(j)$ to $n_2(j)$. It is natural to use a geodesic for each message but this leaves two problems to be addressed. Firstly, there may be many geodesics to choose from, and secondly, in order to minimize the execution time on the hypercube, it is not strictly sufficient to make messages travel along a geodesic. This approach could lead to communication imbalance or "hot spots" and resultant poor concurrent performance. However, we note that if every message travels along a geodesic and the communication is balanced (equal) among processors, then we are guaranteed an optimal implementation. The method of ordered cube geodesics yields a particular choice of geodesics that ensures load balance for many important applications. The algorithms in Chap. 19 used this method as do most of those described subsequently in this chapter. This particular solution is specific to the crystalline communication environment. An alternative approach to this message-routing problem would allow each message to "find" an optimal path dynamically, based upon the changing state of the communication channels in the hypercube. The dynamical approach is inappropriate in the present context since we do not have unpredictable or chaotic message traffic. Rather we have a large number of messages whose movements are highly correlated, so it makes sense to consider the message traffic as a whole and optimize it. This task is straightforward within the synchronous environment provided by the crystalline communication system. Generally speaking, the problems discussed in this book exhibit message traffic that is highly correlated in space and time, so optimizing the overall message traffic, rather than the routing of individual messages, represents a viable approach.

In the next section we present specific examples of the ordered cube geodesic method and relate them to Chap. 19. In Sec. 21-4 and Chap. 22 the discussion is extended to the important class of problems in which a message is to be sent from one node to several other nodes.

The following auxiliary crystalline utilities will be introduced in this chapter:

index
fold
expand
transpose
transfer
scatter
broadcast

In addition, the discussion will include the following routines which have been introduced in Chaps. 11 and 19.

global_reverse
addvec

All these routines are described in the Software Supplement with full implementations in C that employ the CrOS III primitives. In practical applications it may be advisable to optimize these basic implementations for a specific machine environment. In the case of the Caltech Mark II hypercubes, the optimized code runs about twice as fast as the portable routines that are written in C and call CrOS III primitives [Fox 86b].

Figure 21-2 schematically summarizes the action of all the utility routines discussed here and in Chap. 22 on a simple 4-node machine.

Geodesics from n_1 to n_2

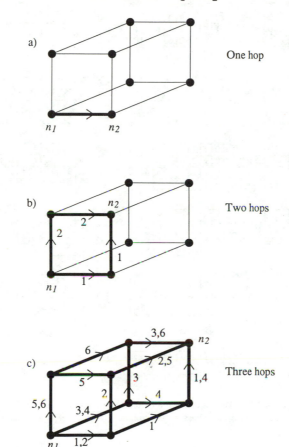

Figure 21-1 Sample geodesics for one, two, and three hop distances between nodes n_1 and n_2.

21-3 Homogeneous Communication Algorithms

21-3.1 Data Structures

Many of the crystalline utilities can be usefully applied to convolutions of the general mathematical form:

$$g(\underline{y}) = F(\underline{y}, f(\underline{x})) \qquad (21\text{-}1)$$

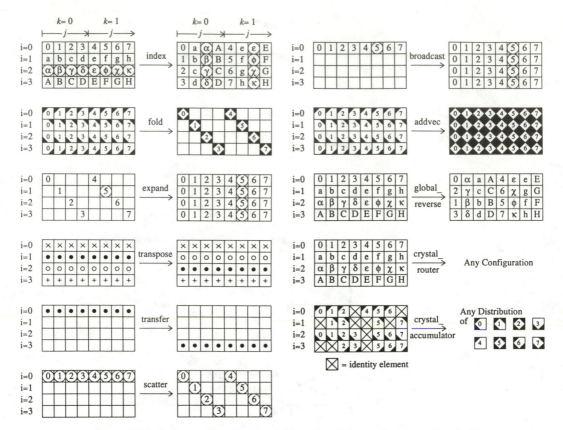

Figure 21-2 A summary for the case of four nodes of the transformations described in this and the following chapter. The indices i, j, and k are described in Sec. 21-3.1.

where F is a functional and f and g functions. The variables $\underline{x}$ and $\underline{y}$ may both be appropriate for decomposition over the nodes of a concurrent computer. As an example, consider the problem of Chap. 19. Dropping the vector notation, and letting y label the distinct sums and x designate the components of each sum, the problem of Chap. 19 can be written:

$$S(y) = \sum_x A(y,x)B(y,x) \qquad (21-2)$$

We start with the range of the variable x fully decomposed and with each node containing all of the y values. However, after the summation stage of the algorithm (called *fold* in Sec. 21-3.3), the variable y is fully decomposed. Problems of this type are intrinsically "long-range" in the sense that data must travel all over the cube. Contrast this example with the standard wave equation problem of Chap. 5. In that case, y and $\underline{x}$ are members of the same domain, where $f(\underline{x})$ is the displacement at time t, and $\overline{g(y)}$ is the same field at time $t+dt$. In the wave equation problem and, in fact, in the majority of problems in this book, one is not faced with two variables with inconsistent decompositions. Usually $f(\underline{x})$ and $g(y)$ naturally share the same decomposition. As a result, we usually only need nearest-neighbor rather than long-range communication. As we will see in the next subsection, the FFT of Chap. 11 is a good example of an exception, in which $\underline{x}$ and $\underline{y}$ actually *do* have different decompositions.

For the most general problem class described by Eq. (21-1), it is natural to label the data (e.g., the A, $B(y,x)$ in Eq. (21-2)) by three indices i, j, and k. The integer i runs from 0 to N-1 and labels the subsets into which $\underline{x}$ is decomposed; j runs from 0 to N-1 and labels the subsets into which $\underline{y}$ is to be decomposed. As usual, N is the number of nodes. The index k supplies any necessary extra labelings. We will typically ignore the k label in discussion since it will usually be used to index only an inner loop of no immediate interest. The situation is illustrated in Fig. 21-3 for the case $N=8$. Each node i holds the data structure labeled by j and k. We will allow degenerate cases in which j does not assume all N values; in general we let j run from 0 to J-1.

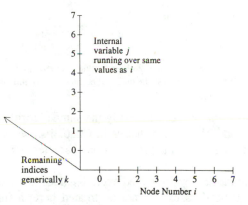

Figure 21-3 The data structure labeled by i, j, and k.

We are now prepared to describe various transformations in the $i-j$ plane which comprise the crystalline communication utilities which are the subject of this chapter.

21-3.2 index

This utility swaps the indices i and j and is illustrated in Fig. 21-4. To take a particular example, after a call to *index*, the original contents of node 3 are spread over the whole hypercube, and stored in the location $j=3$ of each node. Figure 21-5 shows the paths taken by this data with those going to node 3 highlighted. The appropriateness of the name *index* for this utility can be appreciated by considering a database example.

Using the formalism of Sec. 21-3.1, let $\underline{x}$ designate the records in a database and $\underline{y}$ represent the entries in an index to this database. Consider the case in which $\underline{x}$ is decomposed and the contributions to the database index are calculated concurrently. Each node contains contributions to the complete index that need to be assembled together. This assembly action is precisely that performed by *index*, which decomposes the actual index over the hypercube and yields a data structure in which all contributions to a particular index entry are held in a single node.

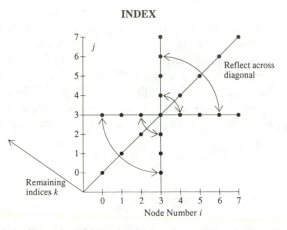

Figure 21-4 An illustration of *index* for the data structure introduced in Fig. 21-3. The routine *index* reflects across the diagonal in the i, j two-dimensional plane.

The routine *index* uses essentially the same algorithm as *addvec* in Chap. 19 and is illustrated in Code 21-1. Note that as in Chap. 19, we systematically run through each channel starting with 0. This procedure is characteristic of the method of ordered cube geodesics.

Note that *index* is well-defined even if j does not assume the full number of values N. Load imbalanced cases will not be treated here; a full discussion will be found in [Fox 86b] and follows reasoning similar to that already given for *addvec* in Chap. 19.

An interesting application of *index* is to a revised concurrent FFT algorithm, as illustrated in Fig. 21-6. This problem represents a convolution of the type given in Eq. (21-1). Consider a 32-node decomposition of a $2^{12} = 4096$ point one-dimensional FFT. As described in Chap. 11, the basic sequential algorithm involves twelve steps, one for each of the binary digits in the representation of a typical $\underline{x}$ or $\underline{y}$ value. In the concurrent FFT problem of Chap. 11, one needs nearest-neighbor communication (in a hypercube) for the first five steps, while the remainder involve no communication. In the revised algorithm, as described in [Fox 86c], *index* is used to swap first the top and bottom five digits in the decomposition of $\underline{x}$ and $\underline{y}$; this operation is shown in Fig. 21-6. Now the first five steps of the conventional FFT are local to each node of the hypercube and may

Cube Geodesics For Index

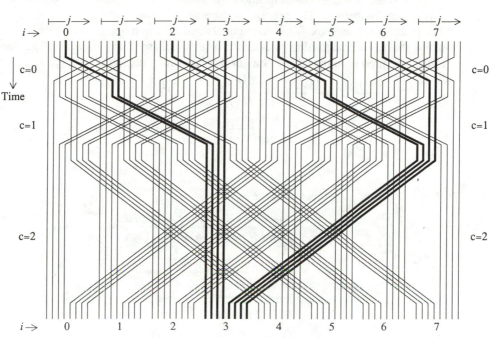

Figure 21-5 The paths followed by the data for *index* in the case *N = 8* shown in Fig. 21-4. There are three basic communication steps labeled by *c* corresponding to the three channels for a three-cube.

```
proc_begin index ( transpose (local index, processor number) array )
declare_int m; ( the number of data items per processor )
declare_buf D; ( array of data items )
     for_begin ( each channel, c, of the hypercube, c = 0,...,(d-1) )
          [ divide D into blocks 2^c data items long ]
          [ let b_c = bit number c of procnum ]
          proc_call vshift ( if b_c = 0 send odd blocks on channel c , else send even
                    blocks; received blocks overwrite those sent )
     for_end
proc_end
```

Code 21-1 The *index* Algorithm

be performed without communication. We now re-apply *index* and complete the last seven steps as before. The relative performance of the two algorithms (Chaps. 11 and 21) is analyzed in [Fox 86b], showing that the communication burdens are identical, while the revised algorithm is actually better because it avoids the calculational load imbalance present in the Chap. 11 algorithm. Defining the ratio, $\tau = t_{comm}/t_{calc}$, we have:

$$f_C = \frac{1}{\varepsilon} - 1 = \frac{[3+2\tau]}{5} \frac{\log N}{\log(Nn)} \qquad (FFT-Chap.\,11) \qquad (21\text{-}3)$$

$$= \frac{2\tau}{5} \frac{\log N}{\log(Nn)} \qquad (revised\ FFT-Chap.\,21) \qquad (21\text{-}4)$$

a) INDEX for the FFT

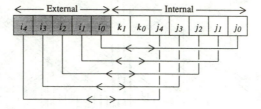

b) GLOBAL REVERSE

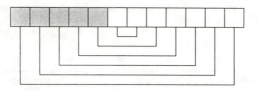

c) DEGENERATE INDEX

d) DEGENERATE GLOBAL REVERSE

Figure 21-6(a) The use of *index* in the concurrent FFT algorithm given in Sec. 21-3.2. This is compared with *global_reverse* in (b) while (c) and (d) illustrate degenerate cases.

It seems remarkable that trading nearest-neighbor communication in the Chap. 11 algorithm for long-distance communication in *index* yields a net gain in efficiency!

The *index* algorithm is very similar to that of *global_reverse* introduced in Chap. 11 to reverse the bits in the decomposition of y. In fact, when j assumes all N values, $(J=N)$, *index* and *global_reverse* differ by only a simple permutation in the local data structure. If J is smaller than N then the two algorithms are completely distinct. The use of *index* in matrix algorithms will be described in Sec. 21-4.2 and 21-5.

21-3.3 fold and expand

Expanding upon our general set of utilities, we will find it useful to divide *addvec* as described in Chap. 19, into two separate functions. The first, *fold*, is illustrated in Fig. 21-7 and combines all data for a given location onto the diagonal of Fig. 21-3 (in the node $j=i$). The routine *fold* can be used with any operation - in Chap. 19 we used simple addition of the partial scalar products of two vectors. The routine *expand* is in some sense the inverse of *fold*, since it takes data stored on the diagonal and broadcasts them horizontally in Fig. 21-3. As illustrated in Fig. 21-8, for a given j all nodes hold the same data values after calling *expand*. In Chap. 19 *fold* was used to accumulate scalar products in a unique node and then the *expand* algorithm was used to ensure that all nodes contained the full set of scalar products. We need not repeat the algorithms for *fold* and *expand* given in Codes 19-1 and 19-2. However, we note that their communication paths are complementary to one another and that they involve the same cycling through channels (characteristic of the method of ordered cube geodesics) shown for *index* in Code 21-1. The performance of *fold* and *expand* has been presented previously in Fig. 19-5, in which the parameter P is the number of values taken by the indices j and k in the notation of Sec. 21-3.1. The routine *expand* can be considered as a special case of *concat*, introduced in Chap. 14, where each node contains the same amount of information. This simplification allows an efficient implementation on the hypercube.

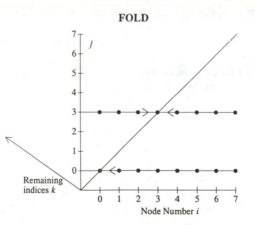

Figure 21-7 An illustration of *fold* for the data structure introduced in Fig. 21-3.

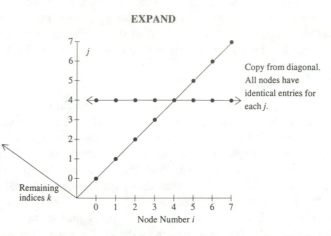

Figure 21-8 An illustration of *expand* for the data structure introduced in Fig. 21-3.

21-3.4 transpose and Matrix-Vector Multiplication

We next illustrate the use of *fold* and *expand* in matrix algorithms by discussing the problem of matrix-vector multiplication:

$$\underline{y} = A\underline{x} \tag{21-5}$$

where $\underline{y}$, and $\underline{x}$ are vectors of length M, and A is an M by M matrix [Fox 86b, 86c, 86e]. We consider the case in which A is a full matrix (few zero entries). We will employ the same decomposition of A as in Chap. 10, with a square $(\hat{m} = M/\sqrt{N}) \times \hat{m}$ submatrix stored in each node of the hypercube. We can write Eq. (21-5) in block form:

$$\hat{y}_i^{\mu} = \sum_{\nu,j} \hat{A}_{ij}^{\mu\nu} \, \hat{x}_j^{\nu} \tag{21-6}$$

where μ and ν are block indices running from 0 to $\sqrt{N} - 1$. The vectors $\hat{y}^{\mu}$ and $\hat{x}^{\nu}$ are $\hat{m}$-dimensional vectors obtained by dividing $\underline{y}$ and $\underline{x}$ respectively into $\sqrt{N}$ separate subvectors:

$$x_{\hat{m}\nu + j} = \hat{x}_j^{\nu} \tag{21-7}$$

$$y_{\hat{m}\mu + i} = \hat{y}_i^{\mu}$$

Figure 21-9(a) illustrates the storage of both A and $\underline{x}$. In the two-dimensional decomposition of processors, the nodes are labeled by the index pair (μ, ν). Let us suppose we start with the initial state shown in Fig. 21-9(a), where the node (μ, ν) holds the block matrix $\hat{A}^{\mu\nu}$ and all elements of $\hat{x}^{\nu}$.

The algorithm for matrix-vector multiplication consists of four stages. In the first, shown in Fig. 21-9(a), we form:

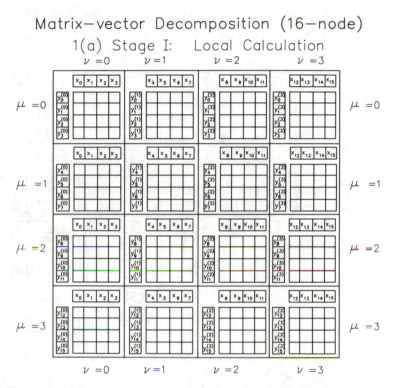

Figure 21-9(a) The first of four stages of matrix-vector multiplication discussed in the text and illustrated for a 16×16 matrix A decomposed on a 16 node hypercube.

$$\hat{y}^{\mu(\nu)} = \sum_j \hat{A}_{ij}^{\mu\nu} \hat{x}_j^{\nu} \qquad (21\text{-}8a)$$

with no summation over the index ν. The $\hat{y}^{\mu(\nu)}$ are partial contributions to the vector $\hat{y}^{\mu}$. This stage is local to each processor and is load-balanced up to differences of at most one row or column in the size of the blocks in each processor.

We now use *fold* as illustrated in Fig. 21-9(b) in each subcube formed by a row of processors. This step completes the sum over ν:

$$\hat{y}^{\mu} = \sum_{\nu} \hat{y}^{\mu(\nu)} \qquad (21\text{-}8b)$$

Next, we call *expand* over the same row of subcubes in order to broadcast $\hat{y}^{\mu}$, so that each processor in a given row holds the vector $\hat{y}^{\mu}$. This step is shown in Fig. 21–9(c). The last step depends on the particular way one wants to use Eq. 21-5. Some applications may involve iterating $y = Ax$ a number of times, replacing x at each iteration with the new y on the right-hand side. In such a case, the implementation is

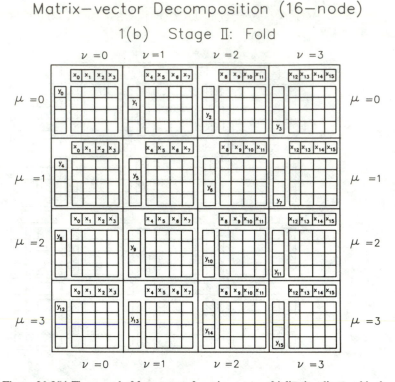

Figure 21-9(b) The second of four stages of matrix-vector multiplication discussed in the text and illustrated for a 16×16 matrix A decomposed on a 16 node hypercube.

completed by ensuring that y is stored in exactly the same manner as $\underline{x}$. This is achieved by adding a stage before the application of *expand*, which transposes the storage of $\hat{y}^{\mu}$ to lie along columns rather than rows [Fox 86b, 86c, Ho 86b]. This introduces the next utility to be discussed. The routine *transpose* transposes matrix data stored in a two-dimensional mesh. After *fold* the vector $\hat{y}^{\mu}$ is distributed so that it forms a matrix $Y^{\mu\nu}$, as illustrated in Fig. 21-9(b). The matrix is initially decomposed so that subblock $Y^{\mu\nu}$ is stored in processor number $\mu + \nu\sqrt{N}$. After application of *transpose* $Y^{\mu\nu}$ is stored in processor $\nu + \mu\sqrt{N}$. The algorithm for this is given in Code 21-2. We use the method of ordered cube geodesics in *transpose* with the usual cycle over communication channels, although in this case it is necessary to run over only half of them.

Not surprising is the form of the communication overhead f_C, which is given via Eq. (5-5) as:

$$f_C = \frac{1}{\varepsilon} - 1 = \frac{1}{\hat{m}} \left[1 - 1/\sqrt{N} + \frac{\log_2 N}{2\sqrt{N}} \right] \frac{t_{comm}}{t_{calc}} \qquad (21\text{-}9)$$

Matrix—vector Decomposition (16—node)
1(c) Stage III: Expand in Rows

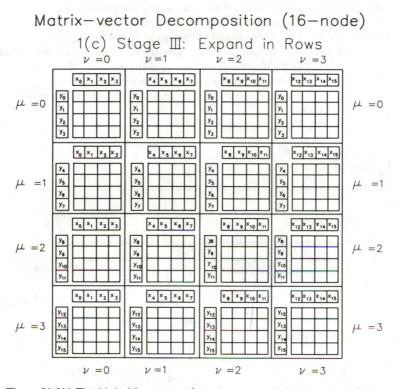

Figure 21-9(c) The third of four stages of matrix-vector multiplication discussed in the text and illustrated for a 16×16 matrix A decomposed on a 16 node hypercube.

with $\hat{m} = \sqrt{n}$ representing the square root of the number of matrix elements stored in each node. This efficiency formula has the usual form for an algorithm of *system dimension* $d = 2$, already seen in Chaps. 10 and 20 for other matrix problems.

Note particularly the timing of *transpose* in Table 21-1. The ratio $\log_2 N / \sqrt{N}$ can be thought of as the ratio of distances in a hypercube to those in a two-dimensional mesh. This ratio is characteristic of the underlying hypercube. It would be replaced by a number of order unity on a two-dimensional mesh architecture in which the *transpose* routine would be required to transmit data through a distance of order $\sqrt{N}$ hops. Figure 21-10 shows the actual speedup obtained for the multiplication of a 16×16 matrix by a vector, as a function of the number of nodes, N.

```
proc_begin transpose ( transpose data stored in 2-D grid of processors )
declare_int μ; ( x co-ordinate of processor in grid of processors )
declare_int ν; ( y co-ordinate of processor in grid of processors )
declare_buf D ; ( buffer for data to be transposed on processor grid )
     for_begin ( each square sub-cube defined by channels c and c+d/2, c=0,...,(d/2-1) )
          if_begin ( bit number c of μ ≠ bit number c of ν ) then
                    proc_call cwrite ( send D channel c + d/2)
                    proc_call cread (receive data on channel c and store in D )
          else
                    proc_call cread ( receive data on channel c + d/2 and forward on channel c )
          if_end
     for_end
proc_end
```

Code 21-2 The transpose Algorithm for a d-Dimensional Hypercube

Action	Time
(a) Local Block Calculation	$(2\hat{m}^2-\hat{m})t_{calc}$
(b) fold	$[1-1/\sqrt{N}]\hat{m}(t_{calc} + t_{comm})$
(c) transpose	$\hat{m}\dfrac{\log_2 N}{\sqrt{N}} t_{comm}$
(d) expand	$(1-1/\sqrt{N})\hat{m}t_{comm}$

Table 21-1 Timing for Steps of Concurrent Matrix-vector Multiplication

21-4 Inhomogeneous Communication Algorithms

We will complete our discussion of the auxiliary crystalline communication routines by considering problems with intrinsic imbalance. Such problems might include the use of *broadcast* to send information from one to all other nodes. The routine *scatter* will be used to distribute information in one node among all others, while *transfer* will send information from one node to a single destination node.

21-4.1 broadcast and forest

We have already encountered the need for *broadcast* in Chaps. 10 and 20, and have commented on its implementation as a tree and pipe algorithm there and in Sec. 14-5.3. The action of *broadcast* on the data structure of Sec. 21-3.1 is shown in Fig. 21-11. In [Fox 85b, Fox 86b and Ho 86a], a detailed discussion of the optimal algorithms for broadcasting on machines without special hardware assistance is given. The optimal

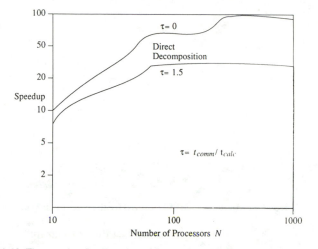

Figure 21-10 The speedup S as function of the number of nodes N for a 16 by 16 matrix A. We show results for both a perfect hypercube ($\tau = t_{comm} = 0$) and a machine similar to the Caltech Mark I, II with $\tau = 1.5$.

algorithm depends greatly upon the ensemble hardware so it is not appropriate to give a detailed discussion here. On the Caltech Mark I and II hypercubes, the best broadcast algorithm depends on the value of $\hat{m}$, the number of words to be sent, and N, the number of nodes. In Fig. 21-12 three "phases" are illustrated with different algorithms dominating in different parameter ranges. The pipe is typically the best algorithm except for short messages. If the hardware imposes significant startup time for messages, as shown in Fig. 4-2 for the initial INTEL iPSC system, then the pipe is no longer attractive, since it requires the message to be broken into several segments, each having its own startup time. Since broadcasts over cubes and subcubes are important, we expect that future hypercubes will include special purpose hardware to support broadcasts. As a result of such modification, the analysis of Fig. 21-12 would be significantly changed.

In Fig. 21-12, one of the phases is dominated by an algorithm referred to as *forest* (see [Fox 86b] and personal communication in [Ho 86a]). The routine *forest* distributes broadcast trees over the hypercube in a way that incurs less startup time than *pipe*. However, the cost per word is lower for the *pipe* routine, which therefore becomes preferable as the message length increases. The routine *forest* is a generalization of the simple *broadcast* algorithm described in Chap. 14 that uses a simple tree decomposed over the hypercube. The routine *forest* takes the several trees formed by different parts (words/packets) of the message to be broadcast and obtains better load balancing by overlapping the different trees. The third phase, *scatter* followed by *expand*, uses an algorithm which is described in the next subsection.

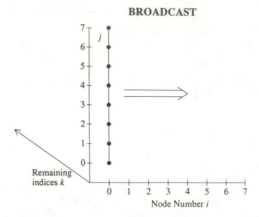

BROADCAST

Figure 21-11 An illustration of *broadcast* for the data structure introduced in Fig. 21-3.

Broadcast Phase Diagram

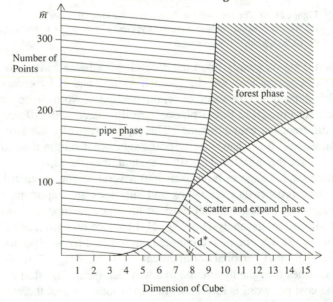

Figure 21-12 A sketch of the domain spanned by $\hat{m}$, the number of words to be broadcast, and $d = \log_2 N$, the dimension of the hypercube. We show three regions where different algorithms dominate. These are the *pipe* discussed in Sec. 20-4; *scatter* followed by *expand* discussed in Sec. 21-4.2 and 21-3.3; *forest* discussed in Sec 21-4.1.

21-4.2 scatter

An important utility, *scatter*, is illustrated in Fig. 21-13. The routine *scatter* takes data stored in a single node and distributes it homogeneously throughout a subcube, which may be the full hypercube, forming the set of destination nodes. The corresponding algorithms given in [Fox 86b] use a combination of ordered cube geodesics and pipes. The *scatter* algorithm is outlined in pseudocode in Code 21-3.

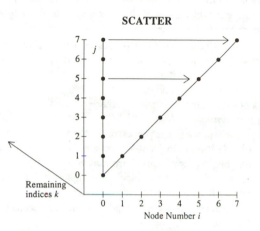

Figure 21-13 An illustration of *scatter* for the data structure introduced in Fig. 21-3.

An obvious application of *scatter* is to distribute a data set stored in a given node, for example node 0, or perhaps in a disk drive attached directly or indirectly to the node. The effect of *scatter* is to divide this data set into N parts and deliver equal portions to each node. Figure 21-14 illustrates another possible use of *scatter*. It will be recalled from Chap. 20 that many sources of load imbalance are associated with banded matrix LU decomposition. In particular, finding the multipliers from the first column of the current window occupied only the $\sqrt{N}$ processors in the first column of the node array. Figure 21-14 shows how we can apply *scatter* to subcubes consisting of rows of nodes and equalize the load on the nodes. Unfortunately, this method is not immediately practical as stated because *scatter* takes time of order $\hat{m}t_{comm}$, where we distribute $\hat{m}$ numbers as $\hat{m}/\sqrt{N}$ packets in $\sqrt{N}$ nodes. The load imbalance that *scatter* is intended to remove involves a calculational cost of order $\hat{m}t_{calc}$. Thus, in the usual situation where $t_{comm} \geq t_{calc}$, no net gain is realized. This approach may be improved, however, by simultaneously applying the idea of Fig. 21-14 to the $\sqrt{N}$ columns involved as the "first column" in the next $\sqrt{N}$ steps. This actually corresponds to applying the *index* algorithm described in Sec. 21-3.2. The routine *index* can be thought of as the homogeneous version of *scatter*, just as *expand* is the homogeneous version of *broadcast*. The *index* calculation requires a time of order $\hat{m}\log_2 N \ t_{comm}$, which is to be compared with the calculational imbalance given by $\hat{m}\sqrt{N} \ t_{calc}$ for the total of $\sqrt{N}$ steps. The use of *index* formally reduces the calculational load imbalance to zero in the limit of large $\sqrt{N}$. Note that the reduction factor of $\log_2 N / \sqrt{N}$ is characteristic of the hypercube, and that these special techniques do not apply to simpler architectures such as the two-dimensional mesh. Another interesting application of *index* to a problem of this general type is the conversion of matrices from the local square subblock to the scattered square subblock decomposition (i.e., from the decomposition of Fig. 20-3(a) to that of 20-3(b)).

Returning to Fig. 21-12 for *broadcast*, we note that for a single transmitted word or a packet of minimum size, *scatter* has no action, and *expand* reduces to the standard *tree* algorithm used in Chap. 14 for *broadcast*. Thus, the low $\hat{m}$ phase of *broadcast* is dominated by a simple generalization of the *tree* algorithm; *scatter* followed by *expand*.

```
proc_begin scatter ( scatter vector in processor 0 among other processors )
declare_buf V; ( a vector; in processor 0 contains data to be scattered )
declare_int M; ( number of items in vector V )
      [ let N = the number of processors ]
      [ let procnum be the processor number]
      [ nloop = minimum of N and M ]
      if_begin( this processor is processor 0 ) then
            [divide V into blocks of N elements (last block may contain less than N) ]
            for_begin ( loop index, i, from nloop −1 to 1 )
                  [ m = number of blocks having an i^{th} data element ]
                  [ c_L = bit number of lowest 1-bit of i ]
                  proc_call vwrite ( send i^{th} item from each of the m blocks on channel c_L )
            for_end
      else_if (procnum < M ) then
            [ c_H = bit number of highest 1-bit of procnum ]
            [ npipes = N/2^{c_H +1} − 1 = number of forwarding pipes ]
            for_begin (i from 1 to npipes)
                  [ c_L = bit number of lowest 1-bit of i ]
                  proc_call vread ( receive data on channel c_H and forward on
                                          channel c_H + c_L + 1 )
            for_end
            proc_call vread ( receive data items on channel c_H and store
                                          in V(procnum), V(procnum + N), etc)
      if_end
proc_end
```

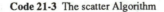

Code 21-3 The scatter Algorithm

21-4.3 transfer

The final utility, *transfer*, is perhaps less generally useful, at least in application to matrix algorithms. As illustrated in Fig. 21–15, it transfers information between two given nodes. This is needed, as shown in Sec. 20-5, when employing pivoting in LU decomposition; *transfer* is used to move the original first row into the position of the chosen pivot row. The latter needs to be broadcast as described in Sec. 20-5, so *transfer* is not required to put the pivot row in the place of the first.

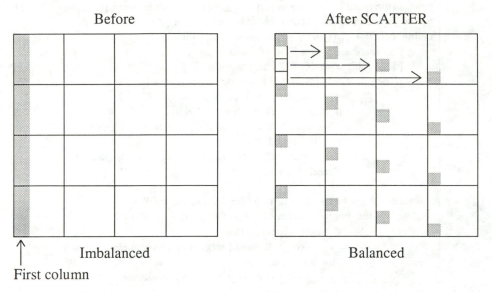

Figure 21-14 A possible use of *scatter* to distribute the first column over a matrix uniformly over all nodes.

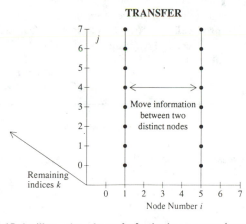

Figure 21-15 An illustration of *transfer* for the data structure introduced in Fig. 21-3.

```
proc_begin transfer ( transfer a vector, V, of m elements between processors S and D )
define_function c_L(i) = bit number of lowest 1-bit of i
define_function c_H(i) = bit number of highest 1-bit of i
     [ let route = bit-wise XOR of S and D ]
     [ let r = bit-wise XOR of S and procnum ]
     if_begin ( r = 0, i.e., this is source processor ) then
          for_begin ( all elements, V_i, of V, i = 0, 1,..., M - 1 )
               if_begin ( i is even ) then
                    proc_call cwrite (send V_i on channel c_L (route))
               else_if ( i is odd ) then
                    proc_call cwrite (send V_i on channel c_H (route))
               if_end
          for_end
     else_if ( r = route, i.e., this is destination processor) then
          for_begin ( all elements, V_i, of V, i = 0, 1,..., M - 1 )
               if_begin ( i is even ) then
                    proc_call cread ( receive V_i on channel c_H (route))
               else_if ( i is odd ) then
                    proc_call cread ( receive V_i on channel c_L (route) )
               if_end
          for_end
     else_if ( r = lowest (c_H(r) + 1) bits of route ) then
          for_begin (all even-numbered elements of V )
               proc_call cread ( receive element on channel c_H(r) and forward on
                         channel c_L(route − r) )
          for_end
     else_if ( r = highest (d−c_L(r)) bits of route ) then
          for_begin (all odd-numbered elements of V)
               proc_call cread (receive element on channel c_L(r) and forward on
                         channel c_H(route − r) )
          for_end
     if_end
     proc_end
```

Code 21-4 The transfer Algorithm

The routine *transfer* can be implemented optimally using two geodesic pipes. In Sec. 20-4, we discussed the best pipe algorithm for *broadcast*, which we can call a *linear (split) pipe*. The pipe connects all nodes in a subcube by decomposing them into a one-dimensional line or ring. If we just wish to connect two nodes, then rather than connecting the nodes by a one-dimensional route, it is better to use a geodesic, and we obtain the dual geodesic pipe outlined in Code 21-4. In an optimized version of this algorithm, pieces of data alternate between the two geodesic pipes.

The optimization used in Code 21-4 is hardware-dependent, and the algorithm assumes a machine for which reading and writing by the intermediate nodes of the pipe take roughly equal time and cannot be overlapped. If message latency is high a better implementation of *transfer* would send all the even and odd elements of the *V* through their respective pipes together using *vread* and *vwrite*, rather than sending one element at a time with *cread* and *cwrite*.

21-5 Comments on General Matrix Algorithms

A great deal of work on matrix algorithms for the hypercube has already been performed; in particular by groups at Caltech [Fox 85b], Yale [Johnsson 85], Oak Ridge [Heath 87] and INTEL [Moler 86]. In this section we extend the results of Chaps. 10 and 20 to other algorithms, and exploit the communication utilities described earlier in this chapter.

We can classify matrix algorithms into three broad classes: (1) those used for full matrices with few zero elements, (2) special techniques that exploit features such as banded or tri-diagonal structure, and (3) iterative algorithms. The latter tend to be used for very sparse matrices since they require less storage and are often more efficient than the direct solution methods. The algorithms used in Chaps. 7 and 8 of this book are of the iterative type.

Let us first consider full matrices and banded matrices where the bandwidth is large compared with $\sqrt{N}$, where N is the number of nodes. These classes of matrices require techniques which are quite similar to those discussed in this book. Three important algorithms are:

Matrix-Vector Multiplication, which is often used as a part of an iterative algorithm. It has been discussed in Sec. 21-3.4.

Matrix Inversion and its generalization, LU decomposition, for solving sets of equations. Some of the relevant algorithms have been described in Chap. 20.

Matrix Eigenvalue and Eigenvector determination, which typically use a technique known as Householder's method to reduce a general symmetric matrix to tri-diagonal form. The fast QR algorithm is then used to diagonalize the resultant tri-diagonal matrix.

We now discuss some of the issues that come up for these algorithms.

1. The decomposition of the matrix into square subblocks is again optimal and to be preferred over row, column, or rectangular decompositions on hypercube hardware without a large message startup time.

2. The scattered decomposition is crucial in both LU decomposition and Householder's method since as these algorithms progress, rows and columns are eliminated or deactivated. We can see this effect in Fig. 20-18 because the full matrix algorithms are structurally similar to the end steps of the banded algorithms. As shown in the examples of Sec. 20-5, approximate load balance is maintained even after pivoting, as long as one uses the scattered decomposition.

3. In [Hipes 86] a particular modification of Gaussian elimination, called the Gauss-Jordan method, is shown to be optimal for full matrix inversion. It naturally preserves load-balance. In Fig. 21-16 we measure the performance of this algorithm on the Caltech/JPL Mark II hypercube. For instance, we find an efficiency of

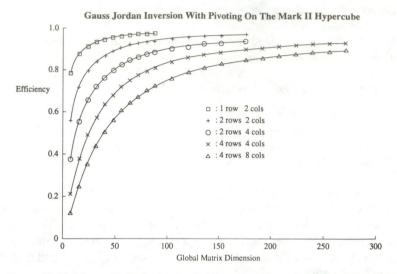

Figure 21-16 Measured efficiencies for the Gauss Jordan matrix inversion algorithm with pivoting. Results are shown on 2, 4, 8, 16, and 32 node hypercubes of the Caltech/JPL Mark II design. The algorithm uses 64-bit arithmetic and the results are plotted against the matrix order M. Each node has a grain size $n = M^2/N$. Even hypercubes use a square and odd hypercubes a rectangular decomposition.

         over 80% on a 16-node hypercube with a grain size corresponding to a 25×25 submatrix in each node, where the full matrix is 100×100. Figure 21-16 shows that the measured efficiency is generally high and indicates the suitability of the hypercube for these problems.

4.   The straightforward subblock decomposition needs another generalization when dealing with symmetric matrices, which are usually the type for which eigenvalues are needed. A square matrix naturally decomposes onto a concurrent processor with the topology of a two-dimensional mesh. One does *not* need a new triangular topology to deal with symmetric matrices. Figure 21-17 shows one of many similar ways that one may decompose a symmetric matrix (or effectively any triangular structure) onto a two-dimensional mesh [Fox 84d]. There is a load imbalance, which is of order $1/\sqrt{n}$, where $\sqrt{n}$ is approximately the number of extra matrix elements in diagonal compared to off-diagonal nodes. For clarity, we show in Fig. 21-17 the local decomposition that is analogous to that of Fig. 20-3(a) for unsymmetric matrices. There is a natural scattered version of this decomposition.

5.   The last stage of the eigenvalue determination, the QR step, only involves a small number of matrix elements since the original $M(M+1)/2$ independent elements have been reduced to $2M-1$ in the tri-diagonalization step. It is interesting that this reduction in the number of variables, which aids the sequential code, makes the concurrent implementation much harder, since there are not enough matrix elements to spread over the nodes. A recent observation by Furmanski has led to a good concurrent algorithm for the QR step [Furmanski 86]. Recent work

[Dongarra 85] has also led to new recursive algorithm called Cuppens Method that may be better than the QR method on sequential computers, and is much easier in its concurrent implementation [Ipsen 87].

6. We always find the typical two-dimensional efficiency form for these matrix algorithms to be:

$$\frac{1}{\varepsilon} - 1 \sim \frac{const}{\sqrt{n}} \tag{21-10}$$

where n is the number of matrix elements stored in each processor and:

$$const = a + b\left(\frac{t_{comm}}{t_{calc}} = \tau\right) \tag{21-11}$$

7. In Eq. (21-11), the nonzero a is due to load-imbalance and was not present in the matrix multiplication algorithm of Chap. 10. However, we see the effect of load-imbalance in Eqs. (20-12, 13) for LU decomposition. One might expect b to depend logarithmically on N for eigenvalue determination because of the need to calculate many scalar products. However, the new algorithm for global scalar products described in Chap. 19 leads to values for a and b that are asymptotically independent of N.

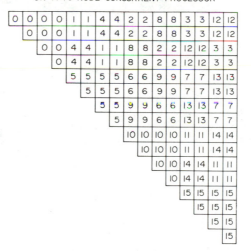

APPROXIMATE LOAD BALANCED STORAGE
OF A SYMMETRIC 16 BY 16 MATRIX
ON A 16 NODE CONCURRENT PROCESSOR

Figure 21-17 A local decomposition appropriate for a symmetric matrix. The nodes are labelled as appropriate for a two dimensional mesh and would be straightforwardly changed on a hypercube.

8. Sparse matrices are surprisingly interesting even for the simple matrix-vector multiplication algorithm described for full matrices in Sec. 21-3.4. In the case of sparse matrices, one is faced with a load-balancing problem that can be tackled with the sophisticated optimization techniques outlined in Chaps. 3 and 17 [Fox 86d].

9. The utilities described in Sec. 21-2, 3, and 4 can be used directly to improve both the methods in Chap. 20 and those of similar algorithms. In particular, using the tricks outlined in Sec. 21-4.2, one can often use *index* to remove the term in a in Eq. (21-11), which is converted into a term proportional to $(\log_2 N / \sqrt{N}) \, t_{comm}$. The results of [Furmanski 86] are presented in Table 21–2. The communication overheads are never large and are comparable, for similar size data sets, to those obtained in simple nearest neighbor problems, such as those in Chaps. 7 and 8.

10. Finally, we note that a key problem in the field of linear programming is an optimization technique involving the solution of many linear inequalities. These can be formulated as a matrix of inequalities. Important strategies for solving these inequalities are the simplex method and an improvement due to Karmarkar [Dantzig 68, Karmarkar 84]. Both of these methods can be implemented efficiently on a hypercube using similar methods to those we have already discussed for other matrix algorithms [Felten 86b].

Algorithm	$Const$ (See Eq. 21-11)
Multiplication - Optimal (Chap. 10)	τ
LU Decomposition + forward reduction	
Naive Square Subblock with Scattered Decomposition and No Pivoting	$\dfrac{9}{4} + \dfrac{3\tau}{2}$
Optimal - No Pivoting	$\dfrac{3}{2}\left[1 + \dfrac{1}{2}\,\dfrac{\log_2 N}{\sqrt{N}}\right]\tau$
Optimal - Pivoting	$\dfrac{3}{2}\left[2 + \dfrac{1}{4}\,\dfrac{\log_2 N}{\sqrt{N}}\right]\tau$
Gauss-Jordan Inversion Optimal	$\left[1 + \dfrac{1}{4}\,\dfrac{\log_2 N}{\sqrt{N}}\right]\tau$
Householder Tridiagonalization Optimal	$\dfrac{3}{4}\left[3 + \dfrac{5\log_2 N}{8\sqrt{N}}\right]\tau$
Banded LU Decomposition + forward reduction	
Naive - No Pivoting but with Scattered Decomposition	$\tau + \dfrac{1}{2}$
Optimal - No Pivoting	$\tau\left[1 + \dfrac{1}{2}\,\dfrac{\log_2 N}{\sqrt{N}}\right]$
Optimal - Pivoting	$\tau\left[2 + \dfrac{1}{4}\,\dfrac{\log_2 N}{3\sqrt{N}}\right]$

Table 21-2 Communication Overheads in Optimal Matrix Algorithms

22

General Message Passing in a
Loosely Synchronous Environment

22-1 Introduction

In the previous chapters of this volume we have seen that the CrOS III communication system can be used to solve a wide range of scientific and engineering problems on concurrent processors. CrOS III is best-suited to problems in which the nature of the communication is known *a priori*, since provision can then be made for any necessary message forwarding. In this chapter we describe the *crystal_router* algorithm, which can be used to pass messages between arbitrary nodes of a hypercube when the need for communication, but not its nature, is known beforehand. The *crystal_router* is therefore useful in irregular problems in which the message traffic changes dynamically and/or involves message passing between non-nearest neighbors. Section 22-3 discusses examples of the use of the *crystal_router* in circuit simulation and the evaluation of non-binary FFTs. The *crystal_accumulator*, introduced in Sec. 22-4, is a modification of the *crystal_router* which allows messages destined for the same processor to be merged *en route* according to some user-specified function.

In Sec. 22-5 we describe the implementation of a virtual concurrent processor, similar to that introduced in Chap. 4, known as the *virtual machine loosely synchronous communication system* (VMLSCS). The CrOS III communication routines are blocking. However, in the VMLSCS this constraint is removed, permitting non-blocking, loosely synchronous communication between arbitrary processors. Details are given of how to implement the VMLSCS by means of the *crystal_router* on a hypercube with a synchronous message passing protocol.

22-2 crystal_router and General Message Traffic in the Crystalline Environment

In this section we shall see that the crystalline environment is quite capable of dealing with rather arbitrary message traffic. The only essential requirement is that the communication calls occur in loose synchronization. In other words, the receiving nodes must know to expect some sort of data. The aim is to be able to transmit messages between arbitrary nodes of the hypercube when the size of the messages is not known *a priori* by the receiving node. All that should be required is a large enough buffer for incoming messages. It seems likely that such a general crystalline router will, in many circumstances, offer equivalent functionality and greater performance over more general message-passing (e.g., interrupt-based) operating systems. In particular, *crystal_router* is useful in irregular problems of the type discussed in Chaps. 8, 16, and 17, where most communication is local and the accommodation of occasional irregularities (both in size and destination) of messages is needed.

Consider first the *ordered cube geodesic* method in the case that a given message must be sent from one node to several others. We have already encountered such cases in Chaps. 9, 10, and 19, where information was broadcast to all nodes of either the cube or a subcube. As shown in these chapters, it is usually not optimal to send one message for each destination node. Rather, it is better to construct a "grand tour" such that the message takes a single path visiting each destination. The routing of multidestination messages is not an easy problem. In general, it involves the solution of a kind of traveling salesman problem, as discussed in Chap. 13, to minimize the path on the hypercube. This point illustrates the fact that it is not simple to extend the methods of Chap. 21 to more general optimal routing methods. Not only is the best route for a given message unknown, but in irregular problems, it is not always obvious how to balance the message traffic. In spite of these reservations, the following discussion presents a natural generalization of the methods of Chap. 21 in the form of the *crystal_router* algorithm.

Consider a concurrent application whose stages of calculation and interprocessor communication are constrained to remain in loose synchronization by the periodic occurrence of expected communication. We will assume that our generic application's communication steps may be characterized as follows:

> *At a given stage of the calculation, each node of the hypercube has a set of messages to be sent to other nodes. The destination nodes expect messages but know neither how many messages will arrive nor the identities of the originating nodes.*

This requirement is termed *need-predictable* in Chap. 16, and is characteristic of loosely synchronous problems. This situation is typical of the message traffic in many problems discussed in this book, but we consider particularly the cases in which the messages are not just sent to nearest-neighbors but also to more distant nodes. Such irregular, but time-synchronized, message traffic occurs in any simulation of an irregular system. Examples follow directly from the problems of Chaps. 7, 8, 16, and 17, when applied to irregular geometries. In addition, the applicability of *crystal_router* to simulations of circuits (Sec. 22-3), and neural networks is of considerable interest.

It is useful to distinguish between two broad categories of the *crystal_router* algorithm. The *dynamic crystal_router*, as described above, routes messages of arbitrary length between arbitrary nodes of the hypercube. The generality of such an algorithm is useful in many applications in which the communication is need-predictable, but of an unknown nature. However, there are applications, such as the circuit simulator described in Sec. 22-3, in which the routing of messages is the same for every call to *crystal_router*. In such cases the communication overhead can be reduced by using the less general *static crystal_router*. Unlike the dynamic *crystal_router*, the static version does not determine *ab initio* whether each message must be sent over each channel every time *crystal_router* is called. Instead the static *crystal_router* has an initialization, or "dry-run", phase during which each node constructs a routing table, which determines how messages are to be routed on subsequent calls to *crystal_router*. The columns of the routing table correspond to individual messages, and the rows to channel numbers. Each entry in the table is assigned one of the three values SEND, KEEP, or BOTH (for messages with multiple destination processors). For each channel the corresponding row of the routing table is scanned, and each message is either sent on that channel (SEND), written to a local buffer (KEEP), or both of these (BOTH), depending on the table entry.

We begin by specifying the structure of messages employed by *crystal_router*. Associated with each message is a set of tickets - one for each destination node. Code 22-1 outlines the dynamic *crystal_router* algorithm.

```
proc_begin crystal_router ( general routing algorithm )
declare_struct mail {  declare_int ndest; ( number of destination processors )
                       declare_buf dest_list;  (integer array of destinations)
                       declare_int nbytes;    ( number of bytes in message )
                       declare_buf message;   ( the message ) };
declare_buf output_mail; ( buffer of mail items to send )
declare_buf input_mail; ( buffer to store mail items received )
declare_buf com_buf; ( communications buffer to store mail items exchanged on
                              specific channel )
    [copy any items in output_mail addressed to this processor to input_mail ]
    for_begin ( each channel, c, of the hypercube, c = 0,..., (d - 1) )
        for_begin ( each mail item in output_mail buffer )
            if_begin ( the cᵗʰ bit of any of the destination processors ≠ the cᵗʰ bit
                          of procnum ) then
                [add mail item to com_buf buffer]
            if_end
        for_end
        [exchange com_buf buffer on channel c, storing received data in com_buf buffer]
        for_begin ( each mail item in com_buf )
            if_begin ( this processor is one of the destination processors ) then
                [copy mail item to input_mail buffer]
            if_end
            if_begin ( mail item must be forwarded ) then
                [copy mail item to output_mail buffer]
            if_end
        for_end
    for_end
proc_end
```

Code 22-1 The crystal_router Algorithm

We see that the *crystal_router* algorithm cycles over each channel and is essentially the *ordered cube geodesic* algorithm. At the end of $\log_2 N$ steps, all messages are guaranteed to have been delivered to their correct addresses. In the case that each message has a ticket to reach every other node, *crystal_router* becomes the *expand* algorithm of Sec. 21-3.3. Furthermore, it reverts to *index* if each message is given the appropriate single destination ticket. Thus, *crystal_router* is optimal for regular hypercube communication in both the distributed broadcast (*expand*) and single destination (*index, transpose,* etc.) limits. However, it is not necessarily optimal in intermediate cases, but its obvious usefulness in irregular simulations makes it a strong contender as the method of choice for communication routing. We have found it to be of use in such diverse applications as non-binary FFT's [Aloisio 87], Kalman filters in a multi-track environment [Gottschalk 87], and circuit simulation. From the point of view of the present section, the routines in Sec. 21-3 may be regarded as simply special cases of *crystal_router*, in which an explicit ticket is unnecessary because it is implied by the positions of the data. In Sec. 22-4 we introduce the *crystal_accumulator* that generalizes *fold* in the same way that the *crystal_router* generalizes *index*.

22-3 Examples of the Use of the Crystal_Router Algorithm

This section presents two examples of the use of the *crystal_router* algorithm. In the first the *crystal_router* is used to communicate circuit information in a spatially decomposed circuit simulation. In the second example, the *crystal_router* is used in performing non-binary FFTs.

22-3.1 Circuit Simulation

The previous section showed how the *crystal_router* provides a general, efficient communication system for the hypercube. Here we sketch out its use in circuit simulations. Although circuit simulations are geometrically quite irregular, the router allows arbitrary nodes of the hypercube to communicate in an efficient, synchronous manner. In addition to the irregularity of communication the balancing of the computational workload among nodes of the hypercube is of equal importance in this example. A simple *recursive bisection* technique [Baden 87, Dippe 84, Dippe 85, Karp 77, Whelan 85] is used to achieve load-balance. Figure 22-1(a) shows the model CAD problem: a VLSI circuit which we wish to simulate (e.g., by using a system similar to SPICE).

The load-balancing problem is illustrated in Fig. 22-1(b). Some types of circuit simulations are dominated by evolution of the transistors, so this is all that is shown in the figure. The challenge is to find a decomposition which puts equal numbers of transistors into each processor (balancing the load), yet groups them into regions of simple, convex shapes (keeping communication overhead reasonable). This is accomplished nicely by the recursive bisection technique. Figure 22-2 shows the decomposition of our model problem onto a 2^5 (32 node) hypercube. The first bisection is given in Fig. 22–2(a), where the data set has been split into two halves, containing an equal number of transistors. The left half of the problem will be simulated via the low half of the hypercube (nodes 0 through 15) while the right half will be handled by the high half of the hypercube (nodes 16 through 31).

The bisection process continues in a recursive manner. Figure 22-2(b) shows the next stage, where each half has been further split into two parts. The process continues through five stages, finally giving the result of Fig. 22-2(c). At this point, each processor of the hypercube is responsible for the transistors of one of the regions of the figure.

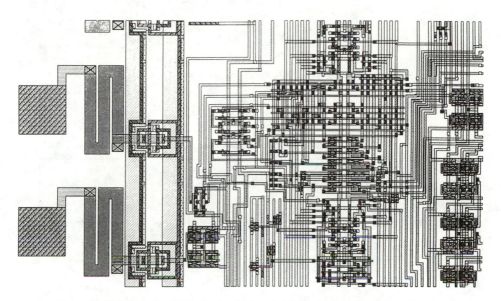

Figure 22-1(a) Part of a VLSI circuit which we wish to simulate (provided by David Gates of Caltech).

Figure 22-1(b) The locations of the dominant computational workload (the transistors).

Figure 22-2(a) The first step of bisection. The circuit to the left of the division will be handled by the low half of the hypercube, the circuit to the right by the high half, (b) The next step of the recursive procedure. Each region is again bisected, (c) The final (fifth) step of bisection. At this point, we have a one-to-one mapping between the 2^5 processors of the hypercube and the 32 regions of the figure.

The major steps of a simple parallel circuit simulator are outlined in Code 22-2. The data, which consists of circuit elements and netlist information, is loaded into the machine and then decomposed by a call to *bisect*. Interprocessor communication is done by means of a static *crystal_router*. Before entering the time evolution loop, initialization is achieved by a call to *dry_run* which takes the netlist as input and sets up routing tables that decide which circuit elements talk to one another when *crystal_router* is called. The main loop consists of a loop over circuit elements. First, the inputs to the element in question from the previous time step are combined. The element is then updated (evolved) and its output placed in the outgoing communications buffer. After looping through all the elements in this processor, a call to *crystal_router* is made which performs all necessary communications in an efficient manner.

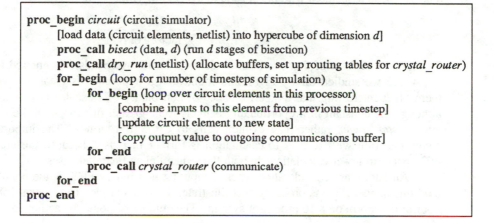

```
proc_begin circuit (circuit simulator)
        [load data (circuit elements, netlist) into hypercube of dimension d]
        proc_call bisect (data, d) (run d stages of bisection)
        proc_call dry_run (netlist) (allocate buffers, set up routing tables for crystal_router)
        for_begin (loop for number of timesteps of simulation)
                for_begin (loop over circuit elements in this processor)
                        [combine inputs to this element from previous timestep]
                        [update circuit element to new state]
                        [copy output value to outgoing communications buffer]
                for_end
                proc_call crystal_router (communicate)
        for_end
proc_end
```

Code 22-2 A circuit simulation algorithm using crystal_router

22-3.2 Non-binary FFTs

In their original formulation of the FFT, Cooley and Tukey [Cooley 65] described the algorithm for any "highly composite" number of points, N_x. In general, the time to compute the Fourier Transform of a vector of length N_x is proportional to N_x times the sum of the prime factors of N_x. In the well known special case in which $N_x = 2^l$, the sum of the prime factors is simply $2l$, or $2\log_2 N_x$. The time to transform the vector is proportional to $N_x \log_2 N_x$. Subsequently, [Rader 68], [Good 58], [Winograd 75, 76], and others introduced improvements to the original algorithm which significantly reduce the number of time consuming complex multiplications. In any event, the overall time to evaluate the transform remains proportional to N_x times the sum of the factors of N_x.

In any of the algorithms, the number of points in the transform is factored into say,

$$N_x = N_1 \times N_2 \times N_3 \times \cdots N_m \qquad (22\text{-}1)$$

A sequence of transformations is applied to the data, first in groups of N_1, then in groups of N_2, and so on. After the last set of transformations is applied, the Fourier Transform has been computed. Non-binary FFTs may be computed efficiently on distributed computers using the static *crystal_router* of Sec. 22–2. The static *crystal_router* is used to move data between processors, so that at the ith stage of the calculation, all the data points in a group of N_i are together in one processor. In general, each time the *crystal_router* is called, all the data in the distributed processor is completely shuffled, requiring approximately:

$$t_{shuffle} = t_{comm} \frac{N_x}{N} \log_2 N \qquad (22\text{-}2)$$

The overhead associated with the m calls to the *crystal_router* is approximately:

$$f_{shuffle} \approx \frac{m t_{comm}}{t_{calc}} \frac{\log_2 N}{(\sum \text{factors of } N_x)} \qquad (22\text{-}3)$$

The functional form of this overhead is identical to the overheads encountered in Chap. 11, where we studied binary FFTs, and found that a hypercube is ideal for evaluating them. It is interesting that the performance of non-binary FFTs scales in a similar way, although the constant of proportionality is likely to be greater due to use of the very general *crystal_router* rather than explicit calls to CrOS III routines. The importance of communication with respect to calculation is further increased because the non-binary FFTs perform fewer calculations in both the sequential and parallel cases.

An additional consideration when computing non-binary FFTs is the possibility of load imbalance. This is probably best illustrated by an example. Consider a 1680 point Fourier transform on a 16 processor system. The number of points is factored as follows:

$$1680 = 7 \times 5 \times 3 \times 16 = 7 \times 5 \times 3 \times 2^4 \qquad (22\text{-}4)$$

The distributed algorithm proceeds as follows:

$7 \times 5 \times 3 = 105$ 16-point transforms
crystal_router
$5 \times 3 \times 16 = 240$ 7-point transforms
crystal_router
$3 \times 16 \times 7 = 336$ 5-point transforms
crystal_router
$16 \times 7 \times 5 = 560$ 3-point transforms

The most imbalanced phase of the calculation is the first, in which 105 transforms are computed on 16 processors. Clearly, 9 processors compute 7 transforms while 7 of the processors compute only 6 transforms. The load imbalance overhead in such a situation is:

$$f_{imbalance} = \frac{t_{slowest} - t_{avg}}{t_{avg}} = \frac{16}{105} = 15\% \qquad (22\text{-}5)$$

It is important to note that the significance of load imbalance decreases rapidly as the number of points in the transform increases. In fact, for a $11760 = 7^2 \times 5 \times 3^2 \times 2^4$ point transform, evaluated on a 128-node system, the load imbalance is only about 2%. Aloisio, Fox, Kim, and Veneziani [Aloisio 87] have compared the performance of the Cooley-Tukey algorithm and the Prime Factor Algorithm on several hypercubes, and concluded that although the Prime Factor Algorithm requires the *crystal_router*, its overall performance is often significantly better than the Cooley-Tukey algorithm.

22-4 The crystal_accumulator Routine

The *crystal_accumulator* is another utility which makes use of the method of ordered cube geodesics. Suppose we have a vector V(i) in each of the nodes, $i = 0, 1, ...,$ $N - 1$, whose elements we wish to combine to form a vector, S, the decomposition of which is arbitrary.

$$S_{q(j)} = V_j(0) \oplus V_j(1) \oplus \cdots \oplus V_j(N-1) \qquad (22\text{-}6)$$

where $j=0,1,...,(M-1)$, labels the vector elements, and $q(j)$ maps the ordering of the elements of S to that of V. Furthermore, let $p(t)$ be the number of the unique processor in which S_t resides. As in the routine *combine* described in Sec. 14-5.4, the combining function $\oplus$ is specified by the user, and must be associative and commutative. An additional feature of the *crystal_accumulator* is that the elements of $V(i)$ which equal the identity element of the combining function do not contribute to S, and so are not communicated between processors.

The pseudocode describing the *crystal_accumulator* algorithm is given in Code 22-5. The algorithm begins by discarding those elements of $V(i)$ equal to the identity element of the combining function. For each of the remaining elements, the channel mask, $c(j)$, required to send V_j to processor $p(q(j))$ is evaluated. The V_j are then arranged in order of increasing $c(j)$ in a data structure called *data_buf*, which also contains the values of $c(j)$ and $q(j)$. Within each group of elements having the same value of $c(j)$, the elements of *data_buf* are stored in order of final storage location, $q(j)$. The algorithm then loops over each channel of the hypercube, starting with the highest, and sends those elements of *data_buf* for which the corresponding bit of $c(j)$ is set. At the same time, elements received on the same channel are stored in a scratch buffer, and each has the bit of $c(j)$ appropriate to that channel set to zero. These elements are then compared with the remaining elements in *data_buf* so that the ordering by channel mask and final storage location is maintained, and elements having the same value of $q(j)$ are combined. After this procedure has been repeated for each channel, the elements remaining in *data_buf* are just the elements of S belonging to each processor, in the order specified by $q(j)$. Figure 22-3 shows how *crystal_accumulator* works for an example on a 2-dimensional hypercube, in which the vector length, M, is 8.

The *crystal_accumulator* provides a useful (although not always optimal) general purpose communication scheme in various complex summation algorithms, where the optimal, custom-designed solution is difficult to find. Modeling complicated, multi-component circuits or neurobiological networks provides various examples of this kind

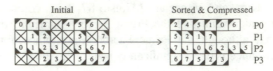

Sort/Compress Stage

Exchange on Channel 1 Followed by Merge/Combine (Step0)

Exchange on Channel 0 Followed by Merge/Combine (Step1)

Figure 22-3 An example of the *crystal_accumulator* for the case *M=8* on a 2-D hypercube. The ordering of S is determined by q(j), and its decomposition over the hypercube by p(j). Here it is assumed that q = (2, 4, 5, 3, 1, 7, 0, 6), and p = (0, 0, 1, 0, 3, 2, 3, 3).

[Furmanski 87a, 87b].

Consider, for example, a neural network with short or medium-range connectivity, and with *patchy* activity patterns such that a domain decomposition would result in poor efficiency in the concurrent algorithm. Patches (i.e., small compact cortical regions with temporal activity excess) might be due to the multi-layer structure arising from the over-lapping in space and time of neuronal sub-populations, or to rhythmic activity in which the enhanced workload area propagates in an oscillatory fashion through a given cortical structure. This type of situation is found, for example, in the hippocampus, cerebellum, and piriform cortex.

Scattered decomposition is the simple, general-purpose solution of the load-balance problem due to patches. If the number of model neurons per patch exceeds the number of nodes on the hypercube, the scattered decomposition results in satisfactory load-balance since each patch is distributed over the whole hypercube. The price to be paid is that the network neighbors are not neighbors in the hypercube topology, and we are faced with the problem of sparse vector summation with non-zero components distributed over a hypercube in a complicated, problem-dependent and time-dependent manner.

This is precisely the problem addressed by the *crystal_accumulator*. Intuitively we can illustrate the action of the algorithm in this case by saying that the dendritic tree of each neuron is distributed over the whole hypercube. In the case of sparse connectivity some, or even many, of the branches may be absent. The *crystal_accumulator* moves signals along the dendrites (represented by hypercube geodesics), concurrently performing partial summations in the nodes in a manner which is statistically homogeneous for all trees. For this example we have M neurons and $V_j(i)$ is the contribution to the input signal of neuron number j coming from all neurons in node i. The calculation of the individual $V_j(i)$ would proceed concurrently, and typically involve a substantial amount of computation.

```
proc_begin crystal_accumulator (combine vectors V(i) to give S)
declare_struct mstruct {declare_int dest_mask, dest_index; declare_buf buf ;};
declare_buf data_buf ; (array of data type mstruct)
declare_buf scratch_buf ; (array of data type mstruct)
declare_buf p; (integer array, maps decomposition of S to processors)
declare_buf q; (integer array, maps ordering of S to that of V(i))
        [copy elements of V not equal to identify element to data_buf]
        [sort elements of data_buf in order of the channel mask needed to get to p(q(i)) ]
        [for each channel mask sort elements of data_buf in order of final decomposition of S]
        for _begin (channel, c, from (d−1) to 0 )
                [send on channel c elements of data_buf with bit number c of dest_mask set,
                    while receiving incoming data on channel c in scratch_buf]
                for_begin (each element in scratch_buf)
                        [set bit number c of dest_mask to zero]
                        if_begin (this element has dest_index
                                equal to that of some element of data_buf) then
                                [combine and overwrite element of data_buf]
                        else
                                [insert element of scratch_buf into data_buf, maintaining
                                    ordering by dest_mask and dest_index ]
                        if_end
                for_end
        for_end
        [copy remaining elements of data_buf to output data buffer]
proc_end
```

Code 22-5 The crystal_accumulator Algorithm

    The irregular nature of the *crystal_accumulator* algorithm makes it difficult to give a performance analysis for the general case. However, instructive results can be obtained for the "random" case, in which each processor contains approximately the same number of non-identity elements in the vector $V(i)$, and the final decomposition of S is uniform over the processors. In this case we denote by $n(c)$ the average number of elements per node, at step c of the algorithm, where $c=0,1,...,d-1$. On the average, at step c each processor exchanges $n(c)/2$ elements over channel $(d-1-c)$. There are $M(c+1)$ possible locations for the elements received, where $M(c+1)=M(0)/2^{c+1}$. Thus, the probability that a particular received element can be combined with another element is

$n(c)/2M(c+1)$, so the number of elements per processor at the next step may be written:

$$n(c+1) = \frac{n(c)}{2} + \left[1 - \frac{n(c)}{2M(c+1)}\right] \frac{n(c)}{2} \qquad (22\text{-}7)$$

where the first term on the right-hand side is the number of "resident" elements at step c, and the second term the number of "new" elements, i.e., the number of elements which were received, but which were not combined with any of the resident elements. The recursion relationship Eq. (22-7) may be solved to give,

$$n(c) = \frac{M}{2^c}\left[1 - \left[1-\gamma\right]^{2^c}\right] \qquad (22\text{-}8)$$

where $\gamma = n/M$ is the initial average fraction of the $V(i)$ not occupied by identity elements, $M = M(0)$ is the length of the vector in each processor, and $n = n(0)$ is the average number of elements per processor not equal to the identity element of the combining function. The total communication time for the *crystal_accumulator* algorithm is,

$$T_{comm} = t_{comm} \sum_{c=0}^{d-1} \frac{n(c)}{2} \qquad (22\text{-}9)$$

so substituting from Eq. (22-3) we have,

$$T_{comm} = t_{comm} \sum_{c=0}^{d-1} \frac{M}{2^{c+1}}\left[1 - \left[1-\gamma\right]^{2^c}\right] \qquad (22\text{-}10)$$

Figure 22-4 shows T_{comm} as a function of n for fixed M. Two limiting cases are of interest. For $n << M$, the communication time is proportional to n, which is the same as for the *crystal_router* algorithm. However, as $n \rightarrow M$ the dependence of T_{comm} on n disappears, and the curve in Fig. 22-4 levels off. This limiting case is the same as the *fold* algorithm. Thus, if the vectors $V(i)$ are sparse the *crystal_accumulator* behaves like the *crystal_router*; however, if the $V(i)$ are full it behaves like the routine *fold*, described in Sec. 21-3.3. Due to the high computational cost of forming the $V_j(i)$, the hypercube implementation in [Furmanski 87a] is very efficient, with the communication dwarfed by calculation.

In [Furmanski 87b], the use of communication algorithms for network simulation was summarized by:

Sparse Regular Network $\rightarrow$ Index
Sparse Irregular Network $\rightarrow$ Crystal_router
Dense Irregular Network $\rightarrow$ Crystal_accumulator
Dense Regular Network $\rightarrow$ Fold

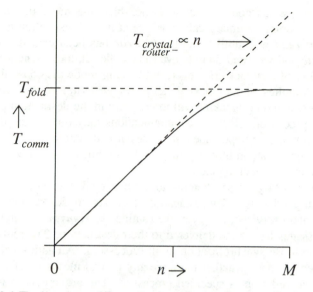

Figure 22-4 The dependence of T_{comm} on n, the average number of non-identity elements per processor, illustrating the two limiting cases.

22-5 An Implementation of the Virtual Concurrent Processor

In Chap. 4 we introduced the concept of the virtual concurrent processor, in which the nodes are fully interconnected and communicate via node-addressed messages. We now consider how such a communication paradigm might be implemented in software on a broad spectrum of real concurrent processors. We call this the *virtual machine loosely synchronous communication system* (VMLSCS). The functionality of the VMLSCS may be modeled by assuming that communication is handled by a separate process, referred to as the *VM process*, which runs in each node. Nodes communicate by making read and write requests to their VM process. Interaction between the VM processes of different nodes actually effects the transfer of messages between the nodes. The user interacts with the VM processes in the nodes only by making read and write requests.

The VM process is initiated by a call to the routine *vm_initproc*, and is terminated by a call to *vm_killproc* (or the end of the program), both of which must be called with loose synchrony. The routine *vm_initproc* allocates buffer space and performs any necessary machine-dependent tasks to initiate the VM process. The routine *vm_killproc* releases the resources assigned to the VM process. Requests to the VM process to read and write messages are made using the routines *vm_read* and *vm_write*, which were introduced in Sec. 4-3. In order to increase the utility of these routines we now add two extra arguments, *message_type* and *mode*. The *message_type* allows processors to exchange messages of a specific type, and the *mode* specifies whether the communication is to be blocking or non-blocking. In Sec. 4-3 *vm_read* and *vm_write* were defined to be blocking communication routines, however this restriction can now be relaxed since these routines only make requests to the VM process, and do not directly send or receive messages. When communicating in non-blocking mode the routine *vm_write* does not wait for a complementary call to *vm_read* in the destination node before returning, nor does *vm_read* wait until a call to *vm_write* has been executed in the source node, thus *vm_write* and *vm_read* do not have to be called in loose synchronization, and there is no possibility of deadlock. However, in blocking mode the constraint of loose synchronization still applies, and a blocking call to *vm_write* in a source processor must be matched by a corresponding blocking call to *vm_read* in the destination processor. On some concurrent processors blocking communications may only be used between certain nodes. For example, on a hypercube only nodes directly connected by a communication channel may communicate in blocking mode. If portability is required all communication should be done in non-blocking mode.

The VM process attempts to service read and write requests made in blocking mode immediately. Communication requests made in non-blocking mode are not immediately serviced, however, the routine *vm_comsync* ensures that all previously written messages have been delivered to their destination. The routine *vm_comsync* must be called in loose synchronization in all processors. An additional routine, *vm_query*, may be called to check whether there are any unread messages of a particular type that have been received from a specified processor. The arguments to *vm_query* are pointers to integers specifying the source processor and message type, either of which may have a "wild card" value to indicate that any value for these quantities is acceptable. If an unread message satisfying the source processor and message type constraints exists, then the actual source processor and message type are stored at the locations pointed to by the routine's arguments. If no such message exists then an error code is returned, otherwise the length of the message in bytes is returned. The routines *vm_write*, *vm_read*, and *vm_query* are defined in Code 22-3.

Having described the functionality of the VMLSCS we now consider how to implement it on different types of concurrent processor. In the case of a hypercube running with an asynchronous communication system, the virtual concurrent processor can be implemented relatively easily since such systems generally provide communication primitives for performing node-addressed communication. In this case a call to *vm_comsync* synchronizes all the nodes, and ensures that all writes have been completed. For a hypercube with a synchronous, channel-addressed communication system, such as CrOS III, the routines *cread* and *cwrite* may be used to implement blocking communication. The *crystal_router* algorithm may be used to implement non-blocking communication, and we will consider this in more detail. For each communication channel there is a corresponding communication buffer, allocated in the routine *vm_initproc*. When a non-blocking write request is made by a call to *vm_write* the message is copied into the communication buffer of the channel on which the message must be sent first. A header containing the number of bytes in the message, the source and destination processors, and the message type is prepended to each message. When *vm_comsync* is called these messages are delivered to their destination processors by means of the *crystal_router* algorithm, as follows. Communication buffers are exchanged over the first communication channel, and the header of each message received is checked to see whether it has reached its destination processor or whether it must be forwarded. If a message is to be forwarded it is copied to the communication buffer of the channel on which it must next be sent. If a message has reached its destination then information about it is copied to an array of data type MESS_DATA referred to as the *read array*. MESS_DATA is defined in Code 22-4. After this process has been repeated for all of the communication channels all messages will have reached their final destination.

```
void vm_write ( message, dest_proc, nbytes, message_type, mode )
char *message;                /* address of message */
unsigned int dest_proc;       /* destination processor*/
int nbytes;                   /* number of bytes in message */
int message_type;
int mode;


int vm_read ( message, source_proc, nbytes, message_type, mode )
char *message;                /* address to store message */
unsigned int source_proc;     /* source processor */
int nbytes;                   /* maximum number of bytes in message */
int message_type;
int mode;


int vm_query ( source_address, type_address )
int *source_address;          /* address to store source processor */
int *type_address;            /* address to store message type */


int vm_comsync ()
```

Code 22-3 VMLSCS Routines

```
declare_struct MESS_DATA {char *message;
                          int nbytes;
                          int source_proc;
                          int dest_proc;
                          int message_type; } ;
```

Code 22-4 The Data Type MESS_DATA

Non-blocking read requests made by *vm_read* cause the read array to be inspected. If an unread message satisfying the source processor and message type constraints is referenced in the read array then the message is copied from the communication buffer to the storage location supplied in the read request, and is flagged for deletion from the communication buffer. Thus read requests are serviced immediately. The routine *vm_query* also inspects the read array, and is similar to a non-blocking read request except that the memory-to-memory copy from the communication buffer to the user-supplied buffer is not performed.

In addition to delivering messages to their destination processors, *vm_comsync* performs another major task. At the start of *vm_comsync* each of the communication buffers is examined, all messages flagged for deletion are removed, and the communication buffer is compacted.

As a further refinement, on some hypercubes with high-speed floating-point units, such as the Caltech/JPL Mark IIIfp hypercube, it is advantageous to split the routine *vm_comsync* into two parts. The first part initiates the exchange of communication buffers whilst the second checks for completion of the exchanges. These two stages can be implemented as distinct routines so that calculation can be performed between the two stages, thereby overlapping communication with calculation. To do this *vm_write* and *vm_read* need to be modified so that the copying of messages in and out of communication buffers is performed as part of the communication step and overlaps calculation. Thus *vm_write* should not copy the message to a communication buffer, but instead maintains a list of pointers to messages in an array of type MESS_DATA. After communication has been initiated this array is inspected, and the messages are then copied to the appropriate message buffers. The routine *vm_read* should be modified so that when a request is issued to read a message that has not yet arrived the request is stored in an array of type MESS_DATA. When the message arrives it is then copied to the location stored in this array.

A full implementation of the virtual concurrent processor should also contain collective communication routines, such as *vm_bcast* for sending messages to more than one destination node, and *vm_combine* for combining data from a set of nodes. Such routines can be implemented quite straightforwardly in terms of *vm_read* and *vm_write*, however we will not go into the details here.

The virtual concurrent processor can also be implemented on shared memory concurrent processors. On such machines an area of shared memory is allocated to contain the messages addressed to each processor. Calls to *vm_write* cause the message and header to be written to the message area of the destination processor. The routines *vm_read* and *vm_query* check through the message headers in the message area for unread messages with the appropriate source processor and message type, and, in the case of *vm_read*, copy any such messages to the storage location supplied in the argument list. The routine *vm_initproc* initializes the message area, and *vm_comsync* synchronizes the processors.

The concept of the virtual concurrent processor was first introduced in Chap. 4 to provide a framework within which to discuss concurrent algorithms. However, it is now apparent that the virtual concurrent processor can be implemented on a wide range of different types of concurrent processor, and provides a common communication system permitting a high degree of software portability.

We emphasize that the virtual concurrent processor with its service routines of Code 22-3 represents an abstract machine model suitable for the general loosely synchronous problem. We have been careful to define VMLSCS so that it can be implemented with either synchronous or asynchronous communication systems. This allows the system implementer to choose the method that gives the desired tradeoff between functionality and performance.

22-6 Portable Programming Environments

We started this book by defining a rather general virtual machine, but used a specific hypercube environment, CrOS III, for much of the detailed algorithmic and performance analysis. Now we have shown how to use CrOS III to build a much more general programming environment - VMLSCS - which realizes the virtual machine concept on a hypercube. The *crystal_router* and *crystal_accumulator* algorithms are the keys to a hypercube implementation of VMLSCS under CrOS III, or more generally under any synchronous system. We have, in fact, ported CrOS III to a variety of different hypercubes and also shared memory machines such as the BBN Butterfly and IBM's RP3. However, VMLSCS is a more appropriate system around which to build a portable environment. VMLSCS can be implemented with either an asynchronous or synchronous message-passing system at the lowest level.

Currently we view CrOS III as a finished product - an optimized synchronous implementation of VMLSCS for the hypercube. In the near future we expect to experiment with VMLSCS and use it with our future concurrent scientific algorithms. We will build VMLSCS on a variety of high performance concurrent machines of different architectures. In particular, we see it as a natural environment for all coarse-grain MIMD machines with either shared or distributed memory.

23

The Hypercube as a Supercomputer in Science and Engineering

23-1 Introduction

This book has covered a large number of algorithms and problems and has shown that in every case there are conditions, i.e., particular values of parameters, under which concurrent computers can be effectively used. Can these examples be convincingly generalized? What are the essential characteristics of the problems? What is the nature of the parameter space? What classes of concurrent computers are covered by our analysis? Can we meaningfully speculate on problems, parameters, or computers that are not natural extrapolations of our examples? We will address these questions in this chapter under the general theme: "When is a hypercube a supercomputer for scientific and engineering computations?"

23-2 Hardware Issues

The essential lessons, as they relate to hardware, have already been summarized in Sec. 3-5 and 3-6, with Chap. 2 describing how the hypercube fits in a taxonomy of parallel computers. The algorithmic chapters (5-13, 16-21) of the book have expanded upon the general algorithmic overview in Chap. 3.

Chap. 2 describes some key choices in the architecture of concurrent computers that are reiterated in Table 23-1.

Table 23-1 Features of Concurrent Computers

Hypercube Characteristics		Other Choices
Distributed Memory	v.	Shared Memory
Large Grain Size	v.	Small Grain Size
MIMD (Asynchronous Nodes)	v.	SIMD (Lockstep Nodes)
General Purpose Node	v.	Special Purpose Node

Of these global choices in Table 23-1, the discussion of this book has leaned heavily toward the left-hand column of Table 23-1. This choice, however, leaves the topology of the node interconnection unspecified. Much applications work can be independent of the topology, but we have frequently chosen to address the hypercube specifically. Chapters 11, 18, 19, 21 and 22 rely on the details of the hypercube topology; the other chapters typically require only a mesh interconnect, which is contained within the hypercube. Inhomogeneous problems and load-balancing (decomposition) techniques rely on a general feature of the hypercube: the short (at most $\log_2 N$) distance between any two nodes in a hypercube network. In the context of current technology, the richness of the hypercube topology seems to justify the additional expense (over a two or three-dimensional mesh) required for its implementation.

According to Eq. (3-22), the speedup on a concurrent machine is given by:

$$S = \frac{N}{1+f_C} \tag{23-1}$$

With the overhead f_C taking the typical form:

$$f_C = [a + b t_{comm}/t_{calc}]/n^{1/d} \tag{23-2}$$

where a, b, and d are constants that we have derived for many of the examples in this book. The values of a, b, and *system dimension d* are determined by the algorithm, and the value of t_{comm}/t_{calc} by the hardware and communication software implementation. Figure 3-5 emphasizes the essential point. As long as the problem is big enough ($n^{1/d} \sim 10$) for typical ranges of parameters ($a + b t_{comm}/t_{calc} \sim 1$), one will obtain a speedup that is close to N and linearly increasing with the number of processors. In general, hypercubes with sufficient memory on each node and with good communication capability ($\tau = t_{comm}/t_{calc}$ comparable in value to that for the original Caltech machines, $\tau \sim 3$) will perform well. We should note that we have tacitly assumed in the previous chapters that communication and calculation cannot be overlapped. In more advanced designs, one can overlap communication with calculation and this leads to a straightforward extension of the performance analysis given in Sec. 3-5. One finds that for typical problems the overlap allows one to relax the condition on τ and find good performance as long as $\tau = t_{comm}/t_{calc}$ is ≤ 15 for the case of overlapped communication and calculation [Fox 87].

It is interesting that we have found no other limiting criteria. All the problems that we have considered have "natural" algorithms that exhibit parallelism. Only in the sorting problem of Chap. 18, did we find that the speedup was significantly reduced by the nonoptimal performance of the concurrent algorithm. Many of the problems discussed in this book are simulations of natural phenomena; clearly nature itself is highly "concurrent" and so it is not surprising that good algorithms can be devised to model this concurrent world.

Throughout this book we have assumed that the communication system between the nodes incurred little startup or latency penalty, i.e., that t_{comm} is roughly independent of the message size. Current commercial hypercubes, however, exhibit the effect illustrated in Fig. 4-2 in which t_{comm} is large for short messages. This effect is a consequence of both hardware and software design differences from the original Caltech hypercubes, which in fact display only a modest dependence of t_{comm} on message size. Some of our conclusions and analysis may require reexamination if machines that exhibit good performance for relatively short messages are not generally available.

Our techniques can be translated straightforwardly to machines that utilize shared memory but also adhere to the "left-hand column" for the last three issues in Table 23-1 (i.e., large grain size, MIMD, and general purpose node). Such machines include those designed by CRAY, ETA, ENCORE, SEQUENT, ALLIANT, BUTTERFLY, ELXSI, etc. In fact, if the shared-memory machine incorporates a large cache on each node, then one can view the caches as the distributed memory and the shared memory as a communication mechanism [Fox 87].

Some of our results apply to fine grain-size machines, but the mapping is not so direct or universal as the correspondence between the hypercube and a large grain-size shared-memory machine.

23-3 Software Issues

We have adopted a conservative approach to the software issues. We have made the minimal necessary extensions to a conventional sequential programming environment. The choices and issues have been reviewed in Sec. 3-4, and here we touch upon the highlights. The software for large grain-size concurrent computers can be very similar in structure to that for sequential machines. One need only add a library of basic communication calls to any standard language. We have discussed C and FORTRAN, but PASCAL, LISP, ADA, PROLOG, BASIC, and even assembly language represent equally acceptable programming languages. The CUBIX environment, described in Chaps. 6 and 15, allows the concurrent programmer access to the same input/output and system facilities of modern sequential systems. It is in many cases quite straightforward to generate concurrent code that with trivial modification may run on both sequential and concurrent machines transparently. Although we have not discussed this point in much detail, the same code may also run on a wide variety of large grain concurrent computers of both distributed and shared memory design. We expect that it will be easier to run hypercube code on a shared-memory machine than vice versa.

The crystalline environment used throughout this book has two important limitations. Firstly, it only addresses the programming of a class of problems that we have termed loosely synchronous in Sec. 3-4; there exists a global synchronization mechanism typically arising from either an iteration count or an overall simulation time. This restriction is apparently not too serious, since it is satisfied by all the examples in this book. Loosely synchronous problems include a large fraction of typical supercomputer applications. Many research groups including our own are working on more general programming environments that will address more extensive problem classes. In Sec. 22-5, we introduced the virtual machine loosely synchronous communication system (VMLSCS) and we believe that this is a natural programming environment for this general problem class. As explained in Sec. 22-5, one can implement VMLSCS with the crystalline system. Other low level message passing paradigms are also appropriate for VMLSCS and could be chosen on the basis of performance/functionality tradeoffs.

The second limitation of the crystalline environment is more subtle. One way of stating this limitation is that the VMLSCS environment is an algorithmic or user communication system but *not* a concurrent operating system. Crystalline communication and CUBIX encompass the necessary message-passing and I/O functionality that a program needs when running application code. This task is accomplished with elegance and high performance. However, the system is incomplete as it does not address many important areas of the programming environment. These areas include sharing the concurrent computer among many users (multi-user environment) and interactive program debugging. These capabilities require a more complete asynchronous operating system that either emulates a crystalline environment or more efficiently transfers control to an optimized crystalline system when the application program is running.

23-4 Scientific Applications on a Concurrent Supercomputer

23-4.1 Introduction

In Chap. 2 we described how an extrapolation of current technology should allow the future construction of large grain-size concurrent computers whose performance will be several orders of magnitude greater than that of current supercomputers. Specialized fine grain-size machines will lead to even greater performance for some problems. The examples discussed in this book have shown how a broad range of problems are capable of effectively using this potential performance, yielding speedups comparable to the number of nodes. At Caltech, we have adopted a somewhat unusual but practical approach to developing the scientific uses of concurrent machines. The research program is based not upon a general theoretical framework, but rather upon experiment. We supplied the necessary support to allow leading computational scientists to use hypercubes, thereby going beyond tryout algorithms and solving significant problems. This approach has had the advantage of ensuring that complete applications were developed so that the total performance could be assessed without neglecting possible hidden sequential bottlenecks that would lower the overall performance. We close this book by describing some of the research applications. This description complements the rest of the book in the sense that the discussion is science-based rather than algorithm-based. Such a compilation is by no means complete, but it is useful as an indicator. We restrict mention to local work with which we are familiar and we choose only to describe those Caltech applications for which the implementation issues are fairly clear-cut. This restriction excludes some exciting work in progress. More details of these implementations can be found in [Fox 86f].

23-4.2 The Hypercube in Biology

Neural Circuit Simulation

There is growing interest in the use of simulation in biological research, and in particular in the study of large systems of neurons. These can either be real neurons as discussed in Chap. 1 when simulating the brain, or "applied" or "theoretical" neurons which comprise computational circuits of the type discussed in [Hopfield 82]. The concurrent decomposition issues in simulating such systems are described in [Furmanski 87b] and are very similar to those involved in the simulation of an array of electronic components such as those in a chip. The best algorithms depend upon the nature of the circuit, but in the cases looked at so far the hypercube can be an excellent circuit simulator. In the case of simulations of the brain, this conclusion is not surprising, since nature's computer, the brain, is a kind of distributed memory system. It should be expected that a general-purpose distributed-memory concurrent computer like the hypercube can be applicable to its simulation.

In many cases, the connectivity between neurons (circuit elements) is so high that one can use the long-range force algorithm of Chap. 9. In this case the input from each neuron is communicated to all nodes. Consider a simulation of a system with N_n neurons on a hypercube with N nodes. Suppose further that on average each neuron is connected to l others. Then if $l >> N$, independent of N_n, the algorithm of Chap. 9 is efficient. In an implementation of the simulation of the piriform cortex on the hypercube, we found that the *fold* algorithm of Chap. 21 was appropriate [Furmanski 87a]. Connectivities with $l \leq N$ may call for the special decomposition or load-balancing techniques which were covered in Sec. 3-8 and Chap. 17. A particularly difficult case with $l = 4$ and random connectivities is discussed in [Fox 86d].

The hypercube is not only appropriate for the simulation of biological and applied neural networks but also in real-time applications such as the controller or "brain" of a robot. This work has been pioneered using a commercial NCUBE hypercube at Oak Ridge National Laboratory [Bahren 87].

Protein Dynamics

An important area of scientific computation in biology and chemistry involves the dynamics of large protein molecules. This is treated as a particle dynamics problem of the type discussed in Chaps. 9 and 16. Since the interatomic electrical forces are long range one can usually employ the algorithm of Chap. 9 even though we may typically ignore the screened potential of atoms that are widely separated. In fact, the implementation issues are not very different from those in a circuit simulation; a protein forms a circuit whose elements are the atoms and whose connection is defined by the interatomic force. This correspondence is an example of the general equivalence given by the theory of complex systems described in Chap. 3.

23-4.3 The Hypercube in Chemistry

Chemical Reactions

The hypercube has been employed in a major new algorithm for the detailed simulation of three- and four-body chemical reactions [Kuppermann 86]. This simulation includes several components. The first step involves the solution of a finite element problem of the type discussed in Chap. 8. This step is followed by the determination of the lowest eigenfunctions of a sparse matrix using the subspace iteration method which can be performed using variants of the general methods described in Chap. 21. The major part of the calculation involves the solution of a coupled-channel Schrödinger equation which uses the logarithmic derivative method and is dominated by the inversion of an $M \times M$ matrix where M is the number of channels. The Gauss-Jordan code described in Sec. 21-5 was developed for this application. Interesting values of M go up to 1000 and such large problems can profitably use hypercubes with several thousand nodes.

23-4.4 The Hypercube in Engineering

Chaos

Two groups have used the hypercube to determine the fractal dimension of data sets; in one case this corresponded to experimental plasma data and in another to trajectories coming from the solutions of ordinary differential equations [Theiler 86, 87 and Lorenz 87]. We have already described the basic idea in Sec. 9-5 where we saw how the long-range force algorithm can be used to calculate the correlation function.

Computational Fluid Dynamics

In general, computational fluid dynamics uses the techniques described in Chaps. 7 and 8 for the solution of partial differential equations. The importance of turbulent flow introduces some important new issues. Investigations have examined flow at high Reynold's number using vortex methods, where the solution of the differential equations is exchanged for a study of the dynamics of independent vortices. These vortices effectively interact with a long-range force and so one can use the method of Chap. 9 to achieve a hypercube implementation of high efficiency [Baden 87, Leonard 80, 87]. We also note that improved sequential algorithms for long-range interactions have recently been developed [Barnes 86] and one may be able to perform this calculation in time complexity $N_v \log N_v$, where N_v is the number of vortices. Preliminary hypercube implementations of Barnes and Hut's algorithm show promising efficiency.

The dynamic nature of the irregularities produced by turbulence poses algorithmic challenges even for sequential machines. It is probably best to use an underlying mesh that changes or adapts as the solution changes. Work is under way on such an adaptive mesh for use on the hypercube in the context of the multigrid solution method [Van de Velde 87a, b]. As discussed in Chap. 8, the multigrid method can be efficiently implemented on the hypercube. One ambitious goal is to combine both the mesh adaption and the hypercube decomposition into a single step, since both need similar optimization methods. Note that the need for adaptive meshes implies that even on a sequential machine, the user can be concerned only with the local problem. This feature renders the transition to the hypercube particularly natural, since domain decomposition has already been enforced by the locally adapting mesh.

A new approach to fluid dynamics has been proposed which models the continuum problem in terms of discrete cellular automata [Wolfram 86]. This leads to algorithms similar to the neural network and statistical physics applications. These are efficiently implemented on the hypercube but the regularity and simplicity of cellular automata suggests that an SIMD approach with an architecture like the Connection Machine would be more cost-effective [Hayot 87].

Earthquake Engineering

The methods of Chap. 8 have applications throughout many disciplines. At Caltech they are being used to solve finite element problems that arise in many structural analysis problems including those occurring in earthquake engineering and at the Jet Propulsion Laboratory in the analysis of spacecraft structures. [Lyzenga 85, Nour–Omid 87a, 87b]

Convolutional Decoding

Convolutional decoding is used in communication, for example between a spacecraft and earth, to decrease the incidence of undetected errors with minimum increase in the volume of information to be transmitted. The Viterbi algorithm is a well-known method of convolutional coding whose complexity increases exponentially with the number of states. It has been shown that the structure of this algorithm is formally identical to that of the FFT, and hence that the hypercube represents an excellent architecture for a parallel implementation of this algorithm [Pollara 85, 86]. The performance analysis is very similar to that in Chap. 11. The algorithm is sufficiently simple that realistic use of it could benefit from a specialized node optimized for this problem.

Ray Tracing in Computer Graphics

Ray tracing is a technique used to render computer graphics images of three-dimensional models. It is time consuming but leads to very realistic images. The picture is divided into a two-dimensional mesh of pixels and several rays are run through each pixel. These rays are propagated according to the laws of optics and interact with the environment by refraction and reflection. Two kinds of decompositions are relevant here. The calculation is rather easily decomposed, since each pixel is independent and each processor can run rays independently. However, one must use the scattered decomposition for the pixels to achieve load balance, because pixels near a complicated part of the picture take longer to process than those in a dull background. On the other hand, the databases describing the model for the image can be very large and in general also require decomposition which is, however, much harder to derive. This issue is related to the general load-balancing problem described in Sec. 3-8 and is a topic of current research. It is expected that the hypercube will still perform well even when the data base is decomposed; the pixel decomposition leads to negligible inefficiencies of 1–2% [Goldsmith 86, 87].

23-4.5 Geophysics

The use of the hypercube in geophysics at Caltech is particularly impressive as the group led by Clayton and Hager has been able to use the hypercube on a day-to-day basis for many different applications [Clayton 87].

Seismic Waves

The example of Chap. 7 is indicative of the application of the hypercube to the study of seismic waves. These are typically solved by finite difference methods which, as described in Chap. 7, work as well on the hypercube for the fourth-order differencing as for the standard second-order approximation. New applications being explored include nonuniform media for which the optimal methods use a mixture of full numeric and partially analytic methods. This combination leads to irregularities in the computational complexity per grid point and to nontrivial load-balancing issues.

Geodynamics

Finite element methods as discussed in Chap. 8 have been employed with a preconditioned conjugate gradient iterative solver. The study of the earth's mantle is reduced to one of thermal convection in an incompressible medium. Three-dimensional problems require large memory to yield good efficiencies for the reasons outlined in Chap. 3.

Tomography and Normal Modes

Two types of geophysical calculations use the hypercube in a different fashion where each node independently calculates part of the answer. In tomography, ray tracing is used to propagate acoustic waves through the earth. The propagation time, which is sensitive to the structure of the earth, is obtained by inversion from the observed timing data. In a normal mode analysis, a set of synthetic seismograms is compiled for a given model of the earth and a particular set of earthquake source parameters. The signal is analyzed into separate modes for each eigenfrequency of the earth, and each mode is calculated separately on a single processor node. These two applications are characterized by essentially 100% concurrent efficiency.

23-4.6 Physics

Computational Astrophysics

One particularly interesting problem involves a study of the evolution of the large-scale structure of the universe on the hypercube [Salmon 86]. This employs the particle in a cell (PIC) algorithm, which involves both particle dynamics (galaxies evolving under Newton's laws) and a mesh-based algorithm. The galaxies are "smeared" to derive a mass density on a mesh, and then the FFT of Chap. 11 is used to calculate the long-range component of the gravitational potential. This reduces a problem of complexity N_g^2 to one that is $N_g \log N_g$, where N_g is the number of galaxies in the simulation. PIC codes involve an interesting conflict between the cell and particle decompositions. These will not be simultaneously load-balanced if the distribution of mesh points does not match the particle density.

In many cases, this presents no serious problem as the easily load balanced FFT dominates the poorly balanced particle stage. Further investigation of a reformulation of the problem using a (galaxy) clustering algorithm to replace the FFT is under way. This approach has the same $N_g \log N_g$ calculational complexity and should be easier to load balance [Appel 85, Barnes 86, Greengard 87].

High-Energy Physics

Lattice gauge theory calculations were described in Chap. 13 and have been a central theme of our hypercube use at Caltech. Roughly twenty separate lattice gauge calculations have been performed on the hypercube, and most of these have been published [Fox 86f]. The theory is very complex, and for this reason lattice gauge calculations make high efficiency use of the hypercube even for small volumes, such as 4×4×4×16 four-dimensional mesh in each node when the surface to volume ratio is high. The regularity of the current numerical formulations leads to rather straightforward concurrent decompositions.

Condensed Matter

The regular nearest-neighbor Monte Carlo algorithm encountered in the lattice gauge theory is neatly complemented by some of the condensed matter Monte Carlo calculations performed on the hypercube. In the study of the melting of a two-dimensional solid, an irregular short-range but not nearest-neighbor problem is involved, and as mentioned in Sec. 13-7, one needs a subtle algorithm to both obtain good efficiency and satisfy the constraint of detailed balance [Johnson 86]. A Monte Carlo study of a long-range force problem in a two-dimensional gas requires a very different algorithm from that in Chap. 9 for the long-range dynamics problem. Detailed balance implies that only one particle can be updated at a time and care is required to ensure that one can efficiently decide which particle to update in a concurrent algorithm [Fucito 85].

Granular Physics

An intuitively appealing application of the hypercube involves the simulation of wind-driven and gravity-driven motion of a collection of sand grains. The conventional continuum approximations are not used, but rather each grain is moved separately in accordance with Newton's laws. This method is intrinsically very time-consuming and is perhaps only worth pursuing if one believes that computer performance will increase substantially in the future. This simulation is a particle dynamics problem of the type discussed in Chap. 16. The sand grains interact by contact only, and define an irregular but pure nearest-neighbor algorithm. The time required to calculate the grain-grain force is typically so large that the node-to-node communication costs are negligible. Load imbalance represents the only serious impact on efficiency, although in practice even this is of small importance. It is amusing to note that the initial hypercube implementation had an efficiency ε of 3! One part of the calculation involves the determination of which sand grains touch, and this was implemented on the sequential machine as a search of a list of all N_g (number of grains) grains, which requires a time of order N_g^2. The concurrent algorithm is implemented with a spatial decomposition which means that this step only needs to search the local and neighboring nodes. Such a search takes a time of order $(N_g/N)^2$ on the hypercube and results in a an algorithmic speedup of order N^2! Of course, this was a case in which the sequential algorithm was intrinsically poor and should also have used a spatial decomposition (or geometric hashing) method. When the concurrent implementation is compared to the sequential version using this improved algorithm, the efficiency assumes a more sensible value near unity with load-imbalance as the dominant overhead [Werner 87].

23-5 The Last Word

We remind readers of our experience that hypercubes exhibit high performance on most large scientific problems. Other concurrent architectures are also successful. If you are interested in cost-effective computing with very high capability (10^{12} flops = 1 Teraflop) in the future, we believe that it would be wise to consider the use of concurrent computers.

References

Note many internal Caltech reports are referred to as C^3P memos. These may be obtained from the Caltech Concurrent Computation Program as explained in the Preamble to this book.

Adams 82   Adams, L. M., "Iterative algorithms for large sparse linear systems on parallel computers," Ph.D. Thesis, University of Virginia (1982).

Adams 84   Adams, L. M. and Voight, R. G., "Design, development, and use of the finite element machine," in *Large Scale Scientific Computation*, Academic Press, New York (1984), 301.

Akl 85   Akl, S. G., *Parallel Sorting Algorithms*, Academic Press, New York (1985).

Aldcroft 87   Aldcroft, T., Cisneros, A., Fox, G. C., Furmanski, W., and Walker, D. W., "LU decomposition of banded matrices and the solution of linear systems on hypercubes," Caltech report C^3P-348, in preparation, 1987.

Allakhverdiyev 81 Allakhverdiyev, N. M., and Sarafuliyeva, S. S., "Choice of multiprocessor system configuration for digital signal processing", translated in *USSR Report - Cybernetics, Computers and Automation Technology*, Foreign Broadcast Information Service, JPRS 83843, July 7, 1983.

Aloisio 87   Aloisio G., Fox, G., Kim, J. S., and Veneziani, N., "A concurrent implementation of the prime factor algorithm on the hypercube," unpublished Caltech report C^3P-468 (1987).

Amdahl 67   Amdahl, G. M., "Validity of the single processor approach to achieving large-scale computing capabilities," in *AFIPS Conference Proceedings 1967, 30*, AFIPS Press, Montvale, N.J. (1967), 483.

ANSI 87   *Draft Proposed American National Standard for Information Systems - Programming Language C*, 1987. Accredited Standards Committee, X3 Secretariat, 311 First St. N.W., Suite 500, Wash. DC 20001.

Appel 85   Appel, A.W., "An efficient program for many-body simulation," *SIAM J. Sci. Stat. Comput., 6*, (1985), 85.

Arvind 87   Arvind and Nikhil, R. S., "Executing a program on the MIT tagged-token dataflow architecture," PARLE Conference, in *Lecture Notes in Computer Science, 259*, edited by G. Goos and J. Hartmanis, Springer-Verlag, New York (1987), 1.

Ashcroft 81   Ashcroft, J., Eldridge, R. H., Paulson, R. W., and Wilson, G. A., *Programming with Fortran 77*, Published by Granada Publishing Ltd., St. Albans, Herts., 1981.

Askew 86   Askew, C. R., Carpenter, D. B., Chalker, J. T., Hey, A. J. G., Nicole, D. A., and Pritchard, D. J., "Monte carlo simulations on transputer arrays", *Computer Physics Communications, 42* (1986), 21.

Athens 87   Proceedings of ICS87, International Conference on Supercomputing, published by Springer-Verlag, New York, as *A Lecture Note in Computer Science*, Edited by C. Polychronoupolos.

ATT 84   *UNIX System V (Release 2.0) Programmer Reference Manual*, sections 2 and 3, 1984.

Baden 87   Baden, S. B., "Run-time partitioning of scientific continuum calculations running on multiprocessors," Ph.D. Dissertation, UC Berkeley, 1987.

Barhen 87   Barhen, J., Einstein, J. R., Jorgensen, C. C., "Advances in concurrent computation for machine intelligence and robotics," in the *Proceedings of the Second International Conference on Supercomputing*, Published by the International Supercomputing Institute Inc., St. Petersburg, Florida, May 1987, Caltech report C^3P -418.

Barkai 84   Barkai, D., Moriarity, K. J. M., and Rebbi C., "A highly optimized vectorized code for Monte Carlo simulations of SU(3) lattice gauge theories," *Computer Physics Communications, 32* (1984), 1.

Barnes 86   Barnes, J. and Hut, P., "A hierarchical O(NlogN) force calculation algorithm," *Nature*, 324, (1986), 446.

Barron 83   Barron, I. M., Cavill, P., May, D., and Wilson, P., "The transputer,"*Electronics* (Nov. 17, 1983), 109.

Batcher 68   Batcher, K. E., "Sorting networks and their applications," in *AFIPS Conference Proceedings 1968, 32,* AFIPS Press, Montvale, N.J. (1968), 307.

Batcher 85   Batcher, K. E., "MPP: A high speed image processor," in *Algorithmically Specialized Parallel Computers*, Academic Press, New York (1985).

Bathe 82   Bathe, K-J., *Finite Element Procedures in Engineering Analysis*, Prentice-Hall, Englewood Cliffs, N.J. (1982).

Baudet 78   Baudet, G. and Stevenson, D., "Optimal sorting algorithms for parallel computers," *IEEE Transactions on Computers, C-27,* (1987), 84.

Beetem 86   Beetem, J., Denneau, M., and Weingarten, D., "GF 11" in *Proceedings of the Conference on Frontiers of Quantum Monte Carlo*, September 3-6, 1985 at Los Alamos, edited by J. E. Gubernatis, *Journal of Statistical Physics 43*, numbers 5/6 (June 1986).

Bell 85   Bell, C. G., "Multis: a new class of multiprocessor computers," *Science, 228*, (1985) 462.

Breaden 86   Breaden, M., Chang, D., Chen, S., and O'Dea, J., "SURFCUBE: the development of a small hypercube for personal computers," (October 1986), Unpublished Caltech report C^3P -374.

Brooks 84   Brooks, E. III, et al., "Pure gauge SU(3) lattice gauge theory on an array of computers," *Phys. Rev. Lett.*, 52, (1984), 2324, Caltech report C^3P -65.

Brown 83   Brown, F. B., "Vectorized Monte Carlo methods for reactor lattice analysis." Talk given at *Conference on Monte Carlo Methods and Future Computer Architectures*, Brookhaven National Laboratory, (April 2-5, 1983).

Buzbee 87   Buzbee, B., "Supercomputers: values and trends," *Int. Journal of Supercomputer Applications 1*, (1987) 100.

Chan 86   Chan, A., Saad, Y., and Schultz, M., "Solving elliptic partial differential equations on the hypercube multiprocessor", *Supercomputer, 13*, (1986), 35.

Chan 87   Chan, T. F. and Tuminaro, R. S., "Implementation of multigrid algorithms on hypercubes," published in *Hypercube Multiprocessors, 1987*, edited by M. T. Heath, SIAM (1987) 730.

Christ 86   Christ, N. H., "Lattice gauge theory with a fast highly parallel computer," in *Proceedings of the Conference on Frontiers of Quantum Monte Carlo*, September 3-6, 1985 at Los Alamos, edited by J. E. Gubernatis, *Journal of Statistical Physics 43*, numbers 5/6 (June 1986).

Chu 87   Chu, E. and George, A., "Gaussian elimination with partial pivoting and load balancing on a multiprocessor," *Parallel Computing, 5*, (1987), 65.

Cisneros 85   Cisneros, A., "Scalar products on the hypercube," Unpublished Caltech report C^3P-199 (1985).

Cisneros 87   Cisneros, A., "A communications system for irregular local interaction problems on a concurrent computer," *Comp. Phys. Comm.*, 46, (1987), 35, Caltech report C^3P-317.

Clayton 84   Clayton, R. W., "Finite difference solutions of the acoustic wave equation on a concurrent processor," Unpublished Caltech report C^3P-89 (1984).

Clayton 87   Clayton, R., Hager, B. and Tanimoto, T., "Applications of concurrent processors in geophysics," in *Proceedings of the Second International Conference on Supercomputing*, Published by the International Supercomputing Institute Inc., St. Petersburg, Florida, (May 1987), Caltech report C^3P-317.

Clementi 87   Clementi, E. and Detrich, J., "Large scale parallel computation on a loosely coupled array of processors," printed in [Dongarra 87].

Cooley 65   Cooley, J. W. and Tukey, J. W., "An algorithm for the machine calculation of complex fourier series", *Mathematics of Computation, 19* (1965), 297.

Creutz 83   Creutz, M., *Quarks, Lattices and Gluons*, Cambridge University Press, Cambridge, Great Britain (1983).

Dally 86   Dally, W., and Seitz, C., "A VLSI architecture for concurrent data structures," *J. Distributed Systems 1* (1986), 187.

Dantzig 68   Dantzig, G. B., *Linear Programming and Extensions*, Princeton University Press, Princeton, N.J. (1968).

DAP 79   "The DAP approach," *Infotech State of the Art Report: Supercomputers, 2* edited by Jesshope, C. R. and Hockney, R. W., Infotech Intl. Ltd., Maidenhead (1979), 311-29.

Dennis 74   Dennis, J. B., "First version of a dataflow procedure language," in *Proc. Programming Symposium, Paris 1974*, edited by G. Goos and J. Hartmanis, Springer-Verlag, New York (1974).

Dewdney 84   Dewdney, A. K., "Computer recreations," *Scientific American*, (December 1984).

Dippe 84   Dippe, M. E. and Swensen, J. A., "An adaptive subdivision algorithm and parallel architecture for realistic image synthesis," *SIGGRAPH '84 Conference Proceedings*, (1984), 149.

Dippe 85   Dippe, M. A. Z. and Wold, E. H., "Antialiasing through stochastic sampling," *Computer Graphics 19*, 69. Also appeared in *SIGGRAPH '85 Conference Proceedings*, (1985).

Dongarra 85   Dongarra, J. J. and Sorensen, D. C. "A fully parallel algorithm for the symmetric eigenvalue problem," *Second SIAM Conference on Vector and Parallel Processing in Scientific Computing*, Virginia, (Nov. 20, 1985).

Dongarra 87   *Experimental Parallel Computing Architectures*, edited by J. J. Dongarra, North-Holland, Amsterdam (1987).

Donath 79   Donath, W. E., "Placement and average interconnection lengths of computer logic," *IEEE Trans. Circuits and Systems 16*, (1979) 272.

Duff 84   Duff, S. I., "Supercomputers in Europe," *Parallel Computing 1*, (1984) 321.

Duff 87   Update of [Duff 84] published in the Proceedings of ICS 87, International Conference on Supercomputing published by Springer-Verlag, New York, as *Lecture Note in Computer Science*, edited by C. Polychronoupolos.

Felten 85a   Felten, E., Karlin, S., and Otto, S., "Sorting on a hypercube," to appear in the *Journal of Parallel and Distributed Computing*, Caltech report, C^3P-244 (1985).

Felten 85b   Felten, E., Karlin, S., and Otto, S., "The traveling salesman problem on a hypercube, MIMD Computer," *Proceedings of 1985 International Conference of Parallel Processing*, St. Charles, IL., 1985, Caltech report C^3P-93b.

Felten 86a   Felten, E., Morison, R., Otto, S., Barish, K., Fätland, R., and Ho, F., "Chess on the hypercube," published in *Hypercube Multiprocessors, 1987*, edited by M. T. Heath, SIAM (1987) 327, Caltech report C^3P-383.

Felten 86b   Felten, E., "Linear programming on a distributed memory multiprocessor," unpublished Caltech report C^3P-467 (1987).

Felten 87   Felten, E., "Parallel branch and bound algorithms," Unpublished Caltech report C^3P-457 (1987).

Feynman 65   Feynman, R. P., and Hibbs, A. R., *Quantum Mechanics and Path Integrals*, McGraw-Hill, New York (1965).

Forty 85   Forty, A. J., "Future facilities for advanced research computing." Joint working party report for Advisory Board for the Research Councils, Computer Board for Universities, and Research Councils University Grants Committee, (June, 1985) Dept. of Education and Science, Elizabeth House, London.

Flower 86   Flower, J., Otto, S. W., and Salama, M., "A preprocessor for finite element problems," to appear in *Proceedings, Symposium on Parallel Computations and Their Impact on Mechanics*, ASME Winter Meeting, Dec. 14-16," Boston, Mass., (1987), Caltech report C^3P-292.

Fox 84a   Fox, G. and Otto, S., "Algorithms for concurrent processors," *Physics Today* (May 1984), Caltech report C^3P-71.

Fox 84b   Fox, G., "Use of concurrent processors in (high-energy physics) data analysis," Unpublished Caltech report, C^3P-129 (1984).

Fox 84c   Fox, G., "On the sequential component of computation," Unpublished Caltech report, C^3P-130 (1984).

Fox 84d   Fox, G., "Square matrix decomposition: symmetric, local, scattered," Unpublished Caltech report, C^3P-97 (1984).

Fox 85a   Fox, G., Otto, S. W., Umland, E. A., "Monte Carlo physics on a concurrent processor" in *Proceedings of the Conference on Frontiers of Quantum Monte Carlo*, September 3-6, 1985 at Los Alamos, edited by J. E. Gubernatis, *Journal of Statistical Physics 43*, numbers 5/6 (June 1986), Caltech report C^3P-214.

Fox 85b   Fox, G., Hey, A. J. G, and Otto, S., "Matrix algorithms on the hypercube I: matrix multiplication," *Parallel Computing, 4,* (1987), 17, Caltech report C^3P-206.

Fox 85c   Fox, G., "The performance of the Caltech hypercube in scientific calculations: A preliminary analysis," *Supercomputers-Algorithms, Architectures, and Scientific Computation*, edited by F. A. Matsen and T. Tajima, University of Texas Press (1987), Caltech report C^3P-161.

Fox 86a   Fox, G. and Otto, S., "Concurrent computation and the theory of complex systems," published in *Hypercube Multiprocessors, 1986*, edited by M. T. Heath, SIAM (1986) 244, Caltech report C^3P-255.

Fox 86b   Fox, G. and Furmanski, W., "Optimal communication algorithms on the Hypercube" Unpublished Caltech report C^3P-314 (1986).

Fox 86c   Fox, G. and Furmanski, W., "Communication algorithms for regular convolutions on the hypercube," published in *Hypercube Multiprocessors, 1987*, edited by M. T. Heath, SIAM (1987) 223, Caltech report C^3P-329.

Fox 86d   Fox, G., "Load balancing and sparse matrix-vector multiplication on the hypercube," to be published in *Proceedings of IMA Workshop, Minnesota* (November 1986), edited by M. Schultz, Caltech report C^3P-327B.

Fox 86e   Fox, G., "Iterative full matrix-vector multiplication on the hypercube," Unpublished Caltech report C^3P-336 (1986).

Fox 86f   Fox, G., "Annual report of the Caltech Concurrent Computation Program 1985-86," published in *Hypercube Multiprocessors, 1987*, edited by M. T. Heath, SIAM (1987) 353, Caltech report C^3P-290B.

Fox 86g   Fox, G., "A review of automatic load balancing and decomposition methods for the hypercube," to be published in *Proceedings of IMA Workshop*, Minnesota (November 1986), edited by M. Schultz, Caltech report C^3P-385.

Fox 86h   Fox, G., Kolawa, A., and Williams, R., "The implementation of a dynamic load balancer," Published in *Hypercube Multiprocessors, 1987*, edited by M. T. Heath, SIAM (1987) 114, Caltech report C^3P-328.

Fox 86i   Fox, G. and Furmanski, W., "Load balancing by a neural network," Unpublished Caltech report, C^3P-363 (1986).

Fox 87   Fox, G., "Domain decomposition in distributed and shared memory environments I," to be published as *Lecture Note in Computer Science*, Springer-Verlag, New York, edited by C. Polychronopoulos, Caltech report C^3P-392 (1987).

Frankel 86   Frankel, A., and Clayton, R. W., "Finite difference simulations of seismic scattering: implications for the propagation of short-period seismic waves in the crust and models of crustal heterogeneity," *J. Geophys. Res. 91*, (1986), 6465, Caltech report C^3P-203.

Frederickson 83   Frederickson, P., Hiromoto, R., Jordan, T., Smith, B., Warnock, T., "Pseudo-random trees in Monte Carlo". proceedings, *Conference on Monte Carlo Methods and Future Computer Architectures*, Brookhaven National Laboratory (April 2-5, 1983).

Frederickson 87   Frederickson P. O. and McBryan O. A., "Parallel superconvergent multigrid," to be published in *Applied Math. Series*, Marcel-Decker, (1987).

Frenkel 86   "Special issue on parallelism; Connection Machine and shared memory," edited by K. A. Frenkel, *Communications of the ACM 29*, (1986), pp. 1168-1239.

Fucito 85   Fucito, F., and Solomon, S., "Monte Carlo parallel algorithm for long-range interactions," *Computer Physics Communications 34*, (1985), 225, Caltech report C^3P-79b.

Furmanski 86   Furmanski, W. and Fox, G., "Matrix", paper in preparation, (1986), Caltech report C^3P-386.

Furmanski 87a   Furmanski, W., Bower, J. M., Nelson, M. E., Wilson, M. A., and Fox, G., "Piriform (Olfactory) cortex model on the hypercube," (February 1987), Caltech report C^3P-404.

Furmanski 87b   Furmanski, W. and Fox, G. C., "Hypercube communication for neural network algorithms," (February 1987), Caltech report C^3P-405.

Gabriel 86   Gabriel, R. P., "Massively parallel computers: the Connection Machine and Non-Von," *Science 231*, (1986) 975.

Gaines 86   Gaines, I., Areti, H., Atac, R., Biel, J., Cook, A., Fischler, M., Hance, R., Husby, D., Nash, T., and Zmuda, T., "The ACP multiprocessor system at Fermilab," invited talk at 1987 Asilomar Conference on Computing in High Energy Physics, published in *Computer Physics Communications 45*, (1987) 323.

Gaines 87   Gaines, I. and Nash, T., "Use of new computer technologies in elementary particle physics," *Ann. Rev. Nucl. Part. Sci.*, 37 (1987), edited by J. D. Jackson, published by Annual Reviews Inc., 4139 El Camino Real, P. O. Box 10139, Palo Alto, CA 94303-0897.

Gehringer 87   Gehringer, E. F., Siewiorek, D. P. and Segall, Z., "Parallel processing: the Cm∗ experience," published by Digital Equipment Corp., Bedford, Mass. (1987).

Geist 86   Geist, G. A. and Heath, M. T., "Matrix factorization on a hypercube multiprocessor," *Hypercube Multiprocessors* 1986, ed. by M. T. Heath, SIAM, Philadelphia (1986), 161.

Geist 87   Geist, G. A. and Romine, C. H., "LU factorization algorithms on distributed-memory multiprocessor architectures," *SIAM J. Sci. Stat. Comput.,* to appear (1987).

Gilbert 58   Gilbert, E. N., "Gray codes and paths on the n-cube," *Bell System Technical Journal, 37,* (May 1958), 815.

Goddard 85   Goddard, W. A. III, "Theoretical chemistry comes alive: Full partner with experiment," *Science 227,* (1985), 917.

Goldsmith 86   Goldsmith, J., and Salmon, J., "Static and dynamic database distribution for graphics ray tracing on the hypercube," Unpublished Caltech report C^3P-360 (1986).

Goldsmith 87   Goldsmith, J. and Salmon, J., "Automatic creation of object hierarchies for ray tracing," *IEEE, CG and A, 14* (1987), Caltech report C^3P-295.

Good 58   Good, I. J., "The interaction algorithm and practical Fourier analysis," *J. Royal Statistical Society 20B,* (1958), 361.

Gottlieb 86   Gottlieb, A., "An overview of the NYU ultracomputer project," printed in [Dongarra 87].

Gottschalk 87   Gottschalk, T. D., "Multiple track initiation on a hypercube," in the *Proceedings of the Second International Conference on Supercomputing,* Published by the International Supercomputing Institute Inc., St. Petersburg, Florida (May 1987), Caltech report C^3P-398.

Grassberger 83   Grassberger, P., and Procaccia, I., "Measuring the strangeness of strange attractors," *Physica 9D* (1983), 189.

Greengard 87   Greengard, L., "The rapid evaluation of potential fields in particle systems," Yale research report YALEU / DCS / RR-533 (April 1987).

Grunwald 87   Grunwald, D. C. and Reed, D. A., "Benchmarking hypercube hardware and software," Published in *Hypercube Multiprocessors, 1987,* Edited by M. T. Heath, SIAM (1987) 169.

Haynes 82   Haynes, L. S., Lau, R. L., Siewiorek, D. P. and Mizell, D. W., "A survey of highly parallel computing," *Computer* (Jan. 1982), 9.

Hayot 87   Hayot, F., Mandal, M. and Sadayappen, P., "Implementation and performance of a binary lattice gas algorithm on parallel processor systems," Ohio State University report (1987).

Heath 87   Heath, M. T., "Hypercube applications at Oak Ridge National Laboratory," in *Hypercube Multiprocessors 1987*, ed. by M. T. Heath, SIAM, Philadelphia (1987), 395.

Held 70   Held, M. and Karp, R. M., "The traveling salesman problem and minimum spanning trees," *Oper. Res. 18,* (1970) 1138.

Held 71   Held, M. and Karp, R. M., "The traveling salesman problem and minimum spanning trees: Part II," *Mathematical Programming 1* (1971) 6.

Hillis 85   Hillis, W. D., *The Connection Machine*, MIT Press, Cambridge, Mass. (1985).

Hillis 87   Hillis, W. D., "The Connection Machine," *Scientific American*, (June 1987) 108.

Hipes 86   Hipes, P. and Kuppermann, A., "Gauss-Jordan matrix inversion with pivoting on the hypercube," Unpublished Caltech report, C^3P-347, (1986).

Ho 86a   Ho, C-T., Johnsson, S. L., "Distributed routing algorithms for broadcasting and personalized communication in hypercubes," *Proceedings of IEEE 1986 International Conference on Parallel Processing*, (1986).

Ho 86b   Ho, C-T., Johnsson, S. L., "Matrix transposition on Boolean n-cube configured ensemble architectures," Yale report YALEU/DCS/TR-494 (September 1986).

Hoare 62   Hoare, C. A. R., "Quicksort," *Computer J. 5*, (October 15, 1962) 10.

Hoare 78   Hoare, C. A. R., "Communicating sequential processes" *Communications of the ACM 21*, (1978) 666.

Hockney 81a   Hockney, R. W., and Eastwood, J. W., Chapter 8, in *Computer Simulation Using Particles*, McGraw-Hill, New York (1981).

Hockney 81b   Hockney, R. W., and Jesshope, C. R., *Parallel Computers*, Adam Hilger, Bristol, Great Britain (1981).

Hopfield 82   Hopfield, J. J., "Neural networks and physical systems with emergent collective computational abilities," *Proc. Natl. Acad. Sci USA, 79* (1982) 2554.

Hopfield 86   Hopfield, J. J. and Tank, D. W., "Computing with neural circuits: a model," *Science 233* (1986), 625.

Hughes 87   Hughes, T. J., *The finite element method: linear static and dynamic finite element analysis*, Prentice-Hall, Englewood Cliffs, N.J. (1987).

Ipsen 87   Ipsen, I. C. F. and Jessup, E., "Two methods for solving the symmetric tridiagonal eigenvalue problem on the hypercube," published in *Hypercube Multiprocessors, 1987*, edited by M. T. Heath, SIAM (1987) 627.

Jefferson 85   Jefferson, D., and Sowizral, H., "Fast concurrent simulation using the time-warp mechanism," *SCG Conference on Distributed Simulation*, San Diego, CA. (January 1985).

Jennings 77   Jennings, A., *Matrix Computation for Engineers and Scientists*, John Wiley & Sons, New York (1977).

Johnson 84   Johnson, S., "Combining parallel and sequential sorting on a Boolean n-cube," *Proceedings, IEEE 1984 International Conference on Parallel Processing*, (1984) 444-48.

Johnson 85   Johnson, M. A., "The interrupt-driven communication system," Unpublished Caltech report C^3P-137 (1985).

Johnson 86   Johnson, M. A., "Concurrent computation and its application to the study of melting in two dimensions," Caltech Ph.D. dissertation (1986), Caltech report C^3P-268.

Johnsson 85   Johnsson, L., "Band-matrix systems solvers on ensemble architectures," in *Supercomputers - Algorithms, Architectures and Scientific Computation*, eds. T. Tajima and F. A. Matsen, University of Texas Press (1987).

Johnsson 87   Johnsson, L. and Ho, C-T., "Matrix multiplication on Boolean cubes using generic communication primitives," to appear in *Proceedings of the ARO Workshop on Parallel Processing and Medium-Scale Multiprocessors,* (1986).

Kalos 86   Kalos, M. H., "Monte Carlo methods and the computers of the future," in *Supercomputers - Algorithms, Architectures, and Scientific Computation,* edited by F. A. Matsen and T. Tajima, University of Texas Press (1987).

Karin 87   Karin, S. and Smith, N. P., *The Supercomputer Era,* Academic Press, New York (1987).

Karlin 85   Karlin, S., Suggs, B., "A 68010 based concurrent processor," Caltech EE91 term paper (fall 1985), unpublished Caltech report C^3P-246.

Karmarkar 84   Karmarkar, N., "A new polynomial time algorithm for linear programming," *Combinatorica 4* (1984), 373.

Karp 77   Karp, R. M., "Probabilistic analysis of partitioning algorithms for the traveling-salesman problem in the plane," *Math. of Operations Res. 2,3* (1977), 209.

Karplus 87   "Multiprocessors and array processors," edited by W. J. Karplus, *Proceedings of the Third Conference on Multiprocessors and Array Processors, Simulation Series, 18,* The Society for Computer Simulation, San Diego (1987).

Kirkpatrick 83   Kirkpatrick, S., Gelatt, C. D., and Vecchi, M. P., "Optimization by simulated annealing," *Science 220,* (May 1983), 671.

Kittel 76   Kittel, C., *Introduction to Solid State Physics,* 5th Ed. John Wiley & Sons, New York (1976), 76-82.

Knuth 73a   Knuth, D. E., *Sorting and Searching, The Art of Computer Programming, Vol. 3,* Addison-Wesley, Reading, Mass. (1973).

Knuth 73b   Knuth, D. E., *Seminumerical Algorithms, The Art of Computer Programming, Vol. 2,* Addison-Wesley, Reading, Mass. (1973).

Knuth 73c   Knuth, D. E., *Fundamental Algorithms, The Art of Computer Programming, Vol. 1*, Addison-Wesley, Reading, Mass. (1973).

Kolawa 85   Kolawa, A. and Otto, S. W., "Performance of the Mark II and INTEL hypercubes," published in *Hypercube Multiprocessors, 1986*, edited by M. T. Heath, SIAM (1986) 272, Caltech report C^3P-254.

Kolawa 86   Kolawa, A. and Fox, G., "Concurrent searching of a database—an application of the hypercube to symbolic quantum chromodynamics," unpublished Caltech report C^3P-182B, (1986).

Krämer 87   Krämer, O. and Mühlenbein, H., "Mapping strategies in message based multiprocessor systems," PARLE Conference, in *Lecture Notes in Computer Science, 258*, edited by G. Goos and J. Hartmanis, Springer-Verlag, New York (1987), 213.

Kung 80   Kung, H. T. and Leiserson, C. E., *Introduction to VLSI systems*, Sec. 8.3, by C. Mead and L. Conway, Addison-Wesley, Reading, Mass. (1980).

Kuck 86   Kuck, D. J., Davidson, E. S., Lawrie, D. H., Sameh, A. H., "Parallel supercomputing today and the Cedar approach," *Science 231*, (1986), 967.

Kuppermann 86   Kuppermann, A., and Hipes, P. G., *J. Chem Phys, 84* (1986), 55.

Landman 71   Landman, B. S. and Russo, R. L., "On a pin versus block relationship for partitions of logic graphs," *IEEE Trans. Comp. C20*, (1971) 1469.

Lazou 87   Lazou, C., *Supercomputers and Their Use*, Oxford University Press, Oxford, Great Britain, (1987).

Leonard 80   Leonard, A. "Vortex methods for flow simulation," *J. Computational Physics 37* (1980), 289.

Leonard 87   Chua K. and Leonard, A., "Three dimensional vortex methods and the vortex reconnection problem," *Bulletin of the American Physical Society*, to be published (1987).

Li 86   Li, P. P., "Parallel sorting on the Ametek/S14," (Sept. 1986) available from the Ametek Corporation, Arcadia, CA.

Lin 65   Lin, S., "Computer solutions of the traveling salesman problem," *The Bell System Technical Journal 44*, (December 1965), 2245.

Lin 73   Lin, S. and Kernighan, B. W., "An effective heuristic algorithm for the traveling salesman problem," *Oper. Res. 21* (1973), 498.

Lorenz 87   Lorenz, J. and Noerdlinger P. D., "Analysis of strange attractors on the hypercube," Unpublished report C^3P-400 (1987).

Luenberger 84   Luenberger, D., *Linear and Nonlinear Programming, 2nd* Ed., Addison-Wesley, Reading, Mass. (1984).

Lyzenga 85   Lyzenga, G. A., Raefsky, A., and Hager, B. H., "Finite elements and the method of conjugate gradients on a concurrent processor," in *Proceedings of the 1985 ASME International Computers in Engineering,* Boston (August 4-8, 1985), Caltech report C^3P-164.

Mandelbrot 79   Mandelbrot, B., *Fractals: Form, Chance, and Dimension,* Freeman, San Francisco, Calif. (1979).

Marinari 86   Marinari, E., "The APE computer and lattice gauge theory," *Proceedings of the Wuppertal Workshop on Lattice Gauge Theory,* edited by R. Burk, K. H. Mütter, and K. Schilling, Plenum Press, New York (1986).

Martin 67   Martin, R. S., and Wilkinson, J. H., "Solution of symmetric and unsymmetric band equations and the calculation of eigenvectors of band matrices," *Numerische Mathematik 9*, (1967), 279.

Mead 80   Mead, C. and Conway L., *Introduction to VLSI Systems*, Addison-Wesley, Reading, Mass. (1980).

Meier 84   Meier, D., "Two-dimensional one-fluid hydrodynamics: an astrophysical test problem for the nearest neighbor concurrent processor," unpublished Caltech report C^3P-90 (1984).

Messina 87   Fox, G. and Messina, P., "Advanced computer architectures," *Scientific American,* (Oct. 1987).

Metropolis 53   Metropolis, N., Rosenbluth, A. W., Rosenbluth, M. N., Teller, A. H., Teller, E., "Equation of state calculations by fast computing machines," *J. Chem Phys 21* (1953), 1087.

Moler 86   Moler, C., "Matrix computation on distributed memory multiprocessors," published in *Hypercube Multiprocessors, 1986*, edited by M. T. Heath, SIAM (1986) 181.

Montry 87   Montry, G. R. and Benner, R. E., "Parallel processing on an ELXSI 6400," in the *Proceedings of the Second International Conference on Supercomputing,* Published by the International Supercomputing Institute Inc., St. Petersburg, Florida (May 1987).

Morison 86   Morison, R. and Otto, S. W., "The scattered decomposition for finite element problems," *Journal of Scientific Computing 2*, (1986), Caltech report C^3P-286.

Muller 85   Muller, A., "Element-by-element iterative procedures in structural finite element analysis," Ph.D. thesis, Stanford University (1985).

Nassimi 79   Nassimi, D., and Sahni, S., "Bitonic sort on a mesh-connected parallel computer," *IEEE Trans. Comp. 27*, (1979), 2.

Noerdlinger 86   Noerdlinger, P. D. and Walker, D. W., "Discrete Fourier transforms on the Mark II Hypercube," (1986), unpublished Caltech report C^3P-337.

Nour-Omid 87a   Nour-Omid, B., and Park, K. C., "Solving structural mechanics problems on the Caltech hypercube machine," *Computer Methods in Applied Mechanics and Engineering 61*, (1987) 161.

Nour-Omid 87b   Nour-Omid, B., Raefsky, A. and Lyzenga, G., "Solving finite element equations on concurrent computers," *Proceedings of the Symposium on Parallel Computations and Their Impact on Mechanics*, ASME, Boston (Dec. 13-18, 1987).

O'Neil 87   O'Neil, E., Allik, H., Moore, S., and Tenenbaum, E., "Finite element analysis on the BBN Butterfly multiprocessor," in the *Proceedings of the Second International Conference on Supercomputing,* published by the International Supercomputing Institute Inc., St. Petersburg, Florida, (May 1987).

Ortega 85 Ortega, J. M. and Voight, R. G., "Solution of partial differential equations on vector and parallel computers," *SIAM Review, 27,* (1985), 149.

Otto 84a Otto, S. W., and Stack, J. D., "SU(3) Heavy-quark potential with high statistics," *Phys. Rev. Lett., 52,* (1984), 2328, Caltech report C^3P-67.

Otto 84b Otto, S., "Lattice gauge theories on a hypercube computer," *Proceedings, Argonne National Laboratory Workshop, Gauge Theory on a Lattice,* (1984), Caltech report C^3P-91.

Palmer 86 Palmer, J., "The NCUBE: A VLSI parallel supercomputer," *Hypercube Multiprocessors, 1986,* edited by M. T. Heath, SIAM (1986) 19.

Papadimitriou 82 Papadimitriou, C. H., and Steiglitz, K., *Combinatorial Optimization: Algorithms and Complexity*, Prentice-Hall, Englewood Cliffs, N.J. (1982).

Percus 87 Percus, O. E. and Kalos, M. H., "Random number generators for ultracomputers," *Ultracomputer Note No. 114* (Feb. 1987), Courant Institute, NYU.

Peterson 85a Peterson, J. C., et al., "The Mark III hypercube ensemble concurrent computer," *IEEE 1985 Conference on Parallel Processing,* St. Charles, IL., (August 1985), Caltech report C^3P-151.

Peterson 85b Peterson, V. L., "Use of supercomputers in computational aerodynamics," *Proceedings of the 1985 Science and Engineering Symposium,* Cray Research Inc., Minneapolis (1985).

Pfister 85 Pfister, G. F., et al., "The IBM research parallel processor prototype (RP3): introduction and architecture," *IEEE 1985 Conference on Parallel Processing,* St. Charles, IL., (August 1985).

Pollara 85 Pollara, F., "Concurrent Viterbi algorithm on a hypercube," in *Proceedings of the 23rd Annual Allerton Conference on Communication Control and Computing,* ed. Hajek, B., Munson Jr., D. C., Univ. of Illinois, (October 85), Caltech report C^3P-208.

Pollara 86   Pollara F., "Concurrent Viterbi algorithm with trace-back," in August 1986 Conference of International Society of Optical Engineering, *Advanced Algorithms and Architectures for Signal Processing*, Vol. 696 of SPIE Proceedings, 204 (1986), Caltech report C^3P -462.

Pritchard 87   Pritchard, D. J., Askew, C. R., Carpenter, D. B., Glendinning, I., Hey, A. J. G. and Nicole, D. A., "Practical parallelism using transputer arrays," PARLE Conference, in *Lecture Notes in Computer Science, 258*, edited by G. Goos and J. Hartmanis, Springer-Verlag, New York (1987), 278.

Quinlan 87   Quinlan, J. and Siewiorek, D., "Baseline measurements of the Mark II hypercube," published in *Hypercube Multiprocessors, 1987*, edited by M. T. Heath, SIAM (1987) 200.

Rader 68   Rader, C. M., "Discrete Fourier transforms when the number of data samples is prime," *Proc. IEEE 56*, (1968) 1107.

Rattner 85   Rattner, J., "Concurrent processing: A new direction in scientific computing," in *Conf. Proc. 1985 National Computing Conference 54*, (1985), 157.

Reed 87   Reed, D. A., Adams, L. M., and Patrick, M. L., "Stencils and problem partitionings: their influence on the performance of multiple processor systems," *IEEE Transactions on Computers, C36*, (1987), 845.

Salmon 86   Salmon, J. and Hogan, C., "Correlation of QSO absorption lines in universes dominated by cold dark matter," *Monthly Notices of the Royal Astronomical Society, 221*, (1986), 93, Caltech report C^3P - 211.

Salmon 87   Salmon, J., "CUBIX: programming hypercubes without programming hosts," published in *Hypercube Multiprocessors, 1987*, edited by M. T. Heath, SIAM (1987), 3, Caltech report C^3P -378.

Sameh 85   Sameh, A., "Numerical algorithms on the Cedar system," *Second SIAM Conference on Vector and Parallel Processing in Scientific Computing*, Virginia, (November 20, 1985).

Schemer 84   Schemer, J. and Neches, P., "The genesis of a database computer," *IEEE Computer Magazine,* (November 1984), 19.

Schilling 87   Schilling, K., "Lattice QCD - a challenge in large scale computing," *Comp. Phys. Comm. 44*, (1987), 261.

Schmidt 87   Schmidt, G. E., "The Butterfly parallel processor," in the *Proceedings of the Second International Conference on Supercomputing,* published by the International Supercomputing Institute inc., St. Petersburg, Florida, May 1987.

Schwartz 80   Schwartz, J. T., "Ultracomputers," *ACM TOPLAS, 2,* (October 1980), 484.

Seitz 84a   Seitz, C. L., and Matisoo, J., "Engineering limits on computer performance," *Physics Today,* (May 1984), 38.

Seitz 84b   Seitz, C. L., "Concurrent VLSI architectures," *IEEE Transactions on Computers, 33,* (1984), 1247.

Seitz 85   Seitz, C. L., "The cosmic cube", *Communications of the ACM 28,* (1985), 22.

Shaw 84   Shaw, "SIMD and MSIMD variants of the non-von supercomputer," *Proceedings of IEEE Compcon 1984*, San Francisco, IEEE Computer Society Press (1984).

Shell 59   Shell, D. L., "A high-speed sorting procedure," *Communications of the ACM, 2,* (1959), 30.

Siegel 79   Siegel, H. J., "Interconnection networks for SIMD machines," *Computer,* (June 1979), 57.

Solomon 84   Solomon, J., Lee, M., and Fox, G. "Image processing and the hypercube —Analysis of initial implementation," unpublished Caltech report C^3P -132, (1984).

Theiler 86   Theiler, J., "Spurious dimension from correlation algorithms applied to limited time-series data," *Phys. Rev. A, 34,* (1986) 2427, Caltech report C^3P -274a.

Theiler 87   Theiler, J., "An efficient algorithm for estimating correlation dimension from a set of discrete points," Phys. Rev. A. to be published, Caltech report (1987).

Thompson 77   Thompson, C. D. and Kung, H. T., "Sorting on a mesh-connected parallel computer," *Communications of the ACM, 20,* 1977, 263.

Tuazon 85   Tuazon, J. et al., "Caltech/JPL hypercube concurrent processor," *IEEE 1985 Conference on Parallel Processing,* St Charles, Illinois, August 1985, Caltech report C^3P-160.

Utku 86   Utku, S., Melosh, R., and Salama, M., "Concurrent Cholesky factorization of positive definite banded Hermitean matrices," *Int. J. Numerical Methods in Engineering, 23* (1986) 2137.

Van de Velde 87a   Van de Velde, E. F. and Keller, H. B., "The design of a parallel multigrid algorithm," in the *Proceedings of the Second International Conference on Supercomputing at Santa Clara,* May 1987, published by the International Supercomputing Institute, Inc., St. Petersburg, Florida (May 1987), Caltech report C^3P-406.

Van de Velde 87b   Van de Velde, E. F. and Keller, H. B., "The parallel solution of nonlinear elliptic equations," Caltech report C^3P-447 (1987).

Vegdahl 84   Vegdahl, S. R., "A survey of proposed architectures for the execution of functional languages," *IEEE Transactions on Computers, C-33,* (1984), 1050.

Wagar 86   Wagar, B., "Hyperquicksort - a fast sorting algorithm for hypercubes," in, *Hypercube Multiprocessors, 1987,* edited by M. T. Heath, SIAM (1987), 292.

Walker 86   Walker, D., Montry, G., Fox, G., and Ho, A., "A comparison of the performance of the Caltech Mark II hypercube and the ELXSI 6400," published in *Hypercube Multiprocessors, 1987,* edited by M. T. Heath, SIAM (1987), 210, Caltech report C^3P-356.

Wallace 84   Wallace, D. J., "Numerical simulation on the ICL distributed array processor," *Phys. Rep 103,* (1984), 191.

Werner 85   Werner, B. T. and Haff, P. K., "Dynamical simulations of granular materials using concurrent processing computers," (1985), Unpublished Caltech report C^3P-242.

Werner 87   Werner, B. T., "A physical model of wind-blown sand transport," Caltech Ph. D. dissertation (1987), unpublished Caltech report C^3P-425.

Whelan 85   Whelan, D., "ANIMAC-a multiprocessor architecture for real-time computer animation," Caltech Ph.D. Thesis (1985).

Wilhelmson 87   *High-speed computing: scientific applications and algorithm design*, edited by Robert Wilhelmson, University of Illinois Press (1987).

Wilson 86   Wilson, K. G., "The Gibbs project," in *Supercomputers - Algorithms, Architectures, and Scientific Computation,* edited by F. A. Matsen and T. Tajima, University of Texas Press (1987).

Winograd 75   Winograd, S., "Some bilinear forms whose multiplicative complexity depends on the field of constraints," *IBM Yorktown Report RC 5669,* (October 10, 1975).

Winograd 76   Winograd, S., "On computing the discrete Fourier Transform," *Proc. Nat. Acad. Sci. 73,* (1976), 1005.

Wolfram 86   Wolfram, S., *Theory and Applications of Cellular Automata,* World Scientific Publishing Co. (1986).

Zweben 83   Zweben, S. J. and Gould, R. W., "Scaling of edge-plasma turbulence in the Caltech tokamak," *Nuclear Fusion 23,* (1983), 1625.

The Glossary

Adaptive Mesh

In problems in which an approximate numerical solution is sought on a **mesh** of **nodal points**, an adaptive mesh is one in which the nodal points change dynamically as the numerical system evolves.

Amdahl's Law

Amdahl's Law states that the maximum concurrent **speedup** attainable for a concurrent algorithm is limited by its sequential components. Thus, if the sequential component takes a fraction, f_{seq}, of the total run time on one **node** of a **concurrent processor**, the maximum possible speedup is $1/f_{seq}$. This law is discussed in Sec. 3-6 and 20-4.

Architecture

The architecture of a computer describes the design of the hardware components of the computer system, and the ways in which these components interact to produce the complete machine. The architecture includes both topology and details of **node** for a **concurrent processor**.

Array or Computer Array

A rather loose term used to describe the set of **nodes** of a **concurrent processor**. This term implies but does not require that the processor has a geometric or matrix like connectivity.

Artificial Intelligence

This defines a class of problems such as pattern recognition, decision making and learning in which humans are clearly very proficient compared with current computers. The definition of artificial intelligence is imprecise and time dependent; some include computer algebra and game playing in this class.

Backsubstitution

See **LU decomposition**

Banded Matrices

A banded matrix is one in which the non-zero elements are clustered around the main diagonal. If all the non-zero elements in the matrix are within m columns of the main diagonal, then $2m+1$ is termed the **bandwidth** of the matrix.

Bandwidth

This is a measure of the speed of information transfer typically used to quantify the communication capability of **concurrent computers**. One can use bandwidth to measure both node to node and collective (bus) communication capability. Bandwidth is usually measured in megabytes of data per second. Also, see **banded matrices** for an entirely different use of bandwidth.

Blocking

Blocking is a term used to describe the action of read and write communication routines that wait until their function is complete. Blocking is usually implemented by means of **polling**, and is described in Chaps. 4, 14, and 22.

Cache

A fast memory used to hold commonly used variables which are automatically fetched by hardware from the slower and larger main computer memory.

Cellular Automaton

A cellular automaton is a collection of objects, cellular automata, each of which has a state that is a function of the state of the other objects, and which is evaluated according to a certain set of rules. The system evolves in a set of discrete steps, with each object evaluating its state at each step according to its rules, which may be different for different objects. A simple example of a cellular automaton is one in which the objects are rectangular cells arranged in a two-dimensional grid so that each cell has four neighbors. The state of a cell may either be 0 or 1, and the rule for all cells is: set your state to 0 if the sum of the states of your four neighbors is odd, otherwise set your state to 1.

Cellular Computer

A term used in Chap. 2 to describe fine grain computers including **neural networks, systolic array** and **SIMD** machines like the **Connection Machine**.

Channel Mask

A channel mask is a non-negative integer specifying a set of **communication channels**. If the numbers of the channels to be specified are $i_0, i_1,..., i_{N-1}$, then the channel mask is the integer for which these bit numbers are set to 1 and all other bits are 0. For example, if the channels to be specified are numbered 0, 1, and 4, the corresponding channel mask is the binary number 10011, or 19, in which bits number 0, 1, and 4 are set to 1.

477

Coarse Grain

> See **grain size.**

Collective Communication Routines

> These are routines which perform commonly used communication sequences as a single unit. Examples for CrOS III are *cshift, broadcast*, and *combine*.

Communication Channel

> A communication channel is a mechanism, such as a wire, a shared bus, or an optical fiber, by which messages may be passed from one node of a concurrent processor to another.

Communication Overhead

> The communication overhead is a measure of the additional workload incurred in a concurrent algorithm due to communication between the **nodes** of the **concurrent processor**. If communication is the only source of overhead, then the communication overhead is given by:

$$f_C = \frac{NT(N) - T(1)}{T(1)} \qquad \text{(G-1)}$$

> where $T(N)$ is the total time to run the algorithm on N nodes.

Complex System

> An abstraction used in Chap. 3 to discuss the global structure of problems and computers. Complex systems are associated with data **domains** which are divided into **grains, granules** and **members.**

Concurrent Computers or Concurrent Processors

> This book is devoted to the use of concurrent processors; these are loosely defined as a collection of individual **Von Neumann**, or **sequential**, nodes joined together to work on the same problem. We use **"concurrent"** and **"parallel"** as synonymous terms in this book. Sometimes concurrent is used to denote asynchronous, and parallel to denote synchronous or lockstep nodes. However, this distinction is not generally accepted. A good taxonomy of concurrent computers is given in [Bell 85]. He defines a **multicomputer** to be a machine like the hypercube which consists of a connected set of complete computers, A **multiprocessor** is defined by Bell to be a shared memory concurrent computer, but others use multiprocessor to be generally synonymous with concurrent processor.

Conjugate Gradient Method

> The conjugate gradient method is a linear algebraic system solver which proceeds by minimizing a quadratic residual error function. The method is iterative but quite powerful: in the absence of roundoff error, the method converges exactly in M steps, where M is the order of the system. The algorithm is specified in Sec. 8-3

and good discussion appears in [Jennings 77].

Connection Machine

An **SIMD** concurrent computer manufactured by the Thinking Machines Corporation with 65536 nodes. The techniques in this book are not directly applicable to this machine but are usually similar to algorithms useable on the Connection Machine.

Contention

Contention occurs when several processes attempt to access the same resource simultaneously. An example is memory contention in shared-memory multiprocessors, which occurs when two processors attempt to read from or write to a location in shared memory in the same clock cycle.

Control Process

The control process controls the execution of a program on a concurrent processor. The major tasks performed by the control process are to initiate execution of the program in each node of the concurrent processor, and to provide I/O facilities for the nodes.

CPU

CPU or central processing unit is used to designate the arithmetic and control portions of a **sequential computer**.

CrOS III Communication System

The CrOS III communication system is a set of routines for performing **loosely synchronous** communication between the **nodes** of a **hypercube concurrent processor**, and between the nodes and the **control process**.

Crystalline Operating System - CrOS - Crystalline Communication System

A crystalline operating system (CrOS) is an operating system which requires interprocessor communication operations between nodes of a **concurrent processor** to occur in a **loosely synchronous** fashion. A corollary to this definition is that crystalline communication operations must always be anticipated by all of the involved processes. This case is distinct from that of an **interrupt-driven system**. Generally CrOS is a synchronous communication system for a loosely synchronous problem. CrOS III is a version of CrOS specific to the hypercube. The calls to a CrOS communication routine synchronize the nodes involved. Sometimes we use the term "operating system" to describe CrOS although communication system is more accurate.

Crystal_Router Algorithm

This algorithm, described in Sec. 22-2, allows messages of arbitrary length to be passed between arbitrary nodes of a hypercube in a **loosely synchronous** environment using **CrOS**.

CUBIX

An extension of the basic **crystalline communication system** to allow the nodes of a **distributed memory concurrent processor** access to UNIX-like system calls; especially those for input/output.

Dataflow

A radical architecture for high performance concurrent computers in which computations are initiated by the arrival of data items; for instance in a dataflow computer, $a=b+c$ would be initiated when the computations of b and c are complete. The techniques of this book would not be directly applicable to such machines.

Deadlock

Deadlock is a situation in which processors of a **concurrent processor** are waiting on an event which will never occur. A simple version of deadlock for a **loosely synchronous** environment arises when **blocking** reads and writes are not correctly matched. For example, if two nodes both execute blocking writes to each other at the same time, deadlock will occur since neither write can complete until a complementary read is executed in the other node.

Dimension

This usually refers to the geometric dimension of a spatial system, but in Chap. 3 we introduce a more general **system dimension** that applies to arbitrary complex systems and quantifies information flow within the system.

Distributed Memory

The memory of a concurrent processor is said to be distributed if it is split up into segments, each of which may be directly accessed by only one node.

Domain

A domain is a set of objects or data which define scope of a computational problem or task. For example, suppose we wish to solve a partial differential equation on a grid. Then the set of grid points constitute the domain of the problem. As another example, suppose we wish to solve an N-body problem. In this case the domain is the set of bodies. Domains are split up into **grains, granules** and **members**.

Domain Decomposition

This term is used in two distinct ways depending on the context. We use it to broadly denote the general method of using concurrent computers by dividing the **domain** associated with the problem into parts, or **grains**; one grain per **node** of the concurrent computer. In the case of domains with a metric, e.g., typical spatial domains, we use domain decomposition in a more specific sense to denote the division of space into locally connected grains. We also call this a **local decomposition**. This is in contrast to a **scattered decomposition**.

Efficiency

The efficiency of a program running concurrently on N nodes is defined as the **speedup** per node. Thus, if T(N) is the time to run on N processors, and T(1) is the time for the best equivalent sequential program to run on one node, then the efficiency is:

$$\varepsilon = \frac{T(1)}{NT(N)} \tag{G-2}$$

Fine Grain

See **grain size**.

Finite Difference Method

This is a method for approximately solving partial differential equations on a discrete grid by approximating derivatives of the unknown quantity ψ on the grid by the difference in ψ between two grid points divided by the separation. For example, for the one-dimensional central differencing technique used in Chap. 5:

$$(\partial^2 \psi / \partial x^2)_i \approx \frac{1}{\Delta x} \left[(\frac{\partial \psi}{\partial x})_{i+1/2} - (\frac{\partial \psi}{\partial x})_{i-1/2} \right] \tag{G-3}$$

$$\approx \frac{1}{\Delta x} \left[(\frac{\psi_{i+1} - \psi_i}{\Delta x}) - (\frac{\psi_i - \psi_{i-1}}{\Delta x}) \right]$$

$$\approx \frac{\psi_{i+1} - 2\psi_i + \psi_{i-1}}{(\Delta x)^2}$$

where Δx is the constant grid spacing in the x direction.

Finite Element Method
>This is an approximate method for solving partial differential equations by replacing continuous functions by piecewise approximations defined on polygons, which are referred to as elements. Usually polynomial approximations are used. The finite element method reduces the problem of finding the solution at the vertices of the polygons to that of solving a set of linear equations. This task may be accomplished by a number of methods, including the **Gaussian Elimination**, **conjugate gradient** and **multigrid methods** which are also listed in this glossary.

Forward Reduction
>See **LU decomposition**.

FFT
>The FFT or Fast Fourier Transform is a technique described in Chap. 11, 21, and 22 for a very fast computation of Fourier series.

Full Matrix
>A full matrix is one in which the number of zero elements is small compared with the total number of elements.

Gauss-Seidel Method
>This is an iterative method for solving partial differential equations on a grid. When updating a grid point the new value depends on the current values at the neighboring grid points, some of which are from the previous iteration and some from the current iteration. Thus updates are performed by sweeping through the grid in a pre-determined manner.

Gaussian Elimination
>This is a method for solving sets of simultaneous equations by eliminating variables from successive equations. Thus the original equation:

$$Ax = b \tag{G-4}$$

>is reduced to:

$$Ux = b' \tag{G-5}$$

>where U is an upper-triangular matrix. The solution vector, x, can then be found be **backsubstitution**. This method is usually formulated as **LU decomposition**.

Gigaflop or Gflop
>See **megaflop**

Grain

When **domain decomposition** is used to subdivide a **domain** the part of the resultant subdomain handled by a single **node** of a **concurrent processor** is called a grain.

Grain Size

Grain size is the number of fundamental entities, or **members**, in a **grain**. For example, if a grid is spatially decomposed into subgrids, then the grain size is the number of grid points in a subgrid. We use the terms **coarse** and **fine grain** to distinguish decompositions using large or small groupings. Grain size can be used to describe either problems or computers.

Granule

A granule is the fundamental grouping of members of a domain (system) into an object manipulated as a unit. In this book we only consider the case when granules and **grains** are identical. If we use multiprogramming at each node, we find several granules in each node.

Gray Code

A Gray Code is a mapping which labels the lattice points on an n-dimensional grid with the integers $0, 1,..., 2^d - 1$, so that the labels at adjacent grid points differ in precisely one bit in their binary representation. A one-dimensional Gray Code can be constructed inductively as follows. Given a Gray Code of length 2^p a Gray Code of length 2^{p+1} may be generated by first writing the numbers in binary and explicitly setting the pth significant bit to zero. The numbers are then written in reverse order, and the pth significant bit is set to 1. The resultant set of 2^{p+1} integers are a Gray Code. For example, the Gray Code of length 2 is:

$$0 \quad 1$$

Setting the second significant bit to 0 we get:

$$00 \quad 01$$

Now writing the original numbers in reverse order we get:

$$00 \quad 01 \quad 1 \quad 0$$

Finally setting the second significant bit of the second half of the sequence to 1 we obtain a Gray Code of length 4:

$$00 \quad 01 \quad 11 \quad 10$$

Gray codes in higher spatial dimensions may be obtained by assigning different sets of bits to each dimension.

Guard Ring

Concurrent algorithms operating on a two-dimensional grid generally store grid values in a two-dimensional array. The guard ring is the additional storage allocated around the edge of the array to hold the values at the grid points lying along the adjacent boundaries of neighboring nodes. These values are obtained by communication between the nodes.

Hypercube

A hypercube is a concurrent processor in which the **nodes** can be imagined to lie at the vertices of an n-dimensional cube. The nodes are linked by **communication channels**, that lie along the edges of the cube. Each node of the hypercube is therefore linked to d neighboring processors, and the entire ensemble contains 2^d nodes. The terms "Boolean n-cube" and "hypercube" are synonymous.

Inhomogeneous Problem

This describes problems whose underlying **domain** contains **members** of different types, e.g., an ecological evolution such as WaTor with different species of fish. Inhomogeneous problems are typically **irregular**, but the converse is not generally true.

Interrupt-Driven System

This term refers to a particular way in which a number of processes communicate by **message passing**. When a message is delivered to its destination process it interrupts execution of the process and initiates execution of an interrupt-handler process, which stores the message for subsequent retrieval. On completion of the interrupt-handler process, the original process resumes execution.

I/O: Input/Output

I/O refers to the hardware and software mechanisms connecting a computer with the "outside world". This includes computer to disk and computer to terminal/network/graphics connections. Standard I/O is a particular software package developed under UNIX for the C language.

Irregular Problem

We use this to describe a problem with a geometrically irregular **domain** containing many similar **members**, e.g, **finite element nodal points**.

Jacobi Method

This is a stationary, iterative, method for solving a partial differential equation on a numerical grid. The update of each grid point depends only on the values at neighboring grid points from the previous iteration. This feature distinguishes the Jacobi from the **Gauss-Seidel** method, in which the most recent grid values are used in performing updates.

Laplace Equation

The Laplace equation is an elliptical partial differential equation of the form:

$$\sum_{i=1}^{N} \frac{\partial^2 \psi}{\partial x_i^2} = 0 \qquad \text{(G-6)}$$

The Laplace equation arises frequently in scientific and engineering problems involving electrostatic potentials and fluid dynamics.

Latency

The latency or **startup time** is the time to send a zero-length message from one **node** of a **concurrent processor** to another. Non zero latency arises from the overhead in initiating and completing the message transfer.

Load Balance

A algorithm on a concurrent processor exhibits load balance if all the nodes perform approximately equal amounts of work, so that no node is idle for a significant amount of time.

Local Decomposition

See **Domain Decomposition**.

Loose Synchronization

A program on a **concurrent processor** is said to be running in loose synchronization if the **nodes** are constrained to intermittently synchronize with each other via communication. Frequently, a global computational parameter such as time or iteration count provides a natural synchronization reference. This parameter divides the computation into compute - communicate cycles.

LU Decomposition

LU decomposition represents a matrix, A, as the product of a lower triangular matrix, L, and an upper triangular matrix, U. This decomposition can be made unique either by stipulating that the diagonal elements of L be unity, or that the diagonal elements of L and U be the same.

LU decomposition is the first stage in the solution of a set of simultaneous equations:

$$Ax=b \qquad\qquad (G\text{-}7)$$

Writing $A=LU$ we have:

$$LUx=b \qquad\qquad (G\text{-}8)$$

We next perform the **forward reduction** step, in which both sides of Eq. (G-8) are multiplied by L^{-1} to give:

$$Ux=L^{-1}b=b_{FR} \qquad\qquad (G\text{-}9)$$

The final stage in the solution is the **backsubstitution** step in which Eq. (G-9) is multiplied by U^{-1} to give the solution:

$$x=U^{-1}b_{FR} \qquad\qquad (G\text{-}10)$$

Full details are given in Sec. 20-2.

Megaflops or MFLOPS

The megaflops of a computer measures its overall performance in units of millions of floating-point operations executed each second. This performance measure depends intricately on the application. A gigaflop or GFLOP is a unit of one thousand times a MFLOP.

Member

We refer in Chap. 3 to the fundamental entities in a **complex system** as members. Members are grouped first into **granules** and then **grains**. In a finite difference problem, the **members** are grid points.

Mesh

A set of interconnected members - grid points or nodal points - arranged geometrically in a physical space. Also sometimes used to denote a grid-like topology of processors or **communication channels**.

Message Passing

Message passing is a communication paradigm in which processes communicate by exchanging messages via **communication channels**.

MIMD

MIMD is an abbreviation for Multiple Instruction, Multiple Data. It refers to a machine **architecture** in which each node operates independently on its own local instruction stream and data. It should be contrasted with **SIMD**, also defined in this glossary.

Monte-Carlo Method

A Monte-Carlo method refers to any modeling or simulation procedure based on the generation of random events to generate samples. Usually viewed as a method of performing integrals over many degrees of freedom.

Multigrid Method

This is a method for solving partial differential equations in which an approximate solution on a coarse grid is used to obtain an improved solution on a finer grid. By iterating between a hierarchy of coarse and fine grids, long wavelength components of the error can be reduced.

Multiprocessor or Multicomputer

See **concurrent processor**.

Multitasking

This refers to the ability of a computer to handle several jobs or processes at one time. None of the applications described in this book use multitasking although both load balancing (Chap. 3) and time sharing by many simultaneous users would require multitasking.

Nearest-Neighbor

Nearest-Neighbor refers to computer architectures or algorithms which involve a connectivity which can be interpreted as that between adjacent **members** in geometric space.

Need Predictable

This term is introduced in Chap. 16 to describe a concurrent algorithm in which the need, but not the nature, of node-to-node communication is known prior to program execution. Need predictable problems are still **loosely synchronous**.

Neural Network

As described in Chap. 1, neurons are the basic computational elements used by the brain. In Chap. 2 we note that man-made devices using interconnects and processing capabilities suggested by the cortex are called neural networks, and seem to be powerful computational systems, especially for optimization problems including content addressable memories and pattern recognition [Hopfield 82, Hopfield 86].

Nodal Point

The solution of partial differential equations described in Chaps. 7 and 8 usually requires discretizing a continuous domain into a set of nodal or grid points. These are often called nodes in the **finite element** literature, but we avoid this term, which we reserve for the elements of a concurrent system.

Node

Concurrent processors are a set of individual **sequential** or **Von Neumann** computers, which are called nodes. We some times refer to these nodes as the "elements" of the concurrent computer.

NP Complete

Formally a problem is NP complete if it can only be solved in polynomial time by non-deterministic methods. In practice such problems are "hard" and are "solved" by a variety of heuristic methods that only give approximate answers near the optimum solution.

OCCAM

An elegant computer language based on the work of [Hoare 78] which implements a **crystalline communication system**. The INMOS **transputer** was designed with this language in mind.

Overhead

In Sec. 3-6 we discussed four contributions to the overhead, f, defined so that the **speedup**, S, is given by:

$$S = N/(1+f) \tag{G-11}$$

where N is the number of **nodes** in the **concurrent processor**. The **communication overhead** and **load balance** contributions are also defined in this glossary. We also meet in the book algorithmic and software contributions to the overhead.

Parallel Processor

See **concurrent processor**.

Pipe

A pipe is a communication primitive discussed in Chaps. 4, 10, 14, 20, and 21. It involves the transmission of information through a linearly connected subset of **nodes** of a **concurrent processor**.

Pivot

Many matrix algorithms need pivoting to reorder operations (typically by swapping rows or columns) to improve numerical accuracy.

Polled Communication

Polling involves a **node** inspecting the communication hardware - typically a flag bit - to see if information has arrived or departed. Polling is an alternative to an **interrupt-driven system** and is typically the basis for implementing **crystalline operating systems**. The natural synchronization of the nodes imposed by polling is used in the implementation of **blocking** communication primitives.

Preconditioner

Many computations, including the solution of partial differential equations, lead to the inversion of matrix equations. Preconditioning is a technique for improving the convergence of iterative inversion techniques, such as the **conjugate gradient method** discussed in Chap. 8, by transforming the equations so that the matrix eigenvalues are redistributed.

Process

The fundamental entity or **member** of the software implementation seen by the computer; it is a sequentially executing piece of code. We simplify the discussion in the book by not considering **multitasking** i.e. only allowing one process on each complete node. Each process represents a **granule** of the data domain associated with the problem.

Relaxation

Relaxation is an iterative method for solving sets of equations, and is typified by the **Jacobi** and **Gauss-Seidel** methods discussed in Chap. 7.

Scattered Decomposition

This is a technique for decomposing data domains that involves scattering, or sprinkling, the elements of the domain (the **members**) over the nodes of the **concurrent processor**. This technique is used when locality, which is preserved by the alternate decomposition into connected domains often called **domain decomposition**, is less important than the gain in **load balance** obtained by associating each node with all parts of the domain.

Sequential Bottleneck

A part of the computation for which there is little or no parallelism is called a sequential bottleneck. **Amdahl's Law**, discussed in Sec. 3-6, points out that one can never attain a **speedup** greater than the inverse of the fraction of the problem forming a sequential bottleneck.

Sequential Computer

A sequential computer architecture is synonymous with a **Von Neumann** computer, and describes a "conventional" computer in which only one **node** works on a given problem at a time.

Shared Memory

A memory that is directly accessed by more than one **node** of a concurrent processor is termed a shared memory. This is an important architectural feature of many supercomputer designs, and is discussed in Sec. 2-6.

SIMD

SIMD is an abbreviation for Single Instruction, Multiple Data, and refers to a computer architecture in which each **node** has local memory but operates in lockstep with the same global instruction stream. It should be contrasted with **MIMD**, also found in this glossary.

Simulated Annealing

This is an optimization technique introduced in [Kirkpatrick 83] which uses statistical physics techniques to find approximate optimizations. Typically one uses a physical analogy for a general system and maps the task of finding a minimum to that of finding the ground state of the physical system.

Sparse Matrix

A matrix, M, is sparse if the majority of its elements are zero. The equations $Mx=b$ solved in Chaps. 7 and 8 are sparse, and parallel solution techniques are discussed there and in Chap. 20.

Speedup

The speedup, S, is the number of times faster a given problem runs on a **concurrent processor** with N **nodes** than on a single node. The ratio S/N is termed the **efficiency**.

Square Decomposition

A strategy in which the array of nodes is decomposed into a two dimensional mesh; as described in Chap. 20, we can then define **scattered** or **local (domain)** versions of this decomposition.

Standard I/O

See **I/O.**

Startup Time

See **latency**.

Subcube

The **hypercube** architecture has a natural recursive definition such that a cube of dimension d_1 includes within it $2^{d_1-d_2}$ lower dimensional sets of nodes, each of which is a hypercube of dimensionality d_2. These subsets of nodes are called subcubes.

Successive Over-Relaxation

This is standard technique for accelerating the convergence of **relaxation** methods for solving sets of simultaneous equations, $Ax=b$. It typically involves adding an appropriate multiple of the unit matrix to the coefficient matrix A.

Supercomputer

This term has no precise definition, but refers to the class of most powerful computers. It is defined pragmatically in Sec. 2-1.

System Dimension

See **Dimension**.

Systolic Array

A class of parallel computers with a fixed array of fine grain nodes through which data is pumped [Mead 80].

t_{calc}

The typical time defined in Sec. 3-5, to perform a floating point operation in a **node**. See Table 2-1 for example values.

t_{comm}

The typical time, defined in Sec. 3-5, to send a word between **nodes** through a **communication channel**. See Table 2-1 for values.

Topology

A **distributed memory concurrent processor** consists of several **nodes** joined by a set of **communication channels**. This defines an interconnection between the nodes which is the topology of the computer.

Transputer

A single chip which contains **CPU, communication channels,** and possibly some memory. INMOS, a British company manufactures a proprietary chip called the transputer and the node of the commercial NCUBE hypercube has similar characteristics.

Virtual Concurrent Processor - or Virtual Machine

The virtual concurrent processor is a programming environment described in Chap. 4 and Sec. 22-5, which allows the user a hardware-independent, portable programming environment within the **message passing** paradigm. The virtual machine is composed of virtual nodes which correspond to individual processes; there may be several process or virtual nodes on the node of a real computer.

Virtual Machine Loosely Synchronous Communication System

A specific realization of a hardware independent programming environment, or the **virtual machine**, which applies to the loosely synchronous problem class. It is derived in Chap. 22 as an abstraction of the methods described in the book.

Von Neumann

John Von Neumann (1903-1957) was a genius who made major contributions to the fields of both pure and applied mathematics. He is credited with the invention of the basic architecture of current sequential computers, which he pioneered with the construction of a computer at the Institute for Advanced Study at Princeton. His interest in numerical methods stemmed from work on hydrodynamics and nuclear energy during the Second World War. In the last years of his life he worked on the general theory of automata, which spanned his interest in logic and computers. A Von Neumann architecture is rather loosely used to describe any computer which does not employ concurrency.

A

Appendix A: A Description of Pseudocode

A-1 Introduction

Pseudocode has been used throughout most of this book to present the structure of algorithms as concisely and clearly as possible. This pseudocode is intended to be representative of high-level languages, such as C and FORTRAN, and is used for two main reasons. Firstly, it allows algorithms to be presented independently of any particular programming language, thereby making them understandable to a wider audience. Secondly, the use of pseudocode permits the salient points of an algorithm to be emphasized without clouding important issues with less pertinent details. Readers interested in the finer details of the algorithms are referred to the Software Supplement, which contains listings in C and FORTRAN 77 of complete programs based on the algorithms presented in this book. The contents of the Software Supplement are listed in Appendix B.

In describing pseudocode the equivalent expression in C and FORTRAN 77 will be given where appropriate. Pseudocode is not intended to be a complete language in the sense that every nuance of C and FORTRAN has a strict pseudocode equivalent, and we define here only those pseudocode constructs that are used in the algorithms of this book. Nor is it true that every statement in pseudocode translates into statements in C or FOR-TRAN code–statements may be inserted into a pseudocode listing merely to clarify a point, or to suggest a way of looking at a problem. Although pseudocode is a fairly informal way of describing algorithms, the introduction of some degree of structure is clearly necessary. The remainder of this appendix will describe the pseudocode constructs of this book.

A-2 Declaration of Variables

It is often convenient to declare the data type and purpose of a variable at the beginning of the routine in which it is used. Pseudocode permits four types of variable to be declared.

(1)   Integers are declared with the following syntax:

   declare_int *variable* ; (description and purpose)

This has a direct equivalent in C :

   int *variable* ; /* description and purpose */

The FORTRAN 77 equivalent is also straightforward:

    INTEGER *variable*

If it is necessary to explicitly specify the length of an integer this may be given inside the parentheses after the variable name.

(2)   Floating-point numbers are declared as follows:

    declare_float *variable* ; (description and purpose)

The corresponding declaration in C is :

    float *variable* ; /* description and purpose */

In FORTRAN 77 this is declared as :

    REAL *variable*

If it is necessary to explicitly specify the length of a float-point number this may be given inside the parentheses after the variable name. Thus, a 64-bit number may be declared in pseudocode as :

    declare_float *variable* ; (a 64-bit floating-point number)

The corresponding declaration in C is :

    double *variable* ; /* description and purpose */

In FORTRAN 77 this is declared as :

    DOUBLE PRECISION *variable*

(3)   In pseudocode a "buffer" is a general way of referring to a set of contiguous memory locations. The syntax for declaring a buffer is :

    declare_buf *buf_name* ; (description and purpose)

There is no single equivalent in C or FORTRAN 77 to a pseudocode buffer. In C a buffer may be referenced by means of a pointer to the location in memory of the start of the buffer. In FORTRAN 77, however, a buffer is referenced simply by a variable name. The pseudocode declaration:

    declare_buf *elk* ; (example of the declaration of a buffer)

could be presented in C by any of the following :

    int elk [ ] ; /* comments */
    float elk [10] ; /* comments */
    char *elk ; /* comments */

FORTRAN 77 equivalents include:

    INTEGER ELK (*)
    CHARACTER*10 ELK
    DOUBLE PRECISION ELK (10)

(4)   A data structure in pseudocode is a special kind of buffer in which the subunits contained in the buffer are explicitly listed. The syntax is as follows :

declare_struct *variable* { list of declarations };

Pseudocode data structures are directly equivalent to structures in C. For example, consider the following data structure :

declare_struct *box* { **declare_int** *height*; (height in feet)
                          declare_int *width*; (width in inches)
                          declare_int *length*; (length in yards) };

This data structure can be represented in C as :

struct   { int height ; /* height in feet */
           int width ; /* width in inches */
           int length ; /* length in yards */ }*box*;

The equivalent data structure in FORTRAN 77 can best be represented with a COMMON block :

INTEGER HEIGHT, WIDTH, LENGTH
COMMON /BOX/ HEIGHT, WIDTH, LENGTH

A-3 Declaring and Calling Routines

In general, all program, subroutine, and function modules have the same general form :

proc_begin *proc_name* (purpose)
declarations
statements
proc_end

A routine is called with the following syntax :

proc_call *proc_name* (purpose)

An exception to this general rule is used in Chap. 4 when defining the communication routines used by the virtual concurrent processor. For these cases the argument list and data type of each routine are given explicitly. Thus a function *func* of integer data type is declared in pseudocode as:

int_fun *func* (arg1, arg2, arg3)

This is equivalent in C to :

int *func* (arg1, arg2, arg3)

and in FORTRAN 77 to :

INTEGER FUNCTION FUNC (ARG1, ARG2, ARG3)

The routine *vm_combine*, described in Sec. 4-4, takes a function as an argument. In pseudocode the argument is declared within *vm_combine* as :

function func ;

In C the argument *func* must be declared within *vm_combine* as a pointer to a function. For example, since *func* is an integer function it would be declared as int (*func)();

In FORTRAN 77 the corresponding declaration is:

INTEGER FUNC

Some FORTRAN 77 compilers require FUNC to be declared EXTERNAL in the calling module.

The **define_function** construct in pseudocode may be used to define a function within a routine, and is similar to the statement function in FORTRAN 77, and the definition of a macro in C by means of a *define* statement. Thus the pseudocode:

define_function $f(x) = x^3 + 2x^2 + 1$

is represented in C by:

#define f(x) (1 + (x)*(2*(x)+(x)*(x)))

and in FORTRAN 77 by:

f(x) = x**3 + 2*x**2 + 1

A-4 Loops

Two types of loop are defined in pseudocode: the *for* and *while* loops. The syntax of the *for* loop is as follows :

for_begin (specification of number of loops)
    statement
for_end

The syntax of the *while* loop is :

while_begin (condition)
    statement
while_end

Throughout this appendix, *statement* should be understood to represent one or more lines of code. The pseudocode *for* loop corresponds directly to the C *for* loop. In FORTRAN 77 the *for* loop may be written as a general loop:

```
10     CONTINUE
       IF ( loop does not terminate yet ) THEN
           statement
           GOTO 10
       ENDIF
```

In many cases, however, a *for* loop may be represented in FORTRAN 77 with a DO loop.

The pseudocode *while* loop is almost exactly the same as that in C, and can also be represented in FORTRAN 77 by a general loop similar to that shown above. A *goto* statement is also provided in pseudocode, though it is rarely of use.

A-5 Conditional Statements

In pseudocode conditional branching is provided by the following construct:

> **if_begin** (*expression 1*) **then**
> > *statement 1*
>
> **else_if** (*expression 2*) **then**
> > *statement 2*
>
> **else**
> > *statement 3*
>
> **if_end**

The above construct causes *statement 1* to be executed if and only if *expression 1* is true; *statement 2* is executed if and only if *expression 1* is false and *expression 2* is true; *statement 3* is executed if and only if *expression 1* and *expression 2* are both false. The equivalent constructs in C and FORTRAN 77 are very similar.

B

Appendix B: The Software Supplement

The chapters in this book contain various fragments of software written in pseudocode. The complete codes from which these fragments were extracted are available on diskette. System software which implements the environments described in Chaps. 6, 14, and 15 is also available. This software exists both as a concurrent processor simulator and as an operating system for a hypercube.

In Table B-2, we refer to the PC-cube which is a collection of IBM PC's connected by RS232 channels so as to emulate a hypercube [Breaden 86]. This is shown in Fig. 2-3(i) and is designed as an educational tool. The Mac-cube is an analogous collection of Apple Macintosh computers using Appletalk to emulate the hypercube. The Ethercube is similarly a set of UNIX workstations using Ethernet to achieve the hypercube connection.

We have also implemented CrOS III on other machines including the BBN Butterfly but we do not intend to distribute this as the portable environment described in Chap. 22 is a more suitable message passing system for general parallel machines.

All the application code and some of the systems codes have been placed in the public domain. Some of the code is covered by copyrights and requires license fees. We expect that the public domain software will be available through a commercial source in supported and enhanced forms.

The public domain software and licensing information is available for a fee to cover expenses from

Tutorial Software

Caltech Concurrent Computation Program, 206-49

California Institute of Technology

Pasadena, CA 91125

The use of this software is covered in Volume 2 - the Software Supplement - of this book.

Table B-1 Available Application Code
All of the following codes are available in both C and FORTRAN 77

Code	Chapter	Comments
Virtual Machine Example 1	4	
Virtual Machine Example 2	4	
Wave Equation	5/6	Available in both CUBIX and CP versions
2D Finite Difference	7	Solves Laplace equation
2D Finite Element	8	Uses conjugate gradient method
Long-Range Force	9	Evaluation of the potential energy of a system of particles evaluation of force on each of a system of particles
Matrix Algorithms	10	Matrix multiplication Naive and pipe broadcasts
Fast Fourier Transform	11	Recursive and iterative algorithms
Generation of Random Nos.	12	Example of random number generation 1D Monte-Carlo integration Evaluation of π
Short-Range Force	16	Lennard-Jones potential used
WaTor	17	A population dynamics model
Sorting	18	Parallel bitonic shellsort and quicksort algorithms
Scalar Products	19	
Banded Matrices	20	Code for solving $Ax = b$ by LU decomposition, forward reduction, back substitution
General Matrix Algorithms	21	Examples of the routines index, fold, expand, transpose, scatter, transfer
General Message Passing	22	The crystal router and crystal accumulator

Table B-2 Systems Software

System	Status	CrOS III C	CrOS III FORTRAN	CUBIX C	CUBIX FORTRAN
Virtual Machine Simulator	Public Domain	X	X	X	X
UNIX Hypercube Simulator	Public Domain	X	X	X	X
VMS Hypercube Simulator	Public Domain	X	X	X	X
INTEL iPSC Hypercube	Caltech Copyright	X	X	X	X
AMETEK S14 Hypercube[**]	AMETEK Copyright	X	X		
NCUBE Hypercube	Caltech Copyright	X	X	X	X
Mark II Hypercube[*]	Caltech Copyright	X	X	X	
Mark III Hypercube[*]	Caltech Copyright	X	X	X	X
PC-cube	Caltech Copyright	X		X	
Mac-cube	Caltech Copyright	X		X	
Ethercube	Public Domain	X		X	

[*] Internal to Caltech/JPL.

[**] Based on a preliminary version of CrOS III

C

APPENDIX C: A Description of FORTRAN CUBIX

This appendix describes the use of FORTRAN CUBIX. The implementation details are not discussed here, but a full description is given in the Software Supplement. Many of the statements discussed here are extensions of FORTRAN 77 statements which are described more fully in textbooks such as [Ashcroft 81]. As in the C version of CUBIX described in Chaps. 6 and 15, a file in FORTRAN CUBIX is either in single or multiple I/O mode.

A file may be opened with the OPEN routine. This routine is the same as the standard FORTRAN 77 OPEN routine, except there is an additional parameter called MODE, which may be set equal to the character string 'single' or 'multi'. If the MODE parameter is omitted the file is opened in the default singular mode. For example, the following call to OPEN opens the file *results.dat* in multiple I/O mode and assigns it to unit number 8:

OPEN (UNIT=8, FILE='results.dat', STATUS='OLD', MODE='multi')

The following two calls to OPEN have the same effect, and open the file *input.dat* in singular I/O mode and assign it to unit number 7:

OPEN (UNIT =7, FILE='input.dat',STATUS='NEW',MODE='single')
OPEN (UNIT =7, FILE='input.dat',STATUS='NEW')

The CLOSE routine may be used to close files, and is used in the same way as the FORTRAN 77 version.

The SINGLE and MULTIPLE statements can be used to switch the I/O mode of a file. Both use an integer unit number to identify the file. The READ, WRITE, and PRINT statements can also make use of the MODE parameter to specify in which mode data is to be read or written. In all other respects these routines are the same as in FORTRAN 77. The FLUSH statement may be used to flush output to a file. FLUSH uses an integer unit number to identify the file.

The I/O mode of a file can be ascertained using the INQUIRE routine. This is the same as the standard FORTRAN 77 routine, except that the mode of the file is returned in a character string, which will have either the value 'single' or 'multi'. The size of the buffer used in performing I/O in multiple mode may be set with the BUFFER statement. The default buffer size is 512 bytes. Some examples of the use of these statements are :

(1)   READ (*, *, END=88, ERR=99, MODE='single') IVAL

(2)   WRITE (8,100, MODE='multi') PROCNU
(3)   FLUSH(UNIT=8)
(4)   INQUIRE(FILE='results.dat',MODE=IOTYPE)
(5)   BUFFER(UNIT=8,SIZE=1024,ERR=999)
(6)   MULTIPLE(UNIT=8,ERR=999)

In example (1) each processor reads in the value of IVAL in singular I/O mode from the default input unit. If the end of the file is encountered the next statement to be obeyed is the one labeled by 88, and if an error occurs while reading then the statement labeled by 99 is next executed in the processor(s) in which the error occurs.

In example (2) the value of PROCNU is output in multiple mode to the file connected to unit number 8 according to the FORMAT statement labeled by 100. This causes each processor to place the value of PROCNU into the output buffer associated with unit number 8. The FLUSH statement, shown in example (3), causes the output buffer of each node to be output to the file connected to unit 8 in *procnum* order.

Example (4) shows how to use the INQUIRE statement to find out the I/O mode of the file *results.dat*. The mode is returned to the program in the character array IOTYPE, and has the value 'single' or 'multi'.

In example (5) the BUFFER statement is used to set the size of the buffer associated with unit number 8 to 1024 bytes. If an error occurs, for example no file is connected to unit 8, then the next statement obeyed is the one labeled by 999.

Lastly in example (6) the multi statement is used to place the file associated with unit number 8 in multiple I/O mode. In the event of an error the statement labeled by 999 is executed next.

An example of FORTRAN CUBIX is given in Code C-1, which is equivalent to the C version given in Code 6-2.

This example illustrates how a common value of INUM can be input to all nodes using the READ statement when in singular I/O mode. However, when in multiple input mode the READ statement causes a distinct value of MYNUM to be input to each node. Likewise in singular output mode an identical WRITE statement in all the nodes causes that data to be output just once, whereas in multiple output mode there is no need for the nodes to write in loose synchronization, and different nodes can output different data. However, the flushing of output buffers by means of FLUSH, CLOSE and STOP must be done in loose synchronization. Code C-2 illustrates the use of the OPEN, CLOSE, FLUSH and INQUIRE statements.

```
      PROGRAM CODEC1
C
C     Example FORTRAN CUBIX program
C
      PARAMETER ( NIN=5, NOUT=6 )
      INTEGER PARAMS(5), PROCNU, DOC
C
      CALL KCPARA (PARAMS)
      DOC = PARAMS(1)
      PROCNU = PARAMS(2)
      NPROC = PARAMS(3)
      PRINT *,'CUBIX is now in singular mode'
      PRINT *,'Please enter a number'
      READ(*, *)INUM
      PRINT *,'CUBIX now switching to multiple input mode'
      MULTIPLE(NIN)
      WRITE (*,100)NPROC
      READ(*, *)MYNUM
      PRINT *,'CUBIX now switching to multiple output mode'
      MULTIPLE(NOUT)
      WRITE(*,101)INUM,MYNUM,PROCNU
      IF (PROCNU.EQ.0) PRINT *,'This message
      came from processor 0'
      STOP
100   FORMAT(/'Enter',I6,'numbers')
101   FORMAT('You gave ',I6,'and',I6,'to processor',I6)
      END
```

Code C-1 Program Illustrating FORTRAN CUBIX

```
      PROGRAM CODEC2
C
      INTEGER PARAMS(5),DOC,PROCNU
      CHARACTER*8 IOTYPE
C
C     Get cube parameters
C
      CALL KCPARA(PARAMS)
      DOC = PARAMS(1)
      PROCNU = PARAMS(2)
      NPROC = PARAMS(3)
C
C     Open output file and check mode
C
      OPEN(UNIT=8,FILE='results.dat',MODE='multi',ERR=999)
      INQUIRE(FILE='results.dat',MODE=IOTYPE)
      WRITE(*,100)IOTYPE
C
C     Output to unit 8 in singular mode
C
      WRITE(8,200,MODE='single')DOC
C
C     Calculate and output square and cube of PROCNU
C
      ITEMP = PROCNU*PROCNU
      WRITE(8,201)ITEMP,PROCNU
      FLUSH(8)
      ITEMP = ITEMP*PROCNU
      WRITE(8,202)ITEMP,PROCNU
      FLUSH(8)
C
C     Output message in singular mode and terminate
C
      PRINT 8,MODE='single',' Program terminating'
      STOP
999   PRINT(/' Error opening output file - program terminated '/)
      STOP
100   FORMAT(/' Output I/O mode is',A/)
200   FORMAT(' The dimensionality of the cube is ',I6)
201   FORMAT(' The square of PROCNU is ',I6)
202   FORMAT(' The cube of PROCNU is ',I6)
      END
```

Code C-2 FORTRAN CUBIX Example Using OPEN, CLOSE, FLUSH and INQUIRE

D

Appendix D:
Code for the One-Dimensional
Wave Equation Example

D-1 Introduction

This appendix contains the C and FORTRAN code for the one-dimensional wave equation application discussed in Chap. 5. Sections D-2 and D-3 contain the control processor and node code, respectively, for the C version. The corresponding FORTRAN code is given in Sec. D-6 and D-7. The CUBIX version of the program, referred to in Sec. 6-3, is presented in Sec. D-4 (C version), and Sec. D-8 (FORTRAN version). As explained in Sec. 6-3, the CUBIX version of the code can be compiled and run on a sequential computer without modifying the parallel code. This is done by implementing sequential versions of the CrOS III routines called in the program, so that they give the correct results for just a single processor. These sequential versions of the C and FOR-TRAN CrOS III routines are assumed to be stored in the files *cros3SEQ.c* and *cros3SEQ.f*, respectively, and are included in the sequential compilation by means of conditional compilation directives. We have assumed that the FORTRAN CUBIX code can be run through the C preprocessor before compilation. If this is not possible some minor alterations to the parallel FORTRAN code are necessary to make it run on a sequential computer. The files *cros3SEQ.c* and *cros3SEQ.f* are listed in Sec. D-5 and D–9, respectively. In this simple example the initial configuration of the string is assumed to be a sine wave.

D-2 Control Processor Code for Wave Equation Example (C Version)

```c
#include <cros.h>
#include <math.h>
#include <stdio.h>

#define MAX_PROCS 16
#define MAX_POINTS 500
#define INITIALIZE 1
#define UPDATE 2
#define OUTPUT 3
#define STOP 4
#define PI 3.14159265
int nproc, doc, ntot, nmin, nleft;
double values[MAX_POINTS+2];

/*--------------------------------------- start of main routine ---------------------------------------*/

main()
{
    int task;

    down_load("waveCNODE");

    while((task=get_task()) != STOP){
        switch(task){
            case INITIALIZE:
                initialize_cp();
                break;
            case UPDATE:
                do_steps();
                break;
            case OUTPUT:
                output_results();
                break;
        }
    }
    exit(0);
}

/*--------------------------------------- end of main routine ---------------------------------------*/

down_load(progname)
char progname[40];
```

```
        {
                printf("\n\nPlease give the hypercube dimensionality ==> ");
                scanf("%d",&doc);

                nproc = 1<<doc;
                cubeld( doc, progname);
        }
```

/*------------------------------------ end of routine down_load --------------------------------*/

```
        int get_task()
        {
                int task;
                char input[40];

                for ( ; ; ){
                        printf("\n\nPlease select one of the following :\n");
                        printf("\n 1...to initialize a new problem");
                        printf("\n 2...to do some updates");
                        printf("\n 3...to output solution");
                        printf("\n 4...to terminate program");
                        printf("\n\n==> ");

                        scanf("%s",input);

                        task = atoi(input);

                        printf("\n");
                        if(task>0 && task<5) break;
                        else printf("\n**** Invalid input–please try again ****\n");
                }

                bcastcp( &task, sizeof(int));

                return task;
        }
```

/*------------------------------------ end of routine get_task --------------------------------*/

```
        initialize_cp()
        {
                double x, delt, fac;
                int i, j, k, npts;
```

```
        for ( ; ; ){
                printf("\n\nPlease give the number of points ==> ");
                scanf("%d",&ntot);

                nmin = ntot/nproc;
                nleft = ntot%nproc;
                if(nmin< MAX_POINTS) break;
                else printf("\n*** Too many points specified ***\n");
        }


        printf("\n\nPlease give the time advance parameter ==> ");
        scanf("%lf",&delt);

        bcastcp( &ntot, sizeof(int));
        bcastcp( &delt, sizeof(double));
}
```

/*------------------------------------ end of routine initialize_cp ---------------------------------*/

```
do_steps()
{
        int nstep, check;

        printf("\nPlease give the number of time steps ==> ");
        scanf("%d",&nstep);

        bcastcp( &nstep, sizeof(int));

        combcp( &check, sizeof(int), 1);
        if(!check) printf("\n\n%d updates completed\n", nstep);
        else printf("\n\nAn error occured in updating\n");
}
```

/*------------------------------------ end of routine do_steps ---------------------------------*/

```
output_results()
{
        int i, j, k, npts, max_bytes, bufmap[MAX_PROCS+1];

        max_bytes = (nmin+1)*sizeof(double);
        for (k=0,i=0; i<nproc; ++i){
```

```
                npts = (i<nleft) ? nmin+1 : nmin;
                mdumpcp( &values[1], max_bytes, bufmap);
                for (j=1; j<=npts; ++j,++k)
                        printf("%7.4f%c",values[j],(k%10==9) ? '\n' : ' ');
        }
}
/*------------------------------------ end of routine output_results --------------------------*/
```

D-3 Node Program for Wave Equation Example (C Version)

```c
#include <cros.h>
#include <math.h>
#include <stdio.h>

#define MAX_POINTS 500
#define INITIALIZE 1
#define UPDATE 2
#define OUTPUT 3
#define STOP 4
#define PI 3.14159265

int nproc, doc, procnum, my_position, left_chan, right_chan;
int ntot, nmin, nleft;
double values[MAX_POINTS+2], oldval[MAX_POINTS+2], newval[MAX_POINTS+2];

/*----------------------------------------- start of main routine -----------------------------------------*/

main()
{
     int len, task;
     double delt;

     get_param();

     decompose();

     while((task=get_task()) != STOP){
          switch(task){
               case INITIALIZE:
                    initialize( &len, &delt);
                    break;
               case UPDATE:
                    do_steps( len, delt);
                    break;
               case OUTPUT:
                    output_results();
                    break;
          }
     }
     exit(0);
}
```

```
/*-------------------------------------- end of main routine -----------------------------------------*/

int add_int( iptr1, iptr2, size)
int *iptr1, *iptr2, size;
{
      *iptr1 += *iptr2;
      return 0;
}

/*-------------------------------------- end of routine add_int --------------------------------------*/

get_param()
{
      struct cubenv env;

      cparam( &env);

      procnum = env.procnum;
      doc = env.doc;
      nproc = env.nproc;
}

/*-------------------------------------- end of routine get_param -----------------------------------*/

decompose()
{
      gridinit( 1, &nproc);
      gridcoord( procnum, &my_position);
      left_chan = gridchan( procnum, 0, -1);
      right_chan = gridchan( procnum, 0, 1);
      if(my_position == 0) left_chan = 0;
      if(my_position == (nproc-1)) right_chan = 0;

}

/*-------------------------------------- end of routine decompose ----------------------------------*/

int get_task()
{
      int task;

      bcastelt( &task, sizeof(int));
```

```
        return task;
}

/*----------------------------------------- end of routine get_task --------------------------------------*/

initialize(len, delt)
int *len;
double *delt;
{
        double x, fac;
        int i, j, k, npts;

        bcastelt( &ntot, sizeof(int));

        nmin = ntot/nproc;
        nleft = ntot%nproc;

        fac = 2.0*PI;
        for ( i=0,k=0; i<nproc; ++i){
                npts = (i<nleft) ? nmin+1 : nmin;
                if(my_position==i){
                        *len = npts;
                        for (j=1; j<=npts; ++j,++k){
                                x = (double)k/(double)(ntot-1);
                                values[j] = sin(fac*x);
                        }
                }
                else k += npts;

        }

        bcastelt( delt, sizeof(double));

        for ( i=1; i<=(*len); ++i) oldval[i]=values[i];
}

/*----------------------------------------- end of routine initialize --------------------------------------*/

do_steps( len, del)
double del;
int len;
{
        double c, delx, pfac;
```

```
                int i, j, sized, nstep, check, add_int();

                bcastelt( &nstep, sizeof(int));

                c = 1.0;
                delx = 1.0;
                pfac =c*del/delx;
                pfac *= pfac;
                sized = sizeof(double);

                for ( i=0; i<nstep; ++i){

                        cshift( &values[0], left_chan, sized, &values[len], right_chan, sized);
                        cshift( &values[len+1], right_chan, sized, &values[1], left_chan, sized);

                        for (j=1; j<=len; ++j){
                            if(my_position==0 && j==1) newval[j] = 0.0;
                            else if (my_position==(nproc-1) && j==len) newval[j]=0.0;
                            else newval[j] = 2.0*values[j] - oldval[j] +
                                    (values[j+1] - 2.0*values[j] + values[j-1])*pfac;
                        }
                        for (j=1; j<=len; ++j){
                                oldval[j] = values[j];
                                values[j] = newval[j];
                        }
                }
                check = 0;
                combelt( &check, add_int ,sizeof(int), 1);
        }

/*------------------------------------ end of routine do_steps ------------------------------------*/

output_results()
{
        int i, npts;

        for ( i=0; i<nproc; ++i){
                npts = (i<nleft) ? nmin+1 : nmin;
                if(my_position !=i)  npts = 0;
                dumpelt( &values[1], sizeof(double)*npts);
        }
}
/*------------------------------------ end of routine output_results ------------------------------------*/
```

D-4 CUBIX Code in C

```c
#ifdef PAR
#include <cros.h>
#else
struct cubenv { int doc, procnum, nproc, cpmask, cubemask;};
#endif
#include <math.h>
#include <stdio.h>

#define MAX_POINTS 500
#define INITIALIZE 1
#define UPDATE 2
#define OUTPUT 3
#define STOP 4
#define PI 3.14159265

int nproc, doc, procnum, my_position, left_chan, right_chan;
int ntot, nmin, nleft;
double values[MAX_POINTS+2], oldval[MAX_POINTS+2], newval[MAX_POINTS+2];

/*--------------------------------- start of main routine ---------------------------------*/

main()
{
    int len, task;
    double delt;

    get_param();

    decompose();

    while((task=get_task()) != STOP){
        switch(task){
            case INITIALIZE:
                initialize( &len, &delt);
                break;
            case UPDATE:
                do_steps( len, delt);
                break;
            case OUTPUT:
                output_results();
                break;
        }
```

```
        }
        exit(0);
}

/*------------------------------------ end of main routine ------------------------------------*/

get_param()
{
        struct cubenv env;

        cparam( &env);

        procnum = env.procnum;
        doc = env.doc;
        nproc = env.nproc;
}

/*------------------------------------ end of routine get_param ------------------------------------*/

decompose()
{
        gridinit( 1, &nproc);
        gridcoord( procnum, &my_position);
        left_chan = gridchan( procnum, 0, -1);
        right_chan = gridchan( procnum, 0, 1);
        if(my_position == 0) left_chan = 0;
        if(my_position == (nproc-1)) right_chan = 0;


}

/*------------------------------------ end of routine decompose ------------------------------------*/

int get_task()
{
        int task;
        char input[40];

        for ( ; ; ){
                printf("\nPlease select one of the following :\n");
                printf("\n 1...to initialize a new problem");
                printf("\n 2...to do some updates");
                printf("\n 3...to output solution");
                printf("\n 4...to terminate program");
```

```
            printf("\n\n=> ");

            scanf("%s",input);

            task = atoi(input);

            printf("\n");
            if(task>0 && task<5) break;
            else printf("\n**** Invalid input-please try again ****\n");
      }

      return task;
}

/*-------------------------------------- end of routine get_task --------------------------------------*/

initialize(len, delt)
int *len;
double *delt;
{
      double x, fac;
      int i, j, k, npts;

      for ( ; ; ){
            printf("\nPlease give the number of points ==> ");
            scanf("%d",&ntot);

            nmin = ntot/nproc;
            nleft = ntot%nproc;
            if(nmin< MAX_POINTS) break;
            else printf("\n***Too many points specified****\n");
      }

      fac = 2.0*PI;
      for ( i=0,k=0; i<nproc; ++i){
            npts = (i<nleft) ? nmin+1 : nmin;
            if(my_position==i){
                  *len = npts;
                  for (j=1; j<=npts; ++j,++k){
                        x = (double)k/(double)(ntot-1);
                        values[j] = sin(fac*x);
                  }
            }
```

```
                    else k += npts;

        }

        printf("\nPlease give the time advance parameter ==> ");
        scanf ( "%lf",delt);

        for ( i=1; i<=(*len); ++i) oldval[i]=values[i];
}

/*------------------------------------ end of routine initialize ------------------------------------*/

do_steps( len, del)
double del;
int len;
{
        double c, delx, pfac;
        int i, j, sized, nstep;

        printf("\nPlease give the number of time steps ==> ");
        scanf("%d",&nstep);

        c = 1.0;
        delx = 1.0;

        pfac =c*del/delx;
        pfac *= pfac;

        sized = sizeof(double);

        for ( i=0; i<nstep; ++i){

                cshift( &values[0], left_chan, sized, &values[len], right_chan, sized);
                cshift( &values[len+1], right_chan, sized, &values[1], left_chan, sized);

                for (j=1; j<=len; ++j){
                        if(my_position==0 && j==1) newval[j] = 0.0;
                        else if (my_position==(nproc-1) && j==len) newval[j]=0.0;
                        else newval[j] = 2.0*values[j] - oldval[j] +
                                (values[j+1] - 2.0*values[j] + values[j-1])*pfac;
                }
                for (j=1; j<=len; ++j){
                        oldval[j] = values[j];
```

```
                            values[j] = newval[j];
                    }
            }
    }

/*------------------------------------ end of routine do_steps ------------------------------------*/

output_results()
{
        int i, j, k, npts;

        fmulti(stdout);

        for (k=0,i=0; i<nproc; ++i){
                npts = (i<nleft) ? nmin+1 : nmin;
                for (j=1; j<=npts; ++j,++k){
                    if(my_position ==i) printf("%7.4f%c",values[j],(k%10==9) ? '\n' : ' ');
                    if (k%60==59) fflush(stdout);
                }
        }
        fsingl(stdout);
}
/*------------------------------------ end of routine output_results ---------------------------*/

#ifdef SEQ
#include "cros3SEQ.c"
#endif
```

D-5 The File Cros3SEQ.c

```
static int dim;

int gridinit( gridim, buff)
int gridim, buff[ ];
{
      dim = gridim;
      return 0;
}
```

/*-- end of routine gridinit --*/

```
int gridcoord( proc, buff)
int proc, buff[ ];
{
      int i;

      for ( i=0; i<dim; ++i) buff[i] = 0;
      return 0;
}
```

/*-- end of routine gridcoord --*/

```
int gridchan( proc, dir, sign)
int proc, dir, sign;
{
      return 0;
}
```

/*-- end of routine gridchan --*/

```
int cshift( inbuf, inchan, inspace, outbuf, outchan, outbytes)
char *inbuf, *outbuf;
int inchan, inspace, outchan, outbytes;
{
      int nbytes;

      if(inchan!=0 || outchan!=0) return -1;
      nbytes = inspace>outbytes ? outbytes : inspace;
      while(nbytes--) *inbuf++ = *outbuf++;

      return nbytes;
```

```
}

/*---------------------------------- end of routine cshift  -------------------------------------*/

fmulti( file)
FILE *file;
{
}

/*---------------------------------- end of routine fmulti -------------------------------------*/

fsingl( file)
FILE *file;
{
}

/*---------------------------------- end of routine fsingl  -------------------------------------*/

cparam( env)
struct cubenv *env;
{
      env->doc =0;
      env->procnum =0;
      env->nproc =1;
      env->cpmask =0;
      env->cubemask = 0;
}
/*---------------------------------- end of routine cparam  -------------------------------------*/
```

D-6 FORTRAN Control Processor Code.

```
            PROGRAM WAVFCP
C
            INTEGER INITIA, UPDATE, OUTPUT, QUIT
            PARAMETER (INITIA=1, UPDATE=2, OUTPUT=3, QUIT=4)
C
            PARAMETER ( MAXSIZ=500 )
C
            INTEGER PROCNU, DOC, NPROC, MYPOS, LCHAN, RCHAN
            COMMON/EXTCOM/ PROCNU, DOC, NPROC, MYPOS, LCHAN, RCHAN
C
            COMMON/NPTCOM/ NMIN, NLEFT, NTOT
C
            INTEGER TASK
C
            CALL DOWNLD('waveFNODE')
C
10          CALL GETASK(TASK)
            IF (TASK.NE.QUIT) THEN
               IF(TASK.EQ.INITIA) THEN
                  CALL INITCP
               ELSEIF (TASK.EQ.UPDATE) THEN
                  CALL DOSTEP
               ELSEIF (TASK.EQ.OUTPUT) THEN
                  CALL OUTRES
               ENDIF
               GOTO 10
            ENDIF
C
            STOP
            END
C
CCCCCCCCCCCCCCCCC  END OF PROGRAM WAVFCP  CCCCCCCCCCCCCCCCCCC
C
            SUBROUTINE DOWNLD(PRGNAM)
            CHARACTER*9 PRGNAM
C
            INTEGER PROCNU, DOC, NPROC, MYPOS, LCHAN, RCHAN
            COMMON/EXTCOM/ PROCNU, DOC, NPROC, MYPOS, LCHAN, RCHAN
C
            PRINT *,' Please give the dimensionality of the hypercube '
            READ(*,*)DOC
C
```

```
              IRESP = KCUBEL (DOC, PRGNAM)
              NPROC = 2**DOC
C
              RETURN
              END
C
CCCCCCCCCCCCCCCCC  END OF PROGRAM DOWNLD  CCCCCCCCCCCCCCCCCCC
C
              SUBROUTINE GETASK(TASK)
C
              INTEGER INITIA, UPDATE, OUTPUT, QUIT
              PARAMETER ( INITIA=1, UPDATE=2, OUTPUT=3, QUIT=4 )
              PARAMETER ( ISIZE=4 )
              INTEGER TASK, STATUS
              CHARACTER*1 RESP
C
10            WRITE(*,100)
              READ(*,200) RESP
              IF (RESP.EQ.'1') THEN
                  TASK = INITIA
              ELSEIF (RESP.EQ.'2') THEN
                  TASK = UPDATE
              ELSEIF (RESP.EQ.'3') THEN
                  TASK = OUTPUT
              ELSEIF (RESP.EQ.'4') THEN
                  TASK = QUIT
              ELSE
                  WRITE(*,101)
                  GOTO 10
              ENDIF
C
              STATUS = KBCSTC(TASK,ISIZE)
C
              RETURN
C
100           FORMAT(/' Please select one of the following:'/
          #   '   1...to initialize a new problem'/
          #   '   2...to do some updates'/
          #   '   3...to output solution'/
          #   '   4...to terminate program'/)
101           FORMAT(/'**** Invalid input–please try again ****'/)
200           FORMAT(A)
C
```

```
          END
C
CCCCCCCCCCCCCCCC  END OF ROUTINE GETASK  CCCCCCCCCCCCCCCCC
C
          SUBROUTINE INITCP
C
          PARAMETER ( MAXSIZ = 500 )
C
          INTEGER PROCNU, DOC, NPROC, MYPOS, LCHAN, RCHAN
          COMMON/EXTCOM/ PROCNU, DOC, NPROC, MYPOS, LCHAN, RCHAN
C
          COMMON/NPTCOM/ NMIN, NLEFT, NTOT
C
          INTEGER DSIZE, STATUS
          DOUBLE PRECISION DELT, PI, FAC, X
          PARAMETER ( PI=3.14159265, DSIZE=8, ISIZE=4 )
C
10        WRITE(*,100)
          READ(*,*)NTOT
          NMIN = NTOT/NPROC
          NLEFT = MOD( NTOT, NPROC )
          IF(NMIN.GE.MAXSIZ) THEN
              WRITE(*,101)
              GOTO 10
          ENDIF
C
          WRITE(*,102)
          READ(*,*) DELT
C
          STATUS = KBCSTC( NTOT, ISIZE)
          STATUS = KBCSTC( DELT, DSIZE)
C
          RETURN
C
100       FORMAT(/' Please give the number of points'/)
101       FORMAT(/' **** Too many points specified ****'/)
102       FORMAT(/' Please give the time advance parameter'/)
C
          END
C
CCCCCCCCCCCCCCCC  END OF ROUTINE INITCP CCCCCCCCCCCCCCCCC
C
          SUBROUTINE DOSTEP
```

```
C
          INTEGER ISIZE, CHECK, STATUS
          PARAMETER ( ISIZE = 4 )
C
          WRITE(*,100)
          READ(*,*)NSTEP
          STATUS = KBCSTC(NSTEP,ISIZE)
C
          STATUS = KCOMBC(CHECK,ISIZE,1)
          IF(CHECK.EQ.0) THEN
              PRINT *,NSTEP,' updates completed'
          ELSE
              PRINT *,' An error occured in update'
          ENDIF
C
          RETURN
C
100       FORMAT(/' Please give the number of time steps'/)
C
          END
C
CCCCCCCCCCCCCCCCC  END OF ROUTINE DOSTEP  CCCCCCCCCCCCCCCCCC
C
          SUBROUTINE OUTRES
C
          PARAMETER ( MAXSIZ = 500 )
C
          INTEGER PROCNU, DOC, NPROC, MYPOS, LCHAN, RCHAN
          COMMON/EXTCOM/ PROCNU, DOC, NPROC, MYPOS, LCHAN, RCHAN
C
          COMMON/NPTCOM/ NMIN, NLEFT, NTOT
C
          DOUBLE PRECISION VALUES(0:MAXSIZ+1)
          PARAMETER ( MAXPRC = 16 )
          INTEGER BUFMAP(MAXPRC+1), DSIZE
          PARAMETER ( DSIZE = 8 )
C
          MAXBYT = (NMIN+1)*DSIZE
          DO 10 I = 0, NPROC-1
              NPTS = NMIN
              IF(I.LT.NLEFT) NPTS = NMIN+1
              STATUS = KMDUMP(VALUES(1),MAXBYT,BUFMAP)
              WRITE(*,100)( VALUES(J), J=1,NPTS)
```

```
10              CONTINUE
C
        RETURN
C
100     FORMAT(F8.4)
C
        END
C
CCCCCCCCCCCCCCCC  END OF ROUTINE OUTRES  CCCCCCCCCCCCCCCCC
C
```

D-7 FORTRAN Node Program

```
          PROGRAM WAVNOD
C
          INTEGER INITIA, UPDATE, OUTPUT, QUIT
          PARAMETER (INITIA=1, UPDATE=2, OUTPUT=3, QUIT=4)
C
          PARAMETER ( MAXSIZ=500 )
C
          INTEGER PROCNU, DOC, NPROC, MYPOS, LCHAN, RCHAN
          COMMON/EXTCOM/ PROCNU, DOC, NPROC, MYPOS, LCHAN, RCHAN
C
          DOUBLE PRECISION VALUES(0:MAXSIZ+1), OLDVAL(0:MAXSIZ+1),
     #    NEWVAL(0:MAXSIZ+1)
          COMMON/VALCOM/ VALUES, OLDVAL, NEWVAL
          COMMON/NPTCOM/ NMIN, NLEFT, NTOT
C
          INTEGER TASK,LEN
          DOUBLE PRECISION DELT
C
          CALL GPARAM
          CALL DECOMP
C
10        CALL GETASK(TASK)
          IF (TASK.NE.QUIT) THEN
             IF(TASK.EQ.INITIA) THEN
                CALL INITZE( LEN, DELT)
             ELSEIF (TASK.EQ.UPDATE) THEN
                CALL DOSTEP(LEN,DELT)
             ELSEIF (TASK.EQ.OUTPUT) THEN
                CALL OUTRES
             ENDIF
             GOTO 10
          ENDIF
C
          STOP
          END
C
CCCCCCCCCCCCCCCCC  END OF PROGRAM WAVNOD  CCCCCCCCCCCCCCCCCCC
C
          INTEGER FUNCTION ADDINT( I1, I2, ISIZE)
C
          I1 = I1+I2
          ADDINT = 0
```

```
          RETURN
          END
C
CCCCCCCCCCCCCCCCC  END OF PROGRAM ADDINT  CCCCCCCCCCCCCCCCCC
C
          SUBROUTINE GPARAM
C
          INTEGER PROCNU, DOC, NPROC, MYPOS, LCHAN, RCHAN
          COMMON/EXTCOM/ PROCNU, DOC, NPROC, MYPOS, LCHAN, RCHAN
          INTEGER ENV(5)
C
          CALL KCPARA( ENV )
          DOC=ENV(1)
          PROCNU=ENV(2)
          NPROC=ENV(3)
C
          RETURN
          END
C
CCCCCCCCCCCCCCCCC  END OF PROGRAM GPARAM  CCCCCCCCCCCCCCCCCC
C
          SUBROUTINE DECOMP
C
          INTEGER PROCNU, DOC, NPROC, MYPOS, LCHAN, RCHAN
          COMMON/EXTCOM/ PROCNU, DOC, NPROC, MYPOS, LCHAN, RCHAN
          INTEGER STATUS
C
          STATUS = KGRDIN( 1, NPROC )
          STATUS = KGRDCO( PROCNU, MYPOS )
C
          LCHAN = KGRDCH( PROCNU, 0, -1)
          RCHAN = KGRDCH( PROCNU, 0, 1)
          IF (MYPOS.EQ.0) LCHAN = 0
          IF (MYPOS.EQ.(NPROC-1)) RCHAN = 0
C
          RETURN
          END
C
CCCCCCCCCCCCCCCCC  END OF ROUTINE DECOMP  CCCCCCCCCCCCCCCCCC
C
          SUBROUTINE GETASK(TASK)
C
          INTEGER TASK, STATUS
```

```
          PARAMETER ( ISIZE=4 )
C
          STATUS = KBCSTE(TASK,ISIZE)
C
          RETURN
          END
C
CCCCCCCCCCCCCCCCC  END OF ROUTINE GETASK  CCCCCCCCCCCCCCCCC
C
          SUBROUTINE INITZE( LEN, DELT )
          INTEGER LEN
          DOUBLE PRECISION DELT
C
          INTEGER PROCNU, DOC, NPROC, MYPOS, LCHAN, RCHAN
          COMMON/EXTCOM/ PROCNU, DOC, NPROC, MYPOS, LCHAN, RCHAN
C
          PARAMETER ( MAXSIZ = 500 )
C
          DOUBLE PRECISION VALUES(0:MAXSIZ+1), OLDVAL(0:MAXSIZ+1),
     #    NEWVAL(0:MAXSIZ+1)
          COMMON/VALCOM/ VALUES, OLDVAL, NEWVAL
          COMMON/NPTCOM/ NMIN, NLEFT, NTOT
C
          INTEGER DSIZE, STATUS
          DOUBLE PRECISION PI, FAC, X
          PARAMETER ( PI=3.14159265, ISIZE=4, DSIZE=8 )
C
          STATUS = KBCSTE(NTOT,ISIZE)
          NMIN  = NTOT/NPROC
          NLEFT = MOD( NTOT, NPROC )
C
          FAC = 2.0*PI
          K = 0
          DO 20 I = 0, NPROC-1
             NPTS = NMIN
             IF(I.LT.NLEFT) NPTS = NMIN+1
             IF (MYPOS.EQ.I) THEN
                LEN = NPTS
                DO 30 J = 1, NPTS
                   X = DBLE(K)/DBLE(NTOT-1)
                   VALUES(J) = DSIN(FAC*X)
                   K = K+1
30              CONTINUE
```

```
                ELSE
                    K = K+NPTS
                ENDIF
20              CONTINUE
C
        STATUS = KBCSTE(DELT,DSIZE)
C
        DO 40 I = 1, LEN
40          OLDVAL(I) = VALUES(I)
C
        RETURN
        END
C
CCCCCCCCCCCCCCCCC  END OF ROUTINE INITZE  CCCCCCCCCCCCCCCCC
C
        SUBROUTINE DOSTEP( LEN, DEL )
        INTEGER LEN
        DOUBLE PRECISION DEL
C
        INTEGER PROCNU, DOC, NPROC, MYPOS, LCHAN, RCHAN
        COMMON/EXTCOM/ PROCNU, DOC, NPROC, MYPOS, LCHAN, RCHAN
C
        PARAMETER ( MAXSIZ = 500 )
C
        DOUBLE PRECISION VALUES(0:MAXSIZ+1), OLDVAL(0:MAXSIZ+1),
     #  NEWVAL(0:MAXSIZ+1)
        COMMON/VALCOM/ VALUES, OLDVAL, NEWVAL
C
        DOUBLE PRECISION C, DELX, PFAC
        INTEGER DSIZE, STATUS, CHECK, ADDINT
        PARAMETER ( ISIZE = 4, DSIZE = 8 )
        EXTERNAL ADDINT
C
        STATUS = KBCSTE(NSTEP, ISIZE)
C
        C  = 1.0
        DELX = 1.0
        PFAC = (C*DEL/DELX)**2
C
        DO 20 I = 0, NSTEP-1
            STATUS = KCSHIF( VALUES(0), LCHAN, DSIZE, VALUES(LEN),
     #                       RCHAN, DSIZE )
            STATUS = KCSHIF( VALUES(LEN+1), RCHAN, DSIZE, VALUES(1),
```

```
      #                         LCHAN, DSIZE )
            DO 30 J = 1, LEN
                IF (MYPOS.EQ.0.AND.J.EQ.1) THEN
                    NEWVAL(J) = 0.0
                ELSEIF (MYPOS.EQ.(NPROC-1).AND.J.EQ.LEN) THEN
                    NEWVAL(J)=0.0
                ELSE
                    NEWVAL(J) = 2.0*VALUES(J) - OLDVAL(J) + (VALUES(J+1)
      #                    -2.0*VALUES(J) + VALUES(J-1))*PFAC
                ENDIF
30          CONTINUE
C
            DO 40 J = 1, LEN
                OLDVAL(J) = VALUES(J)
40              VALUES(J) = NEWVAL(J)
C
20          CONTINUE
C

      CHECK  = 0
      STATUS = KCOMBE(CHECK,ADDINT,ISIZE,1)
C
      RETURN
      END
C
CCCCCCCCCCCCCCCCCC  END OF ROUTINE DOSTEP  CCCCCCCCCCCCCCCCCC
C
      SUBROUTINE OUTRES
C
      PARAMETER ( MAXSIZ = 500 )
 \  C
 )
 ,    INTEGER PROCNU, DOC, NPROC, MYPOS, LCHAN, RCHAN
      COMMON/EXTCOM/ PROCNU, DOC, NPROC, MYPOS, LCHAN, RCHAN
 C
      DOUBLE PRECISION VALUES(0:MAXSIZ+1), OLDVAL(0:MAXSIZ+1),
      # NEWVAL(0:MAXSIZ+1)
      COMMON/VALCOM/ VALUES, OLDVAL, NEWVAL
      COMMON/NPTCOM/ NMIN, NLEFT, NTOT
 C
      INTEGER STATUS, DSIZE
      PARAMETER ( DSIZE = 8 )
 C
      DO 10 I = 0, NPROC-1
          NPTS = NMIN
```

```
                     IF(I.LT.NLEFT) NPTS = NMIN+1
                     IF(MYPOS.NE.I) NPTS = 0
                     STATUS = KDUMPE( VALUES(1), NPTS*DSIZE )
10                   CONTINUE
C
              RETURN
              END
C
CCCCCCCCCCCCCCCCC  END OF ROUTINE OUTRES  CCCCCCCCCCCCCCCCC
C
```

D-8 FORTRAN CUBIX Code

```
        PROGRAM WAVCUB
C
        INTEGER INITIA, UPDATE, OUTPUT, QUIT
        PARAMETER (INITIA=1, UPDATE=2, OUTPUT=3, QUIT=4)
C
        PARAMETER ( MAXSIZ=500 )
C
        INTEGER PROCNU, DOC, NPROC, MYPOS, LCHAN, RCHAN
        COMMON/EXTCOM/ PROCNU, DOC, NPROC, MYPOS, LCHAN, RCHAN
C
        DOUBLE PRECISION VALUES(0:MAXSIZ+1), OLDVAL(0:MAXSIZ+1),
     #  NEWVAL(0:MAXSIZ+1)
        COMMON/VALCOM/ VALUES, OLDVAL, NEWVAL
        COMMON/NPTCOM/ NMIN, NLEFT, NTOT
C
        INTEGER TASK,LEN
        DOUBLE PRECISION DELT
C
        CALL GPARAM
        CALL DECOMP
C
10      CALL GETASK(TASK)
        IF (TASK.NE.QUIT) THEN
            IF(TASK.EQ.INITIA) THEN
                CALL INITZE( LEN, DELT)
            ELSEIF (TASK.EQ.UPDATE) THEN
                CALL DOSTEP(LEN,DELT)
            ELSEIF (TASK.EQ.OUTPUT) THEN
                CALL OUTRES
            ENDIF
            GOTO 10
        ENDIF
C
        STOP
        END
C
CCCCCCCCCCCCCCCCC  END OF PROGRAM WAVCUB  CCCCCCCCCCCCCCCCCCC
C
        SUBROUTINE GPARAM
C
        INTEGER PROCNU, DOC, NPROC, MYPOS, LCHAN, RCHAN
        COMMON/EXTCOM/ PROCNU, DOC, NPROC, MYPOS, LCHAN, RCHAN
```

```
          INTEGER ENV(5)
C
          CALL KCPARA( ENV )
          DOC=ENV(1)
          PROCNU=ENV(2)
          NPROC=ENV(3)
C
          RETURN
          END
C
CCCCCCCCCCCCCCCCC  END OF PROGRAM GPARAM  CCCCCCCCCCCCCCCCCC
C
          SUBROUTINE DECOMP
C
          INTEGER PROCNU, DOC, NPROC, MYPOS, LCHAN, RCHAN
          COMMON/EXTCOM/ PROCNU, DOC, NPROC, MYPOS, LCHAN, RCHAN
          INTEGER STATUS
C
          STATUS = KGRDIN( 1, NPROC )
          STATUS = KGRDCO( PROCNU, MYPOS )
C
          LCHAN = KGRDCH( PROCNU, 0, -1)
          RCHAN = KGRDCH( PROCNU, 0, 1)
          IF (MYPOS.EQ.0) LCHAN = 0
          IF (MYPOS.EQ.(NPROC-1)) RCHAN = 0
C
          RETURN
          END
C
CCCCCCCCCCCCCCCCC  END OF ROUTINE DECOMP  CCCCCCCCCCCCCCCCCC
C
          SUBROUTINE GETASK(TASK)
C
          INTEGER INITIA, UPDATE, OUTPUT, QUIT
          PARAMETER ( INITIA=1, UPDATE=2, OUTPUT=3, QUIT=4 )
          INTEGER TASK
          CHARACTER*1 RESP
C
10        CONTINUE
          WRITE(*,100)
#ifdef PAR
          FLUSH(*)
#endif
```

```
          READ(*,200) RESP
          IF (RESP.EQ.'1') THEN
              TASK = INITIA
          ELSEIF (RESP.EQ.'2') THEN
              TASK = UPDATE
          ELSEIF (RESP.EQ.'3') THEN
              TASK = OUTPUT
          ELSEIF (RESP.EQ.'4') THEN
              TASK = QUIT
          ELSE
              WRITE(*,101)
              GOTO 10
          ENDIF
C
          RETURN
C
100       FORMAT(/' Please select one of the following:'/
     #    '   1...to initialize a new problem'/'   2...to do some updates'/
     #    '   3...to output solution'/'   4...to terminate program'/)
101       FORMAT(/'**** Invalid input–please try again ****'/)
200       FORMAT(A)
C
          END
C
CCCCCCCCCCCCCCCCC  END OF ROUTINE GETASK  CCCCCCCCCCCCCCCCC
C
          SUBROUTINE INITZE( LEN, DELT )
          INTEGER LEN
          DOUBLE PRECISION DELT
C
          PARAMETER ( MAXSIZ = 500 )
C
          INTEGER PROCNU, DOC, NPROC, MYPOS, LCHAN, RCHAN
          COMMON/EXTCOM/ PROCNU, DOC, NPROC, MYPOS, LCHAN, RCHAN
C
          DOUBLE PRECISION VALUES(0:MAXSIZ+1), OLDVAL(0:MAXSIZ+1),
     #    NEWVAL(0:MAXSIZ+1)
          COMMON/VALCOM/ VALUES, OLDVAL, NEWVAL
          COMMON/NPTCOM/ NMIN, NLEFT, NTOT
C
          DOUBLE PRECISION PI, FAC, X
          PARAMETER ( PI=3.14159265 )
C
```

```
10          CONTINUE
            WRITE(*,100)
#ifdef PAR
            FLUSH(*)
#endif
            READ(*,*)NTOT
            NMIN = NTOT/NPROC
            NLEFT = MOD( NTOT, NPROC )
            IF(NMIN.GE.MAXSIZ) THEN
                WRITE(*,101)
#ifdef PAR
                FLUSH(*)
#endif
                GOTO 10
            ENDIF
C
            FAC = 2.0*PI
            K = 0
            DO 20 I = 0, NPROC-1
                NPTS = NMIN
                IF(I.LT.NLEFT) NPTS = NMIN+1
                IF (MYPOS.EQ.I) THEN
                    LEN = NPTS
                    DO 30 J = 1, NPTS
                        X = DBLE(K)/DBLE(NTOT-1)
                        VALUES(J) = DSIN(FAC*X)
                        K = K+1
30                  CONTINUE
                ELSE
                    K = K+NPTS
                ENDIF
20          CONTINUE
C
            WRITE(*,102)
#ifdef PAR
            FLUSH(*)
#endif
            READ(*,*) DELT
C
            DO 40 I = 1, LEN
40              OLDVAL(I) = VALUES(I)
C
            RETURN
```

```
C
100        FORMAT(/' Please give the number of points'/)
101        FORMAT(/' **** Too many points specified ****'/)
102        FORMAT(/' Please give the time advance parameter'/)
C
           END
C
CCCCCCCCCCCCCCCC  END OF ROUTINE INITZE  CCCCCCCCCCCCCCCC
C
           SUBROUTINE DOSTEP( LEN, DEL )
           INTEGER LEN
           DOUBLE PRECISION DEL
C
           INTEGER PROCNU, DOC, NPROC, MYPOS, LCHAN, RCHAN
           COMMON/EXTCOM/ PROCNU, DOC, NPROC, MYPOS, LCHAN, RCHAN
C
           PARAMETER ( MAXSIZ = 500 )
C
           DOUBLE PRECISION VALUES(0:MAXSIZ+1), OLDVAL(0:MAXSIZ+1),
     #     NEWVAL(0:MAXSIZ+1)
           COMMON/VALCOM/ VALUES, OLDVAL, NEWVAL
C
           DOUBLE PRECISION C, DELX, PFAC
           INTEGER DSIZE, STATUS
           PARAMETER ( DSIZE = 8 )
C
           WRITE(*,100)
#ifdef PAR
           FLUSH(*)
#endif
           READ(*,*)NSTEP
C
           C = 1.0
           DELX = 1.0
           PFAC = (C*DEL/DELX)*2
C
           DO 20 I = 0, NSTEP-1
               STATUS = KCSHIF( VALUES(0), LCHAN, DSIZE, VALUES(LEN),
     #                          RCHAN, DSIZE )
               STATUS = KCSHIF( VALUES(LEN+1), RCHAN, DSIZE, VALUES(1),
     #                          LCHAN, DSIZE )
               DO 30 J = 1, LEN
                   IF(MYPOS.EQ.0.AND.J.EQ.1) THEN
```

```
                         NEWVAL(J) = 0.0
                         ELSEIF (MYPOS.EQ.(NPROC-1).AND.J.EQ.LEN) THEN
                         NEWVAL(J)=0.0
                         ELSE
                         NEWVAL(J) = 2.0*VALUES(J) - OLDVAL(J) + (VALUES(J+1)
         #                        -2.0*VALUES(J) + VALUES(J-1))*PFAC
                         ENDIF
30                       CONTINUE
C
              DO 40 J = 1, LEN
                         OLDVAL(J) = VALUES(J)
40                       VALUES(J) = NEWVAL(J)
C
20                       CONTINUE
C
              RETURN
C
100           FORMAT(/' Please give the number of time steps'/)
C
              END
C
CCCCCCCCCCCCCCCCC  END OF ROUTINE DOSTEP  CCCCCCCCCCCCCCCCCC
C
              SUBROUTINE OUTRES
C
              PARAMETER ( MAXSIZ = 500 )
C
              INTEGER PROCNU, DOC, NPROC, MYPOS, LCHAN, RCHAN
              COMMON/EXTCOM/ PROCNU, DOC, NPROC, MYPOS, LCHAN, RCHAN
C
              DOUBLE PRECISION VALUES(0:MAXSIZ+1), OLDVAL(0:MAXSIZ+1),
         #    NEWVAL(0:MAXSIZ+1)
              COMMON/VALCOM/ VALUES, OLDVAL, NEWVAL
              COMMON/NPTCOM/ NMIN, NLEFT, NTOT
C
              INTEGER STDOUT
              PARAMETER ( STDOUT = 6 )
C
#ifdef PAR
              MULTIPLE( STDOUT )
#endif
C
              K = 0
```

```
          DO 10 I = 0, NPROC-1
              NPTS = NMIN
              IF(I.LT.NLEFT) NPTS = NMIN+1
              DO 20 J = 1, NPTS
                  IF(MYPOS.EQ.I) WRITE(*,100) VALUES(J)
                  K = K+1
#ifdef PAR
                  IF(MOD(K,60).EQ.59) FLUSH(STDOUT)
#endif
20                CONTINUE
#ifdef PAR
              FLUSH(STDOUT)
#endif
10            CONTINUE
C
#ifdef PAR
      SINGLE( STDOUT )
#endif
C
      RETURN
C
100   FORMAT(F8.4)
C
      END
C
CCCCCCCCCCCCCCCCC  END OF ROUTINE OUTRES  CCCCCCCCCCCCCCCCC
C
#ifdef SEQ
#include "cros3SEQ.f"
#endif
```

D-9 The File Cros3SEQ.f

```
      FUNCTION KGRDIN(GRIDIM,BUFF)
      INTEGER GRIDIM,BUFF(*)
      COMMON/GRDCOM/IDIM
      SAVE /GRDCOM/
      IDIM = GRIDIM
      KGRDIN = 0
      RETURN
      END
C
CCCCCCCCCCCCCCCCCC  END OF ROUTINE KGRDIN  CCCCCCCCCCCCCCCCCC
C
      FUNCTION KGRDCO(PROC,BUFF)
      INTEGER PROC,BUFF(*)
      COMMON/GRDCOM/IDIM
      SAVE /GRDCOM/
      DO 10 I=1,IDIM
10         BUFF(I) = 0
      KGRDCO = 0
      RETURN
       END
C
CCCCCCCCCCCCCCCCCC  END OF ROUTINE KGRDCO  CCCCCCCCCCCCCCCCCCC
C
      FUNCTION KGRDCH(PROC,DIR,SIGN)
      INTEGER PROC,DIR,SIGN
      KGRDCH = 0
      RETURN
      END
C
CCCCCCCCCCCCCCCCCC  END OF ROUTINE KGRDCH CCCCCCCCCCCCCCCCCCCCC
C
      FUNCTION KCSHIF(INBUF,INCHN,INBYT,OUTBUF,OUTCHN,OUTBYT)
      DOUBLE PRECISION INBUF(*),OUTBUF(*)
      INTEGER INCHN,OUTCHN,INBYT,OUTBYT
      INTEGER SIZED
      PARAMETER (SIZED=8)
C
      IF (INCHN.NE.0.OR.OUTCHN.NE.0) THEN
          KCSHIF = -1
          RETURN
      ENDIF
C
```

```
            INDP = MIN0(INBYT,OUTBYT)/SIZED
            DO 10 I=1,INDP
10              INBUF(I) = OUTBUF(I)
            KCSHIF = MIN0(INBYT,OUTBYT)
C
            RETURN
            END
C
CCCCCCCCCCCCCCCCCCCCC  END OF ROUTINE KCSHIF  CCCCCCCCCCCCCCCCCCC
C
            SUBROUTINE KCPARA(ENV)
            INTEGER ENV(5)
            ENV(1) = 0
            ENV(2) = 0
            ENV(3) = 1
            ENV(4) = 1
            ENV(5) = 1
            RETURN
            END
C
CCCCCCCCCCCCCCCCCCCCC  END OF ROUTINE KCPARA  CCCCCCCCCCCCCCCCCCC
C
```

E

Appendix E:
The CrOS III Operating System

This appendix presents the manual pages for the CrOS III operating described in Chap. 14. The manual pages are divided into four sections. The first section describes the low-level communication routines, such as *cread* and *cwrite*. The second section deals with the higher-level communication routines which allow the user to shift, broadcast, and combine data from different nodes. The third section describes the routines for handling communication between the control processor and the nodes. The final section is a library of utilities. At present the library contains only the *gridmap* routines, but many of the routines described in Chaps. 21 and 22, such as *index, fold, transpose,* and the *crystal_router*, will be included in the Software Supplement, volume 2 of this book.

NAME
   intro–introduction to basic communication system calls

DESCRIPTION
   Section 1 of this manual lists all of the low-level entries into the communication system.

   Many of the basic communication routines are more conveniently used indirectly through the various routines described in Sec. 2 of the manual. For instance, *cshift*(2) is much easier to use than *cread*(1) and *cwrite*(1) because with *cshift*(2) the user does not have to make sure that a write on one side of a channel is complemented by a read on the other side of the channel. However, using *cread*(1) and *cwrite*(1) is certainly more flexible.

   The communication system calls described in this section can be used in both the nodes and the control processor. The file **<cros.h>** defines masks for the channels, the external variable *errcnt*, and the structure *cubenv* that is used by *cparam* (4), and in addition contains macro definitions, such as NULLPTR, used in some of the communication routines.

   All of the communication system calls return −1 to indicate an error. The types of errors that can occur are discussed on the manual pages for each routine. For the C implementation in the external variable *errno* is the same *errno* defined in the UNIX environment and contains the error number, which is used to identify the specific error that occurred. The unix function *perror* can be used to obtain error messages. In addition, some types of errors use the external variable *errcnt* to give additional information about the error. Since *errno* and *errcnt* are not cleared on successful calls, they should be tested only after an error has occurred. The defined values of *errno* and their macros appear in **<errno.h>**. Typical errors are:

   A communication error was detected when data were read from a channel.

   For some reason the buffer address used as a argument to a communication routine is invalid.

   An invalid channel mask was used.

   The byte or item count of the routine is out of range.

   More data was received than could be placed in memory. The maximum amount of data indicated by the routine's arguments has been placed in memory and the rest lost. The amount of data that was actually transmitted is recorded in *errcnt*.

The memory buffer or file being used as the input to *floadcp*(3) or *mloadcp* (3) is invalid. Problems arise if the size of a block of data is out of range or if the number of blocks is less than the number of active nodes.

The return code of the combining function in *combine* (2) returned an error.

A node not directly connected to the control processor tried to write to it.

The communication channels are identified by a *channel mask*. The channel mask is a bit field composed of a one at the bit positions of the desired channels and zeros elsewhere, where the rightmost bit is bit 0. Thus, a channel mask is easily constructed from a channel number, which might be a loop index, by left shifting a 1 by the loop index. For instance, in C $(1 << i)$ converts the channel number i into a channel mask and in Fortran $2**i$ does the same thing. A channel mask indicating several channels is obtained by combining several single channel masks with the bitwise XOR operator.

SEE ALSO
intro(2), intro(3)

NAME
cread—read from a communication channel and forward

C SYNOPSIS
int cread (buffer, inmask, outmask, nbytes)
char *buffer;
unsigned int inmask, outmask;
int nbytes;

C DESCRIPTION
cread may be called from either the nodes or the control processor. *cread* causes at most *nbytes* bytes of data to be read from the communication channel indicated by the channel mask *inmask* and placed in memory starting at *buffer*. In addition, the data is forwarded to the channels indicated by the channel mask *outmask* as it is being read. However, the data cannot be written to the incoming channel *inmask*. It is not guaranteed that *nbytes* bytes will be read; the actual number of bytes read depends on the number written by the transmitting node. If no error occurs, the actual number of bytes read from the communication channel is returned to the calling program.

A call to *cread* must be complemented by a call to *cwrite* on the other side of the channel indicated by *inmask*, and by a call to *cread* on the other side of any channels indicated by *outmask*. Otherwise, deadlock will result.

If more than *nbytes* bytes are written by the transmitting node, only the first *nbytes* bytes are placed in *buffer*. The remaining bytes are read from the channel, so the corresponding call to *cwrite* in the transmitting node can return, but the extra bytes are lost and a −1 is returned to indicate the error. The type of error is identified in the external variable *errno*, and the number of bytes that were transmitted is saved in the external variable *errcnt*. It is considered bad programming style not to make *nbytes* large enough so that all incoming bytes are received and placed in *buffer*. Also, the system slows down when this occurs.

In any case, the whole message is forwarded to the channels indicated in *outmask*. If *buffer* has the special value NULLPTR, the data are not placed in memory; they are only written to the channels indicated by *outmask* and the value of *nbytes* is irrelevant. The number of bytes forwarded is then returned in place of the number of bytes read. If *outmask* is 0, the data are not forwarded to any channels as they are read. If *inmask* is 0, the call to *cread* is ignored, so no call to *cwrite* is needed to complement it. However, if *nbytes* is 0 and *inmask* is nonzero, the call to *cread* must still be complemented by a call to *cwrite* .

Function *cread* can be used to simulate a pipe (i.e., forward a message without saving it in a buffer) by setting *buffer* equal to NULLPTR, and setting the channel mask *outmask* to just a single channel. Similarly, *cread* can be used as a pass (forward a message and save it in *buffer*) by setting *outmask* to just one channel, and setting *buffer* to the location where the data should be stored.

FORTRAN SYNOPSIS
    INTEGER FUNCTION KCREAD (BUFFER, INMSK, OUTMSK, NBYTES)
    INTEGER BUFFER (*), INMSK, OUTMSK, NBYTES

SEE ALSO
    cwrite(1)

DIAGNOSTICS
    If an error occurs in *cread* , it returns a −1 and sets *errno* accordingly. Otherwise,
    it returns the number of bytes actually read. Many conditions can generate an
    error: communication errors, a bad buffer address, an invalid *inmask* or *outmask*, a
    preposterous value of *nbytes*, or reading a message that is longer than *nbytes*. Indi-
    cating more than one channel in the channel mask *inmask* generates an error.
    Communication errors are detected by comparing the checksum of the incoming
    data with the checksum appended to the data by *cwrite* .

NAME
cwrite–write to communication channels

SYNOPSIS
int cwrite (buffer, mask, nbytes)
char *buffer;
unsigned int mask;
int nbytes;

DESCRIPTION
cwrite may be called from either the nodes or the control processor.

cwrite causes *nbytes* bytes of data to be written from memory starting at *buffer* to the communication channels indicated by the channel mask *mask*.

It is guaranteed that *nbytes* bytes will be written; *cwrite* will not return until all *nbytes* bytes of data have been written to each indicated channel and read by the receiving nodes. A call to *cwrite* must be complemented by a call to *cread* on the other side of all of the channels indicated by *mask* . Otherwise, deadlock will result. If *mask* is 0, the call to *cwrite* is ignored, so no call to *cread* is needed to complement it. However, if *nbytes* is 0 and *mask* is nonzero, the call to *cwrite* must still be complemented by a call to *cread*.

FORTRAN SYNOPSIS
INTEGER FUNCTION KCWRIT (BUFFER, MASK, NBYTES)
INTEGER BUFFER (*), MASK, NBYTES

SEE ALSO
cread(1)

DIAGNOSTICS
If an error occurs in *cwrite*, it returns a −1 and sets *errno* accordingly. Otherwise, it returns the number of bytes written. Several conditions can generate an error: a bad buffer address, a nonexistent channel indicated by *mask*, or a preposterous value of *nbytes*. Although no communication errors can be detected by *cwrite*, it appends a checksum to the data when they are written allowing *cread* to detect communication errors when the data are read.

NAME
>   rdstat–check for receive ready

C SYNOPSIS
>   **int rdstat (mask)**
>   **unsigned int mask;**

C DESCRIPTION
>   *rdstat* may be called either from the nodes or the control processor.
>   *rdstat* checks whether the communication channels indicated by the channel mask
>   *mask* have data ready to be read. *rdstat* returns a 1 if messages are ready to be
>   received on all of indicated channels. If the channel mask *mask* contains a channel
>   that does not exist, *rdstat* returns a −1 to indicate the error. Otherwise, it returns a
>   value of 0.
>
>   *rdstat* may be useful for some types of timing routines since a node could incre-
>   ment a counter until *rdstat* indicates that a message has arrived. The value of the
>   counter gives a measure of the amount of time spent waiting for the message and
>   the node can then call either *cread* (1) or *vread*(1) to read the incoming message.

FORTRAN SYNOPSIS
>   INTEGER FUNCTION KRDSTA (MASK)
>   INTEGER MASK

NAME
   vread–read a vector from a communication channel and forward

C SYNOPSIS
   int vread (buffer, inmask, outmask, size, offset, nitems)
   char *buffer;
   unsigned int inmask, outmask;
   int size, offset, nitems;

C DESCRIPTION
   vread may be called from either the nodes or the control processor.

   vread causes at most *nitems* data items to be read from the communication channel indicated by the channel mask *inmask* and placed in memory starting at *buffer* . In addition, the data is forwarded to the channels indicated by the channel mask *outmask* as it is being read. However, the data cannot be written to the incoming channel *inmask*. The size of each data item is *size* bytes, as given by *sizeof(item)*, and the offset between data items is *offset* bytes.

   It is not guaranteed that *nitems* data items will be read; the actual number of items read depends on the number written by the transmitting node. If no error occurs, the actual number of items read from the communication channel is returned to the calling program.

   A call to *vread* must be complemented by a call to *vwrite* on the other side of the channel indicated by *inmask*, and by a call to *vread* on the other side of any channels indicated by *outmask* . In addition, all must specify the same value of *size*. Otherwise, deadlock will result.

   If more than *nitems* data items are written by the transmitting node, only the first *nitems* items are placed in *buffer*. The remaining items are read from the channel, so the corresponding call to *vwrite* in the transmitting node can return, but the extra data items are lost and −1 is returned to indicate the error. The type of error is identified in the external variable *errno*, and the number of items that were transmitted is saved in the external variable *errcnt*. It is considered bad programming style not to make *nitems* large enough so that all incoming data items are received and placed in *buffer*.

   In any case, the whole message is forwarded to the channels indicated in *outmask*. If *buffer* has the special value NULLPTR, the data items are not placed in memory; they are only written to the channels indicated by *outmask* and the value of *nitems* is irrelevant. The number of items forwarded is then returned in place of the number of items read. If *outmask* is 0, the data items are not forwarded to any channels as they are read. If *inmask* is 0, the call to *vread* is ignored, so no call to *vwrite* is needed to complement it. However, if *nitems* is 0 and *inmask* is nonzero, the call to *vread* must still be complemented by a call to *vwrite*.

Function *vread* can be used to forward a message without storing it in a buffer (in technical terms, a *pipe*) by setting *buffer* equal to NULLPTR and setting the channel mask *outmask* to just a single channel. Similarly, *vread* can be used to forward a message and store it in *buffer* (in technical terms, a *pass*) by setting *outmask* to just one channel, and setting *buffer* to the location where the data should be stored.

C EXAMPLE

If the incoming data is to be stored in every fifth element in an array of floats and *sizeof(float)* is 4, then *size* would be 4 and *offset* would be 20. Then, with *buffer* and *nitems* properly set, the function call must be issued, i.e.:

n = vread(buffer, inmask, outmask, size, offset, nitems);

FORTRAN SYNOPSIS

INTEGER FUNCTION KVREAD (BUFFER, INMSK, OUTMSK, SIZE, OFFSET, NITEMS)
INTEGER BUFFER (*), INMSK, OUTMSK, SIZE, OFFSET, NITEMS

SEE ALSO

vwrite(1)

DIAGNOSTICS

If an error occurs in *vread*, it returns a −1 and sets *errno* accordingly. Otherwise, it returns the number of data items actually read. Many conditions can generate an error: communication errors, a bad buffer address, an invalid *inmask* or *outmask*, preposterous values of *size*, *offset*, or *nitems*, or reading a message that is longer than *nitems*. Indicating more than one channel in the channel mask *inmask* generates an error. Communication errors are detected by comparing the checksum of the incoming data with the checksum appended to the data by *vwrite*.

NAME
vwrite–write a vector to communication channels

C SYNOPSIS
int vwrite (buffer, mask, size, offset, nitems)
char *buffer;
unsigned int mask;
int size, offset, nitems;

C DESCRIPTION
vwrite may be called from either the nodes or the control processor.

vwrite writes *nitems* data items from memory starting at *buffer* to the communication channels indicated by the channel mask *mask* . The size of each data item is *size* bytes, as given by *sizeof(item)* and the offset between data items is *offset* bytes. It is guaranteed that *nitems* data items will be written; *vwrite* will not return until all *nitems* items of data have been written to each indicated channel and read by the receiving nodes. A call to *vwrite* must be complemented by a call to *vread* on the other side of all of the channels indicated by *mask*. In addition, all must specify the same value of *size*. Otherwise, deadlock will result. If *mask* is 0, the call to *vwrite* is ignored, so no call to *vread* is needed to complement it. However, if *nitems* is 0 and *mask* is nonzero, the call to *vwrite* must still be complemented by a call to *vread*.

C EXAMPLE
If every third element of an array of integers is to be written and *sizeof(int)* is 2, then *size* would be 2 and *offset* would be 6. Then, with *buffer* and *nitems* properly set, the function call must be issued, i.e.:
n = vwrite(buffer, mask, size, offset, nitems);

FORTRAN SYNOPSIS
INTEGER FUNCTION KVWRIT (BUFFER, MASK, SIZE, OFFSET, NITEMS,)
INTEGER BUFFER (*), MASK, SIZE, OFFSET, NITEMS

SEE ALSO
vread(1)

DIAGNOSTICS
If an error occurs in *vwrite*, it returns −1 and sets *errno* accordingly. Otherwise, it returns the number of data items written. Many conditions can generate an error: a bad buffer address, a nonexistent channel indicated by *mask*, or preposterous values of *size*, *offset*, or *nitems*. Although no communication errors can be detected by *vwrite*, it appends a checksum to the data when they are written allowing *vread* to detect communication errors when the data are read.

NAME

intro–introduction to higher-level communication routines

DESCRIPTION

This section describes communication routines that can be built from the basic communication routines described in Sec. 1. Although the routine in this section are somewhat less flexible than the basic communication routines, they are much easier to use since they implement the collective communications commonly found in application programs. Accordingly, beginning users should master the use of the routines in this section before attempting to implement their own complex communication schemes that require the basic communication routines.

intro(1), intro(3)

DIAGNOSTICS

All of the communication system calls return −1 to indicate that an error occurred. The types of errors that can occur are discussed on the manual pages for each routine. The two external variables, *errno* and *errcnt*, are used to identify the specific error that occurred.

C NAME
broadcast—broadcast data to subcube

C SYNOPSIS
int broadcast (buffer, src, mask, nbytes)
char *buffer;
int src, nbytes;
unsigned int mask;

C DESCRIPTION
broadcast may be called only from the nodes.

broadcast causes *nbytes* bytes of data to be written by processor number *src* from memory starting at *buffer* to all of the other nodes in the subcube defined by the channel mask *mask*. In nodes in the subcube other than the source node, *broadcast* causes at most *nbytes* bytes of data to be read from the source node and placed in memory starting at *buffer*. The source node and the communication channels indicated in the channel mask *mask* uniquely determine the subcube. All nodes in the subcube do not have to use the same value of *nbytes*.

It is guaranteed that *nbytes* bytes will be written to all nodes in the subcube; *broadcast* will not return in the source node until all *nbytes* bytes of data have been written to and read by each node. However, it is not guaranteed that *nbytes* bytes will be read in the nodes other than the source node; the actual number of bytes read depends on the number written by the source node. A call to *broadcast* in the source node must be complemented by a call to *broadcast* in all other nodes in the subcube indicated by the channel mask *mask*. In addition, all must use the same values of *src* and *mask*. Otherwise, deadlock will result.

If the value of *nbytes* is larger in the source node than in a receiving node, only the first *nbytes* bytes are placed in the receiving node's memory starting at *buffer*. The remaining bytes are then read, so the corresponding calls to *broadcast* in the other nodes in the subcube can return, but the extra bytes are lost and −1 is returned to indicate the error. The type of error is identified in the external variable *errno*, and the number of bytes that were transmitted by the source node is saved in the external variable *errcnt*. If *buffer* has the special value NULLPTR in one of the nodes other than the source node, the data are not placed in memory and the value of *nbytes* is irrelevant. The number of bytes transmitted by the source node is then returned in place of the number of bytes read.

FORTRAN SYNOPSIS
INTEGER FUNCTION KBROAD (BUFFER, SRC, MASK, NBYTES)
INTEGER BUFFER (*) , SRC, MASK, NBYTES

SEE ALSO

cread(1), cwrite(1)

DIAGNOSTICS

If an error occurs in *broadcast*, it returns −1 and sets *errno* accordingly. Otherwise, it returns the number of bytes written by the source node. Many conditions can generate an error: communication errors, a bad buffer address, an invalid *src* or *mask*, a preposterous value of *nbytes*, or reading a message that is longer than *nbytes*. Communication errors are detected by comparing the checksum of the incoming data with the checksum appended to the data written by the source node. No communication errors can be detected by the source node.

C NAME
combine—combine data from all nodes

C SYNOPSIS
int combine (buffer, func, size, nitems)
char *buffer;
int (*func)(), size, nitems;

C DESCRIPTION
combine may be called only from the nodes.

combine causes *nitems* data items of size *size* bytes to be taken from memory starting at *buffer* and combined with the data from all other nodes using the combining function given by *func*. The contents of *buffer* are overwritten with the result of the combining operation.

The combining function, which takes three arguments, combines the data items in pairs. It combines the two data items indicated by its first two arguments, which are pointers, to the two data items to be combined, and overwrites the data item indicated by its first argument with the result. The third argument of the combining function is *size*, which allows the possibility of using the same combining function on data items of different size. The maximum value of *size* is dependent on the implementation. In order to avoid making assumptions about the order in which data items from each node are combined, the combining function should be commutative and associative and identical in all of the nodes. For instance, the combining function could return the sum of its input data items, so the result of *combine* would be the sum of the data items from each of the nodes. If the combining function instead returned the maximum of its two arguments, the result of *combine* would then be the maximum of the data item over all nodes. The calling sequence of *func* is:

$$status = (*func)(ptr1, ptr2, size);$$

where the value returned by *func* is a -1 if an error occurred for any reason. Note that even if a function is commutative, floating-point operations may cause rounding errors, and thus the function will not work. Floating-point operations should be avoided, or at least used with caution.

Since the data items from all of the nodes will be combined with *func*, *combine* must be called together by all of the nodes and nodes must use the same values of *size* and *nitems*. Otherwise, deadlock will result.

FORTRAN SYNOPSIS
INTEGER FUNCTION KCOMBI (BUFFER, FUNC, SIZE, NITEMS)
INTEGER BUFFER (*), FUNC, SIZE, NITEMS

SEE ALSO
combelt(3)

DIAGNOSTICS
If an error occurs in *combine*, it returns −1 and sets *errno* accordingly. Otherwise, it returns the number of data items combined. Many conditions can generate an error: communication errors, a bad buffer address, an error returned by *func* or too large a value of *size* or *nitems*. Communication errors are detected by comparing the checksum of the incoming data with the checksum appended to the data when they were written. Since a node must buffer two data items of *size* bytes, some reasonable limit, such as 512 bytes, must be imposed on *size*.

C NAME

concat–concatenate data items from all nodes

C SYNOPSIS

int concat (outbuf, nbytes, inbuf, binsz, szarray)

char *outbuf, *inbuf;
int nbytes, binsz;
int *szarray;

C DESCRIPTION

concat may only be called from the nodes.

concat takes *nbytes* of data, beginning at the pointer *outbuf* , and distributes it to all the nodes of the hypercube. The other nodes are simultaneously distributing their own blocks of data. *concat* places all data blocks into memory, starting at pointer *inbuf*, in procnum order. A maximum of *binsz* bytes of data from each node is concatenated and stored in memory. *concat* then keeps a list of the number of bytes (less than or equal to binsz) of data sent from each node in integer array *szarray* . A call to *concat* in one processor must be complemented by a call to *concat* in all other processors of the hypercube. Otherwise, deadlock will occur.

If a node sends more than *binsz* bytes of data only *binsz* are stored in memory. The remaining bytes are read from the channel so that execution can continue but then a −1 is returned, and the external variable *errcnt* is set to the number of bytes that the node attempted to send.

If *inbuf* has the special value NULLPTR in a node of the hypercube, then data are not placed in memory in that node and the value of *binsz* is irrelevant. Similarly, if *szarray* has the value NULLPTR, the array of sizes is not recorded.

FORTRAN SYNOPSIS

INTEGER FUNCTION KCONCA (OUTBUF, NBYTES, INBUF, BINSZ, SZARRY)
INTEGER OUTBUF (*), INBUF (*), NBYTES, BINSZ, SZARRY

DIAGNOSTICS

If an error occurs in *concat*, it returns a −1 and sets *errno* accordingly. Otherwise, it returns the number of bytes placed in *inbuf* . Many conditions can generate an error: communication errors, bad pointer or array addresses, preposterous values of *nbytes* or *binsz*, or having more than *binsz* bytes sent from a node.

C NAME
cshift—write and read separate data

C SYNOPSIS
int cshift (inbuf, inmask, inbytes, outbuf, outmask, outbytes)
char *inbuf, *outbuf;
unsigned int inmask, outmask;
int inbytes, outbytes;

C DESCRIPTION
cshift may be called only from the nodes.

Calling *cshift* is almost identical to calling *cwrite* and *cread* together, except that a call to *cshift* on one side of a channel is complemented by another call to *cshift* on the other side. *cshift* is easier to use than *cwrite* and *cread* since the application program does not have to decide which nodes call *cwrite* first and which call *cread* first.

cshift causes *outbytes* bytes of data to be written from memory starting at *outbuf* to the channels indicated by the channel mask *outmask*. In addition, it causes at most *inbytes* bytes of data to be read from the channel indicated by the channel mask *inmask* and placed in memory starting at *inbuf*. Since the write and read operations are separate, *inmask* may be one of the channels indicated by *outmask*. Two nodes can exchange data by having the same *inmask* as *outmask*. The buffers for the incoming and outgoing data, *inbuf* and *outbuf*, must not overlap, except in the special case where *inbuf* and *outbuf* are identical. Allowing the incoming data to overwrite the outgoing data is provided for convenience, but may reduce the communication speed on some concurrent processors. Identical input and output buffers may be used even if *inmask* and *outmask* are the same (i.e., incoming data never overwrites the outgoing buffer before it is sent).

It is guaranteed that *outbytes* bytes will be written; *cshift* will not return until all *outbytes* bytes of data have been written to all of the channels indicated by *outmask* and read by the receiving nodes. However, it is not guaranteed that *inbytes* bytes will be read; the actual number of bytes read depends on the number written by the transmitting node. A call to *cshift* on one side of a communication channel must be complemented by another call to *cshift* on the other side. Otherwise, deadlock will result.

If more than *inbytes* bytes are written by the transmitting node, only the first *inbytes* bytes are placed in *inbuf*. The remaining bytes are read from the channel, so the corresponding call to *cshift* that is transmitting the data can return, but the extra bytes are lost and a −1 is returned to indicate the error. The type of error is identified in the external variable *errno*, and the number of bytes that were transmitted is saved in the external variable *errcnt*. The same special cases apply to *cshift* as to *cread* and *cwrite*. Specifically, if *inmask* is 0, no read is performed by *cshift*, and if *outmask* is 0, no write is performed. However, if both *inmask* and *outmask* are 0, the contents of *outbuf* are copied into *inbuf* as if the node had sent a message to itself.

FORTRAN SYNOPSIS

INTEGER FUNCTION KCSHIF (INBUF, INMSK, INBTS, OUTBUF, OUTMSK, OUTBTS)
INTEGER INBUF (*), OUTBUF (*), INMSK, OUTMSK, INBTS, OUTBTS

SEE ALSO

cread(1), cwrite(1)

DIAGNOSTICS

If an error occurs in *cshift*, it returns a −1 and sets *errno* accordingly. Otherwise, it returns the number of bytes actually read. Many conditions can generate an error: communication errors, a bad buffer address, an invalid *inmask* or *outmask*, preposterous values of *inbytes* or *outbytes*, or reading a message that is longer than *inbytes*. Indicating more than one channel in the channel mask *inmask* generates an error. Although no communication errors can be detected by *cshift* on the data it transmits, it appends a checksum to the data when they are written allowing the corresponding *cshift* to detect communication errors when the data are read. Thus, communication errors can be detected only in the incoming data.

C NAME

vshift—write and read separate data

C SYNOPSIS

int vshift (inbuf, inmask, insize, inoffset, initems,
    outbuf, outmask, outsize, outoffset, outitems)
char *inbuf, *outbuf;
unsigned int inmask, outmask;
int insize, outsize, inoffset, outoffset, initems, outitems;

C DESCRIPTION

vshift may only be called from the nodes.

Calling *vshift* is almost identical to calling *vwrite* and *vread* together, except that a call to *vshift* on one side of a channel is complemented by another call to *vshift* on the other side. *vshift* is easier to use than *vwrite* and *vread* since the application program does not have to decide which nodes call *vwrite* first and which call *vread* first.

vshift causes *outitems* data items to be written from memory starting at *outbuf* to the channels indicated by the channel mask *outmask*. In addition, *vshift* causes at most *initems* data items to be read from the channel indicated by the channel mask *inmask* and placed in memory starting at *inbuf*. The size of each incoming data item is *insize* bytes, as given by *sizeof(item)* and the offset between incoming data items is *inoffset* bytes. For example, if the incoming data is to be stored in every fourth element in an array of floats and *sizeof(float)* is 4, then *insize* would be 4 and *inoffset* would be 16. Since the write and read operations are separate, *inmask* may be one of the channels indicated by *outmask*. Two nodes can exchange data by having *inmask* the same as *outmask*. The size of each outgoing data item is *outsize* bytes, as given by *sizeof(item)* and the offset between outgoing data items is *offset* bytes. For example, if every third element in an array of integers is to be written and *sizeof(int)* is 2, then *outsize* would be 2 and *outoffset* would be 6. The buffers for the incoming and outgoing data, *inbuf* and *outbuf*, must not overlap, except in the special case where the three pairs, *inbuf* and *outbuf*, *insize* and *outsize*, and *inoffset* and *outoffset*, are all identical. Allowing the incoming data to overwrite the outgoing data is provided for convenience, but may reduce the communication speed on some concurrent processors. Identical input and output buffers can be used even if *inmask* is the same as *outmask* (i.e., the incoming data never overwrites the outgoing buffer before it is sent).

It is guaranteed that *outitems* data items will be written; *vshift* will not return until all *outitems* items of data have been written to all of the channels indicated by *outmask* and read by the receiving nodes. However, it is not guaranteed that *initems* data items will be read; the actual number of items read depends on the number written by the transmitting node. A call to *vshift* on one side of a communication channel must be complemented by another call to *vshift* on the other side.

Otherwise, deadlock will result.

If more than *initems* data items are written by the transmitting node, only the first *initems* items are placed in *inbuf*. The remaining items are read from the channel, so the corresponding call to *vshift* that is transmitting the data can return, but the extra data items are lost and −1 is returned to indicate the error. The type of error is identified in the external variable *errno*, and the number of items that were transmitted is saved in the external variable *errcnt*. The same special cases apply to *vshift* as to *vread* and *vwrite*. Specifically, if *inmask* is 0, no read is performed by *vshift*, and if *outmask* is 0, no write is performed. However, if both *inmask* and *outmask* are 0, the contents of *outbuf* are copied into *inbuf* as if the node had sent a message to itself.

FORTRAN SYNOPSIS

INTEGER FUNCTION KVSHIF (INBUF, INMSK, INSZE, INOST, INITS, OUT-BUF, OUTMSK, OUTSZE, OUTOST, OUTITS)

INTEGER INBUF (*), OUTBUF (*), INMSK, OUTMSK, INSZE, OUTSZE, INOST, OUTOST, INITS, OUTITS

SEE ALSO

vread(1), vwrite(1), cshift(2)

DIAGNOSTICS

If an error occurs in *vshift*, it returns −1 and sets *errno* accordingly. Otherwise, it returns the number of data items actually read. Many conditions can generate an error: communication errors, a bad buffer address, an invalid *inmask* or *outmask*, preposterous values of *insize*, *outsize*, *inoffset*, *outoffset*, *initems*, or *outitems*, or reading a message that is longer than *initems*. Indicating more than one channel in the channel mask *inmask* generates an error. Although no communication errors can be detected by *vshift* on the data it transmits, it appends a checksum to the data when they are written allowing the corresponding *vshift* to detect communication errors when the data are read. Thus, communication errors can be detected only in the incoming data.

NAME

intro–introduction to node-control processor communication routines

DESCRIPTION

This section describes communication routines that can be built from the basic communication routines described in Sec. 1 and which implement four modes of communication between the nodes and the control processor. The nodes must all communicate together with the control processor when using the routines presented in this section.

The routines include a piece which is called in all of the nodes and a piece which is called in the control processor. The node routines are identified by *elt* (processing *element*) appended to the base name of the routine. The control processor routines are identified by *cp* (control *processor*) appended to the routine name. The *load* routines send data from the control processor to the nodes. The *dump* routines send data from the nodes to the control processor. In addition, the control processor versions of *load* and *dump* come in two versions, one that accesses memory and one that accesses the file system. In the C version of the routines that access the file system, we assume a UNIX environment in which an open file is specified by a *"file descriptor."* In the FORTRAN version an open file is specified by a unit number. The *dump* routines can be used to create files or memory buffers that can be transmitted back to the nodes with the *load* routines.

SEE ALSO

intro(1), intro(2)

DIAGNOSTICS

All of the communication system calls return a −1 to indicate that an error occurred. The types of errors that can occur are discussed on the manual pages for each routine. The two external variables, *errno* and *errcnt*, are used to identify the specific error that occurred.

C NAME

bcastcp—send broadcast data to nodes from control processor

C SYNOPSIS

int bcastcp (buffer, nbytes)
char *buffer;
int nbytes;

C DESCRIPTION

bcastcp causes *nbytes* bytes of data to be broadcast from memory starting at *buffer* to all the nodes.

It is guaranteed that *nbytes* bytes will be written to each node; *bcastcp* will not return until all *nbytes* bytes of data have been written to and read by each node. A call to *bcastcp* in the control processor must be complemented by a call to *bcastelt* in all of the nodes. Otherwise, deadlock will result.

FORTRAN SYNOPSIS

INTEGER FUNCTION KBCSTC (BUFFER, NBYTES)
INTEGER BUFFER (*), NBYTES

SEE ALSO

bcastelt(3)

DIAGNOSTICS

If an error occurs in *bcastcp*, it returns −1 and sets *errno* accordingly. Otherwise, it returns the number of bytes written. Two conditions can generate an error: a bad buffer address or a preposterous value of *nbytes*. Although no communication errors can be detected by *bcastcp*, it appends a checksum to the data when they are written allowing *bcastelt* to detect communicaton errors when the data are read.

C NAME

bcastelt–receive broadcast data from control processor

C SYNOPSIS

    int bcastelt (buffer, nbytes)
    char *buffer;
    int nbytes;

DESCRIPTION

bcastelt causes at most *nbytes* bytes of data to be read from the control processor and placed in memory starting at *buffer*. All nodes must call *bcastelt* together, and each node receives the same block of data from the control processor. The value of *nbytes* does not have to be the same in all nodes.

It is not guaranteed that *nbytes* bytes will be read by each node; the actual number of bytes read depends on the number written by the control processor. A *bcastelt* in all of the nodes must be complemented by a *bcastcp* in the control processor. Otherwise, deadlock will result.

If more than *nbytes* are written by the control processor, only the first *nbytes* bytes are placed in *buffer*. The remaining bytes are then read, so the corresponding calls to *bcastelt* in the other nodes and the call to *bcastcp* in the control processor can return, but the extra bytes are lost and −1 is returned to indicate the error. The type of error is identified in the external variable *errno*, and the number of bytes that were transmitted is saved in the external variable *errcnt*. If *buffer* has the special value NULLPTR the data are not placed in memory and the value of *nbytes* is irrelevant. The number of bytes transmitted by the control processor is then returned in place of the number of bytes read.

FORTRAN SYNOPSIS

    INTEGER FUNCTION KBCSTE (BUFFER, NBYTES)
    INTEGER BUFFER (*), NBYTES

SEE ALSO

bcastcp(3)

DIAGNOSTICS

If an error occurs in *bcastelt*, it returns a −1 and sets *errno* accordingly. Otherwise, it returns the number of bytes actually read. Several conditions can generate an error: communication errors, a bad buffer address, a preposterous value of *nbytes*, or reading a message that is longer than *nbytes*. Communication errors are detected by comparing the checksum of the incoming data with the checksum appended to the data by *bcastcp*.

C NAME
combcp–receive combined data from nodes

C SYNOPSIS
int combcp (buffer, size, nitems)
char *buffer;
int size, nitems;

C DESCRIPTION
combcp causes a single block of at most *nitems* items of size *size* bytes to be read from the nodes and placed in memory starting at *buffer*. The data block is the result of combining data blocks from each node with the combining function used in *combelt*.

It is not guaranteed that *nitems* items will be read; the actual number of items read depends on the number written by the nodes. A call to *combcp* in the control processor must be complemented by a call to *combelt* in all of the nodes. In addition, the value of *size* must be the same as it is in *combelt* in all of the nodes. Otherwise, deadlock will result.

If more than *nitems* items are written by the nodes, only the first *nitems* items are placed in *buffer*. The remaining data items are then read, so the corresponding calls to *combelt* in the nodes can return, but the extra data items are lost and a −1 is returned to indicate the error. The type of error is identified in the external variable *errno*, and the number of items that were transmitted is saved in the external variable *errcnt*.

FORTRAN SYNOPSIS
INTEGER FUNCTION KCOMBC (BUFFER, SIZE, NITEMS)
INTEGER BUFFER (*), SIZE, NITEMS

SEE ALSO
combine(2), combelt(3)

DIAGNOSTICS
If an error occurs in *combcp*, it returns a −1 and sets *errno* accordingly. Otherwise, it returns the number of data items written. Several conditions can generate an error: communication errors, a bad buffer address, a preposterous value of *nbytes* or *nitems*, or reading a message that is longer than *nitems*. Communication errors are detected by comparing the checksum of the incoming data with the checksum appended to the data by *combelt*.

C NAME
combelt–combine data from all nodes and send a copy to the control processor

C SYNOPSIS
int combelt (buffer, func, size, nitems)
char *buffer;
int (*func)(), size, nitems;

C DESCRIPTION
combelt is identical to *combine*, except that the block of *nitems* data items resulting from the combining operation is sent to the control processor in addition to overwriting the contents of *buffer* in each node.

It is guaranteed that *nitems* data items of size *size* bytes will be written; *combelt* will not return until all *nitems* items have been written to and read by the control processor. A call to *combelt* in all of the nodes must be complemented by a call to *combcp* in the control processor. Otherwise, deadlock will result.

FORTRAN SYNOPSIS
INTEGER FUNCTION KCOMBE (BUFFER, FUNC, SIZE, NITEMS)
INTEGER BUFFER (*), FUNC, SIZE, NITEMS

SEE ALSO
combine(2), combcp(3)

DIAGNOSTICS
If an error occurs in *combelt*, it returns −1 and sets *errno* accordingly. Otherwise, it returns the number of data items combined. Many conditions can generate an error: communication errors, a bad buffer address, an error returned by *func* or too large a value of *size* or *nitems*. Communication errors are detected by comparing the checksum of the incoming data with the checksum appended to the data when they were written. Since a node must buffer two data items of *size* bytes, some reasonable limit, such as 512 bytes, must be imposed on *size*.

C NAME

cubeld, cubeldl, cubeldv, cubeldle, cubeldve–load a program into a hypercube

C SYNOPSIS

```
int cubeld (doc, nodeprog)
char *nodeprog;
int doc;

int cubeldl (doc, nodeprog, argv0, argv1, ..., argvN, NULLPTR)
int doc;
char *nodeprog, *argv0, *argv1, ..., *argvN;

int cubeldv (doc, nodeprog, argv)
int doc;
char *nodeprog, *argv[ ];

int cubeldle (doc, nodeprog, argv0, argv1, ..., argvN, NULLPTR, envp)
int doc;
char *nodeprog, *argv0, *argv1, ..., *argvN, *envp[ ];

int cubeldve (doc, nodeprog, argv, envp)
int doc;
char *nodeprog, *argv[ ], *envp[ ];
```

C DESCRIPTION

The *cubeld* subroutines may only be called from the control processor.

cubeld in all its forms begins execution of the program *nodeprog* in a hypercube of dimension *doc*. If another process was executing in the hypercube, that process is halted, and *nodeprog* is loaded in its place. Execution of *nodeprog* is begun at the entry point designated *main*.

When *main* is started, it begins as though called as:

```
main (argc, argv)
int argc;
char *argv[ ];
```

where *argc* will equal $N + 1$ (one more than the number of the last non-null argument), and *argv* will be a vector of the character strings supplied to the *cubeld* subroutines.

cubeld is the simplest of the downloading subroutines because it does not pass any arguments or enivronment to the node program. Thus, the main subroutine of *nodeprog* should look like:

```
main ()
```

instead of:

```
main (argc, argv)
```

cubeldl allows the user to explicitly list the argument strings (*argv0*, *argv1*, ... , *argvN*) in the function call. The argument list must be terminated with a NULLPTR.

cubeldv is useful when pointers to the arguments have already been formed into a vector. As always, the last element of the vector must be NULLPTR (note that this is different from a pointer to a null string.)

Traditionally, the first argument (*argv0*, or *argv[0]*) , is the name of the program being run, i.e., *nodeprog*, although the user is free to disregard this, or use his or her own convention.

The routines *cubeldle* and *cubeldve* also supply an environment to the node program. An environment is a vector of character strings much like *argv*. Usually, each string consists of a sequence of alphanumeric characters, optionally followed by '=' and another sequence of alphanumerics. The vector is terminated by a NULLPTR. In regular C programs (such as the control processor program), the environment that is passed to it by the shell can be found in the external variable:

extern char ∗environ[];

Similarly, the environment that is passed to the node program by the control processor program can be found in the external variable *environ*. Thus, the line

extern char ∗environ[];

must be placed at the beginning of *nodeprog*, and the strings in the vector can be referred to as *environ[0]*, *environ[1]*, etc.

C EXAMPLES

The following statement starts a program (called *myprog*) on a cube of dimension 3. The main routine of *myprog* is called with *argc* set to 2, *argv[0]* set to the character string "myprog", and *argv[1]* set to the character string "horse."

cubeldl(3, ''myprog,'' ''myprog,'' ''horse,'' NULLPTR);

The following is an example of how to relay to the node program the same argument vector and environment vector that are received by the control processor program. The control processor program is called *mycpprog*, and looks something like:

#include headerfiles

extern char ∗environ[];

```
main (cpargc, cpargv)
int cpargc;
char *cpargv[];
{
    cubeldve (atoi(cpargv[1]), cpargv[2], & cpargv[2], environ);
    ...
}
```

Then the node program, which will be called *mynodeprog*, looks something like:

```
#include headerfiles

extern char *environ[];

main (nodeargc, nodeargv)
int nodeargc;
char *nodeargv;
{
  ...
}
```

Finally, after the two programs are compiled and linked properly, the control processor program is executed with the following shell command:

    mycpprog 3 mynodeprog horse dog

This will download and execute *mynodeprog* in a hypercube of dimension 3. The arguments "horse" and "dog" will be passed on to *mynodeprog* and will end up in *nodeargv[0]* and *nodeargv[1]*. Also, the environment of the control processor program is passed intact to the node program.

FORTRAN SYNOPSIS
    INTEGER FUNCTION KCUBEL (DOC, PRGNAM)
    INTEGER DOC
    CHARACTER PRGNAM * (*)

FORTRAN DESCRIPTION
KCUBEL may only be called from the control processor, and upon being called begins execution of the program PRGNAM in a hypercube of dimension DOC. If another process was executing in the hypercube that process is halted, and PRGNAM is loaded in its place.

KCUBEL is the FORTRAN equivalent of *cubeld* in C. There is no FORTRAN equivalent of the C routines *cubeldl, cubeldv, cubeldle, cubeldve*.

DIAGNOSTICS
If an error occurs during any of the *cubeld* routines, −1 is returned, and *errno* is set. Possible sources of error are: an unreasonable value of *doc*, inability to open *nodeprog*, inappropriate data in *nodeprog*, or a communication error during transmission of *nodeprog* to the hypercube.

C NAME

dumpelt–dump data from nodes to control processor

C SYNOPSIS

int dumpelt (buffer, nbytes)
char *buffer;
int nbytes;

C DESCRIPTION

dumpelt may be called only from the nodes.

dumpelt causes *nbytes* bytes of data to be written from memory starting at *buffer* to the control processor. All nodes must call *dumpelt* together, but each node sends a separate block of data that is *nbytes* bytes long. *nbytes* does not have to be the same in all nodes.

It is guaranteed that *nbytes* bytes will be written by each node; *dumpelt* will not return until all *nbytes* bytes of data have been written to and read by the control processor. A call to *dumpelt* in all of the nodes must be complemented by a call to *fdumpcp* or *mdumpcp* in the control processor. Otherwise, deadlock will result.

FORTRAN SYNOPSIS

INTEGER FUNCTION KDUMPE (BUFFER, NBYTES)
INTEGER BUFFER (*), NBYTES

SEE ALSO

fdumpcp(3), mdumpcp(3), loadelt(3)

DIAGNOSTICS

If an error occurs in *dumpelt*, it returns −1 and sets *errno* accordingly. Otherwise, it returns the number of bytes written. Two conditions can generate an error: a bad buffer address or a preposterous value of *nbytes*. Although no communication errors can be detected by *dumpelt*, it appends a checksum to the data when they are written allowing *fdumpcp* or *mdumpcp* to detect communication errors when the data are read.

C NAME

fcread–read from a communication channel

C SYNOPSIS

int fcread (fd, inmask, nbytes)
unsigned int inmask;
int fd, nbytes;

C DESCRIPTION

fcread may be called only from the control processor.

fcread causes at most *nbytes* bytes of data to be read from the communication channel indicated by the channel mask *inmask* and written into the file indicated by *fd*. *fd* is the file descriptor returned from a successful call to one of the UNIX routines: *creat*, *dup*, *open*, or *pipe*.

It is not guaranteed that *nbytes* bytes will be read; the actual number of bytes read depends on the number written by the transmitting node. If no error occurs, the actual number of bytes read from the communication channel is returned to the calling program.

A call to *fcread* must be complemented by a call to *cwrite* on the other side of the channel indicated by *inmask*. Otherwise, deadlock will result.

If more than *nbytes* bytes are written by the transmitting node, only the first *nbytes* bytes are written to file *fd*. The remaining bytes are read from the channel, so the corresponding call to *cwrite* in the transmitting node can return, but the extra bytes are lost and a −1 is returned to indicate the error. The type of error is identified in the external variable *errno*, and the number of bytes that were transmitted is saved in the external variable *errcnt*. It is considered bad programming style not to make *nbytes* large enough so that all incoming bytes are received and placed in file *fd*.

If *inmask* is 0, the call to *fcread* is ignored, so no call to *cwrite* is needed to complement it. However, if *nbytes* is 0 and *inmask* is nonzero, the call to *fcread* must still be complemented by a call to *cwrite*.

FORTRAN SYNOPSIS

INTEGER FUNCTION KFCREA (NUNIT, INMSK, NBYTES)
INTEGER NUNIT, INMSK, NBYTES

FORTRAN DESCRIPTION

KFCREA may only be called from the control processor, and is the direct FORTRAN equivalent of the C routine *fcread*.

The only difference in the arguments of the FORTRAN and C routines is that in the case of KFCREA the argument NUNIT is used to specify the unit number corresponding to the output file.

SEE ALSO

cwrite(1), cread(1), fcwrite(3)

DIAGNOSTICS

If an error occurs in *fcread* , it returns a −1 and sets *errno* accordingly. Otherwise, it returns the number of bytes actually read. Many conditions can generate an error: communication errors, a bad file descriptor, an invalid *inmask,* a preposterous value of *nbytes*, or reading a message that is longer than *nbytes*. Indicating more than one channel in the channel mask *inmask* generates an error. Communication errors are detected by comparing the checksum of the incoming data with the checksum appended to the data by *cwrite*.

C NAME
fcwrite—write to communication channels from a file

C SYNOPSIS
int fcwrite (fd, outmask, nbytes)
unsigned int outmask;
int fd, nbytes;

C DESCRIPTION
fcwrite may be called only from the control processor.

fcwrite causes *nbytes* bytes of data to be written from the file indicated by *fd* to the communication channels indicated by the channel mask *outmask*. *fd* is the file descriptor returned from a successful call to one of the UNIX routines: *creat* , *dup*, *open*, or *pipe* .

It is guaranteed that *nbytes* bytes will be written; *fcwrite* will not return until all *nbytes* bytes of data have been written to each indicated channel and read by the receiving nodes. A call to *fcwrite* must be complemented by a call to *cread* on the other side of all of the channels indicated by *outmask*. Otherwise, deadlock will result. If *outmask* is 0, the call to *fcwrite* is ignored, so no call to *cread* is needed to complement it. However, if *nbytes* is 0 and *mask* is nonzero, the call to *fcwrite* must still be complemented by a call to *cread*.

FORTRAN SYNOPSIS
INTEGER FUNCTION KFCWRI (NUNIT, OUTMSK, NBYTES)
INTEGER NUNIT, OUTMSK, NBYTES

FORTRAN DESCRIPTION
KFCWRI may only be called from the control processor, and is the direct FOR-TRAN equivalent of the C routine *fcwrite*. The only difference in the arguments of the FORTRAN and C routines is that in the case of KFCWRI the argument NUNIT is used to specify the unit number corresponding to the input file.

SEE ALSO
cread(1), fcread(3)

DIAGNOSTICS
If an error occurs in *fcwrite*, it returns −1 and sets *errno* accordingly. Otherwise, it returns the number of bytes written. Several conditions can generate an error: a bad file descriptor, a nonexistent channel indicated by *outmask*, or a preposterous value of *nbytes*. Although no communication errors can be detected by *fcwrite*, it appends a checksum to the data when they are written allowing *cread* to detect communication errors when the data are read.

C NAME
fdumpcp–dump data from nodes to control processor's file system

C SYNOPSIS
int fdumpcp (fd, nbytes, bufmap)
int fd, nbytes;
int *bufmap

C DESCRIPTION
fdumpcp may only be called from the control processor.

fdumpcp causes a separate block of at most *nbytes* bytes of data to be read from each node and written into the file indicated by *fd*. *fd* is the file descriptor returned from a successful call to one of the UNIX routines: *creat*, *dup*, *open*, or *pipe*.

After the call to *fdumpcp*, the file *fd* contains a concatenation of all the blocks of data sent by the nodes, in *procnum* order. Then, a separate map of the data is stored in *bufmap* in order to keep track of which data is from which node. The first integer of the array, *bufmap[0]* contains *nproc*, the total number of nodes in the cube, which is just 2 to the power of *doc*. Then the array elements *bufmap[1]* through *bufmap[nproc]* contain the number of bytes of data sent from each of the nodes. For example, *bufmap[6]* contains the number of bytes of data sent by node 5.

It is guaranteed that a separate block of data will be read from each node; *fdumpcp* will not return until a block of data has been read from each node and written into the file. A call to *fdumpcp* in the control processor must be complemented by a call to *dumpelt* in all of the nodes. Otherwise, deadlock will result.

If more than *nbytes* bytes are written by a node, only the first *nbytes* bytes are placed in the file indicated by *fd*. The remaining bytes are then read, so the corresponding calls to *dumpelt* in the nodes can return, but the extra bytes are lost and −1 is returned to indicate the error. The type of error is identified in the external variable *errno*, and the number of bytes that were transmitted is saved in the external variable *errcnt*. The value of *errcnt* is overwritten each time more than *nbytes* are written by a node, so if several nodes write more than *nbytes* bytes, *errcnt* will contain the value from the last node to write more than *nbytes* bytes of data.

FORTRAN SYNOPSIS
INTEGER KFDUMP (NUNIT, NBYTES, BUFMAP)
INTEGER BUFMAP (*), NUNIT, NBYTES

FORTRAN DESCRIPTION
KFDUMP may only be called from the control processor, and is the direct FORTRAN equivalent of the C routine *fdumpcp*. The only difference in the arguments of the FORTRAN and C routines is that in the case of KFDUMP the argument

NUNIT is used to specify the unit number corresponding to the output file.

SEE ALSO
dumpelt(3), floadcp(3), mdumpcp(3), mloadcp(3)

DIAGNOSTICS
If an error occurs in *fdumpcp*, it returns −1 and sets *errno* accordingly. Otherwise, it returns the number of nodes that sent data. Several conditions can generate an error: physical I/O errors, communication errors, a bad file descriptor, a preposterous value of *nbytes*, or reading a message that is longer than *nbytes*. Communication errors are detected by comparing the checksum of the incoming data with the checksum appended to the data by *dumpelt* .

C NAME

floadcp–load data into nodes from control processor file

C SYNOPSIS

        int floadcp (fd, bufmap)
        int fd, *bufmap;

C DESCRIPTION

floadcp may only be called from the control processor.

floadcp causes a separate block of data to be written to each node from the file indicated by *fd*. *fd* is the file descriptor returned from a successful call to one of the UNIX routines: *creat*, *dup*, *open*, or *pipe*.

Before calling *floadcp*, one block of data for each node in the hypercube must be placed in *fd*, in *procnum* order. Then, a separate map of the data in *fd* must be stored in *bufmap* with the following format: one integer, *nproc*, containing the total number of nodes, followed by one integer for each node, containing the number of bytes of data for that node.

It is guaranteed that a separate block of data will be written to each node; *floadcp* will not return until a block of data has been written to and read by each node. A call to *floadcp* in the control processor must be complemented by a call to *loadelt* in all of the nodes. Otherwise, deadlock will result.

FORTRAN SYNOPSIS

        INTEGER FUNCTION KFLOAD (NUNIT, BUFMAP)
        INTEGER NUNIT, BUFMAP (*)

FORTRAN DESCRIPTION

KFLOAD may only be called from the control processor, and is the direct FORTRAN equivalent of the C routine *floadcp*. The only difference in the arguments of the FORTRAN and C routines is that in the case of KFLOAD the argument NUNIT is used to specify the unit number corresponding to the output file.

SEE ALSO

loadelt(3), fdumpcp(3), mloadcp(3), mdumpcp(3)

DIAGNOSTICS

If an error occurs in *floadcp* it returns −1 and sets *errno* accordingly. Otherwise, it returns the number of nodes to which it sent data. Several conditions can generate an error: physical I/O errors, a bad file descriptor, or invalid contents of the file, such as unreasonable values of *nbytes* or too few data blocks for the number of nodes. Although no communication errors can be detected by *floadcp*, it appends a checksum to the data when they are written allowing *loadelt* to detect communication errors when the data are read.

C NAME

loadelt–load data into nodes from control processor

C SYNOPSIS

int loadelt (buffer, nbytes)
char ∗buffer;
int nbytes;

C DESCRIPTION

loadelt may be called only from the nodes.

loadelt causes at most *nbytes* bytes of data to be read from the control processor and placed in memory starting at *buffer*. All nodes must call *loadelt* together, but each node receives a separate block of data that is at most *nbytes* bytes long. *nbytes* does not have to be the same in all nodes.

It is not guaranteed that *nbytes* bytes will be read by all nodes; the actual number of bytes read depends on the number written by the control processor to each node. A call to *loadelt* in all of the nodes must be complemented by a call to *floadcp* or *mloadcp* in the control processor. Otherwise, deadlock will result.

If more than *nbytes* bytes are written to a node by the control processor, only the first *nbytes* bytes are placed in *buffer*. The remaining bytes are then read, so the corresponding calls to *loadelt* in the other nodes and the call to *floadcp* or *mloadcp* in the control processor can return, but the extra bytes are lost and a −1 is returned to indicate the error. The type of error is identified in the external variable *errno*, and the number of bytes that were transmitted is saved in the external variable *errcnt*. If *buffer* has the special value NULLPTR, the data are not placed in memory and the value of *nbytes* is irrelevant. The number of bytes transmitted by the control processor to the node is then returned in place of the number of bytes read.

FORTRAN SYNOPSIS

INTEGER FUNCTION KLOADE (BUFFER, NBYTES)
INTEGER BUFFER (∗), NBYTES

SEE ALSO

floadcp(3), mloadcp(3), dumpelt(3)

DIAGNOSTICS

If an error occurs in *loadelt*, it returns −1 and sets *errno* accordingly. Otherwise, it returns the number of bytes actually read. Several conditions can generate an error: communication errors, a bad buffer address, a preposterous value of *nbytes*, or reading a message that is longer than *nbytes*. Communication errors are detected by comparing the checksum of the incoming data with the checksum appended to the data by *floadcp* or *mloadcp*.

C NAME
mdumpcp–dump data from nodes to control processor's memory

C SYNOPSIS
int mdumpcp (buffer, nbytes, bufmap)
char *buffer;
int nbytes, *bufmap;

C DESCRIPTION
mdumpcp may only be called from the control processor.

mdumpcp causes a separate block of at most *nbytes* bytes of data to be read from each node and written into memory starting at *buffer*. After the call to *mdumpcp* , *buffer* contains a concatenation of all the blocks of data sent by the nodes, in *procnum* order. Then, a separate map of the data is stored in *bufmap* in order to keep track of which data is from which node. The first integer of the array, *bufmap[0]* contains *nproc*, the total number of nodes in the cube, which is just 2 to the power of *doc*. Then the array elements *bufmap[1]* through *bufmap[nproc]* contain the number of bytes of data sent from each of the nodes. For example, *bufmap[6]* contains the number of bytes of data sent by node 5.

It is guaranteed that a separate block of data will be read from each node; *mdumpcp* will not return until a block of data has been read from each node. A call to *mdumpcp* in the control processor must be complemented by a call to *dumpelt* in all of the nodes. Otherwise, deadlock will result.

If more than *nbytes* bytes are written by a node, only the first *nbytes* bytes are placed in *buffer*. The remaining bytes are then read, so the corresponding calls to *dumpelt* in the nodes can return, but the extra bytes are lost and −1 is returned to indicate the error. The type of error is identified in the external variable *errno*, and the number of bytes that were transmitted is saved in the external variable *errcnt*. The value of *errcnt* is overwritten each time more than *nbytes* are written by a node, so if several nodes write more than *nbytes* bytes, *errcnt* will contain the value from the last node to write more than *nbytes* bytes of data.

FORTRAN SYNOPSIS
INTEGER FUNCTION KMDUMP (BUFFER, NBYTES, BUFMAP)
INTEGER BUFFER (*), BUFMAP (*), NBYTES

SEE ALSO
dumpelt(3), fdumpcp(3), floadcp(3), mloadcp(3)

DIAGNOSTICS
If an error occurs in *mdumpcp*, it returns −1 and sets *errno* accordingly. Otherwise, it returns the number of nodes that sent data. Several conditions can generate an error: communication errors, a bad buffer address, a preposterous value of *nbytes*,

or reading a message that is longer than *nbytes*. Communication errors are detected by comparing the checksum of the incoming data with the checksum appended to the data by *dumpelt*.

C NAME
mloadcp–load data into nodes from control processor

C SYNOPSIS
int mloadcp (buffer, bufmap)
char *buffer;
int *bufmap;

C DESCRIPTION
mloadcp may only be called from the control processor.

mloadcp causes a separate block of data to be written to each node from memory starting at *buffer*. Before calling *mloadcp*, one block of data for each node in the hypercube must be placed in *buffer*, in *procnum* order. Then, a separate map of the data in *buffer* must be stored in *bufmap* with the following format: one integer, *nproc*, containing the total number of nodes, followed by one integer for each node, containing the number of bytes of data for that node.

It is guaranteed that a separate block of data will be written to each node; *mloadcp* will not return until a block of data has been written to and read by each node. A call to *mloadcp* in the control processor must be complemented by a call to *loadelt* in all of the nodes. Otherwise, deadlock will result.

FORTRAN SYNOPSIS
INTEGER FUNCTION KMLOAD (BUFFER, BUFMAP)
INTEGER BUFFER (*), BUFMAP (*)

SEE ALSO
loadelt(3), floadcp(3), fdumpcp(3), mdumpcp(3)

DIAGNOSTICS
If an error occurs in *mloadcp*, it returns −1 and sets *errno* accordingly. Otherwise, it returns the number of nodes to which it sent data. Several conditions can generate an error: a bad buffer address or invalid contents of the buffer, such as unreasonable values of *nbytes* or too few data blocks for the number of nodes. Although no communication errors can be detected by *mloadcp*, it appends a checksum to the data when they are written allowing *loadelt* to detect communication errors when the data are read.

NAME

      intro—introduction to the utility library

DESCRIPTION

      This section describes the utility library that supports the communication routines presented in Sec. 1, 2, and 3. Although this section currently contains few routines, additional routines such as *index, transpose, transfer* and *crystal_router*, will be added as they are implemented.

C NAME
cparam–obtain cube parameters

C SYNOPSIS
cparam (env)
struct cubenv *env;

C DESCRIPTION
cparam may be called either from the nodes or the control processor. *cparam* copies the parameters defining the current node environment into the structure *env*. Irrelevant values may be ignored, i.e. *cpmask* has no meaning in the control processor and will be set to 0. The structure declaration from **<cros.h>** is:

```
struct cubenv {
        int doc;
        int procnum;
        int nproc;
        int cpmask;
        int cubemask;
};
```

doc contains the dimension of the hypercube currently being used. *procnum* contains the unique processor number of a node or 1024 if called in the control processor. *nproc* contains the total number of nodes currently in use. *cpmask* contains the mask of the channel that connects the node to the control processor. *cpmask* is 0 for the control processor and for all nodes that are not directly connected to the control processor. *cubemask* is the channel mask that the control processor uses to talk to the cube (node 0). It is set to 0 when *cparam* is called in the cube.

FORTRAN SYNOPSIS
SUBROUTINE KCPARA (ENV)
INTEGER ENV (5)

FORTRAN DESCRIPTION
KCPARA is the direct FORTRAN quivalent of the C routine *cparam*. Upon return the array ENV contains the parameters defining the current node environment.

```
ENV(1) = doc
ENV(2) = procnum
ENV(3) = nproc
ENV(4) = cpmask
ENV(5) = cubemask
```

C NAME
  gridmap–map interconnection topology onto cartesian grid

C SYNOPSIS
  int gridinit (griddim, num)
  int griddim, *num;

  int gridcoord (proc, coord)
  int proc, *coord;

  int gridproc (coord)
  int *coord;

  int gridchan (proc, dir, sign)
  int proc, dir, sign;

C DESCRIPTION
  The *gridmap* subroutines may be called only from the nodes.

  gridmap collectively refers to four routines that implement the mapping of the interconnection topology of the concurrent processor onto a decomposition topology which is some type of cartesian grid.

  gridinit initializes the other routines and must be called first. The dimension of the cartesian grid is *griddim*, and *num* is a pointer to an array containing the number of nodes in each dimension. *gridinit* returns −1 if it cannot perform the mapping to the indicated decomposition topology. To use the available nodes most efficiently, the number of nodes in each dimension should be a power of two, but even if it is not, the *gridmap* routines will work. However, periodic boundaries, which are normally provided, may not be possible if the number of nodes in each dimension is not a power of two.

  gridcoord converts the processor number *proc* into its cartesian coordinates in the grid. *gridcoord* returns the coordinates by writing them into the array indicated by the pointer *coord*. If node *proc* is not part of the grid, *gridcoord* returns −1.

  The inverse function of *gridcoord* is performed by *gridproc*, which returns the processor number of the node whose coordinates are given in the array *coord*. If the coordinates given by *coord* lie outside the grid initialized by *gridinit*, *gridproc* returns −1.

  gridchan returns the channel mask of the channel in the direction given by *dir* and *sign* relative to processor number *proc*. *dir* labels the particular dimension of the grid and *sign*, which has the allowed values of +1 and −1, and identifies the desired change in the coordinate given by *dir*. Other values of *sign* cause *gridchan* to return −1 to indicate the error.

FORTRAN SYNOPSIS
      INTEGER FUNCTION KGRDIN (GRDDIM, NUM)
      INTEGER GRDDIM, NUM (*)

      INTEGER FUNCTION KGRDCO (PROC, COORD)
      INTEGER PROC, COORD (*)

      INTEGER FUNCTION KGRDPR (COORD)
      INTEGER COORD (*)

      INTEGER FUNCTION KGRDCH (PROC, DIR, SIGN)
      INTEGER PROC, DIR, SIGN

DIAGNOSTICS
      If an error occurs in any of the *gridmap* routines, they return -1. Many conditions can cause an error, such as having a coordinate or processor number out of range or requesting more nodes in the grid than are available.

Index